Star
Commonwealth Stamp ...

Bangladesh, Burma, Pakistan & Sri Lanka

3rd edition 2015

150 YEARS

STANLEY GIBBONS
CATALOGUES
—— 1865 - 2015 ——

Stanley Gibbons Ltd • London and Ringwood

By Appointment to
Her Majesty The Queen
Philatelists
Stanley Gibbons Ltd
London

Published by Stanley Gibbons Ltd
Editorial, Publications Sales Offices
and Distribution Centre:
7 Parkside, Christchurch Road, Ringwood,
Hants BH24 3SH

1st Edition – 2005
2nd Edition – 2011
3rd Edition – 2015

© Stanley Gibbons Ltd 2015

British Library Cataloguing in
Publication Data.
A catalogue record for this book is available
from the British Library.

Errors and omissions excepted
the colour reproduction of stamps is only as
accurate as the printing process will allow.

ISBN-10: 0-85259-942-0
ISBN-13: 978-0-85259-942-6

Item No. R2977-15

Printed by Stephens & George, Wales

Contents

Stanley Gibbons Holdings Plc

Stanley Gibbons Limited, Stanley Gibbons Auctions
399 Strand, London WC2R 0LX
Tel: +44 (0)207 836 8444
Fax: +44 (0)207 836 7342
E-mail: help@stanleygibbons.com
Website: www.stanleygibbons.com
for all departments, Auction and
Specialist Stamp Departments.

Open Monday–Friday 9.30 a.m. to 5 p.m.
Shop. Open Monday–Friday 9 a.m.
to 5.30 p.m. and Saturday 9.30 a.m.
to 5.30 p.m.

Stanley Gibbons Publications Gibbons Stamp Monthly and Philatelic Exporter
7 Parkside, Christchurch Road,
Ringwood, Hampshire BH24 3SH.
Tel: +44 (0)1425 472363
Fax: +44 (0)1425 470247
E-mail: help@stanleygibbons.com
Publications Mail Order.
FREEPHONE 0800 611622

Monday–Friday 8.30 a.m. to 5 p.m.

Stanley Gibbons (Guernsey) Limited
18–20 Le Bordage, St Peter Port,
Guernsey GY1 1DE.
Tel: +44 (0)1481 708270
Fax: +44 (0)1481 708279
E-mail: investment@stanleygibbons.com

Stanley Gibbons (Jersey) Limited
18 Hill Street, St Helier, Jersey,
Channel Islands JE2 4UA.
Tel: +44 (0)1534 766711
Fax: +44 (0)1534 766177
E-mail: investment@stanleygibbons.com

Stanley Gibbons (Asia) Limited
Room 618, 6/F,
100 Queen's Road Central
Central,
Hong Kong
Tel: +852 3180 9370
E-mail: elee@stanleygibbons.com

Benham Collectibles Limited
Unit K, Concept Court,
Shearway Business Park
Folkestone Kent CT19 4RG
E-mail: benham@benham.com

Stanley Gibbons Publications Overseas Representation
Stanley Gibbons Publications are
represented overseas by the following

Australia *Renniks Publications PTY LTD*
Unit 3 37-39 Green Street,
Banksmeadow, NSW 2019, Australia
Tel: +612 9695 7055
Website: www.renniks.com

Canada *Unitrade Associates*
99 Floral Parkway, Toronto,
Ontario M6L 2C4, Canada
Tel: +1 416 242 5900
Website: www.unitradeassoc.com

Germany *Schaubek Verlag Leipzig*
Am Glaeschen 23, D-04420
Markranstaedt, Germany
Tel: +49 34 205 67823
Website: www.schaubek.de

Italy *Ernesto Marini S.R.L.*
V. Struppa, 300, Genova, 16165, Italy
Tel: +3901 0247-3530
Website: www.ernestomarini.it

Japan *Japan Philatelic*
PO Box 2, Suginami-Minami,
Tokyo 168-8081, Japan
Tel: +81 3330 41641
Website: www.yushu.co.jp

Netherlands also covers Belgium Denmark, Finland & France *Uitgeverij Davo BV*
PO Box 411, Ak Deventer, 7400
Netherlands
Tel: +315 7050 2700
Website: www.davo.nl

New Zealand *House of Stamps*
PO Box 12, Paraparaumu,
New Zealand
Tel: +61 6364 8270
Website: www.houseofstamps.co.nz

New Zealand *Philatelic Distributors*
PO Box 863
15 Mount Edgecumbe Street
New Plymouth 4615, New Zealand
Tel: +6 46 758 65 68
Website: www.stampcollecta.com

Norway *SKANFIL A/S*

SPANAV. 52 / BOKS 2030
N-5504 HAUGESUND, Norway
Tel: +47-52703940
E-mail: magne@skanfil.no

Singapore *C S Philatelic Agency*
Peninsula Shopping Centre #04-29
3 Coleman Street, 179804, Singapore
Tel: +65 6337-1859
Website: www.cs.com.sg

South Africa *Mr. Thematic*
737 Redwood Street
Randparkridge Ext 14
Gauteng, South Africa
Tel: +1606 553107
E-mail: ianfrith146@gmail.com,
chrisb@asapcc.co.za

Sweden *Chr Winther Sorensen AB*
Box 43, S-310 20 Knaered, Sweden
Tel: +46 43050743
Website: www.collectia.se

USA *Regency Superior Ltd*
229 North Euclid Avenue
Saint Louis, Missouri 63108, USA

PO Box 8277, St Louis,
MO 63156-8277, USA
Toll Free Tel: (800) 782-0066
Tel: (314) 361-5699
Website: www.RegencySuperior.com
Email: info@regencysuperior.com

General Philatelic Information and Guidelines to the Scope of Stanley Gibbons Commonwealth Catalogues

These notes reflect current practice in compiling the Stanley Gibbons Commonwealth Catalogues.

The Stanley Gibbons Stamp Catalogue has a very long history and the vast quantity of information it contains has been carefully built up by successive generations through the work of countless individuals. Philately is never static and the Catalogue has evolved and developed over the years. These notes relate to the current criteria upon which a stamp may be listed or priced. These criteria have developed over time and may have differed somewhat in the early years of this catalogue. These notes are not intended to suggest that we plan to make wholesale changes to the listing of classic issues in order to bring them into line with today's listing policy, they are designed to inform catalogue users as to the policies currently in operation.

PRICES

The prices quoted in this Catalogue are the estimated selling prices of Stanley Gibbons Ltd at the time of publication. They are, unless it is specifically stated otherwise, for examples in fine condition for the issue concerned. Superb examples are worth more; those of a lower quality considerably less.

All prices are subject to change without prior notice and Stanley Gibbons Ltd may from time to time offer stamps below catalogue price. Individual low value stamps sold at 399 Strand are liable to an additional handling charge. Purchasers of new issues should note the prices charged for them contain an element for the service rendered and so may exceed the prices shown when the stamps are subsequently catalogued. Postage and handling charges are extra.

No guarantee is given to supply all stamps priced, since it is not possible to keep every catalogued item in stock. Commemorative issues may, at times, only be available in complete sets and not as individual values.

Quotation of prices. The prices in the left-hand column are for unused stamps and those in the right-hand column are for used.

A dagger (†) denotes that the item listed does not exist in that condition and a blank, or dash, that it exists, or may exist, but we are unable to quote a price.

Prices are expressed in pounds and pence sterling. One pound comprises 100 pence (£1 = 100p).

The method of notation is as follows: pence in numerals (e.g. 10 denotes ten pence); pounds and pence, up to £100, in numerals (e.g. 4.25 denotes four pounds and twenty-five pence); prices above £100 are expressed in whole pounds with the '£' sign shown.

Unused stamps. Great Britain and Commonwealth: the prices for unused stamps of Queen Victoria to King George V are for lightly hinged examples. Unused prices for King Edward VIII, King George VI and Queen Elizabeth issues are for unmounted mint.

Some stamps from the King George VI period are often difficult to find in unmounted mint condition. In such instances we would expect that collectors would need to pay a high proportion of the price quoted to obtain mounted mint examples. Generally speaking lightly mounted mint stamps from this reign, issued before 1945, are in considerable demand.

Used stamps. The used prices are normally for fine postally used stamps, but may be for stamps cancelled-to-order where this practice exists.

A pen-cancellation on early issues can sometimes correctly denote postal use. Instances are individually noted in the Catalogue in explanation of the used price given.

Prices quoted for bisects on cover or large piece are for those dated during the period officially authorised.

Stamps not sold unused to the public (e.g. some official stamps) are priced used only.

The use of 'unified' designs, that is stamps inscribed for both postal and fiscal purposes, results in a number of stamps of very high face value. In some instances these may not have been primarily intended for postal purposes, but if they are so inscribed we include them. We only price such items used, however, where there is evidence of normal postal usage.

Cover prices. To assist collectors, cover prices are quoted for issues up to 1945 at the beginning of each country.

The system gives a general guide in the form of a factor by which the corresponding used price of the basic loose stamp should be multiplied when found in fine average condition on cover.

Care is needed in applying the factors and they relate to a cover which bears a single of the denomination listed; if more than one denomination is present the most highly priced attracts the multiplier and the remainder are priced at the simple figure for used singles in arriving at a total.

The cover should be of non-philatelic origin; bearing the correct postal rate for the period and distance involved and cancelled with the markings normal to the offices concerned. Purely philatelic items have a cover value only slightly greater than the catalogue value for the corresponding used stamps. This applies generally to those high-value stamps used philatelically rather than in the normal course of commerce. Low-value stamps, e.g. ¼d. and ½d., are desirable when used as a single rate on cover and merit an increase in 'multiplier' value.

First day covers in the period up to 1945 are not within the scope of the system and the multiplier should not be used. As a special category of philatelic usage, with wide variations in valuation according to scarcity, they require separate treatment.

Oversized covers, difficult to accommodate on an album page, should be reckoned as worth little more than the corresponding value of the used stamps. The condition of a cover also affects its value. Except for 'wreck covers', serious damage or soiling reduce the value where the postal markings and stamps are ordinary ones. Conversely, visual appeal adds to the value and this can include freshness of appearance, important addresses, old-fashioned but legible hand-writing, historic town-names, etc.

The multipliers are a base on which further value would be added to take account of the cover's postal historical importance in demonstrating such things as unusual, scarce or emergency cancels, interesting routes, significant postal markings, combination usage, the development of postal rates, and so on.

Minimum price. The minimum catalogue price quoted is 10p. For individual stamps prices between 10p. and 95p. are provided as a guide for catalogue users. The lowest price charged for individual stamps or sets purchased from Stanley Gibbons Ltd is £1

Set prices. Set prices are generally for one of each value, excluding shades and varieties, but including major colour changes. Where there are alternative shades, etc., the cheapest is usually included. The number of stamps in the set is always stated for clarity. The prices for sets containing *se-tenant* pieces are based on the prices quoted for such combinations, and not on those for the individual stamps.

Varieties. Where plate or cylinder varieties are priced in used condition the price quoted is for a fine used example with the cancellation well clear of the listed flaw.

Specimen stamps. The pricing of these items is explained under that heading.

Stamp booklets. Prices are for complete assembled booklets in fine condition with those issued before 1945 showing normal wear and tear. Incomplete booklets and those which have been 'exploded' will, in general, be worth less than the figure quoted.

Repricing. Collectors will be aware that the market factors of supply and demand directly influence the prices quoted in this Catalogue. Whatever the scarcity of a particular stamp, if there is no one in the market who wishes to buy it cannot be expected to achieve a high price. Conversely, the same item actively sought by numerous potential buyers may cause the price to rise.

All the prices in this Catalogue are examined during the preparation of each new edition by the expert staff of Stanley Gibbons and repriced as necessary. They take many factors into account, including supply and demand, and are in close touch with the international stamp market and the auction world.

Commonwealth cover prices and advice on postal history material originally provided by Edward B Proud.

GUARANTEE

All stamps are guaranteed originals in the following terms:

If not as described, and returned by the purchaser, we undertake to refund the price paid to us in the original transaction. If any stamp is certified as genuine by the Expert Committee of the Royal Philatelic Society, London, or by BPA Expertising Ltd, the purchaser shall not be entitled to make any claim against us for any error, omission or mistake in such certificate.

Consumers' statutory rights are not affected by the above guarantee.

The recognised Expert Committees in this country are those of the Royal Philatelic Society, 41 Devonshire Place, London W1G, 6JY, and BPA Expertising Ltd, PO Box 1141, Guildford, Surrey GU5 0WR. They do not undertake valuations under any circumstances and fees are payable for their services.

MARGINS ON IMPERFORATE STAMPS

| Superb | Very fine | Fine | Average | Poor |

GUM

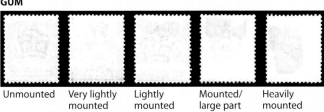

| Unmounted | Very lightly mounted | Lightly mounted | Mounted/ large part original gum (o.g.). | Heavily mounted small part o.g. |

CENTRING

| Superb | Very fine | Fine | Average | Poor |

CANCELLATIONS

| Superb | Very fine | Fine | Average | Poor |

| Superb | Very fine |

| Fine | Average | Poor |

CONDITION GUIDE

To assist collectors in assessing the true value of items they are considering buying or in reviewing stamps already in their collections, we now offer a more detailed guide to the condition of stamps on which this catalogue's prices are based.

For a stamp to be described as 'Fine', it should be sound in all respects, without creases, bends, wrinkles, pin holes, thins or tears. If perforated, all perforation 'teeth' should be intact, it should not suffer from fading, rubbing or toning and it should be of clean, fresh appearance.

Margins on imperforate stamps: These should be even on all sides and should be at least as wide as half the distance between that stamp and the next. To have one or more margins of less than this width, would normally preclude a stamp from being described as 'Fine'. Some early stamps were positioned very close together on the printing plate and in such cases 'Fine' margins would necessarily be narrow. On the other hand, some plates were laid down to give a substantial gap between individual stamps and in such cases margins would be expected to be much wider.

An 'average' four-margin example would have a narrower margin on one or more sides and should be priced accordingly, while a stamp with wider, yet even, margins than 'Fine' would merit the description 'Very Fine' or 'Superb' and, if available, would command a price in excess of that quoted in the catalogue.

Gum: Since the prices for stamps of King Edward VIII, King George VI and Queen Elizabeth are for 'unmounted' or 'never hinged' mint, even stamps from these reigns which have been very lightly mounted should be available at a discount from catalogue price, the more obvious the hinge marks, the greater the discount.

Catalogue prices for stamps issued prior to King Edward VIII's reign are for mounted mint, so unmounted examples would be worth a premium. Hinge marks on 20th century stamps should not be too obtrusive, and should be at least in the lightly mounted category. For 19th century stamps more obvious hinging would be acceptable, but stamps should still carry a large part of their original gum—'Large part o.g.'—in order to be described as 'Fine'.

Centring: Ideally, the stamp's image should appear in the exact centre of the perforated area, giving equal margins on all sides. 'Fine' centring would be close to this ideal with any deviation having an effect on the value of the stamp. As in the case of the margins on imperforate stamps, it should be borne in mind that the space between some early stamps was very narrow, so it was very difficult to achieve accurate perforation, especially when the technology was in its infancy. Thus, poor centring would have a less damaging effect on the value of a 19th century stamp than on a 20th century example, but the premium put on a perfectly centred specimen would be greater.

Cancellations: Early cancellation devices were designed to 'obliterate' the stamp in order to prevent it being reused and this is still an important objective for today's postal administrations. Stamp collectors, on the other hand, prefer postmarks to be lightly applied, clear, and to leave as much as possible of the design visible. Dated, circular cancellations have long been 'the postmark of choice', but the definition of a 'Fine' cancellation will depend upon the types of cancellation in use at the time a stamp was current—it is clearly illogical to seek a circular datestamp on a Penny Black.

'Fine', by definition, will be superior to 'Average', so, in terms of cancellation quality, if one begins by identifying what 'Average' looks like, then one will be half way to identifying 'Fine'. The illustrations will give some guidance on mid-19th century and mid-20th century cancellations of Great Britain, but types of cancellation in general use in each country and in each period will determine the appearance of 'Fine'.

As for the factors discussed above, anything less than 'Fine' will result in a downgrading of the stamp concerned, while a very fine or superb cancellation will be worth a premium.

Combining the factors: To merit the description 'Fine', a stamp should be fine in every respect, but a small deficiency in one area might be made up for in another by a factor meriting an 'Extremely Fine' description.

Some early issues are so seldom found in what would normally be considered to be 'Fine' condition, the catalogue prices are for a slightly lower grade, with 'Fine' examples being worth a premium. In such cases a note to this effect is given in the catalogue, while elsewhere premiums are given for well-centred, lightly cancelled examples.

Stamps graded at less than fine remain collectable and, in the case of more highly priced stamps, will continue to hold a value. Nevertheless, buyers should always bear condition in mind.

The Catalogue in General

Contents. The Catalogue is confined to adhesive postage stamps, including miniature sheets. For particular categories the rules are:

(a) Revenue (fiscal) stamps are listed only where they have been expressly authorised for postal duty.

(b) Stamps issued only precancelled are included, but normally issued stamps available additionally with precancel have no separate precancel listing unless the face value is changed.

(c) Stamps prepared for use but not issued, hitherto accorded full listing, are nowadays foot-noted with a price (where possible).

(d) Bisects (trisects, etc.) are only listed where such usage was officially authorised.

(e) Stamps issued only on first day covers or in presentation packs and not available separately are not listed but may be priced in a footnote.

(f) New printings are only included in this Catalogue where they show a major philatelic variety, such as a change in shade, watermark or paper. Stamps which exist with or without imprint dates are listed separately; changes in imprint dates are mentioned in footnotes.

(g) Official and unofficial reprints are dealt with by footnote.

(h) Stamps from imperforate printings of modern issues which occur perforated are covered by footnotes, but are listed where widely available for postal use.

Exclusions. The following are excluded:

(a) non-postal revenue or fiscal stamps;

(b) postage stamps used fiscally (although prices are now given for some fiscally used high values);

(c) local carriage labels and private local issues;

(d) bogus or phantom stamps;

(e) railway or airline letter fee stamps, bus or road transport company labels or the stamps of private postal companies operating under licence from the national authority;

(f) cut-outs;

(g) all types of non-postal labels and souvenirs;

(h) documentary labels for the postal service, e.g. registration, recorded delivery, air-mail etiquettes, etc.;

(i) privately applied embellishments to official issues and privately commissioned items generally;

(j) stamps for training postal officers.

Full listing. 'Full listing' confers our recognition and implies allotting a catalogue number and (wherever possible) a price quotation.

In judging status for inclusion in the catalogue broad considerations are applied to stamps. They must be issued by a legitimate postal authority, recognised by the government concerned, and must be adhesives valid for proper postal use in the class of service for which they are inscribed. Stamps, with the exception of such categories as postage dues and officials, must be available to the general public, at face value, in reasonable quantities without any artificial restrictions being imposed on their distribution.

For errors and varieties the criterion is legitimate (albeit inadvertent) sale through a postal administration in the normal course of business. Details of provenance are always important; printers' waste and deliberately manufactured material are excluded.

Certificates. In assessing unlisted items due weight is given to Certificates from recognised Expert Committees and, where appropriate, we will usually ask to see them.

Date of issue. Where local issue dates differ from dates of release by agencies, 'date of issue' is the local date. Fortuitous stray usage before the officially intended date is disregarded in listing.

Catalogue numbers. Stamps of each country are catalogued chronologically by date of issue. Subsidiary classes are placed at the end of the country, as separate lists, with a distinguishing letter prefix to the catalogue number, e.g. D for postage due, O for official and E for express delivery stamps.

The catalogue number appears in the extreme left-column. The boldface Type numbers in the next column are merely cross-references to illustrations.

Once published in the Catalogue, numbers are changed as little as possible; really serious renumbering is reserved for the occasions when a complete country or an entire issue is being rewritten. The edition first affected includes cross-reference tables of old and new numbers.

Our catalogue numbers are universally recognised in specifying stamps and as a hallmark of status.

Illustrations. Stamps are illustrated at three-quarters linear size. Stamps not illustrated are the same size and format as the value shown, unless otherwise indicated. Stamps issued only as miniature sheets have the stamp alone illustrated but sheet size is also quoted. Overprints, surcharges, watermarks and postmarks are normally actual size. Illustrations of varieties are often enlarged to show the detail. Stamp booklet covers are illustrated half-size, unless otherwise indicated.

Designers. Designers' names are quoted where known, though space precludes naming every individual concerned in the production of a set. In particular, photographers supplying material are usually named only where they also make an active contribution in the design stage; posed photographs of reigning monarchs are, however, an exception to this rule.

CONTACTING THE CATALOGUE EDITOR

The editor is always interested in hearing from people who have new information which will improve or correct the Catalogue. As a general rule he must see and examine the actual stamps before they can be considered for listing; photographs or photocopies are insufficient evidence.

Submissions should be made in writing to the Catalogue Editor, Stanley Gibbons Publications at the Ringwood office. The cost of return postage for items submitted is appreciated, and this should include the registration fee if required.

Where information is solicited purely for the benefit of the enquirer, the editor cannot undertake to reply if the answer is already contained in these published notes or if return postage is omitted. Written communications are greatly preferred to enquiries by telephone or e-mail and the editor regrets that he or his staff cannot see personal callers without a prior appointment being made. Correspondence may be subject to delay during the production period of each new edition.

The editor welcomes close contact with study circles and is interested, too, in finding reliable local correspondents who will verify and supplement official information in countries where this is deficient.

We regret we do not give opinions as to the genuineness of stamps, nor do we identify stamps or number them by our Catalogue.

TECHNICAL MATTERS

The meanings of the technical terms used in the catalogue will be found in our *Philatelic Terms Illustrated*.

References below to (more specialised) listings are to be taken to indicate, as appropriate, the Stanley Gibbons *Great Britain Specialised Catalogue* in five volumes or the *Great Britain Concise Catalogue*.

1. Printing

Printing errors. Errors in printing are of major interest to the Catalogue. Authenticated items meriting consideration would include: background, centre or frame inverted or omitted; centre or subject transposed; error of colour; error or omission of value; double prints and impressions; printed both sides; and so on. Designs *tête-bêche*, whether intentionally or by accident, are listable. *Se-tenant* arrangements of stamps are recognised in the listings or footnotes. Gutter pairs (a pair of stamps separated by blank margin) are not included in this volume. Colours only partially omitted are not listed. Stamps with embossing omitted are reserved for our more specialised listings.

Printing varieties. Listing is accorded to major changes in the printing base which lead to completely new types. In recess-printing this could be a design re-engraved; in photogravure or photolithography a screen altered in whole or in part. It can also encompass flat-bed and rotary printing if the results are readily distinguishable.

To be considered at all, varieties must be constant.

Early stamps, produced by primitive methods, were prone to numerous imperfections; the lists reflect this, recognising re-entries, retouches, broken frames, misshapen letters, and so on. Printing technology has, however, radically improved over the years, during which time photogravure and lithography have become predominant. Varieties nowadays are more in the nature of flaws and these, being too specialised for this general catalogue, are almost always outside the scope.

In no catalogue, however, do we list such items as: dry prints, kiss prints, doctor-blade flaws, colour shifts or registration flaws (unless they lead to the complete omission of a colour from an individual stamp), lithographic ring flaws, and so on. Neither do we recognise fortuitous happenings like paper creases or confetti flaws.

Overprints (and surcharges). Overprints of different types qualify for separate listing. These include overprints in different colours; overprints from different printing processes such as litho and typo; overprints in totally different typefaces, etc. Major errors in machine-printed overprints are important and listable. They include: overprint inverted or omitted; overprint double (treble, etc.); overprint diagonal; overprint double, one inverted; pairs with one overprint omitted, e.g. from a radical shift to an adjoining stamp; error of colour; error of type fount; letters inverted or omitted, etc. If the overprint is handstamped, few of these would qualify and a distinction is drawn. We continue, however, to list pairs of stamps where one has a handstamped overprint and the other has not.

Albino prints or double prints, one of them being albino (i.e. showing an uninked impression of the printing plate) are listable unless they are particularly common in this form (see the note below Travancore No. 32fa, for example). We do not, however, normally list reversed albino overprints, caused by the accidental or deliberate folding of sheets prior to overprinting (British Levant Nos. 51/8).

Varieties occurring in overprints will often take the form of broken letters, slight differences in spacing, rising spaces, etc. Only the most important would be considered for listing or footnote mention.

Sheet positions. If space permits we quote sheet positions of listed varieties and authenticated data is solicited for this purpose.

De La Rue plates. The Catalogue classifies the general plates used by De La Rue for printing British Colonial stamps as follows:

VICTORIAN KEY TYPE

Die I

1. The ball of decoration on the second point of the crown appears as a dark mass of lines.
2. Dark vertical shading separates the front hair from the bun.
3. The vertical line of colour outlining the front of the throat stops at the sixth line of shading on the neck.
4. The white space in the coil of the hair above the curl is roughly the shape of a pin's head.

Die II

1. There are very few lines of colour in the ball and it appears almost white.

2. A white vertical strand of hair appears in place of the dark shading.

3. The line stops at the eighth line of shading.

4. The white space is oblong, with a line of colour partially dividing it at the left end.

Plates numbered 1 and 2 are both Die I. Plates 3 and 4 are Die II.

GEORGIAN KEY TYPE

Die I

A. The second (thick) line below the name of the country is cut slanting, conforming roughly to the shape of the crown on each side.

B. The labels of solid colour bearing the words "POSTAGE" and "& REVENUE" are square at the inner top corners.

C. There is a projecting "bud" on the outer spiral of the ornament in each of the lower corners.

Die II

A. The second line is cut vertically on each side of the crown.

B. The labels curve inwards at the top.

C. There is no "bud" in this position.

Unless otherwise stated in the lists, all stamps with watermark Multiple Crown CA (w **8**) are Die I while those with watermark Multiple Crown Script CA (w **9**) are Die II. The Georgian Die II was introduced in April 1921 and was used for Plates 10 to 22 and 26 to 28. Plates 23 to 25 were made from Die I by mistake.

2. Paper

All stamps listed are deemed to be on (ordinary) paper of the wove type and white in colour; only departures from this are normally mentioned.

Types. Where classification so requires we distinguish such other types of paper as, for example, vertically and horizontally laid; wove and laid bâtonné; card(board); carton; cartridge; glazed; granite; native; pelure; porous; quadrillé; ribbed; rice; and silk thread.

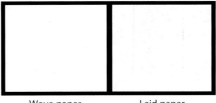

Wove paper   Laid paper

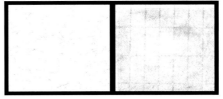

Granite paper   Quadrillé paper

Burelé band

The various makeshifts for normal paper are listed as appropriate. The varieties of double paper and joined paper are recognised. The security device of a printed burelé band on the back of a stamp, as in early Queensland, qualifies for listing.

Descriptive terms. The fact that a paper is handmade (and thus probably of uneven thickness) is mentioned where necessary. Such descriptive terms as "hard" and "soft"; "smooth" and "rough"; "thick", "medium" and "thin" are applied where there is philatelic merit in classifying papers.

Coloured, very white and toned papers. A coloured paper is one that is coloured right through (front and back of the stamp). In the Catalogue the colour of the paper is given in italics, thus:

black/*rose* = black design on rose paper.

Papers have been made specially white in recent years by, for example, a heavy coating of chalk. We do not classify shades of whiteness of paper as distinct varieties. There does exist, however, a type of paper from early days called toned. This is off-white, often brownish or buffish, but it cannot be assigned any definite colour. A toning effect brought on by climate, incorrect storage or gum staining is disregarded here, as this was not the state of the paper when issued.

"Ordinary" and "Chalk-surfaced" papers. The availability of many postage stamps for revenue purposes made necessary some safeguard against the illegitimate re-use of stamps with removable cancellations. This was at first secured by using fugitive inks and later by printing on paper surfaced by coatings containing either chalk or china clay, both of which made it difficult to remove any form of obliteration without damaging the stamp design.

This catalogue lists these chalk-surfaced paper varieties from their introduction in 1905. Where no indication is given, the paper is "ordinary".

The "traditional" method of indentifying chalk-surfaced papers has been that, when touched with a silver wire, a black mark is left on the paper, and the listings in this catalogue are based on that test. However, the test itself is now largely discredited, for, although the mark can be removed by a soft rubber, some damage to the stamp will result from its use.

The difference between chalk-surfaced and pre-war ordinary papers is fairly clear: chalk-surfaced papers being smoother to the touch and showing a characteristic sheen when light is reflected off their surface. Under good magnification tiny bubbles or pock marks can be seen on the surface of the stamp and at the tips of the perforations the surfacing appears "broken". Traces of paper fibres are evident on the surface of ordinary paper and the ink shows a degree of absorption into it.

Initial chalk-surfaced paper printings by De La Rue had a thinner coating than subsequently became the norm. The characteristics described above are less pronounced in these printings.

During and after the Second World War, substitute papers replaced the chalk-surfaced papers, these do not react to the silver test and are therefore classed as "ordinary", although differentiating them without recourse to it is more difficult, for, although the characteristics of the chalk-surfaced paper remained the same, some of the ordinary papers appear much smoother than earlier papers and many do not show the watermark clearly. Experience is the only solution to identifying these, and comparison with stamps whose paper type is without question will be of great help.

Another type of paper, known as "thin striated" was used only for the Bahamas 1s. and 5s. (Nos. 155a, 156a, 171 and 174) and for several stamps of the Malayan states. Hitherto these have been described as "chalk-surfaced" since they gave some reaction to the silver test, but they are much thinner than usual chalk-surfaced papers, with the watermark showing clearly. Stamps on this paper show a slightly 'ribbed' effect when the stamp is held up to the light. Again, comparison with a known striated paper stamp, such as the 1941 Straits Settlements Die II 2c. orange (No. 294) will prove invaluable in separating these papers.

Glazed paper. In 1969 the Crown Agents introduced a new general-purpose paper for use in conjunction with all current printing processes. It generally has a marked glossy surface but the degree varies according to the process used, being more marked in recess-printing stamps. As it does not respond to the silver test this presents a further test where previous printings were on chalky paper. A change of paper to the glazed variety merits separate listing.

Green and yellow papers. Issues of the First World War and immediate postwar period occur on green and yellow papers and these are given separate Catalogue listing. The original coloured papers (coloured throughout) gave way to surface-coloured papers, the stamps having "white backs"; other stamps show one colour on the front and a different one at the back. Because of the numerous variations a grouping of colours is adopted as follows:

Yellow papers

(1) The original *yellow* paper (throughout), usually bright in colour. The gum is often sparse, of harsh consistency and dull-looking. Used 1912–1920.

(2) The *white-backs*. Used 1913–1914.

(3) A bright lemon paper. The colour must have a pronounced greenish tinge, different from the "yellow" in (1). As a rule, the gum on stamps using this lemon paper is plentiful, smooth and shiny, and the watermark shows distinctly. Care is needed with stamps printed in green on yellow paper (1) as it may appear that the paper is this lemon. Used 1914–1916.

(4) An experimental *orange-buff* paper. The colour must have a distinct brownish tinge. It is not to be confused with a muddy yellow (1) nor the misleading appearance (on the surface) of stamps printed in red on yellow paper where an engraved plate has been insufficiently wiped. Used 1918–1921.

(5) An experimental *buff* paper. This lacks the brownish tinge of (4) and the brightness of the yellow shades. The gum is shiny when compared with the matt type used on (4). Used 1919–1920.

(6) A *pale yellow* paper that has a creamy tone to the yellow. Used from 1920 onwards.

Green papers

(7) The original "green" paper, varying considerably through shades of blue-green and yellow-green, the front and back sometimes differing. Used 1912–1916.

(8) The *white backs*. Used 1913–1914.

(9) A paper blue-green on the surface with *pale olive* back. The back must be markedly paler than the front and this and the pronounced olive tinge to the back distinguish it from (7). Used 1916–1920.

(10) Paper with a vivid green surface, commonly called *emerald-green*; it has the olive back of (9). Used 1920.

(11) Paper with *emerald-green* both back and front. Used from 1920 onwards.

3. Perforation and Rouletting

Perforation gauge. The gauge of a perforation is the number of holes in a length of 2 cm. For correct classification the size of the holes (large or small) may need to be distinguished; in a few cases the actual number of holes on each edge of the stamp needs to be quoted.

Measurement. The Gibbons *Instanta* gauge is the standard for measuring perforations. The stamp is viewed against a dark background with the transparent gauge put on top of it. Though the gauge measures to decimal accuracy, perforations read from it are generally quoted in the Catalogue to the nearest half. For example:

Just over perf 12¾ to just under 13¼ = perf 13
Perf 13¼ exactly, rounded up   = perf 13½
Just over perf 13¼ to just under 13¾ = perf 13½
Perf 13¾ exactly, rounded up   = perf 14

However, where classification depends on it, actual quarter-perforations are quoted.

Notation. Where no perforation is quoted for an issue it is imperforate. Perforations are usually abbreviated (and spoken) as follows, though sometimes they may be spelled out for clarity. This notation for rectangular stamps (the majority) applies to diamond shapes if "top" is read as the edge to the top right.

P 14: perforated alike on all sides (read: "perf 14").

P 14×15: the first figure refers to top and bottom, the second to left and right sides (read: "perf 14 by 15"). This is a compound perforation. For an upright triangular stamp the first figure refers to the two sloping sides and second to the base. In inverted triangulars the base is first and the second figure to the sloping sides.

P 14–15: perforation measuring anything between 14 and 15: the holes are irregularly spaced, thus the gauge may vary along a single line or even along a single edge of the stamp (read: "perf 14 to 15").

P 14 *irregular*: perforated 14 from a worn perforator, giving badly aligned holes irregularly spaced (read: "irregular perf 14").

P *comp(ound)* 14×15: two gauges in use but not necessarily on opposite sides of the stamp. It could be one side in one gauge and three in the other; or two adjacent sides with the same gauge. (Read: "perf compound of 14 and 15".) For three gauges or more, abbreviated as "P 12, 14½, 15 *or compound*" for example.

P 14, 14½: perforated approximately 14¼ (read: "perf 14 or 14½"). It does *not* mean two stamps, one perf 14 and the other perf 14½. This obsolescent notation is gradually being replaced in the Catalogue.

Imperf: imperforate (not perforated)

Imperf×P 14: imperforate at top ad bottom and perf 14 at sides.

P 14×*imperf*: perf 14 at top and bottom and imperforate at sides.

Such headings as "P 13×14 (*vert*) and P 14×13 (*horiz*)" indicate which perforations apply to which stamp format—vertical or horizontal.

Some stamps are additionally perforated so that a label or tab is detachable; others have been perforated for use as two halves. Listings are normally for whole stamps, unless stated otherwise.

Imperf×perf

Other terms. Perforation almost always gives circular holes; where other shapes have been used they are specified, e.g. square holes; lozenge perf. Interrupted perfs are brought about by the omission of pins at regular intervals. Perforations merely simulated by being printed as part of the design are of course ignored. With few exceptions, privately applied perforations are not listed.

In the 19th century perforations are often described as clean cut (clean, sharply incised holes), intermediate or rough (rough holes, imperfectly cut, often the result of blunt pins).

Perforation errors and varieties. Authenticated errors, where a stamp normally perforated is accidentally issued imperforate, are listed provided no traces of perforation (blind holes or indentations) remain. They must be provided as pairs, both stamps wholly imperforate, and are only priced in that form.

Stamps imperforate between stamp and sheet margin are not listed in this catalogue, but such errors on Great Britain stamps will be found in the *Great Britain Specialised Catalogue*.

Pairs described as "imperforate between" have the line of perforations between the two stamps omitted.

Imperf between (horiz pair): a horizontal pair of stamps with perfs all around the edges but none between the stamps.

Imperf between (vert pair): a vertical pair of stamps with perfs all around the edges but none between the stamps.

| Imperf between (vertical pair) | Imperf horizontally (vertical pair) |

Where several of the rows have escaped perforation the resulting varieties are listable. Thus:

Imperf vert (horiz pair): a horizontal pair of stamps perforated top and bottom; all three vertical directions are imperf—the two outer edges and between the stamps.

Imperf horiz (vert pair): a vertical pair perforated at left and right edges; all three horizontal directions are imperf—the top, bottom and between the stamps.

Straight edges. Large sheets cut up before issue to post offices can cause stamps with straight edges, i.e. imperf on one side or on two sides at right angles. They are not usually listable in this condition and are worth less than corresponding stamps properly perforated all round. This does not, however, apply to certain stamps, mainly from coils and booklets, where straight edges on various sides are the manufacturing norm affecting every stamp. The listings and notes make clear which sides are correctly imperf.

Malfunction. Varieties of double, misplaced or partial perforation caused by error or machine malfunction are not listable, neither are freaks, such as perforations placed diagonally from paper folds, nor missing holes caused by broken pins.

Types of perforating. Where necessary for classification, perforation types are distinguished.

These include:

Line perforation from one line of pins punching single rows of holes at a time.

Comb perforation from pins disposed across the sheet in comb formation, punching out holes at three sides of the stamp a row at a time.

Harrow perforation applied to a whole pane or sheet at one stroke.

Rotary perforation from toothed wheels operating across a sheet, then crosswise.

Sewing machine perforation. The resultant condition, clean-cut or rough, is distinguished where required.

Pin-perforation is the commonly applied term for pin-roulette in which, instead of being punched out, round holes are pricked by sharp-pointed pins and no paper is removed.

Mixed perforation occurs when stamps with defective perforations are re-perforated in a different gauge.

Punctured stamps. Perforation holes can be punched into the face of the stamp. Patterns of small holes, often in the shape of initial letters, are privately applied devices against pilferage. These (perfins) are outside the scope except for Australia, Canada, Cape of Good Hope, Papua and Sudan where they were used as official stamps by the national administration. Identification devices, when officially inspired, are listed or noted; they can be shapes, or letters or words formed from holes, sometimes converting one class of stamp into another.

Rouletting. In rouletting the paper is cut, for ease of separation, but none is removed. The gauge is measured, when needed, as for perforations. Traditional French terms descriptive of the type of cut are often used and types include:

Arc roulette (percé en arc). Cuts are minute, spaced arcs, each roughly a semicircle.

Cross roulette (percé en croix). Cuts are tiny diagonal crosses.

Line roulette (percé en ligne or en ligne droite). Short straight cuts parallel to the frame of the stamp. The commonest basic roulette. Where not further described, "roulette" means this type.

Rouletted in colour or coloured roulette (percé en lignes colorées or en lignes de coleur). Cuts with coloured edges, arising from notched rule inked simultaneously with the printing plate.

Saw-tooth roulette (percé en scie). Cuts applied zigzag fashion to resemble the teeth of a saw.

Serpentine roulette (percé en serpentin). Cuts as sharply wavy lines.

Zigzag roulette (percé en zigzags). Short straight cuts at angles in alternate directions, producing sharp points on separation. US usage favours "serrate(d) roulette" for this type.

Pin-roulette (originally percé en points and now perforés trous d'epingle) is commonly called pin-perforation in English.

4. Gum

All stamps listed are assumed to have gum of some kind; if they were issued without gum this is stated. Original gum (o.g.) means that which was present on the stamp as issued to the public. Deleterious climates and the presence of certain chemicals can cause gum to crack and, with early stamps, even make the paper deteriorate. Unscrupulous fakers are adept in removing it and regumming the stamp to meet the unreasoning demand often made for "full o.g." in cases where such a thing is virtually impossible.

The gum normally used on stamps has been gum arabic until the late 1960s when synthetic adhesives were introduced. Harrison and Sons Ltd for instance use *polyvinyl alcohol,* known to philatelists as PVA. This is almost invisible except for a slight yellowish tinge which was incorporated to make it possible to see that the stamps have been gummed. It has advantages in hot countries, as stamps do not curl and sheets are less likely to stick together. Gum arabic and PVA are not

distinguished in the lists except that where a stamp exists with both forms this is indicated in footnotes. Our more specialised catalogues provide separate listing of gums for Great Britain.

Self-adhesive stamps are issued on backing paper, from which they are peeled before affixing to mail. Unused examples are priced as for backing paper intact, in which condition they are recommended to be kept. Used examples are best collected on cover or on piece.

5. Watermarks

Stamps are on unwatermarked paper except where the heading to the set says otherwise.

Detection. Watermarks are detected for Catalogue description by one of four methods: (1) holding stamps to the light; (2) laying stamps face down on a dark background; (3) adding a few drops of petroleum ether 40/60 to the stamp laid face down in a watermark tray; (4) by use of the Stanley Gibbons Detectamark, or other equipment, which work by revealing the thinning of the paper at the watermark. (Note that petroleum ether is highly inflammable in use and can damage photogravure stamps.)

Listable types. Stamps occurring on both watermarked and unwatermarked papers are different types and both receive full listing.

Single watermarks (devices occurring once on every stamp) can be modified in size and shape as between different issues; the types are noted but not usually separately listed. Fortuitous absence of watermark from a single stamp or its gross displacement would not be listable.

To overcome registration difficulties the device may be repeated at close intervals *(a multiple watermark),* single stamps thus showing parts of several devices. Similarly, a *large sheet watermark* (or *all-over watermark*) covering numerous stamps can be used. We give informative notes and illustrations for them. The designs may be such that numbers of stamps in the sheet automatically lack watermark: this is not a listable variety. Multiple and all-over watermarks sometimes undergo modifications, but if the various types are difficult to distinguish from single stamps notes are given but not separate listings.

Papermakers' watermarks are noted where known but not listed separately, since most stamps in the sheet will lack them. Sheet watermarks which are nothing more than officially adopted papermakers' watermarks are, however, given normal listing.

Marginal watermarks, falling outside the pane of stamps, are ignored except where misplacement caused the adjoining row to be affected, in which case they may be footnoted.

Watermark errors and varieties. Watermark errors are recognised as of major importance. They comprise stamps intended to be on unwatermarked paper but issued watermarked by mistake, or stamps printed on paper with the wrong watermark. Varieties showing letters omitted from the watermark are also included, but broken or deformed bits on the dandy roll are not listed unless they represent repairs.

Watermark positions. The diagram shows how watermark position is described in the Catalogue. Paper has a side intended for printing and watermarks are usually impressed so that they read normally when looked through from that printed side. However, since philatelists customarily detect watermarks by looking at the back of the stamp the watermark diagram also makes clear what is actually seen.

Illustrations in the Catalogue are of watermarks in normal positions (from the front of the stamps) and are actual size where possible.

Differences in watermark position are collectable varieties. This Catalogue now lists inverted, sideways inverted and reversed watermark varieties on Commonwealth stamps from the 1860s onwards except where the watermark position is completely haphazard.

Great Britain inverted and sideways inverted watermarks can be found in the *Great Britain Specialised Catalogue* and the *Great Britain Concise Catalogue*.

Where a watermark comes indiscriminately in various positions our policy is to cover this by a general note: we do not give separate listings because the watermark position in these circumstances has no particular philatelic importance.

AS DESCRIBED (Read through front of stamp)		AS SEEN DURING WATERMARK DETECTION (Stamp face down and back examined
GvR	Normal	ᴙ v Ɔ
ᴚ v Ɔ	Inverted	Ә ʌ ᴚ
ᴚ v Ɔ	Reversed	GvR
Ә ʌ ᴚ	Reversed and Inverted	ᴚ v Ɔ
GvR (rotated)	Sideways	Ә ʌ ᴚ (rotated)
GvR (rotated)	Sideways Inverted	ᴚ v Ɔ (rotated)

Standard types of watermark. Some watermarks have been used generally for various British possessions rather than exclusively for a single colony. To avoid repetition the Catalogue classifies 11 general types, as under, with references in the headings throughout the listings being given either in words or in the form ("W w **9**") (meaning "watermark type w **9**"). In those cases where watermark illustrations appear in the listings themselves, the respective reference reads, for example, W **153**, thus indicating that the watermark will be found in the normal sequence of illustrations as (type) **153**.

The general types are as follows, with an example of each quoted.

W	Description	Example
w **1**	Large Star	St. Helena No. 1
w **2**	Small Star	Turks Is. No. 4
w **3**	Broad (pointed) Star	Grenada No. 24
w **4**	Crown (over) CC, small stamp	Antigua No. 13
w **5**	Crown (over) CC, large stamp	Antigua No. 31
w **6**	Crown (over) CA, small stamp	Antigua No. 21
w **7**	Crown CA (CA over Crown), large stamp	Sierra Leone No. 54
w **8**	Multiple Crown CA	Antigua No. 41
w **9**	Multiple Script CA	Seychelles No. 158
w **9a**	do. Error	Seychelles No. 158a
w **9b**	do. Error	Seychelles No. 158b
w **10**	V over Crown	N.S.W. No. 327
w **11**	Crown over A	N.S.W. No. 347

CC in these watermarks is an abbreviation for "Crown Colonies" and CA for "Crown Agents". Watermarks w **1**, w **2** and w **3** are on stamps printed by Perkins, Bacon; w **4** onwards on stamps from De La Rue and other printers.

w **1**
Large Star

w **2**
Small Star

w **3**
Broad-pointed Star

Watermark w **1**, *Large Star*, measures 15 to 16 mm across the star from point to point and about 27 mm from centre to centre vertically between stars in the sheet. It was made for long stamps like Ceylon 1857 and St. Helena 1856.

Watermark w **2**, *Small Star* is of similar design but measures 12 to 13½mm from point to point and 24 mm from centre to centre vertically. It was for use with ordinary-size stamps such as Grenada 1863–71.

When the Large Star watermark was used with the smaller stamps it only occasionally comes in the centre of the paper. It is frequently so misplaced as to show portions of two stars above and below and this eccentricity will very often help in determining the watermark.

Watermark w **3**, *Broad-pointed Star*, resembles w **1** but the points are broader.

w **4**
Crown (over) CC

w **5**
Crown (over) CC

Two *Crown (over) CC* watermarks were used:
w **4** was for stamps of ordinary size and w **5** for those of larger size.

w **6**
Crown (over) CA

w **7**
CA over Crown

Two watermarks of *Crown CA* type were used, w **6** being for stamps of ordinary size. The other, w **7**, is properly described as *CA over Crown*. It was specially made for paper on which it was intended to print long fiscal stamps: that some were used postally accounts for the appearance of w **7** in the Catalogue. The watermark occupies twice the space of the ordinary Crown CA watermark, w **6**. Stamps of normal size printed on paper with w **7** watermark show it *sideways*; it takes a horizontal pair of stamps to show the entire watermark.

w **8**
Multiple Crown CA

w **9**
Multiple Script CA

Multiple watermarks began in 1904 with w **8**, *Multiple Crown CA,* changed from 1921 to w **9**, *Multiple Script CA.* On stamps of ordinary size portions of two or three watermarks appear and on the large-sized stamps a greater number can be observed. The change to letters in script character with w **9** was accompanied by a Crown of distinctly different shape.

It seems likely that there were at least two dandy rolls for each Crown Agents watermark in use at any one time with a reserve roll being employed when the normal one was withdrawn for maintenance or repair.

Both the Mult Crown CA and the Mult Script CA types exist with one or other of the letters omitted from individual impressions. It is possible that most of these occur from the reserve rolls as they have only been found on certain issues. The MCA watermark experienced such problems during the early 1920s and the Script over a longer period from the early 1940s until 1951.

During the 1920s damage must also have occurred on one of the Crowns as a substituted Crown has been found on certain issues. This is smaller than the normal and consists of an oval base joined to two upright ovals with a circle positioned between their upper ends. The upper line of the Crown's base is omitted, as are the left and right-hand circles at the top and also the cross over the centre circle.

Substituted Crown

The *Multiple Script CA* watermark, w **9**, is known with two errors, recurring among the 1950–52 printings of several territories. In the first a crown has fallen away from the dandy-roll that impresses the watermark into the paper pulp. It gives w **9a**, *Crown missing*, but this omission has been found in both "Crown only" (*illustrated*) and "Crown CA" rows. The resulting faulty paper was used for Bahamas, Johore, Seychelles and the postage due stamps of nine colonies

w **9a**: Error, Crown missing

w **9b**: Error, St. Edward's Crown

When the omission was noticed a second mishap occurred, which was to insert a wrong crown in the space, giving w **9b**, St. Edward's Crown. This produced varieties in Bahamas, Perlis, St. Kitts-Nevis and Singapore and the incorrect crown likewise occurs in (Crown only) and (Crown CA) rows.

w 10
V over Crown

w 11
Crown over A

Resuming the general types, two watermarks found in issues of several Australian States are: w **10**, *V over Crown*, and w **11**, *Crown over A*.

w 12
Multiple St. Edward's
Crown Block CA

w 13
Multiple PTM

The *Multiple St. Edward's Crown Block CA* watermark, w **12**, was introduced in 1957 and besides the change in the Crown (from that used in Multiple Crown Script CA, w **9**) the letters reverted to block capitals. The new watermark began to appear sideways in 1966 and these stamps are generally listed as separate sets.

The watermark w **13**, *Multiple PTM*, was introduced for new Malaysian issues in November 1961.

w 14
Multiple Crown CA Diagonal

By 1974 the two dandy-rolls the "upright" and the "sideways" for w **12** were wearing out; the Crown Agents therefore discontinued using the sideways watermark one and retained the other only as a stand-by. A new dandy-roll with the pattern of w **14**, *Multiple Crown CA Diagonal,* was introduced and first saw use with some Churchill Centenary issues.

The new watermark had the design arranged in gradually spiralling rows. It is improved in design to allow smooth passage over the paper (the gaps between letters and rows had caused jolts in previous dandy-rolls) and the sharp corners and angles, where fibres used to accumulate, have been eliminated by rounding.

This watermark had no "normal" sideways position amongst the different printers using it. To avoid confusion our more specialised listings do not rely on such terms as "sideways inverted" but describe the direction in which the watermark points.

w 15
Multiple POST OFFICE

During 1981 w **15**, *Multiple POST OFFICE* was introduced for certain issues prepared by Philatelists Ltd, acting for various countries in the Indian Ocean, Pacific and West Indies.

w 16
Multiple Crown Script CA Diagonal

A new Crown Agents watermark was introduced during 1985, w **16**, *Multiple Crown Script CA Diagonal*. This was very similar to the previous w **14**, but showed "CA" in script rather than block letters. It was first used on the omnibus series of stamps commemorating the Life and Times of Queen Elizabeth the Queen Mother.

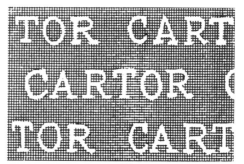

w 17
Multiple CARTOR

Watermark w **17**, *Multiple CARTOR*, was used from 1985 for issues printed by this French firm for countries which did not normally use the Crown Agents watermark.

w **18**

In 2008, following the closure of the Crown Agents Stamp Bureau, a new Multiple Crowns watermark, w **18** was introduced

In recent years the use of watermarks has, to a small extent, been superseded by fluorescent security markings. These are often more visible from the reverse of the stamp (Cook Islands from 1970 onwards), but have occurred printed over the design (Hong Kong Nos. 415/30). In 1982 the Crown Agents introduced a new stock paper, without watermark, known as "C-Kurity" on which a fluorescent pattern of blue rosettes is visible on the reverse, beneath the gum. This paper was used for issues from Gambia and Norfolk Island.

6. Colours

Stamps in two or three colours have these named in order of appearance, from the centre moving outwards. Four colours or more are usually listed as multicoloured.

In compound colour names the second is the predominant one, thus:

orange-red = a red tending towards orange;
red-orange = an orange containing more red than usual.

Standard colours used. The 200 colours most used for stamp identification are given in the Stanley Gibbons Stamp Colour Key. The Catalogue has used the Stamp Colour Key as standard for describing new issues for some years. The names are also introduced as lists are rewritten, though exceptions are made for those early issues where traditional names have become universally established.

Determining colours. When comparing actual stamps with colour samples in the Stamp Colour Key, view in a good north daylight (or its best substitute; fluorescent "colour matching" light). Sunshine is not recommended. Choose a solid portion of the stamp design; if available, marginal markings such as solid bars of colour or colour check dots are helpful. Shading lines in the design can be misleading as they appear lighter than solid colour. Postmarked portions of a stamp appear darker than normal. If more than one colour is present, mask off the extraneous ones as the eye tends to mix them.

Errors of colour. Major colour errors in stamps or overprints which qualify for listing are: wrong colours; one colour inverted in relation to the rest; albinos (colourless impressions), where these have Expert Committee certificates; colours completely omitted, but only on unused stamps (if found on used stamps the information is footnoted) and with good credentials, missing colours being frequently faked.

Colours only partially omitted are not recognised, Colour shifts, however spectacular, are not listed.

Shades. Shades in philately refer to variations in the intensity of a colour or the presence of differing amounts of other colours. They are particularly significant when they can be linked to specific printings. In general, shades need to be quite marked to fall within the scope of this Catalogue; it does not favour nowadays listing the often numerous shades of a stamp, but chooses a single applicable colour name which will indicate particular groups of outstanding shades. Furthermore, the listings refer to colours as issued; they may deteriorate into something different through the passage of time.

Modern colour printing by lithography is prone to marked differences of shade, even within a single run, and variations can occur within the same sheet. Such shades are not listed.

Aniline colours. An aniline colour meant originally one derived from coal-tar; it now refers more widely to colour of a particular brightness suffused on the surface of a stamp and showing clearly on the back.

Colours of overprints and surcharges. All overprints and surcharges are in black unless stated otherwise in the heading or after the description of the stamp.

7. Specimen Stamps

Originally, stamps overprinted SPECIMEN were circulated to postmasters or kept in official records, but after the establishment of the Universal Postal Union supplies were sent to Berne for distribution to the postal administrations of member countries.

During the period 1884 to 1928 most of the stamps of British Crown Colonies required for this purpose were overprinted SPECIMEN in various shapes and sizes by their printers from typeset formes. Some locally produced provisionals were handstamped locally, as were sets prepared for presentation. From 1928 stamps were punched with holes forming the word SPECIMEN, each firm of printers using a different machine or machines. From 1948 the stamps supplied for UPU distribution were no longer punctured.

Stamps of some other Commonwealth territories were overprinted or handstamped locally, while stamps of Great Britain and those overprinted for use in overseas postal agencies (mostly of the higher denominations) bore SPECIMEN overprints and handstamps applied by the Inland Revenue or the Post Office.

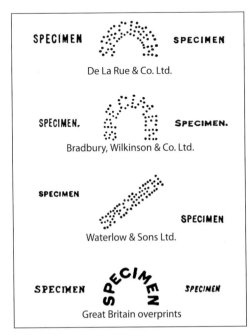

Some of the commoner types of overprints or punctures are illustrated here. Collectors are warned that dangerous forgeries of the punctured type exist.

The *Stanley Gibbons Commonwealth Catalogues* record those Specimen overprints or perforations intended for distribution by the UPU to member countries. In addition the Specimen overprints of Australia and its dependent territories, which were sold to collectors by the Post Office, are also included.

Various Perkins Bacon issues exist obliterated with a "CANCELLED" within an oval of bars handstamp.

Perkins Bacon "CANCELLED"
Handstamp

This was applied to six examples of those issues available in 1861 which were then given to members of Sir Rowland Hill's family. 75 different stamps (including four from Chile) are recorded with this handstamp although others may possibly exist. The unauthorised gift of these "CANCELLED" stamps to the Hill family was a major factor in the loss of the Agent General for the Crown Colonies (the forerunner of the Crown Agents) contracts by Perkins Bacon in the following year. Where examples of these scarce items are known to be in private hands the catalogue provides a price.

For full details of these stamps see *CANCELLED by Perkins Bacon* by Peter Jaffé (published by Spink in 1998).

All other Specimens are outside the scope of this volume.

Specimens are not quoted in Great Britain as they are fully listed in the Stanley Gibbons *Great Britain Specialised Catalogue*.

In specifying type of specimen for individual high-value stamps, "H/S" means handstamped, "Optd" is overprinted and "Perf" is punctured. Some sets occur mixed, e.g. "Optd/Perf". If unspecified, the type is apparent from the date or it is the same as for the lower values quoted as a set.

Prices. Prices for stamps up to £1 are quoted in sets; higher values are priced singly. Where specimens exist in more than one type the price quoted is for the cheapest. Specimen stamps have rarely survived even as pairs; these and strips of three, four or five are worth considerably more than singles.

8. Luminescence

Machines which sort mail electronically have been introduced in recent years. In consequence some countries have issued stamps on fluorescent or phosphorescent papers, while others have marked their stamps with phosphor bands.

The various papers can only be distinguished by ultraviolet lamps emitting particular wavelengths. They are separately listed only when the stamps have some other means of distinguishing them, visible without the use of these lamps. Where this is not so, the papers are recorded in footnotes or headings.

For this catalogue we do not consider it appropriate that collectors be compelled to have the use of an ultraviolet lamp before being able to identify stamps by

our listings. Some experience will also be found necessary in interpreting the results given by ultraviolet. Collectors using the lamps, nevertheless, should exercise great care in their use as exposure to their light is potentially dangerous to the eyes.

Phosphor bands are listable, since they are visible to the naked eye (by holding stamps at an angle to the light and looking along them, the bands appear dark). Stamps existing with or without phosphor bands or with differing numbers of bands are given separate listings. Varieties such as double bands, bands omitted, misplaced or printed on the back are not listed.

Detailed descriptions appear at appropriate places in the listings in explanation of luminescent papers; see, for example, Australia above No. 363, Canada above Nos. 472 and 611, Cook Is. above 249, etc.

For Great Britain, where since 1959 phosphors have played a prominent and intricate part in stamp issues, the main notes above Nos. 599 and 723 should be studied, as well as the footnotes to individual listings where appropriate. In general the classification is as follows.

Stamps with phosphor bands are those where a separate cylinder applies the phosphor after the stamps are printed. Issues with "all-over" phosphor have the "band" covering the entire stamp. Parts of the stamp covered by phosphor bands, or the entire surface for "all-over" phosphor versions, appear matt. Stamps on phosphorised paper have the phosphor added to the paper coating before the stamps are printed. Issues on this paper have a completely shiny surface.

Further particularisation of phosphor – their methods of printing and the colours they exhibit under ultraviolet – is outside the scope. The more specialised listings should be consulted for this information.

9. Coil Stamps

Stamps issued only in coil form are given full listing. If stamps are issued in both sheets and coils the coil stamps are listed separately only where there is some feature (e.g. perforation or watermark sideways) by which singles can be distinguished. Coil stamps containing different stamps *se-tenant* are also listed.

Coil join pairs are too random and too easily faked to permit of listing; similarly ignored are coil stamps which have accidentally suffered an extra row of perforations from the claw mechanism in a malfunctioning vending machine.

10. Stamp Booklets

Stamp booklets are now listed in this catalogue.

Single stamps from booklets are listed if they are distinguishable in some way (such as watermark or perforation) from similar sheet stamps.

Booklet panes are listed where they contain stamps of different denominations *se-tenant*, where stamp-size labels are included, or where such panes are otherwise identifiable. Booklet panes are placed in the listing under the lowest denomination present.

Particular perforations (straight edges) are covered by appropriate notes.

11. Miniature Sheets and Sheetlets

We distinguish between "miniature sheets" and "sheetlets" and this affects the catalogue numbering. An item in sheet form that is postally valid, containing a single stamp, pair, block or set of stamps, with wide, inscribed and/or decorative margins, is a miniature sheet if it is sold at post offices as an indivisible entity. As such the Catalogue allots a single MS number and describes what stamps make it up. The sheetlet or small sheet differs in that the individual stamps are intended to be purchased separately for postal purposes. For sheetlets, all the component postage stamps are numbered individually and the composition explained in a footnote. Note that the definitions refer to post office sale—not how items may be subsequently offered by stamp dealers.

12. Forgeries and Fakes

Forgeries. Where space permits, notes are considered if they can give a concise description that will permit unequivocal detection of a forgery. Generalised warnings, lacking detail, are not nowadays inserted, since their value to the collector is problematic.

Forged cancellations have also been applied to genuine stamps. This catalogue includes notes regarding those manufactured by "Madame Joseph", together with the cancellation dates known to exist. It should be remembered that these dates also exist as genuine cancellations.

For full details of these see *Madame Joseph Forged Postmarks* by Derek Worboys (published by the Royal Philatelic Society London and the British Philatelic Trust in 1994) or *Madame Joseph Revisited* by Brian Cartwright (published by the Royal Philatelic Society London in 2005).

Fakes. Unwitting fakes are numerous, particularly "new shades" which are colour changelings brought about by exposure to sunlight, soaking in water contaminated with dyes from adherent paper, contact with oil and dirt from a pocketbook, and so on. Fraudulent operators, in addition, can offer to arrange: removal of hinge marks; repairs of thins on white or coloured papers; replacement of missing margins or perforations; reperforating in true or false gauges; removal of fiscal cancellations; rejoining of severed pairs, strips and blocks; and (a major hazard) regumming. Collectors can only be urged to purchase from reputable sources and to insist upon Expert Committee certification where there is any kind of doubt.

The Catalogue can consider footnotes about fakes where these are specific enough to assist in detection.

ACKNOWLEDGEMENTS

We are grateful to individual collectors, members of the philatelic trade and specialist societies and study circles for their assistance in improving and extending the Stanley Gibbons range of catalogues. The addresses of societies and study circles relevant to this volume are:

Burma (Myanmar) Philatelic Study Circle
Secretary – Mr M Whittaker, 1 Ecton Leys, Rugby, Warwickshire CV22 5SL

Ceylon Study Circle
Secretary – Mr R W P Frost, 42 Lonsdale Road, Cannington, Bridgwater, Somerset TA5 2JS

Pakistan Study Circle
Membership Secretary – Mr M Robinson, 35 Ethelburt Avenue, Bassett Green, Southampton SO16 3DG

Abbreviations

Printers

A.B.N. Co.	American Bank Note Co, New York.
B.A.B.N.	British American Bank Note Co. Ottawa
B.D.T.	B.D.T. International Security Printing Ltd, Dublin, Ireland
B.W.	Bradbury Wilkinson & Co, Ltd.
Cartor	Cartor S.A., La Loupe, France
C.B.N.	Canadian Bank Note Co, Ottawa.
Continental	Continental Bank Note Co. B.N. Co.
Courvoisier	Imprimerie Courvoisier S.A., La-Chaux-de-Fonds, Switzerland.
D.L.R.	De La Rue & Co, Ltd, London.
Enschedé	Joh. Enschedé en Zonen, Haarlem, Netherlands.
Format	Format International Security Printers Ltd., London
Harrison	Harrison & Sons, Ltd. London
J.W.	John Waddington Security Print Ltd., Leeds
P.B.	Perkins Bacon Ltd, London.
Questa	Questa Colour Security Printers Ltd, London
Walsall	Walsall Security Printers Ltd
Waterlow	Waterlow & Sons, Ltd, London.

General Abbreviations

Alph	Alphabet
Anniv	Anniversary
Comp	Compound (perforation)
Des	Designer; designed
Diag	Diagonal; diagonally
Eng	Engraver; engraved
F.C.	Fiscal Cancellation
H/S	Handstamped
Horiz	Horizontal; horizontally
Imp, Imperf	Imperforate
Inscr	Inscribed
L	Left
Litho	Lithographed
mm	Millimetres
MS	Miniature sheet
N.Y.	New York
Opt(d)	Overprint(ed)
P or P-c	Pen-cancelled
P, Pf or Perf	Perforated
Photo	Photogravure
Pl	Plate
Pr	Pair
Ptd	Printed
Ptg	Printing
R	Right
R.	Row

Recess	Recess-printed
Roto	Rotogravure
Roul	Rouletted
S	Specimen (overprint)
Surch	Surcharge(d)
T.C.	Telegraph Cancellation
T	Type
Typo	Typographed
Un	Unused
Us	Used
Vert	Vertical; vertically
W or wmk	Watermark
Wmk s	Watermark sideways

(†) = Does not exist
(–) (or blank price column) = Exists, or may exist, but no market price is known.
/ between colours means "on" and the colour following is that of the paper on which the stamp is printed.

Colours of Stamps

Bl (blue); blk (black); brn (brown); car, carm (carmine); choc (chocolate); clar (claret); emer (emerald); grn (green); ind (indigo); mag (magenta); mar (maroon); mult (multicoloured); mve (mauve); ol (olive); orge (orange); pk (pink); pur (purple); scar (scarlet); sep (sepia); turq (turquoise); ultram (ultramarine); verm (vermilion); vio (violet); yell (yellow).

Colour of Overprints and Surcharges

(B.) = blue, (Blk.) = black, (Br.) = brown, (C.) = carmine, (G.) = green, (Mag.) = magenta, (Mve.) = mauve, (Ol.) = olive, (O.) = orange, (P.) = purple, (Pk.) = pink, (R.) = red, (Sil.) = silver, (V.) = violet, (Vm.) or (Verm.) = vermilion, (W.) = white, (Y.) = yellow.

Arabic Numerals

As in the case of European figures, the details of the Arabic numerals vary in different stamp designs, but they should be readily recognised with the aid of this illustration.

0	1	2	3	4	5	6	7	8	9

Features Listing

An at-a-glance guide to what's in the Stanley Gibbons catalogues

Area	Feature	Collect British Stamps	Stamps of the World	Thematic Catalogues	Comprehensive Catalogue, Parts 1-22 (including Commonwealth and British Empire Stamps and country catalogues)	Great Britain Concise	Specialised catalogues
General	SG number	√	√	√	√	√	√
General	Specialised Catalogue number						√
General	Year of issue of first stamp in design	√	√	√	√	√	√
General	Exact date of issue of each design				√	√	√
General	Face value information	√	√	√	√	√	√
General	Historical and geographical information	√	√	√	√	√	√
General	General currency information, including dates used	√	√	√	√	√	√
General	Country name	√	√	√	√	√	√
General	Booklet panes				√	√	√
General	Coil stamps				√		√
General	First Day Covers	√				√	√
General	Brief footnotes on key areas of note	√	√	√	√	√	√
General	Detailed footnotes on key areas of note				√	√	√
General	Extra background information				√	√	√
General	Miniature sheet information (including size in mm)	√	√	√	√	√	√
General	Sheetlets				√		
General	Stamp booklets				√	√	√
General	Perkins Bacon "Cancelled"				√		
General	PHQ Cards	√				√	√
General	Post Office Label Sheets				√		
General	Post Office Yearbooks	√				√	√
General	Presentation and Souvenir Packs	√				√	√
General	Se-tenant pairs	√			√	√	√
General	Watermark details - errors, varieties, positions				√	√	√
General	Watermark illustrations	√			√	√	√
General	Watermark types	√			√	√	√
General	Forgeries noted				√		√
General	Surcharges and overprint information	√	√	√	√	√	√
Design and Description	Colour description, simplified		√	√			
Design and Description	Colour description, extended	√			√	√	√
Design and Description	Set design summary information	√	√	√	√	√	√
Design and Description	Designer name				√	√	√
Design and Description	Short design description	√	√	√	√	√	√

Area	Feature	Collect British Stamps	Stamps of the World	Thematic Catalogues	Comprehensive Catalogue, Parts 1-22 (including Commonwealth and British Empire Stamps and country catalogues)	Great Britain Concise	Specialised catalogues
Design and Description	Shade varieties				√	√	√
Design and Description	Type number	√	√		√	√	√
Illustrations	Multiple stamps from set illustrated	√			√	√	√
Illustrations	A Stamp from each set illustrated in full colour (where possible, otherwise mono)	√	√	√	√	√	√
Price	Catalogue used price	√	√	√	√	√	√
Price	Catalogue unused price	√	√	√	√	√	√
Price	Price - booklet panes				√	√	√
Price	Price - shade varieties				√	√	√
Price	On cover and on piece price				√	√	√
Price	Detailed GB pricing breakdown	√			√	√	√
Print and Paper	Basic printing process information	√	√	√	√	√	√
Print and Paper	Detailed printing process information, e.g. Mill sheets				√		√
Print and Paper	Paper information				√		√
Print and Paper	Detailed perforation information	√			√	√	√
Print and Paper	Details of research findings relating to printing processes and history						√
Print and Paper	Paper colour	√	√		√	√	√
Print and Paper	Paper description to aid identification				√	√	√
Print and Paper	Paper type				√	√	√
Print and Paper	Ordinary or chalk-surfaced paper				√	√	√
Print and Paper	Embossing omitted note						√
Print and Paper	Essays, Die Proofs, Plate Descriptions and Proofs, Colour Trials information						√
Print and Paper	Glazed paper				√	√	√
Print and Paper	Gum details				√		√
Print and Paper	Luminescence/Phosphor bands - general coverage	√			√	√	√
Print and Paper	Luminescence/Phosphor bands - specialised coverage						√
Print and Paper	Overprints and surcharges - including colour information	√	√	√	√	√	√
Print and Paper	Perforation/Imperforate information	√	√		√	√	√
Print and Paper	Perforation errors and varieties				√	√	√
Print and Paper	Print quantities				√		√
Print and Paper	Printing errors				√	√	√
Print and Paper	Printing flaws						√
Print and Paper	Printing varieties				√	√	√
Print and Paper	Punctured stamps - where official				√		
Print and Paper	Sheet positions				√	√	√
Print and Paper	Specialised plate number information						√
Print and Paper	Specimen overprints (only for Commonwealth & GB)				√	√	√
Print and Paper	Underprints					√	√
Print and Paper	Visible Plate numbers	√			√	√	√
Print and Paper	Yellow and Green paper listings				√		√
Index	Design index	√			√	√	

International Philatelic Glossary

English	French	German	Spanish	Italian
Agate	Agate	Achat	Agata	Agata
Air stamp	Timbre de la poste aérienne	Flugpostmarke	Sello de correo aéreo	Francobollo per posta aerea
Apple Green	Vert-pomme	Apfelgrün	Verde manzana	Verde mela
Barred	Annulé par barres	Balkenentwertung	Anulado con barras	Sbarrato
Bisected	Timbre coupé	Halbiert	Partido en dos	Frazionato
Bistre	Bistre	Bister	Bistre	Bistro
Bistre-brown	Brun-bistre	Bisterbraun	Castaño bistre	Bruno-bistro
Black	Noir	Schwarz	Negro	Nero
Blackish Brown	Brun-noir	Schwärzlichbraun	Castaño negruzco	Bruno nerastro
Blackish Green	Vert foncé	Schwärzlichgrün	Verde negruzco	Verde nerastro
Blackish Olive	Olive foncé	Schwärzlicholiv	Oliva negruzco	Oliva nerastro
Block of four	Bloc de quatre	Viererblock	Bloque de cuatro	Bloco di quattro
Blue	Bleu	Blau	Azul	Azzurro
Blue-green	Vert-bleu	Blaugrün	Verde azul	Verde azzurro
Bluish Violet	Violet bleuâtre	Bläulichviolett	Violeta azulado	Vioitto azzurrastro
Booklet	Carnet	Heft	Cuadernillo	Libretto
Bright Blue	Bleu vif	Lebhaftblau	Azul vivo	Azzurro vivo
Bright Green	Vert vif	Lebhaftgrün	Verde vivo	Verde vivo
Bright Purple	Mauve vif	Lebhaftpurpur	Púrpura vivo	Porpora vivo
Bronze Green	Vert-bronze	Bronzegrün	Verde bronce	Verde bronzo
Brown	Brun	Braun	Castaño	Bruno
Brown-lake	Carmin-brun	Braunlack	Laca castaño	Lacca bruno
Brown-purple	Pourpre-brun	Braunpurpur	Púrpura castaño	Porpora bruno
Brown-red	Rouge-brun	Braunrot	Rojo castaño	Rosso bruno
Buff	Chamois	Sämisch	Anteado	Camoscio
Cancellation	Oblitération	Entwertung	Cancelación	Annullamento
Cancelled	Annulé	Gestempelt	Cancelado	Annullato
Carmine	Carmin	Karmin	Carmín	Carminio
Carmine-red	Rouge-carmin	Karminrot	Rojo carmín	Rosso carminio
Centred	Centré	Zentriert	Centrado	Centrato
Cerise	Rouge-cerise	Kirschrot	Color de ceresa	Color Ciliegia
Chalk-surfaced paper	Papier couché	Kreidepapier	Papel estucado	Carta gessata
Chalky Blue	Bleu terne	Kreideblau	Azul turbio	Azzurro smorto
Charity stamp	Timbre de bienfaisance	Wohltätigkeitsmarke	Sello de beneficenza	Francobollo di beneficenza
Chestnut	Marron	Kastanienbraun	Castaño rojo	Marrone
Chocolate	Chocolat	Schokolade	Chocolate	Cioccolato
Cinnamon	Cannelle	Zimtbraun	Canela	Cannella
Claret	Grenat	Weinrot	Rojo vinoso	Vinaccia
Cobalt	Cobalt	Kobalt	Cobalto	Cobalto
Colour	Couleur	Farbe	Color	Colore
Comb-perforation	Dentelure en peigne	Kammzähnung, Reihenzähnung	Dentado de peine	Dentellatura e pettine
Commemorative stamp	Timbre commémoratif	Gedenkmarke	Sello conmemorativo	Francobollo commemorativo
Crimson	Cramoisi	Karmesin	Carmesí	Cremisi
Deep Blue	Blue foncé	Dunkelblau	Azul oscuro	Azzurro scuro
Deep bluish Green	Vert-bleu foncé	Dunkelbläulichgrün	Verde azulado oscuro	Verde azzurro scuro
Design	Dessin	Markenbild	Diseño	Disegno

English	French	German	Spanish	Italian
Die	Matrice	Urstempel. Type, Platte	Cuño	Conio, Matrice
Double	Double	Doppelt	Doble	Doppio
Drab	Olive terne	Trüboliv	Oliva turbio	Oliva smorto
Dull Green	Vert terne	Trübgrün	Verde turbio	Verde smorto
Dull purple	Mauve terne	Trübpurpur	Púrpura turbio	Porpora smorto
Embossing	Impression en relief	Prägedruck	Impresión en relieve	Impressione a relievo
Emerald	Vert-eméraude	Smaragdgrün	Esmeralda	Smeraldo
Engraved	Gravé	Graviert	Grabado	Inciso
Error	Erreur	Fehler, Fehldruck	Error	Errore
Essay	Essai	Probedruck	Ensayo	Saggio
Express letter stamp	Timbre pour lettres par exprès	Eilmarke	Sello de urgencia	Francobollo per espresso
Fiscal stamp	Timbre fiscal	Stempelmarke	Sello fiscal	Francobollo fiscale
Flesh	Chair	Fleischfarben	Carne	Carnicino
Forgery	Faux, Falsification	Fälschung	Falsificación	Falso, Falsificazione
Frame	Cadre	Rahmen	Marco	Cornice
Granite paper	Papier avec fragments de fils de soie	Faserpapier	Papel con filamentos	Carto con fili di seta
Green	Vert	Grün	Verde	Verde
Greenish Blue	Bleu verdâtre	Grünlichblau	Azul verdoso	Azzurro verdastro
Greenish Yellow	Jaune-vert	Grünlichgelb	Amarillo verdoso	Giallo verdastro
Grey	Gris	Grau	Gris	Grigio
Grey-blue	Bleu-gris	Graublau	Azul gris	Azzurro grigio
Grey-green	Vert gris	Graugrün	Verde gris	Verde grigio
Gum	Gomme	Gummi	Goma	Gomma
Gutter	Interpanneau	Zwischensteg	Espacio blanco entre dos grupos	Ponte
Imperforate	Non-dentelé	Geschnitten	Sin dentar	Non dentellato
Indigo	Indigo	Indigo	Azul indigo	Indaco
Inscription	Inscription	Inschrift	Inscripción	Dicitura
Inverted	Renversé	Kopfstehend	Invertido	Capovolto
Issue	Émission	Ausgabe	Emisión	Emissione
Laid	Vergé	Gestreift	Listado	Vergato
Lake	Lie de vin	Lackfarbe	Laca	Lacca
Lake-brown	Brun-carmin	Lackbraun	Castaño laca	Bruno lacca
Lavender	Bleu-lavande	Lavendel	Color de alhucema	Lavanda
Lemon	Jaune-citron	Zitrongelb	Limón	Limone
Light Blue	Bleu clair	Hellblau	Azul claro	Azzurro chiaro
Lilac	Lilas	Lila	Lila	Lilla
Line perforation	Dentelure en lignes	Linienzähnung	Dentado en linea	Dentellatura lineare
Lithography	Lithographie	Steindruck	Litografía	Litografia
Local	Timbre de poste locale	Lokalpostmarke	Emisión local	Emissione locale
Lozenge roulette	Percé en losanges	Rautenförmiger Durchstich	Picadura en rombos	Perforazione a losanghe
Magenta	Magenta	Magentarot	Magenta	Magenta
Margin	Marge	Rand	Borde	Margine
Maroon	Marron pourpré	Dunkelrotpurpur	Púrpura rojo oscuro	Marrone rossastro
Mauve	Mauve	Malvenfarbe	Malva	Malva
Multicoloured	Polychrome	Mehrfarbig	Multicolores	Policromo
Myrtle Green	Vert myrte	Myrtengrün	Verde mirto	Verde mirto
New Blue	Bleu ciel vif	Neublau	Azul nuevo	Azzurro nuovo
Newspaper stamp	Timbre pour journaux	Zeitungsmarke	Sello para periódicos	Francobollo per giornali
Obliteration	Oblitération	Abstempelung	Matasello	Annullamento
Obsolete	Hors (de) cours	Ausser Kurs	Fuera de curso	Fuori corso

English	French	German	Spanish	Italian
Ochre	Ocre	Ocker	Ocre	Ocra
Official stamp	Timbre de service	Dienstmarke	Sello de servicio	Francobollo di
Olive-brown	Brun-olive	Olivbraun	Castaño oliva	Bruno oliva
Olive-green	Vert-olive	Olivgrün	Verde oliva	Verde oliva
Olive-grey	Gris-olive	Olivgrau	Gris oliva	Grigio oliva
Olive-yellow	Jaune-olive	Olivgelb	Amarillo oliva	Giallo oliva
Orange	Orange	Orange	Naranja	Arancio
Orange-brown	Brun-orange	Orangebraun	Castaño naranja	Bruno arancio
Orange-red	Rouge-orange	Orangerot	Rojo naranja	Rosso arancio
Orange-yellow	Jaune-orange	Orangegelb	Amarillo naranja	Giallo arancio
Overprint	Surcharge	Aufdruck	Sobrecarga	Soprastampa
Pair	Paire	Paar	Pareja	Coppia
Pale	Pâle	Blass	Pálido	Pallido
Pane	Panneau	Gruppe	Grupo	Gruppo
Paper	Papier	Papier	Papel	Carta
Parcel post stamp	Timbre pour colis postaux	Paketmarke	Sello para paquete postal	Francobollo per pacchi postali
Pen-cancelled	Oblitéré à plume	Federzugentwertung	Cancelado a pluma	Annullato a penna
Percé en arc	Percé en arc	Bogenförmiger Durchstich	Picadura en forma de arco	Perforazione ad arco
Percé en scie	Percé en scie	Bogenförmiger Durchstich	Picado en sierra	Foratura a sega
Perforated	Dentelé	Gezähnt	Dentado	Dentellato
Perforation	Dentelure	Zähnung	Dentar	Dentellatura
Photogravure	Photogravure, Heliogravure	Rastertiefdruck	Fotograbado	Rotocalco
Pin perforation	Percé en points	In Punkten durchstochen	Horadado con alfileres	Perforato a punti
Plate	Planche	Platte	Plancha	Lastra, Tavola
Plum	Prune	Pflaumenfarbe	Color de ciruela	Prugna
Postage Due stamp	Timbre-taxe	Portomarke	Sello de tasa	Segnatasse
Postage stamp	Timbre-poste	Briefmarke, Freimarke, Postmarke	Sello de correos	Francobollo postale
Postal fiscal stamp	Timbre fiscal-postal	Stempelmarke als Postmarke verwendet	Sello fiscal-postal	Fiscale postale
Postmark	Oblitération postale	Poststempel	Matasello	Bollo
Printing	Impression, Tirage	Druck	Impresión	Stampa, Tiratura
Proof	Épreuve	Druckprobe	Prueba de impresión	Prova
Provisionals	Timbres provisoires	Provisorische Marken. Provisorien	Provisionales	Provvisori
Prussian Blue	Bleu de Prusse	Preussischblau	Azul de Prusia	Azzurro di Prussia
Purple	Pourpre	Purpur	Púrpura	Porpora
Purple-brown	Brun-pourpre	Purpurbraun	Castaño púrpura	Bruno porpora
Recess-printing	Impression en taille douce	Tiefdruck	Grabado	Incisione
Red	Rouge	Rot	Rojo	Rosso
Red-brown	Brun-rouge	Rotbraun	Castaño rojizo	Bruno rosso
Reddish Lilac	Lilas rougeâtre	Rötlichlila	Lila rojizo	Lilla rossastro
Reddish Purple	Poupre-rouge	Rötlichpurpur	Púrpura rojizo	Porpora rossastro
Reddish Violet	Violet rougeâtre	Rötlichviolett	Violeta rojizo	Violetto rossastro
Red-orange	Orange rougeâtre	Rotorange	Naranja rojizo	Arancio rosso
Registration stamp	Timbre pour lettre chargée (recommandée)	Einschreibemarke	Sello de certificado lettere	Francobollo per raccomandate
Reprint	Réimpression	Neudruck	Reimpresión	Ristampa
Reversed	Retourné	Umgekehrt	Invertido	Rovesciato
Rose	Rose	Rosa	Rosa	Rosa
Rose-red	Rouge rosé	Rosarot	Rojo rosado	Rosso rosa
Rosine	Rose vif	Lebhaftrosa	Rosa vivo	Rosa vivo
Roulette	Percage	Durchstich	Picadura	Foratura
Rouletted	Percé	Durchstochen	Picado	Forato
Royal Blue	Bleu-roi	Königblau	Azul real	Azzurro reale

English	French	German	Spanish	Italian
Sage green	Vert-sauge	Salbeigrün	Verde salvia	Verde salvia
Salmon	Saumon	Lachs	Salmón	Salmone
Scarlet	Écarlate	Scharlach	Escarlata	Scarlatto
Sepia	Sépia	Sepia	Sepia	Seppia
Serpentine roulette	Percé en serpentin	Schlangenliniger Durchstich	Picado a serpentina	Perforazione a serpentina
Shade	Nuance	Tönung	Tono	Gradazione de colore
Sheet	Feuille	Bogen	Hoja	Foglio
Slate	Ardoise	Schiefer	Pizarra	Ardesia
Slate-blue	Bleu-ardoise	Schieferblau	Azul pizarra	Azzurro ardesia
Slate-green	Vert-ardoise	Schiefergrün	Verde pizarra	Verde ardesia
Slate-lilac	Lilas-gris	Schierferlila	Lila pizarra	Lilla ardesia
Slate-purple	Mauve-gris	Schieferpurpur	Púrpura pizarra	Porpora ardesia
Slate-violet	Violet-gris	Schieferviolett	Violeta pizarra	Violetto ardesia
Special delivery stamp	Timbre pour exprès	Eilmarke	Sello de urgencia	Francobollo per espressi
Specimen	Spécimen	Muster	Muestra	Saggio
Steel Blue	Bleu acier	Stahlblau	Azul acero	Azzurro acciaio
Strip	Bande	Streifen	Tira	Striscia
Surcharge	Surcharge	Aufdruck	Sobrecarga	Soprastampa
Tête-bêche	Tête-bêche	Kehrdruck	Tête-bêche	Tête-bêche
Tinted paper	Papier teinté	Getöntes Papier	Papel coloreado	Carta tinta
Too-late stamp	Timbre pour lettres en retard	Verspätungsmarke	Sello para cartas retardadas	Francobollo per le lettere in ritardo
Turquoise-blue	Bleu-turquoise	Türkisblau	Azul turquesa	Azzurro turchese
Turquoise-green	Vert-turquoise	Türkisgrün	Verde turquesa	Verde turchese
Typography	Typographie	Buchdruck	Tipografia	Tipografia
Ultramarine	Outremer	Ultramarin	Ultramar	Oltremare
Unused	Neuf	Ungebraucht	Nuevo	Nuovo
Used	Oblitéré, Usé	Gebraucht	Usado	Usato
Venetian Red	Rouge-brun terne	Venezianischrot	Rojo veneciano	Rosso veneziano
Vermilion	Vermillon	Zinnober	Cinabrio	Vermiglione
Violet	Violet	Violett	Violeta	Violetto
Violet-blue	Bleu-violet	Violettblau	Azul violeta	Azzurro violetto
Watermark	Filigrane	Wasserzeichen	Filigrana	Filigrana
Watermark sideways	Filigrane couché	Wasserzeichen liegend	Filigrana acostado	Filigrana coricata
Wove paper	Papier ordinaire, Papier uni	Einfaches Papier	Papel avitelado	Carta unita
Yellow	Jaune	Gelb	Amarillo	Giallo
Yellow-brown	Brun-jaune	Gelbbraun	Castaño amarillo	Bruno giallo
Yellow-green	Vert-jaune	Gelbgrün	Verde amarillo	Verde giallo
Yellow-olive	Olive-jaunâtre	Gelboliv	Oliva amarillo	Oliva giallastro
Yellow-orange	Orange jaunâtre	Gelborange	Naranja amarillo	Arancio giallastro
Zig-zag roulette	Percé en zigzag	Sägezahnartiger Durchstich	Picado en zigzag	Perforazione a zigzag

Guide to Entries

A **Country of Issue** – When a country changes its name, the catalogue listing changes to reflect the name change, for example Namibia was formerly known as South West Africa, the stamps in Southern Africa are all listed under Namibia, but split into South West Africa and then Namibia.

B **Country Information** – Brief geographical and historical details for the issuing country.

C **Currency** – Details of the currency, and dates of earliest use where applicable, on the face value of the stamps.

D **Illustration** – Generally, the first stamp in the set. Stamp illustrations are reduced to 75%, with overprints and surcharges shown actual size.

E **Illustration or Type Number** – These numbers are used to help identify stamps, either in the listing, type column, design line or footnote, usually the first value in a set. These type numbers are in a bold type face – **123**; when bracketed (**123**) an overprint or a surcharge is indicated. Some type numbers include a lower-case letter – **123a**, this indicates they have been added to an existing set.

F **Date of issue** – This is the date that the stamp/set of stamps was issued by the post office and was available for purchase. When a set of definitive stamps has been issued over several years the Year Date given is for the earliest issue. Commemorative sets are listed in chronological order. Stamps of the same design, or issue are usually grouped together, for example some of the New Zealand landscapes definitive series were first issued in 2003 but the set includes stamps issued to May 2007.

G **Number Prefix** – Stamps other than definitives and commemoratives have a prefix letter before the catalogue number.
Their use is explained in the text: some examples are A for airmail, D for postage due and O for official stamps.

H **Footnote** – Further information on background or key facts on issues.

I **Stanley Gibbons Catalogue number** – This is a unique number for each stamp to help the collector identify stamps in the listing. The Stanley Gibbons numbering system is universally recognized as definitive.
Where insufficient numbers have been left to provide for additional stamps to a listing, some stamps will have a suffix letter after the catalogue number (for example 214a). If numbers have been left for additions to a set and not used they will be left vacant.
The separate type numbers (in bold) refer to illustrations (see **E**).

J **Colour** – If a stamp is printed in three or fewer colours then the colours are listed, working from the centre of the stamp outwards (see **R**).

K **Design line** – Further details on design variations

L **Key Type** – Indicates a design type on which the stamp is based. These are the bold figures found below each illustration, for example listed in Cameroon, in the West Africa catalogue, is the Key type A and B showing the ex-Kaiser's yacht *Hohenzollern*. The type numbers are also given in bold in the second column of figures alongside the stamp description to indicate the design of each stamp. Where an issue comprises stamps of similar design, the corresponding type number should be taken as indicating the general design. Where there are blanks in the type number column it means that the type of the corresponding stamp

is that shown by the number in the type column of the same issue. A dash (–) in the type column means that the stamp is not illustrated. Where type numbers refer to stamps of another country, e.g. where stamps of one country are overprinted for use in another, this is always made clear in the text.

M **Coloured Papers** – Stamps printed on coloured paper are shown – e.g. "brown/*yellow*" indicates brown printed on yellow paper.

N **Surcharges and Overprints** – Usually described in the headings. Any actual wordings are shown in bold type. Descriptions clarify words and figures used in the overprint. Stamps with the same overprints in different colours are not listed separately. Numbers in brackets after the descriptions are the catalogue numbers of the non-overprinted stamps. The words "inscribed" or "inscription" refer to the wording incorporated in the design of a stamp and not surcharges or overprints.

O **Face value** – This refers to the value of each stamp and is the price it was sold for at the Post Office when issued. Some modern stamps do not have their values in figures but instead it is shown as a letter, for example Great Britain use 1st or 2nd on their stamps as opposed to the actual value.

P **Catalogue Value** – Mint/Unused. Prices quoted for Queen Victoria to King George V stamps are for lightly hinged examples.

Q **Catalogue Value** – Used. Prices generally refer to fine postally used examples. For certain issues they are for cancelled-to-order.

Prices
Prices are given in pence and pounds. Stamps worth £100 and over are shown in whole pounds:

Shown in Catalogue as	Explanation
10	10 pence
1.75	£1.75
15.00	£15
£150	£150
£2300	£2300

Prices assume stamps are in 'fine condition'; we may ask more for superb and less for those of lower quality. The minimum catalogue price quoted is 10p and is intended as a guide for catalogue users. The lowest price for individual stamps purchased from Stanley Gibbons is £1.
Prices quoted are for the cheapest variety of that particular stamp. Differences of watermark, perforation, or other details, often increase the value. Prices quoted for mint issues are for single examples, unless otherwise stated. Those in *se-tenant* pairs, strips, blocks or sheets may be worth more. Where no prices are listed it is either because the stamps are not known to exist (usually shown by a †) in that particular condition, or, more usually, because there is no reliable information on which to base their value.
All prices are subject to change without prior notice and we cannot guarantee to supply all stamps as priced. Prices quoted in advertisements are also subject to change without prior notice.

R **Multicoloured** – Nearly all modern stamps are multicoloured (more than three colours); this is indicated in the heading, with a description of the stamp given in the listing.

S **Perforations** – Please see page xiii for a detailed explanation of perforations.

(A) Country of issue ——•

Bangladesh

In elections during December 1970 the Awami League party won all but two of the seats in the East Pakistan province and, in consequence, held a majority in the National Assembly. On 1 March 1971 the Federal•—— **(B)** Country Information
Government postponed the sitting of the Assembly with the result that unrest spread throughout the eastern province. Pakistan army operations against the dissidents forced the leaders of the League to flee to India from where East Pakistan was proclaimed independent as Bangladesh. In early December the Indian army moved against Pakistan troops in Bangladesh and civilian government was re-established on 22 December 1971.

From 20 December 1971 various Pakistan issues were overprinted by local postmasters, mainly using handstamps. Their use was permitted until 30 April 1973. These are of philatelic interest, but are outside the scope of the catalogue.

(C) Currency ————————•**(Currency. 100 paisa = 1 rupee)**

•—— **(D)** Illustration

5c
N.Z. GOVERNMENT LIFE INSURANCE OFFICE

L 17 •———— **(E)** Illustration or Type number

(F) Date of issue——•**1978** (8 Mar). No. *L* 57 surch with Type *L* **16**. Chalky paper.

L63	L **14**	25c. on 2½c. ultramarine, green and buff	75	1·75

(Des A. G. Mitchell. Litho Harrison)

1981 (3 June). P 14½.

(G) Number prefix——•

L64	L **17**	5c. multicoloured	10	10
L65		10c. multicoloured	10	10
L66		20c. multicoloured	15	15
L67		30c. multicoloured	25	25
L68		40c. multicoloured	30	30
L69		50c. multicoloured	30	45
L64/9 *Set of 6*			1·00	1·25

(H) Footnote ——————• Issues for the Government Life Insurance Department were withdrawn on 1 December 1989 when it became the privatised Tower Corporation.

(Des G. R. Bull and G. R. Smith. Photo Harrison)

1959 (2 Mar). Centenary of Marlborough Province. T **198** and similar horiz designs. W **98** (sideways). P 14½×14.

(I) Stanley Gibbons catalogue number——•

772	2d. green	30	10
773	3d. deep blue	30	10
774	8d. light brown•————	1·25	2·25	•—— **(J)** Colour
772/4 *Set of 3*		1·60	2·25

(K) Design line ——————• Designs:—3d. Shipping wool, Wairau Bar, 1857; 8d. Salt industry, Grassmere.

1915 (12 July). Stamps of German Kamerun. Types *A* and *B*, surch as T **1** (Nos. B1/9) or **2**. (Nos. B10/13) in black or blue.

(L) Key type column ——•

B1•——	*A*	1½d. on 3pf. (No. k7) (B.)	13·00	42·00
		a. Different fount "d"	£150	£350
340	**41**	2d. purple (1903)	£350	£325
341	**28**	3d. bistre-brown (1906)	£700	£600
342	**37**	4d. blue and chestnut/*bluish* (1904)..•——	£300	£350	—— **(M)** Coloured papers
		a. Blue and yellow-brown/*bluish*	£300	£350

(N) Surcharges and overprints ——•

1913 (1 Dec). Auckland Industrial Exhibition. Nos. 387aa, 389, 392 and 40• optd with T **59** by Govt Printer, Wellington.

412	**51**	½d. deep green	20·00•——	55·00	—— **(P)** Catalogue value – Mint
413	**53**	1d. carmine	25·00	48·00
		a. "Feather" flaw	£225	

(O) Face value ——•

414	**52**•——	3d. chestnut	£130	£250
415		6d. carmine	£160	£300•——	•—— **(Q)** Catalogue value – Used
412/15 *Set of 4*			£300	£600

These overprinted stamps were only available for letters in New Zealand and to Australia.

(Des Martin Bailey. Litho Southern Colour Print)

2008 (2 July). Olympic Games, Beijing. T **685** and similar diamond-shaped designs. Multicoloured. Phosphorised paper. P 14½. •——

(R) Multicoloured stamp ——

3056	50c. Type **685**	1·00	85

—— **(S)** Perforations

Stanley Gibbons
Stamp Catalogues

Stamps of the World 1
Simplified Catalogue — 2015 Edition

2015
Stanley Gibbons Stamp Catalogue
COMMONWEALTH & BRITISH EMPIRE STAMPS 1840-1970

New listings of government telegraph stamps
The vital reference work for Commonwealth collectors
Many thousands of price increases
Hundreds of new items listed

We have catalogues to suit every aspect of stamp collecting

Our catalogues cover stamps issued from across the globe - from the Penny Black to the latest issues. Whether you're a specialist in a certain reign or a thematic collector, we should have something to suit your needs. All catalogues include the famous SG numbering system, making it as easy as possible to find the stamp you're looking for.

1 Commonwealth & British Empire Stamps 1840–1970 (117th edition, 2015)

Commonwealth Country Catalogues

Australia & Dependencies (9th Edition, 2014)
Bangladesh, Pakistan & Sri Lanka (3rd edition, 2015)
Belize, Guyana, Trinidad & Tobago (2nd edition, 2013)
Brunei, Malaysia & Singapore (4th edition, 2013)
Canada (5th edition, 2014)
Central Africa (2nd edition, 2008)
Cyprus, Gibraltar & Malta (4th edition, 2014)
East Africa with Egypt & Sudan (3rd edition, 2014)
Eastern Pacific (2nd edition, 2011)
Falkland Islands (6th edition, 2013)
Hong Kong (4th edition, 2013)
India (including Convention & Feudatory States) (4th edition, 2013)
Indian Ocean (2nd edition, 2012)
Ireland (5th edition, 2015)
Leeward Islands (2nd edition, 2012)
New Zealand (5th edition, 2014)
Northern Caribbean, Bahamas & Bermuda (3rd edition, 2013)
St. Helena & Dependencies (5th edition, 2014)
Southern Africa (2nd edition, 2008)
Southern & Central Africa (2nd edition, 2014)
West Africa (2nd edition, 2012)
Western Pacific (3rd edition, 2014)
Windward Islands & Barbados (2nd edition, 2012)

Stamps of the World 2015

Volume 1 Abu Dhabi – Charkhari
Volume 2 Chile – Georgia
Volume 3 German Commands – Jasdan
Volume 4 Jersey – New Republic
Volume 5 New South Wales – Singapore
Volume 6 Sirmoor – Zululand

We also produce a range of thematic catalogues for use with Stamps of the World.

Great Britain Catalogues

Collect British Stamps (65th edition, 201)
Collect Channel Islands & Isle of Man (29th edition, 2014)
Great Britain Concise Stamp Catalogu (29th edition, 2014)

Great Britain Specialised

Volume 1 Queen Victoria (16th edition, 2012)
Volume 2 King Edward VII to King George VI (13th edition, 2009)
Volume 3 Queen Elizabeth II Pre-decimal issues (12th edition, 2011)
Volume 4 Queen Elizabeth II Decima Definitive Issues – Part 1 (10th edition, 2008)
Queen Elizabeth II Decimal Definitive Issues – Part 2 (10th edition, 2010)

Foreign Countries

2 Austria & Hungary (8th edition, 201)
3 Balkans (5th edition, 2009)
4 Benelux (6th edition, 2010)
5 Czech Republic, Slovakia & Polan (7th edition, 2012)
6 France (7th edition, 2010)
7 Germany (11th edition, 2014)
8 Italy & Switzerland (8th edition, 20)
9 Portugal & Spain (6th edition, 20)
10 Russia (7th edition, 2014)
11 Scandinavia (7th edition, 2013)
15 Central America (3rd edition, 200)
16 Central Asia (4th edition, 2006)
17 China (10th edition, 2014)
18 Japan & Korea (5th edition, 2008)
19 Middle East (7th edition, 2009)
20 South America (4th edition, 2008)
21 South-East Asia (5th edition, 201)
22 United States of America (8th edition, 2015)

To order, call **01425 472 363** or for our full range of catalogues, **visit www.stanleygibbons.com**

Bangladesh

In elections during December 1970 the Awami League party won all but two of the seats in the East Pakistan province and, in consequence, held a majority in the National Assembly. On 1 March 1971 the Federal Government postponed the sitting of the Assembly with the result that unrest spread throughout the eastern province. Pakistan army operations against the dissidents forced the leaders of the League to flee to India from where East Pakistan was proclaimed independent as Bangladesh. In early December the Indian army moved against Pakistan troops in Bangladesh and civilian government was re-established on 22 December 1971.

From 20 December 1971 various Pakistan issues were overprinted in English, Bengali or a combination of both by local postmasters, mainly using handstamps. Their use was permitted until 30 April 1973. These are of philatelic interest, but are outside the scope of the catalogue.

(Currency. 100 paisa = 1 rupee)

1 Map of Bangladesh

(2)

(Des B. Mullick. Litho Format)

1971 (29 July). Vert designs as T **1**. P 14×14½.
1	10p. indigo-blue, red-orange and pale blue.		20	10
2	20p. multicoloured		20	10
3	50p. multicoloured		20	10
4	1r. multicoloured		30	10
5	2r. deep greenish blue, light new blue and rose-magenta		30	35
6	3r. apple-green, dull yellowish green and greenish blue		30	65
7	5r. multicoloured		50	1·25
8	10r. gold, rose-magenta and deep greenish blue		1·00	2·25
1/8	*Set of 8*		2·75	4·25

Designs:—20p. "Dacca University Massacre"; 50p. "75 Million People", 1r. Flag of Independence 2r. Ballot box; 3r. Broken chain 5r. Shaikh Mujibur Rahman; 10r. "Support Bangla Desh" and map.

Nos. 1/8 exist imperforate from stock dispersed by the liquidator of Format International Security Printers Ltd.

1971 (20 Dec). Liberation. Nos. 1 and 7/8 optd with T **2**.
9	10p. indigo-blue, red-orange and pale blue.		25	10
10	5r. multicoloured (O.)		2·25	2·50
11	10r. gold, rose-magenta and deep greenish blue		3·25	4·00
9/11	*Set of 3*		5·25	6·00

The remaining values of the original issue were also overprinted and placed on sale in Great Britain but were not issued in Bangladesh. (*Price for the complete set £6 un.*).

On 1 February 1972 the Agency placed on sale a further issue in the flag, map and Shaikh Mujibur designs in new colours and new currency (100 paisas = 1 taka). This issue proved to be unacceptable to the Bangladesh authorities who declared them to be invalid for postal purposes, no supplies being sold within Bangladesh. The values comprise 1, 2, 3, 5, 7, 10, 15, 20, 25, 40, 50, 75p., 1, 2 and 5t. (*Price for set of 15 un.*, £1.).

(New Currency. 100 paisa = 1 taka)

3 "Martyrdom"

4 Flames of Independence

(Des and photo Indian Security Printing Press, Nasik)

1972 (21 Feb). In Memory of the Martyrs. P 13.
12	**3**	20p. dull green and rose-red	30	50

(Des N. Kundu. Photo Indian Security Printing Press, Nasik)

1972 (26 Mar). First Anniv of Independence. P 13.
13	**4**	20p. brown-lake and red	30	10
14		60p. dull ultramarine and red	50	45
15		75p. reddish violet and red	55	55
13/15	*Set of 3*		1·25	1·00

5 Doves of Peace

6 "Homage to Martyrs"

(Litho B.W.)

1972 (16 Dec). Victory Day. P 13½.
16	**5**	20p. multicoloured	20	10
17		60p. multicoloured	30	55
18		75p. multicoloured	30	55
16/18	*Set of 3*		70	1·10

(Des K. Mustafa. Litho B.W.)

1973 (25 Mar). In Memory of the Martyrs. P 13½.
19	**6**	20p. multicoloured	15	10
20		60p. multicoloured	30	40
21		1t.35 multicoloured	65	1·75
19/21	*Set of 3*		1·10	2·00

7 Embroidered Quilt

8 Courts of Justice

(Litho B.W.)

1973 (30 Apr). T **7/8** and similar designs. P 14½×14 (50p., 1t., 5t., 10t.) or 14×14½ (others).
22		2p. black	10	1·00
23		3p. blue-green	50	1·50
		a. Imperf (pair)		
24		5p. light brown	50	10
25		10p. slate-black	30	10
26		20p. yellow-green	50	10
27		25p. bright reddish mauve	3·25	10
28		50p. bright purple	2·25	30
29		60p. greenish blue	2·25	1·25
30		75p. yellow-orange	1·25	1·25
31		90p. orange-brown	1·50	2·00
32		1t. light violet	6·00	30
33		2t. olive-green	6·00	1·25
34		5t. grey-blue	7·50	2·75
35		10t. rose	12·00	6·00
22/35	*Set of 14*		40·00	16·00

Designs: As T **7**—3p. Jute field; 5p. Jack fruit; 10p. Bullocks ploughing; 20p. Rakta jaba (flower); 25p. Tiger; 60p. Bamboo grove; 75p. Plucking tea; 90p. Handicrafts. Horiz as T **8**—5t. Hilsa (fish). Horiz as T **8**—5t. Fishing boat; 10t. Sixty-dome mosque, Bagerhat. Vert as T **8**—2t. Date tree.

See also Nos. 49/51*a*, 64/75 and 711.

9 Flame Emblem

10 Family, Map and Graph

(Des A. Karim. Litho B.W.)

1973 (10 Dec). 5th Anniv of Declaration of Human Rights. P 13½.
36	**9**	10p. multicoloured	10	10
37		1t.25 multicoloured	20	20

(Des A. Karim. Litho B.W.)

1974 (10 Feb). First Population Census. P 13½.
38	**10**	20p. multicoloured	10	10
39		25p. multicoloured	10	10
40		75p. multicoloured	20	20
38/40		Set of 3	30	30

11 Copernicus and Heliocentric System   **12** U.N. H.Q. and Bangladesh Flag

(Des K. Mustafa. Litho B.W.)

1974 (22 July). 500th Birth Anniv of Copernicus. P 13½.
41	**11**	25p. yellow-orange, bluish violet and black	10	10
		a. Imperf (pair)	30·00	
42		75p. orange, yellow-green and black	25	50

(Des A. Karim. Litho B.W.)

1974 (25 Sept). Bangladesh's Admission to the U.N. Multicoloured; frame colour given. P 13½.
43	**12**	25p. light lilac	10	10
44		1t. light greenish blue	35	40

13 U.P.U. Emblem   **14** Courts of Justice

(Des K. Mustafa. Litho B.W.)

1974 (9 Oct). Centenary of Universal Postal Union. T **13** and similar vert designs. Multicoloured; country name on a yellow background (Nos. 45/6) or a blue background (Nos. 47/8). P 13½.
45		25p. Type **13**	10	10
46		1t.25 Mail runner	20	15
47		1t.75 Type **13**	20	25
48		5t. As 1t.25	80	1·60
45/8		Set of 4	1·10	1·75

The above exist imperforate in a miniature sheet from a restricted printing.

1974–76. Nos. 32/5 redrawn with revised value inscriptions as T **14**.
49	1t. light violet	1·50	10
50	2t. olive	3·00	2·00
51	5t. grey-blue (1975)	7·00	70
51a	10t. rose (1976)	26·00	16·00
49/51a	Set of 4	35·00	17·00

For these designs redrawn to 32×20 or 20×32 mm and perforated 14½ see Nos. 72/5, and for the 10t. size 35×22 mm with the same perforation see No. 711.

15 Royal Bengal Tiger   **16** Symbolic Family

(Des and litho B.W.)

1974 (4 Nov). Wildlife Preservation. T **15** and similar vert designs. Multicoloured. P 13½.
52		25p. Type **15**	60	10
53		50p. Tiger whelp	80	70
54		2t. Tiger in stream	1·40	3·25
52/4		Set of 3	2·50	3·50

(Des A. Karim. Litho B.W.)

1974 (30 Dec). World Population Year. "Family Planning for All". T **16** and similar multicoloured designs. P 14.
55		25p. Type **16**	15	10
56		70p. Village family	25	50
57		1t.25 Heads of family (horiz)	40	1·10
55/7		Set of 3	70	1·50

The Bengali numerals on the 70p. resemble "90".

17 Radar Antenna   **18** Woman's Head

(Des and litho B.W.)

1975 (14 June). Inauguration of Betbunia Satellite Earth Station. P 13½.
58	**17**	25p. black, silver and dull red	10	10
59		1t. black, silver and ultramarine	20	70

(Des A. Karim. Litho Asher & Co, Melbourne)

1975 (31 Dec). International Women's Year. P 15.
60	**18**	50p. multicoloured	10	10
61		2t. multicoloured	25	1·00
		a. Vert pair, bottom stamp imperf	£100	

(Litho Asher & Co., Melbourne)

1976 (15 Jan)–**77**. As Nos. 24/31 and 49/51a but redrawn in smaller size and colours changed (5, 75p.). P 14½×15 (50p.), 14½ (1 to 10t.) or 15×14½ (others).

(a) 23×18 mm (50p.) or 18×23 mm (others)
64	5p. deep yellow-green (11.2.76)	20	10
	a. Imperf (pair)	10·00	
65	10p. slate-black (28.4.76)	20	10
66	20p. yellow-green	1·75	10
	a. Imperf (pair)	10·00	
67	25p. bright reddish mauve	6·00	10
	a. Imperf (pair)	10·00	
68	50p. light purple (8.6.76)	3·75	10
69	60p. greenish slate (10.11.76)	40	40
70	75p. yellow-olive (10.11.76)	1·75	3·25
71	90p. orange-brown (10.11.76)	40	60

(b) 20×32 mm (2t.) or 32×20 mm (others)
72	1t. light violet	2·00	10
73	2t. olive-green (8.6.76)	9·50	10
	a. Imperf (pair)	35·00	
74	5t. grey-blue (10.11.76)	3·25	3·00
75	10t. rose (25.2.77)	13·00	5·50
64/75	Set of 12	38·00	11·50

For the 10t. in this perforation, but redrawn to 35×22 mm see No. 711.

19 Telephones, 1876 and 1976   **20** Eye and Nutriments

(Des A. Karim. Litho Asher & Co, Melbourne)

1976 (10 Mar). Telephone Centenary. T **19** and similar vert design. P 15.
76   2t. 25 multicoloured 25   20
77   5t. dull vermilion, apple-green and black... 55   65
   Design:—5t. Alexander Graham Bell.

(Des A. Karim. Litho Asher & Co, Melbourne)

1976 (17 Apr). Prevention of Blindness. P 15.
78   **20**   30p. multicoloured 50   10
79   2t.25 multicoloured .... 1·40   2·75

21 Liberty Bell

(Des E. Roberts. Photo Heraclio Fournier)

1976 (29 May). Bicentenary of American Revolution. T **21** and similar horiz designs. Multicoloured. P 14.
80   30p. Type **21** 10   10
81   2t.25 Statue of Liberty 20   25
82   5t. *Mayflower* 40   40
83   10t. Mount Rushmore 40   70
80/3 *Set of 4* .... 1·00   1·25
MS84 167×95 mm. Nos. 80/3. .... 1·00   2·50
   No. **MS**84 also exists imperforate from a restricted printing.

22 Industry, Science, Agriculture and Education   23 Hurdling

(Des K. Mustafa. Litho Asher & Co, Melbourne)

1976 (29 July). 25th Anniv of the Colombo Plan. P 15.
85   **22**   30p. multicoloured 15   10
86   2t.25 multicoloured 35   1·00

(Des K. Mustafa. Litho Asher & Co, Melbourne)

1976 (29 Nov). Olympic Games, Montreal. T **23** and similar multicoloured designs. P 14½.
87   25p. Type **23** 10   10
88   30p. Running (*horiz*) 10   10
   a. Imperf (pair)
89   1t. Pole vault 15   10
90   2t.25 Swimming (*horiz*) 30   45
91   3t.50 Gymnastics 55   1·25
92   5t. Football .... 1·00   2·00
87/92 *Set of 6* .... 2·00   3·50

24 The Blessing   25 Qazi Nazrul Islam (poet)

(Des and litho Harrison)

1977 (7–17 Feb). Silver Jubilee. T **24** and similar vert designs. Multicoloured. P 14×14½.
93   30p. Type **24** 10   10

94   2t.25 Queen Elizabeth II 20   25
95   10t. Queen Elizabeth and Prince Philip... 70   85
93/5 *Set of 3* 80   1·00
MS96 114×127 mm. Nos. 93/5. P 14½ (17 Feb)...... 80   1·50

(Des K. Mustafa. Litho Harrison)

1977 (29 Aug). Qazi Nazrul Islam Commemoration. T **25** and similar design. P 14.
97   40p. blue-green and black................. 10   10
98   2t.25 sepia, stone and chestnut......... 50   30
   Design: Horiz—2t.25, Head and shoulders portrait.

26 Bird with Letter

(Des A. Karim. Litho Harrison)

1977 (29 Sept). 15th Anniv of Asian-Oceanic Postal Union. P 14.
99   **26**   30p. light rose, new blue and dull green................. 10   10
100   2t.25 light rose, new blue and light grey.. 20   25

27 Sloth Bear   28 Campfire and Tent

(Des K. Mustafa. Litho Harrison)

1977 (9 Nov). Animals. T **27** and similar multicoloured designs. P 13.
101   40p. Type **27** 10   10
102   1t. Spotted Deer 10   10
103   2t.25 Leopard (*horiz*) 20   20
104   3t.50 Gaur (*horiz*) 20   35
105   4t. Indian Elephant (*horiz*) 70   50
106   5t. Tiger (*horiz*) 80   75
101/6 *Set of 6* .... 1·90   1·75
   The Bengali numerals on the 40p. resemble "80", and that on the 4t. resembles "8".

(Des A. Karim. Litho Harrison)

1978 (22 Jan). First National Scout Jamboree. T **28** and similar designs. P 13.
107   40p. red, deep blue and light blue.................. 25   10
108   3t.50 carmine, deep blue and green 80   30
109   5t. reddish lilac, deep blue and bright green................. 95   45
107/9 *Set of 3* .... 1·75   70
   Designs: Horiz—3t.50, Scout stretcher-team. Vert—5t. Scout salute.

29 *Michelia champaca*

(Des and litho Harrison)

1978 (29 Apr). Flowers. T **29** and similar horiz designs. Multicoloured. P 14.
110   40p. Type **29** 10   10
111   1t. *Cassia fistula* 20   15
112   2t.25 *Delonix regia* 25   30
113   3t.50 *Nymphaea nouchali* 30   60
114   4t. *Butea monosperma* 30   80
115   5t. *Anthocephalus indicus* 30   85
110/15 *Set of 6* .... 1·25   2·40

30 St. Edward's Crown
and Sceptres

(Des and litho Harrison)

1978 (20 May). 25th Anniv of Coronation. T **30** and similar vert
designs. Multicoloured. P 14.

116	40p. Type **30**		10	10
117	3t.50 Balcony scene		15	30
118	5t. Queen Elizabeth and Prince Philip		25	50
119	10t. Coronation portrait by Cecil Beaton		45	80
116/19 *Set of 4*			80	1·50
MS120 89×121 mm. Nos. 116/19. P 14½			1·10	1·50

31 Sir Alan Cobham's de Havilland
DH.50J

(Des and litho Harrison)

1978 (15 June). 75th Anniv of Powered Flight. T **31** and similar horiz
designs. P 13.

121	40p. multicoloured		15	10
122	2t.25 blackish brown and light new blue		25	45
123	3t.50 blackish brown and yellow		25	65
124	5t. multicoloured		2·50	3·50
121/4 *Set of 4*			2·75	4·25

Designs:—2t.25, Captain Hans Bertram's Junkers W.33 seaplane
Atlantis; 3t.50, Wright brothers' *Flyer III*; 5t. Concorde.

32 Fenchuganj   33 Tawaf-E-Ka'aba,
Fertilizer Factory   Mecca

(Des P. Mandel (5p.), A. Karim (10p.), Harrison (30, 50p., 1t.). Photo
Harrison)

1978 (6 Nov)–**82**. Designs as T **32**. P 14½.

125	5p. deep brown (25.3.79)		10	10
126	10p. turquoise-blue		10	10
127	15p. orange (1.8.80)		10	10
128	20p. brown-red (15.12.79)		10	10
129	25p. grey-blue (1982)		15	10
130	30p. deep green (10.12.80)		3·50	50
131	40p. maroon (15.12.79)		30	10
132	50p. black (1981)		5·50	1·50
134	80p. brown (1.8.80)		20	10
136	1t. reddish violet (6.81)		9·00	10
137	2t. dull ultramarine (21.10.81)		4·00	3·25
125/37 *Set of 11*			21·00	5·00

Designs: Horiz—5p. Lalbag Fort; 25p. Jute on a boat; 40p., 50p.
Baitul Mukarram Mosque; 1t. Dotara (musical instrument); 2t.
Karnaphuli Dam. Vert—15p. Pineapple; 20p. Bangladesh gas; 30p.
Banana Tree; 80p. Mohastan Garh.

(Des A. Karim. Litho J.W.)

1978 (9 Nov). Holy Pilgrimage to Mecca. T **33** and similar
multicoloured design. P 13.

140	40p. Type **33**		20	10
141	3t.50 Pilgrims in Wuquf, Arafat (*horiz*)		60	45

34 Jasim Uddin

(Des P. Mandel. Litho J.W.)

1979 (14 Mar). Third Death Anniv of Jasim Uddin (poet). P 14.

142	**34**	40p. multicoloured	20	50

35 Moulana Abdul   36 Sir Rowland Hill
Hamid Khan Bhashani

(Des P. Mandel. Litho Harrison)

1979 (17 Nov). Third Death Anniv of Moulana Abdul Hamid Khan
Bhashani (national leader). P 12½.

143	**35**	40p. multicoloured	40	30

(Des A. Karim. Litho Harrison)

1979 (26 Nov). Death Centenary of Sir Rowland Hill. T **36** and similar
designs. P 14.

144	40p. turquoise-blue, Venetian red and pale			
		turquoise-blue	10	10
145	3t.50 multicoloured		35	30
146	10t. multicoloured		80	1·00
144/6 *Set of 3*			1·10	1·25
MS147 176×96 mm. Nos. 144/6			1·75	2·50

Designs: Horiz—3t.50, 1971 10p. definitive stamp and Sir Rowland
Hill; 10t. 1974 1t.25, Centenary of U.P.U. commemorative stamp and
Sir Rowland Hill.

37 Children with Hoops   38 Rotary International
Emblem

(Des P. Mandel. Litho Harrison)

1979 (17 Dec). International Year of the Child. T **37** and similar vert
designs. Multicoloured. P 14×14½.

148	40p. Type **37**		10	10
149	3t.50 Child with kite		35	35
150	5t. Children playing		50	50
148/50 *Set of 3*			80	80
MS151 170×120 mm. Nos. 148/50. P 14½			1·00	2·50

(Des P. Mandel. Litho Rosenbaum Bros, Vienna)

1980 (23 Feb). 75th Anniv of Rotary International. T **38** and similar
vert design showing club emblem. P 13½×14.

152	40p. black, vermilion and bistre-yellow		20	10
153	5t. gold and bright blue		65	1·25

39 Canal Digging

(Des A. Karim. Litho Rosenbaum Bros, Vienna)

1980 (27 Mar). Mass Participation in Canal Digging. P 14×13½.
154   **39**   40p. multicoloured 40   30

40 A. K. Fazlul Huq

(Des P. Mandal. Litho Rosenbaum Bros, Vienna)

1980 (27 Apr). 18th Death Anniv of A. K. Fazlul Huq (national leader). P 13½×14.
155   **40**   40p. multicoloured 30   30
On the face value the Bengali numerals resemble "80".

41 Early forms of Mail Transport   **42** Dome of the Rock

(Des A. Karim. Litho Rosenbaum Bros, Vienna)

1980 (5 May). London 1980 International Stamp Exhibition. T **41** and similar horiz design. Multicoloured. P 14×13½.
156   1t. Type **41** 15   10
157   10t. Modern forms of mail transport .... 1·25   1·60
MS158 140×95 mm. Nos. 156/7 .... 1·40   2·00

(Des A. Karim. Litho Harrison)

1980 (21 Aug). Palestinian Welfare. P 14½.
159   **42**   50p. deep mauve .... 1·00   30
A similar stamp in grey, showing a Palestinian guerilla and the Dome of the Rock, printed by the State Printing Works, Moscow, was prepared in 1980, but not issued due to errors in the Arabic inscription. Quantities of the stamp were subsequently reported stolen. Examples were also issued by Comilla and Kotbari post offices on 27 September 1992 without authority.

43 Outdoor Class

(Des P. Mandal. Litho Rosenbaum Bros, Vienna)

1980 (23 Aug). Education. P 13½×14.
160   **43**   50p. multicoloured 40   30

44 Beach Scene   **45** Mecca

(Des A. Karim. Litho Rosenbaum Bros, Vienna)

1980 (27 Sept). World Tourism Conference, Manila. T **44** and similar horiz design showing different beach scene. P 14.
161   50p. multicoloured 35   50
    a. Horiz pair. Nos. 161/2 .... 1·00   1·60
162   5t. multicoloured 65   1·10

MS163 140×88 mm. Nos. 161/2 .... 1·00   1·60
Nos. 161/2 were printed together, *se-tenant*, in horizontal pairs throughout the sheet.

(Des A. Karim. Litho Rosenbaum Bros, Vienna)

1980 (11 Nov). Moslem Year 1400 A.H. Commemoration. P 14×13½.
164   **45**   50p. multicoloured 50   20

46 Begum Roquiah   **47** Spotted Deer and Scout Emblem

(Des A. Karim. Litho Rosenbaum Bros, Vienna)

1980 (9 Dec). Birth Centenary of Begum Roquiah (campaigner for women's rights). P 14.
165   **46**   50p. multicoloured 10   10
166   2t. multicoloured 35   20

(Des A. Karim. Litho Rosenbaum Bros, Vienna)

1981 (1 Jan). Fifth Asia-Pacific/second Bangladesh Scout Jamboree. P 13½×14.
167   **47**   50p. multicoloured 25   15
168   5t. multicoloured 75   2·00

2nd.
CENSUS
1981
(**48**)

1981 (6 Mar). Second Population Census. Nos. 38/40 optd with T **48**.
169   **10**   20p. multicoloured 10   10
170   25p. multicoloured 10   10
171   75p. multicoloured 20   30
169/71 *Set of 3* 30   40

49 Queen Elizabeth the Queen Mother   **50** Revolutionary with Flag and Sub-machine-gun

(Des R. Granger Barrett. Litho Rosenbaum Bros, Vienna)

1981 (16 Mar). 80th Birthday of Queen Elizabeth the Queen Mother. P 13½×14.
172   **49**   1t. multicoloured 15   15
173   15t. multicoloured .... 1·40   2·50
MS174 95×73 mm. Nos. 172/3 .... 1·40   2·50

(Des P. Mandal. Litho Rosenbaum Bros, Vienna)

1981 (26 Mar). Tenth Anniv of Independence. T **50** and similar vert design. Multicoloured. P 13½×14.
175   50p. Type **50** 15   10
176   2t. Figures on map symbolising Bangladesh life-style 25   45

51 Bangladesh Village and Farm Scenes

(Des A. Karim. Litho Rosenbaum Bros, Vienna)

1981 (1 Sept). U.N. Conference on Least Developed Countries, Paris. P 14×13½.

177	**51**	50p. multicoloured	45	15

52 Kemal Atatürk in Civilian Dress

53 Deaf People using Sign Language

(Des F. Karim and P. Mandal. Litho Rosenbaum Bros, Vienna)

1981 (10 Nov). Birth Centenary of Kemal Atatürk (Turkish statesman). T **52** and similar vert design. Multicoloured. P 13½×14.

178	50p. Type **52**	45	30
179	1t. Kemal Atatürk in uniform...........	80	1·25

(Des F. Karim. Litho Ueberreuter, Austria)

1981 (26 Dec). International Year for Disabled Persons. T **53** and similar multicoloured design. P 13½×14 (50p.) or 14×13½ (2t.).

180	50p. Type **53**	40	20
181	2t. Disabled person writing (*horiz*)	85	2·50

54 Farm Scene and Wheat Ear

55 River Scene

(Des F. Karim. Litho Ueberreuter, Austria)

1981 (31 Dec). World Food Day. P 13½×14.

182	**54**	50p. multicoloured	50	1·00

(Des P. Mandal. Litho Ueberreuter, Vienna)

1982 (22 May). 10th Anniv of Human Environment Conference. P 13½×14.

183	**55**	50p. multicoloured	50	1·00

56 Dr. M. Hussain

57 Knotted Rope surrounding Bengali "75"

(Des F. Karim. Litho Ueberreuter, Vienna)

1982 (9 Oct). First Death Anniv of Dr. Motahar Hussain (educationist). P 13½.

184	**56**	50p. multicoloured	50	1·00

(Des F. Karim and P. Mandal. Litho Ueberreuter, Vienna)

1982 (21 Oct). 75th Anniv of Boy Scout Movement and 125th Birth Anniv of Lord Baden-Powell. T **57** and similar multicoloured design. P 14×13½ (50p.) or 13½×14 (2t.).

185	50p. Type **57**	50	30
186	2t. Lord Baden-Powell (*vert*)...........................	1·50	4·00

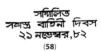

সম্মিলিত
সমস্ত বাহিনী দিবস
২১ নভেম্বর,৮২

(58)

1982 (21 Nov). Armed Forces' Day. No. 175 optd with T **58**.

187	50p. Type **50**	3·50	3·00

59 Capt. Mohiuddin Jahangir

(Litho Ueberreuter, Vienna)

1982 (16 Dec). Heroes and Martyrs of the Liberation. T **59** and similar horiz designs. Multicoloured: background colours of commemorative plaque given. P 14×13½.

188	50p. Type **59** (pale orange)	30	50
	a. Horiz strip of seven. Nos. 188/94............	1·90	3·25
189	50p. Sepoy Hamidur Rahman (apple-green).	30	50
190	50p. Sepoy Mohammed Mustafa Kamal (dull claret)	30	50
191	50p. Muhammed Ruhul Amin (bistre-yellow)	30	50
192	50p. Flt. Lt. M. Matiur Rahman (olive-bistre).	30	50
193	50p. Lance-Naik Munshi Abdur Rob (chestnut)	30	50
194	50p. Lance-Naik Nur Mouhammad (bright green)	30	50
188/94	*Set of 7*	1·90	3·25

Nos. 188/94 were printed together, *se-tenant*, in horizontal strips of seven throughout the sheet.

60 Metric Scales

61 Dr. Robert Koch

(Des F. Karim. Litho Ueberreuter, Vienna)

1983 (10 Jan). Introduction of Metric Weights and Measures. T **60** and similar multicoloured design. P 13½×14 (50p.) or 14×13½ (2t.).

195	50p. Type **60**	40	30
196	2t. Weights, jug and tap measure (*horiz*)....	1·40	2·75

(Des F. Karim. Litho Ueberreuter, Vienna)

1983 (20 Feb). Centenary (1982) of Robert Koch's Discovery of Tubercle Bacillus. T **61** and similar vert design. Multicoloured. P 13½×14.

197	50p. Type **61**	1·00	40
198	1t. Microscope, slide and X-ray	1·75	3·50

 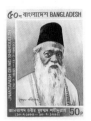

62 Open Stage Theatre

63 Dr. Muhammed Shahidulla

(Des F. Karim and P. Mandal. Litho Ueberreuter, Vienna)

1983 (14 Mar). Commonwealth Day. T **62** and similar horiz designs. Multicoloured. P 14.

199	1t. Type **62**	10	15
200	3t. Boat race	20	30
201	10t. Snake dance	35	90
202	15t. Picking tea	50	1·50
199/202	*Set of 4*	1·00	2·50

(Litho Ueberreuter, Vienna)

1983 (10 July). Dr. Muhammed Shahidulla (Bengali scholar) Commemoration. P 13½×14.

203	**63**	50p. multicoloured	75	1·00

64 Magpie Robin

(Des F. Karim and P. Mandal. Litho Ueberreuter, Vienna)

1983 (17 Aug). Birds of Bangladesh. T **64** and similar multicoloured designs. P 14×13½ (50p., 5t.) or 13½×14 (2t., 3t.75).

204	50p. Type **64**	60	40
205	2t. White-brested Kingfisher (*vert*)	75	1·50
206	3t.75 Lesser Flame-backed Woodpecker (*vert*)	1·00	2·00
207	5t. White-winged Wood Duck	1·10	2·75
204/7	*Set of 4*	3·00	6·00
MS208	165×110 mm. Nos. 204/7 (*sold at* 13t.)	3·75	10·00

65 *Macrobrachium rosenbergii*   Visit of Queen Nov. '83   **(66)**

(Litho Ueberreuter, Vienna)

1983 (31 Oct). Marine Life. T **65** and similar horiz designs. Multicoloured. P 14×13½.

209	50p. Type **65**	30	30
210	2t. White Pomfret	50	1·25
211	3t.75 Rohu	60	1·50
212	5t. Climbing Perch	75	2·25
209/12	*Set of 4*	1·90	4·75
MS213	119×98 mm. Nos. 209/12. Imperf (*sold at* 13t.)	2·00	5·50

1983 (14 Nov). Visit of Queen Elizabeth II. No. 95 optd with T **66** in red.

214	10t. Queen Elizabeth and Prince Philip	10·00	11·00
	a. Optd "Nov '33" (R. 3/10)	85·00	

67 Conference Hall, Dhaka   **68** Early Mail Runner

(Des M. Begum and M. Shamim. Litho Ueberreuter, Vienna)

1983 (5 Dec). 14th Islamic Foreign Ministers' Conference, Dhaka. T **67** and similar horiz design. Multicoloured. P 14×13½.

215	50p. Type **67**	35	30
216	5t. Old Fort, Dhaka	1·25	3·00

(Litho Ueberreuter, Vienna)

1983 (21 Dec). World Communications Year. T **68** and similar multicoloured designs. P 14×13½ (10t.) or 13½×14 (others).

217	50p. Type **68**	40	15
218	5t. Sailing ship, steam train and Boeing 707 airliner	2·25	1·75
219	10t. Mail runner and dish aerial (*horiz*)	3·00	4·75
	a. Gold (on dish aerial) omitted	£120	
217/19	*Set of 3*	5·00	6·00

69 Carrying Mail by Boat   **(70)**

(Des M. Akond, P. Mandal and M. Shamim. Litho State Ptg Wks, Moscow)

1983 (21 Dec)–86. Postal Communications. T **69** and similar designs. P 11½×12½ (5, 25p.), 12×11½ (1, 2, 3, 5t.) or 12½×11½ (others).

220	5p. turquoise-blue	10	50
221	10p. purple	10	50
222	15p. new blue	30	50
223	20p. grey-black	1·75	50
224	25p. slate	50	50
225	30p. brown	50	50
226	50p. light brown	1·75	10
227	1t. dull ultramarine	2·00	10
228	2t. deep bluish green	2·00	10
228a	3t. bistre (11.1.86)	5·50	1·00
229	5t. bright purple	2·25	1·00
220/9	*Set of 11*	15·00	4·50

Designs: Horiz (22×17 *mm*)—10p. Counter, Dhaka G.P.O.; 15p. I.W.T.A. Terminal, Dhaka; 20p. Inside railway travelling post office; 30p. Emptying pillar box; 50p. Mobile post office van. (30×19 *mm*)—1t. Kamalapur Railway Station, Dhaka; 2t. Zia International Airport; 3t. Sorting mail by machine; 5t. Khulna G.P.O. Vert (17×22 *mm*)—25p. Delivering a letter.

1984 (1 Feb). First National Stamp Exhibition (1st issue). Nos. 161/2 optd with T **70** (5t.) or "*First Bangladesh National Philatelic Exhibition—1984*" (50p.), both in red.

230	**44**	50p. multicoloured	1·25	2·00
		a. Horiz pair. Nos. 230/1	2·75	4·75
231	—	5t. multicoloured	1·50	2·75

71 Girl with Stamp Album

(Des P. Mandal. Litho Harrison)

1984 (12 May). First National Stamp Exhibition (2nd issue). T **71** and similar triangular design. Multicoloured. P 14.

232	50p. Type **71**	65	1·25
	a. Pair. Nos. 232/3	1·75	3·50
233	7t.50 Boy with stamp album	1·10	2·25
MS234	98×117 mm. Nos. 232/3 (*sold at* 10t.)	3·00	4·25

Nos. 232/3 were printed together, *se-tenant*, in pairs throughout the sheet.

72 Sarus Crane and Gavial   **73** Eagle attacking Hen with Chicks

(Des P. Mandal and M. Akond. Litho Ueberreuter, Vienna)

1984 (17 July). Dhaka Zoo. T **72** and similar vert design. Multicoloured. P 13½×14.

235	1t. Type **72**	1·75	85
236	2t. Common Peafowl and Tiger	2·50	4·25

(Des K. Mustafa. Litho Harrison)

1984 (3 Dec). Centenary of Postal Life Insurance. T **73** and similar vert design. Multicoloured. P 14.

237	1t. Type **73**	50	25
238	5t. Bangladesh family and postman's hand with insurance cheque	1·25	2·25

74 Abbasuddin Ahmad

(Des K. Mustafa. Litho Harrison)

1984 (24 Dec). Abbasuddin Ahmad (singer) Commemoration. P 14.
239   **74**   3t. multicoloured .... 1·00   1·25

(75)

1984 (27 Dec). "Khulnapex–84" Stamp Exhibition. No. 86 optd with T **75**.
240   **22**   2t.25 multicoloured .... 1·00   1·75

76 Cycling

(Des M. Shamim. Litho Harrison)

1984 (31 Dec). Olympic Games, Los Angeles. T **76** and similar horiz designs. Multicoloured. P 14.
241   1t. Type **76** .... 1·75   30
242   5t. Hockey.. 2·50   2·25
243   10t. Volleyball.. 2·75   4·25
241/3 Set of 3 .... 6·25   6·25

77 Farmer with Rice and Sickle   78 Mother and Baby

(Des M. Shamim. Litho Harrison)

1985 (2 Feb). Ninth Annual Meeting of Islamic Development Bank, Dhaka. T **77** and similar horiz design. Multicoloured. P 14.
244   1t. Type **77** 35   15
245   5t. Citizens of four races................................ 1·25   2·25

(Des M. Akond. Litho Harrison)

1985 (14 Mar). Child Survival Campaign. T **78** and similar vert design. Multicoloured. P 14.
246   1t. Type **78** 30   10
247   10t. Young child and growth graph .... 1·50   3·00

উপজেলা নির্বাচন ১৯৮৫
(79)

1985 (16 May). Local Elections. Nos. 110/15 optd with T **79**.
248   40p. Type **29** 45   65
249   1t. Cassia fistula.. 55   35
250   2t.25 Delonix regia....................................... 75   85
251   3t.50 Nymphaea nouchali............................ 90   1·40
252   4t. Butea monosperma.................................. 90   1·40
253   5t. Anthocephalus indicus 95   1·60
248/53 Set of 6 .... 4·00   5·50

80 Women working at Traditional Crafts

81 U.N. Building, New York, Peace Doves and Flags

(Des M. Akond. Litho Harrison)

1985 (18 July). United Nations Decade for Women. T **80** and similar vert design. Multicoloured. P 14.
254   1t. Type **80**.. 25   10
255   10t. Women with microscope, computer terminal and in classroom .... 1·25   2·25

(Des M. Akond. Litho Harrison)

1985 (14 Sept). 40th Anniv of United Nations Organization and 11th Anniv of Bangladesh Membership. T **81** and similar horiz design. Multicoloured. P 14.
256   1t. Type **81**.. 15   10
257   10t. Map of world and Bangladesh flag .... 1·60   2·00

82 Head of Youth, Flowers and Symbols of Commerce and Agriculture

83 Emblem and Seven Doves

(Des M. Shamim. Litho Harrison)

1985 (2 Nov). International Youth Year. T **82** and similar vert design. Multicoloured. P 14.
258   1t. Type **82**.. 10   10
259   5t. Head of youth, flowers and symbols of industry... 40   60

(Des M. Akond. Litho Harrison)

1985 (8 Dec). First Summit Meeting of South Asian Association for Regional Co-operation, Dhaka. T **83** and similar vert design. Multicoloured. P 14.
260   1t. Type **83**.. 10   10
261   5t. Flags of member nations and lotus blossom... 2·00   1·50

84 Zainul Abedin

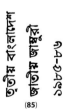

(85)

(Des P. Mandal. Litho Harrison)

1985 (28 Dec). Tenth Death Anniv of Zainul Abedin (artist). P 14.
262   **84**   3t. multicoloured .... 1·00   55
                a. Red-brown ("BANGLADESH" and face value) omitted £180

1985 (29 Dec). Third National Scout Jamboree. No. 109 optd with T **85**.
263   5t. reddish lilac, deep blue and bright green .... 2·75   3·75

86 "Fishing Net" (Safiuddin Ahmed)

(Litho Harrison)

1986 (6 Apr). Bangladesh Paintings. T **86** and similar horiz designs. Multicoloured. P 14.
264		1t. Type **86**	15	10
265		5t. "Happy Return" (Quamrul Hassan)	40	50
266		10t. "Levelling the Ploughed Field" (Zainul Abedin)	70	80
264/6		Set of 3	1·10	1·25

87 Two Players competing for Ball

(Des K. Mustafa. Litho Harrison)

1986 (29 June). World Cup Football Championship, Mexico. T **87** and similar horiz design. Multicoloured. P 15×14.
267		1t. Type **87**	30	10
268		10t. Goalkeeper and ball in net	1·75	3·00
MS269		105×75 mm. 20t. Four players (60×44 mm). Imperf	4·25	6·00

88 General M. A. G. Osmani

SAARC SEMINAR '86

(89)

(Des P. Mandal. Litho Harrison)

1986 (18 Sept). General M.A.G. Osmani (army commander-in-chief) Commemoration. P 14.
270	**88**	3t. multicoloured	1·75	1·00

1986 (3 Dec). South Asian Association for Regional Co-operation Seminar. No. 183 optd with T **89**.
271	**55**	50p. multicoloured	3·75	4·25

90 Butterflies and Nuclear Explosion

CONFERENCE FOR DEVELOPMENT '87

(91)

TK. 1.00

(Des M. Shamim. Litho State Ptg Wks, Moscow)

1986 (29 Dec). International Peace Year. T **90** and similar vert designs. Multicoloured. P 12½×12½.
272		1t. Type **90**	50	25
273		10t. Flowers and ruined buildings	2·25	3·75
MS274		109×80 mm. 20t. Peace dove and soldier	1·50	2·00

1987 (12 Jan). Conference for Development. Nos. 152/3 surch or optd as T **91**.
275	**38**	1t. on 40p. black, vermilion and bistre-yellow	15	20
		a. Surch double		
		b. Surch triple		
		c. Surch sideways		
		d. Surch inverted		
276	—	5t. gold and bright blue	65	1·75
		a. Opt double		
		b. Opt double, one inverted		
		c. Opt inverted		

Stamp booklets containing Nos. 275/6 in strips of three are private productions and were not sold by the Bangladesh Post Office.

92 Demonstrators with Placards **93** Nurse giving Injection

(Des B. Sardar. Litho State Ptg Wks, Moscow)

1987 (21 Feb). 35th Anniv of Bangla Language Movement. T **92** and similar horiz design. Multicoloured. P 12½×12.
277		3t. Type **92**	1·40	2·50
		a. Horiz pair. Nos. 277/8	2·75	5·00
278		3t. Martyrs' Memorial	1·40	2·50

Nos. 277/8 were printed together, se-tenant, in horizontal pairs throughout the sheet, each pair forming a composite design.

(Litho State Ptg Wks, Moscow)

1987 (7 Apr). World Health Day. P 11½×12.
279	**93**	1t. blue-black and deep blue	1·75	2·00

See also No. 295.

94 Pattern and Bengali Script **95** Jute Shika

(Des M. Akond. Litho State Ptg Wks, Moscow)

1987 (16 Apr). Bengali New Year. T **94** and similar vert design. Multicoloured. P 12½×12½.
280		1t. Type **94**	10	10
281		10t. Bengali woman	40	60

(Des P. Mandal, K. Mustafa and M. Akond. Photo State Ptg Wks, Moscow)

1987 (18 May). Export Products. T **95** and similar multicoloured designs. P 12½×12 (5t.) or 12×12½ (others).
282		1t. Type **95**	10	10
283		5t. Jute carpet (horiz)	30	35
284		10t. Cane table lamp	45	70
282/4		Set of 3	70	1·00

96 Ustad Ayet Ali Khan and Surbahar

9

(Litho State Ptg Wks, Moscow)

1987 (2 Sept). 20th Death Anniv of Ustad Ayet Ali Khan (musician and composer). P 12×12½.

285	**96**	5t. multicoloured..	1·50	1·00

97 Palanquin

(Litho State Ptg Wks, Moscow)

1987 (24 Oct). Transport. T **97** and similar horiz designs. Multicoloured. P 12½×12.

286	2t. Type **97**..	35	20
287	3t. Bicycle rickshaw	1·25	45
288	5t. River steamer.....................................	1·50	75
289	7t. Express diesel train	3·50	1·75
290	10t. Bullock cart......................................	70	1·75
286/90	*Set of 5*...	6·50	4·50

98 H.S. Suhrawardy

99 Villagers fleeing from Typhoon

(Des P. Mandal. Litho State Ptg Wks, Moscow)

1987 (5 Dec). Hossain Shahid Suhrawardy (politician) Commemoration. P 12×12½.

291	**98**	3t. multicoloured............................	20	30

(Des M. Akond. Litho State Ptg Wks, Moscow)

1987 (15 Dec). International Year of Shelter for the Homeless. T **99** and similar horiz design. Multicoloured. P 12½×12.

292	5t. Type **99**..	50	70
	a. Horiz pair. Nos. 292/3............................	1·00	1·40
293	5t. Villagers and modern houses...................	50	70

Nos. 292/3 were printed together, *se-tenant*, in horizontal pairs throughout the sheet.

100 President Ershad addressing Parliament

(Des K. Mustafa. Litho State Ptg Wks, Moscow)

1987 (31 Dec). First Anniv of Return to Democracy. P 12½×12.

294	**100**	10t. multicoloured...........................	65	1·00

(Litho State Ptg Wks, Moscow)

1988 (16 Jan). World Health Day. Vert design as T **93**. P 11½×12.

295	25p. brown	1·00	30

Design:—25p. Oral rehydration.

101 Woman Planting Palm Saplings

(Des K. Mustafa. Litho State Ptg Wks, Moscow)

1988 (26 Jan). I.F.A.D. Seminar on Agricultural Loans for Rural Women. T **101** and similar horiz design. Multicoloured. P 12½×12.

296	3t. Type **101**	15	25
297	5t. Village woman milking cow......................	20	75

102 Basketball

(Litho State Ptg Wks, Moscow)

1988 (20 Sept). Olympic Games, Seoul. T **102** and similar diamond-shaped designs. Multicoloured. P 11½.

298	5t. Type **102**	1·50	80
	a. Strip of five. Nos. 298/302.........................	6·75	3·50
299	5t. Weightlifting	1·50	80
300	5t. Tennis..	1·50	80
301	5t. Rifle-shooting...................................	1·50	80
302	5t. Boxing..	1·50	80
298/302	*Set of 5*	6·75	3·50

Nos. 298/302 were printed together, *se-tenant*, in horizontal and vertical strips of five throughout the sheet.

103 Interior of Shait Gumbaz Mosque, Bagerhat

(Litho State Ptg Wks, Moscow)

1988 (9 Oct). Historical Buildings. T **103** and similar horiz designs. Multicoloured. P 12½×12.

303	1t. Type **103**	50	15
304	4t. Paharpur Monastery	1·00	40
305	5t. Kantanagar Temple, Dinajpur	1·00	40
306	10t. Lalbag Fort, Dhaka.............................	1·50	1·25
303/6	*Set of 4*	3·50	2·00

104 Henri Dunant (founder), Red Cross and Crescent

105 Dr. Qudrat-i-Khuda in Laboratory

(Litho State Ptg Wks, Moscow)

1988 (26 Oct). 125th Anniv of International Red Cross and Red Crescent. T **104** and similar vert design. Multicoloured. P 12×12½.

307	5t. Type **104**	1·50	30
308	10t. Red Cross workers with patient	2·25	1·10

(Litho State Ptg Wks, Moscow)

1988 (3 Nov). Dr. Qudrat-i-Khuda (scientist) Commemoration. P 12×12½.

309	**105**	5t. multicoloured............................	1·00	40

106 Wicket-keeper

107 Labourers, Factory and Technician

(Litho State Ptg Wks, Moscow)

1988 (27 Nov). Asia Cup Cricket. T **106** and similar vert designs. Multicoloured. P 12×12½.

310		1t. Type **106**	80	90
		a. Horiz strip of three. Nos. 310/12	3·25	4·00
311		5t. Batsman	1·00	1·25
312		10t. Bowler	1·75	2·25
310/12		Set of 3	3·25	4·00

Nos. 310/12 were printed together, se-tenant, in horizontal strips of three throughout the sheet.

(Litho State Ptg Wks, Moscow)

1988 (29 Nov). 32nd Meeting of Colombo Plan Consultative Committee, Dhaka. P 12×12½.

313	**107**	3t. multicoloured	15	10
314		10t. multicoloured	55	60

108 Dhaka G.P.O. Building

(Litho State Ptg Wks, Moscow)

1988 (6 Dec). 25th Anniv of Dhaka G.P.O. Building. T **108** and similar horiz design. Multicoloured. P 12.

315		1t. Type **108**	20	10
316		5t. Post Office counter	80	40

৫ম জাতীয় রোভার মুট

১৯৮৮-৮৯

(**109**)

1988 (29 Dec). Fifth National Rover Scout Moot. No. 168 optd with T **109**.

317	**47**	5t. multicoloured	4·00	3·25
		a. Opt inverted		

110 Bangladesh Airport

(Des K. Mustafa (3,10t.), N. Islam (5t.), M. Akond (20t.). Litho State Ptg Wks, Moscow)

1989 (1 Jan)–92. Bangladesh Landmarks. T **110** and similar designs. P 12×11½ (3t.), 12×12½ (4, 20t.), 12½×12 (5t.) or 11½×12 (10t.).

318	3t. black and light blue	50	10
318a	4t. steel blue (15.7.92)	50	10
319	5t. black and orange-brown (31.3.89)	1·25	20
320	10t. rosine (1.7.89)	5·00	35
321	20t. multicoloured (1.7.89)	1·75	40
318/21	Set of 5	8·00	1·00

Designs: Vert (22×33 mm)—5t. Curzon Hall. (19½×31½ mm) 10t. Fertiliser factory, Chittagong. Horiz (33×23 mm)—4t. Chittagong port. 20t. Postal Academy, Rajshahi.

For the 3t. redrawn and perforated 14½×14 see No. 709a.

For the 5t. redrawn and perforated 14½ see No. 710.

চতুর্থ দ্বিবার্ষিক এশীয়
চারুকলা প্রদর্শনী
বাংলাদেশ ১৯৮৯

(**111**)

1989 (1 Mar). Fourth Biennial Asian Art Exhibition. No. 266 optd with T **111**.

322		10t. "Levelling the Ploughed Field" (Zainul Abedin)	75	1·00

112 Irrigation Methods and Student with Telescope

113 Academy Logo

(Litho State Ptg Wks, Moscow)

1989 (7 Mar). 12th National Science and Technology Week. P 12×12½.

323	**112**	10t. multicoloured	50	60

(Litho State Ptg Wks, Moscow)

1989 (13 Mar). 75th Anniv of Police Academy, Sardah. P 12×12½.

324	**113**	10t. multicoloured	1·00	60

114 Rejoicing Crowds, Paris, 1789

(Des K. Mustafa (Nos. **MS**327/8). Litho Harrison)

1989 (12 July). Bicentenary of French Revolution. T **114** and similar horiz design. Multicoloured. P 14×14½.

325		17t. Type **114**	70	75
		a. Horiz pair. Nos. 325/6 plus label	1·40	1·50
326		17t. Storming the Bastille, 1789	70	75
MS327		125×125 mm. 5t. Men with pickaxes; 10t. "Liberty guiding the People" (detail) (Delacroix); 10t. Crowd with cannon. P 14	2·00	3·00
MS328		152×88 mm. 25t. Storming the Bastille. Imperf	2·00	3·00

Nos. 325/6 were printed in sheets of 30 (6×5) with No. 325 in vertical columns one and four, labels showing the Bicentenary emblem in columns two and five, and No. 326 in columns three and six.

The design of No. **MS**328 incorporates the three scenes featured on No. **MS**327.

115 Sowing and Harvesting

(Litho State Ptg Wks, Moscow)

1989 (10 Aug). Tenth Anniv of Asia-Pacific Integrated Rural Development Centre. T **115** and similar horiz design. Multicoloured. P 12½×12.

329		5t. Type **115**	75	65
		a. Horiz pair. Nos. 329/30	1·50	1·25
330		10t. Rural activities	75	65

Nos. 329/30 were printed together, se-tenant, in horizontal pairs throughout the sheet, each pair forming a composite design.

116 Helper and Child playing with Baby

(Litho State Ptg Wks, Moscow)

1989 (22 Aug). 40th Anniv of S.O.S. International Children's Village. T **116** and similar horiz design. Multicoloured. P 12½×12.
331   1t. Type **116** 15   10
332   10t. Foster mother with children 85   90

117 U.N. Soldier on Watch   **118** Festival Emblem

(Litho State Ptg Wks, Moscow)

1989 (12 Sept). First Anniv of Bangladesh Participation in U.N. Peace-keeping Force. T **117** and similar vert design. Multicoloured. P 12×12½.
333   4t. Type **117** 50   30
334   10t. Two soldiers checking positions .... 1·00   70

(Litho State Ptg Wks, Moscow)

1989 (17 Nov). Second Asian Poetry Festival, Dhaka. T **118** and similar vert design. P 12×12½.
335   2t. bright scarlet, deep carmine and
            myrtle-green............................. 15   10
336   10t. multicoloured...................................... 85   90
Design:—10t. Festival emblem and hall.

119 State Security Printing Press

(Litho State Security Ptg Press, Gazipur)

1989 (7 Dec). Inauguration of State Security Printing Press, Gazipur. P 13½.
337   **119**   10t. multicoloured.......................... 65   65

120 Water Lilies and T.V. Emblem

(Litho State Ptg Wks, Moscow (5t.), State Security Ptg Press, Gazipur (10t.))

1989 (25 Dec). 25th Anniv of Bangladesh Television. T **120** and similar horiz design. Multicoloured. P 12½×12 (5t.) or 13½ (10t.).
338   5t. Type **120** 35   30
339   10t. Central emblem and water lilies............. 65   80

121 Gharial in Shallow Water   **122** Symbolic Family

(Des K. Mustafa. Litho Harrison)

1990 (31 Jan). Endangered Wildlife. Gharial. T **121** and similar horiz designs. Multicoloured. P 14.
340   50p. Type **121** 80   45
        a. Block of four. Nos. 340/3 .... 4·50   2·40
341   2t. Gharial feeding .... 1·00   60
342   4t. Gharials basking on sand bank .... 1·40   70
343   10t. Two gharials resting .... 1·75   95
340/3 *Set of 4* .... 4·50   2·40
    Nos. 340/3 were printed together, *se-tenant*, in blocks of four throughout the sheet.

(Litho State Ptg Press, Gazipur)

1990 (10 Feb). Population Day. P 13½.
344   **122**   6t. multicoloured........................ 55   35

123 Justice S.M. Murshed

(Des P. Mandal. Litho State Ptg Wks, Moscow)

1990 (3 Apr). Tenth Death Anniv of Justice Syed Mahbub Murshed. P 12½×12.
345   **123**   5t. multicoloured........................ 2·50   1·25

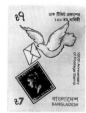

124 Boy learning Alphabet   **125** Penny Black with "Stamp World London 90" Exhibition Emblem

(Litho State Ptg Wks, Moscow)

1990 (10 Apr). International Literacy Year. T **124** and similar vert design. Multicoloured. P 12×12½.
346   6t. Type **124** .... 1·00   50
347   10t. Boy teaching girl to write.................. 1·50   1·25

(Des K. Mustafa. Litho State Security Ptg Press, Gazipur)

1990 (6 May). 150th Anniv of the Penny Black. T **125** and similar vert design. Multicoloured. P 13½.
348   7t. Type **125** .... 1·50   2·00
349   10t. Penny Black, 1983 World
            Communications Year stamp and
            Bengali mail runner .... 1·75   2·50

126 Goalkeeper and Ball

(Des M. Shamim. Litho State Security Ptg Press, Gazipur)

1990 (12 June). World Cup Football Championship, Italy. T **126** and similar horiz designs. Multicoloured. P 13½.
350   8t. Type **126** .... 1·25   1·75
351   10t. Footballer with ball....................... 1·50   2·25
MS352 104×79 mm. 25t. Colosseum, Rome, with
        football. Imperf............................. 13·00   13·00
        a. Country and commemorative inscrs
            inverted..
    On No. **MS**352a "BANGLADESH WORLD CUP FOOTBALL ITALY 1990" at the foot of the design is in white with the same inscriptions in blue inverted at the top of the miniature sheet.

127 Mango   **128** Man gathering Wheat

(Des M. Shamim (1, 2t.), N. Islam (3, 4t.), P. Mandal (5, 10t.). Litho State Ptg Wks, Moscow)

1990 (16 July). Fruit. T **127** and similar vert designs. Multicoloured. P 12×12½.

353	1t. Type **127**	30	20
354	2t. Guava	30	20
355	3t. Water-melon	35	25
356	4t. Papaya	40	30
357	5t. Bread fruit	65	65
358	10t. Carambola	1·25	1·50
353/8 *Set of 6*		3·00	2·75

> **PRINTERS.** The following issues were printed in lithography by the State Security Printing Press, Gazipur, unless otherwise stated.

(Des M. Akond)

1990 (3 Sept). U.N. Conference on Least Developed Countries, Paris. P 14.

359	**128**	10t. multicoloured	1·25	1·25
		a. Blue (U.N. emblem and inscr) inverted		
		b. Blue (U.N. emblem and inscr) omitted	55·00	

On the evidence of the sheet marginal markings it would appear that the blue on No. 359a may be printed correctly and the remainder of the colours inverted. Unequal margins at top and bottom of the sheet also cause the country name and face value, in green, to be displaced.

129 Map of Asia with Stream of Letters   **130** Canoe Racing

(Des K. Mustafa)

1990 (10 Sept). 20th Anniv of Asia-Pacific Postal Training Centre. T **129** and similar vert design. Multicoloured. P 13½×14.

360	2t. Type **129**	1·75	1·75
	a. Horiz pair. Nos. 360/1	3·50	3·50
361	6t. Map of Pacific with stream of letters	1·75	1·75

Nos. 360/1 were printed together, *se-tenant*, in horizontal pairs throughout the sheet, forming a composite map design.

(Des K. Mustafa)

1990 (22 Sept). Asian Games, Beijing. T **130** and similar horiz designs. Multicoloured. P 14×13½.

362	2t. Type **130**	1·00	30
363	4t. Kabaddi	1·25	30
364	8t. Wrestling	1·75	1·50
365	10t. Badminton	3·00	2·00
362/5 *Set of 4*		6·25	3·50

131 Lalan Shah   **132** U.N. Logo and "40"

(Des K. Muatafa)

1990 (17 Oct). 100th Death Anniv of Lalan Shah (poet). P 13½×14.

366	**131**	6t. multicoloured	1·50	1·00

(Des M. Akond)

1990 (24 Oct). 40th Anniv of United Nations Development Programme. P 14×13½.

367	**132**	6t. multicoloured	1·00	70

133 Baby   **134** *Danaus chrysippus*

(Des M. Akond)

1990 (29 Nov). Immunization. P 14½×14.

368	**133**	1t. emerald	50	50
369		2t. brown	50	25

(Des M. Shamim)

1990 (3 Dec). Butterflies. T **134** and similar square designs. Multicoloured. P 13½×12.

370	6t. Type **134**	1·60	1·60
	a. Block of four. Nos. 370/3	6·00	6·00
	ab. Deep blue and chestnut inscr inverted (block of four)		
371	6t. *Precis almana*	1·60	1·60
372	10t. *Ixias pyrene*	1·75	1·75
373	10t. *Danaus plexippus*	1·75	1·75
370/3 *Set of 4*		6·00	6·00

Nos. 370/3 were printed together, *se-tenant*, in blocks of four throughout the sheet.

On No. 370ab the printing of "BANGLADESH", in deep blue on No. 371 and in chestnut on No. 372, is inverted so that the inscription does not occur on these two designs. The inverted deep blue "BANGLADESH" appears on the left sheet margin of No. 373 and the chestnut on No. 370.

135 Drugs attacking Bangladesh

(Des F. Karim (2t.), M. Akond (4t.))

1991 (1 Jan). United Nations Anti-Drugs Decade. T **135** and similar horiz design. Multicoloured. P 14.

374	2t. Type **135**	1·25	50
375	4t. "Drug" snake around globe	1·75	1·25

136 Salimullah Hall   **137** Silhouetted People on Map

(Des P. Mandal)

1991 (30 Jan). P 14½×14.

376	**136**	6t. slate-blue and greenish yellow	1·00	25

(Des P. Mandal)

1991 (12 Mar). Third National Census. P 14.

382	**137**	4t. multicoloured	1·75	1·50

138 "Invincible Bangla"
(statue)

(Des M. Akond)

1991 (26 Mar). 20th Anniv of Independence. T **138** and similar square designs. Multicoloured. P 13½.

383		4t. Type **138**	85	1·00
	a.	Horiz strip of five. Nos. 383/7	3·75	4·50
384		4t. "Freedom Fighter" (statue)	85	1·00
385		4t. Mujibnagar Memorial	85	1·00
386		4t. Eternal Flame	85	1·00
387		4t. National Martyrs' Memorial	85	1·00
383/7		*Set of 5*	3·75	4·50

Nos. 383/7 were printed together, *se-tenant*, in horizontal strips of five throughout the sheet, with the backgrounds forming a composite design.

139 Pres. Rahman Seated

(Des P. Mandal. Litho Ueberreuter, Austria)

1991 (30 May). Tenth Death Anniv of President Ziaur Rahman. T **139** and similar vert design. Multicoloured. P 13½×14.

388		50p. Type **139**	30	15
389		2t. President Rahman's head in circular decoration	1·00	1·10
MS390		146×75 mm. Nos. 388/9 (*sold at* 10t.)	1·90	2·75

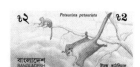

140 Red Giant Flying Squirrel

(Des K. Mustafa)

1991 (16 June). Endangered Species. T **140** and similar multicoloured designs. P 12.

391		2t. Type **140**	2·50	2·50
	a.	Vert pair. Nos. 391 and 394	5·00	5·00
392		4t. Black-faced Monkey (*vert*)	2·50	2·50
	a.	Horiz pair. Nos. 392/3	5·00	5·00
393		6t. Great Indian Hornbill (*vert*)	2·50	2·50
394		10t. Armoured Pangolin	2·50	2·50
391/4		*Set of 4*	9·00	9·00

Nos. 391 and 394, and 392/3 were printed together, *se-tenant*, in vertical (Nos. 391 and 394) or horizontal (Nos. 392/3) pairs throughout separate sheets.

141 Kaikobad

142 Rabindranath Tagore and Temple

(Des K. Mustafa)

1991 (21 July). 40th Death Anniv of Kaikobad (poet). P 14.

395	**141**	6t. multicoloured	1·60	1·25

(Des A. Karim)

1991 (7 Aug). 50th Death Anniv of Rabindranath Tagore (poet). P 14.

396	**142**	4t. multicoloured	1·25	65

143 Voluntary Blood Donation Programme

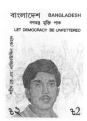

144 Shahid Naziruddin and Crowd

(Des P. Mandal)

1991 (19 Sept). 14th Anniv of "Sandhani" (medical students' association). T **143** and similar vert design. P 14.

397	3t. black and bright carmine	1·00	50
398	5t. multicoloured	2·00	2·25

Design:—5t. Blind man and eye.

1991 (10 Oct). First Death Anniv, of Shahid Naziruddin Jahad (democrat). P 14.

399	**144**	2t. black, emerald and cinnamon	1·00	60
	a.	Emerald ("BANGLADESH" and face value) omitted	£130	

145 Shaheed Noor Hossain with Slogan on Chest

146 Bronze Stupa

(Des K. Mustafa)

1991 (10 Nov). Fourth Death Anniv of Shaheed Noor Hossain (democrat). P 14.

400	**145**	2t. multicoloured	1·00	55

(Des M. Akond)

1991 (26 Nov). Archaeological Relics from Mainamati. T **146** and similar horiz designs. Multicoloured. P 13½.

401		4t. Type **146**	1·50	1·60
	a.	Horiz strip of five. Nos. 401/5	6·75	7·25
402		4t. Earthenware and bronze pitchers	1·50	1·60
403		4t. Remains of Salban Vihara Monastery	1·50	1·60
404		4t. Gold coins	1·50	1·60
405		4t. Terracotta plaque	1·50	1·60
401/5		*Set of 5*	6·75	7·25

Nos. 401/5 were printed together, *se-tenant*, in horizontal strips of 5 throughout the sheet.

147 Demonstrators

148 Munier Chowdhury

(Des. M. Muniruzzaman)

1991 (6 Dec). First Anniv of Mass Uprising. P 13½.

406	**147**	4t. multicoloured	1·25	80

1991 (14 Dec). 20th Anniv of Independence. Martyred Intellectuals (1st series). T **148** and similar vert designs. Each grey-black and reddish brown. P 13½.

407		2t. Type **148**	50	55
	a.	Sheetlet. Nos. 407/16	4·50	5·00
408		2t. Ghyasuddin Ahmad	50	55
409		2t. Rashidul Hasan	50	55
410		2t. Muhammad Anwar Pasha	50	55
411		2t. Dr. Muhammad Mortaza	50	55
412		2t. Shahid Saber	50	55
413		2t. Fazlur Rahman Khan	50	55
414		2t. Ranada Prasad Saha	50	55
415		2t. Adhyaksha Joges Chandra Ghose	50	55
416		2t. Santosh Chandra Bhattacharyya	50	55
417		2t. Dr. Gobinda Chandra Deb	50	55
	a.	Sheetlet. Nos. 417/26	4·50	5·00
418		2t. A. Muniruzzaman	50	55
419		2t. Mufazzal Haider Chaudhury	50	55
420		2t. Dr. Abdul Alim Choudhury	50	55
421		2t. Sirajuddin Hossain	50	55
422		2t. Shahidulla Kaiser	50	55
423		2t. Altaf Mahmud	50	55
424		2t. Dr. Jyotirmay Guha Thakurta	50	55
425		2t. Dr. Muhammad Abel Khair	50	55
426		2t. Dr. Serajul Haque Khan	50	55
427		2t. Dr. Mohammad Fazle Rabbi	50	55
	a.	Sheetlet. Nos. 427/36	4·50	5·00
428		2t. Mir Abdul Quyyum	50	55
429		2t. Golam Mostafa	50	55
430		2t. Dhirendranath Dutta	50	55
431		2t. S. Mannan	50	55
432		2t. Nizamuddin Ahmad	50	55
433		2t. Abul Bashar Chowdhury	50	55
434		2t. Selina Parveen	50	55
435		2t. Dr. Abul Kalam Azad	50	55
436		2t. Saidul Hassan	50	55
407/36 *Set of 30*			13·50	15·00

Nos. 407/16, 417/26 and 427/36 were printed together, *se-tenant*, in sheetlets of 10, the two horizontal rows in each sheetlet being separated by a row of inscribed labels.

See also Nos. 483/92, 525/40, 568/83, 620/35, 656/71, 691/706, 731/46 and 779/94.

149 Penaeus monodon

1991 (31 Dec). Shrimps. T **149** and similar horiz design. Multicoloured. P 14×13½.

437		6t. Type **149**	2·00	2·25
	a.	Horiz pair. Nos. 437/8	4·00	4·50
438		6t. *Metapenaeus monoceros*	2·00	2·25

Nos. 437/8 were printed together, *se-tenant*, in horizontal pairs throughout the sheet.

150 Death of Raihan Jaglu   *151* Rural and Urban Scenes

(Des M. Muniruzzaman)

1992 (8 Feb). Fifth Death Anniv of Shaheed Mirze Abu Raihan Jaglu. P 14×13½.

439	**150**	2t. multicoloured	1·50	60

(Des K. Mustafa (4t.), A. Karim (10t.))

1992 (5 June). World Environment Day. T **151** and similar multicoloured design. P 14.

440		4t. Type **151**	75	25
441		10t. World Environment Day logo (*horiz*)	2·00	2·75

152 Nawab Sirajuddaulah   **153** Syed Ismail Hossain Sirajee

(Des K. Mustafa)

1992 (2 July). 235th Death Anniv of Nawab Sirajuddaulah of Bengal. P 13½.

442	**152**	10t. multicoloured	1·50	2·00
	a.	Emerald ("BANGLADESH" inscr) omitted	£130	

1992 (17 July). 61st Death Anniv of Syed Ismail Hossain Sirajee. P 14.

443	**153**	4t. multicoloured	1·50	60

'PLANT TREES AND SAVE THE ENVIRONMENT'

154 Couple planting Seedling

(Des M. Huq and M. Muniruzzaman)

1992 (19 July). Plant Week. T **154** and similar multicoloured design. P 14.

444		2t. Type **154**	1·00	80
445		4t. Birds on tree (*vert*)	2·00	1·25

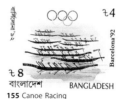

155 Canoe Racing   Banglapex '92 **(156)**

(Des M. Akond, M. Mia and S. Datta)

1992 (25 July). Olympic Games, Barcelona. T **155** and similar horiz designs. Multicoloured. P 14.

446		4t. Type **155**	1·60	1·90
	a.	Block of four. Nos. 446/9	5·75	7·00
447		6t. Hands holding torch with Olympic rings	1·60	1·90
448		10t. Olympic rings and doves	1·60	1·90
449		10t. Olympic rings and multiracial handshake	1·60	1·90
446/9 *Set of 4*			5·75	7·00

Nos. 446/9 were printed together, *se-tenant*, in blocks of four throughout the sheet of 100 with the two 10t. values occurring in the first, third, fifth, seventh and ninth horizontal rows.

1992 (18 Aug). "Banglapex '92", National Philatelic Exhibition (1st issue). No. 290 optd with T **156**.

450		10t. Bullock cart	2·75	3·25

157 Masnad-e-Ala Isa Khan   **158** Ceremonial Elephant (19th-century ivory carving)

1992 (15 Sept). 393rd Death Anniv of Masnad-e-Ala Isa Khan. P 14.
451   **157**   4t. multicoloured ....   1·00   60

(Des M. Begum)

1992 (26 Sept). Banglapex '92, National Philatelic Exhibition (2nd issue). T **158** and similar horiz design. Multicoloured. P 14.
452   10t. Type **158** ....   1·60   2·25
            a. Horiz pair. Nos. 452/3 plus label ....   3·00   4·50
453   10t. Victorian pillarbox between early and
            modern postmen ....   1·60   2·25
MS454 145×92 mm. Nos. 452/3 plus label. Imperf
            (sold at 25t.)..   5·50   6·00
    Nos. 452/3 were printed together, *se-tenant*, in sheets with No. 452 in vertical columns one and four, labels showing the exhibition emblem in columns two and five, and No. 453 in columns three and six.

159 Star Mosque

(Des Md. Jasimuddin)

1992 (29 Oct). Star Mosque, Dhaka. P 14½×13½.
455   **159**   10t. multicoloured ....   2·50   2·25

160 Meer Nisar Ali Titumeer and Fort

(Des M. Akond)

1992 (19 Nov). 161st Death Anniv of Meer Nisar Ali Titumeer. P 14½×13½.
456   **160**   10t. multicoloured ....   1·75   1·75

161 Terracotta Head and Seal

(Des M. Akond, M. Begum and M. Mia)

1992 (30 Nov). Archaeological Relics from Mahasthangarh. T **161** and similar horiz designs. Multicoloured. P 14½×13½.
457   10t. Type **161** ....   1·75   1·90
            a. Horiz strip of four. Nos. 457/60................   6·25   7·00
458   10t. Terracotta panel showing swan................   1·75   1·90
459   10t. Terracotta statue of Surya......................   1·75   1·90
460   10t. Gupta stone column................................   1·75   1·90
457/60 Set of 4..   6·25   7·00
    Nos. 457/60 were printed together, *se-tenant*, in horizontal strips of four throughout the sheet.

162 Young Child and Food

163 National Flags

(Des M. Muniruzzaman)

1992 (5 Dec). International Conference on Nutrition, Rome. P 14½×13½.
461   **162**   4t. multicoloured ....   1·00   55

(Des N. Islam (6t.), M. Akond (10t.))

1992 (5 Dec). Seventh South Asian Association for Regional Co-operation Summit Conference, Dhaka. T **163** and similar vert design. Multicoloured. P 13½×14½.
462   6t. Type **163** ....   1·40   75
463   10t. S.A.A.R.C. emblem................................   1·60   2·00

164 Syed Abdus Samad

165 Haji Shariat Ullah

(Des P. Mandal)

1993 (2 Feb). Syed Abdus Samad (footballer) Commemoration. P 14.
464   **164**   2t. multicoloured..................................   1·50   70

(Des M. Rahman)

1993 (10 Mar). Haji Shariat Ullah Commemoration. P 14½.
465   **165**   2t. multicoloured..................................   1·50   70

166 People digging Canal

(Des M. Rahman)

1993 (31 Mar). Irrigation Canals Construction Project. T **166** and similar horiz design. Multicoloured. P 14.
466   2t. Type **166**   80   80
            a. Horiz pair. Nos. 466/7........................   1·60   1·60
467   2t. Completed canal and paddy-fields........   80   80
    Nos. 466/7 were printed together, *se-tenant*, in horizontal pairs throughout the sheet.

167 Accident Prevention

(Des A. Hussain (6t.), N. Islam (10t.))

1993 (7 Apr). World Health Day. T **167** and similar multicoloured design. P 14.
468   6t. Type **167** ....   2·00   75
469   10t. Satellite photograph and symbols of
            trauma (*vert*) ....   2·25   2·75

168 National Images

169 Schoolchildren and Bengali Script

(Des Md. Shamsuzzoha)

1993 (14 Apr). 1400th Year of Bengali Solar Calendar. P 14.
470   **168**   2t. multicoloured ....   1·00   50

(Des M. Huq (No. 471), M. Mia (No. 472))

1993 (26 May). Compulsory Primary Education. T **169** and similar multicoloured design. P 14×14½ (No. 471) or 14½×14 (No. 472).
471   2t. Type **169**   80   80
472   2t. Books and slate (*horiz*)   80   80

170 Nawab Sir Salimullah and Palace

(Des S. Shaheen)

1993 (7 June). 122nd Birth Anniv of Nawab Sir Salimullah. P 14½×14.
473   **170**   4t. multicoloured ....   1·25   70

171 Fish Production

(Des M. Rahman)

1993 (15 Aug). Fish Fortnight. P 14½×14.
474   **171**   2t. multicoloured   50   40

172 Sunderban   **173** Exhibition Emblem

(Des M. Mia, M. Rahman and B. Biswas)

1993 (30 Oct). Natural Beauty of Bangladesh. T **172** and similar multicoloured designs. P 14½×14 (horiz) or 14×14½ (vert).
475   10t. Type **172** ....   1·00   1·40
476   10t. Kuakata beach ....   1·00   1·40
477   10t. Madhabkunda waterfall (*vert*) ....   1·00   1·40
478   10t. River Piyain, Jaflang (*vert*) ....   1·00   1·40
475/8 *Set of 4* ....   3·50   4·25
MS479 174×102 mm. Nos. 475/8. Imperf. (*sold at* 50t.).   3·50   4·25
No. 476 and the same design in No. **MS**479 also exist with smaller country name and inscr "TOURISM MONTH '93" in English and Bengali. This version was not issued.

(Des Q. Chowdhury)

1993 (2 Nov). Sixth Asian Art Biennale. P 14×14½.
480   **173**   10t. multicoloured   80   1·00

174 Foy's Lake

(Des A. Hussain)

1993 (6 Nov). Tourism Month. P 14½×14.
481   **174**   10t. multicoloured ....   1·00   1·25

175 Burdwan House

(Des N. Islam)

1993 (3 Dec). Foundation Day, Bangla Academy. P 14×14½.
482   **175**   2t. deep brown and emerald ....   1·50   40

1993 (14 Dec). Martyred Intellectuals (2nd series). Vert designs as T **148**. Each grey-black and reddish brown. P 14½.
483   2t. Lt. Cdr. Moazzam Hussain   20   30
       a. Sheetlet. Nos. 483/92 ....   1·75   2·75
484   2t. Muhammad Habibur Rahman...................   20   30
485   2t. Khandoker Abu Taleb........................   20   30
486   2t. Moshiur Rahman................................   20   30
487   2t. Md. Abdul Muktadir...........................   20   30
488   2t. Nutan Chandra Sinha........................   20   30
489   2t. Syed Nazmul Haque   20   30
490   2t. Dr. Mohammed Amin Uddin   20   30
491   2t. Dr. Faizul Mohee...............................   20   30
492   2t. Sukha Ranjan Somaddar   20   30
483/92 *Set of 10* ....   1·75   2·75
Nos. 483/92 were printed together, *se-tenant*, as a sheetlet of 10, the two horizontal rows being separated by a row of inscribed labels.

176 Throwing the Discus

1993 (19 Dec). Sixth South Asian Federation Games, Dhaka. T **176** and similar multicoloured design. P 14½×14 (2t.) or 14×14½ (4t.).
493   2t. Type **176**   20   20
       a. Rose-lilac, yellow-brown and orange (parts of logo) omitted...............   £120
494   4t. Running (*vert*).................................   35   35
       a. Yellow-brown (part of logo) omitted £120

177 Tomb of Sultan Ghiyasuddin Azam Shah

(Des Md. Shamsuzzoha)

1993 (30 Dec). Muslim Monuments. P 14½×14.
495   **177**   10t. multicoloured...................................   75   1·00

178 Scouting Activities and Jamboree Emblem   **179** Emblem and Mother giving Solution to Child

(Des A. Hussain)

1994 (5 Jan). 14th Asian-Pacific and fifth Bangladesh National Scout Jamboree. P 14×14½.
496   **178**   2t. multicoloured   40   30

(Des Md. Shamsuzzoha)

1994 (5 Feb). 25th Anniv of Oral Rehydration Solution. P 14×14½.
497   **179**   2t. multicoloured   65   30

180 Interior of Chhota Sona
Mosque, Nawabgonj

(Des A. Hussain, M. Huq and M. Rahman)

1994 (30 Mar). Ancient Mosques. T **180** and similar horiz designs.
Multicoloured. P 14½×14.

498		4t. Type **180**	40	20
499		6t. Exterior of Chhota Sona Mosque	50	65
500		6t. Exterior of Baba Adam's Mosque, Munshigonj	50	65
498/500	*Set of 3*		1·25	1·40

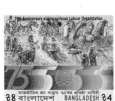

181 Agricultural Workers and
Emblem

182 Priest releasing Peace
Doves

(Des R. Hussain and M. Huq)

1994 (11 Apr). 75th Anniv of International Labour Organization. T **181**
and similar multicoloured design. P 14½×14 (4t.) or 14×14½ (10t.).

501		4t. Type **181**	25	20
	a. Bright blue ("BANGLADESH" inscr) omitted		£160	
502		10t. Worker turning cog (*vert*)	1·00	1·00

(Des A. Hussain)

1994 (14 Apr). 1500th Year of Bengali Solar Calendar. P 14×14½.

503	**182**	2t. multicoloured	55	30

183 Scenes from Baishakhi
Festival

184 Family, Globe and
Logo

(Des A. Hussain)

1994 (12 May). Folk Festivals. T **183** and similar horiz design.
Multicoloured. P 14½×14.

504		4t. Type **183**	50	50
505		4t. Scenes from Nabanna and Paush Parvana Festivals	50	50

(Des M. Huq)

1994 (15 May). International Year of the Family. P 14×14½.

506	**184**	10t. multicoloured	1·00	1·50

185 People planting
Saplings

186 Player kicking Ball

(Des M. Mia and R. Hussain)

1994 (15 June). Tree Planting Campaign. T **185** and similar vert
design. Multicoloured. P 14×14½.

507		4t. Type **185**	50	25
508		6t. Hands holding saplings	75	60

(Des M. Shamim)

1994 (17 June). World Cup Football Championship, U.S.A. T **186** and
similar vert design. Multicoloured. P 14½.

509		20t. Type **186**	2·00	3·00
	a. Horiz strip of three. Nos. 509/10 and label	4·00	6·00
510		20t. Player heading ball	2·00	3·00

Nos. 509/10 were printed together, *se-tenant*, in sheets of 15 (3×5)
with each horizontal row containing one of each design separated by
a label showing the championship mascot.

187 Traffic on Bridge

188 Asian Black-headed
Oriole

(Des A. Rouf)

1994 (24 July). Inauguration of Jamuna Multi-purpose Bridge Project.
P 14½×14.

511	**187**	4t. multicoloured	2·50	60

(Des A. Hussain)

1994 (31 Aug). Birds. T **188** and similar vert designs. Multicoloured.
P 14×14½.

512		4t. Type **188**	40	40
513		6t. Greater Racquet-tailed Drongo (*Dicrurus paradiseus*)	60	80
514		6t. Indian Tree Pie (*Dendrocitta vagabunda*)	60	80
515		6t. Red Junglefowl (*Gallus gallus*)	60	80
512/15	*Set of 4*		2·00	2·50
MS516	165×110 mm. Nos. 512/15 (*sold at 25t.*)		2·25	3·00

189 Dr. Mohammad Ibrahim and
Hospital

190 Nawab Faizunnessa
Chowdhurani

(Des M. Shamim)

1994 (6 Sept). Fifth Death Anniv of Dr. Mohammad Ibrahim (diabetes
treatment pioneer). P 14½×14.

517	**189**	2t. multicoloured	75	20

(Des M. Rahman)

1994 (23 Sept). 160th Birth Anniv of Nawab Faizunnessa
Chowdhurani (social reformer). P 14×14½.

518	**190**	2t. multicoloured	50	20

191 Boxing

(Des A. Hussain)

1994 (2 Oct). Asian Games, Hiroshima, Japan. P 14½×14.

519	**191**	4t. multicoloured	1·75	60

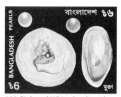

192 Pink and White Pearls with Windowpane Oysters

(Des M. Mia, M. Rahman and Md. Shamsuzzoha)

1994 (30 Oct). Sea Shells. T **192** and similar multicoloured designs. P 14×14½ (No. 523) or 14½×14 (others).

520	6t. Type **192**	1·40	1·60
521	6t. Tranquelous Scallop and other shells....	1·40	1·60
522	6t. Lister's Conch, Asiatic Arabian Cowrie, Bladder Moon and Woodcock Murex.....	1·40	1·60
523	6t. Spotted Tun, Spiny Frog Shell, Spiral Melongena and Gibbous Olive	1·40	1·60
520/3	Set of 4	5·00	5·75

193 Dr. Milon and Demonstrators

(Des M. Akond)

1994 (27 Nov). Fourth Death Anniv of Dr. Shamsul Alam Khan Milon (medical reformer). P 14½×14.

524	**193**	2t. multicoloured	25	20

(Des M. Huq, A. Hussain, M. Mia, A. Moniruzzaman, M. Rahman and Md. Shamsuzzoha)

1994 (14 Dec). Martyred Intellectuals (3rd series). Vert designs as T **148**. Each grey-black and reddish brown. P 14×14½.

525	2t. Dr. Harinath Dey	25	30
	a. Sheetlet. Nos. 525/32	1·75	2·25
526	2t. Dr. A. F. Ziaur Rahman	25	30
527	2t. Mamun Mahmud	25	30
528	2t. Mohsin Ali Dewan	25	30
529	2t. Dr. N. A. M. Jahangir	25	30
530	2t. Shah Abdul Majid	25	30
531	2t. Muhammad Akhter	25	30
532	2t. Meherunnesa	25	30
533	2t. Dr. Kasiruddin Talukder	25	30
	a. Sheetlet. Nos. 533/40	1·75	2·25
534	2t. Fazlul Haque Choudhury	25	30
535	2t. Md. Shamsuzzaman	25	30
536	2t. A. K. M. Shamsuddin	25	30
537	2t. Lt. Mohammad Anwarul Azim	25	30
538	2t. Nurul Amin Khan	25	30
539	2t. Mohammad Sadeque	25	30
540	2t. Md. Araz Ali	25	30
525/40	Set of 16	3·50	4·25

Nos. 525/32 and 533/40 were printed together, *se-tenant*, in sheetlets of eight, the two horizontal rows in each sheetlet being separated by a row of inscribed labels.

194 *Diplazium esculentum*

(Des A. Hussain, N. Islam and Md. Shamsuzzoha)

1994 (24 Dec). Vegetables. T **194** and similar multicoloured designs. P 14½×14 (No. 546) or 14×14½ (others).

541	4t. Type **194**	70	50
542	4t. *Momordica charantia*	70	50
543	6t. *Lagenaria siceraria*	90	70
544	6t. *Trichosanthes dioica*	90	70
545	10t. *Solanum melongena*	1·40	2·00
546	10t. *Cucurbita maxima (horiz)*	1·40	2·00
541/6	Set of 6	5·50	5·75

195 Sonargaon

(Des A. Hussain)

1995 (2 Jan). 20th Anniv of World Tourism Organization. P 14½.

547	**195**	10t. multicoloured	1·75	1·75

196 Exports

(Des M. Huq)

1995 (7 Jan). Dhaka International Trade Fair '95. T **196** and similar horiz design. Multicoloured. P 14½.

548	4t. Type **196**	20	20
549	6t. Symbols of industry	45	65

197 Soldiers of Ramgarh Battalion (1795) and of Bangladesh Rifles (1995)

(Des M. Rahman and Md. Shamsuzzoha)

1995 (10 Jan). Bicentenary of Bangladesh Rifles. T **197** and similar horiz design. Multicoloured. P 14½.

550	2t. Type **197**	1·50	50
551	4t. Riflemen on patrol	1·75	90

198 Surgical Equipment and Lightning attacking Crab (cancer)

(Des M. Rohana)

1995 (7 Apr). Campaign against Cancer. P 14×14½.

552	**198**	2t. multicoloured	40	25

199 Fresh Food and Boy injecting Insulin

(Des N. Islam)

1995 (28 Feb). National Diabetes Awareness Day. P 14.

553	**199**	2t. multicoloured	1·40	30

200 Munshi Mohammad
Meherullah

(Des M. Huq)

1995 (7 June). Munshi Mohammad Meherullah (Islamic educator)
Commemoration. P 14×14½.

554	**200**	2t. multicoloured	30	25

রাজশা।হীপেক্স-৯৫
(**201**)

1995 (23 Aug). Rajshahipex '95 National Philatelic Exhibition. No. 499
optd with T **201** in red.

555		6t. Exterior of Chhota Sona Mosque	2·50	3·00

202 Lagerstroemia
speciosa

203 Aspects of Farming

(Des A. Hussain, Md. Shamsuzzoha, Md.
Jasimuddin, M. Muniruzzaman)

1995 (9 Oct). Flowers. T **202** and similar multicoloured designs.
P 14½.

556		6t. Type **202**	90	90
557		6t. Bombax ceiba (horiz)	90	90
558		10t. Passiflora incarnata	1·25	1·40
559		10t. Bauhinia purpurea	1·25	1·40
560		10t. Canna indica	1·25	1·40
561		10t. Gloriosa superba	1·25	1·40
556/61		Set of 6	6·00	6·75

(Des A. Hussain)

1995 (16 Oct). 50th Anniv of Food and Agriculture Organization.
P 14×14½.

562	**203**	10t. multicoloured	1·00	1·25

A 2t. stamp, in a vertical design, commemorating Shaheed
Khandaker Mosharraf Hossain was due for release on 21 October
1995, but was withdrawn on day of issue although the instructions
may not have reached some offices in time to prevent sale of these
stamps. Some used examples are known.

204 Anniversary Emblem, Peace
Dove and U.N. Headquarters

(Des A. Hussain)

1995 (24 Oct). 50th Anniv of United Nations. T **204** and similar horiz
designs. Multicoloured. P 14½×14.

563		2t. Type **204**	30	20
564		10t. Peace doves circling dates and Globe...	90	1·40
565		10t. Clasped hands and U.N. Headquarters..	90	1·40
563/5		Set of 3	1·90	2·75

205 Diseased Lungs, Microscope,
Family and Map

(Des A. Hussain)

1995 (29 Oct). 18th Eastern Regional Conference on Tuberculosis,
Dhaka. P 14½×14.

566	**205**	6t. multicoloured	1·50	1·00

206 Peace Doves, Emblem
and National Flags

207 Aspects of COMDECA
Projects

(Des A. Hussain)

1995 (8 Dec). Tenth Anniv of South Asian Association for Regional
Co-operation. P 14×14½.

567	**206**	2t. multicoloured	1·40	55

1995 (14 Dec). Martyred Intellectuals (4th series). Vert designs
as T **148**. Each grey-black and reddish brown. P 14×14½.

568		2t. Abdul Ahad	25	30
		a. Sheetlet. Nos. 568/75	1·75	2·25
569		2t. Lt. Col. Mohammad Qadir	25	30
570		2t. Mozammel Hoque Chowdhury	25	30
571		2t. Rafiqul Haider Chowdhury	25	30
572		2t. Dr. Azharul Haque	25	30
573		2t. A. K. Shamsuddin	25	30
574		2t. Anudwaipayan Bhattacharjee	25	30
575		2t. Lutfunnahar Helena	25	30
576		2t. Shaikh Habibur Rahman	25	30
		a. Sheetlet. Nos. 576/83	1·75	2·25
577		2t. Major Naimul Islam	25	30
578		2t. Md. Shahidullah	25	30
579		2t. Ataur Rahman Khan Khadim	25	30
580		2t. A. B. M. Ashraful Islam Bhuiyan	25	30
581		2t. Dr. Md. Sadat Ali	25	30
582		2t. Sarafat Ali	25	30
583		2t. M. A. Sayeed	25	30
568/83		Set of 16	3·50	4·25

Nos. 568/75 and 576/83 were printed together, se-tenant, in
sheetlets of eight, the two horizontal rows in each sheetlet being
separated by a row of inscribed labels.

(Des Md. Shamsuzzoha)

1995 (18 Dec). Second Asia-Pacific Community Development Scout
Camp. P 14×14½.

584	**207**	2t. multicoloured	70	35

208 Volleyball Players

209 Man in Punjabi and
Lungi

(Des A. Hussain)

1995 (25 Dec). Centenary of Volleyball. P 14×14½.

585	**208**	6t. multicoloured	1·00	55

(Des M. Huq, A. Hussain, Md. Shamsuzzoha and M. Rahman)

1995 (25 Dec). Traditional Costumes. T **209** and similar multicoloured designs. P 14½.

586	6t. Type **209**	1·00	1·00
587	6t. Woman in sari	1·00	1·00
588	10t. Christian bride and groom	1·40	1·50
589	10t. Muslim bride and groom	1·40	1·50
590	10t. Buddhist bride and groom (*horiz*)	1·40	1·50
591	10t. Hindu bride and groom (*horiz*)	1·40	1·50
586/91	*Set of 6*	7·00	7·25

210 Shaheed Amanullah Mohammad Asaduzzaman

211 Bowler and Map

(Des A. Hussain)

1996 (20 Jan). 27th Death Anniv. of Shaheed Amanullah Mohammad Asaduzzaman (student leader). P 14×14½.

592	**210**	2t. multicoloured	40	25

(Des M. Huq, A. Hussain and Md. Shamsuzzoha)

1996 (14 Feb). World Cup Cricket Championship. T **211** and similar multicoloured designs. P 14½×14 (10t.) or 14×14½ (others).

593	4t. Type **211**	1·25	55
594	6t. Batsman and wicket keeper	1·50	80
	a. Black and magenta (incl face value) omitted	£110	
595	10t. Match in progress (*horiz*)	2·00	2·25
593/5	*Set of 3*	4·25	3·25

212 Liberation Struggle, 1971

(Des A. Hussain, M. Huq, M. Rahman and Md. Shamsuzzoha)

1996 (26 Mar). 25th Anniv. of Independence. T **212** and similar horiz designs. Multicoloured. P 14½.

596	4t. Type **212**	70	70
597	4t. National Martyrs Memorial	70	70
598	4t. Education	70	70
599	4t. Health	70	70
600	4t. Communications	70	70
601	4t. Industry	70	70
596/601	*Set of 6*	3·75	3·75

213 Michael Madhusudan Dutt

214 Gymnastics

(Des M. Huq)

1996 (29 June). Michael Madhusudan Dutt (poet) Commemoration. P 14×14½.

602	**213**	4t. multicoloured	50	20

(Des M. Huq, Md. Shamsuzzoha and M. Rahman)

1996 (19 July). Olympic Games, Atlanta. T **214** and similar multicoloured designs. P 14×14½ (vert) or 14½×14 (horiz).

603	4t. Type **214**	30	20

604	6t. Judo	40	35
605	10t. Athletics (*horiz*)	45	70
606	10t. High jumping (*horiz*)	45	70
603/6	*Set of 4*	1·40	1·75
MS607	165×110 mm. Nos. 603/6. P 14×14½ (*sold at* 10t.)	1·50	2·00

1996 (29 July). 25th Anniv of Bangladesh Stamps. No. **MS**234 optd "Silver Jubilee Bangladesh Postage Stamps 1971–96" on sheet margin.

MS608	98×117 mm. Nos. 232/3 (*sold at* 10t.)	1·40	1·75

215 Bangabandhu Sheikh Mujibur Rahman

216 Maulana Mohammad Akrum Khan

(Des M. Rahman)

1996 (15 Aug). 21st Death Anniv of Bangabandhu Sheikh Mujibur Rahman. P 14×14½.

609	**215**	4t. multicoloured	40	25

(Des Md. Munirazzaman)

1996 (18 Aug). 28th Death Anniv of Maulana Mohammad Akrum Khan. P 14×14½.

610	**216**	4t. multicoloured	40	20

217 Ustad Alauddin Khan

218 "Kingfisher" (Mayeesha Robbani)

(Des A. Hussain)

1996 (6 Sept). 24th Death Anniv of Ustad Alauddin Khan (musician). P 14×14½.

611	**217**	4t. multicoloured	70	30

1996 (9 Oct). Children's Paintings. T **218** and similar multicoloured design. P 13½×14½ (2t.) or 14½×13½ (4t.).

612	2t. Type **218**	70	45
613	4t. "River Crossing" (Iffat Panchlais) (*horiz*)	90	45
	a. Black and magenta (incl face value) omitted	90·00	

219 Syed Nazrul Islam

220 Children receiving Medicine

(Des M. Rahman)

1996 (3 Nov). 21st Death Anniv of Jail Martyrs. T **219** and similar vert designs. Multicoloured. P 14×14½.

614	4t. Type **219**	30	40
	a. Block of four. Nos. 614/17	1·10	1·40
615	4t. Tajuddin Ahmad	30	40
616	4t. M. Monsoor Ali	30	40
617	4t. A.H.M. Quamaruzzaman	30	40
614/17	*Set of 4*	1·10	1·40

Nos. 614/17 were printed together, *se-tenant*, in blocks of four throughout the sheet.

(Des A. Hussain)

1996 (11 Dec). 50th Anniv of U.N.I.C.E.F. T **220** and similar vert design. Multicoloured. P 14×14½.

618	4t. Type **220**	50	25
619	10t. Mother and child	1·10	1·40

(Des A. Hussain (Nos. 620/1, 625, 632/3), M. Huq (Nos. 622, 624, 627/9, 631) M. Rahman (Nos. 623, 630, 634), T. Hussain (No. 626), N. Islam (No. 635))

1996 (14 Dec). Martyred Intellectuals (5th series). Vert designs as T **148**. Each grey-black and reddish brown. P 14×14½.

620	2t. Dr. Jekrul Haque	45	45
	a. Sheetlet. Nos. 620/7	3·25	3·25
621	2t. Munshi Kabiruddin Ahmed	45	45
622	2t. Md. Abdul Jabbar	45	45
623	2t. Mohammad Amir	45	45
624	2t. A. K. M. Shamsul Huq Khan	45	45
625	2t. Dr. Siddique Ahmed	45	45
626	2t. Dr. Soleman Khan	45	45
627	2t. S. B. M. Mizanur Rahman	45	45
628	2t. Aminuddin	45	45
	a. Sheetlet. Nos. 628/35	3·25	3·25
629	2t. Md. Nazrul Islam	45	45
630	2t. Zahirul Islam	45	45
631	2t. A. K. Lutfor Rahman	45	45
632	2t. Afsar Hossain	45	45
633	2t. Abul Hashem Mian	45	45
634	2t. A. T. M. Alamgir	45	45
635	2t. Baser Ali	45	45
620/35 *Set of 16*		6·50	6·50

Nos. 620/7 and 628/35 were each printed together, *se-tenant*, in sheetlets of eight, the two horizontal rows in each sheetlet being separated by a row of inscribed labels.

221 Celebrating Crowds

(Des Md. Shamsuzzoha)

1996 (16 Dec). 25th Anniv of Victory Day. T **221** and similar multicoloured design. P 14½×14 (4t.) or 14×14½ (6t.).

636	4t. Type **221**	35	30
637	6t. Soldiers and statue (*vert*)	65	70

222 Paul P. Harris

(Des M. Huq)

1997 (18 Feb). 50th Death Anniv of Paul Harris (founder of Rotary). P 14×14½.

638	**222**	4t. multicoloured	35	25
	a. Rotary emblem printed twice		

No. 638a shows the blue and gold Rotary emblem at bottom right printed twice.

223 Shaikh Mujibur Rahman making Speech

(Des A. Hussain)

1997 (7 Mar). 25th Anniv of Shaikh Mujibur's Speech of 7 March (1971). P 12½.

639	**223**	4t. multicoloured	35	25

224 Sheikh Mujibur Rahman

225 Sheikh Mujibur Rahman and Crowd with Banners

(Des M. Mozammel)

1997 (17 Mar). 77th Birth Anniv of Sheikh Mujibur Rahman (first President). P 14×14½.

640	**224**	4t. multicoloured	50	25

(Des M. Rahman)

1997 (26 Mar). 25th Anniv (1996) of Independence. P 12½.

641	**225**	4t. multicoloured	35	25

226 Heinrich von Stephan   **227** Sheep

(Des A. Hussain)

1997 (8 Apr). Death Centenary of Heinrich von Stephan (founder of U.P.U.). P 14×14½.

642	**226**	4t. multicoloured	35	25

(Des A. Hussain)

1997 (10 Apr). Livestock. T **227** and similar horiz designs. Multicoloured. P 14½×14.

643	4t. Type **227**	75	75
644	4t. Goat	75	75
645	6t. Buffalo bull	90	90
646	6t. Cow	90	90
643/6 *Set of 4*		3·00	3·00

228 "Tilling the Field–2" (S. Sultan)

1997 (26 June). Bangladesh Paintings. T **228** and similar horiz design. Multicoloured. P 12½.

647	6t. Type **228**	40	30
648	10t. "Three Women" (Quamrul Hassan)	60	1·25

229 Trophy, Flag and Cricket Ball

(Des A. Hussain)

1997 (4 Sept). Sixth International Cricket Council Trophy Championship, Malaysia. P 12½.

649	**229**	10t. multicoloured	3·75	3·00

230 Kusumba Mosque, Naogaon

(Des Md. Shamsuzzoha)

1997 (4 Sept). Historic Mosques. T **230** and similar horiz designs. Multicoloured. P 14½×14.

650	4t. Type **230**	75	35
651	6t. Atiya Mosque, Tangail	1·00	55
652	10t. Bagha Mosque, Rajshahi	1·60	2·00
650/2 *Set of 3*		3·00	2·50

231 Adul Karim Sahitya Vishard

232 Rover Moot Emblem and Scouts standing on top of World

(Des M. Rahman)

1997 (11 Oct). 126th Birth Anniv of Abdul Karim Sahitya Vishard (scholar). P 14½×14.

653	**231**	4t. multicoloured	40	25

(Des M. Rahman)

1997 (25 Oct). Ninth Asia-Pacific and seventh Bangladesh Rover Moot, Lakkatura. P 14×14½.

654	**232**	2t. multicoloured	50	25

233 Officers and Flag

(Des Md. Jasimuddin)

1997 (21 Nov). 25th Anniv of Armed Forces. P 14½×14.

655	**233**	2t. multicoloured	2·00	70

1997 (14 Dec). Martyred Intellectuals (6th series). Vert designs as T **148**. Each grey-black and reddish brown. P 14×14½.

656	2t. Dr. Shamsuddin Ahmed	65	65
	a. Sheetlet. Nos. 656/63	4·75	4·75
657	2t. Mohammad Salimullah	65	65
658	2t. Mohiuddin Haider	65	65
659	2t. Abdur Rahin	65	65
660	2t. Nitya Nanda Paul	65	65
661	2t. Abdel Jabber	65	65
662	2t. Dr. Humayun Kabir	65	65
663	2t. Khaja Nizamuddin Bhuiyan	65	65
664	2t. Gulam Hossain	65	65
	a. Sheetlet. Nos. 664/71	4·75	4·75
665	2t. Ali Karim	65	65
666	2t. Md. Moazzem Hossain	65	65
667	2t. Rafiqul Islam	65	65
668	2t. M. Nur Husain	65	65
669	2t. Captain Mahmood Hossain Akonda	65	65
670	2t. Abdul Wahab Talukder	65	65
671	2t. Dr. Hasimoy Hazra	65	65
656/71 *Set of 16*		9·50	9·50

Nos. 656/63 and 664/71 were printed together, *se-tenant*, in sheetlets of eight, the two horizontal rows in each sheetlet being separated by a row of inscribed labels.

234 Mohammad Mansooruddin

(Des P. Mandal)

1998 (4 Feb). Professor Mohammad Mansooruddin (folklorist) Commemoration. P 14×14½.

672	**234**	4t. multicoloured	1·40	60

235 Standard-bearer and Soldiers

(Des M. Rahman)

1998 (15 Feb). 50th Anniv of East Bengal Regiment. P 14½×14.

673	**235**	2t. multicoloured	1·00	55

236 Bulbul Chowdhury

237 World Cup Trophy

(Des A. Hussain)

1998 (17 May). Bulbul Chowdhury (traditional dancer) Commemoration. P 14×14½.

674	**236**	4t. multicoloured	40	25

(Des A. Hussain)

1998 (10 June). World Cup Football Championship, France. T **237** and similar vert design. Multicoloured. P 14×14½.

675	6t. Type **237**	75	30
676	18t. Footballer and trophy	2·00	2·50

238 Eastern Approach Road, Bangabandhu Bridge

239 Diana, Princess of Wales

(Des Md. Mia and Md. Shamsuzzoha)

1998 (23 June). Opening of Bangabandhu Bridge. T **238** and similar horiz designs. Multicoloured. P 14½×14.

677	4t. Type **238**	65	30
678	6t. Western approach road	75	40
679	8t. Embankment	95	1·40
680	10t. Main span, Bangabandhu Bridge	1·25	1·60
677/80 *Set of 4*		3·25	3·25

(Des Md. Miah and A. Hussain)

1998 (6 Sept). Diana, Princess of Wales Commemoration. T **239** and similar vert designs. Multicoloured. P 14.

681	8t. Type **239**		1·40	1·40
	a. Horiz strip of three. Nos. 681/3		4·50	4·75
682	18t. Wearing pearl choker		1·75	1·75
683	22t. Wearing pendant necklace		1·75	2·00
681/3 Set of 3			4·50	4·75

Nos. 681/3 were printed together, *se-tenant*, in horizontal strips of three throughout the sheet.

240 Means of collecting Solar Energy

241 World Habitat Day Emblem and City Scene

(Des A. Hussain)

1998 (24 Sept). World Solar Energy Programme Summit. P 14×14½.

684	**240**	10t. multicoloured	1·50	1·50

(Des A. Hussain)

1998 (5 Oct). World Habitat Day. P 14×14½.

685	**241**	4t. multicoloured	1·25	60
		a. Logo at top left in green		

No. 685 normally shows the logo at top left in white.

242 Farmworkers, Sunflower and "20"

243 Batsman

(Des. A. Hussain)

1998 (17 Oct). 20th Anniv of International Fund for Agricultural Development. T **242** and similar vert design. Multicoloured. P 14×14½.

686	6t. Type **242**		65	35
687	10t. Farmworker with baskets and harvested crops		1·10	1·40

(Des A. Hussain)

1998 (24 Oct). Wills International Cricket Cup, Dhaka. P 14×14½.

688	**243**	6t. multicoloured	1·75	1·25

244 Begum Rokeya

(Des A. Hussain)

1998 (9 Dec). Begum Rokeya (campaigner for women's education) Commemoration. P 14½×14.

689	**244**	4t. multicoloured	1·25	60

245 Anniversary Logo

246 Dove of Peace and U.N. Symbols

(Des A. Hussain)

1998 (10 Dec). 50th Anniv of Universal Declaration of Human Rights. P 14×14½.

690	**245**	10t. multicoloured	1·25	1·25

1998 (14 Dec). Martyred Intellectuals (7th series). Vert designs as T **148**. Each grey-black and reddish brown. P 14×14½.

691	2t. Md. Khorshed Ali Sarker		50	50
	a. Sheetlet. Nos. 691/8		3·50	3·50
692	2t. Abu Yakub Mahfuz Ali		50	50
693	2t. S. M. Nural Huda		50	50
694	2t. Nazmul Hoque Sarker		50	50
695	2t. Md. Taslim Uddin		50	50
696	2t. Gulam Mostafa		50	50
697	2t. A. H. Nural Alam		50	50
698	2t. Timir Kanti Dev		50	50
699	2t. Altaf Hossain		50	50
	a. Sheetlet. Nos. 699/706		3·50	3·50
700	2t. Aminul Hoque		50	50
701	2t. S. M. Fazlul Hoque		50	50
702	2t. Mozammel Ali		50	50
703	2t. Syed Akbar Hossain		50	50
704	2t. Sk. Abdus Salam		50	50
705	2t. Abdur Rahman		50	50
706	2t. Dr. Shyamal Kanti Lala		50	50
691/706 Set of 16			7·00	7·00

Nos. 691/8 and 699/706 were each printed together, *se-tenant*, in sheetlets of eight, the horizontal rows in each sheetlet being separated by a row of inscribed labels.

(Des A. Hussain)

1998 (30 Dec). 50th Anniv, of U.N. Peace-keeping Operations. P 14×14½.

707	**246**	10t. multicoloured	1·25	1·50

247 Kazi Nazrul Islam

(Des A. Hussain)

1998 (31 Dec). Birth Centenary (1999) of Kazi Nazrul Islam (poet). P 14½.

708	**247**	6t. multicoloured	1·25	70
		a. Gold (border) omitted		

248 Jamboree Emblem and Scout Activities

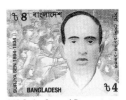

249 Surjya Sen and Demonstrators

(Des A. Hussain)

1999 (6 Feb). Sixth Bangladesh National Scout Jamboree. P 14×14½.

709	**248**	2t. multicoloured	1·00	50

1999 (18 Mar–31 Aug). As Nos. 75 and 318/19, but now printed litho by State Security Ptg Press, Gazipur. P 14½×14 (3t.) or 14½ (5t., 10t.).

709a		3t. black and light blue (2000?) (as No. 318)	55	10
710		5t. black and brown-red (as No. 319)	75	15
711		10t. bright rose (as No. 75, but 35×22 mm)	5·00	1·50

No. 711 has been redrawn so that "SIXTY-DOME MOSQUE" appears above the face value at bottom right instead of below the main inscription at top left.

Nos. 712/4 have been left vacant.

(Des A. Hussain)

1999 (22 Mar). Surjya Sen (revolutionary) Commemoration. P 14½×14.

715	**249**	4t. multicoloured	1·25	60

250 Dr. Fazlur Rahman Khan and Sears Tower

251 National Team Badges

(Des A. Hussain)

1999 (3 Apr). 70th Birth Anniv of Dr. Fazlur Rahman Khan (architect). P 14×14½.

716	**250**	4t. multicoloured	1·00	55

(Des M. Rahman)

1999 (13 May). Cricket World Cup, England. T **251** and similar vert design. Multicoloured. P 14½×14½.

717		8t. Type **251**	1·75	2·00
718		10t. Bangladesh cricket team badge and flag	2·50	2·50
MS719	139×89 mm. Nos. 717/18 (sold at 30t.)		4·75	5·00

252 Mother Teresa

253 Sheikh Mujibur Rahman, New York Skyline and Dove

(Des A. Hussain)

1999 (5 Sept). Mother Teresa Commemoration. P 14×14½.

720	**252**	4t. multicoloured	1·50	65

(Des A. Hussain)

1999 (13 Sept). 25th Anniv of Bangladesh's Admission to U.N. P 14×14½.

721	**253**	6t. multicoloured	1·00	65

254 Shaheed Mohammad Maizuddin

255 Faces in Tree

(Des M. Rahman)

1999 (27 Sept). 15th Death Anniv of Shaheed Mohammad Maizuddin (politician). P 14×14½.

722	**254**	2t. multicoloured	60	30

(Des A. Hussain)

1999 (1 Oct). International Year of the Elderly. P 14×14½.

723	**255**	6t. multicoloured	1·00	60

256 Shanty Town and Modern Buildings between Hands

(Des A. Hussain)

1999 (4 Oct). World Habitat Day. P 14½×14.

724	**256**	4t. multicoloured	1·00	50

257 Mobile Post Office

258 Sir Jagadis Chandra Bose

(Des M. Rahman, A. Hussain and Md. Shamsuzzoha)

1999 (9 Oct). 125th Anniv of Universal Postal Union. T **257** and similar horiz designs. Multicoloured. P 14½×14.

725		4t. Type **257**	80	65
726		4t. Postman on motorcycle	80	65
727		6t. Postal motor launch	1·00	90
728		6t. Two Bangladesh airliners	1·00	90
725/8	Set of 4		3·25	2·75
MS729	141×90 mm. Nos. 725/8 (sold at 25t.)		3·25	3·25

1999 (22 Nov). Sir Jagadis Chandra Bose (physicist and botanist) Commemoration. P 14×14½.

730	**258**	4t. multicoloured	1·50	60

1999 (14 Dec). Martyred Intellectuals (8th series). Vert designs as T **148**. Each grey-black and reddish brown. P 14×14½.

731		2t. Dr. Mohammad Shafi	55	55
		a. Sheetlet. Nos. 731/8	4·00	4·00
732		2t. Maulana Kasimuddin Ahmed	55	55
733		2t. Quazi Ali Imam	55	55
734		2t. Sultanuddin Ahmed	55	55
735		2t. A. S. M. Ershadullah	55	55
736		2t. Mohammad Fazlur Rahman	55	55
737		2t. Captain A.K.M. Farooq	55	55
738		2t. Md. Latafot Hossain Joarder	55	55
739		2t. Ram Ranjan Bhattacharjya	55	55
		a. Sheetlet. Nos. 739/46	4·00	4·00
740		2t. Abani Mohan Dutta	55	55
741		2t. Sunawar Ali	55	55
742		2t. Abdul Kader Miah	55	55
743		2t. Major Rezaur Rahman	55	55
744		2t. Md. Shafiqul Anowar	55	55
745		2t. A. A. M. Mozammel Hoque	55	55
746		2t. Khandkar Abul Kashem	55	55
731/46	Set of 16		8·00	8·00

Nos. 731/8 and 739/46 were each printed together, se-tenant, in sheetlets of eight, the horizontal rows in each sheetlet being separated by a row of inscribed labels.

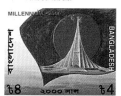

259 Bangladesh Flag and Monument

2000 (1 Jan). New Millennium. T **259** and similar multicoloured design. P 14½×14 (horiz) or 14×14½ (vert).

747		4t. Type **259**	1·25	45
748		6t. Satellite, computer and dish aerial (vert)	1·25	1·40

260 Dr. Muhammad Shamsuzzoha

261 Cub Scouts, Globe and Flag

2000 (8 Feb). 30th Death Anniv. of Dr. Muhammad Shamsuzzoha (1999). P 14×14½.
749   **260**   4t. multicoloured .... 1·00   40

2000 (13 Feb). Fifth Bangladesh Cub Camporee. P 14×14½.
750   **261**   2t. multicoloured 70   40

262 Jibananada Das

263 Shafiur Rahman

2000 (17 Feb). Death Centenary of Jibananada Das (poet) (1999). P 14×14½.
751   **262**   4t. multicoloured .... 1·00   40

2000 (21 Feb). International Mother Language Day. T **263** and similar vert designs. Multicoloured. P 14×14½.
752   4t. Type **263** 75   85
753   4t. Abul Barkat 75   85
754   4t. Abdul Jabbar 75   85
755   4t. Rafiq Uddin Ahmad 75   85
752/5 *Set of 4* .... 2·75   3·00

264 Meteorological Equipment

265 Cricket Week Logo and Web Site Address

2000 (23 Mar). 50th Anniv of World Meteorological Organization. P 14×14½.
756   **264**   10t. multicoloured .... 1·75   1·75

2000 (8 Apr). International Cricket Week. P 14×14½.
757   **265**   6t. multicoloured .... 2·25   1·50

266 Wasp

2000 (18 May). Insects. T **266** and similar square designs. Multicoloured. P 14½.
758   2t. Type **266** 50   30
759   4t. Grasshopper 70   35
760   6t. Bumble bee 90   75
761   10t. Silkworms .... 1·50   2·50
758/61 *Set of 4* .... 3·25   3·50

267 Gecko

268 Batsman

2000 (18 May). Native Fauna. T **267** and similar horiz designs. Multicoloured. P 14½×14.
762   4t. Type **267** 90   90
763   4t. Indian Crested Porcupine 90   90
764   6t. Indian Black-tailed Python .... 1·10   1·10
765   6t. Bengal Monitor .... 1·10   1·10
762/5 *Set of 4* .... 3·50   3·50

2000 (28 May). Pepsi 7th Asia Cricket Cup. P 14×14½.
766   **268**   6t. multicoloured .... 2·25   1·50

269 Water Cock

270 Women's Shotput

2000 (15 July). Birds. T **269** and similar multicoloured designs. P 14½×14 (horiz) or 14×14½ (vert).
767   4t. Type **269** .... 1·25   90
768   4t. White-breasted Waterhen (*Amaurornis phoenicurus*) .... 1·25   90
769   6t. Javanese Cormorant (*Phalacrocorax niger*) (*vert*) .... 1·60   1·40
770   6t. Indian Pond Heron (*Ardeola grayii*) (*vert*) .... 1·60   1·40
767/70 *Set of 4* .... 5·25   4·25

2000 (18 Sept). Olympic Games, Sydney. T **270** and similar vert design. Multicoloured. P 14×14½.
771   6t. Type **270** .... 1·00   50
772   10t. Men's Shotput .... 1·50   1·75

271 Clasped Hands, Landmarks and Flags

2000 (4 Oct). 25th Anniv of Diplomatic Relations with People's Republic of China. P 12½.
773   **271**   6t. multicoloured .... 1·75   75

272 Idrakpur Fort, Munshigonj

2000 (5 Nov). Archaeology. T **272** and similar multicoloured design. P 14½×14 (horiz) or 14×14½ (vert).
774   4t. Type **272** .... 1·00   40
775   6t. Statue of Buddha, Mainamati (*vert*) ... 1·50   1·25

273 Year Emblem **274** Hason Raza

(Des M. Rahman)

2000 (5 Dec). International Volunteers' Year. P 14×14½.
776　**273**　6t. multicoloured ....　1·25　65

(Des M. Rahman)

2000 (6 Dec). 80th Death Anniv of Hason Raza (mystic poet). P 14.
777　**274**　6t. multicoloured ....　1·50　75

275 UNHCR Logo **276** Map of Faces

(Des A. Hussain)

2000 (14 Dec). 50th Anniv of United Nations High Commissioner for Refugees (UNHCR). P 14.
778　**275**　10t. multicoloured ....　1·50　2·00

2000 (14 Dec). Martyred Intellectuals (9th series). Vert designs as T **148**. Each grey-black and reddish brown. P 12½.
779　　2t. M. A. Gofur ....　55　55
　　　a. Sheetlet. Nos. 779/86 ....　4·00　4·00
780　　2t. Faizur Rahman Ahmed ....　55　55
781　　2t. Muslimuddin Miah ....　55　55
782　　2t. Sgt. Shamsul Karim Khan ....　55　55
783　　2t. Bhikku Zinananda ....　55　55
784　　2t. Abdul Jabber ....　55　55
785　　2t. Sekander Hayat Chowdhury ....　55　55
786　　2t. Chishty Shah Helalur Rahman ....　55　55
787　　2t. Birendra Nath Sarker ....　55　55
　　　a. Sheetlet. Nos. 787/94 ....　4·00　4·00
788　　2t. A. K. M. Nurul Haque ....　55　55
789　　2t. Sibendra Nath Mukherjee ....　55　55
790　　2t. Zahir Raihan ....　55　55
791　　2t. Ferdous Dowla Bablu ....　55　55
792　　2t. Capt A. K. M. Nurul Absur ....　55　55
793　　2t. Mizanur Rahman Miju ....　55　55
794　　2t. Dr. Shamshad Ali ....　55　55
779/94 *Set of 16* ....　8·00　8·00
　　Nos. 779/86 and 787/94 were printed together, *se-tenant*, in sheetlets of eight, the two horizontal rows in each sheetlet being separated by a row of inscribed labels.

(Des M. Rahman)

2001 (23 Jan). Population and Housing Census. P 14.
795　**276**　4t. multicoloured ....　1·25　55

277 Producing Food **278** "Peasant Women" (Rashid Chowdhury)

(Des M. Khatun)

2001 (17 Mar). "Hunger-free Bangladesh" Campaign. P 14.
796　**277**　6t. multicoloured ....　1·25　65

2001 (1 Apr). Bangladesh Paintings. P 14×14½.
797　**278**　10t. multicoloured ....　2·00　2·25

279 Lalbagh Kella Mosque

2001 (30 Apr). Historic Buildings. T **279** and similar horiz designs. Multicoloured. P 14.
798　　6t. Type **279** ....　1·00　1·00
　　　a. Block of four. Nos. 798/801 ....　3·50　3·50
799　　6t. Uttara Ganabhavan, Natore ....　1·00　1·00
800　　6t. Armenian Church, Armanitola ....　1·00　1·00
801　　6t. Panam Nagar, Sonargaon ....　1·00　1·00
798/801 *Set of 4* ....　3·50　3·50
　　Nos. 798/801 were printed together, *se-tenant*, in blocks of four throughout the sheet.

280 Smoking Accessories, Globe and Paper People

2001 (31 May). World No Tobacco Day. P 14.
802　**280**　10t. multicoloured ....　1·75　2·00

281 Ustad Gul Mohammad Khan **282** Begum Sufia Kamal

2001 (31 May). Artists. T **281** and similar vert designs. Multicoloured. P 14.
803　　6t. Type **281** ....　80　85
　　　a. Block of four. Nos. 803/6 ....　2·75　3·00
804　　6t. Ustad Khadem Hossain Khan ....　80　85
805　　6t. Gouhar Jamil ....　80　85
806　　6t. Abdul Alim ....　80　85
803/6 *Set of 4* ....　2·75　3·00
　　Nos. 803/6 were printed together, *se-tenant*, in blocks of four throughout the sheet.

2001 (20 June). Begum Sufia Kamal (poet) Commemoration. P 14.
807　**282**　4t. multicoloured ....　75　40

283 Hilsa

2001 (9 July). Fish. T **283** and similar horiz designs. Multicoloured. P 14.
808　　10t. Type **283** ....　1·25　1·40
　　　a. Block of four. Nos. 808/11 ....　4·50　5·00
809　　10t. Tengra ....　1·25　1·40
810　　10t. Punti ....　1·25　1·40
811　　10t. Khalisa ....　1·25　1·40
808/11 *Set of 4* ....　4·50　5·00
　　Nos. 808/11 were printed together, *se-tenant*, in blocks of four throughout the sheet.

284 Parliament House, Dhaka

2001 (13 July). Completion of First Full National Parliamentary Term. P 14.

812	**284**	10t. multicoloured		2·75	2·75

285 Parliament House, Dhaka

2001 (30 Sept). Eighth Parliamentary Elections. P 14.

813	**285**	2t. multicoloured		70	45

286 "Children encircling Globe" (Urska Golob)

287 Meer Mosharraf Hossain

2001 (24 Oct). UN Year of Dialogue among Civilisations. P 14.

814	**286**	10t. multicoloured		1·25	1·50
MS815	95×65 mm. **286** 10t. multicoloured (sold at 30t.)			2·25	3·50

(Des A. Hossain)

2001 (13 Nov). Meer Mosharraf Hossain (writer) Commemoration. P 14.

816	**287**	4t. black, deep rose-red and crimson.		65	40

288 Drop of Blood surrounded by Images

289 Sreshto Medal

(Des A. Hossain)

2001 (1 Dec). World AIDS Day. P 14.

817	**288**	10t. multicoloured		2·25	2·00

(Des M. Akand)

2001 (16 Dec). 30th Anniv of Independence. Gallantry Medals. T **289** and similar vert designs. Multicoloured. P 14.

818	10t. Type **289**		1·25	1·50
	a. Strip of four. Nos. 818/21		4·50	5·00
819	10t. Uttom medal		1·25	1·50
820	10t. Bikram medal		1·25	1·50
821	10t. Protik medal		1·25	1·50
818/21	Set of 4		4·50	5·00

Nos. 818/21 were printed together, se-tenant, as horizontal and vertical strips of four, throughout the sheets of 16.

290 Publicity Poster

(Des Q. Chowdhury)

2002 (9 Jan). Tenth Asian Art Biennale, Dhaka. P 14.

822	**290**	10t. multicoloured		1·00	1·25

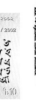
291 Letters from Bengali Alphabet

292 Rokuon-Ji Temple, Japan

(Des Q. Chowdhury (No. **MS**826), A. Hossain (others))

2002 (21 Feb). 50th Anniv of Amar Ekushey (language movement). International Mother Language Day. T **291** and similar designs. P 14.

823	10t. black, gold and vermilion		80	1·10
	a. Horiz strip of three. Nos. 823/5		2·00	3·00
824	10t. black, gold and vermilion		80	1·10
825	10t. black, gold and vermilion		80	1·10
823/5	Set of 3		2·00	3·00
MS826	96×64 mm. 30t. multicoloured		2·00	2·75

Designs: Horiz—No. 823, Type **291**; 824, Language Martyrs' Monument, Dhaka; 825, Letters from Bengali alphabet ("INTERNATIONAL MOTHER LANGUAGE DAY" inscr at right). Vert—No. **MS**826, Commemorative symbol of Martyrs' Monument.

Nos. 823/5 were printed together, se-tenant, in horizontal strips of three throughout the sheets.

2002 (11 Apr). 30th Anniv of Diplomatic Relations with Japan. P 14.

827	**292**	10t. multicoloured		1·00	1·25

293 Silhouetted Goats

(Des S. Basak)

2002 (27 Apr). Goat Production. P 14½×14.

828	**293**	2t. multicoloured		45	25

294 Children

295 Mohammad Nasiruddin

(Des A. Hossain)

2002 (28 Apr). UN Special Session on Children. P 14.

829	**294**	10t. multicoloured		1·25	1·25

(Des A. Hossain)

2002 (21 May). Mohammad Nasiruddin (journalist) Commemoration. P 14.

| 830 | **295** | 4t. black and lake-brown | 75 | 40 |

296 National Flags (trophy at top right)

(Des A. Hossain)

2002 (30 May). World Cup Football Championship, Japan and Korea. T **296** and similar horiz designs. Multicoloured.

831		10t. Type **296**	1·50	1·50
		a. Horiz strip of three. Nos. 831/3	4·00	4·00
832		10t. Pitch markings on world map	1·50	1·50
833		10t. National flags (trophy at top left)	1·50	1·50
831/3 *Set of 3*			4·00	4·00

Nos. 831/3 were printed together, *se-tenant*, as horizontal strips of three throughout the sheets of 90.

297 Children tending Saplings

2002 (15 June). National Tree Planting Campaign. T **297** and similar multicoloured designs. P 14.

834		10t. Type **297**	90	1·00
835		10t. Citrus fruit	90	1·00
836		10t. Trees within leaf symbol (*vert*)	90	1·00
834/6 *Set of 3*			2·40	2·75

298 Children inside Symbolic House

299 Rural Family

2002 (9 July). 30th Anniv of SOS Children's Village in Bangladesh. P 14.

| 837 | **298** | 6t. multicoloured | 1·00 | 45 |

2002 (11 July). World Population Day. P 14.

| 838 | **299** | 6t. multicoloured | 1·00 | 45 |

300 Ompook Pabda (fish)

301 Bangladesh-U.K. Friendship Bridge, Bhairab

2002 (10 Aug). Fish. T **300** and similar horiz design. Multicoloured. P 14.

| 839 | | 4t. Type **300** | 50 | 50 |
| 840 | | 4t. *Labeo gonius* | 50 | 50 |

2002 (10 Sept). Opening of Bangladesh–U.K. Friendship Bridge, Bhairab. P 14.

| 841 | **301** | 4t. multicoloured | 1·00 | 45 |

302 Dhaka City Centre

2002 (7 Oct). World Habitat Day. P 14.

| 842 | **302** | 4t. multicoloured | 70 | 35 |

303 Dariabandha (Tag)

304 Jasimuddin

2002 (10 Nov). Rural Games. T **303** and similar horiz design. P 14.

| 843 | | 4t. Type **303** | 70 | 70 |
| 844 | | 4t. Kanamachee (Blind-man's buff) | 70 | 70 |

(Des A. Sikder)

2003 (1 Jan). Birth Centenary of Jasimuddin (poet). P 14×14½.

| 845 | **304** | 5t. multicoloured | 50 | 35 |

305 Books

306 Footballers and Flags of Participating Countries

(Des A. Hossain)

2003 (1 Jan). National Book Year. P 14×14½.

| 846 | **305** | 6t. multicoloured | 60 | 35 |

(Des A. Hossain)

2003 (10 Jan). Third SAFF Championship, Bangladesh. P 14×14½.

| 847 | **306** | 10t. multicoloured | 2·00 | 2·00 |

ইফাদ-এর ২৫ বছর

25 Years of IFAD

(307)

308 Shefa-ul-Mulk Hakim Habib-ur-Rahman

2003 (19 Feb). 25th Anniv of International Fund for Agricultural Development. No. 687 optd with T **307**.

| 848 | | 10t. Farmworker with baskets and harvested crops | 1·75 | 2·00 |

(Des M. Rahman)

2003 (23 Feb). 56th Death Anniv of Shefa-ul-Mulk Hakim Habib-ur-Rahman. P 14×14½.

849　　**308**　　4t. multicoloured .... 1·50　1·00

309 Ziaur Rahman　　　　　**310** Sapling in Cupped
　　　　　　　　　　　　　　　　Hands and Family

(Des A. Hossain)

2003 (29 May). 22nd Death Anniv of Ziaur Rahman (President 1977–1981). P 14×14½.

850　　**309**　　4t. multicoloured .... 45　25

(Des A. Hossain)

2003 (1 June). National Tree Plantation Campaign. T **310** and similar vert design. Multicoloured. P 14×14½.

851　　　　8t. Type **310** .... 1·25　75
852　　　　12t. Trees, plant, fruit and adult with
　　　　　　　　children inside "petals" .... 1·50　1·75

311 Fruit

(Des Mesbah Uddin Ahmed)

2003 (12 June). Fruit Tree Plantation Fortnight. P 14½×14.

853　　**311**　　6t. multicoloured .... 1·60　1·00

312 *Labeo Calbasu* (Orange-fin　　**313** Train on Jamuna
labeo)　　　　　　　　　　　　　　Bridge and Signals

(Des S. R. Moin)

2003 (12 Aug). Fish Fortnight. P 14½×14.

854　　**312**　　2t. multicoloured .... 75　40

(Des Roop Communication)

2003 (14 Aug). Inauguration of Direct Train Communication between Rajshahi and Dhaka. P 14×14½.

855　　**313**　　10t. multicoloured .... 1·75　1·75

314 Jatiya Sangsad Bhaban
(Parliament House)

(Des A. Hossain)

2003 (7 Oct). 49th Commonwealth Parliamentary Conference. P 14½×14.

856　　**314**　　10t. multicoloured .... 1·25　1·50

315 Mosque　　　　　　　　**316** Emblem

2003 (25 Nov). Eid Mubarak. P 14×14½.

857　　**315**　　4t. multicoloured .... 1·00　65

2003 (7 Dec). International Centre for Diarrhoeal Disease Research, Bangladesh. P 14×14½.

858　　**316**　　10t. multicoloured .... 1·25　1·50

317 Rajshahi University

(Des A. Hossain)

2003 (21 Dec). 50th Anniv of Rajshahi University. P 14½×14.

859　　**317**　　4t. multicoloured .... 1·00　55
　　　　　　　a. Gold (Bangla inscr) omitted £130

318 Books

(Des J. Uddin)

2004 (1 Jan). National Library Year (2003). P 14½×14.

860　　**318**　　6t. multicoloured .... 1·00　70

319 Tents inside Emblem and
Member Flags

(Des S. Bin Salam)

2004 (6 Jan). Seventh Bangladesh and Fourth South Asian Association for Regional Co-operation Jamboree. P 14½×14.

861　　**319**　　2t. multicoloured .... 1·25　45

320 Runner with Olympic Torch

(Des M. Chakraborty)

2004 (10 Jan). Sport and Environment. P 14½×14.
862 **320** 10t. multicoloured .... 1·00 1·25

321 Emblems

(Des S. L. Haq)

2004 (15 Jan). 11th Asian Art Biennale. P 14½×14.
863 **321** 5t. multicoloured 45 25

322 Ziaur Rahman

(Des M. Chakraborty)

2004 (24 Mar). 33rd Anniv of Independence and National Day. P 14½×14.
864 **322** 5t. multicoloured 45 25

323 Road and Emblems

(Des M. Chakraborty)

2004 (7 Apr). World Health Day. P 14½×14.
865 **323** 6t. multicoloured 45 25

Silver Jubilee
Bangladesh National Philatelic Association
(324)

2004 (31 May). 25th Anniv of Bangladesh National Philatelic Association. No. 843 optd with T **324**.
866 4t. Type **303** 45 30

325 Stylized Tree, Fruits and Berries

326 Hafez Shirazi, Iranian Flag and Banay-é Azadi (Freedom Monument), Tehran

(Des A. Hossain)

2004 (1 June). National Tree Plantation Campaign. T **325** and similar vert design. Multicoloured. P 14.
867 10t. Type **325** 65 85
868 10t. Trees and saplings 65 85

(Des M. Chakraborty)

2004 (3 June). Commemoration of Diplomatic Relations with Iran. T **326** and similar horiz design. Multicoloured. P 14½×14.
869 10t. Type **326** .... 80 1·00
870 10t. Nazrul Islam, Bangladeshi flag and War memorial, Dhaka .... 80 1·00

327 Woman planting Tree and Fruit

328 Workers carrying Rice Harvest

(Des Mesbah Uddin Ahmed)

2004 (6 June). Fruit Tree Plantation Campaign. P 14×14½.
871 **327** 10t. multicoloured 75 75

(Des M. Chakraborty)

2004 (21 June). International Year of Rice. P 14½×14.
872 **328** 5t. multicoloured 60 60

329 Man feeding Child and Two Women

330 UN Headquarters and Flags

(Des A. Hossain)

2004 (11 July). World Population Day. P 13½×14½.
873 **329** 6t. multicoloured 45 30

(Des M. Chakraborty)

2004 (16 Sept). 30th Anniv of United Nations Membership. P 14½×14.
874 **330** 4t. multicoloured 30 20

331 Bhasani Novo Theatre, Dhaka

332 Centennial Bell

(Des M. Chakraborty)

2004 (25 Sept). Bhasani Novo Theatre, Dhaka. P 14½×14.
875 **331** 4t. multicoloured 30 20

(Des A. Haque Mallik)

2004 (22 Oct). Centenary of Rotary International. P 14×14½.
876 **332** 4t. multicoloured 30 20

333 *Argemone mexicana*

(Des A. Hossain)

2004 (1 Dec). Wild Flowers. T **333** and similar horiz designs. Multicoloured. P 14½×12½.

877	5t. Type **333**		70	70
	a. Sheetlet. Nos. 877/82		3·75	3·75
878	5t. *Cyanotis axillaris*		70	70
879	5t. *Thevetia peruvians*		70	70
880	5t. *Pentapetes phoenicea*		70	70
881	5t. *Aegle marmelos*		70	70
882	5t. *Datura stramonium*		70	70
877/82 Set of 6			3·75	3·75

Nos. 877/82 were printed together in *se-tenant* sheetlets of six stamps.

334 Rainbow and Emblem   **335** *Sperata aor*

(Des A. Hossain)

2004 (8 Dec). 13th SAARC (South Asian Association for Regional Co-operation) Summit, Dhaka (2005). P 14×14½.

883	**334**	6t. multicoloured	40	25

(Des S.R. Moin Rumi)

2004 (20 Dec). Fish Fortnight. T **335** and similar horiz design. Multicoloured. P 14×13½.

884	10t. Type **335**		1·10	1·25
	a. Horiz pair. Nos. 884/5		2·10	2·50
885	10t. *Notopterus notepturus*		1·10	1·25

Nos. 884/5 were printed together, *se-tenant*, in horizontal pairs throughout the sheet.

336 Cub in Sunflower   **337** Woman Farmer and Microcredit Symbol

(Des A. Hossain)

2004 (26 Dec). Sixth National Cub Camporee. P 14×14½.

886	**336**	6t. multicoloured	40	25

(Des M. Chakraborty)

2005 (15 Jan). United Nations International Year of Microcredit. T **337** and similar horiz design. Multicoloured. P 14½×14.

887	4t. Type **337**		30	45
	a. Horiz pair. Nos. 887/8		1·00	1·25
888	10t. Woman turning lever on coin and microcredit symbol pulley		70	80

Nos. 887/8 were printed together, *se-tenant*, in horizontal pairs throughout the sheet.

338 Beach at Sunset

(Des M. Chakraborty)

2005 (1 Feb). South Asia Tourism Year. P 14½×14.

889	**338**	4t. multicoloured	40	20

339 Major Ziaur Rahman and War Memorial, Dhaka   **340** Sewing Machinist, Fish in Net, Dairy Cattle, Hens and Goats

(Des A. Sikder)

2005 (24 Mar). Independence and National Day. P 14½×14.

890	**339**	10t. multicoloured	75	75

(Des M. Chakraborty)

2005 (31 Mar). Centenary of Co-operative Movement in Bangladesh. P 14×14½.

891	**340**	5t. multicoloured	40	25

341 Family planting Tree   **342** G. A. Mannan (choreographer)

(Des Anowar Hossain)

2005 (1 June). National Tree Plantation Campaign. T **341** and similar horiz design. Multicoloured. P 14½×14.

892	6t. Type **341**		70	75
	a. Horiz pair. Nos. 892/3		1·40	1·50
893	6t. Three trees of different varieties		70	75

Nos. 892/3 were printed together, *se-tenant*, as horizontal pairs in sheets of 100.

(Des Mrinal Chakraborty)

2005 (5 June). Talented Artists. T **342** and similar vert designs. Multicoloured. P 14×14½.

894	6t. Type **342**		60	70
	a. Block of four. Nos. 894/7		2·25	2·50
895	6t. Ustad Phuljhuri Khan (musician)		60	70
896	6t. Ustad Abed Hossain Khan (musician and composer)		60	70
897	6t. Ustad Munshi Raisuddin (musician)		60	70
894/7 Set of 4			2·25	2·50

Nos. 894/7 were printed together, *se-tenant*, as blocks of four stamps in sheets of 100.

343 *Nandus nandus*   **344** Dr. Nawab Ali

2005 (7 Aug). Fish Fortnight. P 14×13½.

898	**343**	10t. multicoloured	1·25	1·25

2005 (4 Dec). Dr. Nawab Ali (physician) Commemoration. P 14×14½.

899	**344**	8t. multicoloured	1·00	80

345 Books, Compass and Dividers

2006 (1 Jan). Science Book Year (2005). P 14½×14.
900 **345** 10t. multicoloured .... 1·00 1·00

346 Emblems, Globe and Computer Screen

2006 (22 Jan). World Summit on the Information Society, Tunis (2005). P 14½×14.
901 **346** 10t. multicoloured .... 1·00 1·00

347 Verwaltungssitz, Vienna and Emblem

2006 (28 Jan). 30th Anniv of OPEC Fund for International Development (2005). P 14½×14.
902 **347** 10t. multicoloured 75 75

348 Palace of Heavenly Peace, Beijing

2006 (6 Mar). 30th Anniv of Bangladesh–China Diplomatic Relations (2005). T **348** and similar horiz designs. Multicoloured. P 12.
903 10t. Type **348** 70 70
a. Horiz strip of four. Nos. 903/6 .... 2·50 2·50
904 10t. Parliament Building, Dhaka 70 70
905 10t. 5th Bangladesh–China Friendship Bridge over Gabkhan River 70 70
906 10t. Great Wall of China 70 70
903/6 Set of 4 .... 2·50 2·50
MS907 140×90 mm. Nos. 903/6 .... 2·50 2·50
Nos. 903/6 were printed together, *se-tenant*, as horizontal strips of four stamps in sheetlets of 16.

349 Major Ziaur Rahman and War Memorial, Dhaka

(Des Amirul Islam Sikder)

2006 (23 Mar). 35th Anniversary of Independence and National Day. P 14½×14.
908 **349** 10t. multicoloured .... 1·00 75

350 Palm Tree

2006 (5 June). National Tree Plantation Campaign and Tree Fair. P 14½×14.
909 **350** 10t. multicoloured .... 1·00 75

351 Mother with Baby and Toddler   **352** Silhouette of Batsman

(Des Anowar Hossain)

2006 (19 July). World Health Day. P 14×14½.
910 **351** 6t. multicoloured .... 1·25 1·00

(Des Anowar Hossain)

2006 (19 July). ICC Under 19 Cricket World Cup (2004), Bangladesh. P 14×14½.
911 **352** 10t. multicoloured .... 1·75 1·25

353 Peace Dove and Modern Buildings and Roads   **354** AIDS Ribbon and Globe

(Des Mrinal Chakraborty)

2006 (25 Oct). Five Years of Peace and Development. P 14×14½.
912 **353** 10t. multicoloured .... 1·00 1·00

(Des Mrinal Chakraborty)

2006 (6 Dec). World AIDS Day. P 14×14½.
913 **354** 10t. multicoloured .... 1·25 1·00

355 Profiles   **356** Family and Jar of Coins ("Invest in health")

(Des Mrinal Chakraborty)

2007 (8 Mar). International Women's Day. P 14×14½.
914 **355** 10t. multicoloured .... 1·00 1·00

(Des Anowar Hossain)

2007 (7 Apr). World Health Day. P 14×14½.
915 **356** 6t. multicoloured .... 1·00 1·00

357 Falling Wicket

358 House and Girls in Plantation

(Des Mrinal Chakraborty and Anowar Hossain)

2007 (19 Apr). World Cup Cricket, West Indies. T **357** and similar multicoloured designs. P 14×14½ (vert) or 14½×14 (horiz).

916		10t. Type **357**	1·75	1·75
		a. Block of four. Nos. 916/19	6·25	6·25
917		10t. Tiger, bowler and trophy (horiz)	1·75	1·75
918		10t. Bangladesh team and Cricket World Cup trophy	1·75	1·75
919		10t. Batsman and trophy (horiz)	1·75	1·75
916/19		Set of 4	6·25	6·25

Nos. 916/19 were printed together, *se-tenant*, as blocks of four stamps in sheets of 100. The two vert designs were laid horizontally in the sheet.

2007 (5 June). National Tree Plantation Campaign. Litho. P 14×14½.

920	**358**	10t. multicoloured	1·00	1·00

359 Md. Habibullah Bahar Choudhury

360 Boy and Girl Scouts

2007 (25 June). Birth Centenary (2006) of Md. Habibullah Bahar Choudhury (politician and writer). P 14×14½.

921	**359**	10t. multicoloured	1·00	1·00

2007 (9 July). Centenary of World Scouting. T **360** and similar horiz design. Multicoloured. P 14½×14.

922		10t. Type **360**	1·00	1·25
		a. Horiz pair. Nos. 922/3	2·00	2·50
923		10t. Lord Baden-Powell (founder)	1·00	1·25

Nos. 922/3 were printed together, *se-tenant*, in horizontal pairs throughout the sheet.

(**361**)

362 Dr. Muhammad Yunus and Peace Medal

2007 (29 July). 20th Anniv of Philatelic Association of Bangladesh. No. 768 optd with T **361**.

924		4t. White-breasted Waterhen (*Amaurornis phoenicurus*)	1·75	1·25

(Des Mrinal Chakraborty)

2007 (29 Aug–7 Sept). Dr. Muhammad Yunus and Grameen Bank– winner of Nobel Peace Prize (2006) as T **362**. P 14×14½.

925	**362**	10t. multicoloured (inscr "Dr. Md. Yunus" and "Awarded Nobel Prize '06")	1·50	1·50
		a. Inscr "Dr. Muhammad Yunus" and "Awarded Nobel Peace Prize '06" (7.9.07)	1·50	1·50

No. 925 was incorrectly inscribed and showed the medal for the Nobel Prize for Physiology or Medicine. It was withdrawn from sale and replaced by No. 925a on 7 September.

363 Children standing in Flood Water

2007 (13 Sept). "In Charity of Flood Victims". T **363** and similar horiz designs. Multicoloured. P 13½.

926		2t. Type **363**	1·00	1·10
		a. Sheetlet. Nos. 926/30	4·50	5·00
927		2t. Children and sheep in flood water	1·00	1·10
928		2t. People and goats taking refuge on corrugated iron roof	1·00	1·10
929		2t. Women queuing for food	1·00	1·10
930		2t. Woman and children with food bowls and flooded houses	1·00	1·10
926/30		Set of 5	4·50	5·00

Nos. 926/30 were printed together, *se-tenant*, in sheetlets of five stamps. Originally the sheetlets contained six stamps, but the upper left stamp showing Prime Minister Fakhruddin Ahmed was removed from all sheetlets before sale because he had not given permission for his image to be used on the stamp.

The exact issue date of Nos. 926/30 is unknown. The date of issue is based on a postmark found on a private first day cover used in Bangladesh.

364 Cricket Match

(Des Syeed Bin Salam)

2007 (24 Sept). ICC World Twenty 20 2007 Cricket Cup, South Africa. T **364** and similar horiz design. Multicoloured. P 14½×14.

931		4t. Type **364**	1·50	1·50
		a. Pair. Nos. 931/2	3·00	3·00
932		4t. Cricketer and map of South Africa	1·50	1·50

Nos. 931/2 were printed together, *se-tenant*, in horizontal and vertical pairs in sheets of 100 (2 panes of 50).

365 Emblem and Globe

366 Soldiers with Flag

(Des Jashim Uddin)

2007 (18 Dec). International Migrants Day. P 14½×14.

933	**365**	10t. multicoloured	1·50	1·50

(Des K. G. Mustafa)

2008 (25 Mar). Independence and National Day. P 14×14½.

934	**366**	10t. multicoloured	1·50	1·50

367 Melting Glacier and Flooded Village

(Des Anowar Hossain)

2008 (7 Apr). World Health Day. "Protecting Health From Climate Change". P 14½×14.

935   **367**   10t. multicoloured .... 1·50   1·50

368 Herd of Spotted Deer   **369** "CELEBRATING 50 YEARS" and Pattern

(Des Anowar Hossain and K. G. Mustafa)

2008 (18 Apr). The Sundarbans World Heritage Site. T **368** and similar horiz designs. Multicoloured. P 14½×14.

936	10t. Type **368**	2·25	2·25
	a. Block of four. Nos. 936/9	8·00	8·00
937	10t. Waterway and mangrove forest	2·25	2·25
938	10t. Collecting bee nests for honey.............	2·25	2·25
939	10t. Tiger	2·25	2·25
936/9 Set of 4		8·00	8·00
MS940 167×95 mm. Nos. 936/9...............		9·00	9·00

Nos. 936/9 were printed together, *se-tenant*, in blocks of four stamps in sheets of 100.

No. **MS**940 also exists imperforate.

(Des Suleman Poonja, Mohammad Adra and Mizaz Nanji)

2008 (19 May). Golden Jubilee of the Aga Khan (2007). T **369** and similar vert design. P 14×14½.

941	**369**	3t. emerald and dull blue-green...........	55	60
942		3t. deep rose-red and dull rose	55	60
943	–	3t. gold pattern on white......................	55	60
944	–	3t. white pattern on gold.....................	55	60
941/4 Set of 4			2·00	2·25

Design: Nos. 943/4 "CELEBRATING 50 YEARS" in circle surrounded by pattern.

370 Athletes on Training Run

(Des Jasim Uddin (25t.) or Aminul Haque Mallick (others))

2008 (6 July). Olympic Games, Beijing. T **370** and similar horiz designs. Multicoloured. P 14½×14.

945	10t. Type **370**.	1·00	1·00
	a. Block of four. Nos. 945/8	4·75	4·75
946	15t. Rifle shooting.............................	1·25	1·25
947	20t. Olympic mascots Beibei, Jingjing, Huanhuan, Yingying and Nini	1·40	1·40
948	25t. Pierre de Coubertin (founder of modern Olympics) and Olympic stamps of Greece (1876) and Bangladesh (1976)............................	1·60	1·60
945/8 Set of 4		4·75	4·75

Nos. 945/8 were printed together, *se-tenant*, as blocks of four stamps in sheets of 100.

371 The First Stamps of Bangladesh, 1971
(Illustration reduced. Actual size 140×90 *mm)*

(Des Jashim Uddin)

2008 (29 July). Stamp Day. Sheet 140×90 mm. Imperf.

MS949   **371**   multicoloured .... 3·75   4·50

372 Khepupara Radar Station, Patuakhali

(Des Jasimuddin)

2008 (23 Sept). Japanese International Cooperation Agency ("Friends from the Birth of Bangladesh"). Sheet 123×75 mm containing T **372** and similar horiz designs. Multicoloured. P 12½×12.

MS950 3t. Type **372**; 7t. Vocational training programme; 10t. Jamuna Multi-purpose Bridge; 10t. Polio vaccination programme .... 2·50   2·75

373 Emblem   **374** Farmer and Workers in Rice Field

(Des K. G. Mustafa)

2008 (31 Oct). 50th Anniv of Dhaka Chamber of Commerce and Industry. P 13½×14.

951   **373**   10t. multicoloured .... 1·50   1·50

2008 (15 Nov). First National Agriculture Day. P 13½×14.

952   **374**   4t. multicoloured 70   50

375 Nimtali Deuri (gateway of Nimtali Palace)

(Des K. G. Mustafa)

2008 (28 Nov). 400th Anniv of Dhaka as Capital of Bengal (1st issue). P 14×13½.

953   **375**   6t. multicoloured 80   60

See also Nos. 1013/6.

376 Cox's Bazar

(Des Jasimuddin)

2008 (30 Nov). Cox's Bazar (world's longest unbroken sea beach). P 12½.

954   **376**   10t. multicoloured .... 1·25   1·25

377 Disabled Man

(Des Anowar Hossain)

2008 (3 Dec). International Day of Persons with Disabilities. P 14×13½.
955 **377** 3t. multicoloured 70 45

378 Women and Child and Emblem

379 1972 "In Memory of the Martyrs" 20p. Stamp

(Des Sajjad Khan)

2008 (24 Dec). International Year of Sanitation. P 13½×14.
956 **378** 3t. multicoloured 70 45

2009 (20 Feb). International Mother Language Day. Sheet 180×119 mm. P 12½×14.
MS957 **379** multicoloured .... 6·00 7·00

380 Sheikh Mujibur Rahman and Children

(Des Anowar Hossain)

2009 (16 Mar). Sheikh Mujibur Rahman Commemoration and National Children's Day. P 12½.
958 **380** 10t. multicoloured .... 1·25 1·25

381 Ziaur Rahman, National Flag and Painting

382 Doctors and Nurses with Patients and Hospital Building

(Des Jashim Uddin)

2009 (25 Mar). Independence and National Day. P 12½.
959 **381** 3t. multicoloured .... 1·00 45

(Des Anowar Hossain)

2009 (7 Apr). World Health Day. P 13½×14.
960 **382** 3t. multicoloured .... 1·25 65

383 China 2009 Emblem

(Des Md. Mominul Azam)

2009 (10 Apr). China 2009 World Stamp Exhibition, Luoyang. Sheet 100×70 mm containing T **383** and similar horiz designs. Multicoloured. P 14×12½.
MS961 10t. Type **383**; 10t. China 2009 "Tree Peony Messenger" mascot; 20t. Ox .... 4·75 4·75
No. **MS961** contains the three stamps and a stamp size label.

384 Shamsun Nahar Mahmud

385 Couple holding Tree Seedlings

(Des Anowar Hossain)

2009 (26 May). Birth Centenary (2008) of Shamsun Nahar Mahmud (writer). P 13½×14.
962 **384** 4t. multicoloured 70 50

(Des Anowar Hossain)

2009 (31 May). National Tree Plantation Campaign and Tree Fair. P 13½×14.
963 **385** 3t. multicoloured 50 35

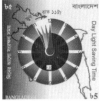

386 Clock

387 Silhouette of Family

2009 (19 June). Day Light Saving Time. P 13½×12.
964 **386** 5t. multicoloured 65 65

2009 (11 July). World Population Day. P 14×13½.
965 **387** 6t. multicoloured 70 70

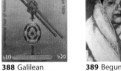

388 Galilean Telescope, 1609

389 Begum Fazilatunnessa Mujib

(Des Anushandhitshu Chokro)

2009 (19 July). International Year of Astronomy. T **388** and similar vert design. Multicoloured. P 12.
966 10t. Type **388** .... 1·50 1·75
     a. Pair. Nos. 966/7 .... 3·00 3·50
967 10t. Andromeda Galaxy .... 1·50 1·75
Nos. 966/7 were printed together, se-tenant, as horizontal and vertical pairs in sheetlets of 16 stamps.

2009 (12 Aug). National Mourning Day. Sheikh Mujibur Rahman and his Family. T **389** and similar horiz designs. Multicoloured. P 12×13½ (No. 968) or 12 (others).
968 3t. Type **389** 35 35
     a. Sheetlet. Nos. 968/84 .... 5·75 5·75
969 3t. Sheikh Kamal 35 35
970 3t. Sheikh Jamal 35 35
971 3t. Sheikh Russel 35 35
972 3t. Sheikh Abu Naser 35 35
973 3t. Sultana Kamal Khuku 35 35
974 3t. Parveen Jamal Rosy 35 35
975 3t. Abdur Rab Serniabat 35 35
976 3t. Sheikh Fazlul Haque Moni 35 35
977 3t. Begum Arju Moni 35 35
978 3t. Colonel Jamiluddin Ahmed 35 35
979 3t. Baby Serniabat 35 35
980 3t. Arif Serniabat 35 35
981 3t. Sukanto Abdullah Babu 35 35
982 3t. Shahid Serniabat 35 35
983 3t. Abdul Nayeem Khan Rintu 35 35
984 15t. Sheikh Mujibur Rahman 35 35
968/84 Set of 17 .... 5·75 5·75
Nos. 968/84 were printed together, se-tenant, in sheetlets of 17 stamps and one triple stamp-size label (at top right).

390 Coin

(Des Jashim Uddin, Mesbah Uddin Ahmed and Badal Chandra Sarker. Eng Amirul Islam Sikder)

2009 (16 Oct). World Food Day. T **390** and similar horiz designs. Multicoloured. P 14×13½.

985	3t. Type **390**		45	45
	a. Block of four. Nos. 985/8		1·60	1·60
986	3t. Bread and agricultural produce		45	45
987	3t. Boat loaded with produce		45	45
988	3t. Fishermen with catch		45	45
985/8 Set of 4			1·60	1·60

Nos. 985/8 were printed together, *se-tenant*, as blocks of four stamps in sheets of 100.

391 Valerie Taylor with Patient

2009 (12 Nov). 30th Anniv of Centre for the Rehabilitation of the Paralysed, Dhaka. P 12½.

989	7t. Type **391**		90	90
	a. Horiz pair. Nos. 989/90		1·75	1·75
990	7t. Rehabilitation		90	90

Nos. 989/90 were printed together, *se-tenant*, as horizontal pairs in sheets of 56.

392 Professor Abdul Moktader

(Des A. T. M. Anowarul Quadir. Litho Security Printing Press, Gazipur)

2009 (27 Dec). Birth Centenary of Professor Abdul Moktader. P 14½×13½.

991	**392**	4t. multicoloured	50	50

393 Scouts saluting

(Des Myhammad Ashraf Shiddike. Litho Security Printing Press, Gazipur)

2010 (16 Jan). Eighth National Scout Jamboree. P 14×13½.

992	**393**	10t. multicoloured	3·25	3·25

394 "Alec's Red"

(Des Jashim Uddin. Litho Security Printing Press, Gazipur)

2010 (11 Feb). Roses: Cultivated Varieties in Bangladesh. T **394** and similar horiz designs. Multicoloured. P 12.

993	10t. Type **394**		2·75	2·75
	a. Sheetlet. Nos. 993/1005		35·00	35·00
994	10t. "Royal Highness"		2·75	2·75
995	10t. "Queen Elizabeth"		2·75	2·75
996	10t. "Ballerina"		2·75	2·75
997	10t. "Alexander"		2·75	2·75
998	10t. "Blue Moon"		2·75	2·75
999	10t. "Papa Meilland"		2·75	2·75
1000	10t. "Double Delight"		2·75	2·75
1001	10t. "Iceberg"		2·75	2·75
1002	10t. "Sonia"		2·75	2·75
1003	10t. "Sunblest"		2·75	2·75
1004	10t. "Piccadilly"		2·75	2·75
1005	10t. "Pascali"		2·75	2·75
993/1005 Set of 13			35·00	35·00

Nos. 993/1005 were printed together, *se-tenant*, in sheetlets of 13 stamps.

395 International Mother Language Institute

(Des Jashim Uddin. Litho Security Printing Press, Gazipur)

2010 (21 Feb). Inauguration of International Mother Language Institute. P 12.

1006	**395**	15t. multicoloured	4·25	4·50

396 Women with Raised Fists

(Des Jashim Uddin. Litho Security Printing Press, Gazipur)

2010 (8 Mar). Centenary of International Women's Day. P 14×13½.

1007	**396**	5t. multicoloured	2·00	2·00

397 1997 4t. Sheikh Mujibur Rahman Stamp

398 Liberation Monument, Public Library Campus, Brahman Baria

(Des Jashim Uddin. Litho Security Printing Press, Gazipur)

2010 (17 Mar). National Children's Day. Sheet 140×100 mm. P 13½×14.

MS1008	**397**	multicoloured (sold for 25t.)	8·50	8·50

(Des Motiur Rahman and Jashim Uddin. Litho Security Printing Press, Gazipur)

2010 (26 Mar). Independence and National Day. Sheet 110×100 mm containing T **398** and similar vert designs. Multicoloured. P 13½×14.
MS1009 **398** 5t.×4 Type **398**; Liberation Monument, Shafipur, Gazipur; Liberation Monument, Jagannath Hall, Dhaka University; Liberation Monument, Vocational Training Institute, Rangpur... 7·00 7·00

399 Cricket Badges **400** Emblem

(Des Aminal Haque Mallick. Litho Security Printing Press, Gazipur)

2010 (22 Apr). ICC World Twenty 20 2010 Cricket Cup. P 13½.
1010 **399** 15t. multicoloured .... 4·25 4·25

(Des Manzare Shamim. Litho Security Printing Press, Gazipur)

2010 (2 May). 12th Anniv of Bangabandhu Sheikh Mujib Medical University. Sheet 140×85 mm. P 13½×12.
1011 **400** 20t. multicoloured .... 7·25 7·25

401 City Park

(Des Anowar Hossain. Litho Security Printing Press, Gazipur)

2010 (1 June). National Tree Plantation Campaign and Tree Fair. P 14½×13½.
1012 **401** 6t. multicoloured .... 1·50 1·50

402 Bara Katra (Mughal Dhaka)

(Des K. G. Mustafa. Litho Security Printing Press, Gazipur)

2010 (16 June). 400th Anniv (2008) of Dhaka as Capital of Bengal (2nd issue). T **402** and similar horiz designs. Multicoloured. P 12×14.
1013 10t. Type **402** .... 3·00 3·00
    a. Block of four. Nos. 1013/16 .... 12·00 12·00
1014 10t. Buriganga River and Buckland Bund (embankment) (British Dhaka) .... 3·00 3·00
1015 10t. Kamlapur Railway Station (Pakistan Period) .... 3·00 3·00
1016 10t. Dhaka City Corporation building and modern Dhaka........................... 3·00 3·00
1013/16 Set of 4 .... 12·00 12·00
Nos. 1013/16 were printed together, se-tenant, as blocks of four in sheets of 16.

403 Anniversary Emblem **404** Two Players

(Des Asem Ansari. Litho Security Printing Press, Gazipur)

2010 (20 June). 50th Anniv of ICDDR'B (International Centre for Diarrhoeal Disease Research, Bangladesh). P 13½.
1017 **403** 5t. gold and black........................... 1·75 1·75

(Des Anowar Hossain. Litho Security Printing Press, Gazipur)

2010 (11 July). World Cup Football Championship, South Africa. T **404** and similar horiz designs. Multicoloured. P 14½×13½.
1018 10t. Type **404** .... 1·50 1·50
    a. Horiz strip of three. Nos. 1018/20 .... 5·50 5·50
1019 10t. Three players pursuing headed ball....... 1·50 1·50
1020 20t. Zakumi mascot .... 1·50 1·50
1018/20 Set of 3 .... 5·50 5·50
Nos. 1018/20 were printed together, se-tenant, as horizontal strips of three with No. 1020 (the 20t. value) forming the central stamp in the strip, in sheets of 90.

405 Chakma Woman **406** Rajban Bihar Pagoda, ('Raj Banbihar'), Rangamati

(Litho)

2010 (2 Aug). Indigenous Peoples in Bangladesh. T **405** and similar vert designs. Multicoloured. P 12.
1021 5t. Type **405** 70 70
    a. Sheetlet. Nos. 1021/40........... 12·00 12·00
1022 5t. Marma woman wearing flower in hair.. 70 70
1023 5t. Mru woman (head and shoulders, wearing red).............. 70 70
1024 5t. Tripura (head and shoulders, wearing red)........................... 70 70
1025 5t. Pangkhua woman........................... 70 70
1026 5t. Chakma woman (full length portrait, wearing sash) 70 70
1027 5t. Marma woman holding bouquet of flowers........................... 70 70
1028 5t. Mru woman (threequarter length portrait, bracelets on arms)........ 70 70
1029 5t. Tripura woman (head and shoulders, wearing white)........................... 70 70
1030 5t. Pangkhua man and woman.......... 70 70
1031 5t. Chakma woman weaving........... 70 70
1032 5t. Two Marma women gathering crops..... 70 70
1033 5t. Two Mru women poundng grain........ 70 70
1034 5t. Two Tripura women carrying firewood. 70 70
1035 5t. Pangkhua man making basket......... 70 70
1036 5t. Two Chakma women........... 70 70
1037 5t. Two Marma women dancing........... 70 70
1038 5t. Mru man spearing pig in pen......... 70 70
1039 5t. Tripura woman dancing.......... 70 70
1040 5t. Pangkhua man with bull's skull........ 70 70
1021/1040 Set of 20........................... 12·00 12·00
Nos. 1021/40 were printed together, se-tenant, in sheetlets of 20.

(Litho)

2010 (2 Aug). Bangkok 2010 25th Asian International Stamp Exhibition, Bangkok, Thailand. Sheet 140×90 mm containing T **406** and similar horiz design. P 12.
MS1041 20t. Type **406**; 20t. Buddha Dhatu Jadi, Bandarban........................... 5·50 6·00

407 Tiger

(Des Motiur Rahman. Litho Security Printing Press, Gazipur)

2010 (28 Sept). 35th Anniv of Diplomatic Relations between Bangladesh and the People's Republic of China. Year of the Tiger. P 13.
1042 **407** 50t. multicoloured .... 7·00 7·00
A miniature sheet issued from Bangladesh was sold in a folder at an exhibition centre in China, but was not issued in Bangladesh.

408 Abu Nayem Mohammed
Nazibuddin Khan (Khurram)

(Des Jasim Uddin. Litho)

2010 (14 Dec). Abu Nayem Mohammed Nazibuddin Khan (Khurram)
(1954–71) Commemoration. P 13.
1043 **408** 3t. multicoloured.............................. 40 30

409 Emblem

410 Children

(Des Aminul Islam Talukder Azad. Litho Security Printing Press,
Gazipur)

2011 (27 Jan). Population and Housing Census. P 13½×14.
1044 **409** 3t. multicoloured................................... 40 30

(Des Muhammad Ashraf Shiddike. Litho Security Printing Press,
Gazipur)

2011 (9 Feb). Seventh National Cub Camporee. P 14×13½.
1045 **410** 10t. multicoloured............................ 1·50 1·25

411 Sheikh Mujibur Rahman
and Followers

(Des Motiur Rahman. Litho Security Printing Press, Gazipur)

2011 (10 Feb). Return to Bangladesh of Sheikh Mujibur Rahman, 1972
("Bangabandhu's Homecoming Day"). T **411** and similar square
designs. Multicoloured. P 13½.
1046   5t. Type **411**................................... 70 70
          a. Horiz strip of three. Nos. 1046/8............. 2·40 2·40
1047   5t. Sheikh Mujibur Rahman waving to
          crowd.. 70 70
1048   10t. Sheikh Mujibur Rahman (1920–75, first
          President of Bangladesh).......................... 1·25 1·25
1046/1048 Set of 3... 2·40 2·40
Nos. 1046/8 were printed together, *se-tenant*, as horizontal strips of
three stamps in sheets of 120 and sheetlets of nine.

412 Mahatma Gandhi at Laksham
Railway Station

(Des Motiur Rahman. Litho Security Printing Press, Gazipur)

2011 (10 Feb). Indipex 2011 World Philatelic Exhibition, New Delhi.
Mahatma Gandhi's Visit to Noakhali, 1946. T **412** and similar
square designs. Multicoloured. P 13½.
1049   10t. Type **412**.............................. 1·75 1·75
          a. Horiz strip of three. Nos. 1049/51 .... 6·00 6·00
1050   15t. Mahatma Gandhi and others at
          Noakhali, 1946.............................. 2·25 2·25
1051   20t. Mahatma Gandhi at Noakhali, 1946....... 2·50 2·50
1049/1051 Set of 3... 6·00 6·00
Nos. 1049/51 were printed together, *se-tenant*, as horizontal strips
of three stamps in sheets of 99 and sheetlets of six.

413 Bowler

414 Emblem

(Des Manzare Shamim. Litho Security Printing Press, Gazipur)

2011 (23 Feb). ICC Cricket World Cup, Bangladesh. T **413** and similar
vert designs. Multicoloured. P 12½.
1052   20t. Type **413**.............................. 3·00 3·00
          a. Horiz strip of four. Nos. 1052/5............... 11·00 11·00
1053   20t. Batsman................................. 3·00 3·00
1054   20t. Wicket-keeper........................... 3·00 3·00
1055   20t. Fielder................................. 3·00 3·00
1052/1055 Set of 4... 11·00 11·00
MS1056 127×91 mm. 50t. Umpire, batsman and
          players. Imperf............................... 7·50 7·50
Nos. 1052/5 were printed together, *se-tenant*, as horizontal strips of
four stamps in sheets of 120.

(Des Sadatuddin Ahmed Amil. Litho Security Printing Press, Gazipur)

2011 (24 Feb). Anti-Corruption Day (9 December 2010). P 12½.
1057 **414** 5t. multicoloured........................... 70 50

415 Bangabandhu Square
Fountain, Dhaka

(Des Motiur Rahman and Jasim Uddin. Litho Security Printing Press,
Gazipur)

2011 (26 Mar). 40th Anniv of Independence. Sheet 110×110 mm
containing T **415** and similar vert designs. Multicoloured. P 12.
MS1058 10t. Type **415**; 10t. Victory of Bangla
          Monument, Chittagong; 10t. Memorial of
          Liberation War, Rajarbagh Police Line, Dhaka;
          10t. Invincible Bhoirab, Kishoreganj; 20t. Sheikh
          Mujibur Rahman (32×84 *mm*)..................... 7·50 7·50

416 Probashi Kallyan Bank, Banknotes
and Globe

(Des Anowar Hossain. Litho Security Printing Press, Gazipur)

2011 (20 Apr). Inauguration of Probashi Kallyan Bank. P 12½.
1059 **416** 10t. multicoloured.......................... 1·50 1·25

417 Rabindranath Tagore and Shlaidaha, Kushtia

(Des Anowar Hossain. Litho Security Printing Press, Gazipur)

2011 (6 May). 150th Birth Anniv of Rabindranath Tagore (poet). T **417** and similar horiz designs. Multicoloured. P 13½.

1060	10t. Type **417**	1·50	1·50
	a. Block of four. Nos. 1060/3	5·50	5·50
1061	10t. Rabindranath Tagore and Shahjadpur, Sirajganj	1·50	1·50
1062	10t. Rabindranath Tagore and Dakkhindihi, Khulna	1·50	1·50
1063	10t. Rabindranath Tagore and Patishar, Naogaon	1·50	1·50
1060/1063	Set of 4	5·50	5·50

Nos. 1060/3 were printed together, se-tenant, as blocks of four stamps in sheetlets of eight.

A miniature sheet containing the four 10t. stamps was sold for 100t., a 60t. premium over face value.

418 Planting Sapling

(Des Begum Rafika Khan. Litho Security Printing Press, Gazipur)

2011 (1 June). National Tree Plantation Campaign. P 14×13½.

1064	**418**	10t. multicoloured	1·50	1·25

419 Kazi Nazrul Islam   **420** Hardella thurjii

(Des Anowar Hossain. Litho Security Printing Press, Gazipur)

2011 (24 June). International Nazrul Conference. 90th Anniv of Publication of Poem *Bidrohi* (The Rebel) by Kazi Nazrul Islam (1899–1976, Bengali poet and musician). T **419** and similar vert designs. Multicoloured. P 13½×14.

1065	10t. Type **419**	1·50	1·50
	a. Block of four. Nos. 1065/8	5·50	5·50
1066	10t. Kazi Nazrul Islam and Nazrul Academy, Trishal	1·50	1·50
1067	10t. Kazi Nazrul Islam wearing hat and building with arches	1·50	1·50
1068	10t. Kazi Nazrul Islam as old man and sculpture at Nazrul Museum	1·50	1·50
1065/1068	Set of 4	5·50	5·50

Nos. 1065/8 were printed together, se-tenant, in blocks of four stamps throughout the sheet.

A miniature sheet containing the four 10t. stamps was sold for 100t., a 60t. premium above face value. This miniature sheet was issued perforated 14×13½ or imperforate.

(Des Anowar Hossain. Litho Security Printing Press, Gazipur)

2011 (17 July). Rare Species of Turtle. T **420** and similar horiz design. Multicoloured. P 14×13½.

1069	10t. Type **420**	2·00	2·00
	a. Horiz pair. Nos. 1069/70	4·00	4·00
1070	10t. Geoclemys hamiltonii	2·00	2·00

Nos. 1069/70 were printed together, se-tenant, as horizontal pairs in sheets of 100.

A Rare Animals of Bangladesh miniature sheet containing four 10t. stamps depicting Frog *Euphilyctis hexadactylus*, Monkey *Trachypithecus phayrei*, River Dolphin *Platanista gangetica* and Fishing Cat *Prionallurus viverrinus* was issued on the same date. It was sold for 100t., a 60t. premium over the face value.

421 Heliopais personata

(Des Anowar Hossain. Litho Security Printing Press, Gazipur)

2011 (17 July). Birds of the Sundarbans. T **421** and similar horiz designs. Multicoloured. P 13½×12.

1071	10t. Type **421**	1·75	1·75
	a. Sheetlet. Nos. 1071/82	19·00	19·00
1072	10t. Leptoptilos javanicus	1·75	1·75
1073	10t. Haliaeetus leucogaster	1·75	1·75
1074	10t. Bubo coromandus	1·75	1·75
1075	10t. Pelargopsis amauroptera	1·75	1·75
1076	10t. Halcyon coromanda	1·75	1·75
1077	10t. Alcedo meninting	1·75	1·75
1078	10t. Halcyon pileata	1·75	1·75
1079	10t. Todiramphus chloris	1·75	1·75
1080	10t. Treron bicincta	1·75	1·75
1081	10t. Gorsachius melanolophus	1·75	1·75
1082	10t. Pitta megarhyncha	1·75	1·75
1071/1082	Set of 12	19·00	19·00

Nos. 1071/82 were printed together, se-tenant, in sheetlets of 12 stamps.

422 Dotara

(Des Anowar Hossain and Jasim Uddin. Litho Security Printing Press, Gazipur)

2011 (21 July). Traditional Musical Instruments of Bangladesh. T **422** and similar horiz designs. Multicoloured. P 14×13½.

1083	5t. Type **422**	70	70
	a. Block of four. Nos. 1083/6	2·50	2·50
1084	5t. Ektara (pale green background)	70	70
1085	5t. Sarinda (pale pink background)	70	70
1086	5r. Sarangi (pale blue background)	70	70
1083/1086	Set of 4	2·50	2·50

Nos. 1083/6 were printed together, se-tenant, as blocks of four stamps in sheets of 100.

423 Coin of Sultan Fakhr al-Din Mubarak Shah (1334–49)

(Des Jashim Uddin. Litho Security Printing Press, Gazipur)

2011 (21 July). Coins of the Independent Sultans of Bengal (1st series). Sheet 140×110 mm containing T **423** and similar horiz designs. Multicoloured. P 13½×12.

MS1087	10t. Type **423**; 10t. Coin of Sultan Shams al-Din Ilyas Shah (1342–57); 10t. Coin of Sultan Ghiyath al-Din Azam Shah (1389–1410); 10t. Coin of Sultan Jalal al-Din Muhammad Shah (1415–32)	5·00	5·50

424 Dhaka Club

(Des Jasim Uddin. Litho Security Printing Press, Gazipur)

2011 (19 Aug). Centenary of Dhaka Club. P 14×13½.
1088 **424** 3t. multicoloured 40 30

425 Emblem and Globe

(Des Jasim Uddin. Litho Security Printing Press, Gazipur)

2011 (1 Dec). E Asia 2011 Conference, Dhaka. P 14×13½.
1089 **425** 10t. multicoloured .... 1·50 1·25

426 Sheikh Mujibur Rahman and
National Memorial, Savar

(Des Anowar Hossain. Litho Security Printing Press, Gazipur)

2011 (16 Dec). 40th Anniv of Victory in War of Independence.
P 14×13½.
1090 **426** 10t. multicoloured .... 1·50 1·25

427 Emblem and Stethoscope

(Des Dr. Pinaki Bhattacharya and Md Tanvier Hasan. Litho Security
Printing Press, Gazipur)

2011 (28 Dec). 40th Anniv of Bangladesh College of Physicians and
Surgeons. P 12½.
1091 **427** 10t. multicoloured .... 1·50 1·25

428 Globe Emblem and Stylised Buildings

(Des Anowar Hossain. Litho Security Printing Press, Gazipur)

2012 (28 Feb). 60th Anniv of Language Movement and International
Mother Language Day. P 13×13½.
1092 **428** 21t. multicoloured .... 3·00 3·00

429 Sheikh Mujibur
Rahman and National Flag

430 City and Trees

(Des Anowar Hossain. Litho Security Printing Press, Gazipur)

2012 (26 Mar). Independence and National Day. P 13½×14.
1093 **429** 26t. multicoloured .... 3·25 3·25

(Des Array. Litho Security Printing Press, Gazipur)

2012 (5 June). National Tree Plantation Campaign. P 14×13½.
1094 **430** 10t. multicoloured .... 1·50 1·25

431 *Ichthyophaga ichthyaetus*

(Des Enam Ul Haque. Litho Security Printing Press, Gazipur)

2012 (14 June). Indonesia 2012 World Stamp Championship and
Exhibition, Jakarta. Birds. T **431** and similar horiz design.
Multicoloured. P 13.
1095 20t. Type **431** .... 3·00 3·00
a. Horiz pair. Nos. 1095/6 with central
label .... 6·00 6·00
1096 20t. *Centropus bengalensis* .... 3·00 3·00
Nos. 1095/6 were printed together, *se-tenant*, in horizontal pairs
with a central Indonesia 2012 label throughout the sheets.
Similar designs depicting *Egretta sacra*, *Otus sunia*, *Chalcoparia
singalensis* and *Serilophus lunatus* were issued in miniature sheets
of four×10t on the same date. These miniature sheets, with the
Indonesia 2012 emblem on the top sheet margin and perforated
12×13½, were sold for 100t., 60t. above face value.

432 Leopard Lacewing

(Des Anowar Hossain. Litho Security Printing Press, Gazipur)

2012 (14 June). Butterflies. T **432** and similar horiz designs.
Multicoloured. P 12½.
1097 10t. Type **432** .... 2·00 2·00
a. Block of four. Nos. 1097/1100 .... 7·25 7·25
1098 10t. Striped Tiger .... 2·00 2·00
1099 10t. Lemon Pansy .... 2·00 2·00
1100 10t. Knight .... 2·00 2·00
1097/1100 Set of 4 .... 7·25 7·25
Nos. 1097/1100 were printed together, *se-tenant*, in blocks of four
stamps in sheets of 200 or sheetlets of 16.

433 *Gyps bengalensis*   **434** *Ploceus philippinus*

(Des Enam El Haque. Litho Security Printing Press, Gazipur)

2012 (14 June). Critically Endangered Animals of Bangladesh. T **433**
and similar horiz design. Multicoloured. P 14×13½.
1101 15t. Type **433** .... 3·00 3·00
a. Horiz pair. Nos. 1101/2 .... 7·50 7·50
1102 25t. *Semnopithecus entellus* .... 4·50 4·50
Nos. 1101/2 were printed together, *se-tenant*, as horizontal pairs in
sheets of 100.
Designs as Nos. 1101/2 were issued in imperforate miniature sheets
sold for 100t., a premium of 60t. over face value.

(Des Enam Ul Haque. Litho Security Printing Press, Gazipur)

2012 (14 June). Bird Nests of Bangladesh. T **434** and similar
octagonal designs. Multicoloured. P 13.
1103 20t. Type **434** .... 3·50 3·50
a. Block of six. Nos. 1103/8 .... 19·00 19·00
1104 20t. *Pycnonotus cafer* .... 3·50 3·50
1105 20t. *Orthotomus sutorius* .... 3·50 3·50
1106 20t. *Dinopium benghalense* .... 3·50 3·50
1107 20t. *Hypothymis azurea* .... 3·50 3·50
1108 20t. *Psittacula krameri* .... 3·50 3·50
1103/1108 Set of 6 .... 19·00 19·00

Nos. 1103/8 were printed together, *se-tenant*, as blocks of six stamps in sheets of 192.

An imperforate miniature sheet containing six 20t. stamps as Nos. 1103/8 was sold for 150t., a 30t. premium over face value.

435 '75' and Emblem

(Des Syed Lutul Haque. Litho Security Printing Press, Gazipur)
2012 (1 July). 75th Anniv of Rotary International in Bangladesh. P 14×13½.
1109 **435** 10t. multicoloured .... 1·50 1·25

436 Heart and National Institute of Cardiovascular Diseases

(Des Dr. Pinaki Bhattacharya and Md. Tanvier Hasan. Litho Security Printing Press, Gazipur)
2012 (12 Sept). 30th Anniv of Open Heart Surgery, National Institute of Cardiovascular Diseases, Dhaka. P 13½.
1110 **436** 10t. multicoloured .... 1·50 1·25

437 Emblem and Trees on Globe

438 Scouts, Conference Emblem and Scouts encircling Globe

(Des Jasim Uddin. Litho Security Printing Press, Gazipur)
2012 (16 Sept). International Ozone Day. 25th Anniv of the Montreal Protocol. P 14×13½.
1111 **437** 10t. multicoloured .... 1·50 1·25

(Des Anowar Hossain. Litho Security Printing Press, Gazipur)
2012 (24 Nov). 24th Asia-Pacific Regional Scout Conference, Bangladesh. P 13½×14.
1112 **438** 20t. multicoloured .... 3·50 3·50

439 Bangladesh Police Academy

(Des Anowar Hossain. Litho Security Printing Press, Gazipur)
2012 (6 Dec). Centenary of Bangladesh Police Academy. P 14×13½.
1113 **439** 12t. multicoloured .... 3·00 2·50

Anser indicus

440 *Anser indicus*

(Des Enam Ul Haque. Litho Security Printing Press, Gazipur)
2013 (13 Jan). Migratory Birds of Bangladesh. T **440** and similar horiz designs. Multicoloured. P 13½×12.
1114 10t. Type **440** .... 2·25 2·25
 a. Block of eight. Nos. 1114/21 .... 16·00 16·00
1115 10t. *Netta rufina* .... 2·25 2·25
1116 10t. *Numenius arquata* .... 2·25 2·25
1117 10t. *Clamator coromandus* .... 2·25 2·25
1118 10t. *Falco tinnunculus* .... 2·25 2·25
1119 10t. *Luscinia calliope* .... 2·25 2·25
1120 10t. *Motacilla citreola* .... 2·25 2·25
1121 10t. *Ciconia nigra* .... 2·25 2·25
1114/1121 *Set of 8* .... 16·00 16·00
MS1122 169×78 mm. Nos. 1114/21 .... 16·00 16·00
 Nos. 1114/21 were printed together, *se-tenant*, as blocks of eight stamps in sheets of 160.

441 '50' and Emblem

442 Woman with Baby

(Des Jasim Uddin. Litho Security Printing Press, Gazipur)
2013 (13 Jan). 50th Anniv of Asian-Pacific Postal Union. P 14×13½.
1123 **441** 3t. multicoloured 40 30

(Des Anowar Hossain. Litho Security Printing Press, Gazipur)
2013 (30 Jan). 40th Anniv of SOS Children's Village International in Bangladesh. P 13½×14.
1124 **442** 10t. multicoloured .... 1·50 1·25

443 Emblem, Audit Reports and Books

444 Sheikh Mujibur Rahman

(Des Anowar Hossain. Litho Security Printing Press, Gazipur)
2013 (7 Feb). Audit Day. P 14×13½.
1125 **443** 5t. multicoloured 50 30

(Des Anowar Hossain. Litho Security Printing Press, Gazipur)
2013 (26 Mar). 42nd Anniv of Independence. P 13½×14.
1126 **444** 10t. multicoloured .... 1·50 1·25

445 Tree Planting and Watering Trees

446 Script

(Des Anowar Hossain. Litho Security Printing Press, Gazipur)

2013 (5 June). National Tree Plantation Campaign and Tree Fair. P 14×13½.
1127 **445** 10t. multicoloured .... 1·50 1·25

(Des Amirul Islam Sikder. Litho Security Printing Press, Gazipur)

2013 (8 July). Centenary of Bangladesh National Museum. P 12½.
1128 **446** 10t. multicoloured .... 1·50 1·25

447 Mimosa pudica

(Des Anowar Hossain. Litho Security Printing Press, Gazipur)

2013 (30 July). Flowers of Bangladesh. T **447** and similar horiz designs. Multicoloured. P 12×13½.
1129 10t. Type **447** .... 2·00 2·00
    a. Block of four. Nos. 1129/32 .... 7·25 7·25
1130 10t. Mesua nagassarium .... 2·00 2·00
1131 10t. Dillenia indica.................................... 2·00 2·00
1132 10t. Wrightia coccinea .... 2·00 2·00
1129/1132 Set of 4.. 7·25 7·25
Nos. 1129/32 were printed together, se-tenant, as blocks of four stamps in sheetlets of eight (2×4).
Designs as Nos. 1129/32 were issued in an imperforate miniature sheet sold for 60t., a premium of 20t. over the face value.

448 Buddha Statue, Dharmarajika Maha Vihara, Dhaka   **449** Tiger

(Des Anowar Hossain. Litho Security Printing Press, Dhaka)

2013 (30 July). Buddha Statue, Dharmarajika Maha Vihara, Dhaka. P 13½×14.
1133 **448** 10t. multicoloured .... 1·50 1·25
A similar design was issued in a miniature sheet for Thailand 2013 World Stamp Exhibition, Bangkok. This miniature sheet was perforated 13 and sold for 40t., a 30t. premium over face value.

(Des Anowar Hossain. Litho Security Printing Press, Gazipur)

2013 (30 July). Save Tiger. Protect Mother-like Sundarbans. T **449** and similar horiz designs. Multicoloured. P 13.
1134 10t. Type **449** .... 2·25 2·25
    a. Block of four. Nos. 1134/7 .... 8·00 8·00
1135 10t. Tigress and cub .... 2·25 2·25
1136 10t. Tiger walking...................................... 2·25 2·25
1137 10t. Tiger laying in long grass................ 2·25 2·25
1134/1137 Set of 4.. 8·00 8·00
Nos. 1134/7 were printed together, se-tenant, as blocks of four stamps in sheetlets of 16 (4×4).
A miniature sheet containing designs as Nos. 1134/7 perforated 12×13½ was sold for 80t., a 40t. premium above face value.
An imperforate miniature sheet issued for Thailand 2013 World Stamp Exhibition containing designs as Nos. 1134/7 was sold for 100t., a 60t. premium.
A miniature sheet depicting Critically Endangered Animals of Bangladesh was also issued on 30 July 2013. It contains 6t. Lutra lutra; 8t. Naja naja; 10t. Nycticebus bengalensis; 12t. Hoolock hoolock, was perforated 13 and sold for 60t., a 24t. premium above face value. An imperforate version of this miniature sheet with the Thailand 2013 World Stamp Exhibition logo on the margin was sold for 70t.

450 Daisies, Family and Woman using Inhaler

(Des Anowar Hossain. Litho Security Printing Press, Gazipur)

2013 (16 Sept). International Ozone Day. CFC Free Inhaler in Bangladesh. P 14×13½.
1138 **450** 10t. multicoloured .... 1·50 1·25

451 Sheikh Mujibur Rahman and Independence Monument   **452** Sheikh Mujibur Rahman, Independence Monument, Computer, Mosque, Technician and Prime Minister Sheikh Hasina Wajed

(Des Anowar Hossain. Litho Security Printing Press, Gazipur)

2013 (16 Dec). 42nd Anniv of Victory Day. P 13½×14.
1139 **451** 10t. multicoloured .... 1·50 1·50

(Des Jasim Uddin. Litho Security Printing Press, Gazipur)

2014 (26 Mar). Independence and National Day. P 14×13½.
1140 **452** 10t. multicoloured .... 1·50 1·50

453 Woman planting Sapling   **454** Emblem

(Des Anowar Hossain. Litho Security Printing Press, Gazipur)

2014 (5 June). National Tree Plantation Campaign and Tree Fair. P 13½×14.
1141 **453** 10t. multicoloured .... 1·50 1·50

(Des Anowar Hossain. Litho Security Printing Press, Gazipur)

2014 (11 July). World Population Day. P 14×13½.
1142 **454** 10t. multicoloured .... 1·50 1·50

455 Dendrobium aphyllum

(Des Anowar Hossain. Litho Security Printing Press, Gazipur)

2014 (4 Aug). Philakorea 2014 World Stamp Exhibition, Seoul. Flowers of Bangladesh. T **455** and similar horiz designs. Multicoloured. P 13½×14.
1143 10t. Type **455** .... 1·50 1·50
    a. Block of four. Nos. 1143/6 .... 5·50 5·50
1144 10t. Rhyncostylis retusa .... 1·50 1·50
1145 10t. Nymphaea nouchali......................... 1·50 1·50
1146 10t. Ochna obtusata .... 1·50 1·50
1143/6 Set of 4... 5·50 5·50
Nos. 1143/6 were printed together, se-tenant, as blocks of four stamps in sheetlets of 16.
A miniature sheet containing the four 10t. stamps was sold for 60t., a 20t. premium above face value. This miniature sheet was issued perforated 12×13½ or imperforate.

456 Emblem, Human Figures and National Flags

457 Sheikh Mujibur Rahman

(Des Anowar Hossain. Litho Security Printing Press, Gazipur)

2014 (13 Sept). BIMSTEC (Bay of Bengal Initiative for Multi-Sectoral Technical and Economic Co-operation) Secretariat, Dhaka. P 13½×14.

| 1147 | **456** | 4t. multicoloured | 50 | 50 |

(Des Anowar Hossain. Litho Security Printing Press, Gazipur)

2014 (17 Sept). 40th Anniv of Bangladesh Membership of United Nations. P 13½×14.

| 1148 | **457** | 5t. multicoloured | 60 | 60 |

OFFICIAL STAMPS

SERVICE (O **1**) **SERVICE** (O **2**) **SERVICE** (O **3**)

1973 (30 Apr). Nos. 22/7, 29/30, 32 and 34 optd with Type O **1**.

O1	**7**	2p. black (R.)	30	1·50
O2	—	3p. blue-green	30	1·75
O3	—	5p. light brown	75	10
O4	—	10p. slate-black (R.)	1·00	10
O5	—	20p. yellow-green	3·00	10
O6	—	25p. bright reddish mauve	4·00	50
O7	—	60p. greenish slate (R.)	4·00	2·25
O8	—	75p. yellow-orange	1·50	75
O9	**8**	1t. light violet	17·00	7·00
O10	—	5t. grey-blue	5·00	10·00
O1/10	Set of 10		32·00	22·00

1974–75. Nos. 49/51 optd with Type O **1**.

O11	**14**	1t. light violet	6·00	50
O12	—	2t. olive	8·00	2·50
O13	—	5t. grey-blue (1975)	22·00	18·00
O11/13	Set of 3		32·00	19·00

1976. Nos. 64/70 and 73 optd with Type O **2** and Nos. 72 and 74 optd with Type O **3**.

O14	5p. deep yellow-green (11.2.76)	1·50	1·00
O15	10p. slate-black (28.4.76)	3·50	1·00
O16	20p. yellow-green (1.76)	3·50	1·25
O17	25p. bright reddish mauve (1.76)	3·50	1·00
O18	50p. light purple (8.6.76)	7·00	60
O19	60p. greenish slate (R.) (10.11.76)	30	3·00
O20	75p. yellow-olive (10.11.76)	30	4·00
O21	1t. ultramarine (1.76)	4·50	70
O22	2t. olive-green (8 6 76)	45	2·75
O23	5t. grey-blue (10.11.76)	45	3·25
O14/23	Set of 10	23·00	17·00

1979–82. Nos. 125/37 optd with Type O **1**.

O24	5p. deep brown	3·25	2·50
O25	10p. turquoise-blue	3·25	3·50
O26	15p. orange (1980)	3·25	3·50
O27	20p. brown-red	1·50	2·75
O28	25p. grey-blue (1982)	80	2·75
O29	30p. deep green	6·00	3·00
O30	40p. maroon	2·75	2·75
O31	50p. black (24.9.81)	30	10
O32	80p. brown	2·25	50
O33	1t. reddish violet (24.9.81)	30	10
O34	2t. dull ultramarine (21.10.81)	50	3·75
O24/34	Set of 11	22·00	23·00

Service (O **4**) **সার্ভিস** (O **5**) (O **6**)

1983 (21 Dec)**–94**. Nos. 220/9 and 318/b optd as Type O **4** in red, diagonally on 1t. to 5t.

O35	5p. turquoise-blue	20	60
O36	10p. purple	20	30
O37	15p. new blue	20	45

O38	20p. grey-black	20	30
O39	25p. slate	20	40
O40	30p. brown	25	40
O41	50p. light brown (opt horiz)	25	20
	a. Opt diagonal (1993)	25	25
O42	1t. dull ultramarine	50	20
O43	2t. deep bluish green	1·75	30
O44	3t. black and light blue (16.7.94)	50	50
O45	4t. slate-blue (28.6.90)	55	55
O46	5t. bright purple (27.7.92)	4·00	1·00
O35/46	Set of 12	8·00	5·00

1989 (31 Mar)**–92**. Nos. 227 and 319 optd with Type O **5**.

O47	1t. ultramarine (R.) (16.9.92)	1·75	50
	a. Opt double		
	b. Opt double, one inverted		
O48	5t. black and orange-brown (B.) (vert opt)	1·75	1·50

Nos. O47a/b show attempts to remove the errors using an eraser.

1990 (29 Nov). Nos. 368/9 (Immunization) optd with Type O **6** in red.

| O49 | **133** | 1t. emerald | 40 | 70 |
| O50 | | 2t. brown | 40 | 70 |

1992 (22 Nov). No. 376 optd as Type O **6**, but horiz in red.

| O51 | **136** | 6t. slate-blue and greenish yellow | 75 | 75 |

(O **6a**)

1994 (16 July). No. 318 optd as Type O **6a**, diagonally in red.

| O51a | **110** | 3t. black and light blue | 1·75 | 1·75 |

1995 (28 Feb). No. 553 (National Diabetes Awareness Day) optd as Type O **6** but horiz in red.

| O52 | **199** | 2t. multicoloured | 1·50 | 1·50 |

সার্ভিস (O **7**) **সার্ভিস** (O **8**)

1996 (23 Aug). Nos. 221 and 223 optd with Types O **7** (nylon block) or O **8** (typo) by Postal Printing Press, Tongi.

O53	O **7**	10p. purple (Blk.)	1·50	1·50
		a. Opt inverted		
		b. Opt double		
		c. Opt double (Types O **8**+O **7**)		
		d. Red opt		
O54		20p. grey-black (R.)	2·50	2·50
		a. Opt inverted		
		b. Opt double		
		c. Black opt		
O55	O **8**	20p. grey-black (R.)		

Similar overprints as Type O **7** in red or black on the 5p. and 50p. (Nos. 220 and 226) were prepared, but not issued.

1999 (31 Aug). No. 710 optd on Type O **5**, but vert in blue.

| O56 | 5t. black and brown-red | 1·00 | 1·00 |

Service (O **9**)

2000 (?). No. 709a optd on Type O **9** in red.

| O57 | 3t. black and light blue | 1·00 | 80 |

Burma

(Currency. 12 pies = 1 anna; 16 annas = 1 rupee)

Stamps of India were used in Burma from 1854 and, after 1856, individual examples can be identified by the use of the concentric octagonal postmarks of the Bengal Postal Circle of which the following were supplied to Burmese post offices:

Type A No. B156
(Rangoon)

Type B No. B5 (Akyab)

B5	Akyab	B146	Pegu
B12*	Bassein	B150	Prome
B22	Nga Thine Khyoung	B156*	Rangoon
B56	Amherst	B159	Sandoway
B108	Kyouk Phyoo	B165	Sarawah (to 1860)
B111	Meeaday	B165	Henzada (from 1861)
B112	Mengyee	B171	Shoay Gyeen
B127	Moulmein	B173	Sittang
B128	Mergui	B179	Thayetmyo
B129	Tavoy	B181	Toungoo
B133	Myanoung	B227	Port Blair
B136	Namayan		

*Exists in black or blue. Remainder in black only.

Akyab, Moulmein and Rangoon used postmarks as both Type A and Type B, Port Blair as Type B only and the remainder as Type A only.

From 1860 various types of duplex cancellations were introduced and Burmese examples can be identified when sufficient of the left-hand portion is visible on the stamp. Such marks were issued for the following offices:

Akyab	Rangoon
Bassein	Rangoon C.R.H. (Cantonment
Mandalay	Receiving House)
Moulmein	Thayetmyo
Port Blair	Toungoo
Prome	

1862 Duplex from Toungoo

1865 Duplex from Akyab

During 1875, a further series of duplex marks was introduced in which the right-hand portion of the cancellation included the office code number, prefixed by the letter "R" for Rangoon:

R–1	Rangoon	R–9	Myanoung
R–1/1	Rangoon Cantonment	R–10	Port Blair
R–2	Akyab	1/R–10	Nancowry
R–3	Bassein	R–11	Prome
R–4	Henzada	R–12	Sandoway
R–5	Kyouk Phyoo	R–13	Shwegyeen
R–6	Mandalay	R–14	Tavoy
R–7	Mergui	R–15	Thayetmyo
R–8	Moulmein	R–16	Tounghoo
1/R–8	Amherst		

1875 type from Rangoon

1875 type from Rangoon Cantonment Receiving House

From 1886 the whole of Burma was united under the Crown and the post offices were supplied with circular date stamps giving the name of the town.

Most Indian stamps, both postage and official, issued during the period were supplied to post offices in Burma. None of the imperforates printed by De La Rue have been seen however, and from the later issues the following have not been recorded with Burma postmarks:

Nos. 39a, 66a, 68, 85a, 92a, 110a/b, 148a, 155a, 165, 192a/c, 195a/b, O15, O38, O40b, O50a/b, O74a, O101a, O102, O103/a, O104/5 and O142.

The value of most India stamps used in Burma coincides proportionally with the used prices quoted for India, but some, especially the provisional surcharges, are extremely rare with Burmese postmarks. Stamps of the face value of 2r. and above from the reigns of Victoria and Edward VII are more common with telegraph cancellations than with those of the postal service.

PRICES FOR STAMPS ON COVER TO 1945		
Nos.	1/18	from × 6
Nos.	18a/33	from × 4
No.	34	from × 5
Nos.	35/50	from × 8
Nos.	O1/27	from × 15

BRITISH ADMINISTRATION

From 1 January 1886 Burma was a province of the Indian Empire but was separated from India and came under direct British administration on 1 April 1937.

BURMA
(1)

BURMA
(1a)

1937 (1 Apr). Stamps of India. (King George V inscr "INDIA POSTAGE") optd with T **1** or **1a** (rupee values). W **69**. P 14.

1	3p. slate	2·50	10
	w. Wmk inverted	16·00	3·00
2	½a. green	1·00	10
	w. Wmk inverted	14·00	3·00
3	9p. deep green (typo)	1·25	10
	w. Wmk inverted	11·00	3·00
4	1a. chocolate	5·00	10
	w. Wmk inverted	12·00	3·00
5	2a. vermilion (small die)	1·00	10
6	2½a. orange	75	10
	w. Wmk inverted	12·00	3·00
7	3a. carmine	5·00	30
	w. Wmk inverted	24·00	4·00
8	3½a. deep blue	8·00	10
	aw. Wmk inverted	8·50	30
	b. Dull blue	25·00	12·00
	bw. Wmk inverted	17·00	4·00
9	4a. sage-green	1·25	10
	w. Wmk inverted	—	£110
10	6a. bistre	1·50	35
	w. Wmk inverted	£180	£110
11	8a. reddish purple	4·25	10
	w. Wmk inverted	£180	

12		12a. claret	16·00	3·50
		w. Wmk inverted	35·00	7·50
13		1r. chocolate and green	65·00	5·50
14		2r. carmine and orange	48·00	27·00
		w. Wmk inverted	75·00	30·00
15		5r. ultramarine and purple	60·00	30·00
		w. Wmk inverted	—	£300
16		10r. green and scarlet	£250	95·00
		w. Wmk inverted	†	—
17		15r. blue and olive (wmk inverted)	£750	£250
18		25r. orange and blue	£1400	£550
		aw. Wmk inverted	£1400	£550
1/18	*Set of* 18		£2350	£850

The opt is at top on all values except the 3a.
The 1a. has been seen used from Yenangyaung on 22 Mar 1937.

2 King George VI and "Chinthes"

3 King George VI and "Nagas"

4 *Karaweik* (royal barge)

5 Burma teak

6 Burma rice

7 River Irrawaddy

8 King George VI and Peacock

9 King George VI and "Nats"

10 Elephants' Heads

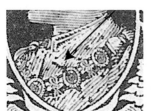

6p. "Medallion" flaw (R. 14/3)

2a.6p. "Birds over trees at left (R. 15/3)

3a.6p. Extra trees flaw (R. 11/8)

3a.6p. "Tick bird" flaw (R. 9/5)

(Des Maung Kyi (2a.6p.), Maung Hline (3a.), Maung Ohn Pe (3a.6p.) and N. K. D. Naigamwalla (8a.). Litho Security Ptg Press, Nasik)

1938 (15 Nov)–**40**. T **2/9**. W **10**. P 14 (vert) or 13½ × 13 (horiz).

18b	**2**	1p. red-orange (1.8.40)	3·50	2·00
19		3p. bright violet	30	3·00
20		6p. bright blue	1·00	10
		a. Medallion flaw	65·00	20·00
21		9p. yellow-green	2·50	2·00
22	**3**	1a. purple-brown	30	10
23		1½a. turquoise-green	2·00	3·75
24		2a. carmine	3·75	1·00
25	**4**	2a.6p. claret	15·00	3·75
		a. Birds over trees	£250	85·00
26	**5**	3a. dull violet	18·00	4·00
27	**6**	3a.6p. light blue and blue	4·25	9·50
		a. Extra trees flaw	£130	
		b. Tick bird flaw	£130	
28	**3**	4a. greenish blue	4·00	20
29	**7**	8a. myrtle-green	4·00	55
30	**8**	1r. purple and blue	4·00	1·00
31		2r. brown and purple	25·00	6·00
32	**9**	5r. violet and scarlet	75·00	65·00
33	**9**	10r. brown and myrtle	80·00	95·00
18b/33	*Set of* 16		£225	£170

The 1a. exists lithographed or typographed, the latter having a "Jubilee" line in the sheet margin.

COMMEMORATION POSTAGE STAMP 6th MAY 1840

(11)

Broken bar (R. 7/8)

1940 (6 May). Centenary of First Adhesive Postage Stamps. No. 25 surch with T **11**.

34	**4**	1a. on 2a.6p. claret	4·25	2·00
		a. Birds over trees	85·00	75·00
		b. Broken bar	85·00	75·00

For stamps issued in 1942–45 see under Japanese Occupation.

CHIN HILLS DISTRICT. This area, in the far north-west of the country, remained in British hands when the Japanese overran Burma in May 1942.

During the period July to December 1942 the local officials were authorised to produce provisional stamps and the letters "OHMS" are known overprinted by typewriter on Nos. 3, 20, 22/4, 28/9 and 31 of Burma or handstamped, in violet, on Nos. 25, 27 and 29. The two types can also occur together or in combination with a handstamped "SERVICE".

From early in 1943 ordinary postage stamps of India were used from the Chin Hills post offices of Falam, Haka, Fort White and Tiddim, this expedient continuing until the fall of Falam to the Japanese on 7 November 1943.

The provisional stamps should only be collected on Official cover (*Price, from* £2250) where dates and the sender's handwriting can be authenticated.

BRITISH MILITARY ADMINISTRATION

Preparations for the liberation of Burma commenced in February 1943 when the Civil Affairs Service (Burma) (CAS(B)) was set up at Delhi as part of the proposed military administration structure. One of the specific tasks assigned to CAS(B) was the operation of a postal service for the civilian population.

Operations against the Japanese intensified during the second half of 1944. The port of Akyab in the Arakan was reoccupied in January 1945. The 14th Army took Mandalay on 29 March and Rangoon was liberated from the sea on 3 May.

Postal services for the civilian population started in Akyab on 13 April 1945, while post offices in the Magwe Division around Meiktila were operating from 4 March. Mandalay post offices opened on 8 June and those in Rangoon on 16 June, but the full network was only completed in December 1945, just before the military administration was wound up.

MILY ADMN	**MILY ADMN**
(12)	(13)

1945 (from 11 Apr). Nos. 18b to 33 optd with T **12** (small stamps) or **13** (others) by Security Printing Press, Nasik.

35	**2**	1p. red-orange	10	10
		a. Opt omitted (in pair with normal)	£1600	
36		3p. bright violet	20	2·00
37		6p. bright blue	20	30
		a. Medallion flaw	32·00	38·00
38		9p. yellow-green	30	2·00
39	**3**	1a. purple-brown (16.6)	20	10
40		1½a. turquoise-green (16.6)	20	15
41		2a. carmine	20	15
42	**4**	2a.6p. claret	2·25	3·75
		a. Birds over trees	60·00	80·00
43	**5**	3a. dull violet	1·50	30
44	**6**	3a.6p. light blue and blue	20	1·00
		a. Extra trees flaw	35·00	
45	**3**	4a. greenish blue	20	70
46	**7**	8a. myrtle-green	20	2·00
47	**8**	1r. purple and blue	50	50
48		2r. brown and purple	50	1·50
49	**9**	5r. violet and scarlet	50	1·50
50		10r. brown and myrtle	50	50
35/50 *Set of* 16			7·00	16·00

Only the typographed version of the 1a., No. 22, received this overprint.

The missing overprints on the 1p. occur on the stamps from the bottom row of one sheet. A further block with two examples of the variety caused by a paper fold also exists.

The exact dates of issue for Nos. 35/50 are difficult to establish.

The initial stock of overprints is known to have reached CAS(B) headquarters, Imphal, at the beginning of April 1945. Postal directives issued on 11 April refer to the use of the overprints in Akyab and in the Magwe Division where surcharged pre-war postal stationery envelopes had previously been in use. The 6p., 1a., 1½a. and 2a.values were placed on sale at Mandalay on 8 June and the 1a. and 2a. at Rangoon on 16 June. It has been suggested that only a limited service was initially available in Rangoon. All values were on sale by 9 August 1945.

HAVE YOU READ THE NOTES AT THE BEGINNING OF THIS CATALOGUE?

These often provide answers to the enquiries we receive

BRITISH CIVIL ADMINISTRATION

3a.6p. Curved plough handle (R. 8/4)

1946 (1 Jan). As Nos. 19/33, but colours changed.

51	**2**	3p. brown	15	4·00
52		6p. deep violet	40	30
53		9p. green	1·75	7·00
54	**3**	1a. blue	1·00	20
55		1½a. orange	50	10
56		2a. claret	40	50
57	**4**	2a.6p. greenish blue	2·75	8·00
		aa. Birds over trees	70·00	
57a	**5**	3a. blue-violet	6·50	12·00
57b	**6**	3a.6p. black and ultramarine	4·00	5·50
		ba. Curved plough handle	95·00	
58	**3**	4a. purple	70	1·50
59	**7**	8a. maroon	1·75	7·50
60	**8**	1r. violet and maroon	3·25	3·75
61		2r. brown and orange	10·00	8·00
62	**9**	5r. green and brown	12·00	32·00
63		10r. claret and violet	25·00	45·00
51/63 *Set of* 15			60·00	£120

No. 54 was printed in typography only.

14 Burman

(Des A. G. I. McGeogh. Litho Nasik)

1946 (2 May). Victory. T **14** and similar vert designs. W **10** (sideways). P 13.

64		9p. turquoise-green	20	20
65		1½a. violet	20	10
66		2a. carmine	20	10
67		3a.6p. ultramarine	50	20
64/7 *Set of* 4			1·00	50

Designs:—1½a. Burmese woman; 2a. Chinthe; 3a.6p. Elephant.

INTERIM BURMESE GOVERNMENT

ကြားဖြတ် အစိုးရ။	၁းဖြတ်ကြ အစိုးရ။	တ်ကြား၀ အစိုးရ။
(**18** *Trans.* "Interim Government")	**18a**	**18b**

Type **18a** shows the first character transposed to the end of the top line (R. 6/15).

Type **18b** shows the last two characters transposed to the front of the top line (R. 14/14).

Some sheets of the 3p. show both errors corrected by a handstamp as Type **18**.

1947 (1 Oct). Stamps of 1946 optd with T **18** (small stamps) or larger opt (others).

68	**2**	3p. brown	1·75	70
		a. Opt Type **18a**	75·00	
		ab. Corrected by handstamp as Type **18**	£200	
		b. Opt Type **18b**	80·00	
		ba. Corrected by handstamp as Type **18**	£200	

69		6p. deep violet	20	30
		a. Opt Type **18a**	65·00	
70		9p. green	20	30
		a. Opt inverted	25·00	38·00
71	**3**	1a. blue	40	30
		a. Vert pair, one with opt omitted	£1600	
72		1½a. orange	3·00	10
73		2a. claret	40	15
		a. Horiz pair, one with opt omitted	£1600	
		b. Opt Type **18a**	90·00	
74	**4**	2a.6p. greenish blue	1·75	1·00
		a. Birds over trees	55·00	55·00
75	**5**	3a. blue-violet	2·75	1·75
76	**6**	3a.6p. black and ultramarine	2·75	3·75
77	**3**	4a. purple	1·75	30
78	**7**	8a. maroon	1·75	3·50
79	**8**	1r. violet and maroon	9·50	3·75
80		2r. brown and orange	11·00	11·00
81	**9**	5r. green and brown	11·00	10·00
82		10r. claret and violet	9·50	10·00
68/82	*Set of 15*		50·00	42·00

The 3p., 6p., 2a., 2a.6p., 3a.6p. and 1r. are also known with overprint inverted.

OFFICIAL STAMPS

BURMA   **BURMA**

SERVICE   **SERVICE**
(O **1**)   (O **1a**)

1937 (Apr–June). Stamps of India. (King George V inscr "INDIA POSTAGE") optd with Type O **1** or O **1a** (rupee values). W **69**. P 14.

O1		3p. slate	4·50	10
		w. Wmk inverted	£130	45·00
O2		½a. green	19·00	10
		w. Wmk inverted	†	—
O3		9p. deep green	5·00	2·50
O4		1a. chocolate	9·50	10
O5		2a. vermilion (*small die*)	20·00	45
		w. Wmk inverted	—	48·00
O6		2½a. orange	9·50	4·00
O7		4a. sage-green	10·00	10
O8		6a. bistre	10·00	19·00
O9		8a. reddish purple (1.4.37)	10·00	4·25
O10		12a. claret (1.4.37)	11·00	18·00
O11		1r. chocolate and green (1.4.37)	30·00	12·00
		w. Wmk inverted	£200	
O12		2r. carmine and orange	50·00	80·00
		w. Wmk inverted	50·00	80·00
O13		5r. ultramarine and purple	£200	90·00
O14		10r. green and scarlet	£550	£300
O1/14	*Set of 14*		£850	£475

For the above issue the stamps were either overprinted "BURMA" and "SERVICE" at one operation or had the two words applied separately. Research has yet to establish if all values exist with both forms of overprinting.

An example of the 4a. in orange is known cancelled at Moulmein.

SERVICE   **SERVICE**
(O **2**)   (O **3**)

1939 (1 Apr). Nos. 19/24 and 28 optd with Type O **2** (typo) and Nos. 25 and 29/33 optd with Type O **3** (litho).

O15	**2**	3p. bright violet	20	20
O16		6p. bright blue	20	20
		a. Medallion flaw	40·00	40·00
O17		9p. yellow-green	4·00	7·00
O18	**3**	1a. purple-brown	20	15
O19		1½a. turquoise-green	3·50	3·75
O20		2a. carmine	1·75	20
O21	**4**	2a.6p. claret	29·00	23·00
		a. Birds over trees	£375	£275
O22	**3**	4a. greenish blue	4·50	2·50
O23	**7**	8a. myrtle-green	20·00	4·00
O24	**8**	1r. purple and blue	16·00	5·50
O25		2r. brown and purple	35·00	20·00
O26	**9**	5r. violet and scarlet	26·00	48·00
O27		10r. brown and myrtle	£130	50·00
O15/27	*Set of 13*		£225	£140

Both versions of the 1a. value exist with this overprint.

1946 (1 Jan). British Civil Administration. Nos. 51/6 and 58 optd with Type O **2** (typo) and Nos. 57 and 59/63 optd with Type O **3** (litho).

O28	**2**	3p. brown	4·00	7·00
O29		6p. deep violet	3·25	2·25
O30		9p. green	2·50	7·50

O31	**3**	1a. blue	40	2·00
O32		1½a. orange	2·50	20
O33		2a. claret	40	2·00
O34	**4**	2a.6p. greenish blue	4·00	14·00
		a. Birds over trees	80·00	
O35	**3**	4a. purple	1·75	70
O36	**7**	8a. maroon	6·00	8·00
O37	**8**	1r. violet and maroon	4·00	12·00
O38		2r. brown and orange	8·50	50·00
O39	**9**	5r. green and brown	22·00	65·00
O40		10r. claret and violet	22·00	75·00
O28/40	*Set of 13*		70·00	£225

1947 (1 Oct). Interim Burmese Government. Nos. O28/40 optd with T **18** (small stamps) or larger opt (others).

O41	**2**	3p. brown	3·50	40
O42		6p. deep violet	5·50	15
O43		9p. green	8·00	90
O44	**3**	1a. blue	8·00	80
O45		1½a. orange	14·00	30
O46		2a. claret	8·00	15
O47	**4**	2a.6p. greenish blue	38·00	23·00
		a. Birds over trees	£400	£250
O48	**3**	4a. purple	27·00	40
O49	**7**	8a. maroon	27·00	4·50
O50	**8**	1r. violet and maroon	17·00	4·00
O51		2r. brown and orange	20·00	22·00
O52	**9**	5r. green and brown	21·00	24·00
O53		10r. claret and violet	21·00	38·00
O41/53	*Set of 13*		£200	£110

TELEGRAPH STAMPS

Indian telegraph stamps were used in Burma up to 1910 and subsequently Indian and then Burmese postage stamps, prior to the issue of the first Burmese telegraph stamps in 1946.

T 1

(Litho Nasik)

1946 (1 Oct?). T **T 1**. W **10**. P 14.

T 1	**1**	1a. carmine-red	3·00
T 2		2a. deep dull blue	3·00
T 3		8a. grey-green	4·00
T 4		12a. bluish grey	5·00
T 5		1r. brown	6·00
T 6		2r. deep dull purple	7·00
T 7		10r. turquoise-blue	8·00
T1/7	*Set of 7*		32·00

Nos. T 1/7 also exist with a one-line "Service" overprint in Burmese script, for official use (*Price, £75, for set of 7, unused*). Their date of issue is unknown.

Later stamp issues will be found listed in Part 21 (*South-East Asia*) of this catalogue.

JAPANESE OCCUPATION OF BURMA

PRICES FOR STAMPS ON COVER	
Nos.	J1/44	—
Nos.	J45/6	*from × 6*
Nos.	J47/56	*from × 8*
No.	J56g	—
Nos.	J57/72	*from × 6*
Nos.	J73/5	*from × 25*
No.	J76	*from × 8*
No.	J77	*from × 20*
Nos.	J78/81	*from × 25*
Nos.	J82/4	*from × 10*
Nos.	J85/7	*from × 40*
No.	J88	*from × 12*
Nos.	J89/97	*from × 30*
Nos.	J98/104	*from × 50*
Nos.	J105/111	*from × 30*

BURMA INDEPENDENCE ARMY ADMINISTRATION

The Burma Independence Army, formed by Aung San in 1941, took control of the Delta area of the Irrawaddy in May 1942. They reopened a postal service in the area and were authorised by the Japanese to overprint local stocks of stamps with the Burmese emblem of a peacock.

Postage and Official stamps with the peacock overprints or handstamps were used for ordinary postal purposes with the probable exception of No. J44.

DISTINGUISHING FEATURES. Type **1**. Body and head of Peacock always clearly outlined by broad uncoloured band. There are four slightly different sub-types of overprint Type **1**.

Type **2**. Peacock with slender neck and more delicately detailed tail. Clear spur on leg at right. Heavy fist-shaped blob of ink below and parallel to beak and neck.

Type **4**. No basic curve. Each feather separately outlined. Straight, short legs.

Type **5**. Much fine detail in wings and tail in clearly printed overprints. Thin, long legs ending in claws which, with the basic arc, enclose clear white spaces in well printed copies. Blob of colour below beak shows shaded detail and never has the heavy fist-like appearance of this portion in Type **2**.

Two sub-types may be distinguished in Type **5**, the basic arc of one having a chord of 14–15 mm and the other 12½–13 mm.

Type **6**. Similar to Type **5**, but with arc deeply curved and reaching nearly to the top of the wings. Single diagonal line parallel to neck below beak.

Collectors are warned against forgeries of these overprints, often in the wrong colours or on the wrong values.

(1)   (2)

(3)

1942 (May). Stamps of Burma overprinted with the national device of a Peacock.

I. Overprinted at Myaungmya
A. With Type 1 in black
On Postage Stamps of King George V.

J1		9p. deep green (No. 3)	£110	
J2		3½a. deep blue (No. 8)	80·00	

On Official Stamp of King George V

J3		6a. bistre (No. O8)	80·00	

On Postage Stamps of King George VI

J4	**2**	9p. yellow-green	£150	
J5	**3**	1a. purple-brown	£550	
J6		4a. greenish blue (opt black on red)	£160	
		a. Triple opt, black on double red	£450	

On Official Stamps of King George VI

J7	**2**	3p. bright violet	42·00	90·00
J8		6p. bright blue	27·00	65·00
J9	**3**	1a. purple-brown	28·00	55·00
J9a		1½a. turquoise-green	£900	£1300
J10		2a. carmine	40·00	£100
J11		4a. greenish blue	40·00	80·00

The overprint on No. J6 was apparently first done in red in error, and then corrected in black. Some stamps have the black overprint so accurately superimposed that the red hardly shows. These are rare.

Nos. J5 and J9 exist with the Peacock overprint on both the typographed and the litho printings of the original stamps.

B. With Types 2 or 3 (rupee values), in black
On Postage Stamps of King George VI

J12	**2**	3p. bright violet	22·00	75·00
J13		6p. bright blue	50·00	£110
J14		9p. yellow-green	27·00	70·00
J15	**3**	1a. purple-brown	17·00	65·00
J16		2a. carmine	28·00	85·00
J17		4a. greenish blue	60·00	£120
		a. Opt double		
		b. Opt inverted	£850	
		c. Opt double, one inverted	£475	
		d. Opt double, both inverted	£750	
J18		1r. purple and blue	£450	£750
J19	**8**	2r. brown and purple	£275	£550

The Myaungmya overprints (including No. J44) are usually clearly printed.

(4)   (5)   (6)

Type **5** generally shows the details of the peacock much less clearly and, due to heavy inking, or careless impression, sometimes appears as almost solid colour.

Type **6** was officially applied only to postal stationery. However, the handstamp remained in the possession of a postal official who used it on postage stamps after the war. These stamps are no longer listed.

II. Handstamped (at Pyapon?) with T 4, in black (so-called experimental type)
On Postage Stamps of King George VI.

J19a	**2**	6p. bright blue	75·00	
J19b	**3**	1a. purple-brown	£100	£250
J20		2a. carmine	£130	£300
J21		4a. greenish blue	£700	£700

Unused specimens of Nos. J20/1 are usually in poor condition.

III. Overprinted at Henzada with T 5 in blue, or blue-black
On Postage Stamps of King George V

J22		3p. slate (No. 1)	4·00	23·00
		a. Opt double	10·00	55·00
J23		9p. deep green (No. 3)	27·00	70·00
		a. Opt double	80·00	
J24		2a. vermilion (No. 5)	£130	£225

On Postage Stamps of King George VI

J25	**2**	1p. red-orange	£225	£375
J26		3p. bright violet	48·00	80·00
J27		6p. bright blue	25·00	55·00
		a. Opt double	£100	£150
		b. Clear opt, on back and front	£350	
J28		9p. yellow-green	£1100	
J29	**3**	1a. purple-brown	9·00	42·00
		a. Opt inverted	£2500	£1200
J30		1½a. turquoise-green	23·00	70·00
		a. Opt omitted (in pair with normal)	£4250	
J31		2a. carmine	23·00	70·00
		a. Opt double	£2750	
J32		4a. greenish blue	45·00	£100
		a. Opt double	£250	
		b. Opt inverted	£3750	

On Official Stamps of King George VI

J33	**2**	3p. bright violet	£140	£275
J34		6p. bright blue	£160	£275
J35	**3**	1½a. turquoise-green	£180	£325
J35a		2a. carmine	£375	£450
J36		4a. greenish blue	£1000	

(**6a**) ("Yon Thon" = "Office use")

V. Official Stamp of King George VI optd at Myaungmya
with Type 6a in black

J44	**7**	8a. myrtle-green	£110	£300

No. J44 was probably for official use.

There are two types of T **6a**, one with base of peacock 8 mm long and the other with base about 5 mm long. The neck and other details also vary. The two types are found se-tenant in the sheet. Stocks of the peacock types were withdrawn when the Japanese Directorate-General took control of the postal services in the Delta in August 1942.

JAPANESE ARMY ADMINISTRATION

7   **8** Farmer

1942 (1 June). Impressed by hand. Thick yellowish paper. No gum. P 12×11.

J45	**7**	(1a.) red	50·00	70·00

This device was the personal seal of Yano Sitza, the Japanese official in charge of the Posts and Telegraphs department of the Japanese Army Administration. It was impressed on paper already perforated by a line machine. Some stamps show part of the papermaker's watermark, either "ABSORBO DUPLICATOR" or "ELEPHANT BRAND", each with an elephant.

Other impressions of this seal on different papers, and showing signs of wear, were not valid for postal purposes.

(Des T. Kato. Typo *Rangoon Gazette* Press)

1942 (15 June). Value in annas. P 11 or 11×11½. Laid bâtonné paper. No gum.

J46	**8**	1a. scarlet	23·00	25·00

Some stamps show part of the papermaker's watermark, either "ELEPHANT BRAND" or "TITAGHUR SUPERFINE", each with an elephant.

½A.   1R.
(9)   (10)

1942 (22 Sept).

*(a) Nos. 314/17, 320/2, 325, 327 and 396 of Japan surch as T **9/10***

J47	**9**	¼a. on 1s. chestnut (Rice harvesting)...	50·00	50·00
		a. Surch inverted	£150	£150
		b. Surch double, one inverted	£190	
J48		½a. on 2s. bright scarlet (General Nogi)	55·00	50·00
		a. Surch inverted	£140	£150
		b. Surch double, one inverted	£190	
J49		¾a. on 3s. green (Power station)	80·00	80·00
		a. Surch inverted	£170	£170
		b. Surch double, one inverted	—	£200
J50		1a. on 5s. claret (Admiral Togo)	80·00	70·00
		a. Surch inverted	£250	£250
		b. Surch double, one inverted	£300	£275
		c. Surch omitted (in pair with normal)	£450	£400
J51		3a. on 7s. green (Diamond Mts)	£130	£150
		a. Surch inverted	£325	
J52		4a. on 4s. emerald (Togo)	60·00	65·00
		a. Surch inverted	£225	
J53		8a. on 8s. violet (Meiji Shrine)	£150	£150
		a. Surch inverted	£325	£325
		b. Surch double, one inverted	£425	
		c. Surch in red	£275	£300
		d. Red surch inverted	£450	
		e. Surch double (black and red)	£1100	
J54	**10**	1r. on 10s. deep carmine (Yomei Gate)	29·00	38·00
		a. Surch inverted	95·00	£110
		b. Surch double	80·00	£100
		c. Surch double (black and red)	£500	£500
		d. Surch omitted (in pair with normal)	£400	£400
		e. Surch omitted (in pair with inverted surch)	£550	
J55		2r. on 20s. ultramarine (Mt Fuji)	55·00	55·00
		a. Surch inverted	£150	£150
		b. Surch double, one inverted	£170	
		c. Surch omitted (in pair with normal black surch)	£275	£275
		d. Surch in red	55·00	55·00
		e. Red surch inverted	£150	£150
		f. Red surch double	£140	£140
		g. Surch omitted (in pair with normal red surch)	£350	£350
		ga. Surch omitted (in pair with double red surch)		
		h. Surch double (black and red)	£500	
J56	**9**	5r. on 30s. turquoise (Torii Shrine)	19·00	27·00
		a. Surch inverted	90·00	
		b. Surch double	£120	
		c. Surch double, one inverted	£160	
		d. Surch omitted (in pair with normal surch)	£325	£325
		e. Surch omitted (in pair with inverted black surch)	£425	
		f. Surch in red	30·00	32·00
		fa. Red surch inverted	95·00	95·00
		fb. J56a and J56fa *se-tenant*	£650	£650
		fc. Surch omitted (in pair with normal red surch)	£325	£325

(b) No. 386 of Japan commemorating the fall of Singapore similarly surch

J56g	**9**	4a. on 4+2s. green and red	£180	£190
		h. Surch omitted (in pair with normal)	£750	
		ha. Surch omitted (in pair with inverted surch)	£800	
		i. Surch inverted	£450	

(New Currency. 100 cents = 1 rupee)

15C.   15C.   15C.
(11)   (12)   (13)

1942 (15 Oct). Previous issues, with "anna" surcharges obliterated, handstamped with new value in cents, as T **11** and **12** (No. J57 handstamped with new value only).

(a) On No. J46

J57		5c. on 1a. scarlet	26·00	30·00
		a. Surch omitted (in pair with normal)	£2000	

(b) On Nos. J47/53

J58		1c. on ¼a. on 1s. chestnut	55·00	55·00
		a. "1 c." omitted (in pair with normal)	£900	
		b. "¼ a." inverted	£275	
J59		2c. on ½a. on 2s. bright scarlet	55·00	55·00
J60		3c. on ¾a. on 3s. green	60·00	60·00
		a. Surch in blue	£225	
J61		5c. on 1a. on 5s. claret	85·00	65·00
J62		10c. on 3a. on 7s. green	£170	£140
J63		15c. on 4a. on 4s. emerald	50·00	55·00
J64		20c. on 8a. on 8s. violet	£900	£700
		a. Surch on No. J53c (surch in red)	£350	£170

The "anna" surcharges were obliterated by any means available, in some cases by a bar or bars, and in others by the butt of a pencil dipped in ink. In the case of the fractional surcharges, the letter "A" and one figure of the fraction, were sometimes barred out, leaving the remainder of the fraction to represent the new value, e.g. the "1" of "½" deleted to create the 2c. surcharge or the "4" of "¾" to create the 3c. surcharge.

1942. Nos. 314/17, 320/1 and 396 of Japan surcharged in cents only as T **13.**

J65		1c. on 1s. chestnut (Rice harvesting)	40·00	20·00
		a. Surch inverted	£140	£140
J66		2c. on 2s. bright scarlet (General Nogi)	60·00	45·00
J67		3c. on 3s. green (Power station)	£100	65·00
		a. Pair, with and without surch	—	£375
		b. Surch inverted	£170	
		c. Surch in blue	£110	£120
		d. Surch in blue inverted	£325	£350
J68		5c. on 5s. claret (Admiral Togo)	£100	55·00
		a. Pair, with and without surch	£450	
		b. Surch in violet	£180	£190
		ba. Surch inverted	—	£350
J69		10c. on 7s. green (Diamond Mts)	£140	80·00
J70		15c. on 4s. emerald (Togo)	29·00	29·00
		a. Surch inverted	£170	£180
		b. Pair, with and without surch	—	£350
J71		20c. on 8s. violet (Meiji Shrine)	£200	95·00
		a. Surch double	£425	

Nos. J67c and J68b were issued for use in the Shan States.

BURMESE GOVERNMENT

On 1 November 1942 the Japanese Army Administration handed over the control of the postal department to the Burmese Government. On 1 August 1943 Burma was declared by the Japanese to be independent.

14 Burma State Crest    **15** Farmer

(Des U Tun Tin and Maung Tin from drawing by U Ba Than. Typo Rangoon)

1943 (15 Feb). No gum. P 11.

J72	**14**	5c. scarlet	29·00	35·00
		a. Imperf	29·00	35·00
		ab. Printed on both sides	95·00	

No. J72 was usually sold affixed to envelopes, particularly those with the embossed 1a. King George VI stamp, which it covered. Unused specimens off cover are not often seen and blocks are scarce.

1943. Typo. No gum. P 11½.

J73	**15**	1c. orange (22 March)	6·00	9·00
		a. Brown-orange	5·00	10·00

J74		2c. yellow-green (24 March)	1·50	1·00
		a. "3" for "2" in face value (R. 2/10)	£350	
		b. Blue-green	15·00	
J75		3c. light blue (25 March)	5·00	1·00
		a. On laid paper	23·00	40·00
		b. Imperf between (horiz pair)	—	£350
J76		5c. carmine (small "c") (17 March)	32·00	21·00
J77		5c. carmine (large "C")	3·50	8·00
		a. Imperf (pair)	£110	
		b. "G" for "C" (R. 2/6)	£180	
J78		10c. grey-brown (25 March)	9·50	9·50
		a. Imperf (pair)	£110	
		b. Imperf between (horiz pair)	—	£350
J79		15c. magenta (26 March)	30	4·50
		b. On laid paper	6·00	23·00
		ba. Inverted "C" in value (R. 2/3)	£200	
J80		20c. grey-lilac (29 March)	30	1·00
J81		30c. deep blue-green (29 March)	1·25	3·00

The 1c., 2c. and 3c. have large "C" in value as illustrated. The 10c. and higher values have small "c". Nos. J73/81 had the face values inserted individually into the plate used for No. J46 with the original face value removed. There were a number of printings for each value, often showing differences such as missing stops, various founts of figures or "c", etc., in the value tablets.

The face value error, No. J74a, was later corrected.

Some sheets of No. J75a show a sheet watermark of Britannia seated within a crowned oval spread across fifteen stamps in each sheet. This paper was manufactured by T. Edmonds and the other half of the sheet carried the watermark inscription "FOOLSCAP LEDGER". No stamps have been reported showing letters from this inscription, but a block of 25 is known on laid paper showing a different sheet watermark "HERTFORDSHIRE LEDGER MADE IN ENGLAND". Examples showing parts of these sheet watermarks are rare.

There are marked varieties of shade in this issue.

16 Soldier carving word "Independence" **17** Rejoicing Peasant

18 Boy with National Flag

Normal   Skyline flaw (R. 5/6)

(Des Maung Ba Thit (**16**), Naung Ohn Maung (**17**), and Maung Soi Yi (**18**). Typo State Press, Rangoon)

1943 (1 Aug). Independence Day. No gum.

(a) P 11

J82	**16**	1c. orange	15·00	20·00
J83	**17**	3c. light blue	15·00	20·00
J84	**18**	5c. carmine	23·00	11·00
		a. Skyline flaw	£140	
J82/4 Set of 3			48·00	45·00

(b) Rouletted

J85	**16**	1c. orange	1·50	1·75
		b. Perf × roul	£150	£150
		c. Imperf (pair)	45·00	55·00
J86	**17**	3c. light blue	2·50	4·00
		b. Perf × roul	£120	£120
		c. Imperf (pair)	45·00	55·00
J87	**18**	5c. carmine	3·50	4·25
		b. Perf × roul	70·00	70·00
		c. Imperf (pair)	45·00	55·00
		d. Skyline flaw	32·00	38·00
J85/7 Set of 3			6·50	9·00

The stamps perf × rouletted may have one, two or three sides perforated.

The rouletted stamps often appear to be roughly perforated owing to failure to make clean cuts. These apparent perforations are very small and quite unlike the large, clean holes of the stamps perforated 11.

A few imperforate sets, mounted on a special card folder and cancelled with the commemorative postmark were presented to officials. These are rare.

19 Burmese Woman   **20** Elephant carrying Log   **21** Watch Tower, Mandalay

(Litho G. Kolff & Co, Batavia)

1943 (1 Oct). P 12½.

J88	**19**	1c. red-orange	20·00	15·00
J89		2c. yellow-green	50	2·00
J90		3c. deep violet	50	2·25
		a. Bright violet	1·75	5·50
J91	**20**	5c. carmine	75	60
J92		10c. blue	2·25	1·10
J93		15c. yellow-green	1·00	3·00
J94		20c. yellow-green	1·00	1·75
J95		30c. olive-brown	1·00	2·00
J96	**21**	1r. red-orange	30	2·00
J97		2r. bright violet	30	2·25
J88/97 Set of 10			26·00	29·00

22 Bullock Cart   **23** Shan Woman   (**24** "Burma State" and value)

(Litho G. Kolff & Co, Batavia)

1943 (1 Oct). Issue for Shan States. P 12½.

J98	**22**	1c. olive-brown	45·00	48·00
J99		2c. yellow-green	50·00	48·00
J100		3c. bright violet	8·00	14·00
J101		5c. ultramarine	3·50	8·50
J102	**23**	10c. blue	17·00	18·00
J103		20c. carmine	48·00	22·00
J104		30c. olive-brown	27·00	65·00
J98/104 Set of 7			£180	£200

The Shan States, except for the frontier area around Keng Tung which was ceded to Thailand on 20 August 1943, were placed under the administration of the Burmese Government on 24 December 1943, and these stamps were later overprinted as T **24** for use throughout Burma.

1944 (1 Nov). Optd as T **24** (the lower characters differ for each value).

J105	**22**	1c. olive-brown	5·00	10·00
J106		2c. yellow-green	60	6·50
		a. Opt inverted	£425	£700
J107		3c. bright violet	2·50	7·00
J108		5c. ultramarine	3·00	4·00
J109	**23**	10c. blue	3·25	2·25
J110		20c. carmine	65	1·50
J111		30c. olive-brown	1·50	1·75
J105/11 Set of 7			15·00	30·00

Pakistan

(Currency. 12 pies = 1 anna; 16 annas = 1 rupee)

DOMINION

PAKISTAN   **PAKISTAN**
(1)   (2)

1947 (1 Oct). Nos. 259/68 and 269a/77 (King George VI) of India optd by litho at Nasik, as T **1** (3p. to 12a.) or T **2** (14a. and rupee values).

1		3p. slate	30	10
2		½a. purple	30	10
		w. Wmk inverted	—	55·00
3		9p. green	30	10
4		1a. carmine	30	10
5		1½a. dull violet	1·75	10
		w. Wmk inverted	—	30·00
6		2a. vermilion	30	20
7		3a. bright violet	35	20
8		3½a. bright blue	1·00	2·25
9		4a. brown	35	20
10		6a. turquoise-green	1·00	1·25
11		8a. slate-violet	45	60
12		12a. lake	1·00	20
13		14a. purple	3·25	3·75
14		1r. grey and red-brown	6·00	1·25
		w. Wmk inverted	80·00	55·00
15		2r. purple and brown	3·50	4·50
16		5r. green and blue	9·00	7·00
17		10r. purple and claret	9·00	11·00
18		15r. brown and green	85·00	£140
19		25r. slate-violet and purple	90·00	90·00
1/19	Set of 19		£190	£225

Numerous provisional "PAKISTAN" overprints, both handstamped and machine-printed, in various sizes and colours, on Postage and Official stamps, also exist.

These were made under authority of Provincial Governments, District Head Postmasters or Local Postmasters and are of considerable philatelic interest.

The 1a.3p. (India No. 269) exists only as a local issue (*Price*, Karachi opt £2 *unused*; £3 *used*).

The 12a., as No. 12 but overprinted at Karachi, exists with overprint inverted (*Price* £70 *unused*).

The 1r. value with Karachi local overprint exists with overprint inverted (*Price* £180 *unused*) or as a vertical pair with one stamp without overprint (*Price* £650 *unused*).

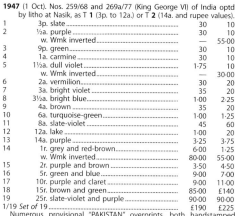

3 Constituent Assembly Building, Karachi   **4** Karachi Airport entrance

5 Gateway to Lahore Fort    **6** Crescent and Stars

(Des A. Chughtai (1r.). Recess D.L.R.)

1948 (9 July). Independence. T **3/6**. P 13½×14 or 11½ (1r.).

20	**3**	1½a. ultramarine	1·25	2·00
21	**4**	2½a. green	1·25	20
22	**5**	3a. purple-brown	1·25	35
23	**6**	1r. scarlet	1·25	70
		a. Perf 14×13½	4·75	24·00
20/3	Set of 4		4·50	3·00

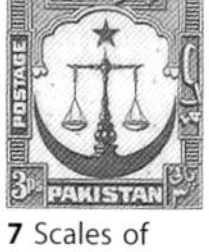

7 Scales of Justice    **8** Star and Crescent    **9** Lloyds Barrage

10 Karachi Airport    **11** Karachi Port Trust

12 Salimullah Hostel, Dacca    **13** Khyber Pass

(Des M. Suharwardi (T **8**). Recess Pakistan Security Ptg Corp Ltd, Karachi (P 13 and 13½), D.L.R. (others))

1948 (14 Aug)–**57**. T **7/13**.

24	**7**	3p. red (P 12½)	10	10
		a. Perf 13½ (5.54)	3·25	1·00
25		6p. violet (P 12½)	1·25	10
		a. Perf 13½ (1954)	6·50	4·50
26		9p. green (P 12½)	50	10
		a. Perf 13½ (1954)	8·00	1·75
27	**8**	1a. blue (P 12½)	20	50
28		1½a. grey-green (P 12½)	20	10
29		2a. red (P 12½)	5·00	70
30	**9**	2½a. green (P 14×13½)	7·00	11·00
31	**10**	3a. green (P 14)	7·50	1·00
32	**9**	3½a. bright blue (P 14×13½)	7·00	5·50
33		4a. reddish brown (P 12½)	1·25	10
34	**11**	6a. blue (P 14×13½)	2·00	50
35		8a. black (P 12)	1·50	1·50
36	**10**	10a. scarlet (P 14)	6·50	12·00
37	**11**	12a. scarlet (P 14×13½)	8·50	1·00
38	**12**	1r. ultramarine (P 14)	20·00	10
		a. Perf 13½ (1954)	18·00	9·50
39		2r. chocolate (P 14)	20·00	75
		a. Perf 13½ (5.54)	26·00	7·00
40		5r. carmine (P 14)	18·00	2·75
		a. Perf 13½ (7.53)	14·00	25
41	**13**	10r. magenta (P 14)	20·00	38·00
		a. Perf 12	£140	10·00
		b. Perf 13 (1951)	19·00	3·25
42		15r. blue-green (P 12)	18·00	28·00
		a. Perf 14	24·00	85·00
		b. Perf 13 (27.7.57)	26·00	32·00
43		25r. violet (P 14)	55·00	£120
		a. Perf 12	42·00	42·00
		b. Perf 13 (1.11.54)	50·00	45·00
24/43a	Set of 20		£160	95·00

For 25r. with W **98**, see No. 210.

The 6p. (No. 25) exists from coils made up from normal sheets.

14 Star and Crescent   **15** Karachi Airport    **15a** Karachi Port Trust

(Recess Pakistan Security Ptg Corp (P 13½), D.L.R. (others).

1949 (Feb)–**53**. Redrawn. Crescent moon with points to left as T **14/15a**.

44	**14**	1a. blue (P 12½)	4·00	85
		a. Perf 13½ (1952)	12·00	10
45		1½a. grey-green (P 12½)	3·75	85
		a. Perf 13½ (1953)	3·50	10
		ab. Printed on the gummed side	65·00	
46		2a. red (P 12½)	4·50	10
		a. Perf 13½ (1952)	7·00	10
47	**15**	3a. green (P 14)	16·00	1·00
48	**15a**	6a. blue (as No. 34) (P 14×13½)	22·00	2·50
49		8a. black (as No. 35) (P 12½)	22·00	2·50
50	**15**	10a. scarlet (P 14)	26·00	3·75
51	**15a**	12a. scarlet (as No. 37) (P 14×13½)	28·00	60
44/51	Set of 8		£110	9·50

The 1a. (No. 44) exists from coils made up from normal sheets.

16   **16a**

(Recess D.L.R.)

1949 (11 Sept). First Death Anniv of Mohammed Ali Jinnah. T **16/a**. P 14.

52	**16**	1½a. brown	3·00	2·00
53		3a. green	3·00	1·50
54	**16a**	10a. black	8·50	8·00
52/4 *Set of 3*			13·00	10·50

17 Pottery   **18** Stylised aeroplane and Hourglass

Two Types of 3½a.:

I   II

19 Saracenic Leaf Pattern   **20** Archway and Lamp

(Des A. Chughtai. Recess D.L.R., later printings, Pakistan Security Ptg Corp)

1951 (14 Aug)–**56**. Fourth Anniv of Independence. P 13.

55	**17**	2½a. carmine	1·75	1·25
56	**18**	3a. purple	1·00	10
57	**17**	3½a. blue (I)	1·25	8·50
57a		3½a. blue (II) (12.56)	4·50	6·00
58	**19**	4a. green	1·50	10
59		6a. brown-orange	1·50	10
60	**20**	8a. sepia	4·50	25
61		10a. violet	2·00	2·25
62	**18**	12a. slate	2·00	10
55/62 *Set of 9*			18·00	16·00

The above and the stamps issued on the 14 August 1954, 1955 and 1956, are basically definitive issues, although issued on the Anniversary date of Independence.

21 "Scinde Dawk" stamp and Ancient and Modern Transport

(Recess D.L.R.)

1952 (14 Aug). Centenary of "Scinde Dawk" Issue of India. P 13.

63	**21**	3a. deep olive/*yellow-olive*	1·00	85
64		12a. deep brown/*salmon*	1·25	15

PRINTERS. All issues up to No. 219 were recess-printed by the Pakistan Security Printing Corporation, unless otherwise stated.

22 Kaghan Valley   **23** Mountains, Gilgit

24 Bahshahi Mosque, Lahore   **25** Mausoleum of Emperor Jehangir, Lahore

26 Tea Plantation, East Pakistan   **27** Cotton plants, West Pakistan

28 Jute fields and River, East Pakistan

1954 (14 Aug). Seventh Anniv of Independence. T **22/8**. P 13½ (14a., 1r., 2r.) or 13 (others).

65	**22**	6p. reddish violet	25	10
66	**23**	9p. blue	3·75	3·00
67	**24**	1a. carmine	30	10
68	**25**	1½a. red	30	10
69	**26**	14a. deep green	6·00	10
70	**27**	1r. green	11·00	10
71	**28**	2r. red-orange	3·00	10
65/71 *Set of 7*			22·00	3·00

29 View of K 2

1954 (25 Dec). Conquest of K 2 (Mount Godwin-Austen). P 13.

72	**29**	2a. deep violet	40	40

30 Karnaphuli Paper Mill, Type I (Arabic fraction on left)   **31** Textile Mill, West Pakistan

32 Jute Mill, East Pakistan   **33** Main Sui gas plant

Type II (Arabic fraction
on right)

1955 (14 Aug)–**56**. Eighth Anniv of Independence. T **30/3**. P 13.

73	**30**	2½a. scarlet (I)	50	1·40
73a		2½a. scarlet (II) (12.56)	1·50	1·40
74	**31**	6a. deep ultramarine	1·50	10
75	**32**	8a. deep reddish violet	3·75	10
76	**33**	12a. carmine and orange	4·00	10
73/6 Set of 5			10·00	2·75

**TENTH
ANNIVERSARY
UNITED NATIONS**

24. 10. 55.

(**34**)

35 Map of West Pakistan

**TENTH
ANNIVERSARY
UNITED NATIONS**

24. 10. 55.

"UNITED NATIONS"
shifted 1 mm to left
(1½a. R. 7/10; 12a. R. 1/8,
3/8, 5/8, 7/8, 9/8)

1955 (24 Oct). Tenth Anniv of United Nations. Nos. 68 and 76 optd
as T **34**.

77	1½a. red (B.)	1·50	5·00
	a. "UNITED NATIONS" 1 mm to left	20·00	30·00
78	12a. carmine and orange (B.)	50	3·50
	a. "UNITED NATIONS" 1 mm to left	6·50	16·00

Forgeries exist of the overprint on No. 77. These are in very
uneven thin type and measure 20×18 mm instead of the genuine
19½×19 mm.

1955 (7 Dec). West Pakistan Unity. P 13½.

79	**35**	1½a. myrtle-green	1·25	1·75
80		2a. sepia	1·00	10
81		12a. deep rose-red	1·50	50
79/81 Set of 3			3·25	2·10

REPUBLIC

36 Constituent Assembly Building,
Karachi

(Litho D.L.R.)

1956 (23 Mar). Republic Day. P 13.

82	**36**	2a. myrtle-green	80	10

37   **38** Map of East Pakistan

1956 (14 Aug). Ninth Anniv of Independence. P 13½.

83	**37**	2a. scarlet	65	10
		a. Printed on the gummed side	7·00	

1956 (15 Oct). First Session of National Assembly of Pakistan at
Dacca. P 13½.

84	**38**	1½a. myrtle-green	40	1·50
85		2a. sepia	40	10
86		12a. deep rose-red	40	1·25
84/6 Set of 3			1·10	2·50

39 Karnaphuli Paper Mill,
East Bengal   **40** Pottery

41 Orange Tree

1957 (23 Mar). First Anniv of Republic. P 13.

87	**39**	2½a. scarlet	25	10
88	**40**	3½a. blue	30	10
89	**41**	10r. myrtle-green and yellow-orange	1·00	25
87/9 Set of 3			1·40	35

The above and No. 95 are primarily definitive issues, although
issued on the Anniversary of Republic Day.

For 10r. with W **98**, see No. 208.

42 Pakistani Flag   **43** Pakistani Industries

(Des Ahsan. Litho D.L.R.)

1957 (10 May). Centenary of Struggle for Independence (Indian
Mutiny). P 13.

90	**42**	1½a. bronze-green	50	10
91		12a. light blue	1·25	10

(Litho D.L.R.)

1957 (14 Aug). Tenth Anniv of Independence. P 14.

92	**43**	1½a. ultramarine	20	30
93		4a. orange-red	45	1·50
94		12a. mauve	45	50
92/4 Set of 3			1·00	2·10

44 Coconut Tree　　　　**45**

1958 (23 Mar). Second Anniv of Republic. P 13.
95　　**44**　15r. red and deep reddish purple .... 2·50　1·50
　This is a definitive issue, see note below No. 89.
　See No. 209 for this stamp with W **98**.

(Photo Harrison)

1958 (21 Apr). 20th Death Anniv of Mohammed Iqbal (poet).
　P 14½×14.
96　　**45**　1½a. yellow-olive and black .... 55　1·00
97　　　　2a. orange-brown and black .... 55　10
98　　　　14a. turquoise-blue and black .... 90　10
96/8 *Set of 3* .... 1·75　1·00

46 UN Charter and
Globe

1958 (10 Dec). Tenth Anniv of Declaration of Human Rights. P 13.
99　　**46**　1½a. turquoise-blue .... 10　10
100　　　　14a. sepia .... 45　10

PAKISTAN
BOY SCOUT
2nd NATIONAL
JAMBOREE

CHITTAGONG
Dec. 58—Jan. 59
(47)

REVOLUTION
DAY
Oct. 27, 1959
(48)

1958 (28 Dec). Second Pakistan Boy Scouts National Jamboree,
　Chittagong. Nos. 65 and 75 optd with T **47**.
101　　　　6p. reddish violet .... 20　10
102　　　　8a. deep reddish violet .... 40　10

1959 (27 Oct). Revolution Day. No. 74 optd with T **48** in red.
103　　　　6a. deep ultramarine .... 80　10

49 "Centenary of An Idea"

1959 (19 Nov). Red Cross Commemoration. Recess; cross typo. P 13.
104　　**49**　2a. red and green .... 30　10
105　　　　10a. red and deep blue .... 55　10

50 Armed Forces Badge　　**51** Map of Pakistan

(Litho D.L.R.)

1960 (10 Jan). Armed Forces Day. P 13½×13.
106　　**50**　2a. red, ultramarine and blue-green.... 50　10
107　　　　14a. red and bright blue .... 1·00　10

1960 (23 Mar). P 13×13½.
108　　**51**　6p. deep purple .... 40　10
109　　　　2a. brown-red .... 60　10
110　　　　8a. deep green .... 1·25　10
111　　　　1r. blue .... 2·00　10
　　　　　a. Printed on the gummed side ....
108/11 *Set of 4* .... 3·75　20

52 Uprooted Tree

1960 (7 Apr). World Refugee Year. P 13.
112　　**52**　2a. rose-carmine .... 20　10
113　　　　10a. green .... 30　10

53 Punjab Agricultural College　　**55** "Land Reforms,
　　　　　　　　　　　　　　　　　Rehabilitation and
　　　　　　　　　　　　　　　　　Reconstruction"

1960 (10 Oct). Golden Jubilee of Punjab Agricultural College,
　Lyallpur. T **53** and similar horiz design. P 12½×14.
114　　　　2a. slate-blue and carmine-red .... 15　10
115　　　　8a. bluish green and reddish violet .... 40　10
Design:—8a. College arms.

(Des M. Hanjra. Photo D.L.R.)

1960 (27 Oct). Revolution Day. P 13×13½.
116　　**55**　2a. green, pink and brown .... 10　10
　　　　　a. Green and pink omitted .... 23·00
　　　　　b. Pink omitted .... 7·00
117　　　　14a. green, yellow and ultramarine .... 50　75

56 Caduceus　　**57** "Economic
　　　　　　　　　　Co-operation"

(Photo D.L.R.)

1960 (16 Nov). Centenary of King Edward Medical College, Lahore.
　P 13.
118　　**56**　2a. yellow, black and blue .... 50　10
119　　　　14a. emerald, black and carmine .... 1·75　1·00

1960 (5 Dec). International Chamber of Commerce CAFEA Meeting,
　Karachi. P 13.
120　　**57**　14a. orange-red .... 75　20

58 Zam-Zama Gun, Lahore ("Kim's
　Gun," after Rudyard Kipling)

(Centre typo, background recess Pakistan Security Ptg Corp)

1960 (24 Dec). Third Pakistan Boy Scouts National Jamboree, Lahore.
　P 12½×14.
121　　**58**　2a. carmine, yellow and deep bluish
　　　　　　green .... 80　30

(New Currency. 100 paisa = 1 rupee)

1 PAISA

(59)

1961 (1 Jan–14 Feb). Nos. 24a, 67/8, 83 and 108/9, surch as T **59**.
Nos. 123/4 and 126 surch by Pakistan Security Ptg Corp and others by the Times Press, Karachi.

122	1p. on 1½a. red (10.1)	40	10
	a. Printed and surch on the gummed side	60·00	
123	2p. on 3p. red	10	10
124	3p. on 6p. deep purple	15	10
	a. "PASIA" for "PAISA"	9·00	
125	7p. on 1a. carmine (14.2)	40	10
126	13p. on 2a. brown-red (14.2)	40	10
	a. "PAIS" for "PAISA"	9·00	
127	13p. on 2a. scarlet (14.2)	30	10
122/7 Set of 6		1·60	30

No. 122. Two settings were used, the first with figure "1" 2½ mm tall and the second 3 mm.
On the 1p. with tall "1" and the 13p. (No. 127), the space between the figures of value and "P" of "PAISA" varies between 1½ mm and 3 mm.
See also Nos. 262/4.

ERRORS. In the above issue and the corresponding official stamps we have listed errors in the stamps surcharged by the Pakistan Security Printing Corp but have not included the very large number of errors which occurred in the stamps surcharged by the less experienced Times Press. This was a very hurried job and there was no time to carry out the usual checks. It is also known that some errors were not issued to the public but came on the market by other means.

NOTE. Stamps in the old currency were also handstamped with new currency equivalents and issued in various districts but these local issues are outside the scope of this catalogue.

60 Khyber Pass

61 Shalimar Gardens, Lahore

62 Chota Sona Masjid (gateway)

(a) (b) (c)

Types (a) and (b) show the first letter in the top right-hand inscription; (a) wrongly engraved, "SH" (b) corrected to "P".
On Nos. 131/2 and 134 the corrections were made individually on the plate, so that each stamp in the sheet may be slightly different.
Type (c) refers to No. 133a only.

1961–63. No wmk. P 13 (T **62**) or 14 (others).

(a) Inscribed "SHAKISTAN" in Bengali
128	**60**	1p. violet (1.1.61)	1·50	10
129		2p. rose-red (12.1.61)	1·50	10
130		5p. ultramarine (23.3.61)	3·00	10

(b) Inscribed "PAKISTAN" in Bengali
131	**60**	1p. violet	1·00	10
		a. Printed on the gummed side		
132		2p. rose-red	1·00	10
133		3p. reddish purple (27.10.61)	75	10
		a. Re-engraved. First letter of Bengali inscription as Type (c) (1963)	8·50	4·00
134		5p. ultramarine	6·50	10
		a. Printed on the gummed side		

135		7p. emerald (23.3.61)	2·00	10
136	**61**	10p. brown (14.8.61)	20	10
137		13p. slate-violet (14.8.61)	20	10
138		25p. deep blue (1.1.62)	5·50	10
139		40p. deep purple (1.1.62)	1·50	10
140		50p. deep bluish green (1.1.62)	35	10
141		75p. carmine-red (23.3.62)	40	70
142		90p. yellow-green (1.1.62)	70	70
143	**62**	1r. vermilion (7.1.63)	6·50	10
		a. Imperf (pair)		
144		1r.25 reddish violet (27.10.61)	1·00	1·25
144a		2r. orange (7.1.63)	5·50	15
144b		5r. green (7.1.63)	6·00	3·00
128/44b Set of 19			40·00	5·50

See also Nos. 170/81 and 204/7.

LAHORE STAMP EXHIBITION 1961
(63)

64 Warsak Dam and Power Station

1961 (12 Feb). Lahore Stamp Exhibition. No. 110 optd with T **63**.
145	**51**	8a. deep green (R.)	1·00	1·75

(Des A. Ghani)
1961 (1 July). Completion of Warsak Hydro-Electric Project. P 12½×14.
146	**64**	40p. black and blue	60	10

65 Narcissus

(Des A. Ghani)
1961 (2 Oct). Child Welfare Week. P 14.
147	**65**	13p. turquoise-blue	50	10
148		90p. bright purple	1·25	20

66 Ten Roses
67 Police Crest and "Traffic Control"

(Des A. Ghani)
1961 (4 Nov). Co-operative Day. P 13.
149	**66**	13p. rose-red and deep green	40	10
150		90p. rose-red and blue	85	90

(Photo D.L.R.)
1961 (30 Nov). Police Centenary. P 13.
151	**67**	13p. silver, black and blue	50	10
152		40p. silver, black and red	1·00	20

68 Locomotive *Eagle*, 1861

(Des M. Thoma. Photo D.L.R.)
1961 (31 Dec). Railway Centenary. T **68** and similar horiz design. P 14.
153		13p. green, black and yellow	75	80
154		50p. yellow, black and green	1·00	1·50

Design:—50p. Diesel locomotive No. 20 and tracks forming "1961".

FIRST JET FLIGHT
KARACHI·DACCA **13**
Paisa

(70)

71 *Anopheles sp* (mosquito)

1962 (6 Feb). First Karachi-Dacca Jet Flight. No. 87 surch with T **70**.
155   **39**   13p. on 2½a. scarlet (R.)............................ 1·75   1·25

(Photo D.L.R.)

1962 (7 Apr). Malaria Eradication. T **71** and similar horiz design. P 14.
156   10p. black, yellow and red.................................. 35   10
157   13p. black, greenish yellow and red.............. 35   10
Design:—13p. Mosquito pierced by blade.

73 Pakistan Map and Jasmine

(Photo Courvoisier)

1962 (8 June). New Constitution. P 12.
158   **73**   40p. yellow-green, bluish green and grey.. 85   10

74 Football

78 Marble Fruit Dish and Bahawalpuri Clay Flask

(Des A. Ghani and M. Bhatti)

1962 (14 Aug). Sports. T **74** and similar horiz designs. P 12½×14.
159   7p. black and blue 10   10
160   13p. black and green 60   2·25
161   25p. black and purple 20   10
162   40p. black and orange-brown..................... 2·00   2·25
159/62 *Set of 4*.. 2·50   4·00
Designs:—13p. Hockey; 25p. Squash; 40p. Cricket.

(Des A. Ghani and M. Bhatti)

1962 (10 Nov). Small Industries. T **78** and similar vert designs. P 13.
163   7p. brown-lake... 10   10
164   13p. deep green.. 2·50   2·50
165   25p. reddish violet.. 10   10
166   40p. yellow-green... 10   10
167   50p. deep red... 10   10
163/7 *Set of 5*.. 2·50   2·50
Designs:—13p. Sports equipment; 25p. Camel-skin lamp and brassware; 40p. Wooden powderbowl and basket-work; 50p. Inlaid cigarette-box and brassware.

83 "Child Welfare"

(Des M. Thoma. Photo D.L.R.)

1962 (11 Dec). 16th Anniv of UNICEF. P 14.
168   **83**   13p. black, light blue and maroon.......... 35   10
169   40p. black, yellow and turquoise-blue... 35   10

Nos. 170, etc.

Nos. 131/42

1962–70. As T **60/1** but with redrawn Bengali inscription at top right. No wmk.
170   **60**   1p. violet (1963) 10   10
171   2p. rose-red (1964)..................... 2·00   10
          a. Imperf (pair)............................. 3·00
172   3p. reddish purple (1970) .... 13·00   6·00
173   5p. ultramarine (1963)................ 10   10
          a. Printed on the gummed side.... 13·00
174   7p. emerald (1964)...................... 7·00   3·50
175   **61**   10p. brown (1963) 10   10
          a. Printed on the gummed side.... 13·00
176   13p. slate-violet............................ 10   10
176a   15p. bright purple (31.12.64)...... 20   10
          ab. Imperf (pair).......................... 4·50
          ac. Printed on the gummed side... 15·00
176b   **61**   20p. myrtle-green (26.1.70) 30   10
          ba. Imperf (pair).......................... 3·50
          bb. Printed on the gummed side... 15·00
177   25p. deep blue (1963).................. 11·00   10
          a. Imperf (pair)............................. 10·00
178   40p. deep purple (1964).............. 15   30
          a. Imperf (pair)............................. 6·50
179   50p. deep bluish green (1964)..... 15   10
          a. Printed on the gummed side.... 13·00
180   75p. carmine-red (1964).............. 50   70
          a. Printed on the gummed side.... 13·00
181   90p. yellow-green (1964)............. 30   1·00
170/81 *Set of 14*.. 32·00   10·50
Other values in this series and the high values (Nos. 204/10) are known imperforate but we are not satisfied as to their status.

U.N. FORCE W. IRIAN

(84)

85 "Dancing" Horse, Camel and Bull

1963 (15 Feb). Pakistan U.N. Force in West Irian. No. 176 optd with T **84**.
182   **61**   13p. slate-violet (R.)................... 10   1·50

(Des S. Jahangir. Photo Courvoisier)

1963 (13 Mar). National Horse and Cattle Show. P 11½.
183   **85**   13p. blue, sepia and cerise...................... 10   10

86 Wheat and Tractor

(Des B. Mirza)

1963 (21 Mar). Freedom from Hunger. T **86** and similar horiz design. P 12½×14.
184   13p. orange-brown .... 3·00   10
185   50p. bistre-brown .... 4·50   55
Design:—50p. Rice.

13 PAISA

INTERNATIONAL
DACCA STAMP
EXHIBITION
1963

(88)

1963 (23 Mar). Second International Stamp Exhibition, Dacca. No. 109 surch with T **88**.
186   **51**   13p. on 2a. brown-red.................... 50   50

89 Centenary Emblem

90 Paharpur

1963 (25 June). Centenary of Red Cross. Recess; cross typo. P 13.
187   **89**   40p. red and deep olive...................... 2·25   15

(Des A. Ghani)

1963 (16 Sept). Archaeological Series. T **90** and similar designs. P 14×12½ (13p.) or 12½×15 (others).

188	7p. ultramarine		55	10
189	13p. sepia		55	10
190	40p. carmine		90	10
191	50p. deep reddish violet		95	10
188/91	Set of 4		2·75	35

Designs: Vert—13p. Moenjodaro; Horiz—40p. Taxila; 50p. Mainamati.

(**94**)

1963 (7 Oct). Centenary of Public Works Department. No. 133 surch with T **94** by typography.

192	**60**	13p. on 3p. reddish purple	10	10

Forged surcharges applied in lithography exist.

95 Atatürk's Mausoleum

(Des A. Ghani)

1963 (10 Nov). 25th Death Anniv of Kemal Atatürk. P 13½.

193	**95**	50p. red	50	10

96 Globe and UNESCO Emblem

(Photo D.L.R.)

1963 (10 Dec). 15th Anniv of Declaration of Human Rights. P 14.

194	**96**	50p. brown, red and ultramarine	40	10

97 Thermal Power Installations

(Des A. Ghani)

1963 (25 Dec). Completion of Multan Thermal Power Station. P 12½×14.

195	**97**	13p. ultramarine	10	10

98 Multiple Star and Crescent

99 Temple of Thot, Queen Nefertari and Maids

1963–79. As Nos. 43b, 89, 95 and 143/4b, but W **98** (sideways* on 15r.).

204	**62**	1r. vermilion	1·25	10
		a. Printed on the gummed side	13·00	
		b. Imperf (pair)	7·50	
		w. Wmk inverted	1·75	

205		1r.25 reddish violet (1964)	2·25	1·50
		aw. Wmk inverted	2·75	
		b. Purple (1975?)	4·75	1·75
		ba. Imperf (pair)	6·00	
206		2r. orange (1964)	1·00	15
		a. Imperf (pair)	8·00	
		w. Wmk inverted	2·00	
207		5r. green (1964)	6·00	1·00
		a. Imperf (pair)	11·00	
		w. Wmk inverted	6·00	
208	**41**	10r. myrtle-green and yellow-orange (1968)	6·50	6·50
		a. Imperf (pair)		
		bw. Wmk inverted		
		c. Wmk sideways	4·00	4·50
209	**44**	15r. red and deep reddish purple (20.3.79)	2·25	4·00
		a. Imperf (pair)	13·00	
		w. Wmk tips of crescent pointing downwards		
210	**13**	25r. violet (1968)	14·00	19·00
		aw. Wmk inverted	17·00	
		b. Wmk sideways	7·50	10·00
		ba. Imperf (pair)	15·00	
204/10b	Set of 7		22·00	19·00

MULTIPLE STAR AND CRESCENT WATERMARKED PAPER. When viewed from the back with the stamp upright, upright and sideways reversed watermarks show the tips of the crescents pointing upwards and to the right; reversed and sideways watermarks show the tips pointing upwards to the left; inverted and sideways inverted and reversed watermarks show the tips pointing downwards and to the left, while sideways inverted and upright inverted and reversed watermarks show them pointing downwards and to the left. Upright and sideways reversed watermarks may be differentiated by the angle of the row of stars which is approximately 60° for the upright and 30° for the sideways reversed.

(Des A. Ghani)

1964 (30 Mar). Nubian Monuments Preservation. T **99** and similar horiz design. P 13×13½.

211	13p. turquoise-blue and red		30	10
212	50p. bright purple and black		70	10

Design:—50p. Temple of Abu Simbel.

101 "Unisphere" and Pakistan Pavilion

103 Shah Abdul Latif's Mausoleum

(Des A. Ghani)

1964 (22 Apr). New York World's Fair. T **101** and similar design. P 12½×14 (13p.) or 14×12½ (1r.25).

213	13p. ultramarine		10	10
214	1r.25 ultramarine and red-orange		40	20

Design: Vert—1r.25 Pakistan Pavilion on "Unisphere".

(Des A. Ghani)

1964 (25 June). Death Bicentenary of Shah Abdul Latif of Bhit. P 13½×13.

215	**103**	50p. bright blue and carmine-lake	1·00	10

104 Mausoleum of Quaid-i-Azam

105 Mausoleum

(Des A. Ghani)

1964 (11 Sept). 16th Death Anniv of Mohammed Ali Jinnah (Quaid-i-Azam). P 13½ (15p.) or 13 (50p.)

216	**104**	15p. emerald-green	1·00	10
217	**105**	50p. bronze-green	2·25	10

106 Bengali and Urdu
Alphabets

107 University Building

(Des N. Rizvi)

1964 (5 Oct). Universal Children's Day. P 13.
218	**106**	15p. brown	10	10

(Des N. Rizvi)

1964 (21 Dec). First Convocation of the West Pakistan University of Engineering and Technology, Lahore. P 12½×14.
219	**107**	15p. chestnut..........................	10	10

PROCESS. All the following issues were lithographed by the Pakistan Security Printing Corporation, unless otherwise stated.

108 "Help the Blind"

(Des A. Chughtai)

1965 (28 Feb). Blind Welfare. P 13.
220	**108**	15p. ultramarine and yellow	20	10

109 ITU Emblem and Symbols

110 ICY Emblem

(Des N. Rizvi. Recess)

1965 (17 May). ITU Centenary. P 12½×14.
221	**109**	15p. reddish purple..........................	1·50	30

1965 (26 June). International Co-operation Year. P 13×13½.
222	**110**	15p. black and light blue	50	15
223		50p. green and yellow....................	1·50	40

111 "Co-operation"

112 Globe and Flags of Turkey, Iran and Pakistan

1965 (21 July). First Anniv of Regional Development Co-operation Pact. P 13½×13 (15p.) or 13 (50p.)
224	**111**	15p. multicoloured..........................	20	10
225	**112**	50p. multicoloured..........................	1·10	10

113 Soldier and Tanks

(Des S. Ghori (7p.), N. Rizvi (15p.), A. Ghani (50p.))

1965 (25 Dec). Pakistan Armed Forces. T **113** and similar horiz designs. Multicoloured. P 13½×13.
226		7p. Type **113**	75	30
227		15p. Naval officer and Tughril (destroyer)......	1·50	10
228		50p. Pilot and Lockheed F-104C Star fighters..	2·50	30
226/8 Set of 3			4·25	60

116 Army, Navy and Air Force Crests

(Des A. Ghani)

1966 (13 Feb). Armed Forces Day. P 13½×13.
229	**116**	15p. royal blue, dull green, bright blue and buff..........................	1·00	10

117 Atomic Reactor, Islamabad

118 Bank Crest

(Des A. Ghani. Recess)

1966 (30 Apr). Inauguration of Pakistan's First Atomic Reactor. P 13.
230	**117**	15p. black..........................	10	10

(Des A. Ghani)

1966 (25 Aug). Silver Jubilee of Habib Bank. P 12½×14.
231	**118**	15p. blue-green, yellow-orange and sepia.	10	10

119 Children

120 UNESCO Emblem

(Des S. Nagi)

1966 (3 Oct). Universal Children's Day. P 13½.
232	**119**	15p. light brown, black, red and pale yellow	10	10

1966 (24 Nov). 20th Anniv of UNESCO. P 14.
233	**120**	15p. multicoloured..........................	3·75	30

121 Flag, Secretariat Building and President Ayub

(Des A. Ghani)

1966 (29 Nov). Islamabad (new capital). P 13.

| 234 | **121** | 15p. deep bluish green, chestnut, light blue and bistre-brown...................... | 35 | 10 |
| 235 | | 50p. deep bluish green, chestnut, light blue and black .... | 65 | 10 |

122 Avicenna   **123** Mohammed Ali Jinnah

(Des A. Ghani)

1966 (3 Dec). Foundation of Health and Tibbi Research Institute. P 13×13½.

| 236 | **122** | 15p. dull green and salmon .... | 40 | 10 |
| | | a. Imperf (pair).. | 75·00 | |

(Des A. Ghani. Recess and litho)

1966 (25 Dec). 90th Birth Anniv of Mohammed Ali Jinnah. T **123** and similar design bearing same portrait, but in different frame. P 13.

| 237 | **123** | 15p. black, orange and greenish blue ... | 15 | 10 |
| 238 | – | 50p. black, purple and ultramarine.......... | 35 | 10 |

124 Tourist Year Emblem   **125** Emblem of Pakistan TB Association

(Des A. Ghani)

1967 (1 Jan). International Tourist Year. P 13½×13.

| 239 | **124** | 15p. black, light blue and yellow-brown .... | 10 | 10 |

1967 (10 Jan). Tuberculosis Eradication Campaign. P 13½×13.

| 240 | **125** | 15p. red, sepia and chestnut .... | 10 | 10 |

126 Scout Salute and Badge   **127** "Justice"

(Des A. Rauf. Photo)

1967 (29 Jan). Fourth National Scout Jamboree. P 12½×14.

| 241 | **126** | 15p. light orange-brown and maroon... | 15 | 10 |

(Des A. Rauf)

1967 (17 Feb). Centenary of West Pakistan High Court. P 13.

| 242 | **127** | 15p. black, slate, light red and slate-blue.. | 10 | 10 |

128 Dr. Mohammed Iqbal (philosopher)

(Des A. Rauf)

1967 (21 Apr). Iqbal Commemoration. P 13.

| 243 | **128** | 15p. sepia and light red.............................. | 15 | 10 |
| 244 | | 1r. sepia and deep green......................... | 35 | 10 |

129 Hilal-i-Isteqlal Flag

(Des A. Rahman)

1967 (15 May). Award of Hilal-i-Isteqlal (for Valour) to Lahore, Sialkot, and Sargodha. P 13.

| 245 | **129** | 15p. multicoloured.. | 10 | 10 |

130 "20th Anniversary"

(Des F. Karim. Photo)

1967 (14 Aug). 20th Anniv of Independence. P 13.

| 246 | **130** | 15p. red and deep bluish green.............. | 10 | 10 |

131 "Rice Exports"   **132** Cotton Plant, Yarn and Textiles

(Des S. Nagi (10p.), F. Karim (others). Photo)

1967 (26 Sept). Pakistan Exports. T **131/2** and similar design. P 13×13½.

247		10p. yellow, deep bluish green and deep blue..	10	15
248		15p. multicoloured	10	10
		a. Pale orange (top panel) omitted..............	23·00	
249		50p. multicoloured	20	15
247/9 *Set of 3*			35	35

Design: Vert as T **132**—50p. Raw jute, bale and bags.

134 Clay Toys

(Des F. Karim)

1967 (2 Oct). Universal Children's Day. P 13.
250   **134**   15p. multicoloured   10   10

135 Shah and Empress of Iran and Gulistan Palace, Teheran

(Des S. Ghori. Recess and litho)

1967 (26 Oct). Coronation of Shah Mohammed Riza Pahlavi and Empress Farah of Iran. P 13.
251   **135**   50p. purple, blue and light yellow-ochre ....   1·25   10

136 "Each For All—All For Each"

(Des A. Rauf)

1967 (4 Nov). Co-operative Day. P 13.
252   **136**   15p. multicoloured   10   10

137 Mangla Dam

(Des S. Nagi)

1967 (23 Nov). Indus Basin Project. P 13.
253   **137**   15p. multicoloured   10   10

138 Crab pierced by Sword   **139** Human Rights Emblem

(Des F. Karim)

1967 (26 Dec). The Fight against Cancer. P 13.
254   **138**   15p. red and black   70   10

1968 (31 Jan). Human Rights Year. Photo. P 14×13.
255   **139**   15p. red and deep turquoise-blue   10   15
256   50p. red, yellow and silver-grey   10   15

140 Agricultural University, Mymensingh
141 WHO Emblem

(Des S. Ghori. Photo)

1968 (28 Mar). First Convocation of East Pakistan Agricultural University. P 13½×13.
257   **140**   15p. multicoloured   10   10

(Des A. Salahuddin. Photo)

1968 (7 Apr). 20th Anniv of World Health Organization. P 14×13.
258   **141**   15p. green and orange-red   10   15
        a. "PAIS" for "PAISA" (R. 4/5) ....   3·25
259   50p. red-orange and indigo   10   15

142 Kazi Nazrul Islam (poet, composer and patriot)

(Des F. Karim. Recess and litho)

1968 (25 June). Nazrul Islam Commemoration. P 13.
260   **142**   15p. sepia and pale yellow   35   15
261   50p. sepia and pale rose-red   65   15
    Nos. 260/1 with a two-line inscription giving the wrong date of birth ("1889") were prepared but not issued. Some are known to have been released in error.

4 PAISA
(143)

1968 (18 July–Aug). Nos. 56, 74 and 61 surch as T **143**.
262   4p. on 3a. purple ....   1·00   1·75
263   4p. on 6a. deep ultramarine (R.) (Aug)........   1·25   1·75
264   60p. on 10a. violet (R.) ....   1·00   35
        a. Surch in black   40   2·50
        b. Surch triple ....   48·00
262/4 Set of 3 ....   3·00   3·50

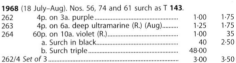

144 Children running with Hoops

(Des A. Rauf)

1968 (7 Oct). Universal Children's Day. P 13.
265   **144**   15p. multicoloured   10   10

145 "National Assembly"

(Des M. Khatoon)

1968 (27 Oct). "A Decade of Development". T **145** and similar horiz designs. P 13.
266   10p. multicoloured   10   10
267   15p. multicoloured   10   10
268   50p. multicoloured ....   2·00   20
269   60p. light blue, dull purple and vermilion.....   50   35
266/9 Set of 4 ....   2·40   65
    Designs:—15p. Industry and agriculture; 50p. Army, Navy and Air Force; 60p. Minaret and atomic reactor plant.

149 Chittagong Steel Mill

(Des M. Khatoon)

1969 (7 Jan). Pakistan's First Steel Mill, Chittagong. P 13.
270　149　15p. grey, light blue and pale yellow-
　　　　　olive .... 10　10

150 "Family"

151 Olympic Gold Medal and Hockey Player

(Des M. Khatoon)

1969 (14 Jan). Family Planning. P 13½×13.
271　150　15p. bright purple and pale greenish
　　　　　blue .... 10　10

(Des S. Ghori. Photo)

1969 (30 Jan). Olympic Hockey Champions. P 13½.
272　151　15p. black, gold, deep green and pale
　　　　　blue .... 75　50
273　　　　1r. black, gold, deep green and flesh-
　　　　　pink .... 2·25　1·00

152 Mirza Ghalib and Lines of Verse

(Des A. Rauf)

1969 (15 Feb). Death Centenary of Mirza Ghalib (poet). P 13.
274　152　15p. multicoloured .... 20　15
275　　　　50p. multicoloured .... 50　15
The lines of verse on No. 275 are different from those in T **152**.

153 Dacca Railway Station

(Des F. Karim)

1969 (27 Apr). First Anniv of New Dacca Railway Station. P 13.
276　153　15p. multicoloured .... 50　10

154 I.L.O. Emblem and "1919–1969"

(Des R-ud Din)

1969 (15 May). 50th Anniv of International Labour Organization. P 13½.
277　154　15p. buff and bluish green .... 10　10
278　　　　50p. cinnamon and cerise .... 40　10

155 "Lady on Balcony"
(18th-cent Mogul)

(Des S. Ghori, A. Rauf, F. Karim, A. Salahuddin,
N. Mohammad and M. Khatoon)

1969 (21 July). Fifth Anniv of Regional Co-operation for Development. T **155** and similar vert designs showing miniatures. Multicoloured. P 13.
279　　20p. Type **155** .... 15　10
280　　50p. "Kneeling Servant" (17th-cent Persian).. 15　10
281　　1r. "Suleiman the Magnificent holding
　　　　Audience" (16th-cent Turkish) .... 20　10
279/81 Set of 3 .... 45　25

158 Eastern Refinery, Chittagong

(Des M. Khatoon. Photo)

1969 (14 Sept). First Oil Refinery in East Pakistan. P 13½×13.
282　158　20p. multicoloured .... 10　10

159 Children playing outside "School"

(Des M. Khatoon. Photo)

1969 (6 Oct). Universal Children's Day. P 13.
283　159　20p. multicoloured .... 10　10

160 Japanese Doll and PIA Air Routes

(Des N. Mohammad)

1969 (1 Nov). Inauguration of PIA Pearl Route, Dacca–Tokyo. P 13½×13.
284　**160**　20p. multicoloured .... 40　10
　　　　　a. Yellow and pink omitted .... 10·00
285　　　　50p. multicoloured .... 60　40
　　　　　a. Yellow and pink omitted .... 10·00

161 "Reflection of Light" Diagram

(Des A. Rauf. Photo)

1969 (4 Nov). Millenary Commemorative of Ibn-al-Haitham (physicist). P 13.
286   **161**   20p. black, lemon and light blue.............   10   10

162 Vickers Vimy and Karachi Airport

163 Flags, Sun Tower and Expo Site Plan

(Des N. Mohammad. Photo)

1969 (2 Dec). 50th Anniv of First England–Australia Flight. P 13½×13.
287   **162**   50p. multicoloured.........................   1·25   35

(Des R-ud Din)

1970 (15 Mar). World Fair, Osaka. P 13.
288   **163**   50p. multicoloured.........................   20   30

164 New U.P.U. HQ Building

(Des R-ud Din)

1970 (20 May). New U.P.U. Headquarters Building. P 13½×13.
289   **164**   20p. multicoloured.........................   15   10
290   50p. multicoloured.........................   25   25
    The above, in a miniature sheet, additionally inscr "U.P.U. Day 9th Oct, 1971", were put on sale on that date in very limited numbers.

165 U.N. HQ Building

(Des A. Rauf)

1970 (26 June). 25th Anniv of United Nations. T **165** and similar horiz design. Multicoloured. P 13×13½.
291   20p. Type **165**.........................   10   10
292   50p. U.N. emblem.........................   15   20

167 IEY Emblem, Book and Pen

(Des M. Khatoon)

1970 (6 July). International Education Year. P 13.
293   **167**   20p. multicoloured   10   10
294   50p. multicoloured   20   20

168 Saiful Malook Lake (Pakistan)

1970 (21 July). Sixth Anniv of Regional Co-operation for Development. T **168** and similar square designs. Multicoloured. P 13.
295   20p. Type **168**.........................   15   10
296   50p. Seeyo-Se-Pol Bridge, Esfahan (Iran).......   20   10
297   1r. View from Fethiye (Turkey).........................   20   15
295/7 *Set of 3*   50   30

171 Asian Productivity Symbol   **172** Dr. Maria Montessori

1970 (18 Aug). Asian Productivity Year. Photo. P 12½×14.
298   **171**   50p. multicoloured.........................   20   20

(Des M. Khatoon)

1970 (31 Aug). Birth Centenary of Dr. Maria Montessori (educationist). P 13.
299   **172**   20p. multicoloured.........................   15   10
300   50p. multicoloured.........................   15   30

173 Tractor and Fertilizer Factory

1970 (12 Sept). Tenth Near East FAO Regional Conference, Islamabad. P 13.
301   **173**   20p. bright green and orange-brown......   15   50

174 Children and Open Book   **175** Pakistan Flag and Text

(Des F. Karim. Photo)

1970 (5 Oct). Universal Children's Day. P 13.
302   **174**   20p. multicoloured.........................   15   10

(Des A. Salahuddin)

1970 (7 Dec). General Elections for National Assembly. P 13½×13.
303   **175**   20p. green and bluish violet.....................   15   10

(Des A. Salauddin)

1970 (17 Dec). General Elections for Provincial Assemblies. As No. 303, but inscr "PROVINCIAL ASSEMBLIES 17TH DEC., 1970".
304   **175**   20p. green and pale magenta..................   15   10

176 Conference Crest and burning Al-Aqsa Mosque

(Des R-ud Din)

1970 (26 Dec). Conference of Islamic Foreign Ministers, Karachi. P 13.
305   **176**   20p. multicoloured   15   15

177 Coastal Embankments

(Des N. Mohammad)

1971 (25 Feb). Coastal Embankments in East Pakistan Project. P 13.
306   **177**   20p. multicoloured   15   15

178 Emblem and United Peoples of the World   **180** Chaharbagh School (Iran)

179 Maple Leaf Cement Factory, Daudkhel

(Des M. Khatoon)

1971 (21 Mar). Racial Equality Year. P 13.
307   **178**   20p. multicoloured   10   15
308   50p. multicoloured   20   45

(Des M. Khatoon)

1971 (1 July). 20th Anniv of Colombo Plan. P 13.
309   **179**   20p. brown, black and reddish violet.....   10   10

(Des A. Raul)

1971 (21 July). Seventh Anniv of Regional Co-operation for Development. T **180** and similar horiz designs. Multicoloured. P 13.
310   10p. Selimiye Mosque (Turkey)   10   15
311   20p. Badshahi Mosque (Lahore)   20   25
312   50p. Type **180**   30   35
310/12 *Set of 3*   55   65

181 Electric Train and Boy with Toy Train

(Des A. Rauf)

1971 (4 Oct). Universal Children's Day. P 13.
313   **181**   20p. multicoloured ....   1·75   50

182 Horseman and Symbols

(Des N. Mohammad)

1971 (15 Oct). 2500th Anniv of Persian Monarchy. P 13.
314   **182**   10p. multicoloured   25   30
315   20p. multicoloured   35   40
316   50p. multicoloured   50   75
314/16 *Set of 3* ....   1·00   1·25
The above exist in a miniature sheet, but only a very limited quantity was placed on sale.

183 Hockey-player and Trophy   **184** Great Bath, Moenjodaro

(Des F. Karim)

1971 (24 Oct). World Cup Hockey Tournament, Barcelona. P 13.
317   **183**   20p. multicoloured ....   1·75   1·00

(Des A. Salahuddin)

1971 (4 Nov). 25th Anniv of UNESCO and Campaign to save the Moenjodaro Excavations. P 13.
318   **184**   20p. multicoloured   20   30

185 UNICEF Symbol

(Des F. Karim)

1971 (11 Dec). 25th Anniv of UNICEF. P 13.
319   **185**   50p. multicoloured   30   60

186 King Hussein and Jordanian Flag

(Des F. Karim)

1971 (25 Dec). 50th Anniv of Hashemite Kingdom of Jordan. P 13.
320   **186**   20p. multicoloured   15   20

187 Badge of Hockey Federation and Trophy

188 Reading Class

(Des F. Karim)

1971 (31 Dec). Hockey Championships Victory. P 13.
321   **187**   20p. multicoloured ....   2·50   1·00

(Des M. Khatoon)

1972 (15 Jan). International Book Year. P 13½.
322   **188**   20p. multicoloured   20   40

OUTSIDE THE COMMONWEALTH

On 30 January 1972 Pakistan left the Commonwealth.

189 View of Venice

(Des A. Salahuddin)

1972 (7 Feb). UNESCO Campaign to Save Venice. P 13.
323   **189**   20p. multicoloured   30   40

190 ECAFE Emblem and Discs

(Des F. Karim)

1972 (28 Mar). 25th Anniv of ECAFE (Economic Commission for Asia and the Far East). P 13.
324   **190**   20p. multicoloured   15   30

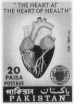

191 Human Heart   **192** "Only One Earth"

(Des M. Khatoon)

1972 (7 Apr). World Health Day. P 13×13½.
325   **191**   20p. multicoloured   20   30

(Des R-ud Din)

1972 (5 June). U.N. Conference on the Human Environment, Stockholm. P 13×13½.
326   **192**   20p. multicoloured   20   30

193 "Fisherman" (Cevat Dereli)

194 Mohammed Ali Jinnah and Tower

(Des F. Karim)

1972 (21 July). Eighth Anniv of Regional Co-operation for Development. T **193** and similar vert designs. Multicoloured. P 13.
327   10p. Type **193**   20   20
328   20p. "Iranian Woman" (Behzad)   35   25
329   50p. "Will and Power" (A. R. Chughtai)   55   70
        a. Brown-ochre (border) omitted ....   24·00
327/9 Set of 3 ....   1·00   1·00

(Des Mukhtar Ahmad and T. Sultana)

1972 (14 Aug). 25th Anniv of Independence. T **194** and similar horiz designs. Multicoloured. P 13 (10 and 60p.) or 14×12½ (20p.).
330   10p. Type **194**   10   10
331   20p. "Land Reform" (46×23½ mm)   20   30
        a. Vert strip of four. Nos. 331/4   70   1·10
332   20p. "Labour Reform" (46×23½ mm)   20   30
333   20p. "Education Policy" (46×23½ mm)   20   30
334   20p. "Health Policy" (46×23½ mm)   20   30
335   60p. National Assembly Building (46×28
        mm)   25   40
330/5 Set of 6 ....   1·00   1·50
Nos. 331/4 were printed vertically se-tenant throughout the sheet, each stamp accompanied by a half stamp-size label.

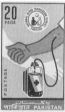

195 Donating Blood   **196** People and Squares

(Des M. Khatoon)

1972 (6 Sept). National Blood Transfusion Service. P 13½×12½.
336   **195**   20p. multicoloured   20   30

(Des Munawar Ahmad)

1972 (16 Sept). Centenary of Population Census. P 13½.
337   **196**   20p. multicoloured   20   20

197 Children from Slums

(Des Mukhtar Ahmad)

1972 (2 Oct). Universal Children's Day. P 13.
338   **197**   20p. multicoloured   20   30

198 People and Open Book

(Des T. Sultana)

1972 (23 Oct). Education Week. P 13.
339   **198**   20p. multicoloured   20   30

199 Nuclear Power Plant

1972 (28 Nov). Inauguration of Karachi Nuclear Power Plant. P 13.
340   **199**   20p. multicoloured   20   40

200 Copernicus in Observatory

(Des M. Sultana)

1973 (19 Feb). 500th Birth Anniv of Nicholas Copernicus (astronomer). P 13.
341   **200**   20p. multicoloured   20   30

201 Moenjodaro Excavations

202 Elements of Meteorology

(Des A. Salahuddin)

1973 (23 Feb). 50th Anniv of Moenjodaro Excavations. P 13×13½.
342   **201**   20p. multicoloured   20   30

(Des T. Sultana)

1973 (23 Mar). IMO/WMO Centenary. P 13.
343   **202**   20p. multicoloured   30   40

203 Prisoners-of-war

(Des Mukhtar Ahmad)

1973 (18 Apr). Prisoners-of-war in India. P 13.
344   **203**   1r.25 multicoloured ....   1·75   2·50

204 National Assembly Building and Constitution Book

(Des Mukhtar Ahmad)

1973 (21 Apr). Constitution Week. P 12½×13½.
345   **204**   20p. multicoloured   70   65

205 Badge and State Bank Building

206 Lut Desert Excavations (Iran)

(Des A. Salahuddin)

1973 (1 July). 25th Anniv of Pakistan State Bank. P 13.
346   **205**   20p. multicoloured   15   30
347   1r. multicoloured   30   50

(Des A. Salahuddin)

1973 (21 July). Ninth Anniv of Regional Co-operation for Development. T **206** and similar vert designs. Multicoloured. P 13×13½.
348   20p. Type **206**   30   20
349   60p. Main Street, Moenjodaro (Pakistan).......   55   50
350   1r.25 Mausoleum of Antiochus I (Turkey).......   75   1·25
348/50 *Set of 3* ....   1·40   1·75

207 Constitution Book and Flag

208 Mohammed Ali Jinnah (Quaid-i-Azam)

(Des Mukhtar Ahmad)

1973 (14 Aug). Independence Day and Enforcement of the Constitution. P 13.
351   **207**   20p. multicoloured   15   30

1973 (11 Sept). 25th Death Anniv of Mohammed Ali Jinnah. P 13.
352   **208**   20p. light emerald, pale yellow and black...........................   15   30

209 Wallago

(Des A. Salahuddin)

1973 (24 Sept). Fish. T **209** and similar horiz designs. Multicoloured. P 13½.
353   10p. Type **209** ....   1·10   1·10
        a. Horiz strip of four. Nos. 353/6...................   4·75   4·75
354   20p. Bohn...........................   1·25   1·25
355   60p. Mozambique Mouthbrooder...........................   1·40   1·40
356   1r. Catla...........................   1·40   1·40
353/6 *Set of 4*...........................   4·75   4·75
Nos. 353/6 were printed within one sheet, horizontally *se-tenant*.

210 Children's Education

1973 (1 Oct). Universal Children's Day. P 13.
357   **210**   20p. multicoloured   15   40

211 Harvesting

(Des A. Salahuddin)

1973 (15 Oct). Tenth Anniv of World Food Programme. P 13.
358   **211**   20p. multicoloured   60   40

212 Ankara and Kemal Atatürk

(Des Mukhtar and Munawar Ahmad)

1973 (29 Oct). 50th Anniv of Turkish Republic. P 13.
359   **212**   50p. multicoloured   45   35

213 Boy Scout   214 "Basic Necessities"

(Des T. Sultana)

1973 (11 Nov). National Silver Jubilee Scout Jamboree. P 13.
360   **213**   20p. multicoloured ....   1·75   50

(Des Munawar Ahmad)

1973 (16 Nov). 25th Anniv of Declaration of Human Rights. P 13.
361   **214**   20p. multicoloured   30   40

215 Al-Biruni and Nandana Hill   216 Dr. Hansen, Microscope and Bacillus

(Des Mukhtar Ahmad)

1973 (26 Nov). Al-Biruni Millennium Congress. P 13.
362   **215**   20p. multicoloured   50   20
363   1r.25 multicoloured ....   1·25   90

1973 (29 Dec). Centenary of Hansen's Discovery of Leprosy Bacillus. P 13.
364   **216**   20p. multicoloured ....   1·00   80

217 Family and Emblem   218 Conference Emblem

(Des M. Saeed)

1974 (1 Jan). World Population Year. P 13.
365   **217**   20p. multicoloured   10   10
366   1r.25 multicoloured   30   40

(Des I. Gilani (20p.), M. Saeed (65p.), A. Salahuddin (No. **MS**369))

1974 (22 Feb). Islamic Summit Conference, Lahore. T **218** and similar design. P 14×12½ (20p.) or 13 (65p.).
367   20p. Type **218**   10   10
368   65p. Emblem on "Sun" (42×30 *mm*)..................   25   60
MS369 102×102 mm. Nos. 367/8. Imperf ....   1·50   4·75

219 Units of Weight and Measurement   220 "Chand Chauthai" Carpet, Pakistan

(Des M. Saeed)

1974 (1 July). Adoption of International Weights and Measures System. P 13.
370   **219**   20p. multicoloured   15   25

(Des I. Gilani)

1974 (21 July). Tenth Anniv of Regional Co-operation for Development. Vert designs as T **220** showing carpets from member countries. Multicoloured. P 13.
371   20p. Type **220**   20   15
372   60p. Persian carpet, 16th-century..................   40   55
373   1r.25 Anatolian carpet, 15th-century..............   65   1·25
371/3 *Set of 3* ....   1·10   1·75

221 Hands protecting Sapling   222 Torch and Map

(Des Munawar Ahmad)

1974 (9 Aug). Tree Planting Day. P 13.
374   **221**   20p. multicoloured   50   60

(Des G. Parwar)

1974 (26 Aug). Namibia Day. P 13.
375   **222**   60p. multicoloured   50   80

223 Highway Map

(Des I. Gilani)

1974 (23 Sept). Shahrah-e-Pakistan (Pakistan Highway). P 13.
376   **223**   20p. multicoloured .... 1·25   1·00

224 Boy at Desk   **225** UPU Emblem

(Des A. Salahuddin)

1974 (7 Oct). Universal Children's Day. P 13.
377   **224**   20p. multicoloured 30   40

(Des T. Sultana (20p.), Mukhtar Ahmad (2r.25))

1974 (9 Oct). Centenary of Universal Postal Union. T **225** and similar vert design. Multicoloured. P 13×13½ (20p.) or 13 (2r.25).
378   20p. Type **225** 20   20
379   2r.25 UPU emblem, Boeing 707 and mail-
            wagon (30×41 *mm*) 55   1·40
MS380 100×101 mm. Nos. 378/9. Imperf .... 1·25   5·00

226 Liaquat Ali Khan   **227** Dr. Mohammed Iqbal
                             (poet and philosopher)

(Des Munawar Ahmad)

1974 (16 Oct). Liaquat Ali Khan (First Prime Minister of Pakistan). P 13×13½.
381   **226**   20p. black and light vermilion 30   40

(Des Munawar Ahmad)

1974 (9 Nov). Birth Centenary of Dr. Iqbal (1977) (1st issue). P 13.
382   **227**   20p. multicoloured 30   40
        See also Nos. 399, 433 and 445/9.

228 Dr. Schweitzer and River Scene

(Des Mukhtar Ahmad)

1975 (14 Jan). Birth Centenary of Dr. Albert Schweitzer. P 13.
383   **228**   2r.25 multicoloured .... 4·50   3·25

229 Tourism Year Symbol

(Des A. Salahuddin)

1975 (15 Jan). South East Asia Tourism Year. P 13.
384   **229**   2r.25 multicoloured 60   1·00

230 Assembly Hall, Flags and Prime Minister Bhutto

(Des A. Salahuddin)

1975 (22 Feb). First Anniv of Islamic Summit Conference, Lahore. P 13.
385   **230**   20p. multicoloured 35   35
386   1r. multicoloured 75   1·40

231 "Scientific Research"   **232** "Globe" and
                                  Algebraic Symbol

(Des A. Salahuddin (20p.), Mukhtar Ahmad (2r.25))

1975 (15 June). International Women's Year. T **231** and similar horiz design. Multicoloured. P 13.
387   20p. Type **231** 25   25
388   2r.25 Girl teaching woman ("Adult
            Education") .... 1·25   2·00

(Des Mukhtar Ahmad)

1975 (14 July). International Congress of Mathematical Sciences, Karachi. P 13.
389   **232**   20p. multicoloured 50   60

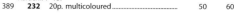

233 Pakistani Camel-skin   **234** Sapling and Dead
Vase   Trees

(Des I. Gilani)

1975 (21 July). 11th Anniv of Regional Co-operation for Development. T **233** and similar multicoloured designs. P 13.

390		20p. Type **233**	30	30
391		60p. Iranian tile (*horiz*)	60	1·00
392		1r.25 Turkish porcelain vase	90	1·50
390/2	*Set of 3*		1·60	2·50

(Des Munawar Ahmad)

1975 (9 Aug). Tree Planting Day. P 13×13½.

393	**234**	20p. multicoloured	35	70

235 Black Partridge

236 "Today's Girls"

(Des A. Salahuddin)

1975 (30 Sept). Wildlife Protection (1st series). P 13.

394	**235**	20p. multicoloured	1·25	35
395		2r. multicoloured	3·50	4·75

See also Nos. 400/1, 411/12, 417/18, 493/6, 560, 572/3, 581/2, 599, 600, 605, 621/2, 691, 702, 752, 780/3, 853 and 1027.

(Des N. Sultana)

1975 (6 Oct). Universal Children's Day. P 13.

396	**236**	20p. multicoloured	30	50

237 Hazrat Amir Khusrau, Sitar and Tabla

(Des A. Salahuddin)

1975 (24 Oct). 700th Birth Anniv of Hazrat Amir Khusrau (poet and musician). P 13½×12½.

397	**237**	20p. multicoloured	20	50
398		2r.25 multicoloured	80	2·00

238 Dr. Mohammed Iqbal

239 Urial (wild sheep)

(Des A. Salahuddin)

1975 (9 Nov). Birth Centenary of Dr. Iqbal (1977) (2nd issue). P 13.

399	**238**	20p. multicoloured	30	50

(Des Munawar Ahmad)

1975 (31 Dec). Wildlife Protection (2nd series). P 13.

400	**239**	20p. multicoloured	30	30
401		3r. multicoloured	1·25	2·75

240 Moenjodaro Remains

241 Dome and Minaret of Rauza-e-Mubarak

(Des A. Salahuddin)

1976 (29 Feb). "Save Moenjodaro" (1st series). T **240** and similar vert designs. Multicoloured. P 13.

402		10p. Type **240**	65	80
		a. Horiz strip of five. Nos. 402/6	3·25	4·00
403		20p. Remains (*different*)	75	90
404		65p. The Citadel	75	90
405		3r. Well inside a house	75	90
406		4r. The "Great Bath"	85	1·00
402/6	*Set of 5*		3·25	4·00

Nos. 402/6 were printed horizontally *se-tenant* within the sheet, the five stamps forming a composite design of the excavations.
See also Nos. 414 and 430.

(Des A. Ghani. Photo)

1976 (3 Mar). International Congress on Seerat. P 13×13½.

407	**241**	20p. multicoloured	15	20
408		3r. multicoloured	55	90

242 Alexander Graham Bell and Telephone Dial

(Des M. Saeed. Photo)

1976 (10 Mar). Telephone Centenary. P 13.

409	**242**	3r. multicoloured	1·25	2·00

243 College Arms within "Sun"

(Des A. Salahuddin)

1976 (15 Mar). Centenary of National College of Arts, Lahore. P 13.

410	**243**	20p. multicoloured	30	50

244 Common Peafowl

(Des A. Salahuddin)

1976 (31 Mar). Wildlife Protection (3rd series). P 13.

411	**244**	20p. multicoloured	1·00	35
412		3r. multicoloured	3·50	4·50

245 Human Eye

(Des M. Saeed)

1976 (7 Apr). Prevention of Blindness. P 13.
413   **245**   20p. multicoloured ....   1·00   70

246 Unicorn and Ruins

(Des I. Gilani)

1976 (31 May). "Save Moenjodaro" (2nd series). P 13.
414   **246**   20p. multicoloured   30   40

247 Jefferson Memorial   **248** Ibex

(Des I. Gilani (90p.), A. Salahuddin (4r.))

1976 (4 July). Bicentenary of American Revolution. T **247** and similar horiz design. Multicoloured. P 13 (90p.) or 13½ (4r.).
415   90p. Type **247**   75   60
416   4r. "Declaration of Independence" (47×36 mm) ....   3·00   5·00

(Des Mukhtar Ahmad)

1976 (12 July). Wildlife Protection (4th series). P 13.
417   **248**   20p. multicoloured   30   35
418   3r. multicoloured ....   1·25   2·50

249 Mohammed Ali Jinnah

(Des A. Salahuddin)

1976 (21 July). 12th Anniv of Regional Co-operation for Development. T **249** and similar diamond-shaped designs. Multicoloured. P 14.
419   20p. Type **249**   65   90
    a. Vert strip of three. Nos. 419/21 ....   1·75   2·40
420   65p. Reza Shah the Great (Iran)........................   65   90
421   90p. Kemal Atatürk (Turkey)............................   65   90
419/21 Set of 3..   1·75   2·40
Nos. 419/21 were printed vertically se-tenant throughout the sheet.

250 Urdu Text   **251** Mohammed Ali Jinnah and Wazir Mansion

(Des A. Salahuddin)

1976 (14 Aug). Birth Centenary of Mohammed Ali Jinnah (1st issue). P 13.

(a) Type **250**
422   5p. black, new blue and yellow   20   25
    a. Block of eight. Nos. 422/9........................   1·75   2·10
423   10p. black, yellow and magenta   20   25
424   15p. black and violet-blue   20   25
425   1r. black, yellow and new blue   30   30

(b) Multicoloured designs as T **251**, *different buildings in the background*
426   20p. Type **251**   20   25
427   40p. Sind Madressah   20   25
428   50p. Minar Qarardad-e-Pakistan   20   25
429   3r. Mausoleum   45   50
422/9 Set of 8..   1·75   2·10
Nos. 422/9 were printed in se-tenant blocks of 8 throughout the sheet.
See also No. 436.

252 Dancing-girl, Ruins and King Priest

(Des A. Salahuddin)

1976 (31 Aug). "Save Moenjodaro" (3rd series). P 14.
430   **252**   65p. multicoloured   35   80

253 U.N. Racial Discrimination Emblem

(Des A. Salahuddin)

1976 (15 Sept). U.N. Decade to Combat Racial Discrimination. P 12½×13½.
431   **253**   65p. multicoloured   30   60

254 Child in Maze and Basic Services

(Des Mukhtar Ahmad)

1976 (4 Oct). Universal Children's Day. P 13.
432   **254**   20p. multicoloured   60   60

Stamps commemorating the visit of King Khalid of Saudi Arabia and showing the Islamabad Mosque were prepared for release on 11 October 1976, but withdrawn before issue. Some are known to have been released in error.

255 Verse from "Allama Iqbal"

(Des M. Javed)

1976 (9 Nov). Birth Centenary of Dr. Iqbal (1977) (3rd issue). P 13.
433　**255**　20p. multicoloured............................. 15　30

256 Mohammed Ali
Jinnah giving Scout
Salute

257 Children Reading

(Des I. Gilani)

1976 (20 Nov). Quaid-i-Azam Centenary Jamboree. P 13½.
434　**256**　20p. multicoloured............................. 1·00　60

(Des Mukhtar Ahmad)

1976 (15 Dec). Children's Literature. P 13.
435　**257**　20p. multicoloured............................. 65　65

258 Mohammed Ali Jinnah

259 Rural Family

(Litho and embossed Cartor S.A., France)

1976 (25 Dec). Birth Centenary of Mohammed Ali Jinnah (2nd issue).
P 12½.
436　**258**　10r. emerald and gold..................... 2·25　3·50

(Des Mukhtar Ahmad)

1977 (14 Apr). Social Welfare and Rural Development Year. P 13.
437　**259**　20p. multicoloured............................. 40　20

260 Turkish Vase, 1800 B.C.

(Des A. Salahuddin)

1977 (21 July). 13th Anniv of Regional Co-operation for
Development. T **260** and similar horiz designs. P 13.
438　　20p. red-orange, violet-blue and black.......... 45　10
439　　65p. multicoloured................................. 65　40
440　　90p. multicoloured................................. 90　1·50

438/40 Set of 3.. 1·75　1·75
　Designs:—65p. Pakistani toy bullock cart, Moenjodaro; 90p. Pitcher
with spout, Sialk Hill, Iran.

261 Forest

262 Desert Scene

(Des A. Ahmed)

1977 (9 Aug). National Tree Plantation Campaign. P 13.
441　**261**　20p. multicoloured............................. 20　30

(Des M. Javed)

1977 (5 Sept). U.N. Conference on Desertification, Nairobi. P 13.
442　**262**　65p. multicoloured............................. 1·25　45

263 "Water for the
Children of the
World"

264 Aga Khan III

(Des A. Salahuddin)

1977 (3 Oct). Universal Children's Day. P 13½×12½.
443　**263**　50p. multicoloured............................. 40　30

(Des A. Rauf)

1977 (2 Nov). Birth Centenary of Aga Khan III. P 13.
444　**264**　2r. multicoloured............................. 55　1·00

265 Iqbal and Spirit of
the Poet Roomi (from
painting by Behzad)

266 The Holy "Khana-Kaaba"
(House of God, Mecca)

(Des A. Ahmed)

1977 (9 Nov). Birth Centenary of Dr. Mohammed Iqbal (4th
issue). T **265** and similar vert designs. Multicoloured. P 13.
445　　20p. Type **265** .... 60　70
　　　a. Horiz strip of five. Nos. 445/9................ 3·00　3·50
446　　65p. Iqbal looking at Jamaluddin Afghani
　　　and Saeed Haleem Pasha at prayer
　　　(Behzad) .... 60　70
447　　1r.25 Urdu verse .... 65　75
448　　2r.25 Persian verse .... 70　85
449　　3r. Iqbal .... 75　95
445/9 Set of 5 .... 3·00　3·50
　Nos. 445, 448/9, 447 and 446 (in that order) were issued in
horizontal *se-tenant* strips of five.

(Des I. Gilani)

1977 (21 Nov). Haj (pilgrimage to Mecca). P 14.
450　**266**　65p. multicoloured............................. 30　30

267 Rheumatic Patient and Healthy Man

268 Woman in Costume of Rawalpindi-Islamabad

(Des T. Hameed)

1977 (19 Dec). World Rheumatism Year. P 13.
451   **267**   65p. turquoise-blue, black and yellow...   30   20

(Des A. Salahuddin)

1978 (5 Feb). Indonesia–Pakistan Economic and Cultural Cooperation Organization. P 12½×13½.
452   **268**   75p. multicoloured..   30   20

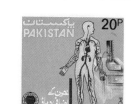

269 Human Body and Sphygmomanometer

270 Henri Dunant

(Des A. Salahuddin)

1978 (20 Apr). World Hypertension Month. P 13.
453   **269**   20p. multicoloured..   25   10
454   –   2r. multicoloured..   75   90
    The 2r. value is as T **269**, but has the words "Down with high blood pressure" instead of the Urdu inscription at bottom left.

(Des A. Salahuddin)

1978 (8 May). 150th Birth Anniv of Henri Dunant (founder of Red Cross). P 14.
455   **270**   1r. black, new blue and vermilion ....   1·00   20

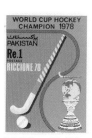

271 Red Roses (Pakistan)

272 "Pakistan, World Cup Hockey Champions"

(Des A. Salahuddin)

1978 (21 July). 14th Anniv of Regional Co-operation for Development. T **271** and similar vert designs. Multicoloured. P 13½.
456   20p. Type **271**   35   25
     a. Horiz strip of three. Nos. 456/8 ....   1·40   1·00
457   90p. Pink roses (Iran)......................................   50   35
458   2r. Yellow rose (Turkey)   75   50
456/8 Set of 3 ....   1·40   1·00
    Nos. 456/8 were printed together, *se-tenant*, in horizontal strips of three throughout the sheet.

(Des Munawar Ahmad)

1978 (26 Aug). "Riccione '78" International Stamp Fair. T **272** and similar vert design. Multicoloured. P 13.
459   1r. Type **272** ....   1·25   25
460   2r. Fountain at Plazza Turismo.........................   50   35

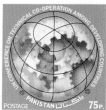

273 Cogwheels within Globe Symbol

274 St. Patrick's Cathedral

(Des A. Salahuddin)

1978 (3 Sept). U.N. Technical Co-operation amongst Developing Countries Conference. P 13.
461   **273**   75p. multicoloured...   25   20

(Des A. Salahuddin)

1978 (29 Sept). Centenary of St. Patrick's Cathedral, Karachi. T **274** and similar vert design. Multicoloured. P 13.
462   1r. Type **274**   15   10
463   2r. Stained glass window..................................   30   30

275 Minar-e-Qarardad-e-Pakistan

276 Tractor

276a Mausoleum of Ibrahim Khan Makli, Thatta

Two Dies of 75p. value:

Die I   Die II

    Die I. Size of design 26½×21½ mm. Figures of value large; "p" small. Plough does not touch left-hand frame.
    Die II. Size of design 25½×21 mm. Smaller figures; larger "p". Plough touches left-hand frame.

(Des A. Salahuddin. Litho (10, 25, 40, 50, 90p.), recess (others))

1978 (7 Nov)–**81**. No wmk (2 to 90p.) or W **98** (1 to 5r.). P 14×13½ (2 to 5p.), 13½×14 (10 to 90p.) or 13 (1 to 5r.).

464	**275**	2p. deep grey-green......................	10	10
		a. Printed on the gummed side......	20·00	
465		3p. black......................................	10	10
		a. Imperf (pair)............................	5·00	
		b. Printed on the gummed side......	20·00	
466		5p. deep ultramarine	10	10
		a. Printed on the gummed side......	20·00	
467	**276**	10p. new blue and greenish blue		
		(7.10.79)................................	10	10
468		20p. deep yellow-green (25.3.79)........	60	10
469		25p. dp green and dull mag (19.3.79)	1·25	10
470		40p. new blue and magenta		
		(16.12.78)...............................	10	10
471		50p. slate-lilac and turquoise-green		
		(19.3.79)................................	30	10
		a. Printed on the gummed side......	15·00	
472		60p. black (16.12.78)......................	10	10
		a. Imperf (pair)............................	5·00	
473		75p. dull vermilion (I) (16.12.78)......	60	10
		a. Imperf (pair)............................	16·00	
		b. Die II (1980).............................	1·75	10
		ba. Imperf (pair)............................	6·00	
		bb. Printed on the gummed side......	25·00	
474		90p. magenta and new blue		
		(16.12.78)...............................	30	10
		a. Printed on the gummed side......	20·00	
475	**276a**	1r. bronze-green (2.8.80)..............	60	10
		a. Imperf (pair)............................	14·00	
		w. Wmk inverted		
476		1r.50 red-orange (17.11.79)............	20	10
		a. Imperf (pair)............................	6·00	
		w. Wmk inverted		
		wb. Printed on the gummed side......		
477		2r. carmine-red (17.11.79)............	20	10
		a. Imperf (pair)............................	8·00	
		b. Printed on the gummed side......	15·00	
		w. Wmk inverted		
478		3r. blue-black (4.6.80)..................	20	10
		a. Imperf (pair)............................	10·00	
		w. Wmk inverted		
479		4r. black (1.1.81).........................	20	10
		a. Imperf (pair)............................	10·00	
		w. Wmk inverted	9·00	
480		5r. sepia (1.1.81).........................	20	10
		a. Imperf (pair)............................	9·00	
		w. Wmk inverted		
464/80 *Set of 17*			4·75	1·25

The remaining values as Type **276** printed in recess, are from Die II. For note regarding watermark orientation see below No. 210.

Postal forgeries exist of the 2r. and 3r. values. These are poorly printed with perforations which do not match those of the genuine stamps.

Later printings of all but the 75p. Type I occur with matt, almost invisible gum of a PVA type, instead of the gum arabic used previously.

277 Emblem and "United Races" Symbol

278 Maulana Mohammad Ali Jauhar

(Des M. Munawar)

1978 (20 Nov). International Anti-Apartheid Year. P 13.

481	**277**	1r. multicoloured..........................	15	15

(Des A. Salahuddin)

1978 (10 Dec). Birth Centenary of Maulana Mohammad Ali Jauhar (patriot). P 13.

482	**278**	50p. multicoloured.......................	50	20

279 Panavia MRCA Tornado, de Havilland DH.89 Dragon Rapide and Wright *Flyer I*

(Des A. Salahuddin)

1978 (24 Dec). 75th Anniv of Powered Flight. T **279** and similar diamond-shaped designs. Multicoloured. P 13.

483		65p. Type **279**	1·00	1·75
		a. Block of four. Nos. 483/6........	4·25	7·00
484		1r. McDonnell Douglas F-4A Phantom		
		II, Lockheed L-1011 TriStar 500 and		
		Wright *Flyer I*........................	1·10	1·75
485		2r. North American X-15, Tupolev Tu-104		
		and Wright *Flyer I*..................	1·25	2·00
486		2r.25 Mikoyan Gurevich MiG-15, Concorde		
		and Wright *Flyer I*..................	1·25	2·25
483/6 *Set of 4*			4·25	7·00

Nos. 483/6 were printed together, *se-tenant*, in blocks of four throughout the sheet.

 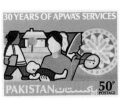

280 "Holy Koran illuminating Globe" and Raudha-e-Mubarak (mausoleum)

281 "Aspects of APWA"

(Des A. Salahuddin)

1979 (10 Feb). "12th Rabi-ul-Awwal" (Prophet Mohammed's birthday). P 13.

487	**280**	20p. multicoloured.......................	40	15

(Des M. Saeed)

1979 (25 Feb). 30th Anniv of APWA (All Pakistan Women's Association). P 13.

488	**281**	50p. multicoloured.......................	75	15

282 Tippu Sultan Shaheed of Mysore

(Des A. Rauf)

1979 (23 Mar). Pioneers of Freedom (1st series). T **282** and similar diamond-shaped designs. Multicoloured. W **98**. P 14.

490		10r. Type **282**	75	1·60
		a. Horiz strip of three. Nos. 490/2	3·00	5·50
491		15r. Sir Syed Ahmad Khan............	1·00	2·25
492		25r. Altaf Hussain Hali.................	1·50	2·25
490/2 *Set of 3*			3·00	5·50

Nos. 490/2 were printed together, *se-tenant*, in the same sheet; there being ten horizontal strips of three values and ten additional 10r. stamps.
See also Nos. 757, 801/27, 838/46, 870/2, 904/6, 921/8, 961/2, 1007, 1019/20 and 1075/7.

283 Himalayan Monal Pheasant

(Des Mukhtar Ahmad)

1979 (17 June). Wildlife Protection (5th series). Pheasants. T **283** and similar horiz designs. Multicoloured. P 13.

493	20p. Type **283**	1·10	60
494	25p. Kalij	1·10	80
495	40p. Koklass	1·40	1·75
496	1r. Cheer	2·50	2·00
493/6 *Set of 4*		5·50	4·75

284 "Pakistan Village Scene" (Ustad Bakhsh)

(Des A. Rauf)

1979 (21 July). 15th Anniv of Regional Co-operation for Development. Paintings. T **284** and similar horiz designs. Multicoloured. P 14×12½.

497	40p. Type **284**	20	25
	a. Vert strip of three. Nos. 497/9	60	70
498	75p. "Iranian Goldsmith" (Kamal al Molk)	20	25
499	1r.60 "Turkish Harvest" (Namik Ismail)	25	30
497/9 *Set of 3*		60	70

Nos. 497/9 were printed together, *se-tenant*, in vertical strips of three throughout the sheet.

285 Guj Embroidered Shirt (detail)

(Des A. Salahuddin)

1979 (23 Aug). Handicrafts (1st series). T **285** and similar horiz designs. Multicoloured. P 14×12½.

500	40p. Type **285**	20	20
	a. Block of four. Nos. 500/3	1·00	1·00
501	1r. Enamel inlaid brass plate	25	25
502	1r.50 Baskets	30	30
503	2r. Chain-stitch embroidered rug (detail)	40	40
500/3 *Set of 4*		1·00	1·00

Nos. 500/3 were printed together, *se-tenant*, in blocks of four throughout the sheet.
See also Nos. 578/9, 595/6 and 625/8.

286 Children playing on Climbing Frame

(Des A. Rauf)

1979 (10 Sept). S.O.S. Children's Village, Lahore (orphanage). P 13.

504	**286**	50p. multicoloured	40	40

287 "Island" (Z. Maloof)

(Des A. Salahuddin)

1979 (22 Oct). International Year of the Child. Children's Paintings. T **287** and similar horiz designs. Multicoloured. P 14×12½.

505	40p. Type **287**	15	15
	a. Block of four. Nos. 505/8	85	85
506	75p. "Playground" (R. Akbar)	25	25
507	1r. "Fairground" (M. Azam)	25	25
508	1r.50 "Hockey Match" (M. Tayyab)	30	30
505/8 *Set of 4*		85	85
MS509	79×64 mm. 2r. "Child looking at Faces in the Sky" (M. Mumtaz) (*vert*). Imperf	1·00	2·00

Nos. 505/8 were printed together, *se-tenant*, in blocks of four throughout the sheet.
Examples of No. **MS**509 are known overprinted in gold for the "PHILEXFRANCE" International Stamp Exhibition in 1982. The Pakistan Post Office has declared such overprints to be bogus.

288 Warrior attacking Crab

289 Pakistan Customs Emblem

(Des A. Salahuddin)

1979 (12 Nov). Fight Against Cancer. P 14.

510	**288**	40p. black, greenish yellow and magenta	70	70

(Des A. Salahuddin)

1979 (10 Dec). Centenary of Pakistan Customs Service. P 13×13½.

511	**289**	1r. multicoloured	30	30

290 Boeing 747-200 and Douglas DC-3 Airliners

291 Islamic Pattern

(Des A. Salahuddin)

1980 (10 Jan). 25th Anniv of Pakistan International Air Lines. P 13.

512	**290**	1r. multicoloured	1·75	90

(Des and litho Secura, Singapore)

1980 (15 Jan–10 Mar). Matt, almost invisible PVA gum. P 12.

513	**291**	10p. slate-green and orange-yellow	10	10
		a. Imperf between (vert pair)		
514		15p. slate-green and bright yellow-green	20	10
515		25p. violet and brown-red (10.3)	30	50
516		35p. carmine and bright yellow-green (10.3)	40	1·00
517	–	40p. rosine and olive-sepia	40	10
		a. Printed on the gummed side		
518	–	50p. violet and dull yellow-green (10.3)	40	50
519	–	80p. bright yellow-green and black (10.3)	60	50
513/19 *Set of 7*			2·25	2·50

The 40 to 80p. values also show different Islamic patterns, the 40p. being horizontal and the remainder vertical.

292 Young Child

293 Conference Emblem

(Des M. Saeed)

1980 (16 Feb). Fifth Asian Congress of Paediatric Surgery, Karachi. P 13.

530	**292**	50p. multicoloured	75	1·50

(Des A. Salahuddin)

1980 (17 May). 11th Islamic Conference of Foreign Ministers, Islamabad. P 13.

531	**293**	1r. multicoloured	1·25	75

294 Karachi Port

(Des A. Salahuddin)

1980 (15 July). Centenary of Karachi Port Authority. P 13×13½.

532	**294**	1r. multicoloured	1·75	2·25

RICCIONE 80

(295)

1980 (30 Aug). Riccione 80 International Stamp Exhibition. Nos. 505/8 optd with T **295** in red.

533		40p. Type **287**	30	80
		a. Block of four. Nos. 533/6	1·60	3·25
534		75p. "Playground" (R. Akbar)	40	90
535		1r. "Fairground" (M. Azam)	45	90
536		1r.50 "Hockey Match" (M. Tayyab)	60	1·10
533/6	*Set of 4*		1·60	3·25

296 College Emblem with Old and New Buildings

(Des Munawar Ahmad)

1980 (18 Sept). 75th Anniv of Command and Staff College, Quetta. P 13.

537	**296**	1r. multicoloured	20	15

WORLD TOURISM CONFERENCE
MANILA 80
(297)

1980 (27 Sept). World Tourism Conference, Manila. No. 496 optd with T **297**.

538		1r. Cheer Pheasant	1·25	40

298 Birth Centenary Emblem

(Des A. Salahuddin)

1980 (5 Oct). Birth Centenary of Hafiz Mahmood Shairani. P 13.

539	**298**	40p. multicoloured	30	1·00

299 Shalimar Gardens, Lahore

(Des A. Salahuddin)

1980 (23 Oct). Aga Khan Award for Architecture. P 13.

540	**299**	2r. multicoloured	40	1·75

300 Rising Sun

(Des S. Ahmed (40p.), J. Sultana (2r.), A. Salahuddin (others))

1980 (10 Nov). 1400th Anniv of Hegira (1st issue). T **300** and similar multicoloured designs. P 14 (2r.) or 13 (others).

541		40p. Type **300**	15	10
542		2r. Ka'aba and symbols of Moslem achievement (34×34 *mm*)	40	45
543		3r. Holy Koran illuminating World (31×54 *mm*)	55	80
541/3	*Set of 3*		1·00	1·25
MS544	106×84 mm. 4r. Candles. Imperf	60	1·00

See also No. 549.

301 Money Order Form

302 Postcards encircling Globe

(Des A. Ahmed)

1980 (20 Dec). Centenary of Money Order Service. P 13.

545	**301**	40p. multicoloured	20	60

(Des A. Ahmed)

1980 (27 Dec). Centenary of Postcard Service. P 13.

546	**302**	40p. multicoloured	20	60

303 Heinrich von Stephan and
UPU Emblem

(Des J. Sultana)

1981 (7 Jan). 150th Birth Anniv of Heinrich von Stephan (founder of
UPU). P 13.
547 **303** 1r. multicoloured 30 20

304 Aircraft and Airmail Letters

(Des J. Sultana)

1981 (15 Feb). 50th Anniv of Airmail Service. P 13.
548 **304** 1r. multicoloured .... 1·00 20

305 Mecca

306 Conference Emblem and
Afghan Refugees

(Des A. Salahuddin)

1981 (7 Mar). 1400th Anniv of Hegira (2nd issue). P 13.
549 **305** 40p. multicoloured 20 60

(Des Z. Akhlaq (Nos. 550 and 552), A. Ahmed (Nos. 551 and
553), M. Jafree (No. 554))

1981 (29 Mar). Islamic Summit Conference (1st issue). T **306** and
similar multicoloured designs. P 13.
550 40p. Type **306** 40 15
551 40p. Conference emblem encircled by flags
and Afghan refugees (28×58 mm) 40 15
552 1r. Type **306** 55 15
553 1r. As No. 551 .... 55 15
554 2r. Conference emblem and map showing
Afghanistan (48×32 mm) 70 50
550/4 Set of 5 .... 2·40 1·00

307 Conference Emblem

308 Kemal Atatürk

(Des A. Salahuddin (Nos. 555, 557), A. Irani (Nos. 556, 558))

1981 (20 Apr). Islamic Summit Conference (2nd issue). T **307** and
similar multicoloured design. P 13.
555 40p. Type **307** 15 15

556 40p. Conference emblem and flags (28×46
mm) 15 15
557 85p. Type **307** 20 40
558 85p. As No. 556 .... 20 40
555/8 Set of 4 .... 65 1·00

(Des A. Salahuddin)

1981 (19 May). Birth Centenary of Kemal Atatürk (Turkish statesman).
P 13.
559 **308** 1r. multicoloured 50 15

309 Green Turtle   **310** Dome of the Rock

(Des Jamal. Litho Secura, Singapore)

1981 (20 June). Wildlife Protection (6th series). Matt, almost invisible
PVA gum. P 12×11½.
560 **309** 40p. multicoloured .... 1·25 40

(Des A. Salahuddin)

1981 (25 July). Palestinian Welfare. P 13.
561 **310** 2r. multicoloured .... 1·50 60

311 Malubiting West

(Des A. Salahuddin. Litho Secura, Singapore)

1981 (20 Aug). Mountain Peaks (1st series). Karakoram Range. T **311**
and similar multicoloured designs. Matt, almost invisible PVA
gum. P 14×13½.
562 40p. Type **311** 35 40
a. Horiz pair. Nos. 562/3 .... 70 80
563 40p. Malubiting West (24×31 mm) 35 40
564 1r. Haramosh 45 75
a. Horiz pair. Nos. 564/5 .... 90 1·50
565 1r. Haramosh (24×31 mm) 45 75
566 1r.50 K6 .... 55 1·10
a. Horiz pair. Nos. 566/7 .... 1·10 2·00
567 1r.50 K6 (24×31 mm) .... 55 1·00
568 2r. K2, Broad Peak, Gasherbrum 4 and
Gasherbrum 2 .... 55 1·40
a. Horiz pair. Nos. 568/9 .... 1·10 2·75
569 2r. K2 (24×31 mm) .... 55 1·40
562/9 Set of 8 .... 3·50 6·50
The two designs of each value were printed together, se-tenant, in
horizontal pairs throughout the sheet.
See also Nos. 674/5.

312 Pakistan Steel "Furnace   **313** Western Tragopan
No. 1"

(Des A. Ahmed)

1981 (31 Aug). First Firing of Pakistan Steel "Furnace No. 1", Karachi. P 13.

570	**312**	40p. multicoloured	20	10
571		2r. multicoloured	60	1·75

(Litho Secura, Singapore)

1981 (15 Sept). Wildlife Protection (7th series). Matt, almost invisible PVA gum. P 14.

572	**313**	40p. multicoloured	2·00	75
573	–	2r. multicoloured	4·00	4·25

The 2r. value is as Type **313** but the background design shows a winter view.

314 Disabled People and IYDP Emblem

315 World Hockey Cup below flags of participating Countries

(Des M. Saeed)

1981 (12 Dec). International Year for Disabled Persons. P 13.

574	**314**	40p. multicoloured	30	50
575		2r. multicoloured	1·10	1·75

(Des A. Salahuddin)

1982 (31 Jan). Pakistan—World Cup Hockey Champions. T **315** and similar vert design. Multicoloured. P 13.

576		1r. Type **315**	2·00	1·50
577		1r. World Hockey Cup above flags of participating countries	2·00	1·50

316 Camel Skin Lamp

(Des A. Salahuddin. Litho Secura, Singapore)

1982 (20 Feb). Handicrafts (2nd series). T **316** and similar vert design. Multicoloured. P 14.

578		1r. Type **316**	70	80
579		1r. Hala pottery	70	80

See also Nos. 595/6.

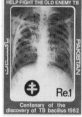

317 Chest X-Ray of Infected Person

318 Indus Dolphin

(Des A. Ahmed)

1982 (24 Mar). Centenary of Robert Koch's Discovery of Tubercle Bacillus. P 13.

580	**317**	1r. multicoloured	1·25	1·50

(Des A. Salahuddin. Litho Secura, Singapore)

1982 (24 Apr). Wildlife Protection (8th series). P 12×11½.

581	**318**	40p. multicoloured	1·50	1·50
582	–	1r. multicoloured	3·00	2·50

The 1r. value is as Type **318** but the design is reversed.

319 "Apollo-Soyuz" Link-up, 1975

(Des A. Salahuddin)

1982 (7 June). Peaceful Uses of Outer Space. P 13.

583	**319**	1r. multicoloured	1·60	1·25

320 Sukkur Barrage

(Des A. Salahuddin)

1982 (17 July). 50th Anniv of Sukkur Barrage. P 13.

584	**320**	1r. multicoloured	30	30

321 Pakistan National Flag and Stylised Sun

(Des A. Ahmed)

1982 (14 Aug). Independence Day. T **321** and similar vert design. Multicoloured. P 13.

585		40p. Type **321**	20	30
586		85p. Map of Pakistan and stylised torch	45	1·25

RICCIONE – 82 –
(322)

1982 (28 Aug). "Riccione 82" International Stamp Exhibition. No. 584 optd with T **322**.

587	**320**	1r. multicoloured	20	20

323 Arabic Inscription and University Emblem

(Des Syed Tanwir Rizvi)

1982 (14 Oct). Centenary of the Punjab University. P 13½×13.

588	**323**	40p. multicoloured	1·25	1·00

324 Scout Emblem and Tents   **325** Laying Pipeline

(Des M. Saeed)

1982 (23 Dec). 75th Anniv of Boy Scout Movement. P 13.
| 589 | **324** | 2r. multicoloured | 50 | 50 |

(Des A. Salahuddin)

1983 (6 Jan). Inauguration of Quetta Natural Gas Pipeline Project. P 13.
| 590 | **325** | 1r. multicoloured | 30 | 30 |

326 *Papilio polyctor*

(Litho Secura, Singapore)

1983 (15 Feb). Butterflies. T **326** and similar horiz designs. Multicoloured. Matt, almost invisible PVA gum. P 13½.
591		40p. Type **326**	1·25	20
592		50p. *Atrophaneura aristolochiae*	1·50	20
593		60p. *Danaus chrysippus*	1·75	60
594		1r.50 *Papilio demoleus*	2·50	2·25
591/4	*Set of 4*		6·25	3·00

(Litho Secura, Singapore)

1983 (9 Mar). Handicrafts (3rd series). Vert designs as T **316**. Multicoloured. Matt, almost invisible PVA gum. P 14.
| 595 | | 1r. Five flower motif needlework, Sind | 15 | 15 |
| 596 | | 1r. Straw mats | 15 | 15 |

327 School of Nursing and University Emblem

(Des A. Salahuddin)

1983 (16 Mar). Presentation of Charter to Aga Khan University, Karachi. P 13½×13.
| 597 | **327** | 2r. multicoloured | 1·50 | 2·00 |

No. 597 was issued in sheets of eight (2×4), each horizontal pair being separated by a different *se-tenant* label showing views of the University.

328 Yak Caravan crossing Zindiharam-Darkot Pass, Hindu Kush

(Des A.Salahuddin)

1983 (28 Apr). Trekking in Pakistan. P 13.
| 598 | **328** | 1r. multicoloured | 1·25 | 1·50 |

329 Marsh Crocodile

(Litho Secura, Singapore)

1983 (19 May). Wildlife Protection (9th series). Matt, almost invisible PVA gum. P 13½.
| 599 | **329** | 3r. multicoloured | 3·50 | 2·00 |

330 Goitred Gazelle

(Litho Secura, Singapore)

1983 (20 June). Wildlife Protection (10th series). Matt, almost invisible PVA gum. P 14×13½.
| 600 | **330** | 1r. multicoloured | 2·50 | 2·00 |

331 Floral Design   **332** Traditional Weaving, Pakistan

(Des A. Ahmed)

1983 (14 Aug). 36th Anniv of Independence. T **331** and similar vert design. Multicoloured. P 13.
| 601 | | 60p. Type **331** | 10 | 10 |
| 602 | | 4r. Hand holding flaming torch | 40 | 45 |

(Des A. Salahuddin)

1983 (19 Aug). Indonesian–Pakistan Economic and Cultural Cooperation Organization, 1969–1983. T **332** and similar horiz design. Multicoloured. P 13.
| 603 | | 2r. Type **332** | 20 | 25 |
| 604 | | 2r. Traditional weaving, Indonesia | 20 | 25 |

333 "Siberian Cranes" (Great White Cranes) (Sir Peter Scott)

1983 (8 Sept). Wildlife Protection (11th series). P 13.
| 605 | **333** | 3r. multicoloured | 3·75 | 3·25 |

334 WCY Emblem

(Des J. Sultana)

1983 (9 Oct). World Communications Year. T **334** and similar multicoloured design. P 13 (2r.) or 14 (3r.).

606	2r. Type **334**	20	25
607	3r. W.C.Y. emblem (*different*) (33×33 *mm*) ..	30	35

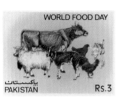

335 Farm Animals

336 Agricultural Produce and Fertiliser Factory

(Des A. Salahuddin)

1983 (24 Oct). World Food Day. T **335** and similar horiz designs. Multicoloured. P 13.

608	3r. Type **335**	1·50	1·75
	a. Horiz strip of four. Nos. 608/11	5·50	6·25
609	3r. Fruit	1·50	1·75
610	3r. Crops	1·50	1·75
611	3r. Sea food	1·50	1·75
608/11	Set of 4	5·50	6·25

Nos. 608/11 were printed together, *se-tenant*, in horizontal strips of four throughout the sheet.

(Des J. Sultana)

1983 (24 Oct). National Fertiliser Corporation. P 13×13½.

612	**336** 60p. multicoloured	20	30

337 Lahore, 1852

338 Winner of "Enterprise" Event

(Des A. Salahuddin)

1983 (13 Nov). National Stamp Exhibition, Lahore. T **337** and similar vert designs showing panoramic view of Lahore in 1852. Multicoloured. P 13×13½.

613	60p. Musti Durwaza Dharmsala	50	75
	a. Horiz strip of six. Nos. 613/18	2·75	4·00
614	60p. Khabgha	50	75
615	60p. Type **337**	50	75
616	60p. Summan Burj Hazuri	50	75
617	60p. Flower Garden, Samadhi Northern Gate	50	75
618	60p. Budda Darya, Badshahi Masjid	50	75
613/18	Set of 6	2·75	4·00

Nos. 613/18 were printed together, *se-tenant* in sheets of twelve, containing two horizontal strips of six.

(Des J. Sultana)

1983 (31 Dec). Yachting Champions, Asian Games, Delhi. T **338** and similar vert design. Multicoloured. P 13.

619	60p. Type **338**	1·25	1·50
620	60p. Winner of "OK" Dinghy event	1·25	1·50

339 Snow Leopard

(Litho Secura, Singapore)

1984 (21 Jan). Wildlife Protection (12th series). Matt, almost invisible PVA gum. P 14.

621	**339**	40p. multicoloured	1·75	90
622		1r.60 multicoloured	4·75	6·00

340 Jahangir Khan (World Squash Champion)

341 PIA Boeing 707 Airliner

(Des A. Salahuddin)

1984 (17 Mar). Squash. P 13.

623	**340**	3r. multicoloured	2·25	1·75

(Des A. Salahuddin)

1984 (29 Apr). 20th Anniv of Pakistan International Airways' Service to China. P 13.

624	**341**	3r. multicoloured	5·00	5·50

342 Glass-work

343 Attock Fort

(Des A. Salahuddin. Litho Secura, Singapore)

1984 (31 May). Handicrafts (4th series). T **342** and similar designs showing glass-work in Sheesh Mahal, Lahore Fort. P 13½.

625	1r. multicoloured (blue frame)	30	20
626	1r. multicoloured (red frame)	30	20
627	1r. multicoloured (green frame) (*horiz*)	30	20
628	1r. multicoloured (violet frame) (*horiz*)	30	20
625/8	Set of 4	1·00	70

(Des S. Hyder (15p.), J. Sultana (others))

1984 (16 June)–**86**. Forts. T **343** and similar horiz designs. P 11.

629	5p. brownish black and brown-pur (1.11.84)..	40	60
630	10p. brownish black and rose-red (25.9.84) ..	40	10
631	15p. reddish violet and bistre-brown (1.12.86)	1·00	10
632	20p. black and bright reddish violet	2·00	10
	a. Black ptd double		
633	50p. sepia and Venetian red (10.4.86)	1·50	10
634	60p. blackish brown and light brown	1·25	10
635	70p. greenish black (3.8.86)	1·50	10
636	80p. bistre-brown and dull scarlet (1.7.86)	1·50	10
629/36	Set of 8	8·50	1·00

Design:—5p. Kot Diji Fort; 10p. Rohtas Fort; 15p. Bala Hissar Fort; 50p. Hyderabad Fort; 60p. Lahore Fort; 70p. Sibi Fort; 80p. Ranikot Fort.

No. 632a appears to have received two distinct impressions of the black plate rather than an offset from the litho "blanket".

No. 636 can be found on the matt, almost invisible PVA gum in addition to the usual gum arabic.

344 Shah Rukn i Alam's Tomb, Multan

(Des A. Salahuddin)

1984 (26 June). Aga Khan Award for Architecture. P 13.
647   **344**   60p. multicoloured.......................................   2·50   2·75

345 Radio Mast and Map of World

(Des J. Sultana)

1984 (1 July). 20th Anniv of Asia–Pacific Broadcasting Union. P 13.
648   **345**   3r. multicoloured.......................................   1·00   60

346 Wrestling

(Des A. Salahuddin)

1984 (31 July). Olympic Games, Los Angeles. T **346** and similar horiz designs. Multicoloured. P 13.
649   3r. Type **346**.......................................   1·00   1·50
650   3r. Boxing.......................................   1·00   1·50
651   3r. Athletics.......................................   1·00   1·50
652   3r. Hockey.......................................   1·00   1·50
653   3r. Yachting.......................................   1·00   1·50
649/53 *Set of 5*.......................................   4·50   6·75

347 Jasmine (National flower) and Inscription

(Des M. Munawar)

1984 (14 Aug). Independence Day. T **347** and similar horiz design. Multicoloured. P 13.
654   60p. Type **347**.......................................   10   10
655   4r. Symbolic torch.......................................   45   50

348 Gearwheel Emblem and Flags of Participating Nations

(Des A. Zafar)

1984 (1 Sept). Pakistan International Trade Fair. P 13.
656   **348**   60p. multicoloured.......................................   1·00   30

349 Interior of Main Dome

(Des A. Salahuddin)

1984 (5 Nov). Tourism Convention. Shahjahan Mosque, Thatta. T **349** and similar horiz designs. Multicoloured. P 13½.
657   1r. Type **349**.......................................   50   60
       a. Horiz strip of five. Nos. 657/61 ....   2·25   2·75
658   1r. Brick and glazed tile work.......................   50   60
659   1r. Gateway.......................................   50   60
660   1r. Symmetrical archways.......................................   50   60
661   1r. Interior of a dome.......................................   50   60
657/61 *Set of 5*.......................................   2·25   2·75
Nos. 657/61 were printed together, *se-tenant*, in horizontal strips of five throughout the sheet.

350 Bank Emblem in Floral Pattern

(Des A. Zafar)

1984 (7 Nov). 25th Anniv of United Bank Ltd. P 13½.
662   **350**   60p. multicoloured.......................................   1·00   1·00

351 Conference Emblem

(Des A. Salahuddin)

1984 (24 Dec). 20th United Nations Conference on Trade and Development. P 14.
663   **351**   60p. multicoloured.......................................   80   40

352 Postal Life Insurance Emblem within Hands

353 Bull (Wall painting)

(Des A. Zafar (60p.), J. Sultana (1r.))

1984 (29 Dec). Centenary of Postal Life Insurance. T **352** and similar vert design. Multicoloured. P 13½.

664	60p. Type **352**	70	15
665	1r. "100" and Postal Life Insurance emblem	90	15

(Des A. Salahuddin and M. Munawar)

1984 (31 Dec). UNESCO Save Moenjodaro Campaign. T **353** and similar vert design. Multicoloured. P 13½.

666	2r. Type **353**	1·40	1·00
	a. Horiz pair. Nos. 666/7	2·75	2·00
667	2r. Bull (seal)	1·40	1·00

Nos. 666/7 were printed together, *se-tenant*, in horizontal pairs throughout the sheet.

354 International Youth Year Emblem and "75"

(Des A. Salahuddin)

1985 (6 Jan). 75th Anniv of Girl Guide Movement. P 13½.

668	**354**	60p. multicoloured	3·25	1·50

355 Smelting Ore **356** Map of Pakistan and Rays of Sun

(Des Munawar Ahmad (60p.), J. Sultana (1r.))

1985 (15 Jan). Inauguration of Pakistan Steel Corporation. T **355** and similar multicoloured design. P 13.

669	60p. Type **355**	65	25
670	1r. Pouring molten steel from ladle (28×46 *mm*)	1·10	25

(Des A. Salahuddin)

1985 (20 Mar). Presidential Referendum of 19 December 1984. P 13.

671	**356**	60p. multicoloured	1·75	55

357 Ballot Box and Voting Paper

(Des A. Salahuddin (No. 672), Sultana Shamim Haider (No. 673))

1985 (23 Mar). March Elections. T **357** and similar multicoloured design. P 13.

672	1r. Type **357**	65	15
673	1r. Minar-e-Qarardad-e-Pakistan Tower, and word "Democracy" (31×43 *mm*)	65	15

(Des and litho Secura, Singapore)

1985 (27 May). Mountain Peaks (2nd series). Horiz designs as T **311**. Multicoloured. Matt, almost invisible PVA gum. P 14×13½.

674	40p. Rakaposhi (Karakoram Range)	1·50	75
675	2r. Nangaparbat (Western Himalayas)	2·75	6·00

358 Trophy and Medals from Olympic Games 1984, Asia Cup 1985 and World Cup 1982

(Des A. Salahuddin)

1985 (5 July). Pakistan Hockey Team "Grand Slam" Success. P 13.

676	**358**	1r. multicoloured	2·50	2·25

359 King Edward Medical College

(Des Sultana Shamim Haider)

1985 (28 July). 125th Anniv of King Edward Medical College, Lahore. P 13.

677	**359**	3r. multicoloured	1·75	1·00

360 Illuminated Inscription in Urdu

(Des A. Salahuddin)

1985 (14 Aug). Independence Day. T **360** and similar horiz design. Multicoloured. P 13.

678	60p. Type **360**	65	1·10
	a. Sheetlet. Nos. 678/9×2	2·25	4·00
679	60p. Illuminated "XXXVIII" (inscr in English)	65	1·10

Nos. 678/9 were issued *se-tenant*, both horizontally and vertically, in sheetlets of four stamps and four stamp-size labels inscribed in Urdu.

361 Sind Madressah-tul-Islam, Karachi

(Des A. Salahuddin)

1985 (1 Sept). Centenary of Sind Madressah-tul-Islam (theological college), Karachi. P 13.

680	**361**	2r. multicoloured	1·75	1·00

362 Jamia Masjid Mosque by Day

(Des A. Salahuddin)

1985 (14 Sept). Inauguration of New Jamia Masjid Mosque, Karachi. T **362** and similar horiz design. Multicoloured. P 13.

681	1r. Type **362**	90	50
682	1r. Jamia Masjid illuminated at night	90	50

363 Lawrence College, Murree

(Des A. Salahuddin)

1985 (21 Sept). 125th Anniv of Lawrence College, Murree. P 13.
683   **363**   3r. multicoloured .... 2·75   3·00

364 United Nations Building, New York

(Des A. Salahuddin)

1985 (24 Oct). 40th Anniv of United Nations Organization. T **364** and similar diamond-shaped design. Multicoloured. P 14.
684   1r. Type **364** 30   15
685   2r. U.N. Building and emblem 40   60

365 Tents and Jamboree Emblem

(Des A. Salahuddin)

1985 (8 Nov). Tenth National Scout Jamboree. P 13.
686   **365**   60p. multicoloured .... 2·00   2·50

366 Islamabad   367 Map of SAARC Countries and National Flags

(Des H. Durrani)

1985 (30 Nov). 25th Anniv of Islamabad. P 14½×14.
687   **366**   3r. multicoloured .... 2·50   1·00

(Des A. Salahuddin)

1985 (8 Dec). First Summit Meeting of South Asian Association for Regional Cooperation, Dhaka, Bangladesh. T **367** and similar multicoloured design. P 13½×13 (1r.) or 13 (2r.).
688   1r. Type **367** .... 1·50   4·00
689   2r. National flags (39×39 mm) 75   2·00
No. 688 is reported to have been withdrawn on 9 December 1985.

368 Globe and Peace Dove

(Des A. Salahuddin)

1985 (14 Dec). 25th Anniv of U.N. General Assembly's Declaration on Independence for Colonial Territories. P 13.
690   **368**   60p. multicoloured .... 1·00   60

369 Peregrine Falcon

(Des and litho Secura, Singapore)

1986 (20 Jan). Wildlife Protection (13th series). Peregrine Falcon. Matt, almost invisible PVA gum. P 13½.
691   **369**   1r.50 multicoloured .... 4·25   4·25

370 ADBP Building, Islamabad

(Des A. Salahuddin)

1986 (18 Feb). 25th Anniv of Agricultural Development Bank of Pakistan. P 13.
692   **370**   60p. multicoloured .... 1·75   50

371 Government S.E. College

(Des Sultana Shamim Haider)

1986 (25 Apr). Centenary of Government Sadiq Egerton College, Bahawalpur. P 13.
693   **371**   1r. multicoloured .... 2·75   50

372 Emblem and Bar Graph   373 "1947 1986"

(Des Sultana Shamim Haider)

1986 (11 May). 25th Anniv of Asian Productivity Organization. P 13½.
694   **372**   1r. multicoloured .... 2·75   30

(Des A. Salahuddin (80p.), M. Munawar (1r.))

1986 (14 Aug). 39th Anniv of Independence. T **373** and similar vert design. Multicoloured. P 14.
695   80p. Type **373** .... 1·50   25
696   1r. Illuminated inscription in Urdu .... 1·50   25

374 Open Air Class   **375** Mother and Child

(Des Sultana Shamim Haider)

1986 (8 Sept). International Literacy Day. P 13.
697   **374**   1r. multicoloured .... 1·75   30

1986 (28 Oct). UNICEF Child Survival Campaign. P 13½×13.
698   **375**   80p. multicoloured .... 2·50   65

376 Aitchison College

(Des A. Salahuddin)

1986 (3 Nov). Centenary of Aitchison College, Lahore. P 13½.
699   **376**   2r.50 multicoloured .... 2·50   1·25

377 Two Doves   **378** Table Tennis Players
carrying Olive
Branches

(Des Sultana Shamim Haider)

1986 (20 Nov). International Peace Year. P 13.
700   **377**   4r. multicoloured 60   75

(Des A. Salahuddin)

1986 (25 Nov). Fourh Asian Cup Table Tennis Tournament, Karachi.
P 14.
701   **378**   2r. multicoloured .... 2·00   1·00

379 Argali

(Des M. Jamal. Litho Secura, Singapore)

1986 (4 Dec). Wildlife Protection (14th series). Argali. Matt, almost
invisible PVA gum. P 14.
702   **379**   2r. multicoloured .... 3·00   3·00

380 Selimiye Mosque,
Edirne, Turkey

(Des A. Salahuddin)

1986 (20 Dec). "Ecophilex '86" International Stamp Exhibition,
Islamabad. T **380** and similar vert designs. Multicoloured. P 13.
703   3r. Type **380** .... 1·40   1·60
    a. Horiz strip of three. Nos. 703/5 .... 3·75   4·25
704   3r. Gawhar Shad Mosque, Mashhad, Iran ... 1·40   1·60
705   3r. Grand Mosque, Bhong, Pakistan .... 1·40   1·60
703/5 *Set of 3* .... 3·75   4·25
    Nos. 703/5 were printed together, *se-tenant*, in horizontal strips of
three within sheetlets of 12.

381 St. Patrick's School

(Des A. Salahuddin)

1987 (29 Jan). 125th Anniv of St. Patrick's School, Karachi. P 13.
706   **381**   5r. multicoloured .... 3·00   1·50

382 Mistletoe Flowerpecker
and Defence Symbols

(Des A. Salahuddin)

1987 (21 Feb). Post Office Savings Bank Week. T **382** and similar vert
designs, each showing a different bird. Multicoloured. P 13.
707   5r. Type **382** .... 1·10   1·25
    a. Block of four. Nos. 707/10 .... 4·00   4·50
708   5r. Spotted Pardalote and laboratory
    apparatus .... 1·10   1·25
709   5r. Black-throated Blue Warbler and
    agriculture symbols .... 1·10   1·25
710   5r. Red-capped Manakin and industrial
    skyline .... 1·10   1·25
707/10 *Set of 4* .... 4·00   4·50
    Nos. 707/10 were printed together, *se-tenant*, in blocks of four
throughout the sheet of 32 which contained six blocks of four and
eight labels in the left and right-hand vertical columns.

383 New Parliament House, Islamabad

(Des A. Salahuddin)

1987 (23 Mar). Inauguration of New Parliament House, Islamabad.
P 13.
711   **383**   3r. multicoloured 50   60

384 Opium Poppies and Flames

(Des A. Salahuddin)

1987 (30 June). Campaign against Drug Abuse. P 13.
712   **384**   1r. multicoloured   75   30

385 Flag and National Anthem Score

(Des A. Salahuddin)

1987 (14 Aug). 40th Anniv of Independence. T **385** and similar horiz design. Multicoloured. P 13.
713   80p. Type **385** ....   1·40   20
714   3r. Text of speech by Mohammed Ali Jinnah, Minar-e-Qarardad-e-Pakistan Tower and arms ....   1·60   80

386 Hawker Tempest Mk II

(Des M. Hussaini and A. Salahuddin)

1987 (7 Sept). Air Force Day. T **386** and similar horiz designs showing military aircraft. Multicoloured. P 13½.
715   3r. Type **386** ....   1·60   1·60
       a. Sheetlet. Nos. 715/24 ....   14·50   14·50
716   3r. Hawker Fury ....   1·60   1·60
717   3r. Supermarine Attacker ....   1·60   1·60
718   3r. North American F-86 Sabre ....   1·60   1·60
719   3r. Lockheed F-104C Starfighter ....   1·60   1·60
720   3r. Lockheed C-130 Hercules ....   1·60   1·60
721   3r. Shenyang/Tianjin F-6 ....   1·60   1·60
722   3r. Dassault Mirage 111 ....   1·60   1·60
723   3r. North American A-5A Vigilante ....   1·60   1·60
724   3r. General Dynamics F-16 Fighting Falcon....   1·60   1·60
715/24 Set of 10 ....   14·50   14·50
Nos. 715/24 were printed together, se-tenant, in sheetlets of ten.

388 Shah Abdul Latif Bhitai Mausoleum

(Des A. Salahuddin)

1987 (8 Oct). Shah Abdul Latif Bhitai (poet) Commemoration. P 13.
729   **388**   80p. multicoloured   30   30

389 D. J. Sind Science College, Karachi

(Des Sultana Shamim Haider)

1987 (7 Nov). Centenary of D. J. Sind Science College, Karachi. P 13.
730   **389**   80p. multicoloured   20   20

726   1r.50 Apricot trees   60   55
727   1r.50 Karakoram Highway   60   55
728   1r.50 View from Khunjerab Pass   60   55
725/8 Set of 4 ....   2·10   2·00
Nos. 725/8 were printed together, se-tenant, in blocks of four throughout the sheet of 24.

390 College Building

391 Homeless People, Houses and Rising Sun

(Des Sultana Shamim Haider)

1987 (9 Dec). 25th Anniv of College of Physicians and Surgeons. P 13.
731   **390**   1r. multicoloured ....   2·25   30

(Des Sultana Shamim Haider)

1987 (15 Dec). International Year of Shelter for the Homeless. P 13.
732   **391**   3r. multicoloured   50   50

392 Cathedral Church of the Resurrection, Lahore

(Des A. Salahuddin)

1987 (20 Dec). Centenary of Cathedral Church of the Resurrection, Lahore. P 13.
733   **392**   3r. multicoloured   50   50

387 Pasu Glacier

(Des A. Salahuddin)

1987 (1 Oct). Pakistan Tourism Convention. T **387** and similar horiz designs showing views along Karakoram Highway. Multicoloured. P 13.
725   1r.50 Type **387**   60   55
       a. Block of four. Nos. 725/8 ....   2·10   2·00

393 Honeycomb and Arms

(Des A. Salahuddin)

1987 (28 Dec). 40th Anniv of Pakistan Post Office. P 13.
734   **393**   3r. multicoloured   50   50

394 Corporation Emblem

(Des A. Salahuddin)

1987 (31 Dec). Radio Pakistan's New Programme Schedules. P 13.
735   **394**   80p. multicoloured   20   15

395 Jamshed Nusserwanjee Mehta and Karachi Municipal Corporation Building

396 Leprosy Symbols within Flower

(Des A. Salahuddin)

1988 (7 Jan). Birth Centenary (1986) of Jamshed Nusserwanjee Mehta (former President of Karachi Municipal Corporation). P 13.
736   **395**   3r. multicoloured   50   50

(Des Sultana Shamim Haider)

1988 (31 Jan). World Leprosy Day. P 13.
737   **396**   3r. multicoloured   75   50

397 WHO Building, Geneva

(Des A. Salahuddin)

1988 (7 Apr). 40th Anniv of World Health Organization. P 13.
738   **397**   4r. multicoloured   60   50

398 Globe

399 Crescent, Leaf Pattern and Archway

1988 (8 May). 125th Anniv of International Red Cross and Crescent. P 13.
739   **398**   3r. multicoloured   50   50

(Des A. Salahuddin)

1988 (14 Aug). Independence Day. P 13½.
740   **399**   80p. multicoloured   20   10
741   **399**   4r. multicoloured   80   70

400 Field Events

(Des A. Salahuddin)

1988 (17 Sept). Olympic Games, Seoul. T **400** and similar horiz designs. Multicoloured. P 13.
742   10r. Type **400** ....   1·10   1·10
      a. Sheetlet. Nos. 742/51 ....   10·00   10·00
743   10r. Track events ....   1·10   1·10
744   10r. Jumping and pole vaulting ....   1·10   1·10
745   10r. Gymnastics ....   1·10   1·10
746   10r. Table tennis, tennis, hockey and baseball ....   1·10   1·10
747   10r. Volleyball, football, basketball and handball ....   1·10   1·10
748   10r. Wrestling, judo, boxing and weightlifting ....   1·10   1·10
749   10r. Shooting, fencing and archery ....   1·10   1·10
750   10r. Water sports ....   1·10   1·10
751   10r. Equestrian events and cycling ....   1·10   1·10
742/51 Set of 10 ....   10·00   10·00
   Nos. 742/51 were issued, se-tenant, in sheetlets of ten stamps and 36 half stamp-size labels.

401 Markhor

(Litho Secura, Singapore)

1988 (29 Oct). Wildlife Protection (15th series). Markhor. Matt, almost invisible PVA gum. P 14.
752   **401**   2r. multicoloured   65   50

402 Islamia College, Peshawar

(Des A. Salahuddin)

1988 (22 Dec). 75th Anniv of Islamia College, Peshawar. P 13½.
753   **402**   3r. multicoloured   50   50

403 Symbols of Agriculture, Industry and Education with National Flags

(Des Sultana Shamim Haider (25r.), G. M. Shaikh (50r.), A. Salahuddin (75r.))

1988 (29 Dec). South Asian Association for Regional Co-operation, fourth Summit Meeting, Islamabad. T **403** and similar multicoloured designs. P 13 (25r.), 14 (50r.) or 13½×13 (75r.).
754	25r. Type **403**		1·50	1·50
755	50r. National flags on globe and symbols of communications (33×33 mm)		4·00	3·25
756	75r. Stamps from member countries (52×29 mm)		2·75	4·50
754/6 Set of 3			7·50	8·25

No. 755 was printed in sheets of eight stamps and one stamp-size label, showing the SAARC emblem, in the central position.

(Des A. Salahuddin)

1989 (23 Jan). Pioneers of Freedom (2nd series). Diamond shaped design as T **282**. Multicoloured. W **98**. P 14.
757	3r. Maulana Hasrat Mohani		45	45

404 Logo **405** Zulfikar Ali Bhutto

(Des A. Salahuddin)

1989 (18 Feb). "Adasia 89" 16th Asian Advertising Congress, Lahore. P 13.
758	**404**	1r. mult ("Pakistan" in yellow)	1·10	1·60
		a. Sheetlet. Nos. 758/60, each×3	8·50	
759		1r. mult ("Pakistan" in turquoise-blue)	1·10	1·60
760		1r. mult ("Pakistan" in white)	1·10	1·60
758/60 Set of 3			3·00	4·25

Nos. 758/60 were printed together, se-tenant, in horizontal and vertical strips of three within the sheetlets of nine.

(Des A. Munir (1r.), A. Salahuddin (2r.))

1989 (4 Apr). Tenth Death Anniv of Zulfikar Ali Bhutto (statesman). T **405** and similar vert design. Multicoloured. P 13.
761	1r. Type **405**		40	10
762	2r. Zulfikar Ali Bhutto (different)		60	50

406 "Daphne" Class Submarine

(Des A. Salahuddin)

1989 (1 June). 25 Years of Pakistan Navy Submarine Operations. T **406** and similar horiz designs. Multicoloured. P 13½.
763	1r. Type **406**		1·60	2·00
	a. Vert strip of three. Nos. 763/5		4·25	5·50
764	1r. "Fleet Snorkel" class submarine		1·60	2·00
765	1r. "Agosta" class submarine		1·60	2·00
763/5 Set of 3			4·25	5·50

Nos. 763/5 were printed together, se-tenant, in vertical strips of three throughout the sheet.

407 "The Oath of the Tennis Court" (David)

(Des A. Salahuddin)

1989 (24 June). Bicentenary of French Revolution. P 13½.
766	**407**	7r. multicoloured	1·75	1·50

408 Pitcher, c. 2200 B.C. **409** Satellites and Map of Asian Telecommunications Network

(Des A. Salahuddin)

1989 (28 June). Archaeological Artifacts. T **408** and similar square designs showing terracotta pottery from Baluchistan Province. Multicoloured. P 14.
767	1r. Type **408**		30	30
	a. Block of four. Nos. 767/70		1·10	1·10
768	1r. Jar, c. 2300 B.C		30	30
769	1r. Vase, c. 3600 B.C		30	30
770	1r. Jar, c. 2600 B.C		30	30
767/70 Set of 4			1·10	1·10

Nos. 767/70 were printed together, se-tenant, in blocks of four throughout the sheet.

(Des G. Shaikh)

1989 (1 July). Tenth Anniv of Asia-Pacific Telecommunity. P 13½.
771	**409**	3r. multicoloured	50	50

410 Container Ship at Wharf

(Des A. Salahuddin)

1989 (5 Aug). Construction of Integrated Container Terminal, Port Qasim. P 14.
772	**410**	6r. multicoloured	3·00	4·00

411 Mohammed Ali Jinnah **412** Mausoleum of Shah Abdul Latif Bhitai

(Des A. Salahuddin. Eng A. Munir. Recess and litho)

1989 (14 Aug). W **98**. P 13.
773	**411**	1r. multicoloured	1·00	10
		a. Wmk sideways	4·00	
		w. Wmk inverted	4·00	
774		1r.50 multicoloured	1·25	50
775		2r. multicoloured	1·50	30
		a. Head omitted	£250	
		b. Wmk sideways		
776		3r. multicoloured	1·75	50
		w. Wmk inverted	5·00	
777		4r. multicoloured	2·00	70
		w. Wmk inverted	3·00	
778		5r. multicoloured	2·00	70
773/8 Set of 6			8·50	2·50

For note regarding watermark orientation see below No. 210.

No. 775a occurs on the last vertical row of a sheet and shows the sepia head completely omitted together with almost all the oval frame.

Examples of Nos. 773/8 overprinted "NATIONAL SEMINAR ON PHILATELY MULTAN 1992" as a continuous pattern were available at this event on 15 and 16 April 1992.

Details of authorisation by the Pakistan Post Offices and of availability at Multan are disputed, but, even if officially sanctioned, these overprints do not fulfil the criteria for catalogue listing due to their limited availability. They were not available from any post office other than Multan and, it is reported, only 45 sheets of each of the three higher values were overprinted.

(Des A. Salahuddin)

1989 (16 Sept). 300th Birth Anniv of Shah Abdul Latif Bhitai (poet). P 13.
779 **412** 2r. multicoloured .... 1·25 70

COMMONWEALTH MEMBER

Pakistan rejoined the Commonwealth on 1 October 1989.

413 Asiatic Black Bear

(Des A. McCoy)

1989 (7 Oct). Wildlife Protection (16th series). Asiatic Black Bear. T **413** and similar horiz designs. Multicoloured. P 13½.
780 4r. Type **413** .... 90 1·25
    a. Block of four. Nos. 780/3 .... 3·25 4·50
781 4r. Bear among boulders .... 90 1·25
782 4r. Standing on rock .... 90 1·25
783 4r. Sitting by trees .... 90 1·25
780/3 Set of 4 .... 3·25 4·00
    Nos. 780/3 were printed together, se-tenant, in blocks of 4 throughout the sheet.

414 Ear of Wheat encircling Globe

415 Games Emblem and Flags of Member Countries

(Des A. Salahuddin)

1989 (16 Oct). World Food Day. P 14×12½.
784 **414** 1r. multicoloured 60 35

(Des A. Salahuddin)

1989 (20 Oct). Fourth South Asian Sports Federation Games, Islamabad. P 13.
785 **415** 1r. multicoloured 35 35

416 Patchwork Kamblee (cloth) entering Gate of Heaven

(Des Farah and Fareeda Batul)

1989 (20 Oct). 800th Birth Anniv of Baba Farid (Muslim spiritual leader). P 13.
786 **416** 3r. multicoloured 50 50

417 Pakistan Television Logo

(Des A. Salahuddin)

1989 (26 Nov). 25th Anniv of Television Broadcasting in Pakistan. P 13½.
787 **417** 3r. multicoloured 50 50

418 Family of Drug Addicts in Poppy Bud

419 Murray College, Sialkot

(Des M. Munawar)

1989 (8 Dec). South Asian Association for Regional Co-operation Anti-Drugs Campaign. P 13.
788 **418** 7r. multicoloured .... 2·25 1·40

(Des A. Salahuddin)

1989 (18 Dec). Centenary of Murray College, Sialkot. P 14.
789 **419** 6r. multicoloured .... 1·50 1·25

420 Government College, Lahore

(Des N. Sheikh)

1989 (21 Dec). 125th Anniv of Government College, Lahore. P 13.
790 **420** 6r. multicoloured .... 1·00 1·25

421 Fields, Electricity Pylons and Rural Buildings

(Des A. Salahuddin)

1989 (31 Dec). Tenth Anniv of Centre for Asia and Pacific Integrated Rural Development. P 13.
791 **421** 3r. multicoloured .... 1·00 75

422 Emblem and Islamic Patterns

(Des A. Salahuddin)

1990 (9 Feb). 20th Anniv of Organization of the Islamic Conference. P 13.

792	**422**	1r. multicoloured	1·75	40

423 Hockey Match

(Des M. Khan)

1990 (12 Feb). Seventh World Hockey Cup, Lahore. P 13½.

793	**423**	2r. multicoloured	4·50	4·25

424 Mohammed Iqbal addressing Crowd and Liaquat Ali Khan taking Oath

(Des A. Zafar (1r.), A. Salahuddin (7r.))

1990 (23 Mar). 50th Anniv of Passing of Pakistan Resolution. T **424** and similar multicoloured designs. P 13 (1r.) or 13½ (7r.).

794	1r. Type **424**		1·00	1·25
	a. Horiz strip of three. Nos. 794/6		2·75	3·25
795	1r. Maulana Mohammad Ali Jauhar and Mohammed Ali Jinnah with banner		1·00	1·25
796	1r. Women with Pakistan flag, and Mohammed Ali Jinnah taking Governor-General's oath, 1947		1·00	1·25
797	7r. Minar-e-Qararadad-e-Pakistan Monument and Resolution in Urdu and English (86×42 *mm*)		2·50	3·00
794/7 Set of 4			5·00	6·00

Nos. 794/6 were printed together, *se-tenant*, in horizontal strips of three throughout the sheet, each strip forming a composite design.

425 Pregnant Woman resting

(Des Family Planning Association of Pakistan)

1990 (24 Mar). "Safe Motherhood" South Asia Conference, Lahore. P 13½.

798	**425**	5r. multicoloured	1·00	1·25

426 "Decorated Verse by Ghalib" (Shakir Ali)

(Des A. Salahuddin)

1990 (19 Apr). Painters of Pakistan (1st series). Shakir Ali. P 13½×13.

799	**426**	1r. multicoloured	2·25	1·25

See also Nos. 856/7.

427 Satellite in Night Sky   **428** Allama Mohammed Iqbal

(Des S. Afsar)

1990 (26 July). Launch of "Badr 1" Satellite. P 13.

800	**427**	3r. multicoloured	3·50	4·00

(Des S. Akhtar)

1990 (14 Aug). Pioneers of Freedom (3rd series). T **428** and similar vert designs. Each brown and green. P 13.

801	1r. Type **428**		40	45
	a. Sheetlet. Nos. 801/9		3·25	3·50
802	1r. Mohammed Ali Jinnah		40	45
803	1r. Sir Syed Ahmad Khan		40	45
804	1r. Nawab Salimullah		40	45
805	1r. Mohtarma Fatima Jinnah		40	45
806	1r. Aga Khan III		40	45
807	1r. Nawab Mohammad Ismail Khan		40	45
808	1r. Hussain Shaheed Suhrawardy		40	45
809	1r. Syed Ameer Ali		40	45
810	1r. Nawab Bahadur Yar Jung		40	45
	a. Sheetlet. Nos. 810/18		3·25	3·50
811	1r. Khawaja Nazimuddin		40	45
812	1r. Maulana Obaidullah Sindhi		40	45
813	1r. Sahibzada Abdul Qaiyum Khan		40	45
814	1r. Begum Jahanara Shah Nawaz		40	45
815	1r. Sir Ghulam Hussain Hidayatullah		40	45
816	1r. Qazi Mohammad Isa		40	45
817	1r. Sir M. Shahnawaz Khan Mamdot		40	45
818	1r. Pir Sahib of Manki Sharif		40	45
819	1r. Liaquat Ali Khan		40	45
	a. Sheetlet. Nos. 819/27		3·25	3·50
820	1r. Maulvi A. K. Fazl-ul-Haq		40	45
821	1r. Allama Shabbir Ahmad Usmani		40	45
822	1r. Sadar Abdur Rab Nishtar		40	45
823	1r. Bi Amma		40	45
824	1r. Sir Abdullah Haroon		40	45
825	1r. Chaudhry Rahmat Ali		40	45
826	1r. Raja Sahib of Mahmudabad		40	45
827	1r. Hassanally Effendi		40	45
801/27 Set of 27			9·50	11·00

Nos. 801/9, 810/18 and 819/27 were printed together, *se-tenant*, in sheetlets of nine.

See also Nos. 838/46, 870/2, 904/6, 921/8, 961/2, 1007, 1019/20 and 1075/7.

429 Cultural Aspects of Indonesia and Pakistan

(Des J. Engineer)

1990 (19 Aug). Indonesia–Pakistan Economic and Cultural Cooperation Organization. P 13.
828   **429**   7r. multicoloured ....   3·75   3·75

430 Globe, Open Book and Pen

(Des S. Afsar)

1990 (8 Sept). International Literacy Year. P 13.
829   **430**   3r. multicoloured ....   1·00   1·50

431 College Crests   **432** Children and Globe

(Des I. Gilani)

1990 (22 Sept). Joint Meeting between Royal College of Physicans, Edinburgh, and College of Physicians and Surgeons, Pakistan. P 13.
830   **431**   2r. multicoloured   60   75

(Des A. Salahuddin)

1990 (29 Sept). U.N. World Summit for Children, New York. P 13.
831   **432**   7r. multicoloured   75   1·25

433 Girl within Members' Flags

(Des A. Salahuddin)

1990 (21 Nov). South Asian Association for Regional Co-operation Year of Girl Child. P 13½.
832   **433**   2r. multicoloured   70   75

434 Paper passing over Rollers   **435** Civil Defence Worker protecting Islamabad

(Des I. Gilani)

1990 (8 Dec). 25th Anniv of Security Papers Limited. P 13.
833   **434**   3r. multicoloured ....   4·50   2·50
        a. Red ("25 YEARS OF SECURITY PAPERS LTD") omitted ....   80·00

(Des I. Gilani)

1991 (1 Mar). International Civil Defence Day. P 13.
834   **435**   7r. multicoloured ....   1·75   1·75

436 Logo and Flags of Member Countries

(Des A. Salahuddin)

1991 (12 Mar). South and West Asia Postal Union Commemoration. P 13.
835   **436**   5r. multicoloured ....   1·60   1·90

437 Globe and Figures

(Des S. Afsar)

1991 (11 July). World Population Day. P 13.
836   **437**   10r. multicoloured ....   1·90   2·50

438 Mentally Handicapped Athlete   **439** Habib Bank Headquarters and Emblem

(Des A. Salahuddin)

1991 (19 July). Pakistan Participation in Special Olympic Games. P 13.
837   **438**   7r. multicoloured ....   1·75   2·50

1991 (14 Aug). Pioneers of Freedom (4th series). Vert designs as T **428**. Each brown and green. P 13.
838   1r. Maulana Zafar Ali Khan   70   80
        a. Sheetlet. Nos. 838/46 ....   5·50   6·50
839   1r. Maulana Mohamed Ali Jauhar   70   80
840   1r. Chaudhry Khaliquzzaman   70   80
841   1r. Hameed Nizami   70   80
842   1r. Begum Ra'ana Liaquat Ali Khan   70   80
843   1r. Mirza Abol Hassan Ispahani   70   80
844   1r. Raja Ghazanfar Ali Khan   70   80
845   1r. Malik Barkat Ali   70   80
846   1r. Mir Jaffer Khan Jamali   70   80
838/46 *Set of 9* ....   5·50   6·50
Nos. 838/46 were printed together, *se-tenant*, as a sheetlet of nine.

(Des I. Gilani)

1991 (25 Aug). 50th Anniv of Habib Bank. P 13.
847   **439**   1r. multicoloured ....   1·25   25
848   5r. multicoloured ....   3·75   4·00

440 St. Joseph's Convent School

(Des A. Salahuddin)

1991 (8 Sept). 130th Anniv (1992) of St. Joseph's Convent School, Karachi. P 13.

| 849 | **440** | 5r. multicoloured | 4·00 | 4·00 |

441 Emperor Sher Shah Suri   **442** Jinnah Antarctic Research Station

(Des S. Akhtar)

1991 (5 Oct). Emperor Sher Shah Suri (founder of road network) Commemoration. Multicoloured. P 13.

| 850 | | 5r. Type **441** | 2·25 | 2·50 |

MS851 92×80 mm. 7r. Emperor on horseback and portrait as Type **441**. Imperf...... 1·75 2·75

(Des I. Gilani)

1991 (28 Oct). Pakistan Scientifc Expedition to Antarctica. P 13.

| 852 | **442** | 7r. multicoloured | 3·00 | 2·75 |

443 Houbara Bustard   **444** Mosque

1991 (4 Nov). Wildlife Protection (17th series). P 13.

| 853 | **443** | 7r. multicoloured | 2·50 | 3·00 |

(Des I. Gilani)

1991 (22 Nov). 300th Death Anniv of Hazrat Sultan Bahoo. P 13.

| 854 | **444** | 7r. multicoloured | 2·50 | 3·25 |

445 Development Symbols and Map of Asia

(Des G. Shaikh)

1991 (19 Dec). 25th Anniv of Asian Development Bank. P 13.

| 855 | **445** | 7r. multicoloured | 3·50 | 3·50 |

(Des A. Salahuddin)

1991 (24 Dec). Painters of Pakistan (2nd series). Horiz designs as T **426**. Multicoloured. P 13½×13.

| 856 | | 1r. "Procession" (Haji Muhammad Sharif) .. | 2·50 | 2·00 |
| 857 | | 1r. "Women harvesting" (Ustad Allah Bux).. | 2·50 | 2·00 |

446 American Express Travellers Cheques of 1891 and 1991

(Des A. Salahuddin)

1991 (26 Dec). Centenary of American Express Travellers Cheques. P 13½.

| 858 | **446** | 7r. multicoloured | 1·75 | 2·50 |
| | | a. Magenta (incl face value) omitted | 60·00 | |

First year of Privatisation

447 Flag, Banknote and Banking Equipment

1992 (8 Apr). First Anniv of Muslim Commercial Bank Privatisation. T **447** and similar horiz design. Multicoloured. P 13.

| 859 | | 1r. Type **447** | 20 | 20 |
| 860 | | 7r. Flag with industrial and commercial scenes | 1·25 | 1·75 |

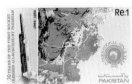

448 Imran Khan (team captain) and Trophy   **449** "Rehber-1" Rocket and Satellite View of Earth

(Des I. Gilani (2r.), A. Salahuddin (5r.), M. Ahmed (7r.))

1992 (27 Apr). Pakistan's Victory in World Cricket Championship. T **448** and similar multicoloured designs. P 13.

861		2r. Type **448**	70	70
862		5r. Trophy and national flags (*horiz*)	1·50	1·50
863		7r. Pakistani flag, trophy and symbolic cricket ball	1·75	2·25
861/3	*Set of 3*		3·50	4·00

(Des I. Gilani (1r.), S. Afsar (2r.))

1992 (7 June). International Space Year. T **449** and similar horiz design. Multicoloured. P 13.

| 864 | | 1r. Type **449** | 40 | 20 |
| 865 | | 2r. Satellite orbiting Earth and logo | 60 | 80 |

450 Surgical Instruments   **451** Globe and Symbolic Family

(Des S. Afsar)

1992 (5 July). Industries. T **450** and similar horiz designs. Multicoloured. P 13½.

866		10r. Type **450**	1·50	2·00
		a. Horiz strip of three. Nos. 866/8	5·50	7·50
867		15r. Leather goods	1·75	2·75
868		25r. Sports equipment	3·00	3·50
866/8	*Set of 3*		5·50	7·50

Nos. 866/8 were printed together, *se-tenant*, in horizontal strips of three throughout the sheet.

(Des S. Afsar)

1992 (25 July). Population Day. P 13.

| 869 | **451** | 6r. multicoloured | 1·25 | 1·50 |

(Des S. Akhtar)

1992 (14 Aug). Pioneers of Freedom (5th series). Vert designs as T **428**. Each brown and green. P 13.

870	1r. Syed Suleman Nadvi	1·75	2·00
	a. Horiz strip of three. Nos. 870/2	4·75	5·50
871	1r. Nawab Iftikhar Hussain Khan Mamdot..	1·75	2·00
872	1r. Maulana Muhammad Shibli Naumani ...	1·75	2·00
870/2 Set of 3		4·75	5·50

Nos. 870/2 were printed together, se-tenant, in horizontal strips of three throughout a sheetlet of nine.

452 Scout Badge and Salute

453 College Building

(Des I. Gilani)

1992 (23 Aug). Sixth Islamic Scout Jamboree and fourth Islamic Scouts Conference. T **452** and similar vert design. Multicoloured. P 14×13.

873	6r. Type **452**	50	75
874	6r. Conference centre and scout salute.......	50	75

(Des I. Gilani)

1992 (1 Nov). Centenary of Islamia College, Lahore. P 13.

875	**453**	3r. multicoloured..	80	1·00

454 Viola odorata (flower) and Symbolic Drug Manufacture

(Des S. Afsar)

1992 (22 Nov). Medicinal Plants (1st series). P 13.

876	**454**	6r. multicoloured..	3·25	2·50

See also Nos. 903, 946, 1010, 1026, 1037, 1099, 1123, 1142, 1159, 1185 and 1333/4.

455 Emblem

(Des A. Salahuddin)

1992 (28 Nov). Extraordinary Ministerial Council Session of Economic Co-operation Organization, Islamabad. P 13.

877	**455**	7r. multicoloured..	1·00	1·75

456 Emblems and Field

457 Alhambra Palace, Granada, Spain

(Des A. Salahuddin)

1992 (5 Dec). International Conference on Nutrition, Rome. P 14.

878	**456**	7r. multicoloured..	70	1·25

(Des A. Salahuddin)

1992 (14 Dec). Cultural Heritage of Muslim Granada. P 13.

879	**457**	7r. multicoloured..	1·00	1·50

458 Mallard

459 Baluchistan Costume

Four different versions of designs as T **458**:
Type A. "Rs.5" at right with rainbow 8 mm beneath "P" of "PAKISTAN"
Type B. "Rs.5" at right with rainbow 2 mm beneath "P"
Type C. "Rs.5" at left with rainbow 2 mm beneath "N" of "PAKISTAN"
Type D. "Rs.5" at left with rainbow 8 mm beneath "N"

(Des A. Salahuddin)

1992 (31 Dec). Water Birds. T **458** and similar vert designs. Multicoloured. P 14×13.

880	5r. Type **458** (A)..	60	70
	a. Sheetlet. Nos. 880/95	8·50	10·00
881	5r. Type **458** (B)..	60	70
882	5r. Type **458** (C)..	60	70
883	5r. Type **458** (D)..	60	70
884	5r. Greylag Goose (A)..................................	60	70
885	5r. As No. 884 (B)..	60	70
886	5r. As No. 884 (C)..	60	70
887	5r. As No. 884 (D)..	60	70
888	5r. Gadwall (A)...	60	70
889	5r. As No. 888 (B)..	60	70
890	5r. As No. 888 (C)..	60	70
891	5r. As No. 888 (D)..	60	70
892	5r. Common Shelduck (A).............................	60	70
893	5r. As No. 892 (B)..	60	70
894	5r. As No. 892 (C)..	60	70
895	5r. As No. 892 (D)..	60	70
880/95 Set of 16		8·50	10·00

Nos. 880/95 were printed together, se-tenant, in sheetlets of 16 (4×4). Stamps in the first two vertical rows show the face value at right and those in the last two show it at left. Each horizontal row shows a rainbow which curves across the tops of the designs. The four different bird designs are repeated in different positions on each horizontal row. Row 1 contains Nos. 880 (A), 885 (B), 890 (C) and 895 (D). Row 2 commences with No. 884 (A) and ends with No. 883 (D) and the sequence continues on the other rows.

(Des S. Rahman)

1993 (10 Mar). Women's Traditional Costumes. T **459** and similar vert designs. Multicoloured. P 13.

896	6r. Type **459**..	1·25	1·50
897	6r. Punjab..	1·25	1·50
898	6r. Sindh..	1·25	1·50
899	6r. North-west Frontier Province..................	1·25	1·50
896/9 Set of 4		4·50	5·50

460 Clasped Hands and Islamic Symbols

461 ITU Emblem

(Des I. Gilani)

1993 (25 Apr). 21st Conference of Islamic Foreign Ministers, Karachi. P 13.

900	**460**	1r. multicoloured..	75	10
901		6r. multicoloured..	2·25	2·75

(Des Pakistan Telecommunication Corporation, Islamabad)

1993 (17 May). 25th Anniv of World Telecommunication Day. P 13.
902   **461**   1r. multicoloured .... 1·50   30

(Des S. Afsar)

1993 (20 June). Medicinal Plants (2nd series). Horiz design as T **454**. Multicoloured. P 13.
903   6r. Fennel and symbolic drug
     manufacture...................... 3·50   2·75

(Des S. Akhtar)

1993 (14 Aug). Pioneers of Freedom (6th series). Vert designs as T **428**. Each brown and vermilion. P 13.
904   1r. Ghulam Mohammad Bhurgri.................. 1·40   1·40
    a. Horiz strip of three. Nos. 904/6 .... 3·75   3·75
905   1r. Mir Ahmed Yar Khan .... 1·40   1·40
906   1r. Mohammad Pir Sahib Zakori Sharif .... 1·40   1·40
904/6 *Set of 3* .... 3·75   3·75
    Nos. 904/6 were printed together, *se-tenant*, in horizontal strips of three throughout a sheetlet of nine.

462 College Building and Arms

(Des Nargis Munir)

1993 (1 Sept). Centenary of Gordon College, Rawalpindi. P 13.
907   **462**   2r. multicoloured.................. 2·25   2·00

463 Juniper Forest   **464** Globe, Produce and Emblem

(Des A. Salahuddin)

1993 (30 Sept)–**95**. Campaign to Save the Juniper Forest, Ziarat. P 13.
907a   **463**   1r. multicoloured (14.2.95) .... 2·50   50
908   7r. multicoloured .... 4·50   3·75

(Des J. Siddiqui)

1993 (16 Oct). World Food Day. P 14.
909   **464**   6r. multicoloured .... 1·50   1·60

465 Burn Hall Institution, Abbottabad   **466** Peace Dove carrying Letter and National Flags

(Des I. Gilani)

1993 (28 Oct). 50th Anniv of Burn Hall Institutions. P 13.
910   **465**   7r. multicoloured .... 3·00   3·25

(Des F. Amir)

1993 (18 Nov). South and West Asia Postal Union Commemoration. P 13.
911   **466**   7r. multicoloured .... 3·25   3·25

467 Congress Emblem   **468** Wazir Mansion (birthplace)

1993 (10 Dec). Pakistan College of Physicians and Surgeons International Medical Congress. P 13.
912   **467**   1r. multicoloured .... 2·50   40

(Des A. Siddique)

1993 (25 Dec). 45th Death Anniv of Mohammed Ali Jinnah. W **98**. P 13½×13.
913   **468**   1r. multicoloured .... 2·00   30
    a. Wmk sideways...............................
    aw. Wmk sideways inverted .... 4·50

469 Emblem and National Flag

(Des A. Salahuddin)

1994 (11 Apr). 75th Anniv of International Labour Organization. W **98** (sideways). P 13.
914   **469**   7r. multicoloured .... 1·75   2·75

470 Ratan Jot (flower)   **471** Silhouette of Family and Emblem

(Des I. Gilani)

1994 (20 Apr). Ratification of International Biological Diversity Convention. T **470** and similar horiz designs. Multicoloured. W **98**. P 13½.
915   6r. Type **470** 50   65
    a. Horiz strip of four. Nos. 915/18................. 1·75   2·40
    aw. Wmk inverted.................................
916   6r. Wetlands habitat........................... 50   65
917   6r. Golden Mahseer (*Tor puttitora*) (fish)...... 50   65
918   6r. Brown Bear................................. 50   65
915/18 *Set of 4* .... 1·75   2·40
    Nos. 915/18 were printed together, *se-tenant*, in horizontal strips of four throughout the sheet.

(Des Nargis Munir)

1994 (15 May). International Year of the Family. W **98**. P 13.
919   **471**   7r. multicoloured 80   1·00

472 Symbolic Globe and Logo

1994 (11 July). World Population Day. W **98**. P 13.
920   **472**   7r. multicoloured .... 1·00   1·00

(Des S. Akhtar)

1994 (14 Aug). Pioneers of Freedom (7th series). Vert designs as T **428**. Each brown and green. P 13.
921   1r. Nawab Mohsin-Ul-Mulk.................... 40   45
     a. Sheetlet. Nos. 921/8.................. 3·00   3·25
922   1r. Sir Shahnawaz Bhutto................... 40   45
923   1r. Nawab Viqar-Ul-Mulk..................... 40   45
924   1r. Pir Ilahi Bux.................................... 40   45
925   1r. Sheikh Abdul Qadir......................... 40   45
926   1r. Dr. Sir Ziauddin Ahmed.................. 40   45
927   1r. Jam Mir Ghulam Qadir Khan 40   45
928   1r. Sardar Aurangzeb Khan 40   45
921/8 *Set of 8* .... 3·00   3·25
    Nos. 921/8 were printed together, *se-tenant*, in sheetlets of eight stamps and one centre label showing the Pakistan flag.

473 Hala Pottery, Pakistan   **474** Boy writing and Globe

(Des A. Siddique (No. 929))

1994 (19 Aug). Indonesia–Pakistan Economic and Cultural Co-operation Organization. T **473** and similar vert design. Multicoloured. W **98** (sideways). P 13.
929   10r. Type **473** .... 2·00   2·50
     a. Horiz pair. Nos. 929/30................ 4·00   5·00
930   10r. Lombok pottery, Indonesia .... 2·00   2·50
    Nos. 929/30 were printed together, *se-tenant*, in horizontal pairs throughout the sheet.

(Des Nargis Munir)

1994 (8 Sept). International Literacy Day. W **98** (sideways). P 13½.
931   **474**   7r. multicoloured............................. 1·00   1·25

475 Mohammed Ali Jinnah and Floral Pattern   **476** Gateway and Emblem

(Des A. Salahuddin. Eng Z. Ali. Recess and litho)

1994 (11 Sept). W **98** (sideways*). P 13.
932   **475**   1r. multicoloured............................. 45   10
933   2r. multicoloured............................. 60   10
934   3r. multicoloured............................. 75   10
935   4r. multicoloured............................. 1·00   10
936   5r. multicoloured............................. 1·00   15
937   7r. multicoloured............................. 1·50   20
938   10r. multicoloured............................. 1·00   30
     w. Wmk tips of crescent pointing
        downwards.................................. 3·00
939   12r. multicoloured............................. 1·25   60
     w. Wmk tips of crescent pointing
        downwards.................................. 18·00
940   15r. multicoloured............................. 1·25   80
     w. Wmk tips of crescent pointing
        downwards.................................. 8·00
941   20r. multicoloured............................. 1·40   1·00
942   25r. multicoloured............................. 1·50   1·25
     w. Wmk tips of crescent pointing
        downwards.................................. 15·00
943   30r. multicoloured............................. 1·60   1·40
     w. Wmk tips of crescent pointing
        downwards..................................

932/43 *Set of 12* .... 12·00   5·50
    *The normal sideways watermark shows the tips of the crescent pointing upwards.

(Des Nargis Munir)

1994 (22 Sept). Second South Asian Association for Regional Co-operation and 12th National Scout Jamborees, Quetta. W **98**. P 13.
944   **476**   7r. multicoloured......................... 1·00   1·10

477 Engraver   **478** Henbane

1994 (7 Oct). First International Festival of Islamic Artisans at Work. W **98** (sideways). P 13½.
945   **477**   2r. multicoloured......................... 1·50   60

(Des F. Amir)

1994 (18 Oct). Medicinal Plants (3rd series). W **98**. P 13.
946   **478**   6r. multicoloured......................... 1·00   1·00

479 Abu-I Kasim Firdausi (poet)   **480** Museum Building

(Des F. Amir)

1994 (27 Oct). Millenary of Shahnama (poem). W **98**. P 13.
947   **479**   1r. multicoloured......................... 35   15
     w. Wmk inverted.............................

(Des A. Siddique)

1994 (27 Dec). Centenary of Lahore Museum. W **98** (sideways). P 13.
948   **480**   4r. multicoloured......................... 60   80

481 World Cup Trophies for 1971, 1978, 1982 and 1994

(Des J. Siddiqui)

1994 (31 Dec). Victory of Pakistan in World Cup Hockey Championship. W **98** (sideways). P 13½×13.
949   **481**   5r. multicoloured......................... 1·25   1·25

482 Tourist Attractions

(Des Nargis Munir)

1995 (2 Jan). 20th Anniv of World Tourism Organization. W **98**. P 13.
950   **482**   4r. multicoloured .... 1·50   1·50

483 Khushal Khan of Khattak and Army

484 ECO Emblem

(Des S. Afsar)

1995 (28 Feb). Khushal Khan of Khattak (poet) Commemoration. W **98**. P 13.
951   **483**   7r. multicoloured .... 2·25   2·25
            a. Wmk sideways...

1995 (14 Mar). Third Economic Co-operation Organization Summit, Islamabad. W **98** (sideways). P 14.
952   **484**   6r. multicoloured .... 1·50   1·50

485 Common Indian Krait

486 Globe and Environments

(Des M-ur Rehman (Nos. 953, 955), A. Siddique (Nos. 954, 956))

1995 (15 Apr). Snakes. T **485** and similar horiz designs. Multicoloured. P 13½.
953   6r. Type **485** 70   90
           a. Block of four. Nos. 953/6 .... 2·50   3·25
954   6r. Indian Cobra... 70   90
955   6r. Indian Python.. 70   90
956   6r. Russell's Viper 70   90
953/6 *Set of* 4 .... 2·50   3·25
  Nos. 953/6 were printed together, *se-tenant*, in blocks of four throughout the sheet.

(Des A. Siddique)

1995 (20 Apr). Earth Day. W **98** (sideways). P 13.
957   **486**   6r. multicoloured 70   80

487 Victoria Carriage, Karachi

(Des F. Amir)

1995 (22 May). Traditional Transport. W **98** (sideways). P 13.
958   **487**   5r. multicoloured .... 1·25   1·00

488 Prime Minister Tansu Ciller of Turkey and Rose

(Des J. Siddiqui)

1995 (1 Aug). First Muslim Women Parliamentarians' Conference, Islamabad. T **488** and similar horiz design. Multicoloured. P 13.
959   5r. Type **488** .... 1·00   1·50
           a. Horiz pair. Nos. 959/60......................... 2·00   6·00
960   5r. Prime Minister Benazir Bhutto and
               jasmine... 1·00   1·50
  Nos. 959/60 were printed together, *se-tenant*, in horizontal pairs throughout the sheet.

(Des S. Akhtar)

1995 (14 Aug). Pioneers of Freedom (8th series). Vert designs as T **428**. Each brown and myrtle-green. P 13.
961   1r. Maulana Shaukat Ali............................. 80   70
           a. Pair. Nos. 961/2.................................. 1·60   1·40
962   1r. Chaudhry Ghulam Abbas..................... 80   70
  Nos. 961/2 were printed together, *se-tenant*, in sheetlets of eight stamps and one centre label showing the Pakistani flag.

489 Oil Sardine

490 *Erasmia pulchella*

(Des Nargis Munir)

1995 (1 Sept). Fishes. T **489** and similar horiz designs. Multicoloured. W **98**. P 13½.
963   6r. Type **489** 70   85
           a. Horiz strip of four. Nos. 963/6.............. 2·50   3·00
          ab. Wmk sideways
964   6r. Mozambique Mouthbrooder ("Tilapia"). 70   85
965   6r. Brown Trout... 70   85
966   6r. Rohu... 70   85
963/6 *Set of* 4 .... 2·50   3·00
  Nos. 963/6 were printed together, *se-tenant*, in horizontal strips of four throughout the sheet.

(Des A. Salahuddin)

1995 (1 Sept). Butterflies. T **490** and similar horiz designs. Multicoloured. W **98** (sideways). P 13½.
967   6r. Type **490** 70   90
           a. Horiz strip of four. No 967/70 .... 2·50   3·25
968   6r. *Callicore astarte* (inscr "CATOGRAMME") 70   90
969   6r. *Ixias pyrene* 70   90
970   6r. *Heliconius* 70   90
967/70 *Set of* 4 .... 2·50   3·25
  Nos. 967/70 were printed together, *se-tenant*, in horizontal strips of four throughout the sheet.

491 Major Raja Aziz Bhatti Shaheed and Medal

(Des A. Zafar)

1995 (6 Sept). Defence Day. W **98**. P 13.
971   **491**   1r.25 multicoloured....................................... 2·00   1·50
            w. Wmk inverted....................................... 6·00

492 Presentation Convent School, Rawalpindi

(Des I. Gilani)

1995 (8 Sept). Centenary of Presentation Convent School, Rawalpindi. W **98**. P 13½.
972   **492**   1r.25 multicoloured....................................... 1·50   1·00

493 Women Soldiers, Golfer and Scientist

494 "Louis Pasteur in Laboratory" (A. Edelfelt)

(Des A. Salahuddin)

1995 (15 Sept). Fourth World Conference on Women, Beijing. T **493** and similar vert designs. Multicoloured. W **98** (sideways*). P 13.

973	1r.25 Type **493**		30	45
	a. Horiz strip of four. Nos. 973/6		1·10	1·60
	aw. Wmk tips of crescent pointing downwards		6·00	
974	1r.25 Women graduates, journalist, computer operator and technicians		30	45
975	1r.25 Sewing machinist and women at traditional crafts		30	45
976	1r.25 Army officer and women at traditional tasks		30	45
973/6	Set of 4		1·10	1·60

*The normal sideways watermark shows the tips of the crescent pointing upwards.

Nos. 973/6 were printed together, se-tenant, in horizontal strips of four throughout the sheet.

1995 (28 Sept). Death Centenary of Louis Pasteur (chemist). W **98** (sideways). P 13.

977	**494**	5r. multicoloured	1·00	1·00

495

1995 (28 Sept)–**96**. P 13½.

978	**495**	5p. blue, yellow-orange and reddish brown (10.10.95)	25	60
979		15p. yellow-orange, dull violet and reddish brown (10.10.95)	50	40
980		25p. cobalt, cerise and purple	50	10
981		75p. bright green, red-brown and reddish brown (15.5.96)	1·40	20
978/81	Set of 4		2·40	1·10

496 Liaquat Ali Khan

(Des A. Salahuddin)

1995 (1 Oct). Birth Centenary (1995) of Liaquat Ali Khan (statesman). W **98**. P 13.

987	**496**	1r.25 multicoloured	1·00	40

497 Village and Irrigated Fields

(Des Nargis Munir)

1995 (16 Oct). 50th Anniv of Food and Agriculture Organization. W **98**. P 13.

988	**497**	1r.25 multicoloured	1·00	40

498 Pakistani Soldier treating Somali Refugees

1995 (24 Oct). 50th Anniv of United Nations. W **98**. P 13½.

989	**498**	7r. multicoloured	1·25	1·60
		a. Wmk sideways		

499 Education Emblem

500 Hand holding Book, Eye and Pen Nib

1995 (3 Nov). 80th Anniv (1993) of Kinnaird College for Women, Lahore. W **98** (sideways). P 14×13.

990	**499**	1r.25 multicoloured	1·00	40
		w. Wmk tips of crescent pointing downwards	6·00	

1995 (30 Nov). International Conference of Writers and Intellectuals, Islamabad. W **98** (sideways). P 14.

991	**500**	1r.25 multicoloured	1·00	40
		w. Wmk tips of crescent pointing downwards	6·00	

501 Children holding Hands and SAARC Logo

502 Jet Skier

(Des Nargis Munir)

1995 (8 Dec). Tenth Anniv of South Asian Association for Regional Co-operation. W **98** (sideways). P 13.

992	**501**	1r.25 multicoloured	60	30

(Des F. Siddiqui and M-ur Rehman)

1995 (14 Dec). National Water Sports Gala, Karachi. T **502** and similar vert designs. Multicoloured. W **98** (sideways*). P 13.

993	1r.25 Type **502**		35	45
	a. Block of four. Nos. 993/6		1·25	1·60
	aw. Wmk tips of crescent pointing downwards			
994	1r.25 Local punts		35	45
995	1r.25 Wind surfers		35	45
996	1r.25 Water skier		35	45
993/6	Set of 4		1·25	1·60

*The normal sideways watermark shows the tips of the crescent pointing upwards.

Nos. 993/6 were printed together, se-tenant, in blocks of four throughout the sheet.

503 Mortar Board and Books

(Des A. Siddique)

1995 (16 Dec). 20th Anniv of Allama Iqbal Open University. W **98**. P 13.

| 997 | **503** | 1r.25 multicoloured | 60 | 30 |
| | | w. Wmk inverted | | |

504 Balochistan Quetta University Building

(Des I. Jillani)

1995 (31 Dec). 25th Anniv of Balochistan Quetta University. W **98**. P 13.

| 998 | **504** | 1r.25 multicoloured | 60 | 30 |

505 Zulfikar Ali Bhutto, Flag and Crowd

(Des A. Salahuddin)

1996 (4 Apr). 17th Death Anniv of Zulfikar Ali Bhutto (former Prime Minister). T **505** and similar multicoloured designs. W **98** (sideways* on 4r.). P 13.

999		1r.25 Type **505**	1·25	20
		w. Wmk inverted	4·50	4·50
1000		4r. Zulfikar Ali Bhutto and flag (53×31 mm)	2·75	2·25
		w. Wmk tips of crescent pointing downwards	4·50	4·50
MS1001		118×74 mm. 8r. Zulfikar Ali Bhutto and crowd. Wmk sideways. Imperf	2·25	2·50
		w. Wmk tips of crescent pointing downwards		

*The normal sideways watermark shows the tips of the crescent pointing upwards.

506 Wrestling

(Des F. Siddiqui and Nargis Munir)

1996 (3 Aug). Olympic Games, Atlanta. T **506** and similar horiz designs. Multicoloured. W **98** (sideways*). P 13.

1002		5r. Type **506**	65	80
1003		5r. Boxing	65	80
1004		5r. Pierre de Coubertin	65	80
		w. Wmk tips of crescent pointing downwards	4·50	
1005		5r. Hockey	65	80
		w. Wmk tips of crescent pointing downwards	4·50	
1002/5		Set of 4	2·40	3·00
MS1006		112×100 mm. 25r. Designs as Nos. 1002/5, but without face values. Imperf	3·00	3·75
		w. Wmk tips of crescent pointing downwards		

*The normal sideways watermark shows the tips of the crescent pointing upwards.

(Des S. Akhtar)

1996 (14 Aug). Pioneers of Freedom (9th series). Vert design as T **425** showing Allama Abdullah Yousuf Ali. P 13.

| 1007 | | 1r. brown and myrtle-green | 40 | 20 |

507 G.P.O. Building, Lahore   **508** Symbolic Open Book and Text

(Des A. Salahuddin)

1996 (21 Aug). Restoration of G.P.O. Building, Lahore. W **98**. P 14.

| 1008 | **507** | 5r. multicoloured | 50 | 60 |

1996 (8 Sept). International Literacy Day. W **98**. P 13.

| 1009 | **508** | 2r. multicoloured | 40 | 30 |
| | | w. Wmk inverted | 3·75 | |

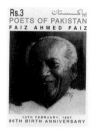

509 Yarrow   **510** Faiz Ahmed Faiz

(Des F. Amir)

1996 (25 Nov). Medicinal Plants (4th series). W **98** (sideways). P 13.

| 1010 | **509** | 3r. multicoloured | 1·75 | 1·00 |

(Des S. Akhtar)

1997 (12 Feb). 86th Birth Anniv of Faiz Ahmed Faiz (poet). P 13.

| 1011 | **510** | 3r. multicoloured | 60 | 60 |

511 Golden Jubilee and OIC Emblems   **512** Amir Timur

1997 (23 Mar). Special Summit Conference of Organization of Islamic Countries commemorating 50th anniv of Pakistan. P 13.

| 1012 | **511** | 2r. multicoloured | 35 | 35 |

1997 (8 Apr). 660th Birth Anniv of Timur (founder of Timurid Empire). P 13.

| 1013 | **512** | 3r. multicoloured | 60 | 60 |

513 Jalal-al-din Moulana Rumi   **514** Apple

(Des J. Siddiqui)

1997 (21 Apr). Pakistan–Iran Joint Issue. T **513** and similar vert design. P 13½.

1014	3r. Type **513**		60	65
1015	3r. Allama Mohammad Iqbal (poet)		50	65

(Des A. Salahuddin)

1997 (8 May). Fruit. P 13.

1016	**514**	2r. multicoloured	35	35

515 People on Globe

516 Stylised Dove of Peace

(Des M-ur Rehman)

1997 (11 July). World Population Day. P 13.

1017	**515**	2r. multicoloured	35	35

(Des Nargis Munir)

1997 (29 July). 40th Anniv of Co-operation between International Atomic Energy Agency and Pakistan Atomic Energy Corporation. P 14.

1018	**516**	2r. multicoloured	70	35

(Des S. Akhtar)

1997 (14 Aug). Pioneers of Freedom (10th series). Vert designs as T **428**. Each deep brown and myrtle-green. P 13.

1019	1r. Mohammad Ayub Khuhro		75	75
1020	1r. Begum Salma Tassaduq Hussain		75	75

517 Mohammed Ali Jinnah

518 College Building

(Des Nargis Munir)

1997 (14 Aug). 50th Anniv of Independence. T **517** and similar vert designs. Multicoloured. P 13.

1021	3r. Type **517**		60	70
	a. Block of four. Nos. 1021/4 with two labels		2·25	2·50
1022	3r. Allama Mohammad Iqbal		60	70
1023	3r. Mohtarma Fatima Jinnah		60	70
1024	3r. Liaquat Ali Khan		60	70
1021/4	Set of 4		2·25	2·50

Nos. 1021/4 were printed together, *se-tenant*, in sheets of 48 stamps and 24 stamp-size labels. The labels, which show either the Pakistan flag or the anniversary logo, alternate in vertical rows 2, 5, 8 and 11. Nos. 1021 and 1023 alternate in vertical rows 1, 4, 7 and 10 with Nos. 1022 and 1024 in vertical rows 3, 6, 9 and 12.

1997 (23 Sept). 75th Anniv of Lahore College for Women. P 13.

1025	**518**	3r. multicoloured	1·50	1·00

519 Garlic

(Des A. Siddique)

1997 (22 Oct). Medicinal Plants (5th series). P 13.

1026	**519**	2r. multicoloured	1·50	65

520 Himalayan Monal Pheasant

521 Globe and Cracked Ozone Layer

(Des A. Salahuddin)

1997 (29 Oct). Wildlife Protection (18th series). P 13.

1027	**520**	2r. multicoloured	2·50	1·25

(Des Nargis Munir)

1997 (15 Nov). Save Ozone Layer Campaign. P 13.

1028	**521**	3r. multicoloured	1·75	1·25

522 Map of Pakistan Motorway Project

(Des A. Salahuddin)

1997 (26 Nov). Pakistan Motorway Project. P 13½.

1029	**522**	10r. multicoloured	2·25	2·50
MS1030	117×97 mm. No. 1029 (*sold at 15r.*)		2·75	3·00

523 Emblem and Disabled People

(Des Nargis Munir)

1997 (3 Dec). International Day for the Disabled. P 13.

1031	**523**	4r. multicoloured	1·50	1·00

524 Karachi Grammar School

525 Mirza Ghalib

(Des F. Amir)

1997 (30 Dec). 150th Anniv of Karachi Grammar School. P 13½.

1032	**524**	2r. multicoloured	1·50	70

(Des F. Siddiqui)

1998 (15 Feb). Birth Bicentenary (1997) of Mirza Ghalib (poet). W **98**. P 13.

1033	**525**	2r. multicoloured	60	30

No. 1033 is inscribed "DEATH ANNIVERSARY".

526 Servicemen, Pakistan Flag and "50"

1998 (23 Mar). 50th Anniv (1997) of Armed Forces. W **98**. P 13½.
1034　**526**　7r. multicoloured .... 1·25　1·25

527 Sir Syed Ahmed Khan

(Des A. Salahuddin)

1998 (27 Mar). Death Centenary of Sir Syed Ahmed Khan (social reformer). W **98**. P 14.
1035　**527**　7r. chocolate, emerald and yellow-
　　　　　ochre .... 1·00　1·25

528 Olympic Torch and Sports

529 Thornapple

(Des A. Salahuddin)

1998 (22 Apr). 27th National Games, Peshawar. W **98**. P 13.
1036　**528**　7r. multicoloured .... 1·00　1·10
　　　　　w. Wmk inverted...

(Des S. Afsar)

1998 (27 Apr). Medicinal Plants (6th series). W **98**. P 13.
1037　**529**　2r. multicoloured .... 1·50　55
　　　　　a. Wmk inverted...

530 Silver Jubilee Emblem

531 Mohammed Ali Jinnah

(Des A. Salahuddin)

1998 (6 Aug). 25th Anniv of Senate. W **98** (sideways). P 13½.
1038　**530**　2r. multicoloured .... 30　15
1039　　　　5r. multicoloured .... 70　85

(Des A. Salahuddin. Eng A. Munir. Recess and litho)

1998 (14 Aug)–**2010**. W **98** (sideways*). P 14.
1039a　**531**　1r. bright carmine and black
　　　　　(20.7.01).. 20　10
　　　　　aa. Wmk tips of crescent pointing
　　　　　　upwards to the right............................ 20　10
1039b　　　　1r. vermilion and black (wmk tips of
　　　　　crescent pointing upwards to the
　　　　　right).. 20
1040　　　　2r. dull ultramarine and carmine.......... 30　10
　　　　　w. Wmk tips of crescent pointing
　　　　　　downwards to the left...................... 2·50
　　　　　y. Wmk tips of crescent pointing
　　　　　　downwards to the right.................... 3·00
1041　　　　3r. deep grey-green and red-brown ... 40　10
　　　　　a. Wmk tips of crescent pointing
　　　　　　upwards to the right........................ 2·50
1042　　　　4r. blackish purple and orange............ 50　10
　　　　　w. Wmk tips of crescent pointing
　　　　　　upwards to the left.......................... 3·00
1043　　　　5r. deep brown and deep green.......... 50　10
　　　　　a. Wmk tips of crescent pointing
　　　　　　upwards to the right........................ 3·00
　　　　　w. Wmk tips of crescent pointing
　　　　　　downwards to the left...................... 2·50
　　　　　y. Wmk tips of crescent pointing
　　　　　　downwards to the right.................... 2·50
1044　　　　6r. deep blue-green and light blue...... 55　20
1045　　　　7r. orange-red and bright violet.......... 65　25
　　　　　y. Wmk tips of crescent pointing
　　　　　　downwards to the right.................... 10·00
1045z　　　　8r. black, emerald and dull orange
　　　　　(1.10.10) .... 1·25　1·00
1039a/45z Set of 9.. 4·00　1·75
*The normal sideways watermark shows the tips of the crescent pointing upwards to the left *when the stamp is vertical and viewed from the back.*
Nos. 1039a/aa, 1040w, 1042w and 1043w are printed on white paper, all others are on cream paper.

532 College Building

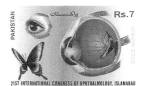

533 "Mohammed Ali Jinnah" (S. Akhtar)

(Des F. Siddiqui)

1998 (14 Aug). Centenary of Government College, Faisalabad. W **98**. P 13.
1046　**532**　5r. multicoloured .... 80　80
　　　　　w. Wmk inverted...

1998 (11 Sept). 50th Death Anniv of Mohammed Ali Jinnah. W **98**. P 13½.
1047　**533**　15r. multicoloured .... 2·25　2·75
MS1048　72×100 mm. **533** 15r. multicoloured. No
wmk *(sold at* 20r.) .... 2·50　3·25

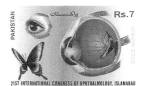

534 Cross-section of Eye

(Des J. Siddiqui)

1998 (12 Sept). 21st International Ophthalmology Congress, Islamabad. W **98** (sideways*). P 13.
1049　**534**　7r. multicoloured...................................... 1·75　1·75
　　　　　w. Wmk tips of crescent pointing
　　　　　　downwards.......................................
*The normal sideways watermark shows the tips of the crescent pointing upwards.

535 United Nations Emblems and Bukhari

(Des A. Salahuddin)

1998 (1 Oct). Birth Centenary of Syed Ahmed Shah Patrus Bukhari. W **98**. P 13.

| 1050 | **535** | 5r. multicoloured | 1·25 | 1·00 |

536 Map, "50 years" and Stamps

537 Mother and Child

(Des J. Siddiqui)

1998 (4 Oct). 50th Anniv of Philately in Pakistan. W **98** (sideways). P 13.

| 1051 | **536** | 6r. multicoloured | 65 | 65 |

(Des Nargis Munir)

1998 (16 Oct). World Food Day. W **98**. P 13.

| 1052 | **537** | 6r. multicoloured | 75 | 75 |

538 Dr. Abdus Salam

539 Satellite Dish Aerial

(Des F. Siddiqui)

1998 (21 Nov). Scientists of Pakistan (1st series). Dr. Abdus Salam. P 13.

| 1053 | **538** | 2r. multicoloured | 50 | 25 |

See also No. 1068.

1998 (27 Nov). "Better Pakistan" Development Plan. T **539** and similar horiz designs. Multicoloured. P 13×14.

1054		2r. Type **539**	55	65
1055		2r. Combine harvester	55	65
1056		2r. Airliner	55	65
1057		2r. Children and doctor	55	65
1054/7 Set of 4			2·00	2·40

540 Globe and Human Rights Emblem

(Des Nargis Munir)

1998 (10 Dec). 50th Anniv of Universal Declaration of Human Rights. W **98**. P 12½×14.

| 1058 | **540** | 6r. multicoloured | 1·25 | 1·25 |

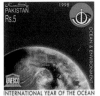

541 Pakistani Woman carrying Water Pot

542 Earth seen from Space

(Des Nargis Munir)

1998 (11 Dec). 50th Anniv of UNICEF in Pakistan. T **541** and similar square designs. Multicoloured. W **98**. P 14.

1059		2r. Type **541**	30	40
		a. Block of four. Nos. 1059/62	1·10	1·40
1060		2r. Woman reading	30	40
1061		2r. Woman with goitre	30	40
1062		2r. Young boy receiving oral vaccine	30	40
1059/62 Set of 4			1·10	1·40

Nos. 1059/62 were printed together, *se-tenant*, in blocks of four with the UNICEF symbol in the centre.

(Des J. Siddiqui)

1998 (15 Dec). International Year of the Ocean. W **98**. P 14.

| 1063 | **542** | 5r. multicoloured | 1·25 | 1·00 |
| | | w. Wmk inverted | | |

543 Marchers and Route Map

(Des F. Afsar)

1998 (16 Dec). Qaumi Parcham March, Khyber to Chaghi. W **98**. P 13.

| 1064 | **543** | 2r. multicoloured | 40 | 25 |

544 Centenary Logo

545 Dr. Salimuzzaman Siddiqui

(Des A. Salahuddin)

1999 (27 Jan). Centenary of Saud Dynasty of Saudi Arabia. T **544** and similar vert design. Multicoloured. P 13½.

1065		2r. Type **544**	30	10
1066		15r. As Type **544**, but with mosaic pattern in corners	1·75	2·00
MS1067 73×100 mm. 15r. No. 1066 (sold at 20r.)			2·50	3·00

(Des M. Siddiqui)

1999 (14 Apr). Scientists of Pakistan (2nd series). Dr. Salimuzzaman Siddiqui. P 13.

| 1068 | **545** | 5r. multicoloured | 60 | 60 |

546 Mountains and Pakistan Flag

(Des A. Salahuddin)

1999 (28 May). "Atoms for Peace". P 13.
1069 **546** 5r. multicoloured 60 60

COMPLETION OF DATA DARBAR
MOSQUE COMPLEX-1999
547 Plan and View of Mosque

548 Fasting Buddha Statue (drapery on left knee)

(Des U. Akhtar)

1999 (31 May). Completion of Data Darbar Mosque Complex, Lahore. P 13.
1070 **547** 7r. multicoloured .... 75 1·00

(Des A. Salahuddin)

1999 (21 July). Archaeological Heritage. T **548** and similar vert designs. Multicoloured. W **98** (sideways). P 13½.
1071 7r. Type **548** 70 85
1072 7r. Fasting Buddha (drapery on right knee) 70 85
MS1073 107×90 mm. Nos. 1071/2. Wmk upright (*sold at* 25r.) .... 2·25 3·00
No. **MS**1073 includes the "China '99" International Stamp Exhibition, Beijing, logo on the margin.

549 Red Cross International Committee Emblem and "50"

(Des A. Salahuddin)

1999 (12 Aug). 50th Anniv of Geneva Conventions. P 13×14.
1074 **549** 5r. orange-red and black 60 50

(Des S. Akhtar)

1999 (14 Aug). Pioneers of Freedom (11th series). Vert designs as T **428**. Each sepia and deep dull green. P 13.
1075 2r. Maulana Abdul Hamid Badayuni 45 50
1076 2r. Chaudhry Muhammad Ali 45 50
1077 2r. Sir Adamjee Haji Dawood 45 50
1075/7 *Set of 3* .... 1·25 1·40

550 Ustad Nusrat Fateh Ali Khan

SILVER JUBILEE CELEBRATIONS OF
ISLAMIC DEVELOPMENT BANK
551 Islamic Development Bank Building

(Des J. Siddiqui)

1999 (16 Aug). Ustad Nusrat Fateh Ali Khan (musician) Commemoration. P 13.
1078 **550** 2r. multicoloured .... 1·25 60

(Des A. Siddique)

1999 (18 Sept). 25th Anniv of Islamic Development Bank. W **98**. P 13.
1079 **551** 5r. multicoloured .... 1·00 1·00

552 Crowd celebrating

553 "Enterprise" Sailing Dinghy

(Des F. Amir (2r.), A. Siddique (15r.))

1999 (21 Sept). 50th Anniv of People's Republic of China. T **552** and similar multicoloured design. W **98**. P 13.
1080 2r. Type **552** 20 20
1081 15r. Bust of Mao Tse-tung (Chinese leader) and emblem (*horiz*) .... 1·25 1·75

(Des A. Salahuddin)

1999 (28 Sept). Ninth Asian Sailing Championship. Sailing Craft. T **553** and similar vert designs. Multicoloured. P 13½.
1082 2r. Type **553** 50 50
 a. Strip of five. Nos. 1082/6 .... 2·25 2·25
1083 2r. "470" dinghy 50 50
1084 2r. "Optimist" dinghy 50 50
1085 2r. "Laser" dinghy 50 50
1086 2r. "Mistral" sail board 50 50
 a. "1999" omitted at right .... 25·00
1082/6 *Set of 5* .... 2·25 2·25
Nos. 1082/6 were printed together, *se-tenant*, as horizontal or vertical strips of five.

554 "Optimist" Sailing Dinghies

(Des. A. Salahuddin)

1999 (7 Oct). Tenth Asian "Optimist" Sailing Championship. P 13½.
1087 **554** 2r. multicoloured 60 40
No. 1087 was printed *se-tenant* with a half stamp-size label showing the Championship emblem.

1874-1999
UNIVERSAL POSTAL UNION
555 UPU Emblem

(Des. F. Amir)

1999 (9 Oct). 125th Anniv of Universal Postal Union. W **98**. P 14.
1088 **555** 10r. multicoloured .... 1·00 1·50
 w. Wmk inverted .... 3·75

556 Hakim Mohammed Said

557 National Bank of Pakistan Building

(Des. F. Amir)

1999 (17 Oct). First Death Anniv of Hakim Mohammed Said. P 13.
1089 **556** 5r. multicoloured 60 60

1999 (8 Nov). 50th Anniv of National Bank of Pakistan. W **98**.
P 13½×14.
1090 **557** 5r. multicoloured .... 1·25 70

558 Evolution of the "Shell" Emblem

559 Profiles of Children in "10"

(Des A. Salahuddin)

1999 (15 Nov). Centenary of Shell in Pakistan. W **98**. P 13.
1091 **558** 4r. multicoloured .... 1·25 75

1999 (20 Nov). Tenth Anniv of United Nations Rights of the Child Convention. P 13×13½.
1092 **559** 2r. emerald, bright green and rosine.. 30 30

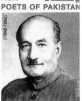

560 Science Equipment, Books and Computer

561 Josh Malihabadi

(Des N. Jawed (2r.), F. Amir (5r.))

1999 (20 Nov). 25th Anniv of Allama Iqbal Open University. T **560** and similar horiz designs. Multicoloured. P 13.
1093 2r. Type **560** 20 15
1094 3r. Scholastic symbols as Type **560** 30 30
1095 5r. Map of Pakistan .... 1·25 90
1093/5 Set of 3 .... 1·60 1·25

(Des. A. Uddin)

1999 (5 Dec). Birth Centenary of Josh Malihabadi (poet). P 13.
1096 **561** 5r. multicoloured 60 60

562 Dr. Afzal Qadri and Locusts

(Des M. Siddiqui)

1999 (6 Dec). 25th Death Anniv of Dr. Afzal Qadri (entomologist). P 13.
1097 **562** 3r. multicoloured 60 40

563 Ghulam Bari Aleeg

564 Plantain

(Des M. Rehman)

1999 (6 Dec). 50th Death Anniv of Ghulam Bari Aleeg (writer). P 13.
1098 **563** 5r. multicoloured .... 1·00 65

(Des G. Khaskheli)

1999 (20 Dec). Medicinal Plants (7th series). P 13.
1099 **564** 5r. multicoloured .... 1·75 1·00

565 Mosque

(Des A. Salahuddin)

1999 (24 Dec). Eid-ul-Fitr Greetings. P 13½.
1100 **565** 2r. multicoloured 40 25
1101 15r. multicoloured .... 2·50 3·25

566 Woman and Young Boy

2000 (12 Mar). 25th Anniv of SOS Children's Villages in Pakistan. P 13.
1102 **566** 2r. multicoloured 65 30

567 Racing Cyclists

(Des A. Salahuddin)

2000 (14 Apr). Centenary of International Cycling Union. P 13½.
1103 **567** 2r. multicoloured .... 2·00 1·00

568 Doves

2000 (21 Apr). Pakistan Convention on Human Rights and Human Dignity. P 13½.
1104 **568** 2r. multicoloured 60 30

569 College Building

2000 (24 Apr). Centenary of Edwardes College, Peshawar. P 13.
1105 **569** 2r. multicoloured 60 30

571 Mahomed Ali Habib

2000 (15 May). Mahomed Ali Habib (founder of Habib Bank Ltd) Commemoration. P 13.
1106   **570**   2r. multicoloured   60   30

571 Emblems and Symbols

2000 (23 June). 50th Anniv of Institute of Cost and Management Accountants. T **571** and similar horiz design. Multicoloured. P 13.
1107   2r. Type **571**   30   20
1108   15r. Emblems, graph, keyboard and globe ..   2·00   2·75

572 Ahmed Jaffer   573 "Sarfaroshaane Tehreeke Pakistan" (detail)

2000 (9 Aug). Tenth Death Anniv of Ahmed Jaffer (prominent businessman). P 13.
1109   **572**   10r. multicoloured ....   1·25   1·25

2000 (14 Aug). "Sarfaroshaane Tehreeke Pakistan" (painting). T **573** and similar vert designs showing different details. Multicoloured. P 13.
1110   Type **573**   50   60
         a. Horiz strip of four. Nos. 1110/13 ....   1·75   2·25
1111   5r. Bullock carts with tree in foreground....   50   60
1112   5r. Bullock carts and crowd carrying
         Pakistan flag   50   60
1113   5r. Unloading bullock cart   50   60
1110/13 Set of 4 ....   1·75   2·25
   Nos. 1110/13 were printed together, se-tenant, in horizontal strips of four throughout the sheets.

574 Captain Muhammad Sarwar

2000 (6 Sept). Defence Day. T **574** and similar horiz design showing winners of Nishan-e-Haider medal. Multicoloured. P 13.
1114   5r. Type **574** ....   1·00   1·25
         a. Horiz pair. Nos. 1114/15 ....   2·00   2·50
1115   5r. Major Tufail Muhammad ....   1·00   1·25
   Nos. 1114/15 were printed together, se-tenant, as horizontal pairs throughout the sheets.

575 Athletics   576 Emblem and Building

2000 (20 Sept). Olympic Games, Sydney. T **575** and similar square designs. Multicoloured. P 14.
1116   4r. Type **575**   70   70
         a. Block of four. Nos. 1116/19 ....   2·50   2·50
1117   4r. Hockey   70   70
1118   4r. Weightlifting   70   70
1119   4r. Cycling   70   70
1116/19 Set of 4 ....   2·50   2·50
   Nos. 1116/19 were printed together, se-tenant, as blocks of four throughout the sheets.

2000 (28 Oct). 125th Anniv of National College of Arts, Lahore. P 14.
1120   **576**   5r. multicoloured   55   65
   No. 1120 was printed in sheets containing two panes of 25 separated by a vertical gutter margin showing various symbols connected to the College.

577 Conference Emblem   578 Exhibition Emblem

2000 (4 Nov). "Creating the Future" Business Conference. P 13½.
1121   **577**   5r. multicoloured ....   1·00   75

2000 (14 Nov). "Ideas 2000" International Defence Exhibition and Seminar. P 13.
1122   **578**   7r. multicoloured ....   1·25   1·25

579 Liquorice   580 Crippled Child and Rotary Emblem

2000 (28 Nov). Medicinal Plants (8th series). P 13.
1123   **579**   2r. multicoloured ....   1·75   55

2000 (13 Dec). "A World Without Polio" Campaign. P 13.
1124   **580**   2r. multicoloured   70   30

581 Refugee Family and Emblems   582 Hafeez Jalandhri

2000 (14 Dec). 50th Anniv of United Nations High Commissioner for Refugees. P 13.

1125	**581**	2r. multicoloured	35	30

2001 (14 Jan). Birth Centenary of Hafeez Jalandhri (poet). P 13.

1126	**582**	2r. multicoloured	1·00	40

583 Habib Bank AG Zurich Head Office

2001 (20 Mar). Habib Bank AG Zurich Commemoration. P 13.

1127	**583**	5r. multicoloured	1·75	1·50

584 Chashma Nuclear Power Station

2001 (29 Mar). Opening of Chashma Nuclear Power Station. P 13.

1128	**584**	4r. multicoloured	1·25	1·00

585 SAF Games Emblem

2001 (9 Apr). Ninth SAF Games, Islamabad. P 13½.

1129	**585**	4r. multicoloured (light blue background)	75	80
1130		4r. multicoloured (pink background)	75	80

586 "Ma Gu's Birthday Offering"

587 Mohammad Ali Jinnah

2001 (12 May). 50th Anniv of Pakistan–China Friendship. T **586** and similar vert designs. P 13.

1131		4r. Type **586**	70	80
		a. Horiz pair. Nos. 1131/2	1·40	1·60
1132		4r. "Two Pakistani Women drawing Water"	70	80
1133		4r. Girls in traditional Yugur and Hunza costumes	70	80
1131/3	*Set of 3*		1·90	2·25

Nos. 1131/2 were printed together, *se-tenant*, as horizontal pairs within the sheets.
No. 1131 is inscribed "BIRTTHDAY" in error.

2001 (14 Aug). 125th Birth Anniv of Mohammad Ali Jinnah ("Quaid-e-Azam"). P 13.

1134	**587**	4r. multicoloured	75	1·00

2001 (6 Sept). Defence Day. Horiz designs as T **574** showing winners of Nishan-e-Haider medal. Multicoloured. P 13.

1135		4r. Major Shabbir Sharif Shaheed	90	1·00
		a. Pair. Nos. 1135/6	1·75	2·00
1136		4r. Major Mohammad Akram Shaheed	90	1·00

Nos. 1135/6 were printed together, *se-tenant*, both horizontally and vertically throughout the sheets.

588 Goat Emblem and Traditional Architecture

2001 (22 Sept). Sindh Festival, Karachi. P 13.

1137	**588**	4r. yellow, black and yellowish green.	60	60

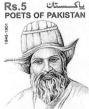 

589 Khawaja Ghulam Farid

590 "Children encircling Globe" (Urska Golob)

2001 (25 Sept). Death Centenary of Khawaja Ghulam Farid (poet). P 13.

1138	**589**	5r. multicoloured	75	60

2001 (9 Oct). UN Year of Dialogue among Civilisations. W **98** (sideways). P 13½.

1139	**590**	4r. multicoloured	50	50

591 Syed Imitaz Ali Taj

592 Pres. Saparmurat Niyazov of Turkmenistan

2001 (13 Oct). Syed Imitaz Ali Taj (writer). Commemoration. P 13.

1140	**591**	5r. multicoloured	75	60

2001 (27 Oct). Tenth Anniv of Turkmenistan Independence. P 13.

1141	**592**	5r. multicoloured	75	60

593 Peppermint

2001 (12 Nov). Medicinal Plants (9th series). W **98** (sideways). P 13.

1142	**593**	4r. multicoloured	2·25	1·25
		w. Wmk tips of crescent pointing downwards	5·00	

594 Convent of Jesus and Mary, Lahore

2001 (15 Nov). 125th Anniv of Convent of Jesus and Mary, Lahore. W **98**. P 13.
1143   **594**   4r. multicoloured...................................... 1·25   1·00

595 Dr. Ishtiaq Husain Qureshi

596 Blue Throat

2001 (20 Nov). 20th Death Anniv of Dr. Ishtiaq Husain Qureshi (historian). P 13.
1144   **595**   4r. multicoloured...................................... 60   50

2001 (26 Nov). Birds. T **596** and similar square designs. Multicoloured. P 13.
1145		4r. Type **596**	1·60	1·60
		a. Block of four. Nos. 1145/8	5·75	5·75
1146		4r. Hoopoe	1·60	1·60
1147		4r. Pin-tailed Sandgrouse	1·60	1·60
1148		4r. Magpie Robin	1·60	1·60
1145/8 Set of 4			5·75	5·75

Nos. 1145/8 were printed together, se-tenant, in blocks of four, throughout the sheets.

597 Handshake beneath Flags of UAE and Pakistan

598 Nishtar Medical College, Multan

2001 (2 Dec). 30th Anniv of Diplomatic Relations between Pakistan and United Arab Emirates. T **597** and similar multicoloured design. P 13.
1149   5r. Type **597** 50   25
1150   30r. Pres. Sheikh Zayed bin Sultan Al Nahyan of UAE and Mohammed Ali Jinnah (horiz)........ 3·25   4·25

2001 (20 Dec). 50th Anniv of Nishtar Medical College, Multan. P 13.
1151   **598**   5r. multicoloured...................................... 1·00   55

599 Mohammad Ali Jinnah taking Oath as Governor General, 1947

600 Troops and Ordnance

2001 (25 Dec). 125th Birth Anniv of Mohammad Ali Jinnah ("Quaid-e-Azam") (2nd issue). T **599** and similar multicoloured designs. P 13.
1152   4r. Type **599** 30   35
| | |a. Horiz strip of three. Nos. 1152/4|80|95|
1153   4r. Opening State Bank, Karachi, 1948........ 30   35

1154   4r. Taking salute, Peshawar, 1948............ 30   35
1155   4r. Inspecting guard of honour, 1948 (55×27 mm)............ 30   35
| | |a. Horiz pair. Nos. 1155/6|60|70|
1156   4r. With anti-aircraft gun crew, 1948 (55×27 mm)............ 30   35
1152/6 Set of 5 .... 1·40   1·60

Nos. 1152/4 and 1155/6 were each printed together, se-tenant, in horizontal strips of three or pairs throughout the sheets.

2001 (28 Dec). 50th Anniv of Pakistan Ordnance Factories. P 13½.
1157   **600**   4r. multicoloured...................................... 1·25   70

601 Samandar Khan Samandar

602 Hyssop

2002 (17 Jan). Samandar Khan Samandar (poet) Commemoration. P 13.
1158   **601**   5r. multicoloured...................................... 60   60

2002 (15 Feb). Medicinal Plants (10th series). P 13.
1159   **602**   5r. multicoloured...................................... 2·00   1·25

603 Statues of Buddha

604 Pakistan and Kyrgyzstan Flags

2002 (28 Apr). 50th Anniv of Diplomatic Relations between Pakistan and Japan. P 14.
1160   **603**   5r. multicoloured...................................... 50   50

2002 (27 May). Tenth Anniv of Diplomatic Relations between Pakistan and Kyrgyzstan. P 14×12½.
1161   **604**   5r. multicoloured...................................... 50   50

605 Anwar Ratol Mangoes

606 Noor us Sabah Begum

2002 (18 June). Fruits of Pakistan. Mangoes. T **605** and similar vert designs. Multicoloured. P 14.
1162   4r. Type **605** 65   75
| | |a. Block of four. Nos. 1162/5|2·40|2·75|
1163   4r. Dushehri mangoes.......... 65   75
1164   4r. Chaunsa mangoes.......... 65   75
1165   4r. Sindhri mango.......... 65   75
1162/5 Set of 4 .... 2·40   2·75

Nos. 1162/5 were printed together, se-tenant, as blocks of four throughout the sheets of 64 (8×8).

2002 (14 Aug). 55th Independence Day Celebrations. Famous People. T **606** and similar vert designs. Multicoloured. P 13.
1166   4r. Type **606** 60   75
1167   4r. Ismail Chundrigar.......... 60   75
1168   4r. Habib Ibrahim Rahimtoola.......... 60   75
1169   4r. Qazi Mureed Ahmed.......... 60   75
1166/9 Set of 4 .... 2·25   2·75

607 Children with
Animals and Pakistan
Flag

2002 (26 Aug). World Summit on Sustainable Development, Johannesburg. T **607** and similar multicoloured designs. P 13 (No. 1170) or 14 (No. 1171).

1170		4r. Type **607**	50	50
1171		4r. Hindu Kush range and cartoon character ("Watershed protection") (37×37 mm)	50	50

608 Mohammad Aly Rangoonwala

609 Muhammad Iqbal in Academic Gown

2002 (31 Aug). Mohammad Aly Rangoonwala (businessman and philanthropist) Commemoration. P 13.

1172	**608**	4r. multicoloured	60	50

2002 (6 Sept). Defence Day. Horiz designs as T **574** showing winners of Nishan-e-Haider medal. Multicoloured. P 13.

1173		4r. Lance Naik Muhammad Mahfuz Shaheed	80	90
		a. Horiz pair. Nos. 1173/3b	1·60	1·75
1173b		4r. Sawar Muhammad Hussain Shaheed	80	90

Nos. 1173/3b were printed together, *se-tenant*, as horizontal pairs throughout the sheets.

2002 (9 Nov). 125th Birth Anniv of Muhammad Iqbal (writer). T **609** and similar vert design. Multicoloured. P 13.

1174		4r. Type **609**	70	90
		a. Horiz pair. Nos. 1174/5	1·40	1·75
1175		4r. Muhammad Iqbal in library	70	90

Nos. 1174/5 were printed together, *se-tenant*, as horizontal pairs throughout the sheet.

610 "Eid Mubarak"

611 Hakim Muhammad Hassan Qarshi and Plants

2002 (14 Nov). Eid-ul-Fitr Festival. W **98** (sideways). P 14.

1176	**610**	4r. multicoloured	50	50

2002 (20 Dec). Hakim Muhammad Hassan Qarshi (pioneer of Tibb homeopathic medicine) Commemoration. P 13½.

1177	**611**	4r. multicoloured	1·25	65

612 Red-legged Partridge, Markhor and White Flowers

2003 (31 Jan). National Philatelic Exhibition, Karachi. W **98**. P 13.

(Des M. ur-Rehman)

1178	**612**	4r. multicoloured	1·50	1·40
		w. Wmk inverted	15·00	

No. 1178 was printed in sheets of 16 containing two vertical rows of eight stamps alternated with two vertical rows of stamp-size labels inscribed with exhibition logo.

613 Anniversary Emblem

614 Minaret Emblem

2003 (15 Feb). 50th Anniv of Pakistan Academy of Sciences. P 14.

1179	**613**	4r. multicoloured	70	70

(Des M. ur-Rehman)

2003 (23 Mar). Centenary Celebrations of North West Frontier Province. W **98** (sideways). P 13½.

1180	**614**	4r. multicoloured	60	60
		w. Wmk tips of crescent pointing downwards		

615 Golden Jubilee Emblem

616 Prof A.B.A. Haleem

(Des M. ur-Rehman)

2003 (31 Mar). 50th Anniv of Pakistan Council of Scientific and Industrial Research, Islamabad. W **98**. P 14.

1181	**615**	4r. yellow-brown, myrtle-green and greenish yellow	60	60
		w. Wmk inverted		

(Des M. ur-Rehman)

2003 (20 Apr). Prof. A.B.A. Haleem (1st Vice Chancellor of Karachi University) Commemoration. W **98** (sideways). P 13½.

1182	**616**	2r. multicoloured	55	35

617 Flowers and Anti Narcotics Force Badge

2003 (21 Apr). "Say No to Drugs". W **98**. P 13.

1183	**617**	2r. multicoloured	1·50	65

618 Sir Syed Memorial, Islamabad

(Des F. Ameer. Litho Pakistan Security Printing Corporation, Karachi)

2003 (30 Apr). Sir Syed Memorial, Islamabad. W **98** (sideways). P 13½.

1184	**618**	2r. multicoloured	45	30

PROCESS. All the following issues were lithographed by the Post Office Foundation Press, Karachi, unless otherwise stated.

619 Rosa damascena   **620** Fatima Jinnah

2003 (14 July). Medicinal Plants (11th series). P 13.
1185 **619** 2r. multicoloured .... 1·50 65

(Des A. Salahuddin)

2003 (31 July). 110th Birth Anniv of Fatima Jinnah (politician and campaigner for women's rights). P 13.
1186 **620** 4r. multicoloured 55 45

621 Abdul Rahman (PO employee killed in raid, 2002)

(Des M. Hanif)

2003 (3 Aug). Commemorations. T **621** and similar horiz design. Multicoloured. P 13.
1187 2r. Type **621** 45 45
1188 2r. M.A. Rahim (trade union leader and philanthropist) 45 45

622 Moulana Abdul Sattar Khan Niazi (politician, 88th)   **623** Emblem

(Des A. Salahuddin)

2003 (14 Aug). Birth Anniversaries. T **622** and similar vert designs. Multicoloured. P 13.
1189 2r. Type **622** 50 60
1190 2r. Muhammad Yousaf Khattak (politician, 86th) 50 60
1191 2r. Moulana Muhammad Ismail Zabeeh (politician, centenary) 50 60
1189/91 Set of 3 .... 1·40 1·60

(Des A. Salahuddin)

2003 (6 Sept). United Nations Literacy Decade. P 13.
1192 **623** 1r. multicoloured 30 20

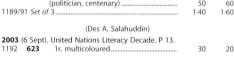

624 Pilot Officer Rashid Minhas and Nishan-e-Haider Medal   **625** Pakistan Academy of Letters, Islamabad

(Des A. Zafar)

2003 (7 Sept). 32nd Death Anniv of Pilot Officer Rashid Minhas. P 14.
1193 **624** 2r. multicoloured .... 1·75 65

(Des M. Hanif)

2003 (24 Sept). 25th Anniv of Pakistan Academy of Letters (2001). P 13.
1194 **625** 2r. multicoloured 50 25

626 Karakoram Highway   **627** Nanga Parbat

(Des A. Salahuddin)

2003 (1 Oct). 25th Anniv of Karakoram Highway. P 12½×13.
1195 **626** 2r. multicoloured .... 1·50 60

(Des A. Salahuddin)

2003 (6 Oct). 50th Anniv of First Ascent of Nanga Parbat Mountain. P 13.
1196 **627** 2r. multicoloured .... 1·25 65

628 PAF Public School, Sargodha   **629** Leather Coats

(Des F. Ameer. Litho Pakistan Security Printing Corporation, Karachi)

2003 (10 Oct). 50th Anniv of PAF Public School, Sargodha. W **98**. P 13×13½.
1197 **628** 4r. multicoloured .... 1·50 1·00

(Des A. Salahuddin)

2003 (20 Oct). Achievement of ten Billion US Dollar Exports Target, 2002–3. T **629** and similar vert designs. Multicoloured. P 13.
1198 1r. Type **629** 35 40
   a. Sheetlet. Nos. 1198/1217 .... 6·00 7·00
1199 1r. Towels 35 40
1200 1r. Readymade garments 35 40
1201 1r. Cargo ship being loaded by crane, Port Qasim 35 40
1202 1r. Fisheries 35 40
1203 1r. Yarn 35 40
1204 1r. Sports equipment 35 40
1205 1r. Fabrics 35 40
1206 1r. Furniture 35 40
1207 1r. Surgical instruments 35 40
1208 1r. Gems and jewellery 35 40
1209 1r. Leather goods 35 40
1210 1r. Information technology 35 40
1211 1r. Rice 35 40
1212 1r. Auto parts 35 40
1213 1r. Carpets 35 40
1214 1r. Marble and granite 35 40
1215 1r. Fruits 35 40
1216 1r. Cutlery 35 40
1217 1r. Engineering goods 35 40
1198/1217 Set of 20 .... 6·00 7·00
Nos. 1198/1217 were printed together, se-tenant, in sheetlets of 20.

INTERNATIONAL DAY FOR DISABLED
630 Boy in Wheelchair with Boy and Girl

2003 (3 Dec). International Day for Disabled. P 13.
1218 **630** 2r. multicoloured .... 1·25 65

631 Globe   **632** Khalid Class Submarine (Agosta 90B)

(Des A. Salahuddin)

2003 (10 Dec). World Summit on the Information Society, Geneva (Switzerland) and Tunis (Tunisia). P 13×12½.
1219 **631** 2r. multicoloured.................................. 75 40

2003 (12 Dec). Submarine Construction in Pakistan. T **632** and similar multicoloured design. P 13.
1220 1r. Type **632** .... 1·00 40
1221 2r. Khalid Class submarine (Agosta 90B) and Pakistan flag (horiz) .... 1·75 1·00

633 Pakistan Air Force Plane, Siachen, 1988–90

634 Emblem

(Des Capt. S.M.A. Hussaini (No. 1222) or S. Ali (No. 1223))

2003 (17 Dec). Centenary of Powered Flight. Pakistan Air Force. T **633** and similar horiz design. Multicoloured. P 13.
1222 2r. Type **633** .... 1·00 1·00
1223 2r. Old and modern Pakistan Air Force planes.. 1·00 1·00

2004 (4 Jan). 12th Summit Meeting of South Asian Association for Regional Cooperation, Islamabad. P 13.
1224 **634** 4r. multicoloured.................................. 50 50

635 Sadiq Public School, Bahawalpur

(Des A. Salahuddin)

2004 (28 Jan). 50th Anniv of Sadiq Public School, Bahawalpur. P 14.
1225 **635** 4r. multicoloured.................................. 60 50

636 South Asian Federation Games Medal

637 Justice Pir Muhammad Karam Shah Al-Azhari

(Des A. Salahuddin)

2004 (29 Mar). Ninth South Asian Federation (SAF) Games, Islamabad. T **636** and similar vert designs. Multicoloured. P 13.
1226 2r. Type **636** 35 40
a. Sheetlet. Nos. 1226/41................ 5·00 5·75
1227 2r. Sprinting.. 35 40
1228 2r. Squash.. 35 40
1229 2r. Boxing... 35 40
1230 2r. Wrestling 35 40
1231 2r. Judo.. 35 40
1232 2r. Javelin throwing.............................. 35 40
1233 2r. Football... 35 40
1234 2r. Rowing.. 35 40
1235 2r. Shooting.. 35 40
1236 2r. Shot-putting..................................... 35 40
1237 2r. Badminton....................................... 35 40
1238 2r. Weight lifting.................................... 35 40
1239 2r. Volleyball... 35 40
1240 2r. Table tennis..................................... 35 40
1241 2r. Swimming.. 35 40
1226/41 Set of 16... 5·00 5·75
Nos. 1226/41 were printed together, se-tenant, in sheetlets of 16.

(Des A. Salahuddin)

2004 (7 Apr). Justice Pir Muhammad Karam Shah Al-Azhari Commemoration. P 13.
1242 **637** 2r. multicoloured.................................. 50 25

638 Cadet College, Hasanabdal

(Des A. Salahuddin)

2004 (8 Apr). 50th Anniv of Cadet College, Hasanabdal. P 13.
1243 **638** 4r. multicoloured.................................. 50 50

639 Central Library, Bahawalpur

640 Bhong Mosque, Rahim Yar Khan

(Des A. Salahuddin)

2004 (26 Apr). 80th Anniv of Central Library, Bahawalpur. P 13.
1244 **639** 2r. multicoloured.................................. 40 25

(Des A. Salahuddin)

2004 (12 May). Bhong Mosque. P 13.
1245 **640** 4r. multicoloured.................................. 70 60

641 Footballer and FIFA Emblem

(Des A. Salahuddin)

2004 (21 May). Centenary of FIFA (Fédération Internationale de Football Association). T **641** and similar horiz designs. Multicoloured. P 14.
1246 5r. Type **641** 75 75
a. Horiz strip of three. Nos 1246/8.............. 2·00 2·00
1247 5r. FIFA emblem.................................... 75 75
1248 5r. As No. 1246 with stadium background extended behind FIFA emblem................ 75 75
1246/8 Set of 3... 2·00 2·00
Nos. 1246/8 were printed together, se-tenant, in horizontal strips of three throughout sheets of 24.

642 Silk Road alongside Indus River

643 Juniper Forest and Emblems

(Des A. Salahuddin)

2004 (7 June). Silk Road. T **642** and similar multicoloured design. P 13.
1249 4r. Type **642** 75 75
1250 4r. Silk Road and Haramosh Peak (vert)....... 75 75

2004 (24 July). 50th Anniv of Sui Southern Gas Company. Protecting National Heritage. P 13.
1251 **643** 4r. multicoloured.................................. 75 55

644 K2   **645** Running

(Des A. Salahuddin)

2004 (31 July). 50th Anniv of First Ascent of K2. T **644** and similar vert designs. Multicoloured. P 13.
1252	5r. Type **644**			70	60
MS1253 96×64 mm. 30r. Views of K2. Imperf				2·75	3·75

(Des A. Salahuddin)

2004 (13 Aug). Olympic Games, Athens. T **645** and similar vert designs. Multicoloured. P 13.
1254	5r. Type **645**	65	75
	a. Horiz strip of four. Nos. 1254/7	2·40	2·75
1255	5r. Boxing	65	75
1256	5r. Hockey	65	75
1257	5r. Wrestling	65	75
1254/7 Set of 4		2·40	2·75

Nos. 1254/7 were each printed together, se-tenant, as horizontal strips of four in sheets of 20.

646 Muhammad Ali Jinnah   **647**

648   **649**

(Des A. Salahuddin)

2004 (14 Aug). 57th Anniv of Independence. P 13.
1258	**646**	5r. multicoloured	45	50
		a. Horiz strip of four. Nos. 1258/61	1·60	1·75
1259	**647**	5r. multicoloured	45	50
1260	**648**	5r. multicoloured	45	50
1261	**649**	5r. multicoloured	45	50
1258/61 Set of 4			1·60	1·75

Nos. 1258/61 were each printed together, se-tenant, as horizontal strips of four stamps in sheets of 20.
Nos. 1258/61 each show Muhammad Ali Jinnah beside Urdu text, which differs on each stamp.

650 Maulvi Abdul Haq   **651** Calligraphic Dove with Olive Branch and Emblem

(Des M. Hanif)

2004 (16 Aug). Maulvi Abdul Haq (scholar) Commemoration. P 13.
1262	**650**	4r. multicoloured	50	40

(Des S. Ali)

2004 (1 Oct). Fourth International Calligraphy and Calligraph-Art Exhibition and Competition. P 13.
1263	**651**	5r. multicoloured	50	40

652 Striped Gourami   **653** Training for Handicapped

(Des A. Salahuddin)

2004 (9 Oct). Fish. T **652** and similar horiz designs. Multicoloured. P 12½×13.
1264	2r. Type **652**	55	60
	a. Horiz strip of five. Nos. 1264/8	2·50	2·75
1265	2r. Black Widow	55	60
1266	2r. Yellow Dwarf Cichlid	55	60
1267	2r. Tiger Barb	55	60
1268	2r. Neon Tetra	55	60
1264/8 Set of 5		2·50	2·75

Nos. 1264/8 were printed, se-tenant, in horizontal rows of five within sheets of 25.

(Des A. Salahuddin)

2004 (8 Nov). 50th Anniv of Japan's International Co-Operation and Assistance. T **653** and similar horiz designs. Multicoloured. Fluorescent security marking on No. **MS**1273. P 13.
1269	5r. Type **653**	75	85
1270	5r. Polio eradication	75	85
1271	5r. Ghazi Barotha hydropower	75	85
1272	5r. Friendship tunnel (Kohat)	75	85
1269/72 Set of 4		2·75	3·00
MS1273 128×68 mm. 30r. Looking down Friendship Tunnel and designs as Nos. 1269/72		2·75	3·50

No. **MS**1273 shows the Pakistan Post emblem visible only under U.V. light.

654 Children and Daffodils   **655** Open University Emblems

2004 (20 Nov). Year of Child Welfare and Rights. P 12½.
1274	**654**	4r. multicoloured	60	45

2004 (6 Dec). 30th Anniv of Allama Iqbal Open University, Islamabad. P 13.
1275	**655**	20r. multicoloured	1·50	2·25

656 Khyber Medical College   **657** Prof. Ahmed Ali

2004 (30 Dec). Centenary of Khyber Medical College. P 13.
1276	**656**	5r. multicoloured	1·00	50

(Des A. Salahuddin)

2005 (14 Jan). 95th Birth Anniv of Prof. Ahmed Ali. Paper with fluorescent fibres. P 13.
1277	**657**	5r. multicoloured	60	50

658 Allama Iqbal (Pakistani), Mihai Emineseu (Romanian) and Monument   **659** Saadat Hasan Manto

(Des A. Salahuddin (No. 1278) or Prof. Dr. E. Ghitulescu))

2005 (14 Jan). Pakistani and Romanian Poets. T **658** and similar vert design. Multicoloured. Paper with fluorescent fibres. P 13.

1278	5r. Type **658**		70	80
1279	5r. Allama Iqbal, Mihai Emineseu and book title		70	80

(Des R. Ahmed)

2005 (18 Jan). 50th Death Anniv of Saadat Hasan Manto (short story writer). Paper with fluorescent fibres. P 13.

1280	**659**	5r. multicoloured	55	45

660 Muhammad Ali Jinnah and Tempest II Airplane

661 Command and Staff College

(Des Adil Salahuddin)

2005 (23 Mar). Air Force. T **660** and similar multicoloured designs. P 13.

1281	5r. Type **660**		1·50	1·50
1282	5r. Visit of Muhammad Ali Jinnah to the Air Force academy (vert)		1·50	1·50
1283	5r. Fighter plane and air force base facilities		1·50	1·50
1284	5r. Roundel and fighter plane		1·50	1·50
1281/4	Set of 4		5·50	5·50

2005 (2 Apr). Centenary of Command and Staff College, Quetta. Paper with fluorescent fibres. P 13.

1285	**661**	5r. multicoloured	1·00	60

662 Muhammad Ali Jinnah and Mustafa Kemal Atatürk

663 Institute of Business Administration, Karachi

2005 (23 Apr). 85th Anniversary of Turkish Grand National Assembly. T **662** and similar horiz design. Multicoloured. Paper with fluorescent fibres. P 14.

1286	10r. Type **662**		1·25	1·75
	a. Pair. Nos. 1286/7		2·50	3·50
1287	10r. Mustafa Kemal Atatürk		1·25	1·75

Nos. 1286/7 were printed together, se-tenant, as horizontal and vertical pairs within the sheet.

(Des R. Ahmed)

2005 (30 Apr). 50th Anniv of Institute of Business Administration, Karachi. T **663** and similar horiz designs. Multicoloured. Paper with fluorescent fibres. P 13.

1288	3r. Type **663**		50	60
1289	3r. Entrance to Institute		50	60

664 School Entrance

665 Akhtar Shairani

(Des R. Ahmed)

2005 (25 May). 95th Anniv of Islamia High School, Quetta. Paper with fluorescent fibres. P 13.

1290	**664**	5r. multicoloured	50	50

(Des R. Ahmed)

2005 (30 June). Birth Centenary of Akhtar Shairani (poet). Paper with fluorescent fibres. P 13.

1291	**665**	5r. multicoloured	50	50

666 Information Society Emblem

667 Abdul Rehman Baba

(Des A. Salahuddin)

2005 (15 July). World Summit on the Information Society, Tunis. Paper with fluorescent fibres. P 13.

1292	**666**	5r. multicoloured	50	50

(Des A. Hai Popalzai)

2005 (4 Aug). Abdul Rehman Baba (poet) Commemoration. Paper with fluorescent fibres. P 13½×13.

1293	**667**	5r. multicoloured	50	50

668 Marathon Runners

(Des A. Salahuddin)

2005 (10 Sept). Lahore Marathon. Paper with fluorescent fibres. P 13.

1294	**668**	5r. multicoloured	50	50

669 Lepiota procera

669a 'HELP EARTHQUAKE VICTIMS'

(Des A. Salahuddin)

2005 (1 Oct). Mushrooms. T **669** and similar vert designs. Multicoloured. Paper with fluorescent fibres. P 13.

1295	5r. Type **669**		75	75
	a. Block of ten. Nos. 1295/1304		6·75	6·75
1296	5r. Tricholoma gambosum		75	75
1297	5r. Amanita caesarea		75	75
1298	5r. Cantharellus cibarius		75	75
1299	5r. Boletus luridus		75	75
1300	5r. Morchella vulgaris		75	75
1301	5r. Amanita vaginata		75	75
1302	5r. Agaricus arvensis		75	75
1303	5r. Coprinus comatus		75	75
1304	5r. Clitocybe geotropa		75	75
1295/1304	Set of 10		6·75	6·75

Nos. 1295/1304 were printed together, se-tenant, in blocks of ten stamps in sheets of 30.

(Des Adil Salahuddin)

2005 (27 Oct). President's Relief Fund for Earthquake Victims. Sheet 174×147 mm. Multicoloured. P 13½.

MS1304a	4r.×8 Type **669a** and 17 stamp size labels (sold for 100r.)	4·50	5·50

No. **MS**1304a contained a central Pakistan Post label, eight stamps in two horizontal and two vertical pairs, and blocks of four labels showing children and ruined buildings in the corners of the sheet. This sheet was sold at 100r., a premium of 60r. for the President's Relief Fund for Earthquake Victims.

670 Silhouettes and Sports Equipment

(Des R. Ahmed)

2005 (5 Nov). International Year of Sports and Physical Education. Paper with fluorescent fibres. P 14.
1305 **670** 5r. multicoloured 50 50

671 Emblem and Clasped Hands   **672** Khwaja Sarwar Hasan

(Des A. Salahuddin)

2005 (12 Nov). 20th Anniv of South Asian Association for Regional Co-operation. Paper with fluorescent fibres. P 13½×13.
1306 **671** 5r. multicoloured 50 50

(Des A. Salahuddin)

2005 (18 Nov). Khwaja Sarwar Hasan (founder of Pakistan Institute of International Affairs) Commemoration. Paper with fluorescent fibres. P 14.
1307 **672** 5r. multicoloured 50 50

673 Emblem and Silhouettes of Children   **674** Emblem and Players

(Des A. Salahuddin)

2005 (20 Nov). 30th Anniv of SOS Children's Villages of Pakistan. Paper with fluorescent fibres. P 13×13½.
1308 **673** 5r. multicoloured 50 50

2005 (8 Dec). 20th World Men's Team Squash Championship, Islamabad. P 14.
1309 **674** 5r. multicoloured .... 1·00 60

675 Supreme Court Building

2006 (23 Mar). 50th Anniv of Supreme Court of Pakistan. T **675** and similar horiz design. Multicoloured. P 14.
1310 4r. Type **675** 60 30
1311 15r. Supreme Court at night.............................. 2·25 3·00

2006 (14 Apr). Muhammad Ali Jinnah's visit to Armoured Corps Centre, Nowshera, 1948. T **676** and similar multicoloured design. P 14.
1312 5r. Type **676** 80 80
1313 5r. Col. Stroud (Commandant), Muhammad Ali Jinnah and Begum Ra'na Liaquat Ali Khan................................ 80 80

676 Muhammed Ali Jinnah inspecting Troops and Tanks   **677** Begum Ra'na Liaquat Ali Khan

(Des Masood ur Rehman)

2006 (13 June). Birth Centenary (2005) of Begum Ra'na Liaquat Ali Khan. P 13½.
1314 **677** 4r. multicoloured.. 60 50

678 Gurdwara Dera Sahib, Lahore

(Des Faizi Amir Siddiqui)

2006 (16 June). 400th Death Anniv of Arjun Dev Ji (Sikh Guru). P 13½.
1315 **678** 5r. multicoloured.. 65 60
    a. Wmk inverted...

679 Polo at Shandur Pass   **680** Hanna Lake, Quetta

2006 (1 July). Shandur Polo Festival, Chitral. P 14.
1316 **679** 5r. multicoloured.. 1·50 75

2006 (20 July). "Visit Pakistan 2006". Lakes. T **680** and similar horiz designs. Multicoloured. P 14.
1317 5r. Type **680** 70 75
    a. Block of four. Nos. 1317/20 .... 2·50 2·75
1318 5r. Lake Payee, Kaghan.................................. 70 75
1319 5r. Lake Saiful Maluk, Kaghan........................ 70 75
1320 5r. Lake Dudi Pat Sar, Kaghan........................ 70 75
1317/20 Set of 4.. 2·50 2·75
    Nos. 1317/20 were printed together, *se-tenant*, as blocks of four stamps in sheetlets of 16.

681 Prof. Shakir Ali

(Des Adil Salahuddin)

2006 (14 Aug). Painters of Pakistan. T **681** and similar horiz designs, each showing the artist and one of their paintings. Multicoloured. P 14.
1321 4r. Type **681** 55 55
    a. Sheetlet. Nos. 1321/30................................ 5·00 5·00
1322 4r. Anna Molka Ahmed................................... 55 55
1323 4r. Sadequain... 55 55
1324 4r. Ali Imam... 55 55
1325 4r. Zubeida Agha.. 55 55
1326 4r. Laila Shahzada... 55 55
1327 4r. Ahmed Parvez.. 55 55
1328 4r. Bashir Mirza... 55 55
1329 4r. Zahooral Akhlaque.................................... 55 55
1330 4r. Askari Mian Irani...................................... 55 55
1321/30 Set of 10.. 5·00 5·00
    3.00 Nos. 1321/30 were printed together, *se-tenant*, in sheetlets of ten stamps.

682 Centenary Emblem   **683** New Houses under Construction

(Des Faizi Ameer)

2006 (25 Aug). Centenary of Hamdard Services. W **98**. P 13½×13.
1331 **682** 5r. multicoloured... 60   50

(Des Masood ur Rehman)

2006 (8 Oct). First Anniv of Earthquake. W **98**. P 13½.
1332 **683** 5r. multicoloured... 60   50

684 Aloe Vera

(Des Masood ur Rehman)

2006 (28 Oct). Medicinal Plants (12th series). T **684** and similar multicoloured design. W **98**. P 13½.
1333   5r. Type **684** .... 1·00   1·00
1334   5r. Chamomilla (vert)... 1·00   1·00

685 UN Emblem

687 Muhammed Ali Jinnah joins Muslim League, 1913

686 Baltit Fort, Karimabad

(Des Faizi Ameer)

2006 (9 Dec). United Nations International Anti-Corruption Day. W **98**. P 13.
1335 **685** 5r. multicoloured... 60   60

(Des Faizi Ameer)

2006 (20 Dec). Tenth Anniv of Baltit Heritage Trust. W **98**. P 13½.
1336 **686** 15r. multicoloured... 2·25   2·75

(Des Adil Salahuddin)

2006 (28 Dec). Centenary of the Muslim League. T **687** and similar vert designs. Multicoloured. W **98**. P 13.
1337   4r. Type **687** 50   50
          a. Sheetlet. Nos. 1337/44.............................. 3·50   3·50
          w. Wmk inverted.. 3·25   3·25
          wa. Sheetlet. Nos. 1337w/44w...................... 25·00 25·00
1338   4r. Muhammed Ali Jinnah ("Quaid") in 1937... 50   50
          w. Wmk inverted.. 3·25   3·25
1339   4r. Addressing Lucknow Session, 1937........ 50   50
          w. Wmk inverted.. 3·25   3·25
1340   4r. With Fatima Jinnah and youth and women of Muslim League, 1938............. 50   50
          w. Wmk inverted.. 3·25   3·25
1341   4r. Hoisting Muslim League flag, Manto Park, Lahore, 1940................................ 50   50
          w. Wmk inverted.. 3·25   3·25
1342   4r. Addressing Lahore session, 1940........... 50   50
          w. Wmk inverted.. 3·25   3·25
1343   4r. Ballot box and crowd (elections victory, 1945–6).. 50   50
          w. Wmk inverted.. 3·25   3·25
1344   4r. Addressing first Constituent Assembly, 1947.. 50   50
          w. Wmk inverted.. 3·25   3·25

1337/44 Set of 8 .... 3·50   3·50
    Nos. 1337/44 were printed together, se-tenant, in sheetlets of eight stamps.

688 Old KMC Building, Karachi

689 Cadet College, Petaro and Arms

(Des Faizi Ameer)

2007 (16 Jan). 75th Anniv of Inauguration of KMC (Karachi Municipal Corporation) Building. P 14.
1345 **688** 10r. multicoloured... 1·50   1·50

(Des Faizi Ameer)

2007 (28 Feb). 50th Anniv of Cadet College, Petaro. P 14.
1346 **689** 10r. multicoloured... 1·00   1·00

690 Women at Work

(Des Faizi Ameer)

2007 (8 Mar). International Women's Day. W **98**. P 13.
1347 **690** 10r. multicoloured... 1·00   1·00

691 Hugh Catchpole

692 Emblem

(Des Masood ur Rehman)

2007 (26 May). Birth Centenary of Hugh Catchpole (educationist). W **98**. P 13.
1348 **691** 10r. multicoloured... 1·00   1·00
          a. Wmk inverted

(Des Spectrum Communications Ltd)

2007 (7 June). "Launch of New Vision of Pakistan Post". W **98**. P 14½.
1349 **692** 4r. orange-vermilion and orange-yellow .... 1·00   1·00

693 JF-17 Thunder

(Des Faizi Ameer)

2007 (6 Sept). Pakistan Air Force Defence Day. W **98**. P 13.
1350 **693** 5r. multicoloured... 1·50   1·00
          w. Wmk inverted

694 Members Flags and Map

2007 (22 Sept). ECO (Economic Co-operation Organization) Postal Authorities Conference, Ankara (2006). W **98**. P 13.
1351 **694** 10r. multicoloured .... 2·00 1·50
No. 1351 is inscr '650 Rials I.R. Iran' at top left and the country name "PAKISTAN" is missing from the stamp.

695 National Assembly Building

(Des Faizi Ameer)

2007 (15 Nov). Completion of Five Years Term of National Assembly of Pakistan. W **98**. P 13.
1352 **695** 15r. multicoloured .... 1·50 2·00

696 Church Building, Medallion and Nave

2007 (19 Nov). Centenary of Catholic Cathedral Church, Lahore. W **98** (sideways). P 13.
1353 **696** 5r. multicoloured .... 1·00 1·00

697 Zulfikar Ali Bhutto, Benazir Bhutto and Crowd

(Des Adil Salahuddin)

2008 (4 Apr). 29th Death Anniv of Zulfikar Ali Bhutto. W **98**. P 13.
1354 **697** 4r. multicoloured .... 1·25 1·00
MS1355 106×70 mm. **696** 20r. multicoloured. Imperf . 2·00 2·50

698 Benazir Bhutto

700 Benazir Bhutto

699 Girls in Class and Rebuilt School

(Des Adil Salahuddin)

2008 (21 June). 55th Birth Anniv of Benazir Bhutto (Prime Minister of Pakistan 1988–90, 1993–6). T **698** and similar multicoloured design. W **98**. P 13 (4r.) or 13×13½ (5r.).
1356 4r. Type **698** .... 1·25 1·00
1357 5r. Benazir Bhutto waving (34×56 *mm*)....... 1·25 1·00
MS1358 67×98 mm. 20r. As No. 1357. Imperf.................. 2·00 2·50
No. **MS**1358 is imperforate with simulated perforations.

(Des Adil Salahuddin)

2008 (8 Oct). Third Anniv of Earthquake. P 13.
1359 **699** 4r. multicoloured .... 1·25 1·00

(Des Adil Salahuddin)

2008 (10 Dec). United Nations Human Rights Award for Benazir Bhutto. W **98** (sideways). P 13.
1360 **700** 4r. multicoloured .... 1·25 1·00

701 Benazir Bhutto and Pakistan Flag

(Des Adil Salahuddin)

2008 (27 Dec). First Death Anniv of Benazir Bhutto. W **98**. P 13.
1361 **701** 4r. multicoloured .... 1·25 1·00
MS1362 99×67 mm. **701** 20r. multicoloured. No wmk. Imperf.................. 2·00 2·50

702 Members Flags

(Des Adil Salahuddin)

2009 (11 Mar). Tenth ECO Summit, Tehran, Iran. W **98**. P 13×13½.
1363 **702** 5r. multicoloured .... 1·00 1·00

703 Deodar

(Des Adil Salahuddin)

2009 (23 Mar). National Year of the Environment. T **703** and similar triangular designs. Multicoloured. W **98** (sideways). P 13.
1364 5r. Type **703** 85 85
1365 5r. Chukar 85 85
1366 5r. Markhor 85 85
1367 5r. Jasmine 85 85
1364/7 Set of 4 .... 3·00 3·00
Each design from Nos. 1364/7 was printed in pairs, giving a square shape within the sheet.

704 Entrance to 'Habib Education Centre'

(Des Aftab Zafar)

2009 (29 Mar). 50th Anniv of Habib Public School, Karachi. W **98**. P 13.
1368 **704** 5r. multicoloured 50   50

705 High School Building, Karachi

(Des Faizi Ameer Siddiqui)

2009 (23 May). 150th Anniv of Bai Virbaiji Soparivala Parsi High School, Karachi. W **98** (sideways). P 13½.
1369 **705** 5r. multicoloured 50   50

706 KCCI Building, Karachi

2009 (30 May). 75th Anniv of Karachi Chamber of Commerce and Industry Building. W **98** (sideways). P 13.
1370 **706** 4r. multicoloured 45   45

707 Ahmad Nadeem Qasmi   **708** Prime Minister holding Refugee Baby

(Des Faizi Ameer)

2009 (10 July). Ahmad Nadeem Qasmi (Urdu poet and writer) Commemoration. W **98** (sideways). P 13.
1371 **707** 5r. multicoloured 50   50

(Des Adil Salahuddin)

2009 (1 Aug). Prime Minister's Relief Fund for Swat Refugees. Sheet 174×153 mm. Multicoloured. P 14.
MS1372 5r.×8 Type **708** and 17 stamp size labels
(*sold for* 100r.) .... 4·50   5·50
No. **MS**1372 contained a central Pakistan Post label, eight stamps in two horizontal and two vertical pairs, and blocks of four labels showing refugee children in the corners of the sheet. This sheet was sold for 100r., a premium of 60r. for the Prime Minister's Relief Fund for Swat Refugees.

709 St. Patrick's Cathedral, Karachi, Gurdwara Dera Sahib, Lahore and Hindu Temple, Taxila

(Des Adil Salahuddin)

2009 (11 Aug). Minorities Week. W **98**. P 13.
1373 **709** 5r. multicoloured 50   50
No. 1373 is incorrectly inscr 'ST. PATARICS'.

710 Teacher, Students and National Flag   **711** Mausoleum of Hazrat Musa Pak Shaheed

(Des Masood ur Rehman)

2009 (14 Aug). Independence Day. W **98**. P 13.
1374 **710** 5r. multicoloured 50   50

(Des Faizi Ameer)

2009 (15 Aug). Mausoleum of Hazrat Musa Pak Shaheed. W **98**. P 13.
1375 **711** 5r. multicoloured 50   50

712 Peace Dove   **713** National Flags of Pakistan and Philippines

(Des Muhammad Abbas)

2009 (16 Aug). "United for Peace". W **98**. P 13½.
1376 **712** 5r. dull violet, azure and black 50   50

(Des Faizi Ameer Siddiqui)

2009 (9 Sept). 60th Anniv of Diplomatic Relations between Pakistan and the Philippines. W **98** (sideways). P 13.
1377 **713** 5r. multicoloured 50   50

714 Sun, Chinese Flag and Outline Map of China

(Des Faizi Ameer Siddiqui)

2009 (1 Oct). 60th Anniv of the People's Republic of China. W **98**. P 13.
1378 **714** 5r. multicoloured 50   50

715 Aseefa Bhutto Zardari and Benazir Bhutto

(Litho Pakistan Security Printing Corporation, Karachi)

2009 (10 Oct). 'Polio Free Pakistan Mother's Vision Daughter's Mission'. T **715** and similar horiz design. Multicoloured. W **98** (sideways). P 13.
1379		5r. Type **715**	50	50
1379*a*		5r. As Type **715** but country name in Urdu and all other inscriptions in English	50	50

716 Mr. Yousaf Raza Gillani, Chief Ministers, Cabinet Members and Portrait of Benazir Bhutto

(Des Adil Salahuddin. Litho Pakistan Security Printing Corporation, Karachi)

2010 (11 Jan). Seventh National Finance Commission Award. W **98**. P 13.
1380	**716**	8r. multicoloured	80	80

717 Gwadar Port

(Des Adil Salahuddin. Litho Pakistan Security Printing Corporation, Karachi)

2010 (12 Jan). 'Aghaz-e-Haqooq-e-Balochistan' (government development package for Balochistan). W **98**. P 13.
1381	**717**	8r. multicoloured	1·10	1·10

718 Pakistan Flag and Navy Rifle Insignia

(Des Adil Salahuddin. Litho Pakistan Security Printing Corporation, Karachi)

2010 (11 Feb). 50th Anniv of the Pakistan Navy Rifle Association. W **98**. P 13½.
1382	**718**	10r. multicoloured	1·50	1·25

719 War Memorial, Nowshera

(Des Masood-ur-Rehman. Litho Pakistan Security Printing Corporation, Karachi)

2010 (22 Feb). Conferment of Hilal-i-Eissar on Cities of Nowshera, Peshawar, Swabi, Mardan and Charsadda. T **719** and similar horiz designs. Multicoloured. W **98**. P 13.
1383	5r. Type **719**		50	50
	a. Vert strip of five. Nos. 1383/7		2·25	2·25
1384	5r. Islamia College, Peshawar		50	50
1385	5r. Judicial Complex, Swabi		50	50
1386	5r. Takht-e-Barhi, Mardan		50	50
1387	5r. Sugar mills, Charsadda		50	50
1383/7	*Set of 5*		2·25	2·25

Nos. 1383/7 were printed together, *se-tenant*, as horizontal strips of five stamps in sheets of 40 (4×10).

720 OICCI Building

(Litho Pakistan Security Printing Corporation, Karachi)

2010 (7 Apr). 150th Anniv of the Overseas Investors Chamber of Commerce and Industry. W **98**. P 13.
1388	**720**	8r. multicoloured	70	70

721 Athletes and Olympic Rings

(Des Faizi Ameer. Litho Pakistan Security Printing Corporation, Karachi)

2010 (14 Aug). Youth Olympic Games, Singapore. W **98** (sideways). P 13½.
1389	**721**	8r. multicoloured	70	70

722 Junior School Building

(Des Gibran Ali Syed. Litho Pakistan Security Printing Corporation, Karachi)

2010 (7 Oct). 150th Anniv of Lawrence College, Ghora Gali, Murree Hills. T **722** and similar horiz designs. Multicoloured. W **98**. P 13.
1390	**722**	8r. Type **722**	70	70
		a. Block of four. Nos. 1390/3 with two central labels showing College arms	2·50	2·50
1391		8r. Lawrence Asylum, 1860	70	70
1392		8r. Aerial view of Senior School building	70	70
1393		8r. Prep School building	70	70
1390/1393		*Set of 4*	2·50	2·50

Nos. 1390/3 were printed together, *se-tenant*, as blocks of four with central labels in sheets of 12 stamps and six labels.

723 Craftswoman (Ilma Tariq)

(Des Adil Salahuddin. Litho Pakistan Security Printing Corporation, Karachi)

2010 (5 Nov). 'Pakistan 2010' National Stamp Exhibition, Karachi. W **98**. P 13.
1394	**723**	8r. multicoloured	70	70

No. 1394 was issued in sheets of eight stamps with eight *se-tenant* Pakistan 2010 Philatelic Exhibition labels.

724 International Islamic University, Islamabad

(Des Faizi Ameer. Litho Pakistan Security Printing Corporation, Karachi)

2010 (15 Dec). 25th Anniv of International Islamic University, Islamabad. W **98**. P 13.
1395 **724** 8r. multicoloured 70 70

725 Islamabad

(Litho Pakistan Security Printing Corporation, Karachi)

2010 (31 Dec). 50th Anniv of Islamabad. W **98**. P 13½.
1396 **725** 5r. multicoloured 70 70

726 Cellular Phone

(Litho Pakistan Security Printing Corporation, Karachi)

2011 (19 Jan). PTA (Pakistan Telecommunication Authority) '100 Million Cellular Subscribers'. W **98**. P 13.
1397 **726** 8r. multicoloured 70 70

727 Census Emblem and Map of Pakistan

(Litho Pakistan Security Printing Corporation, Karachi)

2011 (10 Feb). Sixth Population and Housing Census. W **98**. P 13.
1398 **727** 10r. multicoloured 75 75

728 Train

(Litho Pakistan Security Printing Corporation, Karachi)

2011 (13 May). 150th Anniv of Pakistan Railways. W **98**. P 13.
1399 **728** 8r. multicoloured .... 1·25 75

729 Asif Ali Zardari (Pakistan President) and Hu Jintao (Chinese President)

(Des Adil Salahuddin. Litho Pakistan Security Printing Corporation, Karachi)

2011 (21 May). 60th Anniv of Diplomatic Relations between Pakistan and China (People's Republic). T **729** and similar horiz design. Multicoloured. W **98** (sideways). P 13.
1400 8r. Type **729** 70 70
    a. Horiz pair. Nos. 1400/1 .... 1·40 1·40
    w. Wmk upright......................... 70 70
    wa. Horiz pair. Nos. 1400w/1w .... 1·40 1·40
1401 8r. Yousuf Raza Gilani (Pakistan Prime
    Minister) and Wen Jiabao (Chinese
    Prime Minister)......................... 70 70
    w. Wmk upright......................... 70 70

730 Hands supporting Globe and AIDS Ribbon

(Des Adil Salahuddin. Litho Pakistan Security Printing Corporation, Karachi)

2011 (8 June). 'Uniting for HIV Prevention'. W **98**. P 13×13½.
1402 **730** 8r. multicoloured .... 1·00 70

731 Faisal Mosque, Islamabad and St. Basil's Cathedral, Moscow

(Des Arif Balgamwala. Litho Pakistan Security Printing Corporation, Karachi)

2011 (10 June). Pakistan–Russia Friendship. W **98**. P 13.
1403 **731** 8r. multicoloured 70 70

732 Interior of a House in Swat (Mahnoor Rafi)

(Des Adil Salahuddin. Litho Pakistan Security Printing Corporation, Karachi)

2011 (24 June). Child Art Competition at 'Kurrachee 2011' National Stamp Exhibition, Karachi. T **732** and similar horiz designs. Multicoloured. P 13.
1404 8r. Type **732** 70 70
    a. Sheetlet. Nos. 1404/11 and two labels.. 5·00 5·00
1405 8r. Independence Day Celebrations, with
    traditional dress of the Provinces
    (Khurram Jahangir Khan)......................... 70 70

1406	8r. Historical Monuments of Pakistan (Almen Khan)...........	70	70
1407	8r. Campaign against Pollution in Karachi (Laiba Jawaid)...........	70	70
1408	8r. Bread making in Village in Sindh (Vania Rizvi)...........	70	70
1409	8r. Girls performing Traditional Dance, Kalash Valley (Naveera Jabeen)........	70	70
1410	8r. Sunrise over Beach, Karachi (Mehnur Zahid)...........	70	70
1411	8r. Pollution Free Pakistan (Ali Nazim)	70	70
1404/1411	Set of 8...........	5·00	5·00

Nos. 1404/11 were printed together, se-tenant, in sheetlets of eight stamps containing two blocks of four stamps separated by two stamp-size labels.

733 Anniversary and ICAP Emblems

(Des Adil Salahuddin. Litho Pakistan Security Printing Corporation, Karachi)

2011 (1 July). 50th Anniv of the Institute of Chartered Accountants of Pakistan. W 98. P 13.
1412 733   8r. multicoloured........................... 70 70

734 Al Jama-tus-Saifiyah Building (Dawoodi Bohra university for Islamic Studies)

(Des Arif Balgamwala. Litho Pakistan Security Printing Corporation, Karachi)

2011 (17 July). Birth Centenary Celebrations of Dr. Syedna Mohammed Burhanuddin Saheb (spiritual leader of Dawoodi Bohra community). W 98. P 13.
1413 734   8r. multicoloured........................... 70 70

735 Zarai Taraqiati Bank

(Des Adil Salahuddin. Litho Pakistan Security Printing Corporation, Karachi)

2011 (14 Aug). 50th Anniv of Zarai Taraqiati Bank Ltd. W 98. P 13.
1414 735   8r. multicoloured........................... 70 70

736 Satellite, Radio, Telephones, Television and Satellite Dish

(Des Adil Salahuddin. Litho Pakistan Security Printing Corporation, Karachi)

2011 (18 Aug). 60th Anniv of Managing Radio Frequency Spectrum by Frequency Allocation Board. W 98. P 13.
1415 736   8r. multicoloured........................... 70 70

737 Milad Tower, Tehran

(Des Adil Salahuddin. Litho Pakistan Security Printing Corporation, Karachi)

2011 (29 Aug). Pakistan-Iran Joint Issue. T 737 and similar vert design. Multicoloured. W 98. P 13.
1416 8r. Type 737 .... 70 70
   a. Horiz pair. Nos. 1416/17 plus label at left or right........... 1·40 1·40
1417 8r. Minar-e-Pakistan, Lahore 70 70

Nos. 1416/17 were printed together, se-tenant, as horizontal pairs in sheetlets containing six of each design and six stamp-size labels. Stamps in similar designs were issued by Iran.

738 Satellite and SUPARCO Emblem

(Des Adil Salahuddin. Litho Pakistan Security Printing Corporation, Karachi)

2011 (16 Sept). 50th Anniv of Pakistan Space and Upper Atmosphere Research Commission. W 98. P 13.
1418 738   8r. multicoloured........................... 70 70

739 Karachi Gymkhana

(Des Faizi Ameer. Litho Pakistan Security Printing Corporation, Karachi)

2011 (23 Sept). 125th Anniv of Karachi Gymkhana (club). T 739 and similar horiz designs. Multicoloured. W 98. P 13.
1419 8r. Type 739 .... 90 90
   a. Block of four. Nos. 1419/22 .... 3·25 3·25
1420 8r. Karachi Gymkhana buildings (post at right)........... 90 90
1421 8r. Entrance........... 90 90
1422 8r. Cricket ground 90 90
1419/1422 Set of 4........... 3·25 3·25

Nos. 1419/22 were printed together, se-tenant, as blocks of four in sheets of 96 (8×12).

740 Emblem, Figures and Rainbow

(Des Adil Salahuddin. Litho Pakistan Security Printing Corporation, Karachi)

2011 (30 Nov). Breast Cancer Awareness Campaign in Pakistan. W **98**. P 13.
1423 **740** 8r. multicoloured 70 70

741 Victory Monument, Bangkok and Minar-e-Pakistan, Lahore

742 School Buildings

(Des Adil Salahuddin. Litho Pakistan Security Printing Corporation, Karachi)

2011 (13 Dec). 60th Anniv of Diplomatic Relations between Pakistan and Thailand. W **98**. P 13.
1424 **741** 8r. multicoloured 70 70

(Des Naveed Awan. Litho Pakistan Security Printing Corporation, Karachi)

2011 (31 Dec). 150th Anniv of St. Patrick's High School, Karachi. W **98**. P 13.
1425 **742** 8r. multicoloured 70 70

743 Cabinet Meeting, 25 December 2011

(Des Adil Salahuddin. Litho Pakistan Security Printing Corporation, Karachi)

2012 (18 Jan). 100th Meeting of the Federal Cabinet of Pakistan. W **98**. P 13.
1426 **743** 8r. multicoloured 70 70

744 Arfa Karim Randhawa

(Des Naveed Awan. Litho Pakistan Security Printing Corporation, Karachi)

2012 (2 Feb). Arfa Karim Randhawa (computer genius and World's youngest Microsoft Certified Professional) Commemoration. W **98**. P 13.
1427 **744** 8r. multicoloured 70 70

745 Air Marshal Nur Khan and North American F-86 Sabre Plane

(Des Adil Salahuddin. Litho Pakistan Security Printing Corporation, Karachi)

2012 (22 Feb). Air Marshal Nur Khan Commemoration. W **98**. P 13½.
1428 **745** 8r. multicoloured 70 70

746 Emerald

747 Aitchison College, Lahore

(Des Adil Salahuddin. Litho Pakistan Security Printing Corporation, Karachi)

2012 (24 Feb). Gems and Minerals of Pakistan. T **746** and similar horiz designs. Multicoloured. W **98**. P 13.
1429 8r. Type **746** .... 1·25 1·25
a. Block of four. Nos. 1429/32 ...... 4·50 4·50
1430 8r. Ruby .... 1·25 1·25
1431 8r. Sapphire .... 1·25 1·25
1432 8r. Peridot .... 1·25 1·25
1429/1432 Set of 4 .... 4·50 4·50
Nos. 1429/32 were printed together, se-tenant, as blocks of four stamps in sheets of 24.

(Des Liaquat Ali. Litho Pakistan Security Printing Corporation, Karachi)

2012 (3 Mar). 125th Anniv of Aitchison College, Lahore. W **98**. P 13.
1433 **747** 8r. multicoloured 70 70

748 St. Joseph's Convent School, Karachi

(Des Adil Salahuddin. Litho Pakistan Security Printing Corporation, Karachi)

2012 (19 Mar). 150th Anniv of St. Joseph's Convent School, Karachi. P 13½.
1434 **748** 8r. multicoloured 70 70

749 Emblem

(Des Adil Salahuddin. Litho Pakistan Security Printing Corporation, Karachi)

2012 (1 Apr). 50th Anniv of Asian-Pacific Postal Union (APPU). P 13.
1435 **749** 8r. multicoloured 70 70

750 Government High School No. 1

(Des Naveed Awan. Litho Pakistan Security Printing Corporation, Karachi)

2012 (15 Apr). Centenary of Government High School No. 1, Thana, Malakand Division. P 13½.
1436 **750** 8r. multicoloured 70 70

751 Mountain Troops ('Honour Heroes & Uphold Unity')

(Des Adil Salahuddin. Litho Pakistan Security Printing Corporation, Karachi)

2012 (30 Apr). Martyrs Day. W **98**. P 13.
1437 **751** 8r. multicoloured 70 70

752 King Bhumibol Adulyadej and Queen Sirikit

(Des Adil Salahuddin. Litho Pakistan Security Printing Corporation, Karachi)

2012 (5 May). 50th Anniv of State Visit of King Bhumibol Adulyadej and Queen Sirikit of Thailand to Pakistan. W **98**. P 13.
1438 **752** 8r. multicoloured 70 70

753 Young Boy and Blood Donors

(Des Adil Salahuddin. Litho Pakistan Security Printing Corporation, Karachi)

2012 (8 May). Prevention of Thalassemia Major in Pakistan. W **98**. P 13.
1439 **753** 8r. multicoloured .... 1·00 70

754 Lake Saiful Malook

(Des Adil Salahuddin. Litho Pakistan Security Printing Corporation, Karachi)

2012 (5 June). 40th Anniv of United Nations Environment Programme (UNEP). World Environment Day. T **754** and similar horiz designs. Multicoloured. W **98**. P 13.
1440 8r. Type **754** 70 70
    a. Block of four. Nos. 1440/3 .... 2·50 2·50
1441 8r. Polo at Shandur Pass 70 70
1442 8r. Shalimar Garden, Lahore 70 70
1443 8r. Khyber Gateway 70 70

1440/1443 Set of 4 .... 2·50 2·50
Nos. 1440/3 were printed together, *se-tenant*, as blocks of four stamps in sheetlets of 16 (4×4).

755 Ayub Bridge

(Des Adil Salahuddin. Litho Pakistan Security Printing Corporation, Karachi)

2012 (15 June). 50th Anniv of Ayub Bridge. W **98**. P 13.
1444 **755** 8r. multicoloured 70 70

756 Oven (Priya Parkash Mansha)

(Litho Pakistan Security Printing Corporation, Karachi)

2012 (22 June). Child Art Competition at 'Kurrachee 2012' National Stamp Exhibition, Karachi. T **756** and similar horiz designs. Multicoloured. W **98**. P 13.
1445 8r. Type **756** 70 70
    a. Sheetlet. Nos. 1445/52 and two labels.. 5·00 5·00
1446 8r. Tower, Faisal Mosque, Islamabad and gateway (Ali Muhammad Nizar) 70 70
1447 8r. Narwhal (Samayan Hasan Khan) 70 70
1448 8r. River and wildlife (Sheza Ashraf) 70 70
1449 8r. Independence Monument, dove, crescent and star (Yamna Naveed) 70 70
1450 8r. Monument and child flying kite (Ayesha Qureshi) 70 70
1451 8r. Toucan and parrot (Vania Rizvi) 70 70
1452 8r. Quetzals (Marium Shahzad) 70 70
1445/1452 Set of 8 .... 5·00 5·00
Nos. 1445/52 were printed together, *se-tenant*, in sheetlets of eight stamps containing two blocks of four stamps separated by two stamp-size labels.

757 Pale Yellow Roses

(Des Adil Salahuddin. Litho Pakistan Security Printing Corporation, Karachi)

2012 (13 Aug). Eid Greetings. Roses. T **757** and similar horiz designs. Multicoloured. W **98**. P 13.
1453 8r. Type **757** 70 70
    a. Block of four. Nos. 1453/6 .... 2·50 2·50
1454 8r. Pink roses 70 70
1455 8r. White roses 70 70
1456 8r. Deep yellow roses 70 70
1453/1456 Set of 4 .... 2·50 2·50
Nos. 1453/6 were printed together, *se-tenant*, as blocks of four stamps in sheetlets of 16 (4×4).

758 King Edward Medical University, Lahore

(Des Adil Salahuddin. Litho Pakistan Security Printing Corporation, Karachi)

2012 (28 Aug). 150th Anniv of King Edward Medical University, Lahore. W **98**. P 13.

| 1457 | **758** | 8r. multicoloured | 70 | 70 |

759 Abdur Rahman Chughtai (1897–1975, artist) and 1948 1r. Scarlet Independence Stamp

(Des Adil Salahuddin. Litho Pakistan Security Printing Corporation, Karachi)

2012 (30 Aug). 65th Anniv of Independence. W **98**. P 13×13½.

| 1458 | **759** | 10r. multicoloured | 1·00 | 80 |

760 Sialkot Chamber of Commerce and Industry

(Des Naveed Awan. Litho Pakistan Security Printing Corporation, Karachi)

2012 (26 Sept). 30th Anniv of Sialkot Chamber of Commerce and Industry. W **98**. P 13.

| 1459 | **760** | 8r. multicoloured | 70 | 70 |

761 White Storks

(Des Adil Salahuddin. Litho Pakistan Security Printing Corporation, Karachi)

2012 (27 Sept). Migratory Birds in Pakistan. T **761** and similar horiz designs. Multicoloured. W **98**. P 13.

1460	8r. Type **761**	1·25	1·25
	a. Block of four. Nos. 1460/3	4·50	4·50
1461	8r. Shoveler Ducks	1·25	1·25
1462	8r. Snow Geese	1·25	1·25
1463	8r. Siberian Cranes	1·25	1·25
1460/1463	Set of 4	4·50	4·50

Nos. 1460/3 were printed together, se-tenant, as blocks of four stamps in sheets of 24 (4×6).

762 Fish and Coral Reef

(Des Adil Salahuddin. Litho Pakistan Security Printing Corporation, Karachi)

2012 (4 Oct). Arabian Sea Coral Reefs. T **762** and similar horiz designs. Multicoloured. W **98**. P 13.

1464	8r. Type **762**	75	75
	a. Block of four. Nos. 1464/7	2·75	2·75
1465	8r. Yellow and orange fish and coral reef (face value at top left)	75	75
1466	8r. Orange fish and green coral reef (face value at top right)	75	75
1467	8r. School of silver fish and blue and red corals (face value at top left)	75	75
1464/1467	Set of 4	2·75	2·75

Nos. 1464/7 were printed together, se-tenant, as blocks of four stamps in sheetlets of 16 (4×4).

763 Hameed Naseem

(Des Naveed Awan. Litho Pakistan Security Printing Corporation, Karachi)

2012 (19 Oct). Hameed Naseem (1920–98, poet, writer and broadcaster) Commemoration. W **98**. P 13.

| 1468 | **763** | 8r. multicoloured | 70 | 70 |

764 Department Building

(Des Naveed Awan. Litho Pakistan Security Printing Corporation, Karachi)

2012 (19 Nov). 60th Anniv of Department of Geography, University of Karachi. W **98**. P 13.

| 1469 | **764** | 15r. multicoloured | 1·25 | 1·50 |

765 Certificate

(Des Adil Salahuddin. Litho Pakistan Security Printing Corporation, Karachi)

2012 (21 Nov). 50th Anniv of National Investment Trust Ltd. W **98**. P 13.

| 1470 | **765** | 15r. multicoloured | 1·25 | 1·50 |

766 Muhammad Luthfullah Khan (Prof. Saeed Akhtar)

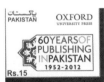

767 Emblem

(Des Adil Salahuddin. Litho Pakistan Security Printing Corporation, Karachi)

2012 (25 Nov). Muhammad Luthfullah Khan (1916–2012, archivist) Commemoration. W **98**. P 13.

1471   **766**   15r. multicoloured .... 1·00   1·00

(Des Afia Batool. Litho Pakistan Security Printing Corporation, Karachi)

2012 (15 Dec). 60th Anniv of Oxford University Press Publishing in Pakistan. W **98**. P 13½×13.

1472   **767**   15r. multicoloured .... 1·00   1·00

768 Wind Farm

(Des Adil Salahuddin. Litho Pakistan Security Printing Corporation, Karachi)

2012 (24 Dec). Commercial Operation of First Wind Farm Project in Pakistan. W **98**. P 13.

1473   **768**   15r. multicoloured .... 1·00   1·00

769 Syed Nasir Raza Kazmi   **770** Qudrat Ullah Shabab

(Des Naveed Awan. Litho Pakistan Security Printing Corporation, Karachi)

2013 (2 Mar). Syed Nasir Raza Kazmi (1925–72, poet) Commemoration. W **98**. P 13.

1474   **769**   15r. multicoloured .... 1·00   1·00

(Des Adil Salahuddin. Litho Pakistan Security Printing Corporation, Karachi)

2013 (23 Mar). Qudrat Ullah Shabab (1917–86, writer) Commemoration. W **98**. P 13.

1475   **770**   15r. multicoloured .... 1·00   1·00

 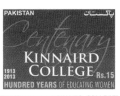

771 Allama Muhammad Asad   **772** 'Centenary KINNAIRD COLLEGE'

(Des Adil Salahuddin. Litho Pakistan Security Printing Corporation, Karachi)

2013 (23 Mar). Allama Muhammad Asad (1900–92, writer) Commemoration. P 13.

1476   **771**   15r. multicoloured .... 1·00   1·00

(Des Faisal Iqbal. Litho Pakistan Security Printing Corporation, Karachi)

2013 (11 Apr). Centenary of Kinnaird College for Women. W **98**. P 13.

1477   **772**   15r. multicoloured .... 1·00   1·00

773 Allama Muhammad Iqbal   **774** Sufi Barkat Ali

(Des Adil Salahuddin. Litho Pakistan Security Printing Corporation, Karachi)

2013 (21 Apr). 75th Death Anniv of Allama Muhammad Iqbal (1877–1938, poet, philosopher and social reformer). W **98**. P 13.

1478   **773**   15r. multicoloured .... 1·00   1·00

(Des Adil Salahuddin. Litho Pakistan Security Printing Corporation, Karachi)

2013 (27 Apr). Sufi Barkat Ali (1911–97, Muslim Sufi saint) Commemoration. W **98**. P 13.

1479   **774**   8r. multicoloured 70   70

775 Statue of Subedar Khuda Dad Khan and Pak Army Museum

(Des Adil Salahuddin. Litho Pakistan Security Printing Corporation, Karachi)

2013 (30 Apr). "Inauguration of Pak Army Museum, Rawalpindi. W **98**. P 13.

1480   **775**   15r. multicoloured .... 1·00   1·00

776 Havildar Lalak Jan Shaheed (1967–99) and Nishan-e-Haider Medal

(Des Adil Salahuddin. Litho Pakistan Security Printing Corporation, Karachi)

2013 (30 Apr). Recipients of Nishan-e-Haider and Hilal-e-Kashmir Medals. T **776** and similar horiz designs. Multicoloured. W **98**. P 13½.

1481	8r. Type **776**	70	70
	a. Strip of three. Nos. 1481/3	1·90	1·90
1482	8r. Captain Karnal Sher Khan Shaheed (1970–99) and Nishan-e-Haider medal	70	70
1483	8r. Naik Saif Ali Janjua Shaheed (1922–48) and Hilal-i-Kashmir medal	70	70
1481/1483	Set of 3	1·90	1·90

Nos. 1481/3 were printed together, *se-tenant*, as horizontal strips of three stamps in sheets of 18 (3×6). The order of stamps within this sheet is as follows:

1481 1482 1483
1483 1481 1482
1481 1482 1483
1483 1481 1482
1482 1483 1481
1481 1482 1483

777 Casting Vote

(Des Adil Salahuddin. Litho Pakistan Security Printing Corporation, Karachi)

2013 (11 May). Election 2013. W **98**. P 13.
1484　**777**　8r. multicoloured ....　70　70

778 Nawab Sadiq　**779** Syed Zamir Jafri
Muhammad Khan Abbasi V

(Des Adil Salahuddin. Litho Pakistan Security Printing Corporation, Karachi)

2013 (24 May). Nawab Sadiq Muhammad Khan Abbasi V (1904–66, Nawab of Bahawalpur) Commemoration. W **98**. P 13.
1485　**778**　8r. multicoloured ....　70　70

(Des Adil Salahuddin. Litho Pakistan Security Printing Corporation, Karachi)

2013 (29 May). Syed Zamir Jafri (1916–99, poet) Commemoration. W **98**. P 13.
1486　**779**　8r. multicoloured ....　70　70

780 Islamia College, Peshawar

(Des Adil Salahuddin. Litho Pakistan Security Printing Corporation, Karachi)

2013 (30 May). Centenary of Islamia College, Peshawar. W **98**. P 13.
1487　**780**　8r. multicoloured ....　70　70

781 Shafiq-ur-Rehman　**782** Mumtaz Mufti

(Des Adil Salahuddin. Litho Pakistan Security Printing Corporation, Karachi)

2013 (6 June). Shafiq-ur-Rehman Commemoration (1920–2000, humorist and short story writer). W **98**. P 13.
1488　**781**　8r. multicoloured ....　70　70

(Des Adil Salahuddin. Litho Pakistan Security Printing Corporation, Karachi)

2013 (12 June). Mumtaz Mufti (1905–95, writer) Commemoration. W **98**. P 13.
1489　**782**　8r. multicoloured ....　70　70
1490　　　　8r. multicoloured ....　70　70

784 Ibn-e-Insha　**785** Society Emblem

(Des Adil Salahuddin. Litho Pakistan Security Printing Corporation, Karachi)

2013 (15 June). Ibn-e-Insha (1927–78, poet) Commemoration. W **98**. P 13.
1491　**784**　8r. multicoloured ....　70　70

(Des Adil Salahuddin. Litho Pakistan Security Printing Corporation, Karachi)

2013 (20 June). 60th Anniv of APNS (All Pakistan Newspaper Society). W **98**. P 13.
1492　**785**　8r. multicoloured ....　70　70

786 Red-vented Bulbul　**787** Pir Meher Ali Shah
(*Pycnonotus cafer*)

(Des Adil Salahuddin. Litho Pakistan Security Printing Corporation, Karachi)

2013 (1 July). Birds of Pakistan. W **98**. P 13½×13.
1493　**786**　8r. multicoloured ....　70　70
Nos. 1494/9 are left for possible additions to this definitive series.

(Des Adil Salahuddin. Litho Pakistan Security Printing Corporation, Karachi)

2013 (30 July). Pir Meher Ali Shah (1859–1937, Sufi saint) Commemoration. W **98**. P 13.
1500　**787**　8r. multicoloured ....　70　70

788 PNS *Aslat* and Pakistan Flag

(Litho Pakistan Security Printing Corporation, Karachi)

2013 (3 Sept). First Indigenously Built F-22P Frigate PNS *Aslat*. W **98**. P 13.
1501　**788**　10r. multicoloured ....　1·25　90

789 Noor Jahan

(Des Adil Salahuddin. Litho Pakistan Security Printing Corporation, Karachi)

2013 (21 Sept). Noor Jahan (1926–2000, singer and actress) Commemoration. W **98**. P 13.
1502 **789** 8r. multicoloured 70 70

790 Jon Elia   **791** Emblem

(Des Adil Salahuddin. Litho Pakistan Security Printing Corporation, Karachi)

2013 (8 Nov). Jon Elia (1931–2002, poet) Commemoration. W **98**. P 13.
1503 **790** 8r. multicoloured 70 70

(Des Adil Salahuddin. Litho Pakistan Security Printing Corporation, Karachi)

2013 (28 Nov). Economic Cooperation Organization 'Two Decades of Extended Cooperation'. W **98**. P 13.
1504 **791** 25r. multicoloured .... 1·40 1·60

792 Perveen Shakir   **794** Habib Jalib

793 Bibles

(Des Adil Salahuddin. Litho Pakistan Security Printing Corporation, Karachi)

2013 (26 Dec). Perveen Shakir (1952–94, poet) Commemoration. W **98**. P 13.
1505 **792** 10r. multicoloured 75 75

(Des Liaquat Ali. Litho Pakistan Security Printing Corporation, Karachi)
2013 (28 Dec). 150th Anniv of the Pakistan Bible Society. W **98**. P 13.
1506 **793** 8r. multicoloured 70 70

(Des Adil Salahuddin. Litho Pakistan Security Printing Corporation, Karachi)

2014 (12 Mar). Habib Jalib (1928-93, poet) Commemoration. W **98**. P 13.
1507 **794** 15r. multicoloured .... 1·00 1·00

795 Air Commodore M. M. Alam

(Des Adil Salahuddin . Litho Pakistan Security Printing Corporation, Karachi)

2014 (20 Mar). Air Commodore M. M. Alam (1935–2013, fighter pilot and recipient of Sitara-e-Jurat) Commemoration. W **98**. P 13½×13.
1508 **795** 8r. multicoloured .... 1·00 70

796 H. M. Habib

(Des Adil Salahuddin. Litho Pakistan Security Printing Corporation, Karachi)

2014 (6 Apr). H. M. Habib the Banker (1936–2013) Commemoration. W **98**. P 13.
1509 **796** 8r. multicoloured 70 70

797 College Entrance

(Des Naveed Awan. Litho Pakistan Security Printing Corporation, Karachi)

2014 (14 May). 150th Anniv of Forman Christian College, Lahore. W **98**. P 13.
1510 **797** 8r. multicoloured 70 70

STAMP BOOKLETS

1956 (23 Mar). Black on green cover. Stapled.
SB1 1r. 08 booklet containing twelve 6p. and 1½a. (Nos. 65, 68) in blocks of 4 .... 9·00

1994 (1 Feb). Maroon on bright greenish blue cover with "window" showing contents. Stamps affixed by selvedge.
SB2 15r. booklet containing fourteen 1r. (No. 913) in block of 14 .... 12·00

OFFICIAL STAMPS

PAKISTAN

PAKISTAN   # SERVICE
(O **1**)   (O **1a**)

1947. Nos. O143, O144b, O145/6, O146b/50 and 259/62 (King George VI) of India, optd as Type O **1** (Nos. O1/9) or as T O **1a** (Nos. O10/13), both in litho by Nasik.
O1 3p. slate .... 3·50 2·75
O2 ½a. purple 60 10
O3 9p. green .... 5·50 4·50
O4 1a. carmine 60 10
 w. Wmk inverted .... — 28·00

O5		1½a. dull violet	60	10
		w. Wmk inverted	28·00	16·00
O6		2a. vermilion	60	60
O7		2½a. bright violet	7·50	15·00
O8		4a. brown	1·50	1·75
O9		8a. slate-violet	2·25	3·25
O10		1r. grey and red-brown	1·25	4·00
O11		2r. purple and brown	11·00	10·00
O12		5r. green and blue	32·00	60·00
O13		10r. purple and claret	85·00	£170
O1/13 Set of 13			£130	£250

See note after No. 19. The 1a.3p. (India No. O146a) exists as a local issue (*Price*, Karachi opt, £14 mint, £35 used).

Whereas the Nasik overprints on the Rupee values were applied to the Indian postage stamps (Nos. 259/62). Those applied at Karachi were on the official stamps (O138/41). The two overprints may be identified by the relative positions of the two words and the shape of the "R" of "SERVICE".

SERVICE SERVICE SERVICE
(O **2**)　　(O **3**)　　(O **4**)

NOTE. Apart from a slight difference in size, Types O **2** and O **3** can easily be distinguished by the difference in the shape of the "c". Type O **4** is taller and thinner in appearance.

PRINTERS. Type O **2** was overprinted by De La Rue and Type O **3** by the Pakistan Security Ptg Corp.

1948 (14 Aug)–**54?** Optd with Type O **2**.

O14	**7**	3p. red (No. 24)	10	10
O15		6p. violet (No. 25) (R.)	10	10
O16		9p. green (No. 26) (R.)	30	10
O17	**8**	1a. blue (No. 27) (R.)	3·75	10
O18		1½a. grey-green (No. 28) (R.)	3·50	10
O19		2a. red (No. 29)	1·50	10
O20	**10**	3a. green (No. 31)	26·00	18·00
O21	**9**	4a. reddish brown (No. 33)	2·50	10
O22	**11**	8a. black (No. 35) (R.)	2·75	10·00
O23	**12**	1r. ultramarine (No. 38)	1·50	10
O24		2r. chocolate (No. 39)	14·00	10·00
O25		5r. carmine (No. 40)	65·00	26·00
O26	**13**	10r. magenta (No. 41)	24·00	80·00
		a. Perf 12 (10.10.51)	32·00	85·00
		b. Perf 13 (1954?)	23·00	90·00
O14/26 Set of 13			£130	£130

1949. Optd with Type O **2**.

O27		1a. blue (No. 44) (R.)	6·00	10
O28		1½a. grey-green (No. 45) (R.)	5·00	10
		a. Opt inverted	£375	60·00
O29		2a. red (No. 46)	7·00	10
		a. Opt omitted (in pair with normal)	—	£180
O30		3a. green (No. 47)	42·00	7·50
O31		8a. black (No. 49) (R.)	65·00	25·00
O27/31 Set of 5			£110	29·00

1951 (14 Aug). 4th Anniv of Independence. As Nos. 56, 58 and 60, but inscr "SERVICE" instead of "PAKISTAN POSTAGE".

O32	**18**	3a. purple	10·00	10·00
O33	**19**	4a. green	2·50	20
O34	**20**	8a. sepia	11·00	8·50
O32/4 Set of 3			21·00	17·00

1953. Optd with Type O **3**.

O35		3p. red (No. 24a)	10	10
O36		6p. violet (No. 25a) (R.)	10	10
O37		9p. green (No. 26a) (R.)	10	10
O38		1a. blue (No. 44a) (R.)	10	10
O39		1½a. grey-green (No. 45a) (R.)	10	10
O40		2a. red (No. 46a) (1953?)	20	10
O41		1r. ultramarine (No. 38a)	10·00	6·50
O42		2r. chocolate (No. 39a)	8·50	30
O43		5r. carmine (No. 40a)	75·00	32·00
O44		10r. magenta (No. 41b) (date?)	28·00	90·00
O35/44 Set of 10			£110	£120

1954 (14 Aug). Seventh Anniv of Independence. Nos. 65/71 optd with Type O **3**.

O45		6p. reddish violet (R.)	10	3·75
O46		9p. blue (R.)	3·00	11·00
O47		1a. carmine	15	2·50
O48		1½a. red	15	2·50
O49		14a. deep green (R.)	1·50	11·00
O50		1r. green (R.)	1·00	10
O51		2r. red-orange	6·50	15
O45/51 Set of 7			11·00	28·00

1955 (14 Aug). Eighth Anniv of Independence. No. 75 optd with Type O **3**.

O52		8a. deep reddish violet (R.)	1·00	10

1957 (Jan)–**59**. Nos. 65/71 optd with Type O **4**.

O53		6p. reddish violet (R.)	10	10
		a. Opt inverted	†	—

O54		9p. blue (R.) (1.59)	15	10
		a. Opt inverted	26·00	
O55		1a. carmine	15	10
		a. Opt inverted	—	60·00
		b. Printed on the gummed side		
O56		1½a. red	15	10
		a. Opt double		
		b. Printed on the gummed side		
O57		14a. deep green (R.) (2.59)	75	5·00
O58		1r. green (R.) (4.58)	75	10
O59		2r. red-orange (4.58)	5·50	10
O53/9 Set of 7			6·75	5·00

1958 (Jan)–**61**. Optd with Type O **4**.

O60	**7**	3p. red (No. 24a)	10	10
O61	–	5r. carmine (No. 40a) (7.59)	7·50	15
O62	**41**	10r. myrtle-green and yellow-orange (No. 89) (R.) (1961)	7·00	11·00
		a. Opt inverted	17·00	
O60/2 Set of 3			14·00	11·00

1958 (Jan)–**61**. Nos. 74/5 optd with Type O **4**.

O63		6a. deep ultramarine (R.) (4.61)	20	10
O64		8a. deep reddish violet (R.)	45	10

1959 (Aug). No. 83 optd with Type O **4**.

O65	**37**	2a. scarlet	10	10

1961 (Apr). Nos. 110/11 optd with Type O **4**.

O66	**51**	8a. deep green	25	10
O67		1r. blue	25	10
		a. Opt inverted	13·00	

NEW CURRENCY. In addition to the local handstamped surcharges mentioned in the note above No. 122, the following typographed surcharges were made at the Treasury at Mastung and issued in the Baluchi province of Kalat: 6p. on 1a. (No. O55), 9p. on 1½a. (No. O56) and 13p. on 2a. (No. O65). They differ in that the surcharges are smaller and "PAISA" is expressed as "Paisa". Being locals they are outside the scope of this catalogue.

1961. Optd with Type O **4**.

O68		1p. on 1½a. (No. 122)	10	10
		a. Optd with Type O **3**	8·50	2·00
O69		2p. on 3p. (No. 123) (1.1.61)	10	10
		a. Surch double		
		b. Optd with Type O **3**	20·00	6·00
O70		3p. on 6p. (No. 124)	10	10
O71		7p. on 1a. (No. 125)	10	10
		a. Optd with Type O **3**	20·00	17·00
O72		13p. on 2a. (No. 126)	10	10
O73		13p. on 2a. (No. 127)	10	10
O68/73 Set of 6			55	30

No. O68 exists with small and large "1" (see note below Nos. 122/7, etc.).

ERRORS. See note after No. 127.

SERVICE
(O **5**)

1961–63. Nos. 128/44b optd with Type O **4** (rupee values) or O **5** (others).

		(a) Inscribed "SHAKISTAN"		
O74		1p. violet (R.) (1.1.61)	10	10
O75		2p. rose-red (R.) (12.1.61)	10	10
O76		5p. ultramarine (R.) (23.3.61)	15	10
		a. Opt inverted		
		(b) Inscribed "PAKISTAN"		
O77		1p. violet (R.)	7·50	10
		a. Printed on the gummed side		
		b. Opt inverted		
O78		2p. rose-red (R.)	50	10
		a. Printed on the gummed side		
O79		3p. reddish purple (R.) (27.10.61)	10	10
O80		5p. ultramarine (R.)	8·00	10
O81		7p. emerald (R.) (23.3.61)	10	10
O82		10p. brown (R.)	10	10
O83		13p. slate-violet (R.) (14.2.61)	10	10
O85		40p. deep purple (R.) (1.1.62)	10	10
O86		50p. deep bluish green (R.) (1.1.62)	15	10
		a. Opt double		
O87		75p. carmine-red (R.) (23.3.62)	20	10
		a. Opt double		
O88		1r. vermilion (7.1.63)	35	10
		a. Opt double	23·00	
		b. Opt as Type O **3**	38·00	29·00
		c. Opt inverted	16·00	
O89		2r. orange (7.1.63)	1·50	20
O90		5r. green (R.) (7.1.63)	4·25	8·50
O74/90 Set of 16			21·00	8·50

1963–78?. Nos. 170, etc., optd with Type O **5**, in red.

O91		1p. violet	10	10
O92		2p. rose-red (1965)	10	10
		a. Opt inverted	3·25	
		b. Albino opt		
		c. Opt double, one albino		
O93		3p. reddish purple (1967)	3·75	1·50
		a. Opt double	17·00	
		b. Opt inverted	3·75	
		c. Printed on the gummed side		
O94		5p. ultramarine	10	10
		a. Opt inverted	2·00	
		ab. Vert pair, top stamp without opt, lower with opt inverted		
O95		7p. emerald (date?)	42·00	17·00
O96		10p. brown (1965)	10	10
		a. Opt inverted	3·75	
O97		13p. slate-violet	10	10
O98		15p. bright purple (31.12.64)	10	2·25
O99		20p. myrtle-green (26.1.70)	10	40
		a. Opt double	26·00	
O100		25p. deep blue (1977)	22·00	5·50
O101		40p. deep purple (1972?)	27·00	11·00
O102		50p. deep bluish green (1965)	15	15
O103		75p. carmine-red (date?)	32·00	26·00
O104		90p. yellow-green (5.78?)	16·00	11·00
O91/104 *Set of 14*			£130	65·00

1968?. Nos. 204, 206 and 207 optd with Type O **4**.

O105	**62**	1r. vermilion	4·50	1·25
		a. Opt inverted	13·00	
		b. Printed and overprinted on the gummed side	16·00	
		w. Wmk inverted	13·00	
O107		2r. orange (date?)	20·00	2·25
		a. Opt inverted	13·00	
O108		5r. green (R.) (date?)	48·00	12·00
		a. Opt inverted	18·00	
O105/8 *Set of 3*			65·00	14·00

1979–85. Nos. 464/72, 473b and 475/80 optd as Type O **5** in black (2r.) or in red (reading vertically downwards on 2, 3 and 5p.) (others).

O109	**275**	2p. deep grey-green	10	30
		a. Opt reading upwards		
		ab. Horiz pair, one with opt reading upwards, the other with opt omitted		
		b. Printed on the gummed side		
O110		3p. black	10	30
		a. Opt reading upwards	3·00	90
O111		5p. deep ultramarine	10	30
		a. Opt reading upwards	1·50	1·50
		b. Vert pair, top stamp without opt	3·00	
O112	**276**	10p. new blue and greenish blue	10	30
O113		20p. deep yellow-green	10	10
O114		25p. deep green and dull magenta	10	10
O115		40p. new blue and magenta	30	10
		a. Opt inverted	8·00	
		b. Albino opt	10·00	
O116		50p. slate-lilac and turquoise-green	10	10
O117		60p. black	1·00	10
		a. Printed on the gummed side		
O118		75p. dull vermilion (Die II) (1980)	1·00	10
O119	**276a**	1r. bronze-green (1980)	2·25	10
O120		1r.50 red-orange (1979)	20	30
		w. Wmk inverted	6·00	
O121		2r. carmine-red (1979)	20	10
		w. Wmk inverted		
O122		3r. blue-black (1980)	30	30
O123		4r. black (1985)	4·00	50
O124		5r. sepia (1985)	4·00	50
O109/24 *Set of 16*			12·50	3·25

Examples of Nos. O109/10, O111a and O115/21 occur with matt, almost invisible gum of a P.V.A. type, as well as the usual gum arabic.

(Des and litho Secura, Singapore)

1980 (15 Jan–10 Mar). As Nos. 513/19 but inscr *"SERVICE"*. P 12.

O125	**291**	10p. slate-green and orange-yellow	1·00	10
O126		15p. slate-green and bright yellow-green	1·00	10
O127		25p. violet and brown-red (10 Mar)	15	1·00
O128		35p. carmine and bright yellow-green (10 Mar)	20	1·50
O129	–	40p. rosine and olive-sepia (10 Mar)	1·00	10
O130	–	50p. violet and dull yellow-green (10 Mar)	20	60
O131	–	80p. bright yellow-green and black (10 Mar)	30	1·50
O125/31 *Set of 7*			3·50	4·25

1984 (25 Sept)–**89**. Nos. 629/30 and 632/6 optd with Type O **6** in red.

O132	–	5p. brownish black and brown-purple (1989?)	10	60

O133	–	10p. brownish black and rose-red	15	40
O135	**343**	20p. black and bright reddish violet (opt at right) (20.11.84)	30	40
		a. Opt at left	10	10
O136	–	50p. sepia and Venetian red (1988?)	40	40
O137	–	60p. light brown and blackish brown (1985)	45	50
O138	–	70p. greenish blue (1988?)	50	70
O139	–	80p. bistre-brown and dull scarlet (1988)	55	70
O132/9 *Set of 7*			2·10	3·00

1989 (24 Dec). No. 773 optd with Type O **5**.

O140	**411**	1r. multicoloured	6·00	1·00

Other values of this series overprinted with a different "SERVICE" are reported to be bogus.

O **7** State Bank of Pakistan Building, Islamabad

1990 (12 Apr)–**99**. W **98** (sideways*). P 13½.

O141	O **7**	1r. carmine and dull green	15	10
		w. Wmk tips of crescent pointing downwards	4·50	
O142		2r. carmine and rose-carmine	25	15
		a. Wmk upright	1·00	
		w. Wmk tips of crescent pointing downwards		
O143		3r. carmine and ultramarine	35	15
		a. Wmk upright	1·00	
O144		4r. carmine and red-brown	45	15
		x. Wmk reversed		
O145		5r. carmine and reddish purple (*wmk tips of crescent pointing downwards*)	50	15
		w. Wmk tips of crescent pointing upwards		
O146		10r. carmine and deep brown (6.2.99)	1·25	40
O141/6 *Set of 6*			2·50	1·00

*The normal sideways watermark for Nos. O141/4 and O146 shows the tips of the crescent pointing upwards and for No. O145 pointing downwards.

1999. No wmk. P 13½.

O150	O **7**	2r. carmine and rose-carmine	40	25
		a. Printed on gummed side	12·00	

BAHAWALPUR

Bahawalpur, a former feudatory state situated to the west of the Punjab, was briefly independent following the partition of India on 15 August 1947 before acceding to Pakistan on 3 October of the same year.

East India Company and later Indian Empire post offices operated in Bahawalpur from 1854. By a postal agreement of 1879 internal mail from the state administration was carried unstamped, but this arrangement was superseded by the issue of Official stamps in 1945.

These had been preceded by a series of pictorial stamps prepared in 1933–34 on unwatermarked paper. It was intended that these would be used as state postage stamps, but permission for such use was withheld by the Indian Government so they were used for revenue purposes. The same designs were utilised for the 1945 Official series, Nos. O1/6, on paper watermarked Star and Crescent. Residual stocks of the unwatermarked 1a., 8a., 1r. and 2r. were used for the provisional Officials, Nos. O7 and O11/13.

A commemorative 1a. Receipt stamp was produced to mark the centenary of the alliance with Great Britain. This may not have been ready until 1935, but an example of this stamp is known used on cover from Deh Rawal to Sadiq Garh and postmarked 14 August 1933. Both this 1a. and the same value from the unwatermarked set also exist with Official Arabic overprint in black. These were not issued for postal purposes although one used example of the latter has been recorded postmarked 22 February 1933 also from Deh Rawal.

Stamps of India were overprinted in the interim period between 15 August and 3 October 1947. After the state joined Pakistan postage stamps were issued for internal use until 1953.

PRICES FOR STAMPS ON COVER

The postage and Official stamps of Bahawalpur are rare used on cover.

Nawab (from 1947 Amir) Sadiq Mohammad Khan Abbasi V, 1907–1966

(1)

1947 (15 Aug). Nos. 265/8, 269a/77 and 259/62 (King George VI) of India optd locally with T **1**.

1		3p. slate (R.)	42·00
2		½a. purple	42·00
3		9p. green (R.)	42·00
4		1a. carmine	42·00
5		1½a. dull violet (R.)	42·00
6		2a. vermilion	42·00
	a.	Opt double	£4750
7		3a. bright violet (R.)	42·00
8		3½a. bright blue (R.)	42·00
9		4a. brown	42·00
10		6a. turquoise-green (R.)	42·00
	a.	Opt double	£4750
11		8a. slate-violet (R.)	42·00
12		12a. lake	42·00
13		14a. purple	85·00
14		1r. grey and red-brown	55·00
	a.	Opt double, one albino	£550
15		2r. purple and brown (R.)	£4250
16		5r. green and blue (R.)	£4250
17		10r. purple and claret (R.)	£4250
1/17		Set of 17	£12000

Nos. 1/17 were issued during the interim period, following the implementation of the Indian Independence Act, during which time Bahawalpur was part of neither of the two Dominions created. The Amir acceded to the Dominion of Pakistan on 3 October 1947 and these overprinted stamps of India were then withdrawn.

The stamps of Bahawalpur only had validity for use within the state. For external mail Pakistan stamps were used.

PRINTERS. All the following issues were recess-printed by De La Rue & Co, Ltd, London.

2 Amir Muhammad Bahawal Khan I Abbasi

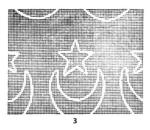

3

1947 (1 Dec). Bicentenary Commemoration. W **3** (sideways). P 12½×11½.

18	**2**	½a. black and carmine	3·75	9·00

4 H.H. the Amir of Bahawalpur

5 The Tombs of the Amirs

6 Mosque in Sadiq-Garh

7 Fort Derawar from the Lake

8 Nur-Mahal Palace

9 The Palace, Sadiq-Garh

10 H.H. the Amir of Bahawalpur

11 Three Generations of Rulers; H.H. the Amir in centre

1948 (1 Apr). W **3** (sideways on vert designs). P 12½ (T **4**), 11½×12½ (T **5**, **7**, **8** and **9**), 12½×11½ (T **6** and **10**) or 13½×14 (T **11**).

19	**4**	3p. black and blue	3·00	20·00
20		½a. black and claret	2·75	20·00
21		9p. black and green	2·75	20·00
22		1a. black and carmine	2·75	20·00
23		1½a. black and violet	4·00	16·00
24	**5**	2a. green and brown	4·00	20·00
25	**6**	4a. orange and brown	4·00	20·00
26	**7**	6a. violet and blue	4·00	20·00
27	**8**	8a. carmine and violet	5·50	20·00
28	**9**	12a. green and carmine	6·50	30·00
29	**10**	1r. violet and brown	19·00	45·00
30		2r. green and claret	55·00	80·00
31		5r. black and violet	55·00	£100
32	**11**	10r. scarlet and black	32·00	£130
19/32		Set of 14	£180	£500

12 H.H. The Amir of Bahawalpur and Mohammed Ali Jinnah

13 Soldiers of 1848 and 1948

1948 (3 Oct). First Anniv of Union of Bahawalpur with Pakistan. W **3**. P 13.

33	**12**	1½a. carmine and blue-green	1·75	7·50

1948 (15 Oct). Multan Campaign Centenary. W **3**. P 11½.

34	**13**	1½a. black and lake	1·25	16·00

1948. As Nos. 29/32, but colours changed.

35	**10**	1r. deep green and orange	1·75	20·00
36		2r. black and carmine	2·00	24·00
37		5r. chocolate and ultramarine	2·00	42·00
38	**11**	10r. red-brown and green	2·00	55·00
35/8		Set of 4	7·00	£130

14 Irrigation

15 Wheat

16 Cotton

17 Sahiwal bull

1949 (3 Mar). Silver Jubilee of Accession of H.H. the Amir of Bahawalpur. T **14/17**. W **3**. P 14.

39	**14**	3p. black and ultramarine	10	8·00
40	**15**	½a. black and brown-orange	10	8·00
41	**16**	9p. black and green	10	8·00
42	**17**	1a. black and carmine	10	8·00
39/42 Set of 4			35	29·00

Nos. 39/42 exist imperforate (*Prices, £27 per pair, unused*).

18 U.P.U. Monument, Berne

1949 (10 Oct). 75th Anniv of Universal Postal Union. W **3**. P 13.

43	**18**	9p. black and green	20	2·25
		a. Perf 17½×17	2·50	24·00
44		1a. black and magenta	20	2·25
		a. Perf 17½×17	2·50	24·00
45		1½a. black and orange	20	2·25
		a. Perf 17½×17	2·50	24·00
46		2½a. black and blue	20	2·25
		a. Perf 17½×17	2·50	24·00
43/6 Set of 4			70	8·00
43a/6a Set of 4			9·00	85·00

Nos. 43/6 exist imperforate (*Prices, £11 per pair, unused*).

OFFICIAL STAMPS

O **1** Panjnad Weir

O **2** Dromedary and Calf

O **3** Blackbuck

O **4** Eastern White Pelicans

O **5** Friday Mosque, Fort Derawar

O **6** Temple at Pattan Munara

Normal

"Sarkark": Part of the overprint at left is missing, altering the word from "Sarkari" (Official) to "Sarkark" (R. 6/3)

1945 (1 Mar). Various horizontal pictorial designs, with red Arabic opt. W **3**. P 14.

O1	O **1**	½a. black and green	13·00	15·00
O2	O **2**	1a. black and carmine	3·75	17·00
		a. Opt omitted	†	£1400
		b. "Sarkark"	£150	
O3	O **3**	2a. black and violet	3·25	14·00
		a. "Sarkark"	£100	
O4	O **4**	4a. black and olive-green	18·00	30·00
O5	O **5**	8a. black and brown	38·00	19·00
		a. "Sarkark"	£350	
O6	O **6**	1r. black and orange	38·00	19·00
O1/6 Set of 6			£100	£100

Permission for the introduction of Nos. O1/6 was granted by the Imperial Government as from 1 January 1945, but the stamps were not used until 1 March. First Day covers exist showing the January date.

Examples of No. O2a come from a sheet used at Rahimya Khan.

It is believed that examples of Nos. O1/2 in different shades and with white gum appeared in 1949 and were included in the Silver Jubilee Presentation Booklet.

O **7** Baggage Camels

(O **8**)

1945 (10 Mar). Revenue stamp with red Arabic opt. No wmk. P 14.

O7	O **7**	1a. black and brown	£100	85·00

1945 (Mar–June). Surch as Type O **8** (at Security Printing Press, Nasik) instead of red Arabic opt. No wmk. P 14.

O11	O **5**	½a. on 8a. black and purple	8·50	7·00
O12	O **6**	1½a. on 1r. black and orange	40·00	11·00
O13	O **1**	1½a. on 2r. black and blue (1 June)	£140	8·50
O11/13 Set of 3			£170	24·00

The stamps used as a basis for Nos. O7 and O11/13 were part of the Revenue series issued in 1933–34.

(O **9**)

O **10** H.H. the Amir of Bahawalpur

1945 (June). Optd with Type O **9** (by D.L.R.) instead of red Arabic opt. No wmk. P 14.

O14	O **1**	½a. black and carmine	1·25	11·00
O15	O **2**	1a. black and carmine	2·00	13·00
O16	O **3**	2a. black and orange	4·00	55·00
O14/16 Set of 3			6·50	70·00

1945 (Sep). P 14.

O17	O **10**	3p. black and blue	8·00	17·00
O18		1½a. black and violet	27·00	8·00

O **11** Allied Banners

(Des E. Meronti. Recess, background litho)

1946 (1 May). Victory. P 14.

O19	O **11**	1½a. green and grey	5·50	4·50

1948. Nos. 19, 22, 24/5 and 35/8 optd as Nos. O1/6.

O20	**4**	3p. black and blue (R.)	80	13·00
O21		1a. black and carmine (Blk.)	80	12·00
O22	**5**	2a. green and carmine (Blk.)	80	13·00
O23	**6**	4a. orange and brown (Blk.)	80	18·00
O24	**10**	1r. deep green and orange (R.)	80	20·00
O25		2r. black and carmine (R.)	80	26·00
O26		5r. chocolate and ultramarine (R.)	80	42·00
O27	**11**	10r. red-brown and green (R.)	80	42·00
O20/7 *Set of 8*			5·75	£170

1949 (10 Oct). 75th Anniv of Universal Postal Union. Nos. 43/6 optd as Nos. O1/6.

O28	**18**	9p. black and green	15	4·50
		aw. Wmk inverted	†	£450
		b. Perf 17½×17	2·50	32·00
O29		1a. black and magenta	15	4·50
		b. Perf 17½×17	2·50	32·00
O30		1½a. black and orange	15	4·50
		b. Perf 17½×17	2·50	32·00
O31		2½a. black and blue	15	4·50
		b. Perf 17½×17	2·50	32·00
O28/31 *Set of 4*			55	16·00
O28b/31b *Set of 4*			9·00	£110

Nos. O28/31 exist imperforate (*Prices, £11 per pair, unused*).

From 1947 stamps of Pakistan were used on all external mail. Bahawalpur issues continued to be used on internal mail until 1953.

Ceylon / Sri Lanka

No.	Type	Description		

CROWN COLONY

PRICES. The prices of the imperf stamps of Ceylon vary greatly according to condition. The following prices are for fine copies with four margins. Poor to medium specimens can be supplied at much lower prices.

1   2   3

NOTE. Beware of stamps of Type **2** which are often offered with corners added.

(Recess P.B.)
1857 (1 Apr). Blued paper. Wmk Star W w **1**. Imperf.

1	**1**	6d. purple-brown	£12000	£450

Collectors should beware of proofs with faked watermark, often offered as originals.

PERKINS BACON "CANCELLED". For notes on these handstamps, showing "CANCELLED" between horizontal bars forming an oval, see Catalogue Introduction.

1857 (2 July)–**59**. Wmk Star, W w **1**. White paper.

(a) Imperf

2	**1**	1d. deep turquoise-blue (24.8.57)	£1100	45·00
		a. Blue	£1200	80·00
		b. Blued paper	—	£225
3		2d. green (shades) (24.8.57)	£200	65·00
		a. Yellowish green	£500	90·00
4	**2**	4d. dull rose (23.4.59)	£70000	£4500
5	**1**	5d. chestnut	£1600	£150
6		6d. purple-brown (1859)	£2750	£140
		a. Brown	£10000	£550
		b. Deep brown	£12000	£1000
		c. Light brown	—	£1500
7	**2**	8d. brown (23.4.59)	£28000	£1500
8		9d. purple-brown (23.4.59)	£60000	£900
9	**3**	10d. dull vermilion	£900	£325
10		1s. slate-violet	£5500	£200

11	**2**	1s.9d. green (H/S "CANCELLED" in oval £9500)	£800	£800
		a. Yellow-green	£5500	£3000
12		2s. dull blue (23.4.59)	£6500	£1300

(b) Unofficial perf 7½ (1s.9d.) or roul (others)

13	**1**	1d. blue	£10000	
14		2d. green	£5000	£2500
15	**2**	1s.9d. green	£16000	

Nos. 13/15 were privately produced, probably by commercial firms for their own convenience.

The 10d. also exists with "CANCELLED" in oval, but no examples are believed to be in private hands.

4

(Typo D.L.R.)
1857 (Oct)–**64**. No wmk. Glazed paper.

(a) Imperf

16	**4**	½d. reddish lilac (blued paper)	£4250	£650
17		½d. dull mauve (1858)	£190	£250
		a. Private roul	£8000	

(b) P 12½

18	**4**	½d. dull mauve (1864)	£225	£180

(Recess P.B.)
1861–**64**. Wmk Star, W w **1**.

(a) Clean-cut and intermediate perf 14 to 15½

19	**1**	1d. light blue	£2500	£300
		a. Dull blue (H/S "CANCELLED" in oval £11000)	£200	13·00
20		2d. green (shades)	£275	28·00
		a. Imperf between (vert pair)	†	—
		b. Yellowish green (H/S "CANCELLED" in oval £12000)	£275	24·00
21	**2**	4d. dull rose (H/S "CANCELLED" in oval £12000)	£2250	£325
22	**1**	5d. chestnut (H/S "CANCELLED" in oval £8000)	£120	8·50
23		6d. brown (H/S "CANCELLED" in oval £9000)	£3000	£180
		a. Bistre-brown	—	£275
24	**2**	8d. brown (H/S "CANCELLED" in oval £10000)	£2500	£500
25		9d. purple-brown	£15000	£250
26	**3**	1s. slate-violet (H/S "CANCELLED" in oval £11000)	£140	13·00
27	**2**	2s. dull blue	£4500	£800

(b) Rough perf 14 to 15½

28	**1**	1d. dull blue	£160	12·00
		a. Blued paper	£800	25·00
29		2d. green	£475	85·00
30	**2**	4d. rose-red	£600	£130
		a. Deep rose-red	£700	£160
31	**1**	6d. deep brown	£1300	£130
		a. Light brown	£2250	£200
		b. Olive-sepia	£1200	£120
32	**2**	8d. brown	£1700	£650
		a. Yellow-brown	£1600	£425
33		9d. deep brown (H/S "CANCELLED" in oval £9000)	£150	£120
		a. Light brown	£1300	£130
		b. Olive-sepia	£850	85·00
34	**3**	10d. dull vermilion	£300	28·00
		a. Imperf vert (horiz pair)	†	—
35		1s. slate-violet	£225	16·00
36	**2**	1s.9d. light green (prepared for use, but not issued)	£750	
37		2s. dull blue (H/S "CANCELLED" in oval £11000)	£750	£160
		a. Deep dull blue	£1100	£190

(c) P 12½ by D.L.R.

38	**3**	10d. dull vermilion (9.64)	£325	22·00

The line machine used for Nos. 19/37 produced perforations of variable quality due to wear, poor cleaning and faulty servicing, but it is generally accepted that the clean-cut and intermediate versions occurred on stamps perforated up to March 1861 and the rough variety when the machine was used after that date.

(Recess D.L.R.)
1862. No wmk. Smooth paper.

(a) P 13

39	**1**	1d. dull blue	£180	7·00
40		5d. lake-brown	£1800	£150
41		6d. brown	£200	29·00
		a. Deep brown	£200	29·00
42	**2**	9d. brown	£1300	£120
43	**3**	1s. slate-purple	£1800	95·00

(b) P 11½, 12

44	**1**	1d. dull blue	£1800	£130
		a. Imperf between (horiz pair)	†	£18000

Nos. 39/44 were printed on paper showing a papermaker's watermark of "T H SAUNDERS 1862", parts of which can be found on individual stamps. Examples are rare and command a premium.

The 1s. is known imperforate, but was not issued in this condition (*Price, £4000, unused*).

5 (23 mm high. "CC" oval)   **6** (21½ mm high. "CC" round and smaller)

(Typo (½d.) or recess (others) D.L.R.)

1863–66. W **5**. Paper medium thin and slightly soft.

(a) P 11½, 12

45	**1**	1d. deep blue	£3500	£325
		x. Wmk reversed	£4750	£550

(b) P 13

46	**1**	6d. sepia	£2750	£250
		x. Wmk reversed		£300
		y. Wmk inverted and reversed	£4000	£700
47	**2**	9d. sepia	£6500	£1000

(c) P 12½

48	**4**	½d. dull mauve (1864)	80·00	50·00
		aw. Wmk inverted	£450	£160
		b. Reddish lilac	90·00	65·00
		c. Mauve	55·00	55·00
49	**1**	1d. deep blue	£180	9·00
		a. Imperf	†	60·00
		w. Wmk inverted	†	60·00
		x. Wmk reversed	£250	9·00
		y. Wmk inverted and reversed	†	90·00
50		2d. grey-green (1864)	£100	15·00
		a. Imperf	†	£5000
		bw. Wmk inverted	£400	£100
		by. Wmk inverted and reversed	†	£200
		c. Bottle-green	†	£4000
		d. Yellowish green	£9000	£400
		dx. Wmk reversed	†	£1100
		e. Emerald (wmk reversed)	£190	£110
		ew. Wmk inverted	£900	£475
51		2d. ochre (wmk reversed) (1866)	£325	£275
		w. Wmk inverted	£950	£800
		y. Wmk inverted and reversed	£850	£600
52	**2**	4d. rose-carmine (1865)	£900	£275
		ax. Wmk reversed	£1300	
		b. Rose	£550	£130
		bx. Wmk reversed	£750	£170
53	**1**	5d. red-brown (shades) (1865)	£325	£110
		w. Wmk inverted	†	£325
		x. Wmk reversed	£450	80·00
54		5d. grey-olive (1866)	£2000	£425
		ax. Wmk reversed	£1600	£350
		b. Yellow-olive	£900	£275
		bx. Wmk reversed	£850	£300
55		6d. sepia	£250	4·50
		aw. Wmk inverted	†	£110
		ax. Wmk reversed		
		b. Reddish brown	£350	14·00
		c. Blackish brown	£300	11·00
		ca. Double print	†	£4250
		cw. Wmk inverted	£425	95·00
		cx. Wmk reversed	£375	70·00
		cy. Wmk inverted and reversed	†	£200
56	**2**	8d. reddish brown (shades) (1864)	£140	75·00
		x. Wmk reversed	£275	£130
		y. Wmk inverted and reversed	£550	£180
57		9d. sepia	£350	50·00
		x. Wmk reversed	£850	£130
58	**3**	10d. vermilion (1866)	£4750	70·00
		ax. Wmk reversed	†	£170
		b. Orange-red	£7500	£450
		bx. Wmk reversed	†	£650
59	**2**	2s. steel-blue (shades) (1864)	£375	40·00
		x. Wmk reversed	£750	£130
		y. Wmk inverted and reversed	£1000	£350

Watermarks as Type **5** were arranged in four panes, each of 60, with the words "CROWN COLONIES" between the panes. Parts of this marginal watermark often appear on the stamps.

De La Rue had considerable difficulty matching the standard Crown CC watermark to the plates received from Perkins Bacon with the result that the watermark W **5** is frequently found misplaced.

A further aid to identifying the two watermarks is the distance between the top of the cross and the foot of "CC", which measures 2 mm on W **5** and 6.5 mm on W **6**.

The ½d. dull mauve, 2d. ochre and 5d. grey-olive with this watermark also exist imperforate, but are not known used. The 6d. sepia and 2s. steel-blue also exist imperforate on wove paper without watermark.

One used example of the 2d. grey-green is known showing private roulettes added to an imperforate stamp (*Price £5000*).

7   **8**

(Typo D.L.R.)

1866–68. Wmk Crown CC.

(a) P 12½

60	**7**	3d. rose	£275	£100

(b) P 14

61	**8**	1d. blue (shades) (1868)	25·00	12·00
		w. Wmk inverted	†	£225
62	**7**	3d. carmine-rose (1867)	90·00	50·00
		a. Bright rose	95·00	55·00

Nos. 60/1 exist imperforate.

(Recess D.L.R.)

1867–70. W **6**. Specially produced hand-made paper. P 12½.

63	**1**	1d. dull blue	£325	17·00
		aw. Wmk inverted	£700	£160
		ax. Wmk reversed	£325	17·00
		ay. Wmk inverted and reversed	†	£275
		b. Deep blue	£275	16·00
		bw. Wmk inverted	—	£160
		bx. Wmk reversed	£450	45·00
64		2d. ochre	£170	14·00
		aw. Wmk inverted		
		ax. Wmk reversed	£300	45·00
		b. Bistre	95·00	9·50
		bw. Wmk inverted	£160	
		c. Olive-bistre	£170	20·00
		cw. Wmk inverted	£170	
		d. Yellow	£130	8·00
		dx. Wmk reversed	85·00	14·00
65	**2**	4d. rose	£300	55·00
		ax. Wmk reversed	£275	45·00
		b. Rose-carmine	85·00	21·00
		bw. Wmk inverted	†	£150
		bx. Wmk reversed	£110	21·00
		by. Wmk inverted and reversed	£700	£225
66	**1**	5d. yellow-olive	£160	23·00
		ax. Wmk reversed	£150	27·00
		ay. Wmk inverted and reversed	†	£150
		b. Olive-green	£150	24·00
		bx. Wmk reversed	†	75·00
		c. Bronze-green	65·00	60·00
67		6d. deep brown (1869)	£140	11·00
		ax. Wmk reversed	£250	
		b. Blackish brown	£190	9·00
		bw. Wmk inverted	†	£170
		bx. Wmk reversed	£225	19·00
		c. Red-brown	60·00	42·00
68	**2**	8d. chocolate	£130	80·00
		ax. Wmk reversed	—	£150
		b. Lake-brown	£140	85·00
		bx. Wmk reversed	£325	£150
69		9d. bistre-brown (12.68)	£950	38·00
		ax. Wmk reversed	£500	25·00
		b. Blackish brown	70·00	7·00
70	**3**	10d. dull vermilion (wmk reversed)	£5500	£150
		ay. Wmk inverted and reversed	†	£350
		b. Red-orange	90·00	18·00
		bx. Wmk reversed	£190	17·00
		by. Wmk inverted and reversed	£1000	
		c. Orange	£150	17·00
71		1s. reddish lilac (1870)	£300	30·00
		ax. Wmk reversed	£500	85·00
		b. Reddish violet	£150	12·00
		bw. Wmk inverted	†	£250
		bx. Wmk reversed	£450	85·00
72	**2**	2s. steel-blue	£275	22·00
		ax. Wmk reversed	†	55·00
		b. Deep blue	£160	16·00
		bx. Wmk reversed	£200	23·00

Watermarks as Type **6** were arranged in one pane of 240 (12×20) with the words "CROWN COLONIES" twice in each side margin.

Unused examples of the 1d. dull blue, 1d. deep blue, 5d. yellow-olive, 6d. deep brown, 9d. blackish brown and 10d. red orange with this watermark exist imperforate.

Nos. 73 to 120 are vacant.

PRINTERS. All stamps from No. 121 to 367 were typographed by De La Rue & Co. Ltd, London.
A wide variety of shades may be found on stamps of this period. We only list the most significant.

(New Currency. 100 cents = 1 rupee)

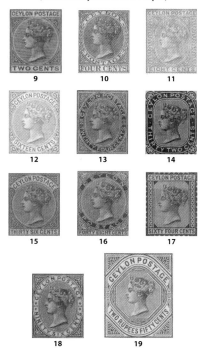

9	10	11

12	13	14

15	16	17

18	19

1872–80. Wmk Crown CC.

(a) P 14

121	9	2c. pale brown (shades)	32·00	4·25
		w. Wmk inverted	£170	95·00
122	10	4c. grey	50·00	1·75
		w. Wmk inverted	£425	95·00
123		4c. rosy-mauve (1880)	75·00	1·50
		w. Wmk inverted	£400	£200
124	11	8c. orange-yellow	55·00	7·00
		a. Yellow	45·00	7·50
		w. Wmk inverted	†	£225
126	12	16c. pale violet	£140	2·75
		w. Wmk inverted	†	£200
127	13	24c. green	80·00	2·25
		w. Wmk inverted	†	£180
128	14	32c. slate (1877)	£180	15·00
		w. Wmk inverted	£600	£200
129	15	36c. blue	£200	30·00
		x. Wmk reversed	£425	£160
130	16	48c. rose	£100	9·50
		w. Wmk inverted	—	85·00
131	17	64c. red-brown (1877)	£300	30·00
132	18	96c. drab	£275	30·00
		w. Wmk inverted	—	£250
121/32 Set of 11			£1300	£150

(b) P 14×12½

133	9	2c. brown	£425	£250
134	10	4c. grey	£2500	38·00
135	11	8c. orange-yellow	£475	55·00
		w. Wmk inverted	†	£400

(c) P 12½

136	9	2c. brown	£4500	£250
		w. Wmk inverted	†	£600
137	10	4c. grey	£3000	£325

(d) P 12½×14

138	19	2r.50 dull-rose (1879)	£800	£425

(e) Prepared for use and sent out to Ceylon, but not issued unsurcharged

139	14	32c. slate (P 14×12½)	£1400	
140	17	64c. red-brown (P 14×12½)	£1600	
141	19	2r.50 dull rose (P 12½)	£3250	

FORGERIES—Beware of forged overprint and surcharge varieties on Victorian issues.

SIXTEEN

16

CENTS
(20)

1882 (Oct). Nos. 127 and 131 surch as T **20** by Govt Printer.

142	13	16c. on 24c. green	42·00	9·50
		a. Surch inverted		
143	17	20c. on 64c. red-brown	14·00	9·00
		a. Surch double	†	£1700

1883–98. Wmk Crown CA.

(a) P 14

146	9	2c. pale brown	70·00	3·50
147		2c. dull green (1884)	3·25	15
		s. Optd "SPECIMEN"	£475	
		w. Wmk inverted	£275	£110
148	10	4c. rosy mauve	6·50	50
		w. Wmk inverted	†	£275
		x. Wmk reversed	†	£350
149		4c. rose (1884)	7·50	13·00
		s. Optd "SPECIMEN"	£450	
150	11	8c. orange-yellow	8·00	14·00
		a. Yellow (1898)	5·50	12·00
151	12	16c. pale violet	£2000	£180

(b) Trial perforation. P 12

151a	9	2c. dull green	£7000	
151b	10	4c. rose	£7000	
151c	13	24c. brown-purple	£7500	

(c) Prepared for use and sent out to Ceylon, but not issued unsurcharged. P 14

152	13	24c. brown-purple	£1700	
		s. Optd "SPECIMEN"	£800	

Although delivered in 1884 it is believed that the 4c. rose, No. 149, was not used until the early 1890s.
See also Nos. 246, 256 and 258 for the 2c. and 4c. in different colours.

Postage &

FIVE CENTS
(21)

TEN CENTS
(22)

Revenue

Twenty Cents
(23)

One Rupee Twelve Cents
(24)

1885 (1 Jan–Mar). T **10/19** surch locally as T **21/24**.

I. Wmk Crown CC

(a) P 14

153	21	5c. on 16c. pale violet	†	£3000
154		5c. on 24c. green	£6500	£110
155		5c. on 32c. slate	70·00	15·00
		a. Surch inverted	†	£2750
		b. Dark grey	£200	45·00
156		5c. on 36c. blue	£300	13·00
		a. Surch inverted	†	£2750
		x. Wmk reversed	†	£180
157		5c. on 48c. rose	£2500	70·00
158		5c. on 64c. red-brown	£140	13·00
		a. Surch double	†	£3500
159		5c. on 96c. drab	£550	70·00
161	22	10c. on 16c. pale violet	£12000	£3000
162		10c. on 24c. green	£500	£140
163		10c. on 36c. blue	£475	£275
164		10c. on 64c. red-brown	£450	£250
165		20c. on 24c. green	80·00	28·00
166	23	20c. on 32c. slate	90·00	75·00
		a. Dark grey	£110	60·00
		aw. Wmk inverted	£400	
167		25c. on 32c. slate	26·00	8·00
		a. Dark grey	28·00	9·00
168		28c. on 48c. rose	40·00	11·00
		a. Surch double	†	£3000
		w. Wmk inverted	†	£400
169	22	30c. on 36c. blue	22·00	16·00
		x. Wmk reversed	16·00	12·00
		xa. Surch inverted	£325	£150
170		56c. on 96c. drab	35·00	26·00

(b) P 14×12½

172	**21**	5c. on 32c. slate	£850	55·00
173		5c. on 64c. red-brown	£950	55·00
		w. Wmk inverted	†	£500
174	**22**	10c. on 64c. red-brown	95·00	£170
		a. Imperf between (vert pair)	£6000	
175	**24**	1r.12 on 2r.50 dull rose (P 12½)	£700	£110
176		1r.12 on 2r.50 dull rose (P 12½×14)	£110	50·00

II. Wmk Crown CA. P 14

178	**21**	5c. on 4c. rose (3.85)	27·00	5·50
		a. Surch inverted	†	£325
179		5c. on 8c. orange-yellow	95·00	11·00
		a. Surch double	†	£3750
		b. Surch inverted	†	£4250
180		5c. on 16c. pale violet	£180	18·00
		a. Surch inverted	†	£250
182		5c. on 24c. brown-purple	—	£500
184	**22**	10c. on 16c. pale violet	£13000	£1700
185		10c. on 24c. brown-purple	18·00	11·00
186		15c. on 16c. pale violet	15·00	11·00

The 5c. on 4c. rosy mauve and 5c. on 24c. green, both watermarked Crown CA, previously catalogued are now known to be forgeries.

REVENUE AND POSTAGE

5 CENTS 10 CENTS 1 R. 12 C.

(25)   (26)   (27)

1885. T **11/15**, **18** and **19** surch with T **25/7** by D.L.R. P 14.

(a) Wmk Crown CA

187	**25**	5c. on 8c. lilac	27·00	1·50
		w. Wmk inverted	†	£140
		x. Wmk reversed	†	£350
188	**26**	10c. on 24c. brown-purple	14·00	8·50
189		15c. on 16c. orange-yellow	60·00	15·00
190		28c. on 32c. slate	28·00	2·50
191		30c. on 36c. olive-green	29·00	16·00
192		56c. on 96c. drab	50·00	17·00

(b) Wmk Crown CC (sideways)

193	**27**	1r.12 on 2r.50 dull rose	60·00	£140
187/93 *Set of 7*			£225	£180
187s/93s Optd "SPECIMEN" *Set of 7*			£1200	

No. 194 is vacant.

28

29

1886. Wmk Crown CA. P. 14.

195	**28**	5c. dull purple	3·75	10
		w. Wmk inverted	£275	£160
196	**29**	15c. sage-green	9·00	2·25
		w. Wmk inverted	£350	£275
197		15c. olive-green	11·00	2·50
198		25c. yellow-brown	6·50	2·00
		a. Value in yellow	£150	85·00
199		28c. slate	26·00	1·60
195s, 197s/9s Optd "SPECIMEN" *Set of 4*			£300	

Six plates were used for the 5c., No. 195, between 1885 and 1901, each being replaced by its successor as it became worn. Examples from the worn plates show thicker lines in the background and masses of solid colour under the chin, in front of the throat, at the back of the neck and at the base.

No. 200 is vacant.

30

1887. Wmk Crown CC (sideways). White or blued paper. P 14.

201	**30**	1r.12 dull rose	30·00	30·00
		aw. Wmk Crown to left of CC	95·00	95·00
		b. Wmk upright	70·00	80·00
		bw. Wmk inverted	£700	£375
		s. Optd "SPECIMEN"	£200	

The normal sideways watermark shows Crown to right of CC, *as seen from the back of the stamp.*

TWO CENTS TWO 2 Cents

(31)   (32)   (33)

Two Cents

2 Cents

(34)   (35)

1888–90. Nos. 148/9 surch with T **31/5**.

202	**31**	2c. on 4c. rosy mauve	1·40	80
		a. Surch inverted	24·00	24·00
		b. Surch double, one inverted	—	£400
203		2c. on 4c. rose	2·50	30
		a. Surch inverted	20·00	21·00
		b. Surch double	—	£425
204	**32**	2(c). on 4c. rosy mauve	1·00	30
		a. Surch inverted	42·00	42·00
		b. Surch double	£120	£130
		c. Surch double, one inverted	95·00	95·00
205		2(c). on 4c. rose	9·00	20
		a. Surch inverted	£450	
		b. Surch double	£110	£130
		c. Surch double, one inverted	£110	£130
206	**33**	2c. on 4c. rosy mauve	80·00	32·00
		a. Surch inverted	£170	42·00
		b. Surch double, one inverted	£225	
207		2c. on 4c. rose	4·25	75
		a. Surch inverted	18·00	9·50
		b. Surch double	£200	£160
		c. Surch double, one inverted	8·00	14·00
		w. Wmk inverted	£200	
208	**34**	2c. on 4c. rosy mauve	65·00	28·00
		a. Surch inverted	£200	30·00
209		2c. on 4c. rose	2·50	1·10
		a. Surch inverted	19·00	8·50
		b. Surch double	£160	£150
		c. Surch double, one inverted	19·00	11·00
210	**35**	2c. on 4c. rosy mauve	65·00	38·00
		a. Surch inverted	95·00	42·00
		b. Surch double, one inverted	£150	£150
		c. Surch double	—	£450
		d. "s" of "Cents" inverted (R. 3/5)	—	£750
		e. As d. Whole surch inverted		
211		2c. on 4c. rose	15·00	1·00
		a. Surch inverted	24·00	7·50
		b. Surch double	£150	£150
		c. Surch double, one inverted	25·00	14·00
		d. "s" of "Cents" inverted (R. 3/5)	£650	£375
		x. Wmk reversed	†	£350
209s, 211s Optd "SPECIMEN" *Set of 2*			65·00	

The 4c. rose and the 4c. rosy mauve are found surcharged "Postal Commission 3 (or "Three") Cents". They denote the extra commission charged by the Post Office on postal orders which had not been cashed within three months of the date of issue. For a short time the Post Office did not object to the use of these stamps on letters.

Nos. 212 to 232 are vacant.

POSTAGE

Five Cents FIFTEEN

REVENUE CENTS

(36)   (37)

1890. No. 197 surch locally with T **36**.

233		5c. on 15c. olive-green	4·00	2·50
		a. Surch inverted	65·00	75·00
		b. Surch double	£120	£140
		c. "Flve" for "Five" (R. 1/1)	£140	95·00
		d. Variety as c, inverted	—	£1800
		e. "REVENUE" omitted	£225	£200
		f. Inverted "s" in "Cents" (R. 10/2)	£130	£120
		g. Variety as f, and whole surch inverted	£2250	
		h. "REVENUE" omitted and inverted "s" in "Cents"	£1800	
		i. "POSTAGE" spaced between "T" and "A" (R. 1/5)	90·00	90·00
		j. Variety as i, and whole surch inverted	£2250	£1800
		s. Optd "SPECIMEN"	35·00	

1891. Nos. 198/9 surch locally with T **37**.

239	**29**	15c. on 25c. yellow-brown	20·00	20·00
240		15c. on 28c. slate	21·00	9·00
		w. Wmk inverted	†	£300

3 Cents

(38)   39

1892. Nos. 148/9 and 199 surch locally with T **38**.

241	**10**	3c. on 4c. rosy mauve	1·25	3·25
242		3c. on 4c. rose	9·00	13·00
		s. Optd "SPECIMEN"	42·00	
		w. Wmk inverted	£200	
		ws. Optd "SPECIMEN"	£150	
243	**29**	3c. on 28c. slate	6·50	6·50
		a. Surch double	£170	
241/3 *Set of 3*			15·00	20·00

1893–99. Wmk Crown CA. P 14.

245	**39**	3c. terracotta and blue-green	7·00	45
246	**10**	4c. carmine-rose (1898)	13·00	15·00
247	**29**	30c. bright mauve and chestnut	5·00	3·25
		a. Bright violet and chestnut	6·50	3·50
249	**19**	2r.50 purple/red (1899)	42·00	65·00
245/9 *Set of 4*			60·00	75·00
245s, 247s/9s Optd "SPECIMEN" *Set of 3*			80·00	

Six Cents
(40)

2 R. 25 C.
(41)

1898 (Dec)–**99**.

(a) No. 196 surch locally with T **40**

250	**29**	6c. on 15c. sage-green	1·25	75

(b) As No. 138, but colour changed and perf 14, surch as T **41**
by D.L.R. (1899)

254	**19**	1r.50 on 2r.50 slate	21·00	55·00
		w. Wmk inverted	£300	£375
255		2r.25 on 2r.50 yellow	50·00	85·00
250s/5s Optd "Specimen" (Nos. 250s) or "SPECIMEN"				
Set of 3			80·00	

43

1899–1900. Wmk Crown CA (1r.50, 2r.25 wmk Crown CC). P 14.

256	**9**	2c. pale orange-brown	5·00	30
257	**39**	3c. deep green	5·00	55
258	**10**	4c. yellow	4·25	3·75
259	**29**	6c. rose and black	3·25	45
		w. Wmk inverted	†	£300
260	**39**	12c. sage-green and rose (1900)	5·50	9·50
261	**29**	15c. blue	8·50	1·25
262	**39**	75c. black and red-brown	11·00	10·00
263	**43**	1r.50 rose	35·00	55·00
		w. Wmk inverted	£400	£400
264		2r.25 dull blue	38·00	55·00
256/64 *Set of 9*			£100	£120
256s/64s Optd "SPECIMEN" *Set of 9*			£225	

44   45   46

47   48

1903 (29 May)–**05**. Wmk Crown CA. P 14.

265	**44**	2c. red-brown (21.7.03)	2·00	20
266	**45**	3c. green (11.6.03)	2·00	1·00
267		4c. orange-yellow and blue	2·25	6·00
268	**46**	5c. dull purple (2.7.03)	2·75	60
		sa. Opt "SPECIMEN" double, one albino	£200	
269	**47**	6c. carmine (5.11.03)	9·50	1·50
		w. Wmk inverted	£130	£150
270	**45**	12c. sage-green and rosine (13.8.03)	5·00	11·00
271	**48**	15c. blue (2.7.03)	6·50	3·50
272		25c. bistre (11.8.03)	5·00	12·00
273		30c. dull violet and green	3·25	4·00
274	**45**	75c. dull blue and orange (31.3.05)	3·50	24·00
275	**48**	1r.50 greyish slate (7.4.04)	65·00	60·00
276		2r.25 brown and green (12.4.04)	95·00	55·00
265/76 *Set of 12*			£180	£160
265s/76s Optd "SPECIMEN" *Set of 12*			£180	

1904 (13 Sept)–**05**. Wmk Mult Crown CA. Ordinary paper. P 14.

277	**44**	2c. red-brown (17.11.04)	2·25	10
278	**45**	3c. green (17.11.04)	1·75	15
279		4c. orange and ultramarine	3·00	1·50
		w. Wmk inverted	—	£250
280	**46**	5c. dull purple (29.11.04)	3·50	1·25
		a. Chalk-surfaced paper (5.10.05)	7·50	70
		ay. Wmk inverted and reversed	—	£300
281	**47**	6c. carmine (11.10.04)	4·75	15
282	**45**	12c. sage-green and rosine (29.9.04)	1·75	1·75
283	**48**	15c. blue (1.12.04)	3·75	60
284		25c. bistre (5.1.05)	6·00	3·75
		w. Wmk inverted	†	£350
285		30c. violet and green (7.9.05)	2·50	3·00
286	**45**	75c. dull blue and orange (25.5.05)	5·25	8·00
287	**48**	1r.50 grey (5.1.05)	29·00	12·00
288		2r.25 brown and green (22.12.04)	22·00	32·00
277/88 *Set of 12*			75·00	55·00

50   51

1908. Wmk Mult Crown CA. P 14.

289	**50**	5c. deep purple (26 May)	7·00	10
290		5c. dull purple	8·50	30
291	**51**	6c. carmine (6 June)	3·00	10
289s, 291s Optd "SPECIMEN" *Set of 2*			70·00	

1910 (1 Aug)–**11**. Wmk Mult Crown CA. P 14.

292	**44**	2c. brown-orange (20.5.11)	1·50	50
293	**48**	3c. green (5.7.11)	1·00	75
294		10c. sage-green and maroon	2·50	3·50
295		25c. grey	2·50	3·00
296		50c. chocolate	4·00	7·50
297		1r. purple/yellow	8·00	13·00
298		2r. red/yellow	15·00	30·00
299		5r. black/green	45·00	£100
300		10r. black/red	£130	£275
292/300 *Set of 9*			£190	£375
292s/300s Optd "SPECIMEN" *Set of 9*			£275	

Examples of Nos. 298/300 are known showing a forged Colombo registered postmark dated '27.1.10'.

52   53

(A)   (B)

Most values in Type **52** were produced by two printing operations, using "Key" and "Duty" plates. Differences in the two Dies of the Key plate are described in the introduction to this catalogue.

In the Ceylon series, however, the 1c. and 5c. values, together with later printings of the 3c. and 6c., were printed from special plates at one operation. These plates can be identified by the large "C" in the value tablet (see illustration A). Examples of these values from Key and Duty plates printing have value tablet as illustration B. The 3c. and 5c. stamps from the single plates *resemble* Die I, and the 1c. and 6c. Die II, although in the latter case the inner top corners of the side panels are square and not curved.

Break in scroll (R. 1/12)

Broken crown and scroll (R. 2/12)

Break in lines below left scroll
(R. 4/9. Ptgs from May 1920)

Damaged leaf at bottom right
(R. 5/6. Ptgs from April 1918)

1912–25. Wmk Mult Crown CA. Chalk-surfaced paper (30c. to 100r.). P 14.

(a) Printed from single plates. Value tablet as A

301	**52**	1c. brown (1919)	1·00	10
		w. Wmk inverted	24·00	
302		3c. blue-green (1919)	5·50	45
		w. Wmk inverted	21·00	42·00
		y. Wmk inverted and reversed	28·00	65·00
303		5c. purple	12·00	2·75
		a. Wmk sideways (Crown to right of CA)	£500	
		x. Wmk reversed	†	£275
		y. Wmk inverted and reversed	£140	
304		5c. bright magenta	1·00	60
		w. Wmk inverted	£180	£150
305		6c. pale scarlet (1919)	14·00	85
		a. Wmk sideways (Crown to left of CA)	45·00	£100
		w. Wmk inverted	32·00	60·00
306		6c. carmine	19·00	1·25
		a. Wmk sideways (Crown to right of CA)	55·00	
		aw. Wmk sideways (Crown to left of CA)	95·00	
		w. Wmk inverted	70·00	
		y. Wmk inverted and reversed	50·00	

(b) Printed from Key and Duty plates.
Die I. 3c. and 6c. have value tablet as B

307	**52**	2c. brown-orange	40	30
		a. Deep orange-brown	30	20
308		3c. yellow-green	6·50	2·25
		a. Deep green (1917)	4·50	1·10
309		6c. scarlet (shades)	1·10	50
		a. Wmk sideways	†	—
310		10c. sage-green	3·00	1·75
		a. Deep sage-green (1917)	6·50	2·50
		w. Wmk inverted	£190	
311		15c. deep bright blue	3·00	1·25
		a. Ultramarine (1918)	1·75	1·25
		aw. Wmk inverted	25·00	
312		25c. orange and blue	7·50	4·50
		a. Yellow and blue (1917)	1·75	1·75
		aw. Wmk inverted	£200	£200
313		30c. blue-green and violet	4·00	3·25
		a. Yellow-green and violet (1915)	7·00	4·00
		ab. Wmk sideways (Crown to right of CA)	32·00	
		abw. Wmk Crown to left of CA	35·00	
		aw. Wmk inverted	50·00	
		awa. Ditto. Duty plate ("CEYLON" and "30c") printed double, one albino and inverted	£375	
314		50c. black and scarlet	1·50	1·75
		w. Wmk inverted	20·00	45·00

315		1r. purple/yellow	5·50	4·50
		a. White back (1913)	6·00	5·00
		as. Optd "SPECIMEN"	50·00	
		b. On lemon (1915)	4·25	8·00
		bs. Optd "SPECIMEN"	45·00	
		c. On orange-buff (1918)	28·00	35·00
		cw. Wmk inverted	80·00	
		d. On pale yellow (1922)	5·00	10·00
		ds. Optd "SPECIMEN"	42·00	
316		2r. black and red/yellow	3·75	16·00
		a. White back (1913)	2·75	16·00
		as. Optd "SPECIMEN"	50·00	
		b. On lemon (1915)	25·00	27·00
		bs. Optd "SPECIMEN"	40·00	
		c. On orange-buff (1919)	40·00	42·00
		cw. Wmk inverted	65·00	
		d. On pale yellow (1921)	40·00	40·00
317		5r. black/green	20·00	45·00
		a. White back (1914)	25·00	42·00
		as. Optd "SPECIMEN"	48·00	
		b. On blue-green (olive back) (1917)	26·00	48·00
		bs. Optd "SPECIMEN"	80·00	
		bw. Wmk inverted	95·00	£140
		c. Die II. On emerald back (1923)	48·00	£110
		cs. Optd "SPECIMEN"	65·00	
318		10r. purple and black/red	70·00	90·00
		aw. Wmk inverted	£250	
		b. Die II (1923)	90·00	£180
		bw. Wmk inverted	£650	
319		20r. black and red/blue	£150	£160
320	**53**	50r. dull purple	£600	
		a. Break in scroll	£1600	
		b. Broken crown and scroll	£1600	
		f. Damaged leaf at bottom right	£1600	
		s. Optd "SPECIMEN"	£225	
321		100r. grey-black	£2750	
		a. Break in scroll	£5000	
		b. Broken crown and scroll	£5000	
		f. Damaged leaf at bottom right	£5000	
		s. Optd "SPECIMEN"	£425	
		w. Wmk inverted	£7000	
322		500r. dull green	£8000	
		a. Break in scroll	£16000	
		b. Broken crown and scroll	£16000	
		f. Damaged leaf at bottom right		
		s. Optd "SPECIMEN"	£700	
323		1000r. purple/red (1925)	£30000	
		b. Broken crown and scroll	£45000	
		e. Break in lines below left scroll		
		f. Damaged leaf at bottom right		
		s. Optd "SPECIMEN"	£1400	
301/18 Set of 14			£100	£140
301s/19s Optd "SPECIMEN" Set of 15			£425	

The 2c. and 5c. exist in coils, constructed from normal sheets, used in stamp-affixing machines introduced in 1915.

Sideways watermark varieties are described *as seen from the back of the stamp.*

The "substituted crown" watermark variety is known on the sheet margin of the 1c., No. 301.

An example of the 1000r. optd "SPECIMEN" is known with the break in scroll variety (R. 1/12).

Nos. 324 to 329 are vacant.

WAR
STAMP
ONE CENT

WAR
STAMP
(54)   (55)

1918 (18 Nov)–**19.**

(a) Optd with T 54 by Govt Printer, Colombo

330	**52**	2c. brown-orange	20	40
		a. Opt inverted	70·00	80·00
		b. Opt double	32·00	45·00
331		3c. blue-green (No. 302) (1919)	3·75	40
		a. Opt double	£140	
332		3c. deep green (No. 308a)	20	50
		a. Opt double	£100	£120
		w. Wmk inverted	†	£190
333		5c. purple	30	30
		a. Opt double	70·00	80·00
		w. Wmk inverted	£120	
334		5c. bright magenta	4·50	3·25
		a. Opt inverted	70·00	80·00
		b. Opt double	50·00	60·00

(b) Surch with T 55

335	**52**	1c. on 5c. purple	50	40
		w. Wmk inverted	£160	
		y. Wmk inverted and reversed	£120	
336		1c. on 5c. bright magenta	3·25	20
330s, 332s/3s, 335s Optd "SPECIMEN" Set of 4			£130	

Collectors are warned against forgeries of the errors in the "WAR STAMP" overprints.

1918. Surch as T **55**, but without "WAR STAMP".

337	**52**	1c. on 5c. purple	15	25
		a. Surch double	£200	
		bs. Optd "SPECIMEN"	42·00	
		by. Wmk inverted and reversed	£160	
337c		1c. on 5c. bright magenta	3·25	4·25

Nick in top right scroll (R. 3/12) (Some printings from 1920 onwards show attempts at repair)

Breaks in scrolls at right (R. 1/3. Ptgs of 12s.6d. from July 1932)

1921–32. Wmk Mult Script CA. Chalk-surfaced paper (30c. to 100r.). P 14.

(a) Printed from single plates. Value tablet as A

338	**52**	1c. brown (1927)	1·00	35
339		3c. green (5.5.22)	5·50	75
		w. Wmk inverted	20·00	48·00
340		3c. slate-grey (1923)	75	20
		a. Wmk sideways	£1700	
		w. Wmk inverted	40·00	
341		5c. purple (1927)	60	15
342		6c. carmine-red (3.8.21)	3·25	75
		w. Wmk inverted	22·00	48·00
		y. Wmk inverted and reversed	70·00	
343		6c. bright violet (1922)	2·50	15
		w. Wmk inverted	42·00	
		y. Wmk inverted and reversed	70·00	

(b) Printed from Key and Duty plates

344	**52**	2c. brown-orange (Die II) (1927)	70	25
345		9c. red/pale yellow (Die II) (1926)	3·00	30
346		10c. sage-green (Die I) (16.9.21)	1·40	40
		aw. Wmk inverted	45·00	
		ay. Wmk inverted and reversed	40·00	65·00
		b. Die II (1924)	1·75	60
		c. Vert gutter pair. Die I and Die II. Nos. 346 and 346b	£375	
347		12c. rose-scarlet (Die I) (1925)	10·00	5·50
		a. Die II	1·25	2·25
		as. Optd "SPECIMEN"	£100	
		b. Vert gutter pair. Die I and Die II. Nos. 347/a	£160	
348		15c. ultramarine (Die I) (30.5.22)	3·75	19·00
349		15c. green/pale yellow (Die I) (1923)	5·50	1·25
		a. Die II (1924)	4·75	1·00
		aw. Wmk inverted	45·00	
		b. Vert gutter pair. Die I and Die II. Nos. 349/a	£325	
350		20c. bright blue (Die I) (1922)	6·00	6·00
		aw. Wmk inverted	70·00	
		b. Die II (1924)	3·50	45
		c. Vert gutter pair. Die I and Die II. Nos. 350 and 350b	£375	
351		25c. orange-yellow and blue (Die I) (17.10.21)	3·00	1·90
		aw. Wmk inverted	75·00	
		b. Die II (1924)	5·00	1·25
		c. Vert gutter pair. Die I and Die II. Nos. 351/a	£190	
352		30c. yellow-green and violet (Die I) (15.3.22)	1·60	5·50
		a. Die II (1924)	6·00	1·25
		b. Vert gutter pair. Die I and Die II. Nos. 352/a	£650	
353		50c. black and scarlet (Die II) (1922)	2·00	80
		a. Die I (1932)	60·00	95·00
354		1r. purple/pale yellow (Die I) (1923)	15·00	45·00
		a. Die II (1925)	25·00	35·00
		b. Vert gutter pair. Die I and Die II. Nos. 354/a	£400	
355		2r. black and red/pale yellow (Die II) (1923)	7·00	14·00
356		5r. black/emerald (Die II) (1924)	50·00	90·00
357		20r. black and red/blue (Die II) (1924)	£300	£375
358	**53**	50r. dull purple (1924)	£750	£1300
		a. Break in scroll	£1500	
		b. Broken crown and scroll	£1500	
		e. Break in lines below left scroll	£1500	
		f. Damaged leaf at bottom right	£1500	
		g. Gash in fruit and leaf	£1500	
		s. Optd "SPECIMEN"	£200	

359		100r. brownish grey (1924)	£2750	
		a. Break in scroll	£4500	
		b. Broken crown and scroll	£4500	
		c. Nick in top right scroll	£4500	
		e. Break in lines below left scroll	£4500	
		f. Damaged leaf at bottom right	£4500	
		h. Grey-black	£2750	
		ha. Break in scroll	£4500	
		hb. Broken crown and scroll	£4500	
		he. Break in lines below left scroll	£4500	
		hf. Damaged leaf at bottom right	£4500	
		s. Optd "SPECIMEN"	£475	
360		100r. dull purple and blue (24.10.27)	£2000	
		a. Break in scroll	£4000	
		b. Broken crown and scroll	£4000	
		e. Break in lines below left scroll	£4000	
		f. Damaged leaf at bottom right	£4000	
		g. Gash in fruit and leaf	£4000	
		s. Optd "SPECIMEN"	£475	
338/56 Set of 19			£100	£140
338s/57s Optd "SPECIMEN" Set of 20			£600	

The 2c. to 30c. and 1r. values produced from Key and Duty plates were printed in sheets of 240 using two plates one above the other. Nos. 346c, 347b, 349b, 350c, 351b, 353b and 354b come from printings in 1924 and 1925 which combined Key Plate 7 (Die I) with Key Plate 12 (Die II).

No. 353a, from Key Plate 23, was a mistake; the "retired" Die I being issued in error when it became necessary to replace Key Plate 21.

(56)   57

(Surch at Ceylon Govt Printing Works)

1926 (27 Nov). Surch as T **56**.

361	**52**	2c. on 3c. slate-grey	3·00	1·00
		a. Surch double	70·00	
		b. Bar omitted	80·00	90·00
362		5c. on 6c. bright violet	1·00	40
361s/2s Optd "SPECIMEN" Set of 2			80·00	

No. 361b comes from the bottom horizontal row of the sheet which was often partially obscured by the selvedge during surcharging.

1927 (27 Nov)–**29**. Wmk Mult Script CA. Chalk-surfaced paper. P 14.

363	**57**	1r. dull and bright purple (1928)	2·50	1·25
364		2r. green and carmine (1929)	3·75	2·75
365		5r. green and dull purple (1928)	17·00	27·00
366		10r. green and brown-orange	65·00	£140
367		20r. dull purple and blue	£250	£500
363/7 Set of 5			£300	£500
363s/7s Optd "SPECIMEN" Set of 5			£250	

No. 364. Collectors are warned against faked 2r. stamps, showing what purports to be a double centre.

58 Tapping Rubber   **59** Adam's Peak

60 Colombo Harbour   **61** Plucking tea

62 Hill paddy (rice)   **63** River scene

64 Coconut Palms   **65** Temple of the Tooth, Kandy

66 Ancient irrigation tank   **67** Wild elephants

68 Trincomalee

(Recess D.L.R. (2, 3, 20, 50c.), B.W. (others))

1935 (1 May)–**36**. T **58**/**68**. Wmk Mult Script CA (sideways on 10, 15, 25, 30c. and 1r.). Various perfs.

368	**58**	2c. black and carmine (P 12×13)	30	40
		a. Perf 14	9·00	40
369	**59**	3c. black and olive-green (P 13×12) (1.10.35)	70	40
		a. Perf 14	38·00	35
370	**60**	6c. black and blue (P 11×11½) (1.1.36)	30	30
371	**61**	9c. green and orange (P 11×11½) (1.1.36)	1·25	65
372	**62**	10c. black and purple (P 11½×11) (1.6.35)	1·25	3·00
373	**63**	15c. red-brown and green (P 11½×11).	1·75	50
374	**64**	20c. black and grey-blue (P 12×13) (1.1.36).	2·75	3·50
375	**65**	25c. deep blue and chocolate (P 11½×11)	1·60	1·25
376	**66**	30c. carmine and green (P 11½×11) (1.8.35)	2·50	3·50
377	**67**	50c. black and mauve (P 14) (1.1.36)	16·00	1·75
378	**68**	1r. violet-blue and chocolate (P 11½×11) (1.7.35)	38·00	29·00
368/78 Set of 11			60·00	40·00
368s/78s Perf "SPECIMEN" Set of 11			£350	

68a Windsor Castle

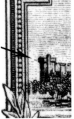 

Diagonal line by turret (Plate 2A R. 10/1 and 10/2)   Dot to left of chapel (Plate 2B R. 8/3)

 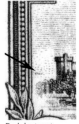

Dot by flagstaff (Plate 4 R. 8/4)   Dash by turret (Plate 4/ R. 3/6)

1935 (6 May). Silver Jubilee. Wmk Mult Script CA. P 13½×14.

379	**68a**	6c. ultramarine and grey	75	30
		f. Diagonal line by turret	80·00	32·00
		g. Dot to left of chapel	£130	50·00
		h. Dot by flagstaff	£110	50·00
		i. Dash by turret	£180	90·00
380		9c. green and indigo	75	2·75
		f. Diagonal line by turret	95·00	£130
		g. Dot to left of chapel	£200	£225
		h. Dot by flagstaff	£170	£200
381		20c. brown and deep blue	4·25	2·75
		f. Diagonal line by turret	£200	£130
		g. Dot to left of chapel	£350	£200
382		50c. slate and purple	5·25	16·00
		f. Diagonal line by turret	£400	£450
		h. Dot by flagstaff	£400	£450
379/82 Set of 4			10·00	20·00
379s/82s Perf "SPECIMEN" Set of 4			£140	

68b King Geroge VI and Queen Elizabeth

1937 (12 May). Coronation. Wmk Mult Script CA. P 11×11½.

383	**68b**	6c. carmine	65	1·00
384		9c. green	2·50	4·50
385		20c. blue	3·50	4·00
383/5 Set of 3			6·00	8·50
383s/5s Perf "SPECIMEN" Set of 3			£120	

69 Tapping Rubber   **70** Sigiriya (Lion Rock)

71 Ancient Guard-stone, Anuradhapura   **72** King George VI

Comma flaw (Pl 2A R. 5/6)

5c. Apostrophe flaw (Frame Pl 1A R. 6/6)
(ptg of 1 Jan 1943 only)

(Recess B.W. (6, 10, 15, 20, 25, 30c., 1r., 2r. (both)), D.L.R. (others) T **72**
typo D.L.R.)

1938–49. T **69/72** and designs as 1935–36, but with portrait of King
George VI instead of King George V, "POSTAGE & REVENUE"
omitted and some redrawn. Wmk Mult Script CA (sideways on
10, 15, 25, 30c. and 1r.). Chalk-surfaced paper (5r.). P 11×11½
(6, 20c., 2r. (both)), 11½×11 (10, 15, 25, 30c., 1r.), 11½×13 (2c.),
13×11½ (3, 50c.), 13½ (5c.) or 14 (5r.).

386	**69**	2c. black and carmine (25.4.38)	22·00	3·25
		aa. Comma flaw	£500	£150
		a. Perf 13½×13 (1938)	£120	1·75
		ab. Comma flaw	£1400	£130
		b. Perf 13½ (25.4.38)	3·00	10
		ba. Comma flaw	£160	75·00
		c. Perf 11×11½ (17.2.44)	1·25	1·50
		cw. Wmk inverted	—	£1500
		d. Perf 12 (22.4.49)	2·25	4·50
387	**59**	3c. black and deep blue-green		
		(21.3.38)	12·00	3·00
		a. Perf 13×13½ (1938)	£275	15·00
		b. Perf 13½ (21.3.38)	6·50	10
		c. Perf 14 (line) (7.41)	£140	1·00
		d. Perf 11½×11 (14.5.42)	1·00	10
		da. "A" of "CA" missing from wmk	£1200	£1200
		dw. Wmk inverted	†	£1700
		e. Perf 12 (14.1.46)	1·50	85
387f	**64**	5c. sage-green and orange (1.1.43)	30	10
		fa. Apostrophe flaw	90·00	45·00
		fb. "A" of "CA" missing from wmk	†	—
		g. Perf 12 (1947)	2·00	30
388	**60**	6c. black and blue (1.1.38)	30	10
		a. "A" of "CA" missing from wmk	†	£1300
389	**70**	10c. black and light blue (1.2.38)	3·50	20
		a. Wmk upright (1.6.44)	2·50	50
390	**63**	15c. green and red-brown (1.1.38)	2·00	20
		a. Wmk upright (23.7.45)	2·75	60
391	**61**	20c. black and grey-blue (15.1.38)	3·25	20
392	**65**	25c. deep blue and chocolate		
		(15.1.38)	5·00	30
		a. Wmk upright (1944)	4·25	20
393	**66**	30c. carmine and green (1.2.38)	12·00	3·50
		a. "A" of "CA" missing from wmk	†	£1400
		b. Wmk upright (16.4.45)	13·00	7·00
394	**67**	50c. black and mauve (25.4.38)	£160	50·00
		a. Perf 13×13½ (25.4.38)	£425	2·75
		b. Perf 13½ (25.4.38)	25·00	1·00
		c. Perf 14 (line) (4.42)	£110	27·00
		d. Perf 11½×11 (14.5.42)	7·50	4·50
		da. "A" of "CA" missing from wmk	£1500	
		e. Perf 12 (14.1.46)	8·00	20
395	**68**	1r. blue-violet and chocolate (1.2.38)	20·00	1·50
		a. Wmk upright (1944)	18·00	2·25
396	**71**	2r. black and carmine (1.2.38)	17·00	4·50
		a. "A" of "CA" missing from wmk	£1700	
396b		2r. black and violet (15.3.47)	4·00	3·00
397	**72**	5r. green and purple (1.7.38)	55·00	18·00
		a. Ordinary paper. Green and pale		
		purple (19.2.43)	38·00	15·00
386/97a (cheapest) Set of 14			£100	25·00
386s/97s Perf "SPECIMEN" Set of 14			£600	

Printings of the 2c., 3c. and 50c. perforated 11×11½ or 11½×11
were produced by Bradbury, Wilkinson after the De La Rue works had
been bombed in December 1940.

(73)　　　　　(74)

1940–41. Nos. 388 and 391 surch by Govt Ptg Office, Colombo.

398	**73**	3c. on 6c. black and blue (10.5.41)	1·00	10
399	**74**	3c. on 20c. black and grey-blue		
		(5.11.40)	6·00	3·50

74a Houses of Parliment, London

1946 (10 Dec). Victory. Wmk Mult Script CA. P 13½×14.

400	**74a**	6c. blue	30	35
401		15c. brown	30	1·75
400s/1s Perf "SPECIMEN" Set of 2			£110	

75 Parliament Building	**76** Adam's Peak

77 Temple of the Tooth	**78** Anuradhapura

(Des R. Tenison and M. S. V. Rodrigo. Recess B.W.)

1947 (25 Nov). Inauguration of New Constitution. T **75/8**. Wmk Mult
Script CA. P 11×12 (horiz) or 12×11 (vert).

402	**75**	6c. black and blue	20	15
403	**76**	10c. black, orange and carmine	30	40
404	**77**	15c. green and purple	30	80
405	**78**	25c. ochre and emerald-green	30	1·75
402/5 Set of 4			1·00	2·75
402s/5s Perf "SPECIMEN" Set of 4			£130	

DOMINION

79 Lion Flag of Dominion	**80** D. S. Senanayake

81 Lotus Flowers and Sinhalese Letters "Sri"

4c. Normal   **4c.** "Short rope" (Pl 1 R. 10/9)

(Recess (flag typo) B.W.)

1949 (4 Feb–5 Apr). First Anniv of Independence.

(a) Wmk Mult Script CA (sideways on 4c.). P 12½×12 (4c.) or 12×12½ (5c.)

406	**79**	4c. yellow, carmine and brown	20	20
		a. "Short rope"	23·00	17·00
407	**80**	5c. brown and green	10	10

*(b) W **81** (sideways on 15c.). P 13×12½ (15c.) or 12×12½ (25c.) (5 April)*

408	**79**	15c. yellow, carmine and vermilion	1·00	1·00
409	**80**	25c. brown and blue	15	1·00
406/9	*Set of 4*		1·25	2·00

The 15c. is larger, measuring 28×12 mm.

82 Globe and Forms of Transport

83   **84**

(Recess D.L.R.)

1949 (10 Oct). 75th Anniv of Universal Postal Union. W **81**. P 13 (25c.) or 12 (others).

410	**82**	5c. brown and bluish green	75	10
411	**83**	15c. black and carmine	1·10	2·75
412	**84**	25c. black and ultramarine	1·10	1·10
410/12	*Set of 3*		2·75	3·50

85 Kandyan Dancer   **86** Kiri Vehera Polonnaruwa

87 Vesak Orchid   **88** Sigiriya (Lion Rock)

89 Octagon Library, Temple of the Tooth   **90** Ruins at Madirigiriya

(Recess B.W.)

1950 (4 Feb). T **85/90**. W **81**. P 11×11½ (75c.), 11½×11 (1r.), 12×12½ (others).

413	**85**	4c. purple and scarlet	15	10
414	**86**	5c. green	15	10
415	**87**	15c. blue-green and violet	3·00	50
416	**88**	30c. carmine and yellow	30	70
417	**89**	75c. ultramarine and orange	9·00	20
418	**90**	1r. deep blue and brown	1·75	30
413/18	*Set of 6*		13·00	1·50

These stamps were issued with redrawn inscriptions in 1958/9. See Nos. 448/65.

91 Sambars, Ruhuna National Park   **92** Ancient Guard-stone, Anuradhapura   **93** Harvesting rice

94 Coconut trees   **95** Sigiriya fresco   **96** Star Orchid

97 Rubber Plantation   **98** Outrigger canoe

99 Tea Plantation   **100** River Gal Dam

101 Bas-relief, Anuradhapura   **102** Harvesting rice

35c. I. No. 424   **35c.** II. No. 424a (Dot added)

(Photo Courvoisier)

1951 (1 Aug)–**54**. T **91**/**102**. No wmk. P 11½.

419	91	2c. brown and blue-green (15.5.54)	10	1·25
420	92	3c. black and slate-violet (15.5.54)	10	1·00
421	93	6c. brown-black and yellow-green (15.5.54)	15	30
422	94	10c. green and blue-grey	1·00	65
423	95	25c. orange-brown and bright blue (15.3.54)	20	20
424	96	35c. red and deep green (I) (1.2.52)	1·50	1·50
		a. Type II (1954)	6·50	60
425	97	40c. deep brown (15.5.54)	5·00	1·00
426	98	50c. indigo and slate-grey (15.3.54)	30	10
427	99	85c. black and deep blue-green (15.5.54)	1·75	30
428	100	2r. blue and deep brown (15.5.54)	11·00	1·25
429	101	5r. brown and orange (15.3.54)	14·00	1·40
430	102	10r. red-brown and buff (15.3.54)	60·00	25·00
419/30		Set of 12	85·00	30·00

Nos. 413/30 (except 422) were reissued in 1958–62, redrawn with 'CEYLON' much smaller and other inscriptions in Sinhalese.
See Nos. 448/65.

103 Ceylon Mace and symbols of Progress   **104** Queen Elizabeth II

(Photo Harrison)

1952 (23 Feb). Colombo Plan Exhibition. Chalk-surfaced paper. W **81** (sideways). P 14½×14.

431	103	5c. green	30	10
432		15c. ultramarine	30	60

(Recess B.W.)

1953 (2 June). Coronation. W **81**. P 12×13.

433	104	5c. green	1·75	10

105 Ceremonial Procession

(Recess D.L.R.)

1954 (10 Apr). Royal Visit. W **81** (sideways). P 13×12½.

434	105	10c. deep blue	1·50	10

106 King Coconuts   **107** Farm Produce

(Photo Courvoisier)

1954 (1 Dec). No wmk. P 11½.

435	106	10c. orange, bistre-brown and buff	10	10

For this design with redrawn inscription see No. 453.

(Photo Harrison)

1955 (10 Dec). Royal Agricultural and Food Exhibition. W **81** (sideways). P 14×14½.

436	107	10c. brown and orange	10	10

108 Sir John Kotelawala and House of Representatives

White stroke to left of "POSTAGE" (R. 2/6)

(Photo Courvoisier)

1956 (26 Mar). Prime Minister's 25 Years of Public Service. P 11½.

437	108	10c. deep bluish green	10	10
		a. White stroke	1·50	

109 Arrival of Vijaya in Ceylon   **110** Lampstand and Dharmachakra

111 Hand of Peace and Dharmachakra   **112** Dharmachakra encircling the Globe

(Photo Courvoisier)

1956. Buddha Jayanti. P 11½.

438	109	3c. blue and brownish grey (23 May)	30	15
439	110	4c. +2c. greenish yellow and deep blue (10 May)	20	75
440	111	10c. +5c. carmine, yellow and grey (10 May)	20	1·00
441	112	15c. bright blue (23 May)	25	10
438/41		Set of 4	85	1·75

113 Mail Transport   **114** Stamp of 1857

(Photo Enschedé (4c., 10c.), Courvoisier (others))

1957 (1 Apr). Centenary of First Ceylon Postage Stamp. P 12½×13 (4c., 10c.) or 11½ (others).

442	**113**	4c. orange-red and deep bluish green	75	50
443		10c. vermilion and blue	75	10
444	**114**	35c. brown, yellow and blue	30	50
445		85c. brown, yellow and grey-green	80	1·60
442/5	*Set of 4*		2·40	2·40

(115)   (116)   117 Kandyan Dancer

1958 (15 Jan). Nos. 439/40 with premium obliterated as T **115** (4c.) or T **116** (10c.).

446	**110**	4c. greenish yellow and deep blue	10	10
		a. Opt inverted	18·00	28·00
		b. Opt double	27·00	40·00
447	**111**	10c. carmine, yellow and grey	10	10
		a. Opt inverted	14·00	19·00
		b. Narrower square (R. 2/3 and R. 10/1)	1·25	

The 4c. exists with opt misplaced to right so that some stamps show the vertical bar on the left (*Price £20 un.*).

On No. 447b the obliterating square is 3 mm. wide instead of 4 mm.

(Recess B.W. (4c., 5c., 15c., 30c., 75c., 1r.). Photo Courvoisier (others))

1958 (14 May)–**62**. As earlier types, but inscriptions redrawn as in T **117**. W **81** (4, 5, 15, 30, 75c., 1r.) or no wmk (others). P 11×11½ (75c.), 11½×11 (1r.), 12×12½ (4, 5, 15, 30c.), or 11½ (others).

448	**91**	2c. brown and blue-green	10	50
449	**92**	3c. black and slate-violet	10	70
450	**117**	4c. purple and scarlet	10	10
451	**86**	5c. green (1.10.58)	10	1·60
		a. Yellow-green (13.6.61)	40	2·25
		b. Deep green (19.6.62)	8·00	4·00
452	**93**	6c. brown-black and yellow-green	10	1·00
453	**106**	10c. orange, bistre-brown and buff (1.10.58)	10	1·00
454	**87**	15c. blue-green and violet (1.10.58)	3·50	1·00
455	**95**	25c. orange-brown and bright blue	25	10
456	**88**	30c. carmine and yellow (1.5.59)	25	1·40
457	**96**	35c. red and deep green (II) (15.7.58)	2·75	30
459	**98**	50c. indigo and slate-grey (15.7.58)	30	10
460	**89**	75c. ultramarine and orange (1.5.59)	9·00	5·00
		a. Ultramarine and brown-orange (3.4.62)	11·00	3·75
461	**99**	85c. black and deep blue-green (1.5.59)	3·75	12·00
462	**90**	1r. deep blue and brown (1.10.58)	60	10
463	**100**	2r. blue and deep brown	5·00	30
464	**101**	5r. brown and orange	17·00	30
465	**102**	10r. red-brown and buff	17·00	1·00
448/65	*Set of 17*		55·00	21·00

118 "Human Rights"

(Photo Enschedé)

1958 (10 Dec). Tenth Anniv of Declaration of Human Rights. P 13×12½.

466	**118**	10c. vermilion and dull purple	10	10
467		85c. vermilion and deep blue-green	30	1·00

119 Portraits of Founders and University Buildings

(Photo Enschedé)

1959 (31 Dec). Institution of Pirivena Universities. P 13×12½.

| 468 | **119** | 10c. red-orange and ultramarine | 10 | 10 |

120 Uprooted Tree   121 S. W. R. D. Bandaranaike

(Des W. A. Ariyasena. Photo Courvoisier)

1960 (7 Apr). World Refugee Year. P 11½.

469	**120**	4c. red-brown and gold	10	85
470		25c. blackish violet and gold	10	15

(Photo Courvoisier)

1961 (8 Jan). Prime Minister Bandaranaike Commemoration. P 11½.

471	**121**	10c. deep blue and greenish blue	10	10
		a. Portrait redrawn (15.6.61)*	10	10

*Earliest known postmark date.

No. 471a can be identified by Mr. Bandaranaike's dark hair at temples.

122 Ceylon Scout Badge   123 Campaign Emblem

(Des W. A. Ariyasena. Photo Courvoisier)

1962 (26 Feb). Golden Jubilee of Ceylon Boy Scouts Association. P 11½.

472	**122**	35c. buff and blue	15	10

(Photo Harrison)

1962 (7 Apr). Malaria Eradication. W **81**. P 14½×14.

473	**123**	25c. red-orange and sepia	10	10

124 de Havilland DH.85 Leopard Moth and Hawker Siddeley Comet 4   125 "Produce" and Campaign Emblem

(Photo Courvoisier)

1963 (28 Feb). 25th Anniv of Airmail. P 11½.

474	**124**	50c. black and light blue	50	50

(Photo Courvoisier)

1963 (21 Mar). Freedom from Hunger. P 11½.

475	**125**	5c. vermilion and blue	1·00	2·00
476		25c. brown and yellow-olive	3·25	30

(126)   127 "Rural Life"

1963 (1 June). No. 450 surch with T **126**.

477	**117**	2c. on 4c. purple and scarlet	10	10
		a. Surch inverted	17·00	
		b. Surch double	50·00	
		c. Surch omitted (in pair with normal)	£300	

(Photo Harrison)

1963 (5 July). Golden Jubilee of Ceylon Co-operative Movement (1962). W **81**. P 14×14½.

478	**127**	60c. rose-red and black	2·00	50

128 S. W. R. D. Bandaranaike

129 Terrain, Elephant and Tree

(Recess Courvoisier)

1963 (26 Sept). P 11½.
479　**128**　10c. light blue................................... 　10　10

(Photo Harrison)

1963 (9 Dec). National Conservation Week. W **81** (sideways). P 14×14½.
480　**129**　5c. sepia and blue......................... 　60　40

130 S. W. R. D. Bandaranaike

131 Anagarika Dharmapala (Buddhist missionary)

(T **130/1**. Photo Courvoisier)

1964 (1 July). P 11½
481　**130**　10c. deep violet-blue and greenish grey .. 　10　10

1964 (16 Sept). Birth Centenary of Anagarika Dharmapala (founder of Maha Bodhi Society). P 11½.
482　**131**　25c. sepia and olive-yellow....................... 　10　10

134 Southern Grackle　**135** D. S. Senanayake　**136**

137 Common Peafowl　**138** Ruins at Madirigiriya

139 Ceylon Junglefowl　**140** Asian Black-headed Oriole　**146** Tea Plantation

147 Girls transplanting rice　**149** Map of Ceylon

(Des A. Dharmasiri (5r.); P. A. Miththapala (10r.). Photo Courvoisier (10c. (486), 20c.), Harrison (10c. (487), 60c., 1r., 5r., 10r.), D.L.R. (others incl sheet))

1964 (1 Oct)–**72**. T **134/140**, **146**, **149** and similar designs. No wmk (Nos. 486, 489). W **81** (others; sideways on Nos. 487, 494 499). P 11½ (Nos. 486, 489), 14½×14 (No. 494) or 14 (others).
485　**134**　5c. multicoloured (5.2.66).................. 　2·00　1·00
486　**135**　10c. myrtle-green (22.3.66)................ 　80　10
487　**136**　10c. myrtle-green (23.9.68)................ 　10　10
　　　　　a. Imperf (pair)................................. 　48·00
　　　　　b. Horiz pair, one stamp imperf 3 sides.. 　£150
488　**137**　15c. multicoloured (5.2.66)................ 　4·50　30
489　**138**　20c. brown-purple and buff.............. 　20　25
494　**139**　60c. multicoloured (5.2.66)................ 　5·00　1·25
　　　　　a. Red omitted................................. 　55·00
　　　　　b. Blue and green omitted*.............. 　45·00
495　**140**　75c. multicoloured (5.2.66)................ 　3·00　70
　　　　　a. No wmk (8.6.72)......................... 　12·00　16·00
497　**146**　1r. brown and bluish green.............. 　1·25　30
　　　　　a. Brown (tea picker, etc) omitted...... 　£1300
　　　　　b. Bluish green omitted................... 　£1400
499　**147**　5r. multicoloured (15.8.69)................ 　11·00　11·00
500　**149**　10r. multicoloured (1.10.69)............... 　28·00　3·00
485/500 Set of 10.. 　50·00　16·00
MS500a　148×174 mm. As Nos. 485, 488, 494 and 495. Imperf... 　8·00　14·00
*Actually only the blue printing is omitted on this sheet, but where this was printed over the yellow to form the leaves it appeared as green.
The 5c., 75c. and 1r. exist with PVA gum as well as gum arabic.
No. 487b comes from a sheet which showed stamps in the third vertical row imperforate at top, bottom and at right.
In the miniature sheet the inscriptions on the 60c. have been rearranged to conform with the style of the other values.

150 Exhibition Buildings and Cogwheels

151 Trains of 1864 and 1964

(Photo State Printing Works, Budapest)

1964 (1 Dec). Industrial Exhibition. T **150** and similar horiz design. No wmk. P 11.
501　　　　5c. multicoloured............................. 　10　75
　　　　　a. Pair. Nos. 501/2........................... 　35　2·50
502　**150**　5c. multicoloured............................. 　10　75
No. 501 is inscribed "INDUSTRIAL EXHIBITION" in Sinhala and Tamil, No. 502 in Sinhala and English. The stamps were issued together se-tenant in alternate vertical rows, producing horizontal pairs.

(Photo Harrison)

1964 (21 Dec). Centenary of Ceylon Railways. T **151** and similar horiz design. W **81** (sideways). P 14×14½.
503　　–　60c. blue, reddish purple and yellow-green.. 　2·75　40
　　　　　a. Vert pair. Nos. 503/4..................... 　5·50　5·50
504　**151**　60c. blue, reddish purple and yellow-green.. 　2·75　40
No. 503 is inscribed "RAILWAY CENTENARY" in Sinhala and Tamil, No. 504 in Sinhala and English. The stamps were issued together se-tenant in alternate horizontal rows, producing vertical pairs.

152 I.T.U. Emblem and Symbols　**153** I.C.Y. Emblem

(Photo Harrison)

1965 (17 May). I.T.U. Centenary. W **81** (sideways). P 14½.
505　**152**　2c. bright blue and red...................... 　1·00　1·10
506　　　　30c. brown and red.......................... 　3·25　45
　　　　　a. Value omitted............................... 　£190
No. 506a was caused by the misplacement of the red.

(Photo Courvoisier)

1965 (26 June). International Co-operation Year. T **153** and similar horiz design. P 11½.
507　　　　3c. deep blue and rose-carmine.............. 　1·25　1·00
508　　　　50c. black, rose-carmine and gold............. 　3·25　50
No. 508 is similar to T **153** but has the multilingual inscription "CEYLON" rearranged.

154 Town Hall, Colombo

(Photo Courvoisier)

1965 (29 Oct). Centenary of Colombo Municipal Council. P 11×11½.
509   **154**   25c. myrtle-green and sepia 20   20

5 ■

(155)

1965 (18 Dec). No. 481 surch with T **155**.
510   **130**   5c. on 10c. deep violet-blue and
                greenish grey 10   2·00

157 Kandy and Council Crest   **158** W.H.O. Building

(Photo Harrison)

1966 (15 June). Kandy Municipal Council Centenary. W **81**. P 14×13½.
512   **157**   25c. multicoloured 20   20

(Litho D.L.R.)

1966 (8 Oct). Inauguration of W.H.O. Headquarters. Geneva. P 14.
513   **158**   4c. multicoloured .... 3·50   3·00
514   1r. multicoloured .... 8·00   1·50

159 Rice Paddy and   **160** Rice Paddy and
Map of Ceylon   Globe

(Photo Courvoisier)

1966 (25 Oct). International Rice Year. P 11½.
515   **159**   6c. multicoloured 20   75
516   **160**   30c. multicoloured 30   15

161 U.N.E.S.C.O. Emblem

(Litho State Ptg Wks, Vienna)

1966 (3 Nov). 20th Anniv of U.N.E.S.C.O. P 12.
517   **161**   3c. multicoloured .... 2·75   3·75
518   50c. multicoloured .... 8·00   50

162 Water-resources   **163** Devotees at Buddhist
Map   Temple

(Litho D.L.R.)

1966 (1 Dec). International Hydrological Decade. P 14.
519   **162**   2c. orange-brown, greenish yellow
               and blue 30   85
520   2r. orange-brown, greenish yellow,
               blue and yellow-green ...... 2·25   2·25

(Photo State Ptg Wks, Vienna)

1967 (2 Jan). Poya Holiday System. T **163** and similar horiz designs. Multicoloured. P 12.
521   5c. Type **163** 20   60
522   20c. Mihintale 30   10
523   35c. Sacred Bo-tree, Anuradhapura 30   15
524   60c. Adam's Peak 30   10
521/4 *Set of 4* .... 1·00   85

167 Galle Fort and Clock Tower

(Litho Rosenbaum Brothers, Vienna)

1967 (5 Jan). Centenary of Galle Municipal Council. P 13½.
525   **167**   25c. multicoloured 70   20

168 Field Research

(Litho Rosenbaum Bros, Vienna)

1967 (1 Aug). Centenary of Ceylon Tea Industry. T **168** and similar horiz designs. Multicoloured. P 13½.
526   4c. Type **168** 60   80
527   40c. Tea-tasting equipment .... 1·75   1·50
528   50c. Leaves and bud .... 1·75   20
529   1r. Shipping tea .... 1·75   10
526/9 *Set of 4* .... 5·25   2·25

169 Elephant Ride

(Litho Rosenbaum Bros, Vienna)

1967 (15 Aug). International Tourist Year. P 13½.
530   **169**   45c. multicoloured .... 2·25   80

1967 (16 Sept). First National Stamp Exhibition. No. **MS**500a optd "FIRST NATIONAL STAMP EXHIBITION 1967".
MS531 148×174 mm. Nos. 485, 488, 494/5.
  Imperf .... 7·00   9·00

170 Ranger, Jubilee Emblem   **171** Col. Olcott and Buddhist Flag
and Flag

(Litho D.L.R.)

1967 (19 Sept). Golden Jubilee of Ceylon Girl Guides Association. P 12½×13.
532   **170**   3c. multicoloured 50   20
533   25c. multicoloured 75   10

(Litho Rosenbaum Bros, Vienna)

1967 (8 Dec). 60th Death Anniv of Colonel H. S. Olcott (theosophist). P 13½.

534	**171**	15c. multicoloured	30	20

172 Independence Hall   **173** Lion Flag and Sceptre

(Photo Harrison)

1968 (2 Feb). 20th Anniv of Independence. W **81** (sideways). P 14.

535	**172**	5c. multicoloured	10	55
536	**173**	1r. multicoloured	50	10

174 Sir D. B.   **175** Institute of Hygiene
Jayatilleke

(Litho D.L.R.)

1968 (14 Feb). Birth Centenary of Sir Baron Jayatilleke (scholar and statesman). P 14.

537	**174**	25c. yellow-brown and sepia	10	10

(Litho B.W.)

1968 (7 Apr). 20th Anniv of World Health Organization. W **81**. P 12.

538	**175**	50c. multicoloured	10	10

176 Vickers Super VC-10   **177** Open Koran and "1400"
Aircraft over Terminal Building

(Des and litho B.W.)

1968 (5 Aug). Opening of Colombo Airport. W **81**. P 13½.

539	**176**	60c. grey-blue, chestnut, red and yellow	1·00	10

(Des M. I. M. Mohideen. Photo Harrison)

1968 (14 Oct). 1400th Anniv of the Holy Koran. W **81**. P 14.

541	**177**	25c. multicoloured	10	10

178 Human Rights Emblem   **179** All Ceylon Buddhist Congress
Headquarters

(Photo Pakistan Security Printing Corp)

1968 (10 Dec). Human Rights Year. P 12½×13½.

542	**178**	2c. multicoloured	10	30
543		20c. multicoloured	10	10
544		40c. multicoloured	10	10
545		2r. multicoloured	80	4·75
542/5	*Set of 4*		1·00	4·75

(Des A. Dharmasiri. Litho Rosenbaum Bros, Vienna)

1968 (19 Dec). Golden Jubilee of All Ceylon Buddhist Congress. P 13½.

546	**179**	5c. multicoloured	10	50

A 50c. value showing a footprint was prepared but its release was stopped the day before it was due for issue. However, some are known to have been released in error at rural offices (*Price £38 mint*).

180 E. W. Perera   **181** Symbols of
(patriot)   Strength in Savings

(Photo Harrison)

1969 (17 Feb). E. W. Perera Commemoration. W **81**. P 14×13½.

547	**180**	60c. brown	10	30

(Des A. Dharmasiri. Photo Harrison)

1969 (20 Mar). Silver Jubilee of National Savings Movement. W **81**. P 14.

548	**181**	3c. multicoloured	10	30

182 Seat of   **183** Buduresmala
Enlightenment under   (Six fold Buddha-
Sacred Bodhi Tree   Rays)

(Des L. T. P. Manjusree. Litho D.L.R.)

1969 (10 Apr). Vesak Day (inscr "Wesak"). W **81** (sideways). P 15.

549	**182**	4c. multicoloured	10	50
550	**183**	6c. multicoloured	10	50
551	**182**	35c. multicoloured	10	10
549/51	*Set of 3*		25	1·00

No. 549 exists with the gold apparently omitted. Normally the gold appears (without a seperate plate number) over an underlay of olive-green on carmine. In one sheet we have seen, the gold only shows as tiny specks under a strong magnifying glass and as there may be intermediate stages of faint printing we do not list this.

184 A. E.   **185** I.L.O. Emblem
Goonesinghe

(Des and photo Harrison)

1969 (29 Apr). Commemoration of Goonesinghe (founder of Labour Movement in Ceylon). W **81**. P 14.

552	**184**	15c. multicoloured	10	10

(Photo Harrison)

1969 (4 May). 50th Anniv of International Labour Organisation. W **81** (sideways). P 14.

553	**185**	5c. black and turquoise-blue	10	10
554		25c. black and carmine-red	10	10

186 Convocation Hall,   **187** Uranium Atom
University of Ceylon

(Des Ahangama Edward (35c.); L. D. P. Jayawardena (50 c.);
A. Dharmasiri (60c.); 4c. from photograph. Litho Rosenbaum Bros,
Vienna)

1969 (1 Aug). Educational Centenary. T **186**, **187** and similar
multicoloured designs. P 13½.

555	4c. Type **186**	10	80
556	35c. Lamp of Learning, Globe and flags		
	(horiz)	20	10
557	50c. Type **187**	20	10
558	60c. Symbols of Scientific education	30	10
555/8 Set of 4		70	1·00

188 Ath Pana
(Elephant Lamp)

189 Rock Fortress
of Sigiriya

(Des from photographs. Litho Rosenbaum Bros, Vienna)

1969 (1 Aug). Archaeological Centenary. P 13½.

559	**188**	6c. multicoloured	25	1·50
560	**189**	1r. multicoloured	25	10

A 50c. stamp showing the footprint of Buddha was due to be
issued on 19 December 1969 in commemoration of the 50th
anniversary of the All Ceylon Buddhist Congress. Following objections
from religious leaders, the stamp was withdrawn before issue date;
nevertheless, examples are known on first day cover.

190 Leopard

191 Emblem and Symbols

(Litho Rosenbaum Bros, Vienna)

1970 (11 May). Wildlife Conservation. T **190** and similar horiz designs.
Multicoloured. P 13½.

561	5c. Water Buffalo	1·25	1·25
	a. Magenta omitted	£160	
562	15c. Slender Loris	2·00	1·25
	a. Magenta omitted	£200	
563	50c. Spotted Deer	1·40	1·25
	a. Imperf (in vert pair with stamp perf 3 sides)	£600	
564	1r. Type **190**	1·40	1·75
561/4 Set of 4		5·50	5·00

In No. 561a the Buffalo are predominantly green instead of brown
and in No. 562a the sky is blue instead of violet and the animal is in
green and yellow only.

(Des A. Dharmasiri. Litho Rosenbaum Bros, Vienna)

1970 (17 June). Asian Productivity Year. P 13½.

565	**191**	60c. multicoloured	10	10

192 New U.P.U. HQ Building

193 Oil Lamp and Caduceus

(Litho Rosenbaum Bros, Vienna)

1970 (14 Aug). New U.P.U. Headquarters Building. P 13½.

566	**192**	50c. yellow-orange, black and new blue	50	10
		a. New blue (Building) omitted	£200	
567		1r.10 vermilion, black and new blue	4·50	40

(Des A. Dharmasiri. Litho Rosenbaum Bros, Vienna)

1970 (1 Sept). Centenary of Colombo Medical School. P 13½.

568	**193**	5c. multicoloured	1·25	80
		a. Vert pair, bottom stamp imperf	£500	
569		45c. multicoloured	1·50	60

194 Victory March and
S. W. R. D. Bandaranaike

(Des A. Dharmasiri. Litho D.L.R.)

1970 (25 Sept). Definitive issue marking establishment of United
Front Government. P 13½.

570	**194**	10c. multicoloured	10	10

195 U.N. Emblem and Dove
of Peace

196 Keppetipola
Dissawa

(Des A. Dharmasiri. Photo Pakistan Security Printing Corp)

1970 (24 Oct). 25th Anniv of United Nations. P 12½×13½.

571	**195**	2r. multicoloured	2·00	4·25

(Des A. Dharmasiri. Litho Harrison)

1970 (26 Nov). 152nd Death Anniv of Keppetipola Dissawa (Kandyan
patriot). P 14×14½.

572	**196**	25c. multicoloured	10	10

197 Ola Leaf Manuscript

(Des A. Dharmasiri. Photo Pakistan Security Printing Corp)

1970 (21 Dec). International Education Year. P 13.

573	**197**	15c. multicoloured	2·75	1·25

198 C. H. de Soysa

199 D. E. H. Pedris
(patriot)

200 Lenin

(Des L. D. P. Jayawardena. Litho Pakistan Security Printing Corp)

1971 (3 Mar). 135th Birth Anniv of C. H. de Soysa (philanthropist).
P 13½.

574	**198**	20c. multicoloured	15	50

(Des L. D. P. Jayawardena. Litho Harrison)

1971 (8 July). D. E. H. Pedris Commemoration. P 14×14½.

575	**199**	25c. multicoloured	15	50

(Des L. D. P. Jayawardena. Litho Harrison)

1971 (31 Aug). Lenin Commemoration. P 14½.

576	**200**	40c. multicoloured	25	50

201 Ananda
Rajakaruna

5 **X**

(202)

(Des A. Dharmasiri (Nos. 577 and 579), P. A. Miththapala (Nos. 578 and 580), L. D. P. Jayawardena (No. 581). Litho Harrison)

1971 (29 Oct). Poets and Philosophers. T **201** and similar vert designs. P 14×13½.

577		5c. royal blue	10	15
578		5c. lake-brown	10	15
579		5c. red-orange	10	15
580		5c. deep slate-blue	10	15
581		5c. brown	10	15
577/81 *Set of 5*			30	70

Portraits: No. 577, Type **207**; No. 578, Arumuga Navalar; No. 579, Rev. S. Mahinda; No. 580, Ananda Coomaraswamy; No. 581, Cumaratunga Munidasa.

1971 (26 Nov). Nos. 549/50, 555, 559 and 570 surch as T **202** (obliterating shape differs).

582	**182**	5c. on 4c. multicoloured	6·00	1·75
		a. Surch inverted	6·00	
		b. Pair, one with "X" omitted	65·00	
		c. Surch double, one inverted	11·00	
		d. Ditto. Pair one with "X" omitted	45·00	
583	**186**	5c. on 4c. multicoloured	10	1·25
		a. Surch inverted	2·75	
		b. Surch double, one inverted	8·50	
584	**194**	15c. on 10c. multicoloured (2 Dec)	15	30
		a. Surch inverted	2·75	
		b. Surch double	8·00	
		c. Surch and dot transposed		
		d. Surch at right, dot omitted		
585	**183**	25c. on 6c. multicoloured	30	60
		a. Surch double, one inverted	20·00	
		b. Surch inverted	21·00	
586	**188**	25c. on 6c. multicoloured	30	2·25
		a. Surch inverted	2·75	
582/6 *Set of 5*			7·00	5·50

Nos. 584c/d were caused by a misplacement of the surcharge on one sheet.

203 Colombo Plan Emblem and Ceylon

(Des P. A. Miththapala. Litho Harrison)

1971 (28 Dec). 20th Anniv of Colombo Plan. P 14×14½.

587	**203**	20c. multicoloured	20	30

204 Globe and CARE Package

205 WHO Emblem and Heart

(Des A. Dharmasiri. Litho Harrison)

1971 (28 Dec). 20th Anniv of CARE (Co-operative for American Relief Everywhere). P 14×13½.

588	**204**	50c. new blue, lilac and violet	35	30

(Des A. Miththapala. Litho D.L.R.)

1972 (2 May). World Health Day. P 13×13½.

589	**205**	25c. multicoloured	2·50	60

206 Map of Asia and UN Emblem

(Des L. D. P. Jayawardena. Litho B.W.)

1972 (2 May). 25th Anniv of ECAFE (Economic Commission for Asia and the Far East). P 13.

590	**206**	85c. multicoloured	4·75	2·75

SRI LANKA

REPUBLIC

Ceylon became the Republic of Sri Lanka on 22 May 1972.

208 National Flower and Mountain of the Illustrious Foot

209 Map of World with Buddhist Flag

(Des L. D. P. Jayawardena. Litho D.L.R.)

1972 (22 May). Inauguration of the Republic of Sri Lanka. P 13.

591	**208**	15c. multicoloured	30	30

(Des L. D. P. Jayawardena. Litho Harrison)

1972 (26 May). Tenth Conference of the World Fellowship of Buddhists. P 14×13.

592	**209**	5c. multicoloured	30	60
		a. "1972" ptd double		
		b. "1972" ptd double, one inverted	20·00	

This stamp was scheduled for release in May 1971, and when finally released had the year "1972" additionally overprinted in red. Sheets are known without this overprint but their status has not been established.

210 Book Year Emblem

211 Emperor Angelfish

(Des L. D. P. Jayawardena. Photo Pakistan Security Printing Corp)

1972 (8 Sept). International Book Year. P 13.

593	**210**	20c. light yellow-orange and lake-brown	20	50

(Des G. D. Kariyawasam. Litho Rosenbaum Bros, Vienna)

1972 (12 Oct). T **211** and similar horiz designs showing fish. Multicoloured. P 13×13½.

594		2c. Type **211**	10	1·25
		a. Plum colour omitted	3·00	
595		3c. Green Chromide	10	1·25
596		30c. Skipjack Tuna	1·25	30
597		2r. Black Ruby Barb	3·50	5·25
594/7 *Set of 4*			4·50	7·25

On No. 594a the stripes of the fish are in green instead of plum.

212 Memorial Hall

(Des R. B. Mawilmada. Litho D.L.R.)

1973 (17 May). Opening Bandaranaike Memorial Hall. P 14.

598	**212**	15c. light cobalt and deep grey-blue	30	30

213 King Vessantara giving away his Children

(Des P. Wanigatunga. Litho D.L.R.)

1973 (3 Sept). Rock and Temple Paintings. T **213** and similar vert designs. Multicoloured. P 13½×14.

599		35c. Type **213**	35	10
600		50c. The Prince and the Grave-digger	40	10
601		90c. Bearded old man......................................	60	85
602		1r. 55 Two female figures..............................	70	2·00
599/602		*Set of* 4	1·90	2·75
MS603		115×141 mm. Nos. 599/602	3·25	3·50

214 Bandaranaike Memorial Conference Hall

215 Prime Minister Bandaranaike

(Des and litho Harrison)

1974 (6 Sept). 20th Commonwealth Parliamentary Conference, Colombo. P 14½.

604	**214**	85c. multicoloured	30	30

(Des and photo Harrison)

1974 (25 Sept). P 14½.

605	**215**	15c. multicoloured	15	10
		a. Red (face value) omitted	10·00	
		b. Pale blue (background) omitted	5·50	
		c. Ultramarine (country inscr) omitted.	15·00	
		d. Black omitted...................................		
		e. Imperf (pair).....................................	£130	

216 "UPU" and "100"

217 Sri Lanka Parliament Building

(Des P. Jayatillake. Litho German Bank Note Ptg Co, Leipzig)

1974 (9 Oct). Centenary of Universal Postal Union. P 13½×13.

606	**216**	50c. multicoloured	1·00	75

(Litho Toppan Printing Co, Japan)

1975 (1 Apr). Inter-Parliamentary Meeting. P 13.

607	**217**	1r. multicoloured	30	50

218 Sir Ponnambalam Ramanathan (politician)

219 D. J. Wimalasurendra (engineer)

(Des A. Rasiah. Litho Toppan Ptg Co, Japan)

1975 (4 Sep). Ramanathan Commemoration. P 13.

608	**218**	75c. multicoloured	30	80

(Des A. Dharmasiri. Litho Toppan Ptg Co, Japan)

1975 (17 Sept). Wimalasurendra Commemoration. P 13.

609	**219**	75c. blue-black and new blue	30	80

220 Mrs. Bandaranaike, Map and Dove

221 Ma-ratmal

(Des B. U. Ananda Somatilaka. Litho Toppan Ptg Co, Japan)

1975 (22 Dec). International Women's Year. P 13.

610	**220**	1r. 15 multicoloured	2·25	1·25

(Des and litho Toppan Ptg Co, Japan)

1976 (1 Jan). Indigenous Flora. T **221** and similar vert designs. Multicoloured. P 13.

611		25c. Type **221**	10	10
		a. Imperf (pair).....................................	90·00	
612		50c. Binara	10	10
613		75c. Daffodil orchid	15	15
614		10r. Diyapara...	3·00	4·50
611/14		*Set of* 4.	3·00	4·50
MS615		153×153 mm. Nos. 611/14..........................	12·00	16·00

A used example of No. 613 has been seen with the yellow printing apparently omitted. This results in the leaves appearing blue instead of green.

222 Mahaweli Dam

223 Dish Aerial

(Des R. B. Mawilmada. Litho German Bank Note Ptg Co, Leipzig)

1976 (8 Jan). Diversion of the Mahaweli River. P 13×12½.

616	**222**	85c. turquoise, violet-blue and azure	30	1·25

Stamps in this design with a face value of 60c. were not issued to post offices.

(Des P. A. Miththapala. Litho German Bank Note Ptg Co, Leipzig)

1976 (6 May). Opening of Satellite Earth Station, Padukka. P 14×13½.

617	**223**	1r. multicoloured...	65	1·25

224 Conception of the Buddha

(Des P. Wanigatunga. Litho Toppan Ptg Co, Japan)

1976 (7 May). Vesak. T **224** and similar horiz designs showing paintings from the Dambava Temple. Multicoloured. P 13.

618		5c. Type **224**	10	90
619		10c. King Suddhodana and the astrologers .	10	90
620		1r.50 The astrologers being entertained..........	90	95
621		2r. The Queen in a palanquin........................	1·00	95
622		2r.25 Royal procession	1·10	1·90
623		5r. Birth of the Buddha................................	1·60	3·25
618/23		*Set of* 6	4·25	8·00
MS624		161×95 mm. Nos. 618/23	9·50	13·00

225 Blue Sapphire

226 Prime Minister Mrs. S. Bandaranaike

(Des State Gem Corporation. Litho Tappan Ptg Co, Japan)

1976 (16 June). Gems of Sri Lanka. T **225** and similar horiz designs. Multicoloured. P 12×12½.

625		60c. Type **225**	4·75	30
626		1r.15 Cat's Eye	7·50	1·50
627		2r. Star Sapphire	9·00	3·25
628		5r. Ruby	11·00	11·00
625/8		*Set of* 4	29·00	14·50
MS629		152×152 mm. Nos. 625/8............................	42·00	27·00

(Photo Harrison)

1976 (3 Aug). Non-aligned Summit Conference, Colombo. P 14×14½.

630	**226**	1r.15 multicoloured	25	50
631		2r. multicoloured	40	1·00

227 Statue of Liberty

228 Bell, Early Telephone and Telephone Lines

(Des A. Harischandra. Litho German Bank Note Ptg Co, Leipzig)

1976 (29 Nov). Bicentenary of American Revolution. P 13½.

632 **227** 2r.25 cobalt and indigo .... 65 1·50

(Des A. Harischandra. Litho German Bank Note Ptg Co, Leipzig)

1976 (21 Dec). Telephone Centenary. P 13.

633 **228** 1r. multicoloured 60 20

229 Maitreya (pre-carnate Buddha)

230 Kandyan Crown

(Des P. Wanigatunga. Litho German Bank Note Ptg Co, Leipzig)

1977 (1 Jan). Centenary of Colombo Museum. T **229** and similar Vert designs showing statues. Multicoloured. P 12½.

634 50c. Type **229** 25 15
635 1r. Sundara Murti Swami (Tamil psalmist).. 30 30
636 5r. Tara (goddess)........................ 2·25 4·50
634/6 Set of 3 .... 2·50 4·50

(Des R. B. Mawilmada. Litho Toppan Ptg Co, Japan)

1977 (18 Jan). Regalia of the Kings of Kandy. T **230** and similar vert design. Multicoloured. P 13.

637 **230** 1r. Type **230** 50 40
638 2r. Throne and footstool .... 1·10 3·25

231 Sri Rahula Thero (poet)

232 Sir Ponnambalam Arumachalam (social reformer)

(Des S. Dissanayaka. Litho Toppan Ptg Co, Japan)

1977 (23 Feb). Sri Rahula Commemoration. P 13.

639 **231** 1r. multicoloured .... 75 1·00

(Litho Toppan Ptg Co, Japan)

1977 (10 Mar). Ponnambalam Arunachalam Commemoration. P 13.

640 **232** 1r. multicoloured .... 50 1·00

233 Brass Lamps

234 Siddi Lebbe (author and educationalist)

(Des A. Hanschandra. Litho Toppan Ptg Co, Japan)

1977 (7 Apr). Handicrafts. T **233** and similar vert designs. Multicoloured. P 13.

641 20c. Type **233** 20 15
642 25c. Jewellery box....................... 20 15
643 50c. Caparisoned elephant............. 45 20
644 5r. Mask............................... 1·40 3·25
641/4 Set of 4 .... 2·00 3·25
MS645 205×89 mm. Nos. 641/4............ 3·75 4·50

(Des Sarasvati Rockwood. Litho Toppan Ptg Co, Japan)

1977 (11 June). Siddi Lebbe Commemoration. P 13½.

646 **234** 1r. multicoloured .... 30 1·00

235 Girl Guide

(Des and litho Asher & Co, Melbourne)

1977 (13 Dec). 60th Anniv of Sri Lanka Girl Guides Association. P 14½×15.

647 **235** 75c. multicoloured 85 30

236 Parliament Building and "Wheel of Life"

237 Youths Running

(Des R. B. Mawilmada. Photo Enschedé)

1978 (4 Feb). Election of New President. P 12×12½.

648 **236** 15c. gold, bright yellow-green and emerald 20 10

No. 648 was re-issued on 7 September 1978 additionally dated "1978.09.07" to mark the Promulgation of the Constitution for the Democratic Socialist Republic of Sri Lanka. This re-issue was only available on First Day Covers (Price on F.D.C. £2).

See also Nos. 680/c.

(Des M. Dissanayake. Litho Asher & Co, Melbourne)

1978 (27 Apr). National Youth Service Council. P 15×14½.

649 **237** 15c. multicoloured 30 70

238 Prince Siddhartha's Renunciation

(Des P. Wanigatunga. Litho Metal Box Singapore Ltd)

1978 (16 May). Vesak. Rock Carvings from Borobudur Temple. T **238** and similar horiz design in buff, brown and ultramarine. P 13.

650 15c. Type **238** 75 30
651 50c. Prince Siddharta shaving his hair......... 1·00 1·75

(239)

240 Veera Puran Appu

1978 (18 May). Nos. 559, 601/2, 605 and 648/9 surch as T **239**.
652	5c. on 90c. Bearded old man (26.6)	2·00	3·50
	a. Surch inverted	12·00	
653	10c. on 35c. Type **213**	50	50
	a. Surch inverted	12·00	
654	25c. on 15c. Type **215** (20.11)	4·25	4·25
	a. Dot after "25" (R.3/4)	18·00	
655	25c. on 15c. Type **236** (20.11)	4·25	4·25
	a. Surch inverted	10·00	
	b. Surch quadruple		
656	25c. on 15c. Type **237** (Blk & Pink) (20.11)	4·25	4·25
	a. Surch and obliterating square inverted	9·00	
	ab. Surch only inverted	8·50	
657	1r. on 1r.55 Two female figures (17.11)	1·25	45
	a. Surch inverted		
652/7	Set of 6	15·00	16·00

No. 656 has the surcharge applied in black on a pink square, previously printed over the original face value.

(Des A. Dharmasiri. Litho Metal Box Singapore Ltd)

1978 (8 Aug). 130th Death Anniv of Veera Puron Appu (revolutionary). P 13.
658	**240**	15c. multicoloured	20	35

SRI LANKA

241 *Troides helena*   (**242**)

(Des G. Ratnavira. Litho J. W. or Questa (ptgs of 25c. from 5 Jan 1990))

1978 (28 Nov). Butterflies. T **241** and similar vert designs. Multicoloured. P 14.
659	25c. Type **241**	55	10
660	50c. *Cethosia nietneri*	1·00	10
661	5r. *Kallima horsfieldi* (s sp *philarchus*)	1·75	1·25
662	10r. *Papilio polymnestor*	1·75	2·50
659/62	Set of 4	4·50	3·50
MS663	203×147 mm. Nos. 659/62	11·00	7·00

1979 (22 Mar). No. 486 surch with T **242** in black and turquoise-blue.
664	15c. on 10c. myrtle-green	2·75	1·75
	a. Surch double	13·00	
	b. Turquoise-blue surch omitted	22·00	

Type **242** shows only part of the turquoise-blue section of the overprint ("SRI LANKA"), which also includes a rectangle obliterating the original face value. The new value is printed on this rectangle in black.

243 Prince Danta and Princess Hema Mala bringing the Sacred Tooth Relic from Kalinga

244 Piyadasa Sirisena

(Des A. Dharmasin. Litho J. W.)

1979 (3 May). Vesak. Kelaniya Temple Paintings. T **243** and similar vert designs. Multicoloured. P 13×13½.
665	25c. Type **243**	10	10
666	1r. Theri Sanghamitta bringing the Bodhi Tree branch to Sri Lanka	15	15
667	10r. King Kirti Sri Rajasinghe offering fan of authority to the Sangha Raja	1·50	2·75
665/7	Set of 3	1·50	2·75
MS668	120×80 mm. Nos. 665/7	2·75	3·75

(Des P. Jayatillake. Litho Toppan Ptg Co, Japan)

1979 (22 May). Piyadasa Sirisena (writer) Commemoration. P 13.
669	**244**	1r.25 multicoloured	40	40

245 Wrestlers   **246** Dudley Senanayake

(Des R. B. Mawilmada. Litho Metal Box Singapore Ltd)

1979 (28 May). Wood Carvings from Embekke Temple. T **245** and similar vert design. P 14.
670	20r. chocolate, ochre and deep green	1·25	1·25
671	50r. agate, bistre-yellow and deep green	1·50	2·75

Design:—50r. Dancer.

(Photo Heraclio Fournier)

1979 (19 June). Dudley Senanayake (former Prime Minister) Commemoration. P 14.
672	**246**	1r.25 bottle green	15	20

Examples of this design exist with a face value of 25c., but there is no evidence that such stamps were issued for postal purposes.

247 Mother with Child   **248** Ceylon 1857 6d. Stamp and Sir Rowland Hill

(Des A. Dharmasiri and R. Mawilmada. Litho Metal Box Singapore Ltd)

1979 (31 July). International Year of the Child. T **247** and similar horiz designs. Multicoloured. P 12½.
673	5c. Type **247**	10	10
674	3r. Superimposed heads of children of different races	40	1·10
675	5r. Children playing	50	1·40
673/5	Set of 3	80	2·40

(Des A. Dharmasiri. Litho Toppan Ptg Co, Japan)

1979 (27 Aug). Death Centenary of Sir Rowland Hill. P 13.
676	**248**	3r. multicoloured	30	1·25

249 Conference Emblem and Parliament Building   **250** Airline Emblem on Aircraft Tail-fin

(Des A. Harischandra. Litho Toppan Ptg Co, Japan)

1979 (28 Aug). International Conference of Parliamentarians on Population and Development, Colombo. P 13.
677	**249**	2r. multicoloured	70

(values 70   1·50)

(Des S. Saparamadu. Litho Metal Box Singapore Ltd)

1979 (1 Sept). Inauguration of "Airlanka" Airline. P 12½.
678	**250**	3r. black, deep blue-green and vermilion	1·00 1·75

251 Coconut Tree   **252** Swami Vipulananda

(Des G. Wathuwalagedara. Litho Metal Box Singapore Ltd)

1979 (10 Sept). Tenth Anniv of Asian and Pacific Coconut Community. P 14.

679	**251**	2r. multicoloured	1·00	1·75

1979 (10 Oct)–**87**. Design as No. 648 but smaller, 20×24 mm. P 12½×13.

680	**236**	25c. gold, bright yellow-green and emerald	30	20
680a		50c. gold, bright yellow-green & emerald (6.6.81)	3·00	10
680b		60c. gold, bright yellow-green and emerald (30.12.83)	14·00	2·25
680c		75c. gold, bright yellow-green and emerald (1.7.87)	15	10
680/c Set of 4			16·00	2·25

(Des R. B. Mawilmada. Litho Metal Box Singapore Ltd)

1979 (18 Nov). Swami Vipulananda (philosopher) Commemoration. P 12½.

681	**252**	1r. 25 multicoloured	30	60

253 Inscription and Crescent

(Des Q. V. Saldin. Litho Metal Box Singapore Ltd)

1979 (22 Nov). 1500th Anniv of the Hegira (Mohammedan religion). P 12½.

682	**253**	3r. 75 black, deep green and blue-green	35	2·00

254 "The Great Teacher" (Institute emblem)

255 Ceylon Blue Magpie

(Des H. P. Rupasinghe. Litho Metal Box Singapore Ltd)

1979 (29 Nov). 50th Anniv of Institute of Ayurveda (school of medicine). P 13×12½.

683	**254**	15c. multicoloured	30	70

(Des G. Ratnavira. Litho German Bank Note Ptg Co, Leipzig)

1979 (13 Dec). Birds (1st series). T **255** and similar vert designs. Multicoloured. P 13½×14.

684	**255**	10c. Type **255**	10	1·25
685		15c. Ceylon Hanging Parrot ("Ceylon Lorikeet")	1·00	10
686		75c. Ceylon Whistling Thrush ("Ceylon Arrenga")	15	15
687		1r. Ceylon Spurfowl	15	15
688		5r. Yellow-fronted Barbet	75	1·75
689		10r. Yellow-tufted Bulbul	75	1·75
684/9 Set of 6			2·50	4·50
MS690 151×151 mm. Nos. 684/9			5·50	7·00

See also Nos. 827/31, 985/9 and 1242/6.

256 Rotary International Emblem and Map of Sri Lanka

(Des A. Harischandra. Litho Metal Box Singapore Ltd)

1979 (27 Dec). 50th Anniv of Sri Lanka Rotary Movement and 75th Anniv of Rotary International. P 14.

691	**256**	1r.50 multicoloured	70	2·00

257 A. Ratnayake   (**258**)   **259** Tank and Stupa (symbols of Buddhist culture)

(Photo Govt Ptg Works, Rome)

1980 (7 Jan). 80th Birth Anniv of A. Ratnayake (politician). P 13½.

692	**257**	1r.25 deep grey-green	20	30

1980 (17 Mar). No. 680 surch with T **258**.

693	**236**	35c. on 25c. gold, bright yellow-green and emerald	15	15
		a. Surch ".33" (R. 6/1)	20·00	
		b. Dot omitted (R. 7/6)	6·00	
		c. Obliterating square misplaced (R. 6/9)	6·00	

On No. 693c the obliterating square falls below the decimal point, thus exposing the original value.

(Des R. B. Mawilmada. Photo Govt Ptg Works, Rome)

1980 (25 Mar). 60th Anniv of All Ceylon Buddhist Congress. T **259** and similar horiz design showing symbols of Buddhist culture. Multicoloured. P 13½.

694		10c. Type **259**	25	1·50
695		35c. Bo-leaf wheel and fan	25	20

260 Colonel Olcott   **261** Patachara's Journey through Forest

(Des S. Senevirante. Litho J.W.)

1980 (17 May). Centenary of Arrival of Colonel Olcott (campainer for Buddhism). P 14.

696	**260**	2r. multicoloured	1·00	1·75

(Des A. Dharmasiri. Litho Metal Box Singapore Ltd)

1980 (23 May). Vesak. Details from Temple Paintings, Purvaramnya Kataluwa. T **261** and similar horiz design. Multicoloured. P 13 ½.

697		35c. Type **261**	30	15
698		1r.60 Patachara crossing river	1·25	2·50

262 George E. de Silva   **263** Dalada Maligawa

(Des A. Rasiah. Litho German Bank Note Ptg Co, Leipzig)

1980 (8 June). George E. de Silva (politician) Commemoration. P 13.

699	**262**	1r.60 multicoloured	30	60

(Des A. Dharmasiri and R. B. Mawilmada. Litho Metal Box Singapore Ltd)

1980 (25 Aug). UNESCO–Sri Lanka Cultural Triangle Project. T **263** and similar horiz designs. P 13.

700		35c. claret	15	40
701		35c. grey	15	40
702		35c. rose-carmine	15	40
703		1r.60 olive-green	45	1·10
704		1r.60 slate-green	45	1·10
705		1r.60 sepia	45	1·10
700/5 Set of 6			1·60	4·00
MS706 215×115 mm. Nos. 700/5			2·50	5·50

Designs:—No. 701, Dambulla; No. 702, Alahana Pirivena; No. 703, Jetavanarama; No. 704, Abhayagiri; No. 705, Sigiri.

264 Co-operation Symbols
265 Lanka Mahila Samiti Emblem

(Des R. B. Mawilmada. Litho Metal Box Singapore Ltd)
1980 (1 Oct). 50th Anniv of Co-operative Department. P 13.
707　**264**　20c. multicoloured .... 10　30

(Des R. B. Mawilmada. Photo Govt Ptg Works, Rome)
1980 (7 Nov). 50th Anniv of Lanka Mahila Samiti (Rural Women's Movement). P 14×13.
708　**265**　35c. violet, rosine and yellow.................. 15　65

266 The Holy Family
267 Colombo Public Library

(Des L. Priyantha Silva. Litho Metal Box Singapore Ltd)
1980 (20 Nov). Christmas. T **266** and similar vert design. Multicoloured. P 12×11½.
709　35c. Type **266** .... 10　10
710　3r.75 The Three Wise Men.............................. 60　1·75
MS**711** 125×75 mm. Nos. 709/10. P 13.................... 1·25　2·00

(Des P. Jayatillake. Litho Toppan Ptg Co, Japan)
1980 (17 Dec). Opening of Colombo Public Library. P 12×12½.
712　**267**　35c. multicoloured...................................... 10　10

268 Flag of Walapane Disown
269 Fishing Cat

(Des Mrs. J. L. M. Fernando. Litho Toppan Ptg Co, Japan)
1980 (18 Dec). Ancient Flags. T **268** and similar horiz designs. P 13.
713　10c. black, green and brown-purple.............. 10　10
714　25c. black, greenish yellow and brown-
　　　purple .... 10　10
715　1r.60 black, greenish yellow and brn-purple.. 15　20
716　20r. black, greenish yellow and brown-
　　　purple .... 85　2·50
713/16 Set of 4.. 1·00　2·50
MS**717** 215×140 mm. Nos. 713/16.......................... 1·75　3·50
　Designs:—25c. Flag of the Gajanayaka, Huduhumpola, Kandy; 1r.60, Sinhala Royal Flag; 20r. Sinhala Royal Flag, Ratnapura.

(Des L. Ranasinghe. Litho J.W.)
1981 (10 Feb). Animals. T **269** and similar horiz designs. Multicoloured. P 13½×14.
718　2r.50 on 1r.60 Type **269** .... 25　15
719　3r. on 1r.50 Golden Palm Civet .... 25　20
720　4r. on 2r. Indian Spotted Chevrotain .... 25　30
721　5r. on 3r.75 Rusty-spotted Cat .... 35　45
718/21 Set of 4.. 1·00　1·00
MS**722** 165×89 mm. Nos. 718/21.......................... 1·00　2·50
　Nos. 718/21 are previously unissued stamps surcharged as in T **269**. No. 718 without surcharge exists, but its status is not known.
　For redrawn designs with revised face values see Nos. 780/3 and No. 1081.

270 Heads and Houses on Map of Sri Lanka
271 Sri Lanka Light Infantry Regimental Badge

(Des D. Hemaratna. Litho Toppan Ptg Co, Japan)
1981 (2 Mar). Population and Housing Census. P 12½×12.
723　**270**　50c. multicoloured.................................. 75　1·50

(Des D. Karunaratne. Litho Metal Box Singapore Ltd)
1981 (1 Apr). Centenary of Sri Lanka Light Infantry. P 12×11½.
724　**271**　2r. multicoloured.................................... 1·00　1·50

272 Panel from "The Great Stupa" in Honour of the Buddha, Sanci India, 1st-century A.D.
273 St. John Baptist de la Salle

(Des P. Jayatillake. Litho German Bank Note Ptg Co, Leipzig)
1981 (5 May). Vesak. T **272** and similar vert designs. P 13×13½.
725　35c. black, blackish green and sage-green.... 10　10
726　50c. multicoloured.. 10　10
727　7r. black and flesh.. 2·00　4·50
725/7 Set of 3.. 2·00　4·50
MS**728** 147×108 mm. Nos. 725/7. P 13×14.............. 3·50　5·00
　Designs:—50c. Silk banner representing a Bodhisattva from "Thousand Buddhas", Tun-Huang, Central Asia; 7r. Bodhisattva from Fondukistan, Afghanistan.

(Des Grant Kenyon and Eckhardt Ltd. Litho State Printing Works, Moscow)
1981 (15 May). 300th Anniv of De La Salle Brothers (Religious Order of the Brothers of the Christian Schools). P 12½×12.
729　**273**　2r. bright rose, deep violet-blue and
　　　new blue .... 1·50　2·25

274 Rev. Polwatte Sri Buddadatta
275 Dr. Al-Haj T. B. Jayah

(Des G. Fernando. Litho Metal Box Singapore Ltd)
1981 (22 May). National Heroes. T **274** and similar vert designs, each showing scholar, writer and Buddhist campaigner. P 12.
730　50c. bistre .... 60　1·25
731　50c. brown-rose .... 60　1·25
732　50c. deep mauve .... 60　1·25
730/2 Set of 3.. 1·60　3·25
　Designs:—No. 731, Rev. Mohottiwatte Gunananda; No. 732, Dr. Gnanaprakasar.

(Des P. Jayatillake. Litho Metal Box Singapore Ltd)
1981 (31 May). Dr. Al-Haj T. B. Jayah (statesman) Commemoration. P 12.
733　**275**　50c. grey-green .... 70　1·25

276 Dr. N. M. Perera   **277** Stylised Disabled Person and Globe

(Des P. Jayatillake. Litho Metal Box Singapore Ltd)

1981 (6 June). Dr. N. M. Perera (campaigner for social reform) Commemoration. P 12.

734	**276**	50c. rose-red..........................	1·00	1·50

(Des A. Adhikari. Litho State Printing Works, Moscow)

1981 (19 June). International Year for Disabled Persons. P 12×12½.

735	**277**	2r. vermilion, black and grey.................	1·10	2·00

278 Hand placing Vote into Ballot Box

(Des J. Vincent (50c.), R. Mawilmada (7r.). Litho State Printing Works, Moscow)

1981 (7 July). 50th Anniv of Universal Franchise. T **278** and similar multicoloured design. P 12½×12 (50c.) or 12×12½ (7r.).

736		50c. Type **278**	25	15
737		7r. Ballot box, and people forming map of Sri Lanka (vert)......................	1·75	3·25

279 T. W. Rhys Davids (founder)   **280** Federation Emblem and "25"

(Des P. Jayatillake. Litho State Printing Works, Moscow)

1981 (14 July). Centenary of Pali Text Society. P 12½×12.

738	**279**	35c. stone, deep brown and orange-brown......................	70	65

(Des R. Mawilmada. Litho Secura, Singapore)

1981 (21 July). 25th Anniv of All Ceylon Buddhist Students' Federation. P 13½.

739	**280**	2r. black, greenish yellow and dull vermilion......................	1·00	1·50

281 "Plan for Happiness"   **282** Dove Symbol with Acupuncture Needle and "Yin-Yang" (Chinese universe duality emblem)

(Des D. Wijesinghe. Litho Secura, Singapore)

1981 (25 Sept). Population and Family Planning. P 13½×13.

740	**281**	50c. multicoloured......................	1·00	1·75

(Des F. Perera. Litho State Printing Works, Moscow)

1981 (20 Oct). World Acupuncture Congress. P 12×12½.

741	**282**	2r. black, yellow and red-orange..........	2·75	3·75

283 Union and Sri Lanka Flags   **284** "Conserve our Forests"

(Des and litho J.W.)

1981 (21 Oct). Royal Visit. P 14.

742	**283**	50c. multicoloured......................	50	25
743		5r. multicoloured	1·75	4·00
MS744		165×90 mm. Nos. 742/3.................	2·25	4·00

(Des Ravi Advertising. Litho German Bank Note Co, Leipzig)

1981 (27 Nov). Forest Conservation. T **284** and similar horiz designs. P 13.

745	35c. multicoloured......................	15	10
746	50c. olive-brown and stone.................	20	20
747	5r. multicoloured	1·90	3·75
745/7	Set of 3	2·00	3·75
MS748	180×90 mm. Nos. 745/7. P 14×13......................	1·50	3·75

Designs:—50c. "Plant a tree"; 5r. Jak (tree).

285 Sir James Peiris   **286** F. R. Senanayaka

(Des P. Jayatillake. Litho Metal Box Singapore Ltd)

1981 (20 Dec). Birth Centenary of Sir James Peiris (politician). P 12.

749	**285**	50c. light brown......................	60	1·00

(Des M. Katugampola. Litho J.W.)

1982 (1 Jan). Birth Centenary of F. R. Senanayaka (national hero). P 14.

750	**286**	50c. olive-brown......................	1·00	1·25

287 Philip Gunawardhane   **288** Department of Inland Revenue Building, Colombo

(Des P. Jayatillake. Litho J.W.)

1982 (11 Jan). Tenth Death Anniv of Philip Gunawardhane (politician). P 14.

751	**287**	50c. cerise......................	70	1·25

(Des S. Mallikerachchi. Litho J.W.)

1982 (9 Feb). 50th Anniv of Department of Inland Revenue. P 14.

752	**288**	50c. black, blue-black and reddish orange......................	70	1·25

289 Rupavahini Emblem   **290** Cricketer and Ball

(Des G. Arthasad. Litho J.W.)

1982 (15 Feb). Inauguration of Rupavahini (national television service). P 14.
753	**289**	2r.50 lemon, purple-brown and grey	2·25	4·00

(Des R. Mawilmada. Litho J.W.)

1982 (17 Feb). First Sri Lanka-England Cricket Test Match, Colombo. P 14.
754	**290**	2r.50 multicoloured..	4·50	5·50

291 Obsbeckia wightiana

(Des P. Jayatillake. Litho Security Printers (M), Malaysia)

1982 (1 Apr). Flowers. T **291** and similar horiz designs. Multicoloured. P 12.
755	35c.	Type **291**	10	10
756	2r.	*Mesua nagassarium*	20	20
757	7r.	*Rhodomyrtus tomentosa*	50	1·25
758	20r.	*Phaius tancarvilleae*	1·40	4·50
755/8	Set of 4		2·00	5·50
MS759	180×110 mm. Nos. 755/8		6·00	7·50

292 Mother breast-   **293** Conference
feeding Child   Emblem

(Des A. Ratnapala. Litho Pakistan Security Printing Corp)

1982 (6 Apr). Food and Nutrition Policy Planning. P 13.
760	**292**	50c. multicoloured..	1·50	1·75

(Des M. Hussain. Litho J.W.)

1982 (21 Apr). World Hindu Conference. P 14.
761	**293**	50c. multicoloured..	1·00	1·75

294 King Vessantara giving away magical, rain-making White Elephant

(Des A. Dharmasiri. Litho J.W.)

1982 (23 Apr). Vesak. Legend of Vessantara Jataka. Details of Cloth Painting from Arattana Rajamaha Vihara (temple), Hanguranketa, District of Nuwara Eliya. T **294** and similar horiz designs. Multicoloured. P 14.
762	35c. Type **294**		45	10

763	50c. King Vessantara with family in Vanka giri Forest..		55	15
764	2r.50 Vessantara giving away his children as slaves..		2·00	2·25
765	5r. Vessantara and family returning to Jetuttara in royal chariot		2·75	3·50
762/5	Set of 4		5·25	5·50
MS766	160×115 mm. Nos. 762/5		7·00	7·00

295 Parliament Buildings, Sri   **296** Dr. C. W. W.
Jayawardanapura   Kannangara

(Des M. Katugampola. Litho J.W.)

1982 (29 Apr). Opening of Parliament Building Complex, Sri Jayawardanapura, Kotte. P 14.
767	**295**	50c. multicoloured..	1·00	1·50

(Des M. Katugampola. Litho State Printing Works, Moscow)

1982 (22 May). Dr. C. W. W. Kannangara ("Father of Free Education") Commemoration. P 12×12½.
768	**296**	50c. yellow-olive	1·00	1·75

297 Lord Baden-Powell   **298** Dr. G. P.
Malalasekara

(Des W. Rohana. Litho State Printing Works, Moscow)

1982 (24 May). 125th Birth Anniv of Lord Baden-Powell. P 12½×12.
769	**297**	50c. multicoloured..	1·75	1·75

(Des A. Rasiah. Litho State Printing Works, Moscow)

1982 (26 May). Dr. G. P. Malalasekara (founder of World Fellowship of Buddhists) Commemoration. P 12×12½.
770	**298**	50c. deep bluish green	1·00	1·50

299 Wheel encircling Globe

(Des A. Ratnapala. Litho State Printing Works, Moscow)

1982 (1 June). World Buddhist Leaders Conference. P 12½×12.
771	**299**	50c. multicoloured..	1·00	1·50

300 Wildlife   **301** Sir Waitialingam
Duraiswamy

(Des U. Karunaratna. Litho State Printing Works, Moscow)

1982 (5 June). World Environment Day. P 12½×12.
772   **300**   50c. multicoloured... 1·90   1·75

(Des A. Rasiah. Litho State Printing Works, Moscow)

1982 (14 June). Sir Waitialingam Duraiswamy (statesman and educationalist) Commemoration. P 12×12½.
773   **301**   50c. blackish brown and brown.............. 1·00   1·50

302 YMCA Emblem

(Des R. Mawilmada. Litho State Printing Works, Moscow)

1982 (24 June). Centenary of Colombo YMCA. P 11½×11.
774   **302**   2r.50 multicoloured...................................... 3·00   4·50

303 Rev. Weliwita   **304** Maharagama Sasana Sevaka
Sri Saranankara   Samithiya Emblem
Sangharaja

(Des M. Katugampola. Litho State Printing Works, Moscow)

1982 (5 July). Rev. Weliwita Sri Saranankara Sangharaja (Buddhist leader) Commemoration. P 12×12½.
775   **303**   50c. brown and yellow-orange................ 1·00   1·50

(Des A. Ratnapala. Litho Toppan Ptg Co, Japan)

1982 (4 Aug). Silver Jubilee of Maharagama Sasana Sevaka Samithiya (Buddhist Social Reform Movement). P 12×12½.
776   **304**   50c. multicoloured... 1·40   1·75

305 Dr. Robert Koch

(Des W. Rohana. Litho Toppan Ptg Co, Japan)

1982 (21 Sept). Centenary of Robert Koch's Discovery of Tubercle Bacillus. P 12×12½.
777   **305**   50c. multicoloured... 2·00   1·75

306 Sir John   **307** Eye Donation Society
Kotelawala   and Lions Club Emblems

(Des A. Rasiah. Litho State Printing Works, Moscow)

1982 (2 Oct). Second Death Anniv of Sir John Kotelawala. P 12×12½.
778   **306**   50c. deep olive.. 1·00   1·50

(Des Grant Kenyon and Eckhardt Ltd. Litho State Printing Works, Moscow)

1982 (16 Nov). World-Wide Sight Conservation Project. P 12×12½.
779   **307**   2r.50 multicoloured...................................... 3·00   4·75

308 1859 4d. Dull Rose and 1948 15c.
Independence Commemorative

(Des L. Ramasinghe. Litho Questa (5r.) or J.W. (others))

1982 (16 Nov)–**89**. As Nos. 718/21, but without surcharges and showing revised face values. P 14.
780   2r.50 Type **269** (1.6.83).............................. 1·00   20
781   3r. Golden Palm Civet (21.6.83)............... 8·00   6·50
782   4r. Indian Spotted Chevrotain................. 75   40
783   5r. Rusty-spotted Cat (1.12.89)................ 75   50
780/3 Set of 4 .... 9·50   7·00
For the 3r. in similar design, but printed by Questa with imprint date see No. 1081.

(Des D. Karunaratne. Litho Security Printers (M), Malaysia)

1982 (2 Dec). 125th Anniv of First Postage Stamps. T **308** and similar horiz design. Multicoloured. P 13×13½.
784   50c. Type **308** 75   75
785   2r.50 1859 1s.9d. green and 1981 50c. "Just
         Society" stamp....................................... 2·00   3·50
MS786 59×84 mm. Nos. 784/5 (sold at 5r.) ...... 2·50   4·25

309 Sir Oliver   **310** Sarvodaya Emblem
Goonetilleke

(Des A. Ratnapala. Litho State Printing Works, Moscow)

1982 (17 Dec). Fourth Death Anniv of Sir Oliver Goonetilleke (statesman). P 12×12½.
787   **309**   50c. olive-grey, bistre-brown and black 60   1·50

(Des P. Gunasinghe. Litho Secura, Singapore)

1983 (1 Jan). 25th Anniv of Sarvodaya Movement. P 13×13½.
788   **310**   50c. multicoloured... 1·00   1·50

311 Morse Key, Radio Aerial and   **312** Customs Co-
Amateur Radio Society Emblem   operation Council
                              Emblem and Sri Lanka
                              Flag

(Des W. Rohana. Litho Secura, Singapore)

1983 (17 Jan). Amateur Radio Society. P 13×13½.
789   **311**   2r.50 multicoloured...................................... 3·00   5·00

(Des W. Rohana. Litho Secura, Singapore)

1983 (26 Jan). 30th Anniv of International Customs Day. P 12×11½.
790   **312**   50c. multicoloured... 50   40
791   5r. multicoloured... 3·00   6·00

313 Bottle-nosed Dolphin

(Des G. Ratnavira. Litho Harrison)

1983 (22 Feb). Marine Mammals. T **313** and similar horiz designs. P 14½×14.

792	50c. black, new blue and grey-green	50	20
793	2r. multicoloured	1·00	1·00
794	2r.50 black, dp grey-blue and dp bluish grey	2·50	2·50
795	10r. multicoloured	6·00	7·50
792/5 *Set of 4*		9·00	10·00

Designs:—2r. Dugongs; 2r.50, Humpback Whale; 10r. Sperm Whale.

314 *Lanka Athula* (container ship)

(Des Vision Ltd. Litho Security Printers (M), Malaysia)

1983 (1 Mar). Ships of the Ceylon Shipping Corporation. T **314** and similar horiz designs. Multicoloured. P 11½×12.

796	50c. Type **314**	25	15
797	2r.50 Map of routes	90	70
798	5r. *Lanka Kalyani* (freighter)	1·25	1·60
799	20r. *Tammanna* (tanker)	2·00	7·00
796/9 *Set of 4*		4·00	8·50

315 Woman with IWD Emblem and Sri Lanka Flag

316 Waterfall

(Des R. Mawilmada. Litho Secura, Singapore)

1983 (8 Mar). International Women's Day. T **315** and similar vert design. Multicoloured. P 13.

800	50c. Type **315**	20	25
801	5r. Woman, emblem, map and symbols of progress	80	2·75

(Des S. Lankatilake. Litho Secura, Singapore)

1983 (14 Mar). Commonwealth Day. T **316** and similar horiz designs. Multicoloured. P 13.

802	50c. Type **316**	10	10
803	2r.50 Tea plucking	15	25
804	5r. Harvesting rice	25	40
805	20r. Decorated elephants	80	2·00
802/5 *Set of 4*		1·10	2·50

317 Lions Club International Badge

318 "The Dream of Queen Mahamaya"

(Des U. Karunaratna. Litho J.W.)

1983 (7 May). 25th Anniv of Lions Club International in Sri Lanka. P 14.

806	**317** 2r.50 multicoloured	2·50	2·50

(Des G. Keyt and A. Dharmasiri. Litho Toppan Ptg Co, Japan)

1983 (13 May). Vesak. Life of Prince Siddhartha from temple murals at Gotami Vihara. T **318** and similar vert designs. Multicoloured. P 12½×12.

807	35c. Type **318**	15	10
808	50c. "Prince Siddhartha given to Maha Brahma"	15	10
809	5r. "Prince Siddhartha and the Sleeping Dancers"	85	1·50
810	10r. "The Meeting with Mara"	1·40	3·50
807/10 *Set of 4*		2·25	4·50
MS811 150×90 mm. Nos. 807/10		2·25	4·50

319 First Telegraph' Transmission, Colombo to Galle, 1858

320 Henry Woodward Amarasuriya (philanthropist)

(Des W. Rohana. Litho Toppan Ptg Co, Japan)

1983 (17 May). 125th Anniv of Telecommunications in Sri Lanka (2r.) and World Communications Year (10r.). T **319** and similar horiz design. Multicoloured. P 12×12½.

812	2r. Type **319**	65	60
813	10r. World Communications Year emblem	2·50	5·00

(Litho Security Printers (M), Malaysia (No. 810), Pakistan Security Printing Corp (others))

1983 (22 May). National Heroes. T **320** and similar vert designs. P 12×11½ (No. 814) or 13 (others).

814	50c. bright emerald	30	1·00
815	50c. new blue	30	1·00
816	50c. magenta	30	1·00
817	50c. turquoise-green	30	1·00
814/17 *Set of 4*		1·10	3·50

Designs:—No. 815, Father Simon Perera (historian); No. 816, Charles Lorenz (lawyer and newspaper editor); No. 817, Noordeen Abdul Cader (first President of All-Ceylon Muslim League).

A fifth design to commemorate C. W. Tharnotheram Pillai was prepared for this set, but was withdrawn at the last moment when it was realised that the wrong portrait had been used. It is understood, however, that supplies were sold at some rural post offices where the instruction was not received in time. A corrected version was later issued, see No. 825.

321 Family and Village

322 Caravan of Bulls

(Des K. Gunasiri and U. Karuninatna. Litho Toppan Ptg Co, Japan)

1983 (23 June). Gam Udawa (Village Re-awakening Movement). T **321** and similar horiz design. Multicoloured. P 12×12½.

818	50c. Type **321**	10	25
819	5r. Village view	55	2·25

(Des A. Rasiah (35c., 2r.), D. Hemaratna (2r.50), U. Karunaratna (5r.). Litho State Printing Office, Budapest)

1983 (22 Aug). Transport. T **322** and similar horiz designs. Multicoloured. P 12.

820	35c. Type **322**	10	10
821	2r. Steam train	2·00	1·75
822	2r.50 Ox and cart	1·00	2·25
823	5r. Ford motor T touring car	2·25	4·25
820/3 *Set of 4*		4·75	7·50

323 Sir Tikiri Banda Panabokke

324 C. W. Thamotheram Pillai

(Des and litho Harrison)

1983 (2 Sept). 20th Death Anniv of Adigar Sir Tikiri Banda Panabokke. P 14×14½.

824	**323**	50c. Indian red	1·00	1·50

(Des and litho Pakistan Security Printing Corp)

1983 (1 Oct). C. W. Thamotheram Pillai (Tamil scholar) Commemoration. P 13.

825	**324**	50c. orange-brown	1·00	1·50

See note below No. 817.

325 Arabi Pasha

326 Sri Lanka Wood Pigeon

(Des and litho Pakistan Security Printing Corp)

1983 (13 Nov). Centenary of the Exile to Ceylon of Arabi Pasha. (Egyptian nationalist). P 13×13½.

826	**325**	50c. green	1·00	1·50

(Des G. Ratnavira. Litho Format)

1983 (22 Nov)–**88**. Birds (2nd series). T **326** and similar horiz designs. Multicoloured. P 14½.

827	25c. Type **326**	1·00	1·75
828	35c. Large Sri Lanka White Eye	1·00	1·00
829	2r. Sri Lanka Dusky Blue Flycatcher	1·00	40
829a	7r. As 35c. (28.9.88)	50	30
830	20r. Ceylon Coucal	1·50	4·00
827/30	Set of 5	4·50	6·75
MS831	183×93 mm. Nos. 827/9 and 830	2·75	6·50

Special packs prepared for the S.A.A.R.C. "Philex 96" stamp exhibition at Colombo contained the block of stamps from No. **MS**831 with the sheet margins removed.

No. 829 exists imperforate from stock dispersed by the liquidator of Format International Security Printers Ltd.

327 Pelene Siri Vajiragnana

328 Mary praying over Jesus and St. Joseph welcoming Shepherds

(Des and litho Harrison)

1983 (25 Nov). Pelene Siri Vajiragnana (scholar) Commemoration. P 14×14½.

832	**327**	50c. red-brown	1·50	1·75

(Des P. de Silva. Litho German Bank Note Co, Leipzig)

1983 (30 Nov). Christmas. P 12½×13.

833	**328**	50c. multicoloured	10	15
834		5r. multicoloured	30	2·00
MS835	85×141 mm. Nos. 833/4	65	2·50

. 60 (329)   . 60 (330)

1983 (1 Dec). No. 680a surch with T **329/30** by Aitken Spence Ptg (Pte) Ltd, Sri Lanka.

836	**236**	60c. on 50c. gold, bright yellow-green and emerald (surch T **329**)	6·00	2·00
		a. Surch inverted		
837		60c. on 50c. gold, bright yellow-green and emerald (surch T **330**)	9·50	7·50

331 Paddy Field, Globe and F.A.O. Emblem

(Des R. Mawilmada. Litho State Ptg Works, Moscow)

1984 (2 Jan). World Food Day. P 12½×12.

838	**331**	3r. multicoloured	45	2·00

332 Modern Tea Factory

333 Students and University

(Des M. Ratnapala. Litho State Ptg Works, Moscow)

1984 (31 Jan). Centenary of the Colombo Tea Auctions. T **332** and similar horiz designs. Multicoloured. P 12½×12.

839	**332**	1r. Type **332**	25	15
840		2r. Logo	45	45
841		5r. Girl picking tea	1·00	2·25
842		10r. Auction in progress	1·60	4·50
839/42	Set of 4		3·00	6·50

(Des R. Mawilmada. Litho Security Printers (M), Malaysia)

1984 (10 Feb). Fourth Anniv of Mahapola Scheme for Development and Education. T **333** and similar vert designs. Multicoloured. P 12.

843	**333**	60c. Type **333**	10	15
844		1r. Teacher with Gnana Darsana class	10	15
845		5r.50 Student with books and microscope	45	2·00
846		6r. Mahapola lamp symbol	50	2·00
843/6	Set of 4		1·00	3·75

334 King Daham Sonda instructing Angels

(Des A. Dharmasiri. Litho D.L.R.)

1984 (27 Apr). Vesak. The Story of King Daham Sonda from ancient casket paintings. T **334** and similar horiz designs. Multicoloured. P 14.

847	**334**	35c. Type **334**	30	10
		a. Perf 13×13½	60	20
848		60c. Elephant paraded with gift of gold	65	25
		a. Perf 13×13½	70	35
849		5r. King Daham Sonda leaps into mouth of God Sakra	1·50	3·00
		a. Perf 13×13½	1·75	3·25
850		10r. God Sakra carrying King Daham Sonda	1·90	5·00
		a. Perf 13×13½	2·25	5·50
847/50	Set of 4		4·00	7·50
847a/50a	Set of 4		4·75	8·50
MS851	154×109 mm. Nos. 847/50. P 13	4·00	7·00

335 Development Programme Logo

336 Dodanduwe Siri Piyaratana Tissa Mahanayake Thero (Buddhist scholar)

(Des R. Mawilmada. Litho Harrison)

1984 (5 May). Sri Lanka Lions Clubs' Development Programme. P 14×14½.

852	**335**	60c. multicoloured	1·40	1·00

(Litho State Ptg Works, Moscow)

1984 (22 May). National Heroes. T **336** and similar vert designs. P 12×12½.

853	60c. yellow-bistre	35	1·00
854	60c. yellow-green	35	1·00
855	60c. emerald-green	35	1·00
856	60c. red	35	1·00
857	60c. deep yellow-brown	35	1·00
853/7 Set of 5		1·60	4·50

Designs:—No. 853, Type **336**; 854, G. P. Wickremarachchi (physician); 855, Sir Mohamed Macan Markar (politician); 856, Dr. W. Arthur de Silva (philanthropist), 857, K. Balasingham (lawyer).

337 Association Emblem

(Des A. Harischandra. Litho Govt Printing Bureau, Tokyo)

1984 (16 June). Centenary of Public Service Mutual Provident Association. P 13×13½.

858	**337**	4r.60 multicoloured	70	2·50

Imperforate examples of No. 858 exist, but their status is unknown.

338 Sri Lanka Village

339 World Map showing APBU Countries

(Des S. Herath. Litho State Ptg Wks, Moscow)

1984 (23 June). Sixth Anniv of "Gam Udawa" (Village Reawakening Movement). P 12×12½.

859	**338**	60c. multicoloured	30	1·00

(Des G. Arthasad. Litho State Ptg Wks, Moscow)

1984 (30 June). 20th Anniv of Asia-Pacific Broadcasting Union. P 12½×12.

860	**339**	7r. multicoloured	2·25	3·75

340 Drummers and Elephant carrying Royal Instructions

(Des R. Mawilmada. Litho State Ptg Wks, Moscow)

1984 (11 Aug). Esala Perahera (Procession of the Tooth), Kandy. T **340** and similar horiz designs. Multicoloured. P 12½×12.

861	4r.60 Type **340**		1·25	2·10
	a. Horiz strip of four. Nos. 861/4		4·50	7·50
862	4r.60 Dancers and elephants		1·25	2·10
863	4r.60 Elephant carrying Tooth Relic		1·25	2·10
864	4r.60 Custodian of the Sacred Tooth and attendants		1·25	2·10
861/4 Set of 4			4·50	7·50
MS865 223×108 mm. Nos. 861/4			4·50	7·50

Nos. 861/4 were printed together, se-tenant, in horizontal strips of four throughout the sheet, forming a composite design.

341 *Vanda memoria* Ernest Soysa (orchid)

342 Symbolic Athletes and Stadium

(Des G. Ratnavira. Litho D.L.R.)

1984 (22 Aug). 50th Anniv of Ceylon Orchid Circle. T **341** and similar vert designs, showing orchids. Multicoloured. P 14.

866	60c. Type **341**	2·25	30
	a. Perf 13½×13	1·00	1·25
867	4r.60 *Acanthephippium bicolor*	3·50	4·50
	a. Perf 13½×13	2·00	4·00
868	5r. *Vanda tessellate* var. *rufescens*	4·25	4·75
	a. Perf 13½×13	1·25	4·00
869	10r. *Anoectochilus setaceus*	4·00	6·00
866/9 (cheapest) Set of 4		7·50	13·00
MS870 115×110 mm. Nos. 866/9. P 13		7·00	12·00

(Des M. Heenkenda. Litho Govt Printing Bureau, Tokyo)

1984 (5 Oct). First National School Games. P 13½×13.

871	**342**	60c. black, grey and bright new blue	1·75	1·75

343 D. S. Senanayake, Temple and Fields

(Des L. Jayawardena (35c.), G. Fernando (60c.), N. Lasantha (4r.60), R. Mawilmada (6r.). Litho J.W.)

1984 (20 Oct). Birth Centenary of D. S. Senanayake (former Prime Minister). T **343** and similar horiz designs. Mulicoloured. P 14.

872	35c. Type **343**	10	10
873	60c. Senanayake and statue	10	10
874	4r.60 Senanayake and irrigation project	40	60
875	6r. Senanayake and House of Representatives	55	80
872/5 Set of 4		1·00	1·40

344 Lake House

345 Agricultural Workers and Globe

(Des Grant Kenyon and Eckhardt Ltd. Litho State Printing Office, Budapest)

1984 (19 Nov). 150th Anniv of the "Observer" Newspaper. P 13×13½.

876	**344**	4r.60 multicoloured	2·75	4·00

(Des M. Ratnapala. Litho German Bank Note Ptg Co, Leipzig)

1984 (10 Dec). 20th Anniv of World Food Programme. P 13×13½.
877　345　7r. multicoloured.................................... 2·25　1·50

346 College
Emblem

347 Dove and Stylized
Figures

(Des S. Herath. Litho J.W.)

1984 (24 Dec). Centenary of Baari Arabic College, Weligama.
P 13×12½.
878　346　4r.60 blackish olive, turquoise-green
　　　　　　　and turquoise-blue .... 1·25　3·25

(Des S. Chandrajeewa (4r.60), O. Weerakkody (20r.). Litho J.W.)

1985 (1 Jan). International Youth Year. T **347** and similar horiz design.
Multicoloured. P 12½×13.
879　　　4r.60 Type **347**　　　　　　　　　　75　75
880　　　20r. Dave, stylized figures and flower............ 2·25　4·00

348 Religious Symbols

349 College Crest

(Des R. Mawilmada. Litho Security Printers (M), Malaysia)

1985 (20 Jan). World Religion Day. P 12.
881　348　4r.60 multicoloured.................................... 3·00　3·75

(Des G. Arthasad. Litho J.W.)

1985 (29 Jan). 150th Anniv of Royal College, Colombo. T **349** and
similar vert design. P 13×12½.
882　　　60c. bright yellow and deep ultramarine ...... 25　25
883　　　7r. multicoloured.. 2·75　4·50
　　Design:—7r. Royal College.

350 Banknotes, Buildings,
Ship and "Wheel of Life"

351 Wariyapola Sri
Sumangala Thero

(Des R. Mawilmada. Litho J.W.)

1985 (7 Feb). Fifth Anniv of Mahapola Scheme. P 14.
884　350　60c. multicoloured.................................... 1·00　1·75

(Des G. Fernando. Litho State Printing Office, Budapest)

1985 (2 Mar). Wariyapola Sri Sumangala Thero (Buddhist priest and
patriot) Commemoration. P 13×13½.
885　351　60c. black, reddish brown and
　　　　　　　greenish yellow .... 70　1·50

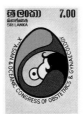
352 Victoria Dam

353 Cover of
50th Edition of
International
Buddhist Annual,
Vesak Sirisara

(Des G. Arthasad. Litho State Ptg Wks, Moscow)

1985 (12 Apr). Inauguration of Victoria Hydro-electric Project. T **352**
and similar multicoloured design. P 12½×12 (60c.) or 12½×12½ (7r.).
886　　　60c. Type **352**　　　　　　　　　　1·00　50
887　　　7r. Map of Sri Lanka enclosing dam and
　　　　　　　power station (*vert*) .... 5·50　7·50

(Des B. Harischandra (35 c.), R. Mawilmada (others). Litho J.W.)

1985 (26 Apr). Centenary of Vesak Poya Holiday. T **363** and similar
vert designs. Multicoloured. P 13×12½.
888　　　35c. Type **353**　　　　　　　　　　10　10
889　　　60c. Buddhists worshipping at temple .... 10　10
890　　　6r. Buddhist Theosophical Society
　　　　　　　Headquarters, Colombo...................... 75　1·50
891　　　9r. Buddhist flag .... 2·00　3·00
888/91 Set of 4 .... 2·75　4·25
MS892 180×110 mm. Nos. 888/91 .... 4·00　6·50

354 Ven. Waskaduwe
Sri Subhuthi (priest
and scholar)

355 Stylised Village and
People

(Des S. Silva. Litho J.W.)

1985 (22 May). Personalities. T **364** and similar vert designs.
P 13×12½.
893　　　60c. black, yellow-orange and lake-brown.... 30　90
894　　　60c. black, yellow-orange and deep mauve . 30　90
895　　　60c. black, yellow-orange and light brown... 30　90
896　　　60c. black, yellow-orange and emerald.......... 30　90
893/6 Set of 4 .... 1·10　3·25
Designs:—No. 893, Type **354**; 894, Revd. Fr. Peter A. Pillai
(educationist and social reformer); 895, Dr. Senarath Paranavitane
(scholar); 896, A. M. Wapche Marikar (architect and educationist).

(Des S. Herath. Litho German Bank Note Co, Leipzig)

1985 (23 June). Gam Udawa' 85 (Village Re-awakening Movement).
P 13½×13.
897　355　60c. multicoloured.................................... 1·00　1·50

356 Emblem

357 Kothmale Dam and Reservoir

(Des B. Harischandra. Litho German Bank Note Co, Leipzig)

1985 (25 June). 50th Anniv of Colombo Young Poets' Association.
P 14.
898　356　60c. multicoloured.................................... 1·75　2·00

(Des R. Mawilmada. Litho J.W.)

1985 (24 Aug). Inauguration of Kothmale Hydro-electric
Project. T **367** and similar horiz design. Multicoloured. P 14.
899　　　60c. Type **357**　　　　　　　　　　75　25
900　　　6r. Kothmale Power Station .... 3·75　5·00

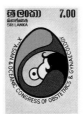
358 Federation Logo

359 Breast Feeding

(Des R. Mawilmada. Litho J.W.)

1985 (2 Sept). Tenth Asian and Oceanic Congress of Obstetrics and
Gynaecology. P 14.
901　358　7r. multicoloured...................................... 3·25　4·50

(Des B. Harischandra. Litho Cartor)

1985 (5 Sept). UNICEF Child Survival and Development Programme. T **359** and similar vert designs. Multicoloured. W w **17**. P 13½.

902		35c. Type **359**	30	10
903		60c. Child and oral rehydration salts	45	30
904		6r. Weighing child (growth monitoring)	2·25	3·50
905		9r. Immunization	2·75	5·50
902/5 *Set of 4*			5·25	8·50
MS906	99×180 mm. Nos. 902/5. P 12½		4·50	6·50
	w. Wmk inverted		4·50	6·50

360 Blowing Indian Chunk Shell

361 Casket containing Land Grant Deed

(Des G. Malaviachi. Litho Heraclio Fournier, Spain)

1985 (27 Sept). Tenth Anniv of World Tourism Organization. T **360** and similar horiz designs. Multicoloured. P 14.

907		1r. Type **360**	30	10
908		6r. Parliamentary Complex, Jayawardhanapura, Kotte	90	90
909		7r. Tea plantation	1·00	1·10
910		10r. Ruwanveliseya (Buddhist shrine), Anuradhapura	1·60	1·75
907/10 *Set of 4*			3·50	3·50
MS911	179×89 mm. Nos. 907/10. P 13½		3·50	3·75

(Des B. Harischandra. Litho Harrison)

1985 (15 Oct). 50th Anniv of Land Development Ordinance. P 14×15.

912	**361**	4r.60 multicoloured	2·00	3·75

362 Koran and Map of Sri Lanka

363 "Our Lady of Matara" Statue

(Des R. Mawilmada. Litho Cartor)

1985 (17 Oct). Translation of The Koran into Sinhala. W w **17**. P 13½.

913	**362**	60c. gold and bright violet	2·50	2·00

(Des S. Silva. Litho Security Printers (M), Malaysia)

1985 (5 Nov). Christmas. T **363** and similar vert design. Multicoloured. P 12.

914		60c. Type **363**	30	15
915		9r. "Our Lady of Madhu" statue	1·50	3·00
MS916	180×100 mm. Nos. 914/15		7·00	8·50

(**364**)

365 Linked Arms and Map of SAARC Countries

1985 (1 Dec)–86. Nos. 680b, 780, 823, 860 and 879 surch as T **364** by Aitken Spence Ptg (Pte) Ltd, Sri Lanka.

917	**236**	75c. on 60c. gold, bright yellow-green and emerald (G.)	40	10
		a. Surch double	†	—
918	**347**	1r. on 4r.60 mult (29.4.86)	13·00	5·00
919	**339**	1r. on 7r. multicoloured (20.1.86)	14·00	5·00

920	**269**	5r.75 on 2r.50 multicoloured (Br)	3·50	3·00
921	–	7r. on 35c. mult (No. 828) (10.3.86)	11·00	1·50
		a. Surch inverted		
		b. Surch double		
		c. Surch triple		
917/21 *Set of 5*			38·00	13·00

(Des B. Harischandra. Litho J.W.)

1985 (8 Dec). First Summit Meeting of South Asian Association for Regional Co-operation, Dhaka, Bangladesh. T **365** and similar horiz design. Multicoloured. P 14.

922		60c. Type **365**	6·50	9·00
923		5r.50 Logo and flags of member countries	5·00	5·00

No 922 was, reportedly, withdrawn on 11 December after Pakistan objected to the boundaries shown on the map.

366 "Viceroy Special" Train

(Des G. Malaviachi. Litho Format)

1986 (2 Feb). Inaugural Run of "Viceroy Special" Train from Colombo to Kandy. P 12½.

924	**366**	1r. multicoloured	75	1·50

367 Girl and Boy Students

(Des S. Silva. Litho Heraclio Fournier, Spain)

1986 (14 Feb). Sixth Anniv of Mahapola Scheme. P 14.

925	**367**	75c. multicoloured	50	1·50

368 D. R. Wijewardena

369 Ven Welitara Gnanatillake Maha Nayake Thero

(Des S. Silva. Litho J.W.)

1986 (23 Feb). Birth Centenary of D. R. Wijewardena (newspaper publisher). P 14×14½.

926	**368**	75c. orange-brown and deep olive	30	1·50

(Des S. Silva. Litho Cartor)

1986 (26 Feb). Ven. Welitara Gnanatillake Maha Nayake Thero (scholar) Commemoration. W w **17**. P 13½.

927	**369**	75c. multicoloured	70	1·00

370 Red Cross Flag and Personnel

(Des W. Rohana. Litho Format)

1986 (31 Mar). 50th Anniv of Sri Lanka Red Cross Society. P 12½.

928	**370**	75c. multicoloured	2·00	1·75

371 Comet depicted as Goddess visiting Sun-god

372 Woman lighting Lamp

(Des W. Rohana. Litho Format)

1986 (5 Apr). Appearance of Halley's Comet. T **371** and similar horiz designs. Multicoloured. P 12½.

929	50c. Type **371**	15	20
930	75c. Comet and constellations of Scorpius and Sagittarius	15	20
931	6r.50 Comet's orbit	30	1·50
932	8r.50 Edmond Halley	55	2·50
929/32	Set of 4	1·00	4·00
MS933	180×115 mm. Nos. 929/32	5·50	11·00

(Des B. Harischandra. Litho Format)

1986 (10 Apr). Sinhalese and Tamil New Year. T **372** and similar vert designs. Multicoloured. P 12½.

934	50c. Type **372**	15	20
935	75c. Woman and festive foods	15	20
936	6r.50 Women playing drum	30	2·00
937	8r.50 Anointing and making offerings at temple	55	2·50
934/7	Set of 4	1·00	4·50
MS938	178×108 mm. Nos. 934/7	1·75	6·00

373 The King donating Elephant to the Brahmin

374 Ven. Kalukondayave Sri Prajnasekhara Maha Nayake Thero (Buddhist leader and social reformer)

(Des N. Bulathsinhala. Litho Format)

1986 (16 May). Vesak. Wall paintings from Samudragiri Temple, Mirissa. T **373** and similar horiz designs. Multicoloured. P 12½.

939	50c. Type **373**	10	20
940	75c. The Bodhisattva in the Vasavarthi heaven	10	20
941	5r. The offering of milk rice by Sujatha	50	2·00
942	10r. The offering of parched corn and honey by Thapassu and Bhalluka	55	2·75
939/42	Set of 4	1·00	4·75

(Des S. Silva. Litho Format)

1986 (22 May). National Heroes. T **374** and similar vert designs. Multicoloured. P 12½.

943	75c. Type **374**	15	80
944	75c. Brahmachari Walisinghe Harischandra (social reformer) (birth centenary)	15	80
945	75c. Martin Wickramasinghe (author and scholar)	15	80
946	75c. G. G. Ponnambalam (politician)	15	80
947	75c. A. M. A. Azeez (Islamic scholar) (75th birth anniv)	15	80
943/7	Set of 5	65	3·50

375 Stylised Village and People

(Des S. Herath. Litho German Bank Note Co, Leipzig)

1986 (23 June). Gam Udawa '86 (Village Re-awakening Movement). P 13½×13.

948	**375**	75c. multicoloured	1·50	2·00

376 Co-op Flag and Emblem

377 Arthur V. Dias

(Des A. Harischandra. Litho Format)

1986 (5 July). 75th Anniv of Sri Lanka Co-operative Movement. P 12½.

949	**376**	1r. multicoloured	1·00	2·00

(Des S. Silva. Litho Harrison)

1986 (31 July). Birth Centenary of Arthur V. Dias (philanthropist). P 14×15.

950	**377**	1r. chestnut and dull violet-blue	1·50	2·25

378 Bull Elephant

379 Congress Logo

(Des G. Ratnavira. Litho Harrison)

1986 (5 Aug). Sri Lanka Wild Elephants. T **378** and similar horiz designs. Multicoloured. P 15×14.

951		5r. Type **378**	12·00	8·00
		a. Horiz strip of four. Nos. 951/4	42·00	29·00
952		5r. Cow elephant and calf	12·00	8·00
953		5r. Cow elephant	12·00	8·00
954		5r. Elephants bathing	12·00	8·00
951/4	Set of 4		42·00	29·00

Nos. 951/4 were printed, together, se-tenant, in horizontal strips of four throughout the sheet.

(Des S. Silva. Litho Govt Printing Bureau, Tokyo)

1986 (14 Aug). Second Indo-Pacific Congress on Legal Medicine and Forensic Sciences. P 13½×13.

955	**379**	8r.50 multicoloured	3·00	3·50

380 Map showing Route of Cable and Telephone Receiver

(Des R. Mawilmada. Litho Security Printers (M), Malaysia)

1986 (8 Sept). SEA-ME-WE Submarine Cable Project. P 13½×14.

956	**380**	5r.75 multicoloured	6·00	3·00

381 Anniversary Logo

382 Logo on Flag

(Des R. Mawilmada. Litho Format)

1986 (20 Sept). 25th Anniv of Dag Hammarskjold Award. P 12½.
957   **381**   2r. multicoloured ....   1·40   1·50

(Des A. Harischandra. Litho Security Printers (M), Malaysia)

1986 (22 Sept). Second National School Games. P 12.
958   **382**   1r. multicoloured ....   3·25   2·50

383 Logo   **384** College Building and Crest

(Des W. Rohana. Litho Govt Printing Bureau, Tokyo)

1986 (27 Sept). 60th Anniv of Surveyors' Institute of Sri Lanka. P 13½×13.
959   **383**   75c. red-brown and cinnamon   60   1·50

(Des W. Rohana. Litho Security Printers (M), Malaysia)

1986 (1 Nov). Centenary of Ananda College, Colombo. T **384** and similar horiz designs. P 12.
960   75c. multicoloured   10   15
961   5r. multicoloured   30   1·10
962   5r.75 multicoloured   35   1·10
963   6r. carmine-red, gold and rose-lilac   40   1·40
960/3 Set of 4 ....   1·00   3·25
Designs:—5r. Sports field and college crest; 5r.75, Col. H. S. Olcott (founder), Ven. Migettuwatte Gunananda, Ven. Hikkaduwe Sri Sumangala (Buddhist leaders) and Buddhist flag; 6r. College flag.

385 Mangrove Swamp   **386** Family and Housing Estate

(Des G. Ratnavira. Litho Security Printers (M), Malaysia)

1986 (11 Nov). Mangrove Conservation. T **385** and similar horiz designs. Multicoloured. P 12.
964   35c. Type **385** ....   1·25   30
965   50c. Mangrove tree ....   1·40   40
966   75c. Germinating mangrove flower ....   1·50   50
967   6r. Fiddler Crab ....   9·00   10·00
964/7 Set of 4 ....   11·50   10·00

(Des R. Mawilmada. Litho Govt Printing Bureau, Tokyo)

1987 (1 Jan). International Year of Shelter for the Homeless. P 13×13½.
968   **386**   75c. multicoloured ....   1·75   70

387 Ven. Ambagahawatte Indasabhawaragnana– samy Thero   **388** Proctor John de Silva

(Des S. Silva. Litho Security Printers (M), Malaysia)

1987 (29 Jan). Ven. Ambagahawatte Indasabhawaragnanasamy Thero (Buddhist monk) Commemoration. P 12.
969   **387**   5r.75 multicoloured ....   2·50   1·25

(Des S. Silva. Litho Security Printers (M), Malaysia)

1987 (31 Jan). Proctor John de Silva (playwright) Commemoration. P 12.
970   **388**   5r.75 multicoloured ....   1·00   1·00

389 Mahapola Logo and Aspects of Communication   **390** Dr. R. L. Brohier

(Des R. Mawilmada. Litho Security Printers (M), Malaysia)

1987 (6 Feb). Seventh Anniv of Mahapola Scheme. P 12.
971   **389**   75c. multicoloured   75   1·50

(Des S. Silva. Litho Security Printers (M), Malaysia)

1987 (10 Feb). Dr. Richard L. Brohier (historian and surveyor) Commemoration. P 12.
972   **390**   5r.75 multicoloured ....   2·00   1·40

391 Tyre Corporation Building, Kelaniya, and Logo

(Des A. Harischandra. Litho Questa)

1987 (23 Mar). 25th Anniv of Sri Lanka Tyre Corporation. P 14.
973   **391**   5r.75 black, lake and bright orange   50   70

392 Logo

(Des A. Harischandra. Litho Govt Printing Bureau, Tokyo)

1987 (24 Mar). Centenary of Sri Lanka Medical Association. P 13×13½.
974   **392**   5r.75 lake-brown, greenish yellow and black ....   2·25   3·50

393 Clasped Hands, Farmer and Paddy Field   **394** Exhibition Logo

(Des B. Harischandra. Litho Questa)

1987 (29 Mar). Inauguration of Farmers' Pension and Social Security Benefit Scheme. P 14.
975   **393**   75c. multicoloured ....   1·25   1·50

(Des W. Rohana. Litho Security Printers (M), Malaysia)

1987 (2 Apr). Mahaweli Maha Govíya Contest and Agra Mahaweli Exhibition. P 12.
976   **394**   75c. multicoloured   30   30

395 Young Children with WHO and Immunization Logos

(Des B. Harischandra. Litho Questa)

1987 (7 Apr). World Health Day. P 14.

977	**395**	1r. multicoloured	2·50	1·50

396 Girls playing on Swing

397 Lotus Lanterns

(Des G. Fernando. Litho Security Printers (M). Malaysia)

1987 (9 Apr). Sinhalese and Tamil New Year. T **396** and similar vert design. Multicoloured. P 12.

978		75c. Type **396**	10	10
979		5r. Girls with oil lamp and sun symbol........	50	50

(Des W. Rohana. Litho Security Printers (M). Malaysia)

1987 (4 May). Vesak. T **397** and similar horiz designs. Multicoloured. P 12.

980		50c. Type **397**	10	10
981		75c. Octagonal lanterns..................................	10	10
982		5r. Star lanterns..	35	30
983		10r. Gok lanterns.......................................	60	65
980/3	*Set of 4*		1·00	1·00
MS984	150×90 mm. Nos. 980/3		1·00	1·00

398 Emerald-collared Parakeet

399 Ven. Heenatiyana Sri Dhammaloka Maha Nayake There (Buddhist monk)

(Des G. Ratnavira. Litho Questa)

1987 (18 May)–**91**. Birds (3rd series). T **398** and similar horiz designs. Multicoloured. P 14.

A. With imprint date at bottom right

985A	50c. Type **398**	50	10
986A	1r. Legge's Flowerpecker................................	75	10
987A	5r. Ceylon White-headed Starling	1·10	1·60
988A	10r. Ceylon Jungle Babbler............................	1·40	2·75
985A/8A	*Set of 4*	3·25	4·00
MS989A	140×80 mm. Nos. 985A/8A..........................	8·00	9·00

B. Without imprint date

987B	5r. Ceylon White-headed Starling	4·00	1·50
988B	10r. Ceylon Jungle Babbler............................	2·50	2·75

Imprint dates: "1987", Nos. 985A/9A; "1989", No. 986A; "1990", No. 988A.

1987 (22 May). National Heroes. T **399** and similar vert designs. Multicoloured. P 12.

990		75c. Type **399**	40	40
991		75c. P. de S. Kularatne (educationist).............	40	40
992		75c. M. C. Abdul Rahuman (legislator)...........	40	40
990/2	*Set of 3*		1·10	1·10

400 Peasant Family and Village

401 *Mesua nagassarium*

(Des J. Semage. Lithe Security Printers (M), Malaysia)

1987 (23 June). Gam Udawa '87 (Village Re-awakening movement). P 12.

993	**400**	75c. multicoloured...	30	30

(Des P. Hewabettage 175c.), B. Harischandra (5r.), Litho Security Printers (M), Malaysia)

1987 (25 June). Forest Conservation. T **401** and similar horiz design. Multicoloured. P 12.

994	75c. Type **401**	10	10
995	5r. Elephants in forest	1·50	1·25

402 Dharmaraja College, Crest and Col. H. Olcott (founder)

403 Youth Services Logo

(Des C. Kandewela. Litho Security Printers (M), Malaysia)

1987 (30 June). Centenary of Dharmaraja College, Kandy. P 12.

996	**402**	75c. multicoloured...	2·25	30

(Des H. Drayaratne. Litho Security Printers (M), Malaysia)

1987 (15 July). 20th Anniv of National Youth Services. P 12.

997	**403**	75c. multicoloured...	20	20

404 Arm holding Torch and Mahaweli Logo

405 Open Bible and Logo

(Des W. Rohana. Litho Security Printers (M), Malaysia)

1987 (5 Sept). Mahaweli Games. P 12.

998	**404**	75c. multicoloured...	3·25	3·00

(Des C. Beling. Litho Security Printers (M), Malaysia)

1987 (2 Oct). 175th Anniv of Ceylon Bible Society. P 12.

999	**405** 5r.75 multicoloured...	40	40

406 Hurdler and Committee Symbol

(Des R. Mawilmada. Litho Heraclio Fournier, Spain)

1987 (8 Oct). 50th Anniv of National Olympic Committee. P 13.

1000	**406**	10r. multicoloured...	2·50	1·25

407 Madonna and Child, Flowers and Oil Lamp

408 Sir Ernest de Silva

(Des B. Mendis. Litho Security Printers (M), Malaysia)

1987 (17 Nov). Christmas. T **407** and similar vert design. Multicoloured. P 12 (75c.) or 12½×13 (10r.).
1001		75c. Type **407**	10	10
1002		10r. Christ Child in manger, star and dove...	35	40
MS1003		145×82 mm. Nos. 1001/2. P 12	60	70

(Des P. Gunasinghe. Litho German Bank Note Co, Leipzig)

1987 (25 Nov). Birth Centenary of Sir Ernest de Silva (philanthropist and philatelist). P 13×13½.
1004	**408**	75c. multicoloured	30	30

409 Society Logo

(Des W. Rohana. Litho German Bank Note Co, Leipzig)

1987 (28 Nov). 150th Anniv of Kandy Friend-in-Need Society. P 13½×13.
1005	**409**	75c. multicoloured	30	30

410 University Flag and Graduates

411 Father Joseph Vaz

(Des R. Samarasinghe. Litho Security Printers (M), Malaysia)

1987 (14 Dec). First Convocation of Buddhist and Pali University. P 12.
1006	**410**	75c. multicoloured	30	30

(Des S. Silva. Litho Security Printers (M), Malaysia)

1987 (15 Dec). 300th Anniv of Arrival of Father Joseph Vaz in Kandy. P 12.
1007	**411**	75c. multicoloured	30	30

412 Wheel of Dhamma, Dagaba and Bo Leaf

413 Dharmayatra Truck

(Des W. Rohana. Litho Security Printers (M), Malaysia)

1988 (1 Jan). 30th Anniv of Buddhist Publication Society, Kandy. P 12.
1008	**412**	75c. multicoloured	30	30

(Des B. Harischandra. Litho German Bank Note Co, Leipzig)

1988 (4 Jan). Fifth Anniv of Mahapola Dharmayatra Service. P 13½×13.
1009	**413**	75c. multicoloured	60	30

414 Society Logo

415 National Youth Centre, Maharagama

(Des R. Samarasinghe. Litho Security Printers (M), Malaysia)

1988 (8 Jan). Centenary of Ceylon Society of Arts. P 12.
1010	**414**	75c. multicoloured	30	30

(Des R. Chandrajeewa. Litho German Bank Note Co, Leipzig)

1988 (31 Jan). Opening of National Youth Centre, Maharagama. P 13½×13.
1011	**415**	1r. multicoloured	3·50	30

416 Citizens with National Flag and Map of Sri Lanka

417 Graduates, Clay Lamp and Open Book

(Des R. Samarasinghe. Litho Security Printers (M), Malaysia)

1988 (4 Feb). 40th Anniv of Independence. T **416** and similar vert design. Multicoloured. P 12.
1012		75c. Type **416**	10	10
1013		8r. 50 "40" in figures and lion emblem	90	90

(Des R. Samarasinghe. Litho Security Printers (M), Malaysia)

1988 (11 Feb). Eighth Anniv of Mahapola Scheme. P 12.
1014	**417**	75c. multicoloured	30	30

418 Bus and Logo

419 Ven. Weligama Sri Sumangala Maha Nayake Thero

(Des W. Rohana. Litho Security Printers (M), Malaysia)

1988 (19 Feb). 30th Anniv of Sri Lanka Transport Board. P 12.
1015	**418**	5r.75 multicoloured	1·00	80

(Des S. Silva. Litho Security Printers (M), Malaysia)

1988 (13 Mar). Ven. Weligama Sri Sumangala Maha Nayake Thero (Buddhist monk) Commemoration. P 12.
1016	**419**	75c. multicoloured	30	30

420 Regimental Colour

(Des W. Rohana. Litho Security Printers (M), Malaysia)

1988 (20 Apr). Centenary of Regiment of Artillery. P 12.

1017 **420** 5r.75 multicoloured.. 2·50 80

421 Chevalier I. X. Pereira

422 Invitation to the Deities and Brahmas

(Des S. Silva. Litho Security Printers (M), Malaysia)

1988 (26 Apr). Birth Centenary of Chevalier I. X. Pereira (politician). P 12.

1018 **421** 5r.75 multicoloured.. 50 50

(Des N. Bulathsinhala. Litho State Ptg Wks, Moscow)

1988 (13 May). Vesak. Paintings from Narendrarama Rajamaha Temple, Suriyagoda. T **422** and similar horiz design. Multicoloured. P 12½×12.

1019 50c. Type **422**.. 15 15
1020 75c. Bodhisathva at the Seventh Step........... 15 15
MS1021 150×92 mm. Nos. 1019/20......................... 2·00 2·50

423 Father Ferdinand Bonnet (educationist)

424 Stylized Figures and Reawakened Village

(Des S. Silva. Litho State Ptg Wks, Moscow)

1988 (22 May). National Heroes. T **423** and similar vert designs. Multicoloured. P 12½×12½.

1022 75c. Type **423**.. 15 25
1023 75c. Sir Razik Fareed (politician)................ 15 25
1024 75c. W. F. Gunawardhana (scholar)............ 15 25
1025 75c. Edward Nugawela (politician)............. 15 25
1026 75c. Chief Justice Sir Arthur
          Wijeyewardene.. 15 25
1022/6 *Set of 5*.. 60 1·00

(Des P. Gunasinghe. Litho Security Printers (M), Malaysia)

1988 (23 June). Tenth Anniv of Gam Udawa (Village Re-awakening Movement). P 12.

1027 **424** 75c. multicoloured.. 30 30

425 Maliyadeva College, Kurunegala, and Crest

426 M. J. M. Lafir, Billiard Game and Trophy

(Des W. Rohana. Litho German Bank Note Co, Leipzig)

1988 (30 June). Centenary of Maliyadeva College, Kurnnegala. P 13½×13.

1028 **425** 75c. multicoloured.. 30 30

(Des S. Silva, Litho State Ptg Wks, Moscow)

1988 (5 July). Mohamed Junaid Mohamed Lafir (World Amateur Billiards Champion, 1973) Commemoration. P 12½×12.

1029 **426** 5r.75 multicoloured.. 45 55

427 Flags of Australia and Sri Lanka, Handclasp and Map of Australia

(Des R. Samarasinghe. Litho Security Printers (M), Malaysia)

1988 (19 July). Bicentenary of Australian Settlement. P 12.

1030 **427** 8r.50 multicoloured.. 1·25 1·00

428 Ven. Kataluwe Sri Gunaratana Maha Nayake Thero

429 Athlete, Rice and Hydro-electric Dam

(Des S. Silva. Litho State Ptg Wks, Moscow)

1988 (11 Aug). Ven. Kataluwe Sri Gunaratana Maha Nayake Thero (Buddhist monk) Commemoration. P 12×12½.

1031 **428** 75c. multicoloured.. 30 30

(Des P. Gunaeinghe. Litho Security Printers (M), Malaysia)

1988 (3 Sept). Mahaweli Games. P 12.

1032 **429** 75c. multicoloured.. 30 30

430 Athletics

431 Outline Map of Sri Lanka and Anniversary Logo

(Des P. Gunasinghe. Litho State Ptg Wks, Moscow)

1988 (6 Sept). Olympic Games, Seoul. T **430** and similar vert designs. Multicoloured. P 12½×12½.

1033 75c. Type **430**.. 10 10
1034 1r. Swimming.. 10 10
1035 5r.75 Boxing.. 40 40
1036 8r.50 Map of Sri Lanka and logos of Olympic
          Committee and Seoul Games................... 70 70
1033/6 *Set of 4*.. 1·10 1·10
MS1037 181×101 mm. Nos. 1033/6......................... 1·10 1·40

(Des S. Silva. Litho Security Printers (M), Malaysia)

1988 (12 Sept). 40th Anniv of World Health Organization. P 12.

1038 **431** 75c. multicoloured.. 30 30

432 Games Logo

433 Mahatma Gandhi

(Des A. Harischandra. Litho Security Printers (M), Malaysia)

1988 (20 Sept). Third National School Games. P 12.
1039   **432**   1r. black, gold and mauve...................... 2·75   25

(Des S. Silva. Litho Security Printers (M), Malaysia)

1988 (2 Oct). 40th Death Anniv of Mahatma Gandhi. P 12.
1040   **433**   75c. multicoloured............................ 2·50   1·00

434 Globe with Forms of
Transport and Communications

(Des R. Samarasinghe. Litho State Ptg Wks, Moscow)

1988 (28 Oct). Asia–Pacific Transport and Communications Decade. T **434** and similar horiz design. P 12½×12.
1041   75c. multicoloured.................................. 1·00   20
1042   5r.75 magenta, royal blue and black................ 3·00   1·60
   Design:—5r.75, Antenna tower with dish aerials and forms of transport.

435 Woman with Rice Sheaf
and Hydro-electric Project

(Des B. Harischandra. Litho Security Printers (M), Malaysia)

1988 (31 Oct). Commissioning of Randeingala Project. T **435** and similar horiz design. Multicoloured. P 12.
1043   75c. Type **435** 10   10
1044   5r.75 Randenigala Dam and reservoir.............. 90   90

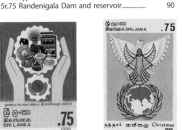

436 Handicrafts and
Centre Logo in Cupped
Hands

437 Angel, Dove. Olive
Branch and Globe

(Des R. Samarasinghe. Litho Secura. Singapore)

1988 (17 Nov). Opening of Gramodaya Folk Art Centre, Colombo. P 13½.
1045   **436**   75c. multicoloured.......................... 30   30

(Des B. Mendis. Litho State Ptg Wks, Moscow)

1988 (21 Nov). Christmas. T **437** and similar vert design. Multicoloured. P 12×12½.
1046   75c. Type **437** 10   10
1047   8r.50 Shepherds and Star of Bethlehem.......... 70   90
MS1048 175×100 mm. Nos. 1046/7 .... 1·00   1·00

438 Dr. E. W. Adikaram

439 Open Book in Tree and
Children reading

(Des S. Silva. Litho Security Printers (M), Malaysia)

1988 (28 Dec). Dr. E. W. Adikaram (educationrist) Commemoration. P 12.
1049   **438**   75c. multicoloured.......................... 30   30

(Des Lakmini Amararatne. Litho German Bank Note Co, Leipzig)

1989 (23 Jan). Tenth Anniv of Free Distribution of School Text Books. P 13½×13.
1050   **439**   75c. multicoloured.......................... 30   30

440 Wimalaratne
Kumaragama

441 Logo and New
Chamber of Commerce
Building

(Des S. Silva. Litho German Bank Note Co, Leipzig)

1989 (27 Jan). Poets of Sri Lanka. T **440** and similar vert designs. Multicoloured. P 13×13½.
1051   75c. Type **440** 20   30
1052   75c. G. H. Perera.................................. 20   30
1053   75c. Sagara Palansuriya.......................... 20   30
1054   75c. P. B. Alwis Perera.......................... 20   30
1051/4 Set of 4.. 70   1·00

(Des Mel Ads Ltd. Litho Security Printers (M), Malaysia)

1989 (25 Mar). 150th Anniv of Ceylon Chamber of Commerce. P 12.
1055   **441**   75c. multicoloured.......................... 30   30

442 Bodhisatva at Lunch and
Funeral Pyre

(Des N. Bulathsinhala. Litho State Ptg Wks, Moscow)

1989 (15 May). Vesak. Wall Paintings fron Medawala Monastery, Harispattuwa. T **442** and similar horiz designs. Multicoloured. P 12½×12.
1056   50c. Type **442** 10   10
1057   75c. Rescue of King Vessantara's children by god Sakra 10   10
1058   5r. Bodhisatva ploughing and his son attacked by snake 30   40
1059   5r.75 King Vessantara giving away his children 30   55
1056/9 Set of 4.. 70   1·00
MS1060 150×90 mm. Nos. 1056/9........................ 1·00   1·00

443 Parawahera
Vajiragnana Thero
(Buddhist monk)

444 College Crest

(Des S. Silva. Litho Security Printers (M), Malaysia)

1989 (22 May). National Heroes. T **443** and similar multicoloured designs. P 12.
1061   75c. Type **443** 25   25
1062   75c. Father Maurice Jacques Le Goc (educationist)................................ 25   25
1063   75c. Hemapala Munidasa (author).................. 25   25
1064   75c. Ananda Samarakoon (composer)............ 25   25
1065   75c. Simon Casie Chitty (scholar) (horiz)........ 25   25
1061/5 Set of 5.. 1·10   1·10

445 Dramachakra, Lamp, Buddhist Flag and Map

(Des W. Rohana. Litho Security Printers (M), Malaysia)
1989 (5 June). 150th Anniv of Hartley College, Point-Pedro (1988). P 12.
1066   **444**   75c. multicoloured 30   30

(Des P. Gunasinghe. Litho State Ptg Wks, Moscow)
1989 (18 June). Establishment of ministry of Buddha Sasana. P 12½×12.
1067   **445**   75c. multicoloured 30   30

446 Hands holding Brick and Trowel, House and Family   **447** Two Families and Hand turning Cogwheel

(Des P. Gunasinghe. Litho State Ptg Wks, Moscow)
1989 (23 June). Gam Udama '89 (Village Re-awakening Movement). P 12½×12.
1068   **446**   75c. multicoloured 30   30

(Des P. Gunasinghe. Photo State Ptg Works, Moscow)
1989 (23 June)–**90**. Janasaviya Development Programme. "1989" (75c.) or "1990" (1r.) imprint date at bottom right. P 12×11½.
1069   **447**   75c. multicoloured 20   20
1070   1r. multicoloured (31.1.90) 30   20
                 a. Without imprint date at bottom
                 right (4.12.90) .... 1·00   60

448 Dunhinda Falls   **449** Rev. James Chater (missionary) and Baptist Church

(Des S. Silva. Litho State Ptg Works, Moscow)
1989 (11 Aug). Waterfalls. T **448** and similar vert designs. Multicoloured. P 12.
1071   75c. Type **448** 20   10
1072   1r. Rawana Falls 20   10
1073   5r.75 Laxapana Falls 55   50
1074   8r.50 Diyaluma Falls 65   85
1071/4 Set of 4 .... 1·40   1·40

(Des S. Silva. Litho State Ptg Works, Moscow)
1989 (19 Aug). 177th Anniv of Baptist Church in Sri Lanka. P 12½×12.
1075   **449**   5r.75 multicoloured 50   50

450 Bicentenary Logo   **451** Old and New Bank Buildings and Logo

(Des R. Samarasinghe. Litho German Bank Note Co, Leipzig)
1989 (26 Aug). Bicentenary of French Revolution. P 13½×13.
1076   **450**   8r.50 black, deep blue and bright
                 carmine 80   80

(Des W. Rohana. Litho German Bank Note Co, Leipzig)
1989 (31 Aug). 50th Anniv of Bank of Ceylon. T **451** and similar horiz design. Multicoloured. P 13½×13.
1077   75c. Type **451** 10   10
1078   5r. "Bank of Ceylon" orchid and logo 50   50

452 Water Lily, Dharma Chakra and Books   **453** Wilhelm Geiger

(Des P. Gunasinghe. Litho Security Printers (M), Malaysia)
1989 (22 Sept). State Literary Festival. P 12.
1079   **452**   75c. multicoloured 30   30

(Des S. Silva. Litho German Bank Note Co, Leipzig)
1989 (30 Sept). Wilhelm Geiger (linguistic scholar) Commemoration. P 13×13½.
1080   **453**   75c. multicoloured 30   30

(Litho Questa)
1989 (11 Oct). As No. 781, but different printer. Face value and inscriptions in black. "1989" imprint date. P 14.
1081   3r. Golden Palm Civet .... 2·75   30
No. 781 has face value and inscriptions in red-brown and is without imprint date.

454 H. V. Perera, Q.C.   **455** Sir Cyril de Zoysa

(Des S. Silva. Litho Security Printers (M), Malaysia)
1989 (16 Oct). Constitutional Pioneers. T **454** and similar vert design. Multicoloured. P 12.
1082   75c. Type **454** 20   20
1083   75c. Prof Ivor Jennings 20   20

(Des S. Silva. Litho German Bank Note Co, Leipzig)
1989 (26 Oct). Sir Cyril de Zoysa (Buddhist philanthropist) Commemoration. P 13×13½.
1084   **455**   75c. multicoloured 30   30

456 Map of South-east Asia and Telecommunications Equipment   **457** Members with Offerings and Water Lily on Map of Sri Lanka

(Des W. Rohana. Litho State Ptg Works, Moscow)
1989 (1 Nov). Tenth Anniv of Asia-Pacific Telecommunity. P 12×12½.
1085   **456**   5r.75 multicoloured .... 1·00   70

(Des P. Gunasinghe. Litho Security Printers (M), Malaysia)

1989 (9 Nov). 50th Anniv of Sri Sucharitha Welfare Movement. P 13.
1086   **457**   75c. multicoloured 30   30

458 "Apollo 11" Blast-off and Astronauts

459 Shepherds

(Des W. Rohana. Litho State Ptg Works, Moscow)

1989 (10 Nov). 20th Anniv of First Manned Landing on Moon. T **458** and similar vert designs. Multicoloured. P 12×12½.
1087   75c. Type **458** 15   10
1088   1r. Armstrong leaving lunar module
          Eagle 20   10
1089   2r. Astronaut on Moon 35   30
1090   5r.75 Lunar surface and Earth from Moon...... 60   70
1087/90 *Set of 4* .... 1·10   1·10
MS1091 100×160 mm. Nos. 1087/90.......................... 2·50   2·50

(Des Father P. Silva. Litho Secura, Singapore)

1989 (21 Nov). Christmas. T **459** and similar vert design. Multicoloured. P 13½.
1092   75c. Type **459** 10   10
1093   8r.50 Magi with gifts................................... 60   2·25
MS1094 160×100 mm. Nos. 1092/3 .... 1·50   2·50

460 Ven. Sri Devananda Nayake Thero

461 College Building, Crest and Revd. William Ault (founder)

(Des S. Silva. Litho Security Printers (M), Malaysia)

1989 (25 Nov). Ven. Sri Devananda Nayake Thero (Buddhist monk) Commemoration. P 12.
1095   **460**   75c. multicoloured 30   30

(Des W. Rohana. Litho Security Printers (M), Malaysia)

1989 (29 Nov). 175th Anniv of Methodist Central College, Batticaloa. P 12.
1096   **461**   75c. multicoloured 30   30

462 Golf Ball, Clubs and Logo

463 "Raja"

(Des G. Bozell. Litho Pakistan Security Ptg Corp, Karachi)

1989 (8 Dec). Centenary of Nuwara Eliya Golf Club. T **462** and similar horiz design. Multicoloured. P 13½.
1097   75c. Type **462** .... 3·00   50
1098   8r.50 Course and club house .... 11·00   9·50

(Litho German Bank Note Co, Leipzig)

1989 (12 Dec). "Raja" Royal Ceremonial Elephant, Kandy, Commemoration. P 13×13½.
1099   **463**   75c. multicoloured .... 3·50   75

464 College Building and G. Wickremarachchi (founder)

465 Ven. Udunuwara Sri Sarananda Thero

(Des S. Silva. Litho German Bank Note Co, Leipzig)

1989 (14 Dec). 60th Anniv of Gampaha Wickremarachchi Institute of Ayurueda Medicine. P 13½×13.
1100   **464**   75c. multicoloured 30   30

(Des S. Silva. Litho State Ptg Wks, Moscow)

1989 (20 Dec). Ven. Udunuwara Sri Sarananda Thero (Buddhist monk) Commemoration. P 12×12½.
1101   **465**   75c. multicoloured 50   30

466 Diesel Train on Viaduct, Ella-Demodara Line

467 Cardinal Thomas Cooray

(Des R. Mawilmada. Litho Security Printers (M), Malaysia)

1989 (27 Dec). 125 Years of Sri Lanka Railways. T **466** and similar horiz designs. Multicoloured. P 12.
1102   75c. Type **466** .... 1·50   25
1103   2r. Diesel train at Maradana Station .... 2·50   30
          a. Perf 13 .... 2·50   30
1104   3r. Steam train and semaphore signal........ 2·50   75
          a. Perf 13 .... 2·50   75
1105   7r. Steam train leaving station, 1864........... 3·50   2·00
1102/5 *Set of 4* .... 9·00   3·00

(Des S. Silva. Litho German Bank Note Co, Leipzig)

1989 (28 Dec). Cardinal Thomas Cooray Commemoration. P 13×13½.
1106   **467**   75c. multicoloured .... 1·50   30

468 Farmer and Wife with Dagaba and Dam

(Des P. Gunasinghe. Litho Security Printers (M), Malaysia)

1989 (29 Dec). Agro Mahaweli Development Programme. P 12.
1107   **468**   75c. multicoloured 30   30

469 Justin Wijayawardena

(469a)

(Des S. Silva. Litho State Ptg Wks, Moscow)

1990 (14 Jan). Justin Wijayawardena (scholar) Commemoration. P 12×12½.
1108 **469** 1r. multicoloured .... 2·50 30

1990 (16 Feb). No. 1059 surch with T **469a**.
1108a 25c. on 5r.75 King Vessantara giving away
his children .... 1·25 30

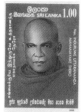

470 Ven. Induruwe Uttarananda Mahanayake Thero

(Des S. Silva. Litho Security Printers (M), Malaysia)

1990 (15 Mar). Fourth Death Anniv. of Ven. Induruwe Uttarananda Mahanayake Thero (Buddhist theologian). P 12.
1109 **470** 1r. multicoloured .... 1·40 1·25

(470a)

1990 (22 Mar). No. 1069 surch with T **470a**.
1109a **447** 1r. on 75c. multicoloured .... 2·00 1·25

471 Two Graduates, Lamp and Open Book

(Des P. Gunasinghe. Litho Secura, Singapore)

1990 (25 Mar). Ninth Anniv of Mahapola Scheme. P 13½.
1110 **471** 75c. multicoloured 30 30

472 Traditional Drums

(Des R. Samarasinha. Litho Security Printers (M), Malaysia)

1990 (2 Apr). 25th Anniv of Laksala Traditional Handicrafts Organization. T **472** and similar horiz designs. Multicoloured. P 12.
1111 1r. Type **472** 35 10
1112 2r. Silverware 60 15
1113 3r. Lacquerware 80 30
1114 8r. Dumbara mats .... 2·50 2·75
1111/14 Set of 4 .... 3·75 3·00

473 King Mahn Prathapa visiting Queen Chandra

474 Father T. Long (educationist)

(Des N. Bulathsinhala. Litho State Ptg Wks, Moscow)

1990 (2 May). Vesak. Wall Paintings from Buduraja Mahn, Viharaya, Wewurukannala. T **473** and similar horiz designs. Multicoloured. P 12½×12.
1115 75c. Type **473** 10 10
1116 1r. Execution of Prince Dharmapala 15 10
1117 2r. Prince Mahinsasaka with the Water Demon 25 20
1118 8r. King Dahamsonda with the God Sakra disguised as a demon .... 1·00 1·00
1115/18 Set of 4 .... 1·40 1·25
MS1119 160×99 mm. Nos. 1115/18 .... 1·60 1·50

(Des S. Silva. Litho Security Printers (M), Malaysia (No. 1120), State Ptg Wks, Moscow (others))

1990 (22 May). National Heroes. T **474** and similar vert designs. Multicoloured. P 12 (No. 1120) or 12×12½ (others).
1120 1r. Type **474** 50 35
1121 1r. Prof M. Ratnasuriya (37×25 mm) 50 35
1122 1r. D. Wijewardene (patriot) (37×25 mm) ... 50 35
1123 1r. L. Manjusri (artist) (37×25 mm) 50 35
1120/3 Set of 4 .... 1·75 1·25

475 Janasaviya Workers

476 Gold Reliquary

(Des P. Dissanayake. Litho State Ptg Wks, Moscow)

1990 (23 June). 12th Anniv of Gam Udawa and Opening of Janasaviya Centre, Pallekele. P 12½×12.
1124 **475** 1r. multicoloured .... 2·00 30

(Des N. Bulathsinhala. Litho Security Printers (M), Malaysia)

1990 (7 July). Centenary of Department of Archaeology. T **476** and similar vert designs. P 13 (8r.) or 12 (others).
1125 1r. black and orange-yellow 40 10
1126 2r. black and greenish grey 65 15
1127 3r. black, apple-green and ochre 90 35
a. Perf 13 .... 90 35
1128 8r. black and ochre .... 2·00 1·50
1125/8 Set of 4 .... 3·50 1·90
Designs:—2r. Statuette of Ganesh; 3r. Terrace of the Bodhi-tree, Isurumumiya Vihara; 8r. Inscription of King Nissankamalla.

477 Male Tennis Player at Left

478 Spotted Loach

(Des W. Rohana. Litho Pakistan Security Ptg Corp, Karachi)

1990 (14 Aug). 75th Anniv of Sri Lanka Tennis Association. T **477** and similar horiz designs. Multicoloured. P 13½.
1129 1r. Type **477** .... 1·00 1·00
a. Horiz pair. Nos. 1129/30 .... 2·00 2·00
1130 1r. Male tennis player at right .... 1·00 1·00
1131 8r. Male tennis players .... 2·75 2·75
a. Horiz pair. Nos. 1131/2 .... 5·50 5·50
1132 8r. Female tennis players .... 2·75 2·75
1129/32 Set of 4 .... 6·75 6·75
Nos. 1129/30 and 1131/2 were each printed together, se-tenant, in horizontal pairs throughout the sheets, each pair forming a composite design of a singles (1r.) or doubles (8r.) match.

(Des R. Samarasinghe. Litho State Ptg Wks, Moscow)

1990 (14 Sept). Endemic Fishes. T **478** and similar horiz designs. Multicoloured. P 11½.
1133 25c. Type **478** 10 10
1134 2r. Spotted Gourami ("Ornate Paradise Fish") 40 20
1135 9r. Mountain Labeo .... 95 1·25
1136 20r. Cherry Barb .... 1·75 3·50
1133/6 Set of 4 .... 2·75 4·50
MS1137 150×90 mm. Nos. 1133/6 .... 2·75 4·50

479 Rukmani Devi

480 Innkeeper turning away Mary and Joseph

(Litho Security Printers (M), Malaysia)

1990 (28 Oct). 12th Death Anniv of Rukmani Devi (actress and singer). P 12.

1138	**479**	1r. multicoloured	2·75	1·25

(Des P. Silva. Litho Security Printers (M), Malaysia)

1990 (28 Nov). Christmas. T **480** and similar vert design. Multicoloured. P 13.

1139		1r. Type **480**	50	10
1140		10r. Adoration of the Magi	4·50	5·00
MS1141	190×114 mm. Nos. 1139/40. P 12		6·00	7·00

481 Health Worker talking to Villagers

(Des W. Rohana. Litho Security Printers (M), Malaysia)

1990 (30 Nov). World Aids Day. T **481** and similar horiz design. Multicoloured. P 12.

1142		1r. Type **481**	75	15
1143		8r. Emblem and Aids virus	4·00	4·50

482 Main College Building and Flag

483 Peri Sundaram

(Des P. Gunasinghe. Litho Security Printers (M), Malaysia)

1990 (8 Dec). 50th Anniv of Dharmapala College, Pannipitiya. P 12.

1144	**482**	1r. multicoloured	3·00	1·25

(Des W. Rohana. Litho Security Printers (M), Malaysia)

1990 (14 Dec). Birth Centenary of Peri Sundaram (lawyer and politician). P 12.

1145	**483**	1r. red-brown and yellow-green	3·00	1·25

484 Letter Box, Galle, 1904

485 Chemical Structure Diagram, Graduating Students and Emblem

(Des W. Rohana. Litho Security Printers (M), Malaysia)

1990 (26 Dec). 175th Anniv of Sri Lanka Postal Service. T **484** and similar vert designs. Multicoloured. P 12.

1146		1r. Type **484**	75	10
1147		2r. Mail runner, 1815	1·25	30
1148		5r. Mail coach, 1832	2·50	2·00
1149		10r. Nuwara-Eliya Post Office, 1894	3·25	4·50
1146/9	Set of 4		7·00	6·25

(Des W. Rohana. Litho Security Printers (M), Malaysia)

1991 (25 Jan). 50th Anniv of Institute of Chemistry. P 12.

1150	**485**	1r. multicoloured	3·00	1·25

486 Kastavahana on Royal Elephant

(Des U. Karunaratne. Litho Security Printers (M), Malaysia)

1991 (17 May). Vesak. Temple Paintings from Karagampitiya Subodarama. T **486** and similar horiz designs. Multicoloured. P 12.

1151		75c. Type **486**	55	20
1152		1r. Polo Janaka in prison	55	10
1153		2r. Two merchants offering food to Buddha	90	45
1154		11r. Escape of Queen	3·25	6·50
1151/4	Set of 4		4·75	6·50
MS1155	150×90 mm. Nos. 1151/4		5·50	7·00

487 Narada Thero (Buddhist missionary)

488 Society Building

(Des S. Silva. Litho State Ptg Works, Moscow)

1991 (22 May). National Heroes. T **487** and similar vert designs. Multicoloured. P 12×12½.

1156		1r. Type **487**	50	60
1157		1r. Wallewatta Silva (novelist)	50	60
1158		1r. Sir Muttu Coomaraswamy (lawyer and politician)	50	60
1159		1r. Dr. Andreas Nell (opthalmic surgeon)	50	60
1156/9	Set of 4		1·75	2·25

(Des R. de Silva. Litho Security Printers (M), Malaysia)

1991 (31 May). Centenary of Maha Bodhi Society. P 12.

1160	**488**	1r. multicoloured	1·25	1·00

489 Women working at Home

490 Globe and Plan Symbol

(Des T. Kariyawasam. Litho Security Printers (M), Malaysia)

1991 (23 June). 13th Anniv of Gam Udawa Movement. P 12½.

1161	**489**	1r. multicoloured	2·00	80

(Des R. Mawilmada. Litho Security Printers (M), Malaysia)

1991 (1 July). 40th Anniv of Colombo Plan. P 12.

1162	**490**	1r. bright violet and new blue	2·25	80

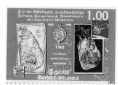

491 17th-century Map and Modern Satellite Photo of Sri Lanka

492 Ven. Nayak Henpitagedera Gnanaseeha Nayake Thero

(Des P. Miththapala. Litho Security Printers (M), Malaysia)

1991 (1 Aug). 190th Anniv of Sri Lanka Survey Department. P 12½.
1163   **491**   1r. multicoloured .... 2·25   80

(Des S. Silva. Litho Security Printers (M), Malaysia)

1991 (1 Aug). Tenth Death Anniv of Ven. Nayak Henpitagedera Gnanaseeha Nayake Thero (Buddhist theologian). P 12½.
1164   **492**   1r. multicoloured .... 1·75   80

493 Police Officers of 1866 and 1991 with Badge

(Des S. Silva. Litho Security Printers (M), Malaysia)

1991 (3 Sept). 125th Anniv of Sri Lankan Police Force. P 12½.
1165   **493**   1r. multicoloured .... 1·40   70

494 Kingswood College

(Des W. Rohana. Litho State Ptg Wks, Moscow)

1991 (26 Oct). Centenary of Kingswood College, Kandy. P 12½×12.
1166   **494**   1r. multicoloured 65   30

495 The Annunciation

496 Early Magneto Telephone

(Des P. Silva. Litho Security Printers (M), Malaysia)

1991 (19 Nov). Christmas. T **495** and similar vert design. Multicoloured. P 12½.
1167   1r. Type **495** 20   20
1168   10r. The Presentation of Jesus in the Temple.......................... 1·10   2·25
MS1169 90×150 mm. Nos. 1167/8.......................... 1·50   2·50

(Des W. Rohana. Litho Security Printers (M), Malaysia)

1991 (23 Nov). Inauguration of Sri Lankan Telecom Corporation. T **498** and similar vert designs. Multicoloured. P 12½.
1170   1r. Type **496** 20   10
1171   2r. Manual switchboard and telephonist.... 25   15
1172   8r. Satellite communications system............ 55   1·40
1173   10r. Fibre optics cable and mobile phone.... 70   1·40
1170/3 *Set of 4*.......................... 1·50   2·75

497 SAARC Logo and Bandaranaike Memorial Hall

498 "Pancha" (Games mascot)

(Des W. Rohana (1r.), S. Silva (8r.). Litho Security Printers (M), Malaysia)

1991 (21 Dec). Sixth South Asian Association for Regional Cooperation Summit, Colombo. T **497** and similar horiz design. P 12½.
1174   1r. Type **497** 15   10
1175   8r. Logo and Hall surrounded by national flags.......................... 60   1·75

(Des Sri Lanka National Design Centre. Litho Secura, Singapore)

1991 (22 Dec). Fifth South Asian Federation Games. T **498** and similar horiz designs. P 13½×14.
1176   1r. Type **498** 25   10
1177   2r. Games logo.......................... 45   20
1178   4r. Sugathadasa Stadium.......................... 85   1·25
1179   11r. Asia map on globe and national flags.. 1·75   4·00
1176/9 *Set of 4*.......................... 3·00   5·00

499 Crate, Boeing 737-300/400 Airliner and Container Ship

500 Plucking Tea

(Des W. Rohana. Litho Security Printers (M), Malaysia)

1992 (13 Jan). Exports Year. P 12.
1180   **499**   1r. multicoloured .... 1·75   80

(Des R. Mawilmada. Litho Secura, Singapore)

1992 (12 Feb). 125th Anniv of Tea Industry. T **500** and similar horiz designs. Multicoloured. P 14.
1181   1r. Type **500** 50   10
1182   2r. Healthy family, tea and tea estate.......... 85   20
1183   5r. Ceylon tea symbol.......................... 2·25   2·25
1184   10r. James Taylor (founder) .... 3·00   4·75
1181/4 *Set of 4*.......................... 6·00   6·50

501 General Ranjan Wijeratne

502 Olcott Hall, Mahinda College

(Des W. Rohana. Litho State Ptg Wks, Moscow)

1992 (2 Mar). First Death Anniv of General Ranjan Wijeratne. P 12×12½.
1185   **501**   1r. multicoloured 50   20

(Des W. Rohana. Litho Security Printers (M), Malaysia)

1992 (2 Mar). Centenary of Mahinda College, Galle. P 12.
1186   **502**   1r. multicoloured 30   20

503 Newstead College and Logo

SRI LANKA

(Des S. Silva. Litho Security Printers (M), Malaysia)
1992 (13 Mar). 175th Anniv of Newstead Girls' College, Negombo (1991). P 12.
1187 **503** 1r. multicoloured 30 20

504 Student and Oil Lamp
505 Sama's Parents leaving for Forest

(Des S. Perera. Litho Security Printers (M), Malaysia)
1992 (30 Mar). 11th Anniv of Mahapola Scholarship Fund. P 12.
1188 **504** 1r. multicoloured 30 20

(Des N. Bulathsinhala. Litho Security Printers (M), Malaysia)
1992 (5 May). Vesak Festival. Sama Jataka Paintings from Kottimbulwala Cave Temple. T **505** and similar horiz designs. Multicoloured. P 12.
1189 75c. Type **505** 20 10
1190 1r. Sama and parents in forest 20 10
1191 8r. Sama leading blind parents .... 1·40 1·75
1192 11r. Sama's parents grieving for wounded son .... 1·75 2·50
1189/92 *Set of 4* .... 3·25 4·00
MS1193 151×91 mm. Nos. 1189/92 .... 3·25 4·75

506 Ven. Devamottawe Amarawansa (Buddhist missionary)
507 Map of Sri Lanka, Flag and Symbol

(Des S. Silva. Litho Leigh-Mardon Ltd, Melbourne)
1992 (22 May). National Heroes. T **506** and similar vert designs. Multicoloured. P 14.
1194 1r. Type **506** 15 30
1195 1r. Richard Mirando (Buddhist philanthropist) 15 30
1196 1r. Gate Mudaliyar N. Canaganayagam (Buddhist social reformer) 15 30
1197 1r. Abdul Azeez (Moorish social reformer). 15 30
1194/7 *Set of 4* .... 55 1·10

(Des S. Silva. Litho State Ptg Wks, Moscow)
1992 (14 June). 2300th Anniv of Arrival of Buddhism in Sri Lanka. P 12×12½.
1198 **507** 1r. multicoloured 30 20

508 Family in House

(Des P. Miranda. Litho Security Printers (M), Malaysia)
1992 (23 June). 14th Anniv of Gam Udawa Movement. P 12.
1199 **508** 1r. multicoloured 30 20

509 Postal Activities and Award
510 Narilata Mask

(Des W. Robson. Litho Leigh-Mardon Ltd, Melbourne)
1992 (11 July). Postal Service Awards. T **509** and similar horiz design. Multicoloured. P 14.
1200 1r. Type **509** 50 10
1201 10r. Medals and commemorative cachet...... 3·00 3·50

(Des A. Dharmasiri. Litho Secura, Singapore)
1992 (19 Aug). Kolam Dance Masks. T **510** and similar vert designs. Multicoloured. P 12½.
1202 1r. Type **510** 25 10
1203 2r. Mudali mask 35 20
1204 5r. Queen mask 75 75
1205 10r. King mask .... 1·25 2·25
1202/5 *Set of 4* .... 2·40 3·00
MS1206 150×90 mm. Nos. 1202/5 .... 3·50 4·00
Special packs prepared for the S.A.A.R.C. "Philex '96" stamp exhibition at Colombo contained the strip of stamps from No. **MS**1206 with the sheet margins removed.

511 19th and 20th-century Players and Match of 1838

(Des W. Rohana. Litho Secure, Singapore)
1992 (8 Sept). 160th Anniv of Cricket in Sri Lanka. P 13.
1207 **511** 5r. multicoloured .... 3·75 3·00

512 Running
513 Vijaya Kumaratunga

(Litho Questa)
1992 (15 Sept). Olympic Games, Barcelona. T **512** and similar vert designs. Multicoloured. P 14.
1208 1r. Type **512** 30 10
1209 11r. Shooting .... 1·75 2·50
1210 13r. Swimming .... 2·00 3·00
1211 15r. Weight-lifting .... 2·50 3·25
1208/11 *Set of 4* .... 6·00 8·00
MS1212 91×151 mm. Nos. 1208/11 .... 7·00 8·50

(Litho Secura, Singapore)
1992 (9 Oct). Vijaya Kumaratunga (actor) Commemoration. P 13.
1213 **513** 1r. multicoloured 40 20

514 College Building and Crest

170

(Des W. Rohana. Litho Security Printers (M), Malaysia)

1992 (24 Oct). Centenary of Al-Bahjathhul Ibraheemiyyah Arabic College. P 12.

1214 **514** 1r. multicoloured.......................... 40 20

515 Official Church Seal   **516** Nativity

(Des W. Rohana. Litho Security Printers (M), Malaysia)

1992 (25 Oct). 350th Anniv of Dutch Reformed Church in Sri Lanka. P 12.

1215 **515** 1r. black, yellowish green and greenish yellow...................... 1·50 60

(Des S. Purnajith. Litho Security Printers (M), Malaysia)

1992 (17 Nov). Christmas. T **516** and similar vert design. Multicoloured. P 12.

1216		1r. Type **516**	15	10
1217		9r. Family going to church	1·60	2·50
MS1218	150×90 mm. Nos. 1216/17		1·75	3·00

517 Fleet of Columbus   (**518**)

(Des and litho Questa)

1992 (1 Dec). 500th Anniv of Discovery of America by Columbus. T **517** and similar horiz designs. Multicoloured. P 14.

1219	1r. Type **517**		50	10
1220	11r. Columbus landing in New World		1·25	1·50
1221	13r. Wreck of *Santa Maria*		1·50	2·25
1222	15r. Columbus reporting to Queen Isabella and King Ferdinand		1·50	2·25
1219/22	*Set of 4*		4·25	5·50
MS1223	155×95 mm. Nos. 1219/22		4·25	6·50

1992 (1 Dec). No. 684 surch with T **518**.

1224 **255** 2r. on 10c. multicoloured.................. 9·00 1·00

519 Ven. Sumedhankara Thero and Dagoba   **520** University Logo, Students and Building

(Des S. Silva. Litho Security Printers (M), Malaysia)

1992 (10 Dec). Birth Centenary of Ven. Dambagasare Sumedhankara Nayake Thero. P 12.

1225 **519** 1r. multicoloured.......................... 30 20

(Des W. Rohana. Litho Security Printers (M), Malaysia)

1992 (22 Dec). 50th Anniv of University Education in Sri Lanka (1st issue). P 12.

1226 **520** 1r. multicoloured.......................... 30 20

521 University of Colombo Building and Logo   **522** College Building and Crest

(Des W. Rohana. Litho Secura, Singapore)

1993 (23 Mar). 50th Anniv of University Education in Sri Lanka (2nd issue). P 12½.

1227 **521** 1r. multicoloured.......................... 75 20

(Des W. Rohana. Litho Secura, Singapore)

1993 (7 Apr). Centenary of Zahira College, Colombo. P 12½.

1228 **522** 1r. multicoloured.......................... 75 30

523 Magandiya being presented to Buddha   **524** Girl Guide, Badge and Camp

(Des S. Silva. Litho Security Printers (M), Malaysia)

1993 (30 Apr). Vesak Festival. Verses from the Dhammapada. T **523** and similar vert designs. Multicoloured. P 12.

1229	75c. Type **523**		20	10
1230	1r. Kisa Gotami carrying her dead baby		20	10
1231	3r. Patachara and her dying family		60	70
1232	10r. Angulimala praying		1·25	2·50
1229/32	*Set of 4*		2·00	3·00
MS1233	180×101 mm. Nos. 1229/32. P 12×12½		2·50	3·50

(Des W. Rohana. Litho Security Printers (M), Malaysia)

1993 (10 May). 75th Anniv of Sri Lanka Girl Guides Association. T **524** and simlar vert design. Multicoloured. P 12.

1234	1r. Type **524**		50	10
1235	5r. Girl Guide activities		1·50	2·00

525 Ven. Yagirala Pagnananda Maha Nayaka Thero (scholar)   **526** Family arriving at New Home

(Des S. Silva. Litho Leigh-Mardon Ltd, Melbourne)

1993 (22 May). National Heroes. T **525** and similar vert designs. Multicoloured. P 14.

1236	1r. Type **525**		40	50
1237	1r. Charles de Silva (politician)		40	50
1238	1r. Wilmot A. Perera (politician)		40	50
1239	1r. Abdul Caffoor (philanthropist)		40	50
1236/9	*Set of 4*		1·40	1·75

(Des R. de Silva. Litho Secura, Singapore)

1993 (23 June). "Gam Udawa '93". P 12½.

1240 **526** 1r. multicoloured.......................... 1·25 30

527 Consumer Movement Flag and Logo   **528** Ashy-headed Laughing Thrush

(Des S. Perera. Litho Secura, Singapore)

1993 (3 July). 50th Anniv of Co-operative Consumer Movement (1992). P 12½.

1241 **527** 1r. multicoloured.......................... 1·50 30

(Des G. Ratnavira. Litho State Ptg Wks, Moscow)

1993 (14 July). Birds (4th series). T **528** and similar horiz designs. Multicoloured. P 12½×12.

1242	3r. Type **528**		40	20
1243	4r. Brown-capped Jungle Babbler		40	20
1244	5r. Red-faced Malkoha		50	55
1245	10r. Ceylon Grackle ("Ceylon Hill-Mynah")		95	1·40
1242/5 Set of 4			2·00	2·10
MS1246 151×121 mm. Nos. 1242/5			3·25	4·00

529 Talawila Church

(Des W. Rohana. Litho Secura, Singapore)

1993 (26 July). 150th Anniv of Talawila Church. P 13.

1247	**529**	1r. multicoloured	1·00	30

530 Rosette and Mail Delivery   531 College and Flag

(Des W. Rohana. Litho Secura, Singapore)

1993 (22 Aug). Sri Lanka Post Excellent Service Awards. P 13.

1248	**530**	1r. multicoloured	1·00	30

(Des W. Rohana. Litho Secura, Singapore)

1993 (15 Nov). Centenary of Musaeus College. P 13.

1249	**531**	1r. multicoloured	1·75	30

532 Presentation of Jesus in the Temple

(Des S. Silva. Litho Pakistan Security Ptg Corporation, Karachi)

1993 (30 Nov). Christmas. T **532** and similar horiz design. Multicoloured. P 13½.

1250	1r. Type **532**		10	10
1251	17r. Boy Jesus with the Jewish teachers		1·25	2·50
MS1252 180×102 mm. Nos. 1250/1			1·25	2·50

533 Healthy Youth and Drug Addict

(Des W. Robson. Litho Pakistan Security Ptg Corp, Karachi)

1993 (16 Dec). Youth and Health Campaign. P 14.

1253	**533**	1r. multicoloured	70	30

534 Maradana Technical College Building and Emblems   535 Trinity College Logo

(Des W. Rohana. Litho Secura, Singapore)

1993 (17 Dec). Centenary of Technical Education. P 13.

1254	**534**	1r. multicoloured	1·00	30

(Des W. Rohana. Litho Secura, Singapore)

1994 (11 Feb). Centenary of Trinity College, Kandy, Old Boys' Association. P 13.

1255	**535**	1r. multicoloured	30	20

536 College Flag

(Des W. Rohana. Litho Secura, Singapore)

1994 (10 Mar). 150th Anniv of St. Thomas' College, Matara. P 13.

1256	**536**	1r. lake-brown and pale new blue	30	20

537 Ven. Siyambalangamuwe Sri Gunaratana Thero

(Des S. Silva. Litho Secura, Singapore)

1994 (2 Apr). Ven. Siyambalangamuwe Sri Gunaratana Thero (educationist) Commemoration. P 12½.

1257	**537**	1r. multicoloured	2·00	40

538 College Building and Arms

(Des S. Silva. Litho Secura Singapore)

1994 (4 Apr). 125th Anniv of St. Joseph's College, Trincomalee. P 13.

1258	**538**	1r. multicoloured	30	20

539 Man distributing Water   540 I.L.O. Monument, Geneva, Logo and Workers

(Des S. Silva. Litho Secura, Singapore)

1994 (7 May). Vesak Festival. Dasa Paramita (Ten Virtues). T **539** and similar horiz designs. Multicoloured. P 13.

1259	1r. Type **539**		20	10
1260	2r. Man and elephant		1·25	40
1261	5r. Man surrounded by women		1·00	1·00
1262	17r. Ruler with snake charmer		2·75	5·00
1259/62	Set of 4		4·75	6·00
MS1263	162×88 mm. Nos. 1259/62		4·25	6·50

(Des W. Rohana. Litho Secura, Singapore)

1994 (12 May). 75th Anniv of International Labour Organization. P 13.

1264	**540**	1r. multicoloured	1·25	40

541 Mahakavindra Dhammaratana Thero (Buddhist theologian)

542 Conference Logo

(Des S. Silva. Litho Leigh-Mardon Ltd, Melbourne)

1994 (22 May). National Heroes. T **541** and similar horiz designs. Multicoloured. P 14.

1265	1r. Type **541**	30	40
1266	1r. Ranasinghe Premadasa (former President)	30	40
1267	1r. Dr. Colvin de Silva (trade union leader)	30	40
1268	1r. E. Periyathambipillai (Tamil poet)	30	40
1265/8	Set of 4	1·00	1·40

A 1r. stamp for "Gam Udawa '94" was prepared for issue on 23 June 1994, but was not released due to the assassination of President Premadasa. Unused stamps exist from publicity examples circulated before the decision to cancel the issue was taken.

This Gam Udawa stamp was eventually issued (on 17 May 2002) due to a shortage of 1r. stamps.

See No. 1577c.

(Des R. de Silva. Litho Secura, Singapore)

1994 (9 July). 13th International Federation of Social Workers World Conference, Colombo. P 13.

1269	**542**	8r. multicoloured	3·00	3·00

543 Ven. Sri Somaratana Thero and Temple

544 Communication Technology and Logo

(Des S. Silva. Litho Secura, Singapore)

1994 (2 Aug). Tenth Death Anniv of Ven. Sri Somaratana Thero (Buddhist religious leader). P 13.

1270	**543**	1r. multicoloured	2·25	50

(Des W. Rohana. Litho Secura, Singapore)

1994 (8 Sept). "INFOTEL LANKA '94" International Computers and Telecommunications Exhibition. P 13.

1271	**544**	10r. multicoloured	3·00	3·25

545 Veddah Tribesman stringing Bow

546 Luca Pacioli (pioneer), Logo and Equipment inside "500"

(Des R. de Silva. Litho Security Printers (M), Malaysia)

1994 (12 Sept). Year of Indigenous People (1993). T **545** and similar vert design. Multicoloured. P 12.

1272	1r. Type **545**	35	10
1273	17r. Veddah artist and rock paintings	4·50	5·00

(Des W. Rohana. Litho Secura, Singapore)

1994 (11 Oct). 500th Anniv of Accountancy. P 13.

1274	**546**	1r. multicoloured	2·25	50

547 Society Emblem

(Des P. Miththapala. Litho Secura, Singapore)

1994 (24 Nov). Centenary of Wildlife and Nature Society of Sri Lanka. T **547** and similar horiz designs. P 13.

1275	1r. bronze-green and black		20	10
1276	2r. multicoloured		70	20
1277	10r. multicoloured		2·00	2·00
1278	17r. multicoloured		3·00	5·00
1275/8	Set of 4		5·50	6·50
MS1279	130×96 mm. Nos. 1275/8		5·00	6·50

Designs:—2r. Horned Lizard; 10r. Giant Squirrel; 17r. Sloth Bear.

548 Airliner, ICAO Logo and Globe

(Des W. Rohana. Litho Secura, Singapore)

1994 (7 Dec). 50th Anniv of International Civil Aviation Organization. P 13.

1280	**548**	10r. multicoloured	4·00	3·50

549 Christmas Crib

550 Map of Sri Lanka and Aspects of Science

(Des S. Silva. Lithe Secura, Singapore)

1994 (8 Dec). Christmas. T **549** and similar horiz design. Multicoloured. P 13.

1281	1r. Type **549**	20	10
1282	17r. St. Joseph's carpentry workshop, Nazareth	3·25	4·00
MS1283	145×81 mm. Nos. 1281/2	3·00	4·00

(Des D. Gunasekera. Litho Secura, Singapore)

1994 (19 Dec). 50th Anniv of Sri Lankan Association for the Advancement of Science. P 13.

1284	**550**	1r. multicoloured	2·75	60

551 College Building and Arena

552 Dendrobium maccarthiae

(Des P. Nimal de Silva. Litho Secura, Singapore)

1994 (24 Dec). Centenary of Richmond College Old Boys' Association. P 13.
1285 **551** 1r. black, carmine-vermilion and
violet-blue.. 30 20

(Des P. Miththapala. Litho Secura, Singapore)

1994 (27 Dec). 60th Anniv of Orchid Circle of Ceylon. T **552** and
similar vert designs. Multicoloured. P 13.
1286 50c. Type **552**.. 30 10
1287 1r. *Cottonia peduncularis* 45 10
1288 5r. *Bulbophyllum wightii*......................... 1·00 1·00
1289 17r. *Habenaria crinifera*............................ 2·50 4·00
1286/9 *Set of 4* .... 3·75 4·50
MS1290 127×95 mm. Nos. 1286/9................... 3·25 5·00

553 Father Joseph Vaz and
Pope John Paul II

(Des S. Silva. Litho Japanese Govt Ptg Bureau, Tokyo)

1995 (20 Jan). Papal Visit and Beatification of Father Joseph Vaz. P 13.
1291 **553** 1r. multicoloured........................... 3·50 1·00

554 Blue Water Lily
(*Nymphaea stellata*)
555 College Building and Arms

(Des S. Silva. Litho Leigh-Mardon Ltd, Melbourne)

1995 (22 Feb). P 14½×14.
1292 **554** 1r. multicoloured........................... 1·00 10

(Des W. Rohana. Litho Secura, Singapore)

1995 (2 Mar). Centenary of St. Joseph's College, Colombo. P 13.
1293 **555** 1r. multicoloured........................... 1·50 50

556 Sirimavo Bandaranaike
and National Flag

(Des W. Rohana. Litho Security Printers (M), Malaysia)

1995 (17 Apr). Election of Sirimavo Bandaranaike as Prime Minister.
P 12½×12.
1294 **556** 2r. multicoloured........................... 2·25 1·25

557 Man offering Water
to Crew of Outrigger
Canoe
558 14th-century Map
ofSri Lanka and Society
Arms

(Des S. Silva. Litho Security Printers (M), Malaysia)

1995 (29 Apr). Vesak Festival. Dasa Paramita (ten virtues). T **557** and
similar vert designs. Multicoloured. P 12×12½.
1295 1r. Type **557** 20 10
1296 2r. Catching falling man..................... 35 15

1297 10r. Teacher with students .... 1·25 1·50
1298 17r. Stopping man digging .... 2·00 3·25
1295/8 *Set of 4*... 3·50 4·50
MS1299 170×90 mm. Nos. 1295/8. P 12½ .... 4·50 5·00

(Litho Secura, Singapore)

1995 (17 May). 150th Anniv of Royal Asiatic Society of Sri Lanka. P 12½.
1300 **558** 1r. multicoloured........................... 2·50 75

559 Abdul Coder
560 College Building

(Des S. Silva. Litho Bank Note Corporation of America, New York)

1995 (3 June). 120th Birth Anniv of Abdul Coder (lawyer). P 11.
1301 **559** 2r. multicoloured........................... 2·25 1·25

(Des A. Hopman. Litho Security Printers (M), Malaysia)

1995 (21 June). Centenary of St. Aloysius's College, Galle. P 12½×12.
1302 **560** 2r. multicoloured........................... 2·25 1·25

561 Tikiri Ilangaratna
562 Lamps and Schools Flag

(Des S. Silva. Litho Secura, Singapore)

1995 (7 July). Tikiri Bandara Ilangaratna (politician and author)
Commemoration. P 12½×13.
1303 **561** 2r. multicoloured........................... 2·25 1·25

(Des P. Gunasinghe. Litho Secura, Singapore)

1995 (3 Aug). Centenary of Dhamma Schools Movement. P 12½.
1304 **562** 2r. multicoloured........................... 2·25 1·25

563 GPO Building

(Des S. Silva. Litho Pakistan Security Ptg Corp, Karachi)

1995 (22 Aug). Centenary of General Post Office, Colombo. P 13½.
1305 **563** 1r. multicoloured........................... 2·00 45

564 Young Hands
surrounding Old Hand
565 Sri Lankan Parliament
Building and CPA Logo

(Des S. Purnajith. Litho Enschedé)

1995 (1 Oct). International Day for the Elderly. P 14×13½.
1306 **564** 2r. multicoloured........................... 2·25 1·25

(Des W. Rohana. Litho Pakistan Security Ptg Corp, Karachi)

1995 (8 Oct). 41st Commonwealth Parliamentary Conference,
Colombo. P 13½.
1307 **565** 2r. multicoloured........................... 2·25 1·25

566 Anniversary
Emblem and Map of
Sri Lanka

567 Money falling into
Globe Money Box

(Des S. Purnajith. Litho Pakistan Ptg Corp, Karachi)

1995 (24 Oct). 50th Anniv of United Nations. P 13½.

1308	**566**	2r. multicoloured	2·25	1·25

(Des S. Purnajith. Litho Pakistan Ptg Corp, Karachi)

1995 (31 Oct). 71st Anniv of World Thrift Day and 110th Anniv of National Savings Bank. P 13½.

1309	**567**	2r. multicoloured	2·25	1·25

568 Diocesan Arms of Colombo
and Kurunegala

(Des S. Purnajith. Litho Secura, Singapore)

1995 (30 Nov). Christmas. 150th Anniv of Anglican Diocese of Colombo. T **568** and similar horiz design. Multicoloured. P 13.

1310		2r. Type **568**	25	10
1311		20r. Nativity scene and hands surrounding map	3·00	4·50
MS1312 150×90 mm. Nos. 1310/11			3·00	4·50

569 Flags of Member
Countries

570 School Emblem

(Des S. Purnajith. Litho Secura, Singapore)

1995 (8 Dec). Tenth Anniv of South Asian Association for Regional Co-operation. P 12½×13.

1313	**569**	2r. multicoloured	2·75	1·25

(Des S. Pumajith. Litho Secura, Singapore)

1996 (17 Jan). 175th Anniv of Vincent Girls' High School, Batticaloa. P 12½×13.

1314	**570**	2r. multicoloured	2·25	1·25

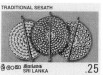

571 Little Basses
Lighthouse

572 Traditional Sesath
(umbrellas)

(Des S. Purnajith. Litho State Ptg Wks, Moscow)

1996 (22 Jan)–**97**. Lighthouses. T **571** and similar vert designs. Multicoloured. P 12.

1315		50c. Type **571**	60	35

1316		75c. Great Basses	70	35
1317		2r. Devinuwara	1·50	45
1317a		2r.50 As 2r. (12.2.97)	8·50	2·75
1318		20r. Galle	3·25	4·75
1315/18 Set of 5			13·00	7·25
MS1319 151×91 mm. Nos. 1315/17 and 1318			7·00	8·00

Nos. 1315/18 were printed in sheets of 50. During 1997 a printing of the 2 r. value appeared in sheets of 36.

Special packs for the SAARC "Philex '96" stamp exhibition at Colombo contained the strip of stamps from No. **MS**1319 with the sheet margins removed.

(Des P. Gunasinghe. Litho State Ptg Wks, Moscow)

1996 (13 Mar). Traditional Handicrafts. T **572** and similar horiz designs. Multicoloured. P 12.

1320		25c. Type **572**	10	10
1321		8r.50 Pottery	50	55
1322		10r.50 Mats	65	75
1323		17r. Lace	1·00	1·75
1320/3 Set of 4			2·00	2·75
MS1324 150×90 mm. Nos. 1320/3			3·25	3·75

573 School Emblem
and Trees

574 Upaka and Capa

(Des S. Purnajith. Litho Security Printers (M), Malaysia)

1996 (21 Mar). Centenary of Chundikuli Girls' College, Jaffna. P 12×12½.

1325	**573**	2r. multicoloured	2·25	1·25

(Des S. Silva. Litho Security Printers (M), Malaysia)

1996 (3 Apr). Vesak Festival. T **574** and similar vert designs. Multicoloured. P 12.

1326		1r. Type **574**	15	10
1327		2r. Dantika and elephant	40	15
1328		5r. Subha removing her eye	60	70
1329		10r. Poona and the Brahmin	85	1·50
1326/9 Set of 4			1·75	2·25
MS1330 170×90 mm. Nos. 1326/9. P 12×12½			1·75	2·50

The 2r. value exists on ordinary paper with normal ink, on phosphorised paper in either normal or phosphorised ink and on paper with luminescent fibres.

575 Diving

(Des S. Purnajith. Litho Enschedé)

1996 (22 July). Olympic Games, Atlanta. T **575** and similar multicoloured designs. P 14×13½ (vert) or 13½×14 (horiz).

1331		1r. Type **575**	40	10
1332		2r. Volleyball	90	20
1333		5r. Rifle shooting (horiz)	1·25	1·00
1334		17r. Running (horiz)	2·25	4·00
1331/4 Set of 4			4·25	4·75

576 Bowler

(Des S. Purnajith. Litho Enschedé)

1996 (18 Aug). Sri Lanka's Victory in World Cup Cricket Tournament. T **576** and similar triangular designs. Multicoloured. P 13½.

1335		2r. Type **576**	45	25
1336		10r.50 Wicket-keeper	80	90
1337		17r. Batsman	1·25	1·75
1338		20r. World Cup Trophy	1·40	2·00
1335/8 *Set of 4*			3·50	4·50
MS1339 150×90 mm. Nos. 1335/8			3·50	4·50

577 Main Building, Jaffna Central College

(Des S. Purnajith. Litho Pakistan Security Printing Corp, Karachi)

1996 (7 Sept). 180th Anniv of Jaffna Central College. P 13½×13.

1340	**577**	2r. multicoloured	2·25	1·25
		a. Black ("SRI LANKA", upper and lower panels, etc) omitted	£100	

578 Globe in Flames and White Dove

579 Jesus washing the Disciples' Feet

(Des S. Herath. Litho Pakistan Security Ptg Corp, Karachi)

1996 (4 Nov). 50th Anniv of UNESCO. P 13½.

1341	**578**	2r. multicoloured	2·50	1·25

(Litho Oriental Press, Bahrain)

1996 (2 Dec). Christmas. T **597** and similar vert design showing murals by David Paynter from Trinity College Chapel, Kandy. Multicoloured. P 13½×13.

1342		2r. Type **579**	10	10
1343		17r. Parable of the Good Samaritan	1·50	2·00
MS1344 150×90 mm. Nos. 1342/4			1·50	2·25

580 Cupped Hands holding Child

581 Swami Vivekananda and Globe

(Des P. Gunasinghe. Litho Pakistan Security Ptg Corp, Karachi)

1996 (12 Dec). 50th Anniv of UNICEF. P 13×13½.

1345	**580**	5r. multicoloured	70	1·00

(Des S. Silva. Litho Oriental Press, Bahrain)

1997 (15 Jan). Centenary of Swami Vivekananda's Visit to Sri Lanka. P 13½×13.

1346	**581**	2r.50 multicoloured	1·50	1·00

2.50	**2.50**	**2.50**	**2.50**
(**582**)	(**583**)	(**584**)	(**585**)

1997 (12 Feb). No. 1317 surch with T **582**/5.

1347	**582**	2r.50 on 2r. multicoloured	15·00	1·50
1348	**583**	2r.50 on 2r. multicoloured	15·00	1·50
1349	**584**	2r.50 on 2r. multicoloured	4·00	1·25
1350	**585**	2r.50 on 2r. multicoloured	4·00	1·25
1347/50 *Set of 4*			21·00	5·00

Nos. 1347/50 occur in separate sheets. Nos. 1347 and 1349 were surcharged by the State Ptg Corporation and Nos. 1348 and 1350 by Lakmini Printers Ltd.

586 Venerable Welivitiye Sorata Thero (scholar)

(Des S. Silva. Litho Oriental Press, Bahrain)

1997 (4 Apr). National Heroes (1st series). T **586** and similar vert designs. Multicoloured. P 13½×13.

1351		2r. Type **586**	75	75
1352		2r. Mahagama Sekera (writer and artist)	75	75
		a. Asterisk ovpt double		
		b. Asterisk ovpt omitted		
1353		2r. Dr. S. A. Wickremasinghe (physician)	75	75
1354		2r. Lt.-Gen. Denzil Kobbekaduwa	75	75
1351/4 *Set of 4*			2·75	2·75

No. 1352 was issued with the inscriptions at the top right and bottom left corners obliterated by rows of asterisks. A small quantity without the overprint is known to have been sold at one post office.

See also Nos. 1373/6.

11.00 ▬▬▬	**11.00** ▬▬▬
(**587**)	(**588**)

1997 (6 May). No. 1322 surch with T **587**/8 by State Ptg Corporation.

1355	**587**	11r. on 10r.50 multicoloured	6·00	6·00
1356	**588**	11r. on 10r.50 multicoloured	6·00	6·00
		a. Surch omitted (in horiz pair with normal)	25·00	25·00

The surcharge omitted error occurs in the last vertical row. The stamp next to it has the obliterating block missing.

589 Thuparama Stupa, 3rd-century B.C.

590 Don Johannes Kumarage

(Des P. Gunasinghe. Litho Security Printers (M), Malaysia)

1997 (7 May). Vesak Festival. Anauradhapura Sites. T **589** and similar vert designs. Multicoloured. No wmk. P 12×12½ (2 r. 50) or 12 (others).

1357		1r. Type **589**	15	10
		a. Perf 12×12½	5·00	10
1358		2r.50 Ruwanvalisaya stupa, 161–137 B.C.	25	10
1359		3r. Abhayagiri Dagaba,103–102 B.C.	30	15
		a. Perf 12×12½	50	20
1360		17r. Jethavana Dagaba, 276–303 A.D.	1·50	2·25
1357/60 *Set of 4*			2·00	2·25
MS1361 170×90 mm. Nos. 1357/60. P 12×12½			1·75	2·25

For 1r. watermarked "SPM", Type **613a** see No. 1421.

(Des W. Rohana. Litho Pakistan Security Ptg Corp, Karachi)

1997 (10 June). Birth Centenary of D. J. Kumarage (Buddhist teacher). P 13×13½.

1362	**590**	2r. 50 multicoloured	1·75	1·00

591 *Munronia pinnata*

592 Tourist Board Logo, Airliner and Holiday Resorts

(Des D. Gunatilake. Litho Pakistan Security Ptg Corp, Karachi)

1997 (17 June). Medicinal Herbs. T **591** and similar vert design. Multicoloured. P 13½×14.

1363	2r.50 Type **591**	25	10
1364	14r. *Rauvolfia serpentina*	1·00	1·75

(Des S. Kalupahana. Litho Security Printers (M), Malaysia)

1997 (11 Sept). Visit Sri Lanka. P 12.

1365	**592** 20r. multicoloured	2·75	3·25

1.00

(593)

594 Lyre Head Lizard

1997 (22 Sept). No. 1321 surch with T **593** by State Ptg Corporation.

1366	1r. on 8r.50 Pottery	6·00	55

(Des V. Perera. Litho Security Printers (M), Malaysia)

1997 (18 Oct). Reptiles. T **594** and similar horiz designs. Multicoloured. P 12½×12 (20r.) or 12 (others).

1367	2r.50 Type **594**	10	10
1368	5r. Boie's Roughside (snake)	20	25
1369	17r. Common Lanka Skink	75	1·40
1370	20r. Great Forest Gecko	1·00	1·75
1367/70	*Set of 4*	1·75	3·00
MS1371	170×90 mm. Nos. 1367/70. P 12	1·75	3·00

595 St. Servatius' College, Matara

596 The Nativity

(Des P. Gunasinghe. Litho Security Printers (M), Malaysia)

1997 (1 Nov). Centenary of St. Servatius' College, Matara. P 12½×12.

1372	**595** 2r.50 multicoloured	60	30
	a. Perf 12×12½	60	30

(Des S. Silva. Litho Secura, Singapore)

1997 (11 Nov). National Heroes (2nd series). Vert designs as T **586**. Multicoloured. P 12½×13.

1373	2r.50 Sri Indasara Nayake Thero (Buddhist leader)	30	40
	a. Block of four. Nos. 1373/6	1·00	1·40
1374	2r.60 Abdul Aziz (trade union leader)	30	40
1375	2r.50 Prof Subramaniam Vithiananthan	30	40
1376	2r.50 Vivienne Goonewardene (politician)	30	40
1373/6	*Set of 4*	1·00	1·40

Nos. 1373/6 were printed together, *se-tenant*, in blocks of four throughout the sheet.

(Des S. Silva. Litho Security Printers (M), Malaysia)

1997 (20 Nov). Christmas. T **596** and similar vert design. Multicoloured. P 12½.

1377	2r.50 Type **596**	15	10
1378	20r. Visit of the Three Kings	1·25	1·75
MS1379	170×90 mm. Nos. 1377/8	1·40	2·00

597 Young Men's Buddhist Association Building, Colombo

(Des P. Ediriweera. Litho Security Printers (M), Malaysia)

1998 (8 Jan). Centenary of Young Men's Buddhist Association, Colombo. P 12½×13.

1380	**597** 2r. 50 multicoloured	40	30

598 Sri Jayawardenapura Vidyalaya School

599 Children and Mathematical Symbols

(Des P. Gunasinghe. Litho Security Printers (M), Malaysia)

1998 (28 Jan). 175th Anniv of Sri Jayawardenapura Vidyalaya School, Kotte. P 12½.

1381	**598** 2r.50 multicoloured	40	30

(Des P. Gunasinghe (No. 1383), R. Mawilmada (others). Litho Pakistan Security Ptg Corp (No. 1383), Secura, Singapore (others))

1998 (4 Feb). 50th Anniv of Independence. T **599** and similar horiz designs. Multicoloured. P 13½ (No. 1383) or 12½ (others).

1382	2r. Type **599**	40	10
1383	2r.50 Flag and 1949 4c. Independence stamp (38×28 *mm*)	1·00	65
1384	2r.50 People with technological and industrial symbols	60	65
1385	5r. Dancers with arts and music symbols	80	80
1386	10r. Women with cultural and historical symbols	1·00	1·50
1382/6	*Set of 5*	3·50	3·25

600 Scouts raising Flag and Jamboree Logo

601 WHO Emblem in "50" and Flag of Sri Lanka

(Des W. Rohana. Litho Pakistan Security Ptg Corp, Karachi)

1998 (18 Feb). Fifth National Scout Jamboree, Kandy. T **600** and similar vert design. Multicoloured. P 13½.

1387	2r.50 Type **600**	50	10
1388	17r. Scout saluting and Jamboree emblem	1·60	2·50

(Des P. Gunasinghe. Litho Security Printers (M), Malaysia)

1998 (7 Apr). 50th Anniv of World Health Organization. P 12½.

1389	**601** 2r.50 multicoloured	50	20

602 Chunam Box

603 Kelani River and Stupa

(Des P. Ediriweera. Litho Pakistan Security Ptg Corp, Karachi)

1998 (24 Apr). Traditional Jewellery and Crafts. T **602** and similar vert designs. Multicoloured. P 13½.

1390	2r.50 Type **602**	20	10
1391	5r. Agate necklace	30	20
1392	10r. Bangle and hairpin	50	60
1393	17r. Sigiri earring	80	1·25
1390/3	*Set of 4*	1·60	1·90
MS1394	151×91 mm. Nos. 1390/3	1·50	2·25

(Des P. Gunasinghe. Litho Security Printers (M), Malaysia)

1998 (30 Apr). Vesak Festival. Wall Paintings from Kelaniya Temple. T **603** and similar vert designs. Multicoloured. P 12½.

1395	1r. Type **603**	10	10
1396	2r.50 Crown Prince Mahanaga and his court on way to Magampura	20	10
1397	4r. Mahanaga and wife with baby Yatala Tissa	35	30
1398	17r. Prince Mahanaga with King's minister	80	1·40
1395/8	*Set of 4*	1·25	1·60
MS1399	170×90 mm. Nos. 1395/8	1·25	2·00

604 School Building and Emblem

(Des P. Gunasinghe. Litho Thai British Security Ptg Co Ltd, Thailand)

1998 (7 May). 175th Anniv of St. John's College, Jaffna. P 14½×14.

1400	**604**	2r.50 multicoloured	30	15

605 Elephants in River

(Des W. Perera. Litho Japanese Govt Ptg Bureau, Tokyo)

1998 (28 May). Elephants. T **605** and similar horiz designs. Multicoloured. P 13×13½.

1401	2r.50 Type **605**	45	15
1402	10r. Cow and calf	75	50
1403	17r. Family group	1·00	1·25
1404	50r. Bull elephant	1·75	4·00
1401/4	*Set of 4*	3·50	5·50
MS1405	150×90 mm. Nos. 1401/4	3·50	5·50

606 SAARC Flags and Logo

606a

(Des D. Paul. Litho Thai British Security Ptg Co Ltd, Thailand)

1998 (29 July). Tenth Anniv of South Asian Association for Regional Co-operation. W **606a** (sideways). P 14½×14.

1406	**606**	2r.50 multicoloured	55	25

607 William Gopallawa   **608** Satellite and Computer

(Des S. Silva. Litho Pakistan Security Ptg Corp, Karachi)

1998 (17 Sept). William Gopallawa (first President of Sri Lanka) Commemoration. P 13½.

1407	**607**	2r.50 multicoloured	30	15

(Des P. Gunasinghe. Litho Pakistan Security Ptg Corp, Karachi)

1998 (7 Oct). Year of Information Technology. P 13½.

1408	**608**	2r.50 multicoloured	30	15

609 Ven. Kotahene Panmakitti Nayaka Thero (Buddhist scholar)   **610** Flag of Sri Lanka and Lions Club Emblem

(Des S. Silva. Litho Secura, Singapore)

1998 (11 Nov). Distinguished Personalities. T **609** and similar vert designs. Multicoloured. P 13.

1409	2r.50 Type **609**	30	30
1410	2r.50 Prof Ediriweera Sarachchandra (scholar)	30	30
1411	2r.50 Sir Nicholas Attygalle (medical pioneer)	30	30
1412	2r.50 Dr. Samuel Fisk Green (Tamil scholar)	30	30
1409/12	*Set of 4*	1·00	1·00

(Des P. Ediriweera. Litho Thai British Security Ptg Ltd, Thailand)

1998 (20 Nov). Lions Clubs International 26th South Asia, Africa and Middle East Forum, Colombo. P 14×14½.

1413	**610**	2r.50 multicoloured	2·00	1·25

611 "50" and Meteorological Symbols

(Des W. Rohana. Litho Pakistan Security Ptg Corp, Karachi)

1998 (7 Dec). 50th Anniv of Department of Meteorology. P 13½.

1414	**611**	2r.50 multicoloured	1·00	55

612 Virgin Mary and the Infant Jesus   **613** S. W. Bandaranaike as a Young Man

(Des L. Priyantha Silva. Litho Pakistan Security Ptg Corp, Karachi)

1998 (10 Dec). Christmas. T **612** and similar vert design. Multicoloured. P 13½.

1415	2r.50 Type **612**	15	10
1416	20r. The Annunciation	1·25	1·75
	a. Black omitted		
MS1417	90×150 mm. Nos. 1415/16	1·40	2·00

The missing black, No. 1416a, shows on the hair, costumes and in the omission of the brown on the curtain.

Des S. Silva. Litho Security Printers (M), Malaysia)

1999 (8 Jan). Birth. Centenary of S. W. Bandaranaike. T **613** and similar vert design. Multicoloured. P 12.

1418	3r.50 Type **613**	1·25	1·25
1419	3r.50 Bandaranaike as Prime Minister	1·25	1·25
MS1420	81×100 mm. Nos. 1418/19. P 12½	2·75	3·00

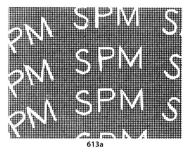

613a

(Litho Security Printers (M), Malaysia)

1999 (18 Jan). No. 1357 redrawn with inscriptions in slightly different position. W **613a** (sideways). P 12½.

1421	1r. Type **589**	6·50	75

614 Traditional Dancer

614a Traditional Dancer

615 Sir Arthur C. Clarke (author) and Spacecraft

(Des P. Ediriweera)

1999 (3 Feb)–**2000**.

(a) Photo Courvoisier. P 11½ (1r. to 4r.) or 11½×12 (5r. to 20r.)

1422	**614**	1r. sepia	10	10
1423		2r. greenish blue	10	10
1424		3r. purple	15	10
1425		3r.50 ultramarine	20	10
1426		4r. rose-carmine	20	10
1427		5r. dull yellowish green	20	10
1428		10r. bluish violet	30	20
1429		13r.50 bright vermilion	40	30
1430		17r. deep turqoise-green	45	40
1431		20r. bistre	55	50
1422/31		Set of 10	2·40	1·50

The 5r. to 20r. are larger, 21×26 mm.

(b) Photo Enschedé. Phosphorised paper. P 13½×13 (with one elliptical hole on each vertical side)

1431a	**614a**	50r. blackish brown and bright orange (5.10.2000)	75	70
1431b		100r. blackish brown and ochre (5.10.2000)	1·25	1·40
1431c		200r. deep lavender and new blue (5.10.2000)	2·50	2·75
1431a/c	Set of 3		4·00	4·25

(Des W. Rohana. Litho Security Printers (M), Malaysia)

1999 (19 Feb). Fifty Years of Communications Improvement. T **615** and similar vert design. Multicoloured. P 12.

1432	3r.50 Type **615**	1·00	1·00
	a. Horiz pair. Nos. 1432/3	2·00	2·00
1433	3r.50 Sir Arthur C. Clarke with spacecraft orbiting earth	1·00	1·00

Nos. 1432/3 were printed together, se-tenant, in horizontal pairs throughout the sheet, each pair forming a composite design.

616 Salvation Army Badge, Bible and Cross

(Des P. Gunasinghe. Litho Security Printers (M), Malaysia)

1999 (28 Apr). 116th Anniv of Salvation Army in Sri Lanka. P 12.

1434	**616**	3r.50 multicoloured	1·00	70

617 Activities of British Council

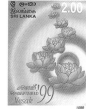

618 "Birth of Prince Siddhartha"

(Des A. Dharmasiri. Litho Security Printers (M), Malaysia)

1999 (20 May). 50th Anniv of British Council. P 12.

1435	**617**	3r.50 multicoloured	60	50

(Des P. Gunasinghe. Litho Security Printers (M), Malaysia)

1999 (25 May). Vesak Festival. T **618** and similar vert designs. Multicoloured. P 12½ (13r.50) or 12 (others).

1436	2r. Type **618**	10	10
1437	3r.50 "The Enlightenment"	15	15
1438	13r.50 "The Maha Parinirvana"	60	85
1439	17r. Celebrating Vesak	80	1·25
1436/9	Set of 4	1·50	2·00
MS1440	151×90 mm. Nos. 1436/9. P 12½	1·50	2·25

619 Dish Aerial and Transmitting Tower

620 Sumithrayo Logo

(Des P. Gunasinghe. Litho Secura, Singapore)

1999 (5 June). 20th Anniv of Independent Television. P 13.

1441	**619**	3r.50 multicoloured	80	40

(Des W. Rohana. Litho Secura, Singapore)

1999 (14 June). 25th Anniv of Sumithrayo (humanitarian charity). P 13.

1442	**620**	3r.50 multicoloured	1·25	60

621 Scene from Handaya and Camera Crew

622 Vidyodaya Pirivena

(Des W. Rohana. Litho Secura, Singapore)

1999 (17 Sept). Fifty Years of Sri Lankan Cinema. T **621** and similar vert designs. Multicoloured. P 13.

1443	3r.50 Type **621**		20	10
1444	4r. Scene from *Nidhanaya* and film societies' emblems		20	10
1445	10r. Scene from *Gamperaliya* and camera crew		50	50
1446	17r. Two scenes from *Kadawunu Poronduwa*		90	1·60
1443/6 *Set of 4*			1·60	2·00
MS1447 109×183 mm. Nos. 1443/6			1·60	2·25

(Des P. Gunasinghe. Litho Secura, Singapore)

1999 (17 Sept). 125th Anniv of Vidyodaya Pirivena (Buddhist education foundation). P 13.

1448	**622**	3r.50 multicoloured	45	30

623 Hector Kobbekaduwa

624 Hands holding Emblem, Fountain Pen and Magazine

(Des S. Silva. Litho Security Printers (M), Malaysia)

1999 (18 Sept). Hector Kobbekaduwa (former Minister of Agriculture and Lands) Commemoration. W **613a** (sideways). P 12½.

1449	**623**	3r.50 multicoloured	45	30

(Des E. Amitha. Litho Security Printers (M), Malaysia)

1999 (23 Sept). Centenary of Bhakthi Prabodanaya (religious magazine). P 12.

1450	**624**	3r.50 multicoloured	45	30
		a. Perf 12½×12	5·00	

No. 1450, occurs on some sheets which show the stamps in the first vertical column perforated 12 and the remainder of the sheet perforated 12½×12.

625 Army Emblem and Flags

626 Emblem and Scenery within Segments of Circle

(Des W. Rohana. Litho Secura, Singapore)

1999 (10 Oct). 50th Anniv of Sri Lankan Army. P 13.

1451	**625**	3r.50 multicoloured	65	40

(Des P. Gunasinghe. Litho Security Printers (M), Malaysia)

1999 (16 Nov). 50th Anniv of Sri Lankan National Commission for U.N.E.S.C.O. W **613a** (sideways). P 12½.

1452	**626**	13r.50 multicoloured	3·00	3·50

627 Two Children on Globe within Hands

628 Ven. Balangoda Ananda Maitreya

(Des B. Horischandra. Litho Security Printers (M), Malaysia)

1999 (20 Nov). Tenth Anniv of United Nations Rights of the Child Convention. W **613a** (sideways). P 12½.

1453	**627**	3r.50 multicoloured	1·25	80

(Des S. Silva. Litho Secura, Singapore)

1999 (26 Nov). Ven. Balangoda Ananda Maitreya (Buddhist monk and teacher). P 13.

1454	**628**	3r.50 multicoloured	40	30

629 The Nativity

(Des S. Nanayakkara. Litho Security Printers (M), Malaysia)

1999 (30 Nov). Christmas. T **629** and similar horiz design. Multicoloured. W **613a**. P 12½.

1455	3r.50 Type **629**		40	10
1456	20r. Visit of Three Wise Men		1·90	2·50
MS1457 150×90 mm. Nos. 1455/6. Wmk inverted			2·25	2·75

630 Sunil Santha

(631)

(Des S. Silva. Litho Security Printers (M), Malaysia)

1999 (3 Dec). 85th Birth Anniv of Sunil Santha (musician and teacher). W **613a** (sideways). P 12½.

1458	**630**	3r.50 multicoloured	1·75	1·00

1999 (3 Dec). No. 1317a surch with T **631**.

1459	2r. on 2r.50 Devinuwara Lighthouse		8·00	1·25

632 Dr. Pandithamani Kanapathipillai

633 Emblem, Figures and Inscriptions

(Des S. Silva. Litho Security Printers (M), Malaysia)

1999 (4 Dec). Birth Centenary of Dr. Pandithamani Kanapathipillai (Tamil scholar). W **613a** (sideways). P 12½.

1460	**632**	3r.50 multicoloured	1·50	80

(Des W. Rohana. Litho Security Printers (M), Malaysia)

1999 (6 Dec). Bicentenary of State Audit Department. W **613a**. P 12½.

1461	**633**	3r.50 multicoloured	1·00	60

634 Dr. Badiudin Mahmud

635 "Christian Family" (David Paynter)

(Des S. Silva. Litho Security Printers (M), Malaysia)

1999 (8 Dec). 95th Birth Anniv of Dr. Badiudin Mahmud (Islamic politician). W **613a** (sideways). P 12½.
1462   **634** 3r.50 multicoloured............................. 1·75   80

(Des P. Gunasinghe. Litho Secura, Singapore)

1999 (12 Dec). Sri Lankan Paintings. T **635** and similar vert designs. Multicoloured. P 13.
1463   3r.50 Type **635** 20   15
1464   4r. "Sri Lankan Woman" (Justin Daraniyagala)............................. 20   15
1465   17r. "Waiting for the Fishermen" (Ivan Peries)............................. 70   1·25
1466   20r. "Composing the 'Tripitaka" (Soliyas Mendis)............................. 80   1·50
1463/6 *Set of 4*............................. 1·60   2·75
MS1467 150×91 mm. Nos. 1463/6............................. 1·50   2·75

636 Kumar Anandan swimming Palk Strait

637 Striped Albatross (butterfly)

(Des R. de Silva. Litho Secura, Singapore)

1999 (30 Dec). Sporting Achievements. T **636** and similar multicoloured designs. P 13.
1468   1r. Type **636** 25   10
1469   3r.50 Batsman and trophy (One Day Cricket World Champions, 1996) (*vert*) 70   30
1470   13r.50 Athletics (*vert*)............................. 1·25   2·00
1468/70 *Set of 3*............................. 2·00   2·10

(Des P. Ediriweera. Photo Courvoisier)

1999 (30 Dec). Butterflies. T **637** and similar vert designs. Multicoloured. Granite paper. P 12×11½.
1471   3r.50 Type **637** 55   10
1472   13r.50 Ceylon Tiger .... 1·25   1·25
1473   17r. Three-spot Grass Yellow............................. 1·60   1·75
1474   20r. Great Orange Tip .... 1·75   2·00
1471/4 *Set of 4*............................. 4·75   4·50
MS1475 90×148 mm. Nos. 1471/4............................. 4·50   4·50

638 Doves at Nest and Religious Symbols

639 Cathedral Church, Kurunagala

(Des P. Gunasinghe. Photo Courvoisier)

2000 (1 Jan). New Millennium. T **638** and similar square designs. Multicoloured. Granite paper. P 11½×12.
1476   10r. Type **638** 75   25
1477   100r. Girl reading within hands, Scales of Justice and Red Cross .... 2·75   4·50
1478   100r. Man using computer, airliner and dish aerial............................. 2·75   4·50
1479   100r. People within open cupped hands......... 2·75   4·50
1476/9 *Set of 4*............................. 8·00   12·00
MS1480 148×90 mm. Nos. 1476/9............................. 8·50   12·00

(Des S. Nanayakkara. Litho Security Printers (M), Malaysia)

2000 (2 Feb). 50th Anniv of Diocese of Kuranagala. P 12½.
1481   **639** 13r.50 multicoloured............................. 1·50   2·00

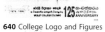

640 College Logo and Figures around Globe

(Des P. Gunasinghe. Litho Security Printers (M), Malaysia)

2000 (2 Mar). 125th Anniv of Wesley College, Colombo. P 12.
1482   **640** 3r.50 multicoloured............................. 45   30

641 Buddhist Monk and Temple

(Des P. Ediriweera. Litho Security Printers (M), Malaysia)

2000 (12 Mar). Centenary of Saddharmakara Pirivena (Buddhist college), Panadura. P 12.
1483   **641** 3r.50 multicoloured............................. 45   30

642 Boulder Coral

643 Arrival of Cutting from Jaya Sri Maha Bodhi (sacred tree)

(Des J. Jinasena. Photo Courvoisier)

2000 (18 Mar). Corals. T **642** and similar horiz designs. Multicoloured. Granite paper. P 12.
1484   3r.50 Type **642** 55   10
1485   13r.50 Blue-tipped Coral............................. 1·25   1·50
1486   14r. Brain-boulder Coral............................. 1·25   1·50
1487   22r. Elk-horn Coral............................. 1·75   2·50
1484/7 *Set of 4*............................. 4·25   5·00
MS1488 148×90 mm. Nos. 1484/7............................. 4·25   5·00

(Des B. Harischandra. Litho Security Printers (M), Malaysia)

2000 (28 Apr). Vesak Festival. T **643** and similar vert designs. Multicoloured. P 12½.
1489   2r. Type **643** 20   10
1490   3r.50 King Devanampiyatissa carrying Jaya Sri Mahn Bodhi............................. 35   20
1491   10r. Venerating the Jaya Sri Maha Bodhi 80   90
1492   13r.50 Planting the cutting at Anuradhapura .. 1·10   1·50
1489/92 *Set of 4*............................. 2·25   2·40
MS1493 98×166 mm. Nos. 1489/92. W **613a** (sideways). P 12............................. 2·00   2·50
   It is understood that Nos. 1489/92, perf 13×12½, previously listed as 1489a/92a, were used on first day covers.

644 Bar Association Logo and Courts

(Des P. Gunasinghe. Litho Security Printers (M), Malaysia)

2000 (10 June). 25th Anniv of Sri Lanka Bar Association. P 12.
1494   **644** 3r.50 multicoloured............................. 45   30

645 C.W.E Emblem and People in Supermarket

(**646**)

(Des W. Rohana. Litho Secura, Singapore)

2000 (1 July). 50th Anniv of Co-operative Wholesale Establishment. P 12½.
1495 **645** 3r.50 multicoloured.............................. 45 30

2000 (21 July). No. 1135 surch with T **646**.
1496 50c. on 8r. Mountain Labeo............................... 7·00 3·25

647 St. Patrick's College

(Des S. Nanayakkara. Litho Secura, Singapore)

2000 (21 July). 150th Anniv of St. Patrick's College, Jaffna. P 12½.
1497 **647** 3r.50 multicoloured.............................. 1·50 80

648 Surveyors at Work

(Des P. Ediriweera. Litho Secura, Singapore)

2000 (2 Aug). Bicentenary of Survey Department, Sri Lanka. P 12½.
1498 **648** 3r.50 multicoloured.............................. 45 30

649 Central Bank of Sri Lanka

(Des P. Gunasinghe. Litho Security Printers (M), Malaysia)

2000 (27 Aug). 50th Anniv of Central Bank of Sri Lanka. P 13.
1499 **649** 3r.50 multicoloured.............................. 45 40

650 Dr. Maria Montessori | **651** "2" with Olympic Rings and Maps

(Des P. Ediriweera. Photo Courvoisier)

2000 (31 Aug). 130th Birth Anniv of Dr. Maria Montessori (educator). P 12.
1500 **650** 3r.50 multicoloured.............................. 45 30

(Des W. Rohana. Photo Courvoisier)

2000 (7 Sept). Olympic Games, Sydney. T **651** and other vert designs. Multicoloured. P 12.
1501 10r. Type **651**.............................. 90 1·00
    a. Horiz strip of four. Nos. 1501/4................. 3·25 3·50
1502 10r. Running .... 90 1·00
1503 10r. Olympic flame............................ 90 1·00
1504 10r. Hurdling .... 90 1·00
1501/4 *Set of 4*.............................. 3·25 3·50
MS1505 172×96 mm. Nos. 1501/4. P 12×11½.. 3·25 3·50
    Nos. 1501/4 were printed together, *se-tenant*, as horizontal strips of four, the complete sheet showing "2000" as part of the Olympic rings.

652 Association Flag and Conference Hall | **653** Beach, Hotel and Birds

(Des P. Gunasinghe. Photo Courvoisier)

2000 (16 Sept). 50th Anniv of All Ceylon Young Men's Muslim Association Conference. P 12.
1506 **652** 3r.50 multicoloured........................ 45 30

(Des W. Perera. Litho Secura, Singapore)

2000 (18 Sept).25th Anniv of Modern Hotel Industry. P 13×12½.
1507 **653** 10r. multicoloured......................... 2·50 2·50

654 Airliner, Ship and Globe | **655** Saumiyamoorthy Thondaman

(Des S. Jayawardena. Photo Courvoisier)

2000 (2 Oct). 50th Anniv of Dept of Immigration and Emigration. P 12.
1508 **654** 3r.50 multicoloured......................... 1·25 80

(Des P. Ediriweera. Litho Secura, Singapore)

2000 (30 Oct). Saumiyamoorthy Thondaman (politician) Commemoration. P 13.
1509 **655** 3r.50 multicoloured......................... 75 50

656 Baddegama Siri Piyaratana Nayake Thero (Buddhist educator) | **657** Journey to Bethlehem

(Des S. Silva. Litho Security Printers (M), Malaysia)

2000 (14 Nov). Distinguished Personalities. T **656** and similar vert designs. Multicoloured. Phosphorised paper. P 12½.
1510 3r.50 Type **656**.............................. 40 50
1511 3r.50 Aluthgamage Simon de Silva (novelist). 40 50
1512 3r.50 Desigar Ramanujam (trade unionist)...... 40 50
1510/12 *Set of 3* .... 1·10 1·40

(Des S. Nanayakkara. Litho Security Printers (M), Malaysia)

2000 (23 Nov). Christmas. T **657** and similar vert design. Multicoloured. Phosphorised paper. P 12½.
1513 2r. Type **657**.............................. 40 10
1514 17r. The Nativity............................. 2·50 2·75
MS1515 150×91 mm. Nos. 1513/14. P 12......... 2·50 3·00

658 Lalith Athulathmudali

(Des Grant Advertising. Litho Security Printers (M), Malaysia)

2000 (30 Nov). Lalith Athulathmudali (politician) Commemoration. Phosphorised paper. P 12½.

1516	**658**	3r.50 multicoloured	45	30
		a. Perf 12		

659 Five Elements and Butterfly

(Des P. Gunasinghe. Litho Secura, Singapore)

2000 (1 Dec). 38th Anniv of Medicina Alternativa (alternative medicine society). P 13.

1517	**659**	13r.50 multicoloured	4·00	4·50

660 Chapel of Hope of the World **661** Patrol Boat

(Des P. Ediriweera. Litho Secura, Singapore)

2000 (7 Dec). Centenary of Ladies' College, Colombo. P 13.

1518	**660**	3r.50 multicoloured	45	30

(Des. W. Rohana. Litho Secura, Singapore)

2000 (9 Dec). 50th Anniv of Sri Lanka Navy. P 12½.

1519	**661**	3r.50 multicoloured	1·25	70

662 Peliyagoda Vidyalankara Pirivena Building **663** Bishop's College

(Des P. Gunasinghe. Litho Enschedé)

2000 (30 Dec). 125th Anniv of Peliyagoda Vidyalankara Pirivena (Buddhist university). P 12.

1520	**662**	3r.50 multicoloured	45	30

(Des P. Gunasinghe. Litho People's Printing Works, Beijing)

2001 (19 Jan). 125th Anniv of Bishop's College, Colombo. P 12.

1521	**663**	3r.50 multicoloured	45	30

664 St. Thomas' College **665** Woman with Basket of Vegetables and Logo

(Des P. Gunasinghe. Litho Secura, Singapore)

2001 (3 Feb). 150th Anniv of St. Thomas' College, Mount Lavinia. P 13.

1522	**664**	3r.50 multicoloured	45	30

(Des S. Jayawardena. Litho Secura, Singapore)

2001 (15 Feb). 70th Anniv of Lanka Mahili Samiti (rural women's society). P 13.

1523	**665**	3r.50 multicoloured	45	30

666 Air Force Crest and Aircraft

(Des S. Jaywardena. Litho Secura, Singapore)

2001 (9 Mar). 50th Anniv of Sri Lanka Air Force. Phosphorised paper. P 13.

1524	**666**	3r.50 multicoloured	1·25	70

667 St. Lawrence's School

(Des D. Somapala. Litho Secura, Singapore)

2001 (15 Mar). Centenary of St. Lawrence's School, Wellawatta (2000). Phosphorised paper. P 13.

1525	**667**	3r.50 multicoloured	45	30

668 Bernard Soysa **669** Nagadeepa Stupa, Jaffna

(Des P. Ediriweera. Litho Secura, Singapore)

2001 (20 Mar). Bernard Soysa (politician) Commemoration. Phosphorised paper. P 13.

1526	**668**	3r.50 multicoloured	45	30

(Des W. Rohanna. Litho Security Printers (M), Malaysia)

2001 (7 Apr). Vesak Festival. Buddhist shrines. T **669** and similar vert designs. Multicoloured. Phosphorised paper. P 13½ (2r.) or 14½×14 (others).

1527		2r. Type **669**	10	10
1528		3r.50 Muthiyangana Chaithya, Badulla.............	20	10
1529		13r.50 Kirivehera Stupa, Kataragama	65	75
1530		17r. Temple of the Tooth, Kandy....................	90	1·25
1527/30	*Set of 4*		1·60	2·00
MS1531	179×99 mm. Nos. 1527/30. P 14½×14		1·60	2·25

670 "Hansa Jataka" (George Keyt)

(Des P. Ediriweera. Litho Security Printers (M), Malaysia)

2001 (24 Apr). Birth Centenary of George Keyt (painter). Phosphorised paper. P 13.

1532	**670**	13r.50 multicoloured	1·60	2·00

671 Gold Kahavanu Coin (9th Century) **672** Colombo Plan Emblem

(Des P. Ediriweera. Litho Security Printers (M), Malaysia)

2001 (18 June). Sri Lanka Coins. T **671** and similar horiz designs. Multicoloured. Phosphorised paper. P 13½ (13r.50) or 14×14½ (others).
1533	3r.50	Type **671**	40	10
	a. Perf 13½			
1534	13r.50	Silver coin of Vijayabahu I, (11th-12th century)	1·00	1·00
1535	17r.	Copper Sethu coin from Jaffna (13th-14th century)	1·40	1·60
1536	20r.	Silver commemorative five rupee coin (1957)	1·60	1·75
	a. Perf 13½			
1533/6	Set of 4		4·00	4·00
MS1537	155×95 mm. Nos. 1533/6. P 13½		4·00	4·25

(Des P. Ediriweera. Litho Security Printers (M), Malaysia)

2001 (2 July). 50th Anniv of Colombo Plan. Phosphorised paper. P 13½.
1538	**672**	10r. multicoloured	85	1·00

673 Flags of Sri Lanka and USA
674 Lance-Corporal Gamini Kularatne and Attack on Tank

(Des D. Somapala. Litho Secura, Singapore)

2001 (3 July). 150th Anniv of Bilateral Relations with USA. Phosphorised paper. P 13.
1539	**673**	10r. multicoloured	85	1·00

(Des S. Jaywardena. Litho Security Printers (M), Malaysia)

2001 (14 July). Tenth Death Anniv of Gamini Kularatne (war hero). Phosphorised paper. P 13½.
1540	**674**	3r.50 multicoloured	50	30

(675)
676 Prince and Princess of Wales Colleges, Moratuwa

2001 (7 Sept). No. 630 surch as T **675** by State Printing Corporation.
1541	226	5r. on 1r.15 multicoloured	5·50	2·00
1542		10r. on 1r.15 multicoloured	8·00	6·00

(Des P. Gunasinghe. Litho Madras Security Printers)

2001 (14 Sept). 125th Anniv of Prince and Princess of Wales Colleges, Moratuwa. Phosphorised paper. P 13½×13.
1543	**676**	3r.50 multicoloured	45	30

677 Congress Building

(Des P. Gunasinghe. Litho Secura, Singapore)

2001 (17 Sept). All-Ceylon Buddhist Congress National Awards Ceremony. Phosphorised paper. P 13.
1544	**677**	3r.50 multicoloured	1·50	80

678 Children encircling Globe
679 Hand protecting Globe from Harmful Rays

(Des Urska Golob. Litho Madras Security Printers)

2001 (9 Oct). UN Year of Dialogue among Civilisations. Phosphorised paper. P 13×13½.
1545	**678**	10r. multicoloured	85	1·00

(Des P. Ediriweera. Litho Madras Security Printers Ltd, India)

2001 (18 Oct). 13th Meeting of the Montreal Protocol Group (protection of Ozone Layer), Colombo. P 13×13½.
1546	**679**	13r.50 multicoloured	1·50	1·75

680 Ramakrishna Mission Students' Home, Batticaloa

(Des S. Rohana. Litho Secura, Singapore)

2001 (19 Oct). 75th Anniv of Ramakrishna Mission Students' Home, Batticaloa. P 12½.
1547	**680**	3r.50 multicoloured	45	30

681 Daul Drummer
682 Bandaranaike Memorial International Conference Hall, Colombo

(Litho Madras Security Printers, India)

2001 (8 Nov)–**03**. Drummers. T **681** and similar vert designs. P 12½×13 (1r. to 3r.50), 13½×12½ (16r.50) or 13×12½ (others).
1548	1r.	bright rose-red	10	10
1549	2r.	bright emerald	15	10
1550	3r.	deep cinnamon	25	10
1551	3r.50	bright blue	30	10
1552	4r.	bright rose	30	10
		a. Printed on the gummed side	5·00	40
1552b	4r.50	bright blue (16.8.02)	7·00	40
1553	5r.	bright orange	35	10
1554	10r.	violet	65	20
1555	13r.50	reddish violet	80	50
1555a	16r.50	reddish violet (17.2.03)	1·10	75
1556	17r.	yellow-orange	1·10	55
1557	20r.	bright turquoise-blue	1·10	60
1548/57	Set of 12		12·00	3·00

Designs: (18×23 mm)—1r. to 3r.50, Type **681**. (23×28 mm)—4r. to 10r. Kandyan drummer; 13r.50 to 20r. Low Country drummer.
No. 1552a was caused by a paper fold. Seven complete stamps were affected.

(Des P. Gunasinghe. Litho Enschedé)

2001 (27 Nov). 25th Anniv of SWRD Bandaranaike National Memorial Foundation. P 14×13½.
1558	**682**	3r.50 multicoloured	50	25

683 Jesus with Children
684 Conical Wart Pygmy Tree-frog

(Des Sibil Wettasinghe. Litho Security Printers (M), Malaysia)

2001 (28 Nov). Christmas. T **683** and similar square design. Multicoloured. P 13.

1559	3r.50 Type **683**	15	10
1560	17r. Angel Gabriel appearing to Mary	85	1·25
MS1561	150×120 mm. Nos. 1557/8	1·00	1·40

(Des Jayantha Jinasena. Litho Calcutta Security Printers Ltd, Kanpur)

2001 (3 Dec). Fourth World Congress of Herpetology. Frogs. T **684** and similar horiz designs. Multicoloured. P 13½×13.

1562	3r.50 Type **684**	25	10
1563	13r.50 Sharp-snout Saddle Tree-frog	70	75
1564	17r. Round-snout Pygmy Tree-frog	85	1·00
1565	20r. Sri Lanka Wood Frog	95	1·25
1562/5	Set of 4	2·50	2·75
MS1566	180×120 mm. Nos. 1560/3	2·50	3·25

685 St. Bridget's Convent   686 Front Page from First Edition of *Ceylon Government Gazette*, 1802

(Des D. Jayawardena. Litho Madras Security Printers, India)

2002 (1 Feb). Centenary of St. Bridget's Convent, Colombo. P 13½×13.
1567 **685** 3r.50 multicoloured ... 45 30

(Des P. Ediriweera. Litho Dept of Govt Printing)

2002 (15 Mar). Bicentenary of Ceylon Government Gazette. P 13½×14.
1568 **686** 3r.50 multicoloured ... 45 30

687 Prime Minister D. Senanayake   688 Gamini Dissanayake and Victoria Dam

(Des P. Ediriweera. Litho Dept of Govt Printing)

2002 (22 Mar). 50th Death Anniv of D. Senanayake (first Sri Lankan Prime Minister). P 14×13½.
1569 **687** 3r.50 multicoloured ... 45 30

(Des. D. Jayawardena. Litho Dept of Govt Printing)

2002 (27 Mar). 60th Birth Anniv of Gamini Dissanayake (former government minister). P 13½×14.
1570 **688** 3r.50 multicoloured ... 45 30

689 Lester James Peries and Awards

(Des S. Rohana Wickremasinghe. Litho Madras Security Printers, India)

2002 (5 Apr). Lester James Peries (film director). P 13½×13.
1571 **689** 3r.50 multicoloured ... 45 30

690 Sinharaja Forest Reserve

(Des D. Sudath Jayawardena. Litho Madras Security Printers, India)

2002 (10 Apr). Natural Beauty of Sri Lanka. T **690** and similar horiz designs. Multicoloured. P 13×13½.

1572	5r. Type **690**	20	15
1573	10r. Horton Plains National Park	35	30
1574	13r.50 Knuckles Range	45	60
1575	20r. Rumassala Cliff and Bonavista Coral Reef	70	1·25
1572/5	Set of 4	1·50	2·10

691 Mount Fuji and Flags of Sri Lanka and Japan   692 President Ranasinghe Premadasa and Modern Housing Development

(Des S. Rohana Wickremasinghe. Litho Dept of Govt Printing)

2002 (21 Apr). 50th Anniv of Sri Lanka–Japan Diplomatic Relations. P 14×13½.
1576 **691** 16r.50 multicoloured ... 85 1·10

(Des P. Ediriweera. Litho Dept of Govt Printing)

2002 (29 Apr). Ninth Death Anniv of Ranasinghe Premadasa (President 1989–93). P 13½×14.
1577 **692** 4r.50 multicoloured ... 30 25

(692a)   .25   4.50 (692b)

2002 (17 May). Nos. 1075 and 1551 surch with T **692a/b**.

1577a	**449**	25c. on 5r.75 multicoloured	50	50
1577b	–	4r.50 on 3r.50 bright blue	6·00	1·50

692c Trees, Crops and Village

(Des G. Withanage. Litho Secura, Singapore)

2002 (17 May). "Gam Udawa '94". P 12½.
1577c **692c** 1r. multicoloured ... 60 15

No. 1577c was prepared for issue on 23 June 1994, but not released due to the assassination of President Premadasa. It was issued on 17 May 2002 due to a shortage of 1r. stamps caused by the revision of postal rates.

693 Queen Mahamaya's Dream   694 Madihe Pamasiha Maha Nayaka Thera

(Des N. Bulathsinhala. Litho Dept of Govt Printing)

2002 (17 May). Vesak. Dambulla Raja Maha Vihara Rock Paintings. T **693** and similar horiz designs. Multicoloured. P 13½×14.

1578	3r. Type **693**	10	10
1579	4r.50 Birth of Prince Siddhartha	15	10
1580	16r.50 Prince Siddhartha demonstrating his archery skills	70	90
1581	23r. Ordination of Prince Siddhartha	80	1·25
1578/81	Set of 4	1·60	2·00
MS1582	150×93 mm. Nos. 1578/81	1·60	2·00

(Des P. Ediriweera. Litho Dept of Govt Printing)

2002 (23 June). 90th Birthday of Most Venerable Madihe Pamasiha Maha Nayaka Thera (Supreme Patriarch of Sri Lanka Amarapura Maha Nikaya). P 14×13½.
1583   **694**   4r.50 multicoloured 40   25

695 Buddhist Monk with Pen and Scroll and Society Emblem

(Des P. Ediriweera. Litho Dept of Govt Printing)

2002 (24 July). Centenary of Sri Lanka Oriental Studies Society. P 13½×14.
1584   **695**   4r.50 multicoloured 40   25

696 Anniversary Emblem and Association Headquarters

(Des B. Ghouse. Litho Dept of Govt Printing, Sri Lanka)

2002 (26 July). 125th Anniv of Rifai Thareeq Association of Sri Lanka. P 13½×14.
1585   **696**   4r.50 multicoloured 40   25

697 Discus Thrower   **698** Carved Stone Lion of 12th Century (squatting)

(Des Kumara Jayakantha. Litho Dept of Govt Printing, Sri Lanka)

2002 (8 Aug). 14th Asian Athletic Championships, Colombo. T **697** and similar horiz designs. Multicoloured. P 13½×14.
1586		4r.50 Type **697**	15 10
1587		16r.50 Sprinter	60 65
1588		23r. Hurdler	80 1·25
1589		26r. Long jumper	80 1·25
1586/9		*Set of 4*	2·10 2·75

(Des P. Gunasinghe. Litho Dept of Govt Printing, Sri Lanka)

2002 (27 Aug). 125th Anniv of National Museum, Colombo. T **698** and similar horiz design. Multicoloured. P 13½×14.
1590   4r.50 Type **698** 75   90
       a. Horiz pair. Nos. 1590/1 .... 1·50   1·75
1591   4r.50 Carved stone lion of 12th century (standing) 75   90
Nos. 1590/1 were printed together, *se-tenant*, in horizontal pairs throughout the sheets, each pair forming a composite design.

699 "Sapu Mudra" Logo of   **700** Dr. A. C. S. Hameed
Sri Lanka Tourist Board

(Des P. Gunasinghe. Litho Dept of Govt Printing, Sri Lanka)

2002 (28 Aug). Tourism. "Sri Lanka. A land like no other". P 14×13½.
1592   **699**   10r. multicoloured 70   75

(Des P. Ediriweera. Litho Dept of Govt Printing, Sri Lanka)

2002 (3 Sept). Third Death Anniv of Dr. A. C. S. Hameed (Foreign Minister 1977–92). P 14×13½.
1593   **700**   4r.50 multicoloured 40   25

701 Freemasons Hall, Colombo

(Des D. Sudath Jayawardena. Litho Dept of Govt Printing, Sri Lanka)

2002 (5 Sept). Centenary of Freemasons Hall (Victoria Masonic Temple), Colombo (2001). P 13½×14.
1594   **701**   4r.50 multicoloured .... 1·00   70

702 Holy Cross College, Kalutara   **703** Berlin Buddhist Vihara (temple)

(Des P. Gunasinghe. Litho Dept of Govt Printing, Sri Lanka)

2002 (13 Sept). Centenary of Holy Cross College, Kalutara. P 13½×14.
1595   **702**   4r.50 multicoloured 40   25

(Des P. Gunasinghe. Litho Dept of Govt Printing, Sri Lanka)

2002 (21 Sept). 50th Anniv of German Dharmaduta Society. P 14×13½.
1596   **703**   4r.50 multicoloured 40   25

704 Images from   **705** Dr. M. C. M.
Children's Paintings   Kaleel

(Des D. Sudath Jayawardena. Litho Dept of Govt Printing, Sri Lanka)

2002 (1 Oct). International Children's Day. P 14×13½.
1597   **704**   4r.50 multicoloured 40   25

(Des D. Sudath Jayawardena. Litho Dept of Govt Printing, Sri Lanka)

2002 (18 Oct). Al-Haj Dr. M. C. M. Kaleel Commemoration. P 14×13½.
1598   **705**   4r.50 deep grey-green 40   25

706 College Entrance, Arms and   **707** Dr. Wijayananda
Building   Dahanayake

(Des Harsha Maduranga Jayasekara. Litho Dept of Govt Printing, Sri Lanka)

2002 (19 Oct). 150th Anniv of Uduppiddy American Mission College. P 13½×14.
1599   **706**   4r.50 multicoloured 40   25

(Des P. Ediriweera. Litho Dept of Govt Printing, Sri Lanka)

2002 (22 Oct). Birth Centenary of Dr. Wijayananda Dahanayake (politician and educational reformer). P 14×13½.
1600　**707**　4r.50 purple-brown.. 40　25

708 Meeting of King of Kandy and Admiral van Spilbergen, 1602 (from painting by C. L. Beling)

709 Virgin and Child

(Des P. Gunasinghe. Litho Dept of Govt Printing, Sri Lanka)

2002 (22 Nov). 400th Anniv of Sri Lanka–Netherlands Relations. P 13½×14.
1601　**708**　16r.50 multicoloured.. 1·00　1·50

(Des D. Sudath Jayawardena. Litho Madras Security Printers, India)

2002 (15 Dec). Christmas. T **709** and similar design showing stained glass windows. Multicoloured. P 13×13½.
1602　　4r.50 Type **709**.. 15　10
1603　　26r. Holy Family... 1·10　1·40
MS1604 190×130 mm. Nos. 1602/3 .... 1·25　1·75

710 Woman harvesting Rubber and Chinese Rice Farmer

(Des P. Gunasinghe. Litho Dept of Govt Printing, Sri Lanka)

2002 (20 Dec). 50th Anniv of Ceylon–China Rubber–Rice Pact. P 13½×14.
1605　**710**　4r.50 multicoloured.. 40　25

711 Kopay Christian College

(Des M. Fonseka. Litho Dept of Govt Printing, Sri Lanka)

2002 (28 Dec). 150th Anniv of Kopay Christian College. P 13½×14.
1606　**711**　4r.50 multicoloured.. 40　25

712 Teacher and Class

713 Stained Glass Window

(Des D. Sudath Jayawardena. Litho Dept of Govt Printing, Sri Lanka)

2003 (21 Jan). Centenary of Teachers' College, Maharagama. P 13½×14.
1607　**712**　4r.50 multicoloured.. 40　25

(Des G. Andree. Litho Dept of Govt Printing, Sri Lanka)

2003 (3 Feb). Centenary of Holy Family Convent, Bambalapitiya. P 14×13½.
1608　**713**　4r.50 multicoloured.. 40　25

(**714**)

715 M. D. Banda and Rice Fields

2003 (17 Feb). No. 1556 surch with T **714**.
1609　　50c. on 17r. yellow-orange............................... 1·25　65

(Des P. Gunasinghe. Litho Dept of Govt Printing, Sri Lanka)

2003 (14 Mar). 30th Death Anniv (2004) of M. D. Banda (politician). P 13½×14.
1610　**715**　4r.50 multicoloured.. 40　25

716 Scholar and Buildings

(Des N. Bulathsinhala. Litho Dept of Govt Printing, Sri Lanka)

2003 (6 Apr). Centenary of Balagalle Saraswati Maha Pirivena. P 13½×14.
1611　**716**　4r.50 multicoloured.. 40　25

717 D. B. Welagedara

718 Children paying Obeisance to Parents

(Des P. Ediriweera. Litho Dept of Govt Printing, Sri Lanka)

2003 (22 Apr). D. B. Welagedara (politician) Commem. P 14×13½.
1612　**717**　4r.50 multicoloured.. 40　25

(Des B. Harischandra. Litho Dept of Govt Printing, Sri Lanka)

2003 (26 Apr). Vesak. T **718** and similar vert designs. Multicoloured. P 14×13½.
1613　　2r.50 Type **718** .... 10　10
1614　　3r. Dhamma school .... 15　15
1615　　4r.50 Bhikku on alms round .... 20　15
1616　　23r. Meditation .... 1·25　1·60
1613/16 *Set of 4* .... 1·50　1·75
MS1617 93×152 mm. Nos. 1613/16 .... 1·50　1·75

719 Stupa

720 Emblem

(Des D. Sudath Jayawardena. Litho Madras Security Printers, India)

2003 (28 Apr). Features of Construction of Dagobas in Ancient Sri Lanka. T **719** and similar multicoloured designs. P 13×13½ (4r.50, 16r.50) or 13½×13 (50r.).
1618　　4r.50 Type **719** .... 15　10
1619　　16r.50 Guard stones and flight of steps (57×28 *mm*) .... 70　70
1620　　50r. Moonstone (*horiz*) .... 1·40　1·75
1618/20 *Set of 3* .... 2·00　2·25
MS1621 155×116 mm. Nos. 1618/20...................... 2·00　2·75

(Des D. Sudath Jayawardena. Litho Dept of Govt Printing, Sri Lanka)

2003 (2 May). Second World Hindu Conference, Sri Lanka. P 14×13½.
1622 **720** 4r.50 multicoloured... 40 25

721 Nurses carrying Lamps and Florence Nightingale

(Des P. Gunasinghe. Litho Dept of Govt Printing, Sri Lanka)

2003 (12 May). International Nursing Day. P 13½×14.
1623 **721** 4r.50 multicoloured... 55 25

722 Sirimavo Bandaranaike Memorial Exhibition Centre and Mrs. Bandaranaike (former Prime Minister)

(Des P. Gunasinghe. Litho Dept of Govt Printing, Sri Lanka)

2003 (17 May). Opening of Sirimavo Bandaranaike Memorial Exhibition Centre. Joint issue with People's Republic of China. P 13½×12.
1624 **722** 4r.50 multicoloured... 40 25

723 Al-Haj H. S. Ismail   **724** Plantation Workers, Port, Cogwheels and Computer

(Des P. Ediriweera. Litho Dept of Govt Printing, Sri Lanka)

2003 (18 May). Al-Haj H. S. Ismail (former Speaker of Parliament) Commemoration. P 14×13½.
1625 **723** 4r.50 multicoloured... 40 25

(Des D. Sudath Jayawardena. Litho Dept of Govt Printing, Sri Lanka)

2003 (21 May). 25th Anniv of Board of Investment of Sri Lanka. P 13½×12.
1626 **724** 4r.50 multicoloured... 40 25

725 Pidurutalagala Mountain Range

(Des D. Sudath Jayawardena. Litho Dept of Govt Printing, Sri Lanka)

2003 (22 May). World Bio-diversity Day. T **725** and similar horiz designs. Multicoloured. P 13½×12.
1627   4r. Type **725** 20 15
1628   4r.50 Seven Maidens Mountain Range............. 20 15
1629   16r.50 Kirigalpoththa Mountain .... 75 1·00
1630   23r. Ritigala Mountain .... 1·00 1·50
1627/30 Set of 4 .... 2·00 2·50

726 College Arms

(Des H. Dayaratne. Litho Dept of Govt Printing, Sri Lanka)

2003 (6 June). Centenary of G/Gonapinuwala Saralankara College. P 13½×14.
1631 **726** 4r.50 multicoloured... 40 25

727 Masjidul Abrar   **728** Healthy People
Jummah Mosque   and Drug Addicts
(central section)

(Des P. Edirweera. Litho Dept of Govt Printing, Sri Lanka)

2003 (8 June). First Arab Settlement in Sri Lanka, Beruwala. T **727** and similar multicoloured design. P 14×13½ (4r.50) or 14×13½ (23r.).
1632   4r.50 Type **727** 15 10
1633   23r. Masjidul Abrar Jummah Mosque,
          Beruwala (57×22 mm)............................ 85 1·50

(Des K. Gunasekara. Litho Dept of Govt Printing, Sri Lanka)

2003 (23 June). Anti Narcotic Week. P 14×13½.
1634 **728** 4r.50 multicoloured... 1·00 50

729 Malwathu Maha Viharaya

(Des P. Gunasinghe. Litho Dept of Govt Printing, Sri Lanka)

2003 (13 July). 250th Anniv of Buddhist Higher Ordination in Sri Lanka. T **729** and similar horiz design. Multicoloured. P 13½×14.
1635   4r.50 Type **729** 50 50
1636   4r.50 Asgiri Maha Viharaya............................ 50 50

730 Two Cow Elephants with Calves

(Des D. Sudath Jayawardena. Litho Madras Security Printers, India)

2003 (13 July). Elephant Orphanage, Pinnawala. T **730** and similar horiz designs. Multicoloured. P 13½×13.
1637   4r.50 Type **730** 50 20
1638   16r.50 Keeper hand feeding milk to young
          elephant.. 1·00 1·00
1639   23r. Young elephant and calf .... 1·25 1·60
1640   26r. Tusker... 1·25 1·60
1637/40 Set of 4 .... 3·50 4·00
MS1641 183×100 mm. Nos. 1637/40.......................... 3·50 4·50

731 Emblem and Mother with Children looking at Stamp Album

(Des P. Ediriweera. Litho Dept of Govt Printing, Sri Lanka)

2003 (31 July). "Lanka Philex 2003" Stamp Exhibition, Colombo. 25th Anniv of Philatelic Society of Sri Lanka. P 13½×12.
1642 **731** 16r.50 multicoloured...................................... 1·00 1·50
MS1643 111×92 mm. **731** 16r.50 multicoloured............ 1·50 2·00

732 Dr. Ananda Tissa de Alwis

(Des P. Ediriweera. Litho Dept of Govt Printing, Sri Lanka)

2003 (21 Aug). Dr Ananda Tissa de Alwis (first Speaker of New Parliament, Kotte) Commemoration. P 13½×14.

1644 **732** 4r.50 multicoloured 50 35

733 Ven. Mohottiwatte Gunananda Thero, Wheel and Globe

734 Ven. Haldanduwana Dhammarakkitha Thero

(Des B. Harischandra. Litho Dept of Govt Printing, Sri Lanka)

2003 (24 Aug). 130th Anniv of the Great Panadura Controversy (debate between Buddhists and Christians. P 14×13½.

1645 **733** 4r.50 multicoloured 50 35

(Des P. Ediriweera. Litho Dept of Govt Printing, Sri Lanka)

2003 (3 Sept). Ven. Haldanduwana Dhammarakkitha Thero (Chief Sanganayake and Buddhist philosopher) Commemoration. P 14×13½.

1646 **734** 4r.50 multicoloured 50 35

735 Shrine in Procession

736 M. H. M. Ashraff

(Des S. Wickramasinghe. Litho Dept of Govt Printing, Sri Lanka)

2003 (10 Sept). 75th Anniv of Poson Maha Perahara (cultural pageant). P 13½×14.

1647 **735** 4r.50 multicoloured .... 1·00 50

(Des W. Kulakulasooriya. Litho Dept of Govt Printing, Sri Lanka)

2003 (18 Sept). M. H. M. Ashraff (leader of National Unity Alliance) Commemoration. P 14×13½.

1648 **736** 4r.50 multicoloured 70 40

737 Convent of Sisters of the Holy Angels

738 Black-necked Stork

(Des P. Gunasinghe. Litho Dept of Govt Printing, Sri Lanka)

2003 (27 Sept). Centenary of the Sisters of the Holy Angels. P 13½×14.

1649 **737** 4r.50 multicoloured 35 35

(Des K. Gunasekara. Litho Dept of Govt Printing, Sri Lanka)

2003 (27 Sept). Resident Birds of Sri Lanka. T **738** and similar vert designs. Multicoloured. P 14×13½.

1650	4r.50 Type **738**	40	40
	a. Sheetlet. Nos. 1650/74	9·00	9·00
1651	4r.50 Purple Swamphen	40	40
1652	4r.50 Grey Heron	40	40
1653	4r.50 White-throated Kingfisher	40	40
1654	4r.50 Black-crowned Night Heron	40	40
1655	4r.50 Scarlet Minivet	40	40
1656	4r.50 White-rumped Shama	40	40
1657	4r.50 Malabar Trogon	40	40
1658	4r.50 Asiatic Paradise Flycatcher	40	40
1659	4r.50 Little Green Bee Eater	40	40
1660	4r.50 Brown Wood Owl	40	40
1661	4r.50 Crested Serpent Eagle	40	40
1662	4r.50 Asian Crested Goshawk	40	40
1663	4r.50 Jungle Owlet	40	40
1664	4r.50 Chestnut-bellied Hawk Eagle ("Rufous-bellied Eagle")	40	40
1665	4r.50 Chestnut Mannikin ("Black-headed Munia")	40	40
1666	4r.50 Pompadour Green Pigeon	40	40
1667	4r.50 Plum-headed Parakeet	40	40
1668	4r.50 Crimson-breasted Barbet ("Coppersmith Barbet")	40	40
1669	4r.50 Emerald Dove	40	40
1670	4r.50 Blue-faced Malkoha	40	40
1671	4r.50 Travancore Scimitar Babbler	40	40
1672	4r.50 Painted Partridge ("Painted Francolin") .	40	40
1673	4r.50 Lesser Flame-backed Woodpecker ("Red-backed Woodpecker")	40	40
1674	4r.50 Malabar Pied Hornbill	40	40
1650/74	Set of 25	9·00	9·00

Nos. 1650/74 were printed together, *se-tenant*, in sheetlets of 25.

739 Globe and City

(Des P. Ediriweera. Litho Dept of Govt Printing, Sri Lanka)

2003 (6 Oct). World Habitat Day. P 13.

1675 **739** 4r.50 multicoloured 40 25

740 Globe, Post, Computer, Fax and Telephone

741 Blue Sapphire

(Des D. Sudath Jayawardena. Litho Dept of Govt Printing, Sri Lanka)

2003 (9 Oct). World Post Day. P 14×13½.

1676 **740** 23r. multicoloured .... 1·25 1·75

(Des D. Sudath Jayawardena. Litho Dept of Govt Printing, Sri Lanka)

2003 (21 Oct)–**04**. National Gem Stone of Sri Lanka (Blue Sapphire). P 12×13½.

1677 **741** 4r.50 multicoloured 50 10
1677a 5r. multicoloured (14.12.04) 50 10

742 Pope John Paul II

743 Couple with Candle and Sacred Cow

(Des W. Vasantha Perera. Litho Dept of Govt Printing, Sri Lanka)

2003 (22 Oct). 25th Anniv of the Pontificate of Pope John Paul II. P 13.
1678   **742**   4r.50 multicoloured 75   45

(Des N. S. Gnanakurubaran. Litho Dept of Govt Printing, Sri Lanka)

2003 (23 Oct). Deepavali Festival. P 13.
1679   **743**   4r.50 multicoloured 40   25

744 Ramboda
Waterfall

745 Hon. U. B.
Wanninayake

(Des P. Ediriweera. Litho Dept of Govt Printing, Sri Lanka)

2003 (11 Nov). Waterfalls of Sri Lanka. T **744** and similar vert designs.
Multicoloured. P 14×13½.
1680   2r.50 Type **744** 10   10
1681   4r.50 Saint Clair Waterfall 20   10
1682   23r. Bopath Ella Waterfall 70   1·00
1683   50r. Devon Waterfall .... 1·40   2·25
1680/3 Set of 4 .... 2·10   3·00

(Des W. S. Kulakulasooriya. Litho Dept of Govt Printing, Sri Lanka)

2003 (23 Nov). Hon. U. B. Wanninayake (Minister of Finance, 1965–70)
Commemoration. P 13.
1684   **745**   4r.50 multicoloured 40   25

746 St. Philipnery Church,
Katukurunda, Kalutara

(Des W. S. Kulakulasooriya. Litho Dept of Govt Printing, Sri Lanka)

2003 (30 Nov). Christmas. T **746** and similar multicoloured design. P 13.
1685   4r.50 Type **746** 15   10
1686   16r.50 Angel and shepherds (*vert*) 60   80

747 Dr. Pandith Amaradeva

(Des P. Ediriweera. Litho Dept of Govt Printing, Sri Lanka)

2003 (5 Dec). Sri Lankan Artists' Day. Dr. Pandith W. D. Amaradeva
(musician). P 13.
1687   **747**   4r.50 multicoloured 50   35

748 Gangarama
Seemamalakaya

749 Pushparamaya Temple,
Malegoda

(Des P. Gunasinghe. Litho Dept of Govt Printing, Sri Lanka)

2003 (20 Dec). Sri Jinaratana Vocational Training Centre. P 13.
1688   **748**   4r.50 multicoloured 40   25

(Des Palitha Gunasinghe. Litho Dept of Govt Printing, Sri Lanka)

2003 (31 Dec). Daham Pahana (Buddhist Religious Ceremony). P 13.
1689   **749**   4r.50 multicoloured 40   25

750 Jummah Mosque, Beruwala

751 Emblem of
Chavakachcheri
Hindu College

(Des P. Ediriweera. Litho Dept of Govt Printing, Sri Lanka)

2004 (6 Jan). 140th Anniv of Shazuliyathul Fassiya Tharika. P 13.
1690   **750**   18r. multicoloured 80   1·10

(Des S. Wickramasinghe. Litho Dept of Govt Printing, Sri Lanka)

2004 (30 Jan). Centenary of Chavakachcheri Hindu College.
P 12×13½.
1691   **751**   4r.50 multicoloured 40   30

752 Cricket Match

753 D. B. Wijetunga

(Des S. Wickramasinghe. Litho Dept of Govt Printing, Sri Lanka)

2004 (30 Jan). 125th Cricket Match between The Royal and S. Thomas
Colleges. P 13.
1692   **752**   4r.50 multicoloured .... 1·00   55

(Des W. Shrinath. Litho Dept of Govt Printing, Sri Lanka)

2004 (15 Feb). 82nd Birth Anniv of D. B. Wijetunga (President
1993–94). P 13.
1693   **753**   4r.50 multicoloured 40   30

754 Old and Young Trees

(Des K. Gunasekara. Litho Dept of Govt Printing, Sri Lanka)

2004 (17 Feb). 150th Anniv of Inauguration of the Planters
Association. P 13½×14.
1694   **754**   4r.50 multicoloured 75   50

755 Mapalagama
Vipulasara Thero (artist)

756 Batsman, Ball
and Emblems

(Des P. Ediriweera, Sudath Jayawardena and S. Wickramasinghe. Litho Madras Security Printers, India)

2004 (28 Feb). Distinguished Personalities. T **755** and similar vert designs. Multicoloured. P 13×13½.

1695	3r.50 Type **755**	20	20
1696	3r.50 Cathiravelu Sittampalam (politician).......	20	20
1697	3r.50 Maithripala Senanayeke (politician)........	20	20
1698	3r.50 M.G. Mendis (politician)	20	20
1695/8 Set of 4...		70	70

(Des P. Ediriweera. Litho Dept of Govt Printing, Sri Lanka)

2004 (7 Mar). 75th Anniv of Ananda and Nalanda Cricket Matches. "Battle of the Maroons". P 12×13½.

1699	**756**	4r.50 multicoloured...	1·00	60

757 St. Anthony's College, Kandy

(Des Palitha Gunasinghe. Litho Dept of Govt Printing, Sri Lanka)

2004 (12 Mar). 150th Anniv of St. Anthony's College, Kandy. P 13½×12.

1700	**757**	4r.50 multicoloured...	40	30

758 Sucharita going to Pandit Vidhura

(Des Palitha Gunasinghe. Litho Dept of Govt Printing, Sri Lanka)

2004 (30 Apr). Vesak. T **758** and similar horiz designs. Multicoloured. P 13½×12.

1701	4r. Type **758**	15	10
1702	4r.50 Sucharita meeting with Pandit Vidhura	15	10
1703	16r.50 Sucharita introduced to Badraka by Pandit Vidhura..	60	80
1704	20r. Sucharita going to Sanjaya, who advises meeting Prince Sambava	75	1·00
1701/4 Set of 4...		1·50	1·75
MS1705 122×81 mm. 26r. Sucharita meeting Badraka and Sanjaya...		1·00	1·50

759 "Gongalegoda Banda"

760 Stylised Figure in Blood Droplet and Globe

(Des R. de Silva. Litho Dept of Govt Printing, Sri Lanka)

2004 (22 May). 155th Death Anniv of Wansapurna Deva David "Gongalegoda Banda" (leader of 1848 Rebellion). P 14×13½.

1706	**759**	4r.50 multicoloured...	40	30

(Des Sudath Jayawardena. Litho Dept of Govt Printing, Sri Lanka)

2004 (15 June). World Blood Donor Day (14th June). P 13.

1707	**760**	4r.50 multicoloured...	75	30

761 Swimming

(Des V. Shrinath Kurukulasooriya. Litho Dept of Govt Printing, Sri Lanka)

2004 (6 Aug). Olympic Games, Athens. T **761** and similar diamond-shaped designs. Multicoloured. P 13.

1708	4r.50 Type **761**	15	10
1709	16r.50 Woman sprinting	60	75
1710	17r. Shooting	60	75
1711	20r. Men's athletics	70	90
1708/11 Set of 4...		1·90	2·25

762 Sri Siddartha Buddharakkhita

763 Robert Gunawardena

(W. Kurukulasooriya, Litho Dept of Govt Printing, Sri Lanka)

2004 (16 Aug). Most Venerable Sri Siddartha Buddharakkhita (the first Maha Nayaka of the Malwatta Chapter) Commemoration. P 13.

1712	**762**	4r.50 purple-brown...	40	30

(Des P. Ediriweera. Litho Dept of Govt Printing, Sri Lanka)

2004 (23 Aug). Robert Gunawardena (revolutionary politician) Commemoration. P 14.

1713	**763**	4r.50 multicoloured...	40	30

764 Junius Richard Jayewardene

765 Dove

(Des W. Kulakulasooriya. Litho Dept of Govt Printing, Sri Lanka)

2004 (17 Sept). 98th Birth Anniv of Junius Richard Jayewardene (first Executive President of Sri Lanka). P 13.

1714	**764**	4r.50 multicoloured...	40	30

(Des Mevan Fonseka. Litho Dept of Govt Printing, Sri Lanka)

2004 (21 Sept). International Day of Peace. P 13.

1715	**765**	4r.50 multicoloured...	40	30

766 Sri Chandraratne Manawasinghe

767 Government Service Buddhist Association Headquarters

(Des P. Ediriweera. Litho Dept of Govt Printing, Sri Lanka)

2004 (6 Oct). 40th Death Anniv of Sri Chandraratne Manawasinghe (writer). P 12×13½.

1716   **766**   4r.50 multicoloured 40   30

(Des Palitha Gunasinghe. Litho Dept of Govt Printing, Sri Lanka)

2004 (7 Oct). 50th Anniv of the Government Service Buddhist Association. P 13.

1717   **767**   4r.50 multicoloured 40   30

768 Two Different Postal Workers

769 Raddelle Sri Pannaloka Anunayaka Thero

(Des Sudath Jayawardena. Litho Dept of Govt Printing, Sri Lanka)

2004 (9 Oct). World Post Day. P 12×13½.

1718   **768**   4r.50 multicoloured 40   30

(Des W. Kulakulasooriya. Litho Dept of Govt Printing, Sri Lanka)

2004 (20 Oct). 60th Death Anniv of Most Venerable Raddelle Sri Pannaloka Anunayaka Thero (priest). P 13.

1719   **769**   4r.50 multicoloured 40   30

770 The Nativity and Dove of Peace

771 Stylised Buildings, Computer Terminals, Houses, Screen with Atlas and Satellite Dish

(Des Mevan Fonseca. Litho Dept of Govt Printing, Sri Lanka)

2004 (27 Nov). Christmas. T **770** and similar multicoloured design. P 14 (No. 1720) or 13½×12 (No. 1721).

1720   5r. Type **770** 35   20
1721   20r. Rev. Fr. Jacome Gonsalves, Bolawatta Roman Catholic Church and Rt. Rev. Dr. Edmond Peiris (60×25 *mm*) 90   1·25

(Des Sudath Jayawardena. Litho Dept of Govt Printing, Sri Lanka)

2004 (29 Nov). Information and Communication Technology Week. P 14.

1722   **771**   5r. multicoloured 40   30

772 De Soysa Hospital for Women

773 Thalalle Siri Dhammananda Maha Nayaka Thero

(Des K. Gunasekara. Litho Dept of Govt Printing, Sri Lanka)

2004 (11 Dec). 125th Anniv of De Soysa Hospital for Women. P 14.

1723   **772**   5r. multicoloured 50   30

(Des W. Kurukulasooriya. Litho Dept of Govt Printing, Sri Lanka)

2005 (13 Mar). Most Venerable Thalalle Siri Dhammananda Maha Nayaka Thero (academic) Commemoration. P 14.

1724   **773**   5r. multicoloured 40   30

.50   .50   .50
(**774**)   (**775**)   (**776**)

2005 (21 Mar). No. 684 surch as T **774**.

1725   50c. on 10c. Type **255** .... 2·50   1·25

2005 (21 Mar). No. 964 surch as T **775** and No. 967 surch as T **776**.

1726   50c. on 35c. Type **385** .... 2·25   1·25
1727   50c. on 6r. Fiddler Crab .... 2·25   1·25

.50
(**777**)

2005 (21 Mar). No. 1090 surch as T **777**.

1728   50c. on 5r.75 Lunar surface and Earth from Moon .... 2·25   1·25

778 Prof. Hammalawa Saddhatissa Nayaka Maha Thero

779 T. B. Tennakoon

(Des Pulasthi Ediriweera. Litho Dept of Govt Printing, Sri Lanka)

2005 (22 Mar). 15th Death Anniv of Prof. Hammalawa Saddhatissa Nayaka Maha Thero (academic). P 14.

1729   **778**   5r. multicoloured 40   30

(Des W. Kurukulasooriya. Litho Dept of Govt Printing, Sri Lanka)

2005 (25 Mar). 25th Death Anniv of T. B. Tennakoon (poet and politician). P 14.

1730   **779**   5r. multicoloured 40   30

780 Don Alwin Rajapaksa

781 Ambulatory Meditation

(Des Sanjeewa Siribaddana. Litho Dept of Govt Printing, Sri Lanka)

2005 (25 Mar). Birth Centenary of Don Alwin Rajapaksa (politician). P 13½×14.

1731   **780**   5r. multicoloured 40   30

(Des S. Wickramasinghe. Litho Dept of Govt Printing, Sri Lanka)

2005 (12 May). Vesak (Buddha Day). T **781** and similar vert designs. Multicoloured. P 14.

1732   4r.50 Type **781** 30   20
1733   5r. Spiritual bliss through Buddhism 35   25
1734   10r. Meditation in standing posture 65   65
1735   50r. Sedentary meditation .... 3·00   3·50
1732/5 *Set of 4* .... 3·75   4·25
MS1736 98×149 mm. Nos. 1732/5 .... 3·75   4·50

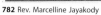

782 Rev. Marcelline Jayakody

783 Stylised Family under Helmet

(Des W. Kurukulasooriya. Litho Dept of Govt Printing, Sri Lanka)

2005 (3 June). Rev. Marcelline Jayakody (Catholic Priest, film personality and song writer) Commemoration. P 13.

1737	**782**	20r. multicoloured		1·50	2·00

(Des W. Kurukulasooriya. Litho Dept of Govt Printing, Sri Lanka)

2005 (7 June). National Rana Viru Day. P 14×13½.

1738	**783**	50r. multicoloured		2·50	3·00

Nos. 1739, T **784** are vacant.

785 Deshamanya M. A. Bakeer Markar

786 Most Ven. Matara Kithalagama Sri Seelalankara Nayaka Thero

(Des P. Ediriweera. Litho Dept of Govt Printing, Sri Lanka)

2005 (20 July). Deshamanya M. A. Bakeer Markar (former Speaker of Parliament and Governor of Southern Province) Commemoration. P 14.

1740	**785**	5r. multicoloured		40	30

(Des P. Ediriweera. Litho Dept of Govt Printing, Sri Lanka)

2005 (21 July). Most Ven. Matara Kithalagama Sri Seelalankara Nayaka Thero (Buddhist monk) Commemoration. P 14.

1741	**786**	25r. multicoloured		1·25	1·75

787 South Asian Scenes

(Des W. Perera. Litho Dept of Govt Printing, Sri Lanka)

2005 (29 July). SAARC South Asia Tourism Year. P 13.

1742	**787**	100r. multicoloured		5·00	6·00

788 Kalutara Bodhi and Dagoba

(Des S. R. Wickramasinghe. Litho Dept of Govt Printing, Sri Lanka)

2005 (6 Aug). Kalutara Bodhi and Dagoba. P 13½×14.

1743	**788**	5r. multicoloured		40	30

789 New Postal Headquarters, Colombo

(**790**)

(Des W. Wasantha Perera. Litho Dept of Govt Printing, Sri Lanka)

2005 (12 Sept). Opening of New Postal Headquarters, Colombo. P 14.

1744	**789**	5r. multicoloured		40	30

2005 (16 Sept). No. 1549 surch with T **790**.

1745		50c. on 2r. bright emerald		2·00	1·00

791 National Seminary, Ampitiya

792 Letter and Parcel encircling Globe

(Des K. Gunasekara. Litho Dept of Govt Printing, Sri Lanka)

2005 (1 Oct). 50th Anniv of National Seminary of Our Lady of Sri Lanka, Ampitiya, Senkadagala. P 14.

1746	**791**	10r. multicoloured		60	70

(Des P. Gunasinghe. Litho Dept of Govt Printing, Sri Lanka)

2005 (9 Oct). World Post Day. P 13½×14.

1747	**792**	5r. multicoloured		40	30

793 Emblem

(Des S. Jayawardena. Litho Dept of Govt Printing, Sri Lanka)

2005 (11 Oct). 25th Anniv of the General Sir John Kotelawala Defence Academy. P 13.

1748	**793**	5r. multicoloured		50	35

794 Mary, Baby Jesus and Angel

(Des P. Ediriweera. Litho Dept of Govt Printing, Sri Lanka)

2005 (3 Dec). Christmas. T **794** and similar horiz design. Multicoloured. P 14.

1749		5r. Type **794**		35	15
1750		30r. Nativity		1·75	2·25
MS1751		93×132 mm. Nos. 1749/50		2·10	2·40

795 UN Emblem and Sri Lanka Flag

796 Higher Ordination (Upasampada) Ceremony

(Des Sudath Jayawardena. Litho Dept of Govt Printing, Sri Lanka)

2005 (13 Dec). 50th Anniv of Sri Lanka's Admission to the United Nations. P 14.

| 1752 | **795** | 20r. multicoloured | 1·40 | 1·75 |

(Des P. Gunasinghe. Litho Dept of Govt Printing, Sri Lanka)

2005 (20 Dec). Bicentenary of Sri Lanka Amarapura Maha Nikaya. P 14.

| 1753 | **796** | 10r. multicoloured | 60 | 70 |

797 Minihagalkanda Area and Stone Tools

(Des Pulasthi Ediriweera. Litho Dept of Govt Printing, Sri Lanka)

2005 (21 Dec). Ancient Sri Lanka (1st series). Prehistoric Era. T **797** and similar horiz designs. Multicoloured. P 13½×12.

1754	5r. Type **797**	40	30
1755	20r. Extinct elephant, hippo and rhinoceros and bone fragments	1·50	1·50
1756	25r. Kuruwita, Batadomba-lena and human skull	1·50	1·75
1757	30r. Horton Plains and fossilised barley pollen	1·60	2·00
1754/7	Set of 4	4·50	5·00

798 Wrecked Vehicles and Post Office Ruins, Kalmunai

(Des Mevan Fonseka. Litho Dept of Govt Printing, Sril Lanka)

2005 (26 Dec). First Anniv of Tsunami Disaster. T **798** and similar horiz designs. Multicoloured. P 13½×14.

1758	5r. Type **798**	45	15
1759	20r. Wreckage of train	1·50	1·50
1760	30r. Tsunami wave	1·60	2·00
1761	33r. Tsunami waves and lighthouse	2·00	2·50
1758/61	Set of 4	5·00	5·50

799 *Muntiacus muntjak* ("Barking Deer")

(Des K. Gunasekara. Litho Dept of Govt Printing, Sri Lanka)

2006 (4 Jan). National Parks of Sri Lanka (1st series). Wilpattu National Park. T **799** and similar horiz designs. Multicoloured. P 13½×12.

1762	5r. Type **799**	40	15
1763	10r. White-bellied Sea Eagle	1·25	75
1764	20r. Sloth Bear	1·40	1·40
1765	50r. Leopard	2·75	4·00
1762/5	Set of 4	5·25	5·50

MS1766 Four sheets, each 99×69 mm. (a) No. 1762. (b) No. 1763. (c) No. 1764. (d) No. 1765 *Set of 4 sheets* ... 5·25 6·00

800 Emblem

801 1957 First Ceylon Postage Stamp Centenary 35c. Stamp

(Des Mevan Fonseka. Litho Dept of Govt Printing, Sri Lanka)

2006 (6 Jan). Centenary of The Institution of Engineers, Sri Lanka. P 12×13½.

| 1767 | **800** | 5r. new blue and black | 40 | 30 |

(Des Studio Labranda. Litho Enschedé)

2006 (2 Feb). 50th Anniv of First Europa Stamp. T **801** and similar vert designs. Multicoloured. P 13×13½.

1768	100r. Type **801**	2·50	2·75
1769	500r. Map of Europe and galleon	10·00	13·00
MS1770	100×72 mm. Nos. 1768/9	12·00	16·00

802 Most Ven. Madithiyawala Vijithasena Anunayaka Thero

803 Cricket Balls and Match

(Des Wasantha Shrinath Kurukulasooriya. Litho Dept of Govt Printing, Sri Lanka)

2006 (5 Mar). Most Ven. Madithiyawala Vijithasena Anunayaka Thero Commemoration. P 14.

| 1771 | **802** | 17r. multicoloured | 1·00 | 1·00 |

(Des Sanath Rohana Wickramasinghe. Litho Dept of Govt Printing, Sri Lanka)

2006 (24 Mar). Centenary Cricket Match between Kingswood College and Dharmaraja College, Kandy. P 14.

| 1772 | **803** | 4r.50 multicoloured | 1·50 | 1·00 |

804 Anagarika Dharmapala (founder) and First *Sinhala Baudhhaya* Newspaper

805 Cadet Corps Emblem

(Des N. Sangabo Dias. Litho Dept of Govt Printing, Sri Lanka)

2006 (7 May). Centenary of *Sinhala Baudhhaya* (Buddhist newspaper). P 14.

| 1773 | **804** | 5r. multicoloured | 40 | 30 |

(Des M. Fonseka. Litho Dept of Govt Printing, Sri Lanka)

2006 (18 May). 125th Anniv of National Cadet Corps. P 12×13½.

| 1774 | **805** | 2r. multicoloured | 30 | 20 |

806 "A Plea to the Master to descend from the Heaven" (wall painting) and Tivamka Image House, Polonnaruva

(Litho Dept of Govt Printing, Sri Lanka)

2006 (5 May). 2550th Anniv of Buddha Jayanthi (Vesak). T **806** and similar horiz designs. Multicoloured. P 13½×12.

1775	2r.50	Type **806**	20	25
		a. Sheet. Nos. 1775/1824	20·00	22·00
		b. Sheetlet. Nos. 1775/84	2·00	2·75
1776	2r.50	"Queen Mahamaya on her Way to Visit her Parents" (bas relief) and Jetavana Vihara, Anuradhapura	20	25
1777	2r.50	"The Great Birth of Prince Siddhartha" (wall painting) and Shailabimbarama Vihara, Dodanduwa	20	25
1778	2r.50	"Asita, the Royal Teacher visits Prince Siddhartha" (wall painting) and Purwarama Viharaya, Kataluva	20	25
1779	2r.50	"The Great Renunciation" (bas relief) and Girihandu Vihara, Ambalantota	20	25
1780	2r.50	"Defeat of Maras (evils) by the Master" (rock painting) and Hindagala Vihara, Hindagala	20	25
1781	2r.50	"The First Sermon of Dhammachakka pavattana sutta" (rock painting) and Rangiri Dambulu Vihara, Dambulla	20	25
1782	2r.50	"The Conversion of Alavaka, a Demon" (wall painting) and Sapugoda Vihara, Beruvala	20	25
1783	2r.50	"The Great Funeral Pyre of the Master" (wall painting) and Veheragalla Samudragiri Vihara, Mirissa	20	25
1784	2r.50	"Tapassu and Bhalluka arriving in Sri Lanka with the Relics of the Master" and Girihandu seya, Tiriyaya	20	25
1785	4r.50	"Perfection of generosity: Vessantara Jataka" (wall painting) and Bodhirukkharama Vihara, Eluvapitiya	30	35
		b. Sheetlet. Nos. 1785/94	3·50	4·00
1786	4r.50	"Perfection of wisdom: Paduma Jataka" (rock painting) and Kaballelena Vihara, Wariyapola	30	35
1787	4r.50	"Perfection of renunciation: Sutasoma Jataka" (wall painting) and Degaldoruva Vihara, Kandy	30	35
1788	4r.50	"Perfection of Equanimity: Sivi Jataka" (wall painting) and Paramakanda Vihara, Anamaduwa	30	35
1789	4r.50	"Perfection of Loving-kindness: Sachchankira Jataka" (wall painting) and Sunandarama Vihara, Ambalangoda	30	35
1790	4r.50	"Recitation of Chullahastipadopama sutta by Arhat Mahinda" and the Stupa at Mihintale	30	35
1791	4r.50	Establishment of Buddhism in Sri Lanka and the Rajagiri lena, Mihintale	30	35
1792	4r.50	Sri Maha Bodhi entering the City and the Sri Maha Bodhi at Anuradhapura	30	35
1793	4r.50	Writing Dhamma on ola leafs and Alu Vihara, Matale	30	35
1794	4r.50	Arrival of the tooth relic of the Master and coast at Lankapattana in Trincomalee	30	35
1795	5r.	"The practice of Aranyaka tradition" (drawing) and Situlpavuva Vihara	30	35
		b. Sheetlet. Nos. 1795/1804	3·50	4·00
1796	5r.	Lovamahapaya Abhayagiri vihara, Vajra symbol and lotus	30	35
1797	5r.	Emergence of katikavatas (treaty) and Vatadage in Polonnaruwa	30	35
1798	5r.	Buddhist discourse between Sri Lanka and south east Asia and Tooth Relic Temple, Kandy	30	35
1799	5r.	Translation of the Tripitaka into Sinhala and the Buddhajayanti Vihara, Columbo	30	35
1800	5r.	Vesak festival and Deepaduttarama Vihara, Kothana	30	35
1801	5r.	Serving food to Buddhist clergy and the refectory at Abhayagiriya, Anuradhapura	30	35
1802	5r.	Chanting Paritta and the Nishshanka Lata Mandapa in Polonnaruwa	30	35
1803	5r.	Village, temple, tank and Tissamaharama Stupa	30	35
1804	5r.	Veneration of the Bodhi tree and Bodhighara, Nillakgama	30	35
1805	10r.	Hatthikuchchi Vihara in Galgamuva and a Padhanaghara in Anuradhapura	50	55
		b. Sheetlet. Nos. 1805/14	5·50	6·00
1806	10r.	A ritual performance for the tooth relic and Atadage, Polonnaruva	50	55
1807	10r.	"Perahara" (painting) and Subodharama Vihara, Karagampitiya	50	55
1808	10r.	Street market (wall painting), Mulgirigala Vihara and ancient coin	50	55

1809	10r.	Sanctity of the temple (painting) and Namal Uyana in Ranava	50	55
1810	10r.	Great Stupas in Rajarata: Ruvanvalisaya and Thuparama in Anuradhapura	50	55
1811	10r.	Great Stupas in Ruhuna: Kirivehera at Kataragama and Stupa at Seruvila	50	55
1812	10r.	Great Stupas in Uva and the north: at Mahiyangana and Nagadipa, Jaffna	50	55
1813	10r.	Stupa at Kelaniya and the Samantakuta	50	55
1814	10r.	Mutiyangana Stupa at Badulla and Stupa at Deeghavapi	50	55
1815	17r.	Painted Stupas: Hanguranketa Raja Maha Vihara and ancient stupas at Kandarodai	75	80
		b. Sheetlet. Nos. 1815/24	8·00	9·00
1816	17r.	Façade of stupa at Mihintale and "Bahiravas" (bas-relief)	75	80
1817	17r.	The Twin-pond at Anuradhapura and Punkalasa (lotus pond) at Polonnaruva	75	80
1818	17r.	Ruins of Mangul Maha Vihara in Lahugala and moonstone	70	80
1819	17r.	Ruins of Muhudumaha Vihara in Potuvil and Bodhisattva Avalokiteshvara (statue)	75	80
1820	17r.	Nalanda Gedige at Naula and Satmahal Prasada at Polonnaruva	75	80
1821	17r.	Ruins and drawing of Lankatilaka Vihara, Polonnaruva	75	80
1822	17r.	Tampita Vihara, Menikkadawara and Thuparama Image House, Polonnaruva	75	80
1823	17r.	"The Buddhist Cosmos" (wall painting) and Omalpe Vihara, Kolonne	75	80
1824	17r.	Madanvala Vihara, Hanguranketa and Makara Torana motif	75	80
1775/1824 Set of 50			20·00	22·00

Nos. 1775/824 were printed together, *se-tenant*, in sheets of 50 (5×10). Nos. 1775/84, 1785/94, 1795/1804, 1805/14 and 1815/24 were also each printed together, *se-tenant*, in sheetlets of ten stamps of the same value.

807 Kotte Sri Kalyani Samagridharma Maha Sanga Sabha

808 Sri Lanka Ramanna Maha Nikaya

(Des K. Gunasekara. Litho Dept of Govt Printing, Sri Lanka)

2006 (25 June). 150th Anniv of First Higher Ordination Ceremony of Kotte Sri Kalyani Samagridharma Maha Sanga Sabha. P 14.

1825	**807**	4r.50 multicoloured	40	30

(Des S. Dias. Litho Dept of Govt Printing, Sri Lanka)

2006 (29 June). 65th Upasampada (Higher Ordination) Ceremony of Sri Lanka Ramanna Maha Nikaya. P 14.

1826	**808**	4r.50 multicoloured	40	30

809 Boys

810 Lakshman Kadirgamar

(Des B. Cooray. Litho Dept of Govt Printing, Sri Lanka)

2006 (15 July). 125th Anniv of St. Vincent's Boys Home, Maggona. P 14.

1827	**809**	10r. multicoloured	60	70

(Des V. S. Kurukulasooriya. Litho Dept of Govt Printing, Sri Lanka)

2006 (10 Aug). Lakshman Kadirgamar (Minister of Foreign Affairs 1994–2001, 2004–5) Commemoration. P 14.

1828	**810**	10r. multicoloured	60	70

811 St. John Dal Bastone and St. John Dal Bastone Church

812 St. John Ambulance and Volunteers with Casualty

(Des P. Ediriweera. Litho Dept of Govt Printing, Sri Lanka)

2006 (13 Aug). 125th Anniv of St. John Dal Bastone Church, Talangama South. P 14.

1829	**811**	5r. multicoloured	40	30

(Des G. Abeykoon. Litho Dept of Govt Printing, Sri Lanka)

2006 (15 Aug). Centenary of St. John Ambulance in Sri Lanka. P 14.

1830	**812**	5r. multicoloured	1·00	80

813 High Jump

814 St. Joseph's Church, Wennappuwa

(Des M. Fonseka. Litho Dept of Govt Printing, Sri Lanka)

2006 (17 Aug). Tenth South Asian Games, Colombo. T **813** and similar horiz designs. Multicoloured. P 14.

1831		10r. Type **813**	60	40
1832		100r. Cycling	5·00	6·00

(Des R. De Silva. Litho Dept of Govt Printing, Sri Lanka)

2006 (23 Aug). 125th Anniv of St. Joseph's Church, Wennappuwa. P 13½×14.

1833	**814**	2r. multicoloured	25	20

815 Professor Senaka Bibile

816 Children and Globe

(Des V. S. Kurukulasooriya. Litho Dept of Govt Printing, Sri Lanka)

2006 (29 Sept). Professor Senaka Bibile (founder of State Pharmaceuticals Corporation) Commemoration. P 12×13½.

1834	**815**	10r. multicoloured	60	70

(Des P. U. Samaraweera. Litho Dept of Govt Printing, Sri Lanka)

2006 (1 Oct). World Children's Day. P 13½×14.

1835	**816**	5r. multicoloured	40	30

817 *Nelumbo nucifera* (Sacred Lotus), Western Province

818 "Post for All–For All Places" (Kanchana Imesha Gimhani)

(Des K. Gunasekara. Litho Dept of Govt Printing, Sri Lanka)

2006 (2 Oct). Provincial Flowers of Sri Lanka. T **817** and similar vert designs. Multicoloured. P 14.

1836		4r.50 Type **817**	50	30
	a.	Sheetlet. No. 1836 and 1838, each ×4	18·00	
1837		4r.50 *Cassia fistula* (Indian laburnum), North-Central Province	50	30
	a.	Sheetlet. No. 1837 and 1839, each ×4	18·00	
1838		50r. *Murraya paniculata* (orange jessmine), North-Western Province	4·50	5·00
1839		50r. *Rhynchostylis retusa* (foxtail orchid), Uva-Province	4·50	5·00
1836/9	*Set of 4*		9·00	9·50

Nos. 1836/9 were issued in separate sheets of 100.

Nos. 1836 and 1838, and 1837 and 1839, respectively, were also each printed together, *se-tenant*, in sheetlets of eight stamps.

2006 (9 Oct). World Post Day. Winning Entry in Children's Art Competition. P 14.

1840	**818**	40r. multicoloured	3·00	3·50

(**819**)

820 "Birth of Holy Jesus" (Ann Ruchini Prasanika Fernando)

2006 (27 Oct). No. 1550 surch with T **819**.

1841	20r. on 3r. deep cinnamon	3·00	3·00

(Des B. Cooray. Litho Dept of Govt Printing, Sri Lanka)

2006 (13 Nov). Christmas. T **820** and similar multicoloured design. P 14×13½ (5r.) or 13½×14 (20r.).

1842	5r. Type **820**	50	25
1843	20r. St. Anthony's Shrine, Wahakotte (*horiz*)	1·60	2·00

821 Rugby Players

(Des W. Perera. Litho Dept of Govt Printing, Sri Lanka)

2006 (8 Dec). 125 Years (2004) of Rugby Football in Sri Lanka. P 13.

1844	**821**	4r.50 multicoloured	75	40

822 D. M. Rajapaksa

823 Vee Bissakara Govijana Chaityaya, Ambuluwawa

(Des N. Sangabo Dias. Litho Dept of Govt Printing, Sri Lanka)

2006 (14 Dec). D. M. Rajapaksa (peasants leader, educationist and member of Hambantota District Council 1936–45) Commemoration. P 14×13½.

1845	**822**	5r. multicoloured	40	30

(Des S. Jayawardena. Litho Dept of Govt Printing, Sri Lanka)

2006 (18 Dec). Biodiversity Complex and Religious Centre, Ambuluwawa. T **823** and similar multicoloured design. P 12×13½ (5r.) or 13½×14 (25r.).

1846	5r. Type **823**	35	25
1847	25r. Biodiversity Complex, Ambuluwawa (40×30 mm)	1·40	1·75

10.00

(824)

2006 (28 Dec). No. 1355 surch with T **824**.

1848	10r. on 11r. on 10r.50 Mats	5·00	3·00

825 Kande Viharaya, Aluthgama

(Des G. Abaykoon. Litho Dept of Govt Printing, Sri Lanka)

2007 (6 Jan). Inauguration of New Giant Buddha Statue at Kande Vihara, Aluthgama. P 13½×14.

1849	**825**	5r. multicoloured	40	30

50.00

(826)

2007 (8 Jan). No. 715 surch with T **826**.

1850	50r. on 1r.60 black, greenish yellow and brown-purple	8·00	8·00

4.50   **4.50**

(827)   (828)

2007 (29 Jan). Nos. 459 and 518 of Ceylon and Nos. 610, 1042 and 1487 surch as Types **827** or **828**.

1851	4r.50 on 50c. indigo and slate-grey (No. 459 of Ceylon) (as T **827**)	1·00	80
1852	4r.50 on 50c. Type **161** (T **827**)	1·00	80
1853	4r.50 on 1r.15 Type **220** (T **828**)	1·00	80
1854	4r.50 on 5r.75 magenta, royal blue and black (No. 1042) (as T **828**)	1·00	80
1855	4r.50 on 22r. Elk-horn coral (No. 1487) (as T **827**)	1·00	80
1851/5 *Set of 5*		4·50	3·50

829 Sigiriya, Sri Lanka and Great Wall of China

(Des Sudath Jayawardena. Litho Dept of Govt Printing, Sri Lanka)

2007 (7 Feb). 50th Anniv of Sri Lanka–China Diplomatic Relations. P 13½×12.

1856	**829**	50r. multicoloured	3·75	4·25

5.00

(830)

2007 (13 Feb). Nos. 457 and 524 of Ceylon and Nos. 1085, 1321 and 1640 surch as T **777** and No. 1552 surch with T **830**.

1857	50c. on 35c. red and deep green (No. 457)	1·25	1·25
1858	50c. on 60c. Adam's Peak (No. 524)	1·25	1·25
1859	50c. on 5r.75 Type **456** (No. 1085)	1·25	1·25
1860	50c. on 8r.50 Pottery (No. 1321)	1·25	1·25
1861	50c. on 26r. Tusker (No. 1640)	1·25	1·25
1862	5r. on 4r. bright rose (No. 1552)	2·50	2·50
1857/62 *Set of 6*		8·00	8·00

831 Batsman and Ball

(Des Sudath Jayawardena. Litho Dept of Govt Printing, Sri Lanka)

2007 (23 Feb). World Cup Cricket, West Indies. T **831** and similar diamond-shaped design. Multicoloured. P 13.

1863	5r. Type **831**	70	40
1864	50r. Sri Lanka team and national flag	5·00	6·00

832 I. M. R. A. Iriyagolle   **833** Ceylon 1857 6d. Stamp and Mail Steamship

(Des Wasantha Srinath Kurukulasooriya. Litho Dept of Govt Printing, Sri Lanka)

2007 (20 Mar). Birth Centenary of Imiya Mudiyanselage Raphiel Abayawansa Iriyagolle (Minister of Education and Culture, 1965–70). P 14½×14.

1865	**832**	5r. multicoloured	40	30

(Des Pulasthi Ediriweera. Litho Dept of Govt Printing, Sri Lanka)

2007 (1 Apr). 150th Anniv of the First Sri Lanka (Ceylon) Stamps. T **833** and similar horiz designs. Multicoloured. P 13½×14.

1866	5r. Type **833**	35	25
1867	10r. Ceylon 1857 5d., 10d. and 1s. stamps and mail runner	75	85
1868	20r. Ceylon 1857 1d., and 2d. stamps and mail canoe	1·40	1·60
1869	45r. Ceylon 1857 ½d. stamp and mail coach	3·50	4·25
1866/9 *Set of 4*		5·50	6·25
MS1870 130×112 mm. Nos. 1866/9		6·00	7·00

834 King and Queen (kneeling), King with Courtiers and House with Sivavatuka (bird) Figure

(Des Palitha Gunasinghe. Litho Dept of Govt Printing, Sri Lanka)

2007 (20 Apr). Vesak. T **834** and similar horiz designs showing "Thelpattha Jathaka" wall paintings from Sri Sudharshanaramaya Vihara. Multicoloured. P 13½×14.

1871	5r. Type **834**		35	55
	a. Horiz pair. Nos. 1871/2		70	1·10
1872	5r. King with courtiers and house with woman levitating and unconscious man		35	55
1873	20r. King on throne and riding elephant in procession led by drummers		1·40	2·00
	a. Horiz pair. Nos. 1873/4		2·75	4·00
1874	20r. Couple in bedroom, people tempted and devoured by demons of sensual pleasure and King on throne and riding elephant		1·40	2·00
1871/4 Set of 4			3·25	4·50
MS1875 100×170 mm. Nos. 1871/4			3·50	4·50

835 Sri Lanka Team and Stadium **836** Textile Cone

(Des Sanath Rohana Wickramasinghe. Litho Dept of Govt Printing, Sri Lanka)

2007 (30 Apr). Sri Lanka–Runner Up In World Cup Cricket, West Indies. T **835** and similar horiz design. Multicoloured. P 13½×14.

1876	15r. Type **835**	2·50	2·75
1877	15r. Mahela Jayawardena (team captain) and cricketers in action	2·50	2·75

(Des W. Vasantha Perera. Litho Dept of Govt Printing, Sri Lanka)

2007 (22 May). Seashells of Sri Lanka. T **836** and similar horiz designs. Multicoloured. P 14.

1878	5r. Type **836**	35	25
1879	12r. Aquatile Hairy Triton	90	1·00
1880	15r. Rose Branched Murex	1·10	1·25
1881	45r. Trapezium Horse-conch	3·50	4·25
1878/81 Set of 4		5·25	6·00
MS1882 228×137 mm. Nos. 1878/81		5·75	6·75

No. **MS**1882 was cut around in the shape of a trapezium horse-conch shell.

837 Scout Leader, Rover Scout, Senior Scout and Cub Scout **838** Shield

(Des Kumudu Tharaka. Litho Dept of Govt Printing, Sri Lanka)

2007 (26 May). Centenary of World Scouting. P 13½×12.

1883	**837**	5r. multicoloured	40	30

(Des Kelum Gunasekara. Litho Dept of Govt Printing, Sri Lanka)

2007 (17 June). Centenary of Sri Sangamitta Balika Maha Vidyalaya (girls' school), Matale. P 12×13½.

1884	**838**	5r. multicoloured	40	30

839 Flowers and Temples

(Des Mevan Fonseka. Litho Dept of Govt Printing, Sri Lanka)

2007 (26 June). 50th Anniv (2006) of the Sri Lanka–Japan Friendship Society. P 13½×12.

1885	**839**	15r. multicoloured	1·10	1·40

840 Emblem **841** Bogambara and Welikada Prisons and Rehabilitation Emblem

(Des Gamini Abeykoon. Litho Dept of Govt Printing, Sri Lanka)

2007 (3 July). 50th Anniv of Ceylon Baithulmal Fund. P 12×13½.

1886	**840**	5r. multicoloured	40	30

(Des Sanath Rohana Wickramasinghe. Litho Dept of Govt Printing, Sri Lanka)

2007 (16 July). Sri Lanka Prisons Day. P 14.

1887	**841**	5r. multicoloured	40	30

842 Emblem **843** Founding of Buddhist Vihara in Berlin

(Des Kelum Gunasekara. Litho Dept of Govt Printing, Sri Lanka)

2007 (27 July). 104th Anniv of K/Jabbar Central College, Galagedara. P 13½×12.

1888	**842**	5r. multicoloured	40	30

(Des Nihal Sangabo Dias. Litho Dept of Govt Printing, Sri Lanka)

2007 (22 Aug). 50th Anniv of First Buddhist Mission to Germany. P 13.

1889	**843**	5r. multicoloured	40	30

844 Queen Mahamaya Sculpture, Adam's Peak, Mount Everest and Mayadevi Sculpture

(Des Kelum Gunasekara. Litho Dept of Govt Printing, Sri Lanka)

2007 (1 Sept). 50th Anniv of Sri Lanka–Nepal Diplomatic Relations. P 13.

1890	**844**	15r. multicoloured	1·40	2·00

845 Statue and Shrine of Our Lady of Matara

(Des Kelum Gunasekara. Litho Dept of Govt Printing, Sri Lanka)

2007 (9 Sept). Centenary of the Shrine of Our Lady of Matara. P 13.
1891　**845**　5r. multicoloured .... 40　30

846 Basket-maker, Ayurvedic Medicine, Dancer and Chef　　**847** Emblem

(Des Palitha Gunasinghe. Litho Dept of Govt Printing, Sri Lanka)

2007 (27 Sept). World Tourism Day. "Tourism opens Doors for Women". P 13.
1892　**846**　5r. multicoloured .... 40　30

(Des Ruwan Upasena. Litho Dept of Govt Printing, Sri Lanka)

2007 (6 Oct). 50th Anniv of Lions International in Sri Lanka. P 12×13½.
1893　**847**　5r. multicoloured .... 40　30

848 IMS Ribbon connecting Letter Recipients Worldwide

(Des W. Vasantha Perera. Litho Dept of Govt Printing, Sri Lanka)

2007 (9 Oct). World Post Day. P 13½×12.
1894　**848**　5r. multicoloured .... 40　30

849 Aries　　**850** Young Farmers and Produce

(Des Sudath Jayawardena and Pulasthi Ediriweera. Litho Dept of Govt Printing, Sri Lanka)

2007 (9 Oct). Constellations. T **849** and similar vert designs. Multicoloured. P 13 (50c. to 25r.) or 12×13½ (30 to 45r.).

(a) 19×24 mm

1895A	50c. Type **849**	10	10
1896A	1r. Taurus	10	10
1897A	2r. Gemini	15	10
1898A	3r. Cancer	20	15
1899A	4r. Leo	30	20
1900A	4r.50 Virgo	35	25
1901A	5r. Libra	35	25
1902A	10r. Scorpius	80	85
1903A	12r. Sagittarius	90	95
1904A	15r. Capricornus	1·10	1·25
1905A	20r. Aquarius	1·50	1·75
1906A	25r. Pisces	2·10	2·25

(b) Size 25×30 mm

1907	30r. Centaurus	2·25	2·50
1908	35r. Ursa major	2·50	2·75
1909	40r. Ophiuchus	2·75	3·00
1910	45r. Orion	3·50	3·75
1895A/1910 *Set of 16*		17·00	18·00
MS1911 100×95 mm. Nos. 1895A/1906A. P 13 ...		16·00	17·00
MS1912 119×50 mm. Nos. 1907/10. P 12×13½		27·00	28·00

(c) As Nos. 1895A/1906A but on granite paper with fluorescent fibres and perf 13 with one elliptical hole in each horiz side an one notched elliptical hole in each vert side

1895B	50c. Type **849**	10	10
1896B	1r. Taurus	10	10

1897B	2r. Gemini	15	10
1898B	3r. Cancer	20	15
1899B	4r. Leo	30	20
1900B	4r.50 Virgo	35	25
1901B	5r. Libra	35	25
1902B	10r. Scorpius	80	85
1903B	12r. Sagittarius	90	95
1904B	15r. Capricornus	1·10	1·25
1905B	20r. Aquarius	1·50	1·75
1906B	25r. Pisces	2·10	2·25
1895B/1906B *Set of 12*		7·25	7·50

Nos. 1895A/1906A were on paper with shiny gum, 1895B/1906B had matt gum: some of the higher values have also been reported with matt as well as shiny gum.

(Des Nihal Sangabo Dias. Litho Dept of Govt Printing, Sri Lanka)

2007 (16 Oct). National Farmers Day. P 13.
1913　**850**　5r. multicoloured .... 40　30

851 Water Buffaloes

(Des Sudath Jayawardene (5, 45r., **MS**1918(a) or Pulasthi Ediriweera (15, 40r., **MS**1918(b). Litho Dept of Govt Printing, Sri Lanka)

2007 (31 Oct). National Parks of Sri Lanka (2nd series). Udawalawe National Park. T **851** and similar horiz designs. Multicoloured. P 13.

1914	5r. Type **851**	45	25
1915	15r. Elephants.	1·75	1·50
1916	40r. Ruddy Mongoose	3·00	3·50
1917	45r. Common Langur	3·50	4·00
1914/17 *Set of 4*		8·00	8·25

MS1918 Two sheets, each 126×85 mm. (a) As Type **851**; As No. 1917. (b) As Nos. 1915/16. Both P 14.. 9·00　9·50

852 Leslie Goonewardene　　**853** Emblem and Traditional Musician

(Des Vasantha Srinath Kurukulasooriya. Litho Dept of Govt Printing, Sri Lanka)

2007 (6 Nov). Birth Centenary (2009) of Leslie Goonewardene (Minister of Transport and Communications 1970–5). P 13.
1919　**852**　5r. multicoloured .... 40　30

(Des Sudath Jayawardene. Litho Dept of Govt Printing, Sri Lanka)

2007 (7 Nov). Commonwealth Games Federation General Assembly, Colombo. T **853** and similar horiz design. Multicoloured. P 13.

1920	5r. Type **853**	35	25
1921	45r. Emblem and winged figures............	3·50	4·00

854 St. Henry's College, Ilavalei

(Des Basil Cooray. Litho Dept of Govt Printing, Sri Lanka)

2007 (10 Nov). Centenary of St. Henry's College, Ilavalei. P 13.
1922　**854**　5r. multicoloured .... 40　30

855 Nativity (Minura Senal Bandara Ranatunge)

856 Muthiah Muralidaran

(Des Basil Cooray. Litho Dept of Govt Printing, Sri Lanka)

2007 (18 Nov). Christmas. T **855** and similar horiz design. Multicoloured. P 13.

1923	5r. Type **855**		35	25
1924	30r. St. James' Church, Mutwal		1·40	1·75

No. 1923 was the winning design in a children's Christmas stamp design competition on the theme of "Christmas and Unity".

(Des Pulasthi Ediriweera. Litho Dept of Govt Printing, Sri Lanka)

2007 (3 Dec). Muthiah Muralidaran (highest wicket taker in test cricket). Granite paper with fluorescent fibres. P 14.

1925	**856**	5r. multicoloured	1·50	1·00

No. 1925 is perforated in a circle enclosed in an outer perforated square. It was issued in sheets of 100 and also in sheetlets of 12 stamps containing two blocks of six (3×2) separated by a gutter containing three circular stamp-size labels.

857 Hare and Tortoise at Start of Race

858 St. Mary's Church, Maggona

(Des Bandula Harischandra. Litho Dept of Govt Printing, Sri Lanka)

2007 (9 Dec). Children's Stories (1st series). International Children's Broadcasting Day. The Race between the Hare and the Tortoise. T **857** and similar square designs. Multicoloured. P 12×13½.

1926	5r. Type **857**		35	40
	a. Horiz strip of three. Nos. 1926/8		1·00	1·10
1927	5r. Tortoise passing sleeping Hare		35	40
1928	5r. Tortoise laughing at finish and running Hare		35	40
1926/8 Set of 3			1·00	1·10

Nos. 1926/8 were printed together, se-tenant, as horizontal strips of three stamps in sheetlets of 12.

(Des Basil Cooray. Litho Dept of Govt Printing, Sri Lanka)

2007 (9 Dec). 150th Anniv of St. Mary's Church, Maggona. P 13.

1929	**858**	5r. multicoloured	40	30

859 Placard "Say No to Corruption"

(Des Sanath Rohana Wickramasinghe. Litho Dept of Govt Printing, Sri Lanka)

2007 (10 Dec). International Anti-Corruption Day. Granite paper with fluorescent fibres. P 13.

1930	**859**	5r. black and new blue	40	30

860 Rural Landscape, Map and Satellite

(Litho Dept of Govt Printing, Sri Lanka)

2008 (4 Jan). Nenasala 500 Initiative, (to provide Information and Communication Technology access to rural areas). P 13½×12.

1931	**860**	5r. multicoloured	40	30

861 Most Ven. Halgasthota Sri Devananda Mahanayaka Thero

862 National Flag and "60"

(Des Pulasthi Ediriweera. Litho Dept of Govt Printing, Sri Lanka)

2008 (30 Jan). Most Ven. Halgasthota Sri Devananda Mahanayaka Thero Commemoration. P 14.

1932	**861**	5r. multicoloured	40	30

(Des Pulasthi Ediriweera. Litho Dept of Govt Printing, Sri Lanka)

2008 (4 Feb). 60th Independence Day. P 12×13½.

1933	**862**	5r. multicoloured	40	30

863 Deshamanya N. U. Jayawardena

(Des Pulasthi Ediriweera. Litho Dept of Govt Printing, Sri Lanka)

2008 (25 Feb). Birth Centenary of Deshamanya N. U. Jayawardena (first Sri Lankan Governor of Central Bank of Sri Lanka, businessman and financier). P 13½×14.

1934	**863**	5r. multicoloured	40	30

864 Young Man and Woman releasing Peace Dove

865 St. Mary's Convent School, Matara

(Des Gamini Abeykoon. Litho Dept of Govt Printing, Sri Lanka)

2008 (26 Apr). Seventh Commonwealth Youth Ministers Meeting, Colombo. P 13½×13 (with one star-shaped perforation on each vertical side).

1935	**864**	5r. multicoloured	40	30

(Des Pulasthi Ediriweera. Litho Dept of Govt Printing, Sri Lanka)

2008 (29 Apr). Centenary of St. Mary's Convent School, Matara. P 13×13½ (with one star shaped hole on each horiz side).

1936	**865**	5r. multicoloured	40	30

866 Megalithic Cist Burial and Necklace of Beads (600–400BC)

867 King Daham Sonda and Courtiers

(Des Sudath Jayawardana. Litho Dept of Govt Printing, Sri Lanka)

2008 (30 Apr). Ancient Sri Lanka (2nd series). Proto-historic and Early Anuradhapura Periods. T **866** and similar square designs. Multicoloured. P 12×13½.

1937	5r. Type **866**	35	25
1938	10r. Abhaya (Basawakkulama) Veva (earth bank for irrigation) (3BC)	80	85
1939	12r. Vallipuram gold plate (letters in Brahmi characters) (1AD)	90	95
1940	15r. Alakolaveva iron furnace (1–2AD)	1·10	1·50
1941	30r. Gajalakshmi coin (1BC–4AD) and punch mark coin (3BC–4AD)	1·40	1·75
1942	40r. Sigiri painting (5AD)	1·60	2·00
1937/42	Set of 6	5·50	6·50

(Pulasthi Ediriweera. LItho Dept of Govt Printing, Sri Lanka)

2008 (9 May). Vesak. T **867** and similar horiz designs showing wall paintings from Reswehera Raja Maha Vihara, Kudakatnoruwa, Meegalewa. Multicoloured. P 13½×14.

1943	4r.50 Type **867**	35	25
1944	5r. Procession with elephant	35	25
1945	15r. Goddess and demon	1·10	1·40
1946	40r. King Daham Sonda	1·60	2·00
1943/6	Set of 4	3·00	3·50
MS1947	143×110 mm. Nos. 1943/6. P 13½	3·50	3·75

868 Pistol Shooting

(Des Kumudu Tharaka. Photo UAB Garsu Pasaulis, Lithuania)

2008 (23 July). Olympic Games, Beijing. T **868** and similar trapezoid designs. Multicoloured. P 13.

1948	5r. Type **868**	45	25
1949	15r. Javelin throwing	1·25	1·25
1950	40r. Boxing	1·75	2·25
1951	45r. Running	1·75	2·40
1948/51	Set of 4	4·75	5·50

869 Sigiri Painting (5AD), Flags of Member Countries and Emblem

(Des Anuruddhika Kobbekaduwa. Litho Dept of Govt Printing, Sri Lanka)

2008 (2 Aug). 15th SAARC (South Asian Association for Regional Co-operation) Summit, Colombo. P 13.

1952	**869**	15r. multicoloured	1·10	1·40

870 Takiko Yoshida

871 Clasped Hands

(Des V. Srinath Kurukulasooriya. Litho Dept of Govt Printing, Sri Lanka)

2008 (16 Aug). Birth Centenary of Takiko Yoshida (educationist and philanthropist). P 13½×13 (with one star-shaped hole on each vertical side).

1953	**870**	5r. multicoloured	40	30

(Des Mevan Fonseka. Litho Dept of Govt Printing, Sri Lanka)

2008 (11 Sept). 50th Anniv of Employees Provident Fund. P 14×13½.

1954	**871**	5r. multicoloured	40	30

872 Middle Age Gold Coin, its Mould and Gold Ingot (8–10th century AD)

(Des Basil Cooray (5, 20r.) or Gamini Abeykoon (others). Litho Dept of Govt Printing, Sri Lanka)

2008 (16 Sept). Ancient Sri Lanka (3rd series). Late Anuradhapura Era. T **872** and similar horiz designs. Multicoloured. P 13×12.

1955	5r. Type **872**	45	25
1956	10r. Remnants of Medirigiriya Vatadage and conjectural drawing of it in 7th century	90	85
1957	15r. Urinal stone at Western Monasteries, Anuradhapura and cross-section of sanitary system (7th–9th century AD)	1·25	1·40
1958	20r. Bangle, pendant, anklet and necklace of terracotta beads (8th–9th century AD)	1·50	1·75
1959	30r. Bodhisattva Vajrapani and Avalokithesvara statues at Buduruvagala and carved tableau of King Dutugemunu and family at Isurumuniya Vihara Museum (8th–9th century AD)	1·75	2·25
1955/9	Set of 5	5·25	6·00

873 Lion

874 Post Boxes

(Des Sudath Jayawardena. Photo and recess Garsu Pasulis, Lithuania)

2008 (24 Sept). Multicoloured, background colour given. Granite paper with fluorescent fibres. P 12½ (with one elliptical perforation on each side).

1960	**873**	50r. magenta	3·75	2·50
1961		70r. pale blue	4·00	3·25
1962		100r. olive-bistre	4·50	3·00
1963		500r. pale orange	7·00	7·25
1964		1000r. lavender	13·00	13·50
1965		2000r. turquoise-green	21·00	22·00
1960/5	Set of 6		50·00	45·00

(Des Kelum Gunasekara. Litho Dept of Govt Printing, Sri Lanka)

2008 (9 Oct). World Post Day. P 13½×14.

1966	**874**	5r. multicoloured	40	30

875 Dutch Burgher Union Hall`   **876** Anton Jayasuriya

(Des Kelum Gunasekara. Litho Dept of Govt Printing, Sri Lanka)

2008 (22 Oct). Centenary of the Dutch Burgher Union of Ceylon. P 13½×14.

1967	**875**	5r. multicoloured	40	30

(Des Pulasthi Ediriweera. Litho Dept of Govt Printing, Sri Lanka)

2008 (7 Nov). Professor Anton Jayasuriya (founder of Medicine Alternativa and the Open International University for Complementary Medicine) Commemoration. P 13×12½ (with one star-shaped hole on each vertical side).

1968	**876**	5r. multicoloured	40	30

877 Pieter Keuneman   **878** Scene from the Story

(Des V. Srinath Kurukulasooriya. Litho Dept of Govt Printing, Sri Lanka)

2008 (1 Dec). Pieter Keuneman (founder General Secretary of the Communist Party of Sri Lanka, MP 1947–77, Minister of Housing and Construction 1970–7) Commemoration. P 13×12½ (with one star-shaped hole on each vertical side).

1969	**877**	5r. multicoloured	40	30

(Des Sanath Rohana Wickramasinghe. Litho Dept of Govt Printing, Sri Lanka)

2008 (5 Dec). Childrens' Stories (2nd series). Lanka Philex 2008 National Stamp Exhibition. *The Story of Two Men and the Bear.* P 12½×13 (with two star-shaped perforations on each horizontal side).

1970	**878**	5r. multicoloured	40	30

879 Most Ven. Weweldeniye Medhalankara Mahanayake Mahathero   **880** *Christmas is the Peace Bridge Join the North and South of Sri Lanka* (Isuri Dileka Tittagalle)

2008 (7 Dec). Birth Centenary of Most Ven. Weweldeniye Medhalankara Mahanayake Mahathero. P 13×12½ (with one star-shaped hole on each vertical side).

1971	**879**	5r. multicoloured	40	30

(Des Ruwan Upasena (5r. adapted from child's painting)

2008 (9 Dec). Christmas. T **880** and similar multicoloured design. P 12½×13 (with one star-shaped hole on each horizontal side) (5r.) or 13×12½ (with one star-shaped hole on each vertical side) (30r.).

1972		5r. Type **880**	35	25
1973		30r. St. Mary's Cathedral, Kaluwella, Galle (vert)	1·60	2·00

881 People enclosed in Cupped Hands   **882** Transport Board Emblem

(Des Kelum Gunasekara. Litho Dept of Govt Printing, Sri Lanka)

2008 (10 Dec). 60th Anniv of the Universal Declaration of Human Rights. P 13½×14.

1974	**881**	5r. multicoloured	40	30

(Des Pulasthi Ediriweera. Litho Dept of Govt Printing, Sri Lanka)

2008 (30 Dec). 50th Anniv of Sri Lanka Transport Board. P 13×12.

1975	**882**	5r. multicoloured	40	30

883 River Channel of Madu Ganga   **884** Students with English Books, using Computers and Standing on Top of Globe

(Des Palitha Gunasingha. Litho Dept of Govt Printing, Sri Lanka)

2009 (2 Feb). World Wetland Day. Madu Ganga RAMSAR Wetland. T **883** and similar horiz design. Multicoloured. P 13½×14.

1976		5r. Type **883**	35	25
1977		25r. Mangroves of Madu Ganga	1·50	2·00

(Des Ruwan Upasena. Litho Dept of Govt Printing, Sri Lanka)

2009 (13 Feb). Year of English and Information Technology. P 14×13½.

1978	**884**	5r. multicoloured	40	30

885 University of Sri Jayewardenepura   **886** F. R. Jayasuriya

(Des Gamini Abeykoon. Litho Dept of Govt Printing, Sri Lanka)

2009 (18 Feb). 50th Anniv of University of Sri Jayewardenepura. P 13½×14.

1979	**885**	5r. multicoloured	40	30

(Des Sanath Rohana Wickramasinghe. Litho Dept of Govt Printing, Sri Lanka)

2009 (25 Feb). Birth Centenary of Professor Felix Reginald Jayasuriya (former Professor of Economics at University of Kelaniya). P 14×13½.

1980	**886**	5r. multicoloured	40	30

887 A. P. de Zoysa

(Des Pulasthi Ediriweera. Litho Dept of Govt Printing, Sri Lanka)

2009 (5 Mar). Agampodi Paulus de Zoysa (social reformer and Buddhist scholar) Commemoration. P 13½×14.

1981	**887**	5r. multicoloured	40	30

888 Pavilion, Moors Sports Club

(Des Sudath Jayawardene. Litho Dept of Govt Printing, Sri Lanka)

2009 (5 Mar). Centenary (2008) of Moors Sports Club, Colombo. P 12½×13 (with one notched elliptical hole on each horiz side).

1982	**888**	5r. multicoloured	75	40

889 Steam Locomotive, Canadian Locomotive M-2/591 and Running Shed

890 Mahmoud Shamsuddeen Kariapper

(Des Sudath Jayawardena. Litho Dept of Govt Printing, Sri Lanka)

2009 (9 Mar). Centenary of Railway Running Shed, Dematagoda. P 12½×13 (with one notched elliptical hole on each horiz side).

1983	**889**	5r. multicoloured	1·00	55

(Des Kumudu Tharaka. Litho Dept of Govt Printing, Sri Lanka)

2009 (13 Mar). Mahmoud Shamsuddeen Kariapper (politican and philanthropist) Commemoration. P 12×13.

1984	**890**	5r. multicoloured	40	30

891 Students and University Building

892 Natural Rubber Research and Development

(Litho Dept of Govt Printing, Sri Lanka)

2009 (31 Mar). Inauguration of University of Vocational Technology, Colombo. P 13×12½ (with one notched elliptical hole on each vert side).

1985	**891**	5r. multicoloured	40	30

(Litho Dept of Govt Printing, Sri Lanka)

2009 (2 Apr). Centenary of Natural Rubber Research and Development in Sri Lanka. P 12½×13 (with one notched elliptical hole on each horiz side).

1986	**892**	5r. multicoloured	40	30

893 Jeyaraj Fernandopulle

894 Hand holding Flower and Plaque

(Litho Dept of Govt Printing, Sri Lanka)

2009 (7 Apr). First Death Anniv of Jeyaraj Fernandopulle (Minister of Highways and Road Development). P 13×12½ (with one notched elliptical hole on each vert side).

1987	**893**	5r. multicoloured	40	30

(Litho Dept of Govt Printing, Sri Lanka)

2009 (23 Apr). 300th Anniv (2008) of Leprosy Hospital, Hendala. P 13½×14.

1988	**894**	5r. multicoloured	60	35

895 Sri Sumangala College, Panadura

896 Handupelpola Sri Punnaratana Nayaka Maha Thero

(Litho Dept of Govt Printing, Sri Lanka)

2009 (23 Apr). Centenary of Sri Sumangala College, Panadura. P 12½×13 (with one notched elliptical hole on each horiz side).

1989	**895**	5r. multicoloured	40	30

(Des Kumudu Taraka. Litho Dept of Govt Printing, Sri Lanka)

2009 (2 May). Birth Centenary of Handupelpola Sri Punnaratana Nayaka Maha Thero (Professor of Archaeology and founder of Nalanda University College, Kudauduwa). P 13×12½ (with one notched elliptical hole on each vert side).

1990	**896**	5r. multicoloured	40	30

897 A Visit to the Temple

898 Most Ven. Welithara Sri Gnanawimala Tissa Mahanayake Thero

(Des Bandula Harischandra. Litho Dept of Govt Printing, Sri Lanka)

2009 (5 May). Vesak. T **897** and similar horiz design. Multicoloured. P 13½×14 (4r.) or 12½×13 (with one notched elliptical hole on each horiz side) (5r. only).

1991		4r. Type **897**	45	50
1992		5r. Meditation	55	60

(Des Sanath Rohana Wickramasinghe. Litho Dept of Govt Printing, Sri Lanka)

2009 (5 May). Most Ven. Welithara Sri Gnanawimala Tissa Mahanayake Thero Commemoration. P 13×12½ (with one notched elliptical hole on each vert side).

1993	**898**	5r. multicoloured	40	30

899 Hon. Nimal Siripala de Silva and Nurse with Baby

(Des Sudath Jayawardena. Litho Dept of Govt Printing, Sri Lanka)

2009 (8 June). Appointment of Hon. Nimal Siripala de Silva as President of World Health Assembly, 2009–10. P 13½×14.

1994	**899**	5r. multicoloured	40	30

900 Galpotha Inscription of King Nissankamalla
and Coin of Queen Leelawathi

(Des Sudath Jayawardena (5, 15, 30r.) or Kelum Gunasekara (10, 25,
40r.). Litho Dept of Govt Printing, Sri Lanka)

2009 (23 June). Ancient Sri Lanka (4th series). Polonnaruwa Era
(1017–1235AD). T **900** and similar horiz designs. Multicoloured.
P 12½×13 (with two notched elliptical holes on each horiz side).

1995	5r. Type **900**	30	20
1996	10r. Siva Temple and artefacts from temple	50	50
1997	15r. Parakrama Samudra reservoir and stone statue in Pothgul Vihara	70	70
1998	25r. Palace of King Parakramabahu and Audience Hall of King Nissankamalla	1·10	1·40
1999	30r. Ancient hospital with medicinal bath, surgical instrument and grinding stone	1·10	1·60
2000	40r. Hindu sculptures of Siva, Uma and Saint Karaikkal Ammaiyar	1·50	1·90
1995/2000 Set of 6		4·75	5·50

901 Mahmood Hasarath

902 Hameed Al Husseinie
College, Colombo

(Des Sudath Jayawardena. Litho Dept of Govt Printing, Sri Lanka)

2009 (25 July). Mahmood Hasarath (Mahmood Abdul Majeed)
(Principal of Cassimiyya Arabic College, 1944–85)
Commemoration. P 14×13½.

2001	**901**	5r. deep grey-green	40	30

(Des Sanath Rohana Wickramasinghe. Litho Dept of Govt Printing,
Sri Lanka)

2009 (30 July). 125th Anniv of Hameed Al Husseinie College,
Colombo. P 13½×14.

2002	**902**	5r. multicoloured	40	30

903 Vidyalankara Pirivena and Modern Kelaniya
University

(Des Mevan Fonseka. Litho Dept of Govt Printing, Sri Lanka)

2009 (31 July). 50th Anniv of University of Kelaniya. P 13×12.

2003	**903**	5r. multicoloured	40	30

904 Bank of Ceylon

905 Most Rev. Dr. Oswald
Gomis

(Des Chamath Enterprises. Litho Dept of Govt Printing, Sri Lanka)

2009 (3 Aug). 70th Anniv of the Bank of Ceylon. P 14×13½.

2004	**904**	5r. multicoloured	40	30

(Des Pulasthi Ediriweera. Litho Dept of Govt Printing, Sri Lanka)

2009 (10 Aug). Most Rev. Dr. Oswald Gomis, Archbishop of Colombo
and Chancellor of the University of Colombo. P 14×13½.

2005	**905**	15r. multicoloured	1·00	1·25

906 Globe, Ships, Airliner and
Bullock Cart

907 Sree Narayana
Gurudev

(Des Ruwan Upasena. Litho Dept of Govt Printing, Sri Lanka)

2009 (25 Aug). Bicentenary of Sri Lanka Customs. P 12½×13 (with
one notched elliptical hole on each horiz side).

2006	**906**	15r. multicoloured	1·50	1·50

(Des Basil Cooray. Litho Dept of Govt Printing, Sri Lanka)

2009 (4 Sept). 155th Birth Anniv of Sree Narayana Gurudev
(Malayalee spiritual leader and social reformer). P 14×13½.

2007	**907**	5r. chestnut and lake-brown	40	30

908 Sivali Central College, Ratnapura

(Des Kelum Gunasekara. Litho Dept of Govt Printing, Sri Lanka)

2009 (25 Sept). Centenary of Sivali Central College, Ratnapura.
P 13×12.

2008	**908**	15r. multicoloured	1·00	1·40

909 Earth, Planets and
Lines of Communication

910 Soldiers, Tanks and Arms
and Flags of Sri Lanka

(Des Anuruddhika Kobbekaduwa. Litho Dept of Govt Printing, Sri
Lanka)

2009 (9 Oct). World Post Day. P 14×13½.

2009	**909**	15r. multicoloured	1·00	1·40

(Des Sanath Rohana Wickramasinghe. Litho Dept of Govt Printing,
Sri Lanka)

2009 (10 Oct). 60th Anniv of Sri Lanka Army. P 13.

2010	**910**	15r. multicoloured	1·40	1·40

911 Community Dog

912 Nativity (Isuru
Sadara Miranda)

(Des Basil Cooray. Litho Dept of Govt Printing, Sri Lanka)

2009 (5 Nov). Humane Eradication of Rabies. P 14×13½.

2011	**911**	15r. multicoloured	1·40	1·40

(Des Basil Cooray. Litho Dept of Govt Printing, Sri Lanka)
2009 (8 Nov). Christmas. T **912** and similar multicoloured design.
P 14×13½ (vert) or 13½×14 (horiz).
| 2012 | | 5r. Type **912** | 30 | 25 |
| 2013 | | 15r. St. Mary's Cathedral, Badulla (*horiz*) | 90 | 1·25 |

A miniature sheet containing No. 2012×2 was sold for 20r.
A miniature sheet containing No. 2013×2 was sold for 40r.

913 Mahogany Tree planted by Che Guevara at Horana

914 Man in Wheelchair

(Des Sudath Jayawardena. Litho Dept of Govt Printing, Sri Lanka)
2009 (9 Nov). 50th Anniv of Diplomatic Relations between Sri Lanka and Cuba. P 12×13.
| 2014 | **913** | 5r. multicoloured | 40 | 30 |

(Des Pulasthi Ediriweera. Litho Dept of Govt Printing, Sri Lanka)
2009 (3 Dec). International Day of Persons with Disabilities. P 13½×14.
| 2015 | **914** | 10r. multicoloured | 65 | 75 |

915 Johannes Voet (Dutch jurist and Society founder)

916 P. H. William De Silva

(Des Gamini Abeykoon. Litho Dept of Govt Printing, Sri Lanka)
2009 (4 Dec). 110th Anniv of Voet Lights Society of Sri Lanka. P 13½×14.
| 2016 | **915** | 15r. multicoloured | 1·00 | 1·40 |

(Des Ruwan Upasena. Litho Dept of Govt Printing, Sri Lanka)
2009 (15 Dec). Birth Centenary (2008) of Peduru Hewage William De Silva (Minister of Industries and Fisheries, 1956–9). P 13×12½ (with one notched elliptical hole on each vert side).
| 2017 | **916** | 10r. multicoloured | 65 | 75 |

917 Dr. Hudson Silva

918 D. M. Dasanayake

(Des Basil Cooray. Litho Dept of Govt Printing, Sri Lanka)
2009 (21 Dec). 80th Birth Anniv of Dr. Hudson Silva (founder of Sri Lanka Eye Donation Society and Human Tissue Bank). P 14×13½.
| 2018 | **917** | 10r. multicoloured | 65 | 75 |

(Des Nihal Sangabo Dias. Litho Dept of Govt Printing, Sri Lanka)
2010 (8 Jan). Second Death Anniv of Dasanayake Mudiyanselage Dasanayake (politician and Minister of Nation Building). P 14.
| 2019 | **918** | 10r. multicoloured | 65 | 75 |

919 Thurstan College, Colombo

(Des Sudath Jayawardena. Litho Dept of Govt Printing, Sri Lanka)
2010 (11 Jan). 60th Anniv of Thurstan College, Colombo. P 13½×12.
| 2020 | **919** | 10r. multicoloured | 65 | 75 |

No. 2021, T **920** are vacant.

Two sheetlets of Deyata Kirula personalised stamps, each containing 6×5r. stamps and six labels, were issued on 4 February 2010. They were sold at 500r. per sheetlet.

921 Trainees in Workshops and College Building

(Des Ruwan Upasena. Litho Dept of Govt Printing, Sri Lanka)
2010 (15 Feb). 50th Anniv of Ceylon—German Technical Training Institute, Moratuwa. P 13½×14.
| 2022 | **921** | 10r. multicoloured | 65 | 75 |

922 Emblem and Government Officers

923 Rotary Emblem

(Des Ruwan Upasena. Litho Dept of Govt Printing, Sri Lanka)
2010 (20 Feb). Centenary of The Government Officers Benefits Association. P 13½×14.
| 2023 | **922** | 5r. multicoloured | 40 | 30 |

(Des Pulasthi Ediriweera. Litho Dept of Govt Printing, Sri Lanka)
2010 (18 Mar). 80th Anniv of Rotary in Sri Lanka. P 14×13½.
| 2024 | **923** | 10r. multicoloured | 65 | 75 |

924 M. J. C. Fernando and Buddhist Hall, Moratuwa

925 Buddhist Flag and Globe

(Des Pulasthi Ediriweera. Litho Dept of Govt Printing, Sri Lanka)
2010 (27 Mar). 125th Birth Anniv of M. J. C. Fernando (founder of Sri Lanka Bauddha Samitiya for Buddhist education in Moratuwa). P 13½×14.
| 2025 | **924** | 10r. multicoloured | 70 | 75 |

(Des Gamini Abeykoon. Litho Dept of Govt Printing, Sri Lanka)

2010 (28 Apr). 125th Anniv of the Buddhist Flag. P 14×13½.

2026   **925**   5r. multicoloured   50   50

926 Arrival of Lord Buddha to Mahiyanganaya

927 St. Anthony's Shrine, Kochchikade, Colombo

(Des Ratnapala de Silva and Palitha Gunasinghe. Litho Dept of Govt Printing, Sri Lanka)

2010 (24 May). Vesak. T **926** and similar multicoloured designs. P 14×13½ (vert) or 13½×14 (horiz).

2027	4r. Type **926**	30	25
2028	5r. Mahiyangana Stupa	35	25
2029	10r. Mirisawetiya Stupa, Anuradhapura (*horiz*)	65	75
2030	30r. Jetawana Stupa, Anuradhapura (*horiz*)..	1·75	2·25
2027/30	Set of 4	3·00	3·25
MS2031	117×180 mm. Nos. 2027/30..................	3·00	3·25

(Des Pulasthi Ediriweera. Litho Dept of Govt Printing, Sri Lanka)

2010 (12 June). 175th Anniv of Consecration of St. Anthony's Shrine, Kochchikade, Colombo. P 14×13½.

2032   **927**   5r. multicoloured   40   30

928 Sri Kalyaniwansa Nikaya

(Des Palitha Gunasinghe. Litho Dept of Govt Printing, Sri Lanka)

2010 (17 June). Bicentenary of Sri Kalyaniwansa Nikaya. P 13½×14.

2033   **928**   10r. multicoloured   70   75

929 Mahajana College, Tellippalai

(Des Basil Cooray. Litho Dept of Govt Printing, Sri Lanka)

2010 (18 June). Centenary of Mahajana College, Tellippalai. P 13½×14.

2034   **929**   10r. multicoloured   70   75

930 Pepiliyana Sunethra Mahadevi Piriven Rajamaha Viharaya

(Des Sanath Rohana Wickramasinghe. Litho Dept of Govt Printing, Sri Lanka)

2010 (20 June). 600th Anniv of Pepiliyana Sunethra Mahadevi Piriven Rajamaha Viharaya. P 13½×12.

2035   **930**   5r. multicoloured   40   30

931 Dove with Olive Branch flying over Map of Sri Lanka (V. Jeyarajasinham)

932 Postmen's Uniforms and Pillar Boxes, National Postal Museum

(Des Sanath Rohana Wickramasinghe. Litho Dept of Govt Printing, Sri Lanka)

2010 (6 July). First Anniv of Victory and Peace. Winning Entry from Art Competition. P 14×13½.

2036   **931**   5r. multicoloured   40   30

(Des Pulasthi Ediriweera. Litho Dept of Govt Printing, Sri Lanka)

2010 (6 July). Inauguration of National Postal Museum and Philatelic Exhibition Centre, Colombo. P 13½×14.

2037	5r. Type **932**	50	50
	a. Horiz pair. Nos. 2037/8	1·00	1·00
2038	5r. Early Ceylon stamps and stamp exhibits, Philatelic Exhibition Centre	50	50

Nos. 2037/8 were printed together, *se-tenant*, as horizontal pairs in sheets of 100.

A miniature sheet containing Nos. 2037/8 was sold for 60r., a premium of 50r. above the face value of the stamps.

933 Early and Modern Hospitals, Anuradhapura

(Des Sanath Rohana Wickramasinghe. Litho Dept of Govt Printing, Sri Lanka)

2010 (10 July). 50th Anniv of Teaching Hospital, Anuradhapura. P 13½×14.

2039   **933**   5r. multicoloured   40   30

934 Royal College, Colombo (Lahiru Anuradha Jayakody)

(Des Sanath Rohana Wickramasinghe. Litho Dept of Govt Printing, Sri Lanka)

2010 (16 July). 175th Anniv of Royal College, Colombo. Winning Entry from School Children's Design Competition. P 13½×14.

2040   **934**   10r. multicoloured   70   75

935 Kokuvil Hindu College

936 M. P. De Zoysa

(Des Basil Cooray. Litho Dept of Govt Printing, Sri Lanka)

2010 (22 July). Centenary of Kokuvil Hindu College. P 13½×14.

2041   **935**   10r. multicoloured   70   75

(Des Basil Cooray. Litho Dept of Govt Printing, Sri Lanka)

2010 (9 Aug). Birth Centenary of M. P. De Zoysa (politician). P 14×13½.

2042   **936**   10r. multicoloured.. 70   75

937 '1ST YOG', Mascots and Emblems

(Des Sanath Rohana Wickramasinghe. Litho Dept of Govt Printing, Sri Lanka)

2010 (12 Aug). First Youth Olympic Games, Singapore. P 12½×13½ (with two notched elliptical holes on each horiz side).

2043   **937**   10r. multicoloured.. 70   75

938 Central Bank of Sri Lanka on Banknote

(Des Kelum Gunasekara. Litho Dept of Govt Printing, Sri Lanka)

2010 (27 Aug). 60th Anniv of Central Bank of Sri Lanka. P 13½×12.

2044   **938**   10r. multicoloured.. 70   75

939 Pasikudah Beach

(Des Pulasthi Ediriweera and Sangabo Dias. Litho Garsu Pasaulis, Lithuania)

2010 (7 Sept). Beaches. T **939** and similar horiz designs. Multicoloured. P 13×13½.

2045	15r. Type **939**		1·50	1·50
2046	25r. Rocky headland, Trincomalee Beach		2·25	2·50
2047	40r. Surfer at Arugam Bay Beach		3·50	4·00
2045/7	*Set of 3*		6·50	7·25

A set of three miniature sheets containing Nos. 2045/7 were sold at 100r. each, a premium above the face values of the stamps.

940 Sri Lanka Whistling Thrush

(Des W. Vasantha Perera. Litho Garsu Pasaulis, Lithuania)

2010 (7 Sept). National Parks of Sri Lanka (3rd series). Horton Plains National Park. T **940** and similar multicoloured designs. P 13½×13 (vert) or 13×13½ (horiz).

2048	5r. Type **940**		1·25	45
2049	15r. Sambur (*horiz*)		1·50	1·50
2050	25r. Rhinohorn Lizard (*horiz*)		2·25	2·50
2051	40r. Purple-faced Leaf Monkey		3·50	4·00
2048/51	*Set of 4*		7·75	7·75
MS2052	130×90 mm. No. 2049		1·75	2·00

Three other miniature sheets containing Nos. 2048, 2050 and 2051 were sold at 15r., 35r. and 50r., all at a premium above face value.

941 Faculty of Engineering, University of Peradeniya

942 Ozone Layer with Parasol

(Des Ruwan Upasena. Litho Dept of Govt Printing, Sri Lanka)

2010 (9 Sept). 60th Anniv of Engineering Faculty, University of Peradeniya. P 13½×14.

2053   **941**   15r. multicoloured.. 1·00   1·25

(Des Isuru Sadara Mirendo and Gamini Abeykoon. Litho Dept of Govt Printing, Sri Lanka)

2010 (16 Sept). 25th Anniv of Vienna Convention for Ozone Layer Protection. P 14×13½.

2054   **942**   5r. multicoloured.. 40   30

943 Indigenous People

944 St. Michael's Church, Koralawella

(Des Ruwan Upasena. Litho Dept of Govt Printing, Sri Lanka)

2010 (25 Sept). World Indigenous People's Day. P 13½×14.

2055	5r. Type **943**		50	50
	a. Horiz pair. Nos. 2055/6		1·00	1·00
2056	5r. Cave painting		50	50

Nos. 2055/6 were printed together, *se-tenant*, in sheets of 100 (2 panes of 50).

A miniature sheet containing Nos. 2055/6 was issued, sold at 60r., a premium of 50r. above face value.

(Des Mevan Fonseka. Litho Dept of Govt Printing, Sri Lanka)

2010 (29 Sept). 150th Anniv of St. Michael's Church, Koralawella. P 14×13½.

2057   **944**   5r. multicoloured.. 40   30

945 Hands supporting Children

(Des Anuruddika Kobbekaduwa. Litho Dept of Govt Printing, Sri Lanka)

2010 (3 Oct). World Children's Day. P 13.
2058   **945**   5r. multicoloured   40   30

946 Cranes carrying Tortoise

(Des Anuruddhika Kobbekaduwa. Litho Dept of Govt Printing, Sri Lanka)

2010 (3 Oct). Chidren's Stories (3rd series). *How the Tortoise Flew.* P 13½×14.
2059   **946**   5r. mutlicoloured ....   1·00   55

947 Globe and Letter

(Des Gamini Abeykoon Litho Dept of Govt Printing, Sri Lanka)

2010 (9 Oct). World Post Day. P 13½×14.
2060   **947**   5r. multicoloured   40   30

948 Rankot Viharaya, Panadura

(Des Bandula Harischandra. Litho Dept of Govt Printing, Sri Lanka)

2010 (10 Oct). Bicentenary of Rankot Viharaya, Panadura. P 13½×14.
2061   **948**   5r. multicoloured   40   30

949 Anglican Church

(Des Nihal Sangabo Dias. Litho Dept of Govt Printing, Sri Lanka)

2010 (14 Oct). 125th Anniv of Diocesan Council for Diocese of Colombo. P 13½×14.
2062   **949**   5r. multicoloured   40   30

950 Louis Braille

(Des Kumudu Tharaka. Litho Dept of Govt Printing, Sri Lanka)

2010 (15 Oct). Birth Bicentenary of Louis Braille (inventor of Braille writing for the blind) and World White Cane Day. P 13½×14.
2063   **950**   5r. multicoloured   40   30

951 Buddhists praying

(Des Ruwan Upasena. Litho Dept of Govt Printing, Sri Lanka)

2010 (14 Nov). World Fellowship of Buddhists. P 13½×12.
2064   **951**   5r. multicoloured   40   30

952 Magam Ruhunupura Port, Map of Southeast Asia and Pres. Rajapaksa

(Des Pulasthi Ediriweera. Litho Dept of Govt Printing, Sri Lanka)

2010 (18 Nov). Inauguration of Magam Ruhunupura Port. P 13½×14.
2065   **952**   5r. multicoloured ....   1·00   50

953 Family around Christmas Tree
(R. P. G. Savinda Shyamal Karunathilake)

(Des Kumudu Tharaka. Litho Dept of Govt Printing, Sri Lanka)

2010 (28 Nov). Christmas. T **953** and similar horiz design. Multicoloured. P 13½×14.
2066   5r. Type **953**   40   15
2067   15r. St. Mary's Church, Kegalle ....   1·00   1·25
  Type **953** shows the winning entry children's Christmas stamp designing competition.
  A miniature sheet containing Nos. 2066/7 was sold at 35r., a premium of 15r. above face value.

954 Gunboat   **955** Holy Emmanuel Church, Moratuwa

(Des Mevan Fonseka. Litho Dept of Govt Printing, Sri Lanka)

2010 (9 Dec). 60th Anniv of the Sri Lanka Navy. P 13.
2068   **954**   5r. multicoloured ....   1·00   60

(Des Kumudu Tharaka. Litho Dept of Govt Printing, Sri Lanka)

2010 (27 Dec). 150th Anniv of Holy Emmanuel Church, Moratuwa. P 14×13½.
2069   **955**   5r. multicoloured   40   30

956 Labugama Reservoir

(Des Pulasthi Ediriweera. Litho Dept of Govt Printing, Sri Lanka)

2011 (18 Jan). 125th Anniv of Labugama Reservoir. P 14×13½.

| 2070 | **956** | 5r. multicoloured | 40 | 30 |

957 Dr. P. R. Anthonis

958 Marie Curie, Prof. Sultanbawa and Structure of Aluminium Oxide

(Des Basil Cooray. Litho Dept of Govt Printing, Sri Lanka)

2011 (21 Jan). Birth Centenary of Dr. Polwatte Arachchige Romeil Anthonis (surgeon). P 14×13½.

| 2071 | **957** | 5r. multicoloured | 40 | 30 |

(Des Mevan Fonseka. Litho Dept of Govt Printing, Sri Lanka)

2011 (30 Jan). International Year of Chemistry. P 12×13½.

| 2072 | **958** | 5r. multicoloured | 40 | 30 |

959 'Viceroy Special' Steam Locomotive B8 240

960 St. Mary's Church, Dehiwala

(Des Ruwan Upasena. Litho Dept of Govt Printing, Sri Lanka)

2011 (2 Feb). 25th Anniv of *Viceroy Special* Steam Train. T **959** and similar horiz designs. Multicoloured. Granite paper. P 12½×13½ (with one notched elliptical hole on each horiz side).

2073		5r. Type **959**	70	70
		a. Horiz strip of four. Nos. 2073/6	2·50	2·50
2074		5r. 'Viceroy Special' locomotive B2 213	70	70
2075		5r. Sentinel Camel steam rail car V2 331	70	70
2076		5r. Narrow gauge steam locomotive J1 220	70	70
2073/76 Set of 4			2·50	2·50

Nos. 2073/6 were printed together, *se-tenant*, in horizontal strips of four throughout the sheets.

Nos. 2073/6 were also sold in booklets containing eight 5r. (Nos. 2073/6) in a block containing two of each design. These booklets were sold at 50r., a premium of 10r. above the face value.

A miniature sheet containing a 45r. stamp was issued, sold at 60r, a premium of 15r. above face value.

(Des Kumudu Tharaka. Litho Dept of Govt Printing, Sri Lanka)

2011 (6 Feb). 175th Anniv of St. Mary's Church, Dehiwala. P 13½×14.

| 2077 | **960** | 5r. multicoloured | 40 | 30 |

961 Southlands College, Galle

(Des Kelum Gunasekara. Litho Dept of Govt Printing, Sri Lanka)

2011 (18 Feb). 125th Anniv of Southlands College, Galle. P 13½×12.

| 2078 | **961** | 5r. multicoloured | 40 | 30 |

We understand that No. 2078 was released early at a number of offices.

962 Fighter Aircraft

(Des Gamini Abeykoon. Litho Dept of Govt Printing, Sri Lanka)

2011 (2 Mar). 60th Anniv of Sri Lanka Air Force. P 13½×14.

| 2079 | **962** | 5r. multicoloured | 1·00 | 60 |

| 15.00 | 15.00 |
| (963) | (964) |

2011 (1 Apr). No. 1552*b* (Daul drummer) surch with T **963/4**.

| 2080 | | 15r. bright blue (Type **963**) | 1·25 | 1·00 |
| 2081 | | 15r. bright blue (Type **964**) | 1·25 | 1·00 |

965 Yuri Gagarin

(Des Sanath Rohana Wickramasinghe. Litho Dept of Govt Printing, Sri Lanka)

2011 (26 Apr). 50th Anniv of First Manned Space Flight. P 13½.

| 2082 | **965** | 5r. multicoloured | 60 | 35 |

No. 2082 was perforated in a circle contained within an outer perforated square showing flags of Soviet Union and Sri Lanka, launch of *Vostok I* and Yuri Gagarin on visit to Sri Lanka, December 1961

966 'Buddhism is a universal doctrine'

(Des Kelum Gunasekara, Kumudu Tharaka, Palitha Gunasinghe and Ratnapala de Silva. Litho Dept of Govt Printing, Sri Lanka)

2011 (29 Apr). 2600th Sambuddhatva Jayantiya Vesak (1st issue). T **966** and similar horiz designs. P 13×12.

2083		5r. Type **966**	40	40
		a. Block of six. Nos. 2083/8	2·25	2·25
2084		5r. 'Let us practise Buddhist principles'	40	40
2085		5r. 'Let us take care of our parents and respect them'	40	40
2086		5r. 'Let us help the sick'	40	40
2087		5r. 'Person who practises Buddhism illuminates the entire world'	40	40
2088		5r. 'Let us build an antinarcotic society'	40	40
2083/88 Set of 6			2·25	2·25

Nos. 2083/8 were printed together, *se-tenant*, as blocks of six in sheets of 12 stamps.

967 Rabindranath Tagore

968 Lumbini

(Des Pulasthi Ediriweera. Litho Dept of Govt Printing, Sri Lanka)

2011 (7 May). 150th Birth Anniv of Rabindranath Tagore (Bengali poet, writer and musician). P 14×13½.

2089	**967**	5r. multicoloured	60	35

(Des Kelum Gunasekara (2090, 2092) or Pulasthi Ediriweera (2091, 2093). Litho Dept of Govt Printing, Sri Lanka)

2011 (14 May). 2600th Sambuddhatva Jayanthi Vesak (2nd issue). T **968** and similar vert designs. Multicoloured. P 14×13½.

2090		5r. Type **968**	40	40
		a. Block of four. Nos. 2090/3	1·40	1·40
2091		5r. Temple at Buddhagaya	40	40
2092		5r. Baranesa Isipathanarama	40	40
2093		5r. Kusinara	40	40
2090/93	*Set of 4*		1·40	1·40

Nos. 2090/3 were printed together, *se-tenant*, as blocks of four stamps throughout the sheet.

A miniature sheet containing Nos. 2090/3 was sold at 35r., a premium of 15r. above the face value of the stamps.

969 Ancient Stone Bridge, Mahakanadarawa

(Des Kelum Gunasekara (2094, 2096) or Sudath Jayawardena (2095, 2097). Litho Dept of Govt Printing, Sri Lanka)

2011 (27 May). Bridges of Sri Lanka. T **969** and similar horiz designs. Multicoloured. P 13½×12.

2094		10r. Type **969**	70	80
		a. Vert pair. Nos. 2094/5	1·40	1·60
2095		10r. Suspension bridge, Peradeniya	70	80
2096		15r. Wooden bridge, Bogoda	1·10	1·40
		a. Vert pair. Nos. 2096/7	2·10	2·75
2097		15r. Steel arch bridge, Ruwanwella	1·10	1·40
2094/97	*Set of 4*		3·25	4·00

Nos. 2094/5 and 2096/7 were each printed together, *se-tenant*, as vertical pairs throughout the sheets.

Two miniature sheets, containing either Nos. 2094 and 2096 or 2095 and 2097, were issued, sold at 40r. each, a premium of 15r. above the face value of the stamps.

970 Bank Building and Anniversary Emblem

971 Radampala Sri Sumangala Central College

(Des Kelum Gunasekara. Litho Dept of Govt Printing, Sri Lanka)

2011 (1 July). 50th Anniv of People's Bank. P 12½×13½ (with one notched elliptical hole on each horiz side).

2098	**970**	5r. multicoloured	40	30

(Des Kelum Gunasekara. Litho Dept of Govt Printing, Sri Lanka)

2011 (15 July). Centenary of Radampala Sri Sumangala Central College, Matara. P 13½×14.

2099	**971**	5r. multicoloured	40	30

972 Emblem encircled by Flags of Member Countries

973 Buddhist Temple ('Heritage')

(Des Ruwan Upasena. Litho Dept of Govt Printing, Sri Lanka)

2011 (21 July). 50th Anniv of the Non Aligned Movement. P 13½×12½ (with one notched elliptical hole in each vert side).

2100	**972**	5r. multicoloured	40	30

(Des Wasantha Perera (2102, 2108), Sangabo Dias (2103/4), Pulasthi Ediriweera (2105, 2109/10) and Kelum Gunasekara (2101, 2106/7). Litho Dept of Govt Printing, Sri Lanka)

2011 (27 Sept). World Tourism Day. T **973** and similar square designs. Multicoloured. P 13.

2101		5r. Type **973**	40	40
		a. Sheetlet. Nos. 2101/10 and two central labels x 3	11·50	12·50
2102		5r. Stone lion paws and staircase, Sigiriya Rock Fortress ('Heritage')	40	40
2103		5r. Kandyan dancers ('Festive')	40	40
2104		5r. Sinhala, Tamil, Muslim and Burgher girls ('Essence')	40	40
2105		15r. Woman in bath of flowers ('Bliss')	1·00	1·10
2106		15r. Waterfall ('Scenic')	1·00	1·10
2107		30r. Elephants ('Wild')	2·25	2·50
2108		35r. Leopard ('Wild')	2·25	2·50
2109		40r. Beach with boat offshore ('Pristine')	2·25	2·50
2110		45r. White water rafting ('Thrills')	2·25	2·50
2101/10	*Set of 10*		11·50	12·50

Nos. 2101/10 were printed together, *se-tenant*, in sheetlets of ten stamps and two central stamp-size labels, and also in separate sheets of 80.

974 Children and Sri Lanka Flag on Globe

975 Pillar Box and Postman delivering Letter

(Des V. Sakun Chandeepa Niranjaya. Litho Dept of Govt Printing, Sri Lanka)

2011 (1 Oct). World Children's Day. P 13½×12½ (with one notched elliptical hole on each vert side).

2111	**974**	5r. multicoloured	75	35

(Des Sangabo Dias. Litho Dept of Govt Printing, Sri Lanka)

2011 (9 Oct). World Post Day. P 12½×13½.

2112	**975**	5r. multicoloured	75	35

976 Handball, Football and Volleyball Players on Beach

(Des Sudath Jayawardena. Litho Dept of Govt Printing, Sri Lanka)

2011 (11 Oct). First South Asian Beach Games, Hambantota. P 13½×14.

2113	**976**	5r. multicoloured	60	30

977 Dudley Senanayake

978 '1919' (telephone number)

(Des Isuru Chathuranga. Litho Dept of Govt Printing, Sri Lanka)

2011 (14 Oct). Birth Centenary of Hon. Dudley Senanayake (Prime Minister 1965–70). P 13½×12½ (with one notched elliptical hole on each vert side).

2114	**977**	5r. light brown and black	40	30

(Des Sudath Jayawardana. Litho Dept of Govt Printing, Sri Lanka)

2011 (17 Oct). Government Information Centre. P 12½×13½ (with one notched elliptical hole on each horiz side).

2115	**978**	5r. multicoloured	40	30

979 Austin 12, 1928

(Des Amila Perera. Litho Dept of Govt Printing, Sri Lanka)

2011 (28 Oct). Vintage and Classic Cars of Sri Lanka. T **979** and similar horiz designs. Black and grey. P 12½×13½ (with one notched elliptical hole in each horiz side).

2116		5r. Type **979**	50	50
2117		5r. Rolls-Royce 20/25, 1934	50	50
2118		5r. Jaguar SS 100, 1937	50	50
2119		5r. Morris Minor, 1949	50	50
2116/19 Set of 4			1·75	1·75

Two miniature sheets containing Nos. 2116/19, one with and one without the Lanka Philex 2011 emblem, were issued on the same date. They were sold at 40r. each, a 20r. premium above face value.

980 Shrine of Our Lady of Lourdes, Kalaoya

981 Most Ven. Kotagama Wachissara Thero

(Des Kelum Gunasekara (5r.) or Lasith Christopher Rubera (20r.). Litho Dept of Govt Printing, Sri Lanka)

2011 (27 Nov). Christmas. T **980** and similar vert design. Multicoloured. P 13½×12½ (with one notched elliptical hole on each vert side).

2120		5r. Type **980**	40	15
2121		20r. Peace dove with Sri Lanka flag on wings enfolding nativity scene	1·25	1·50

A miniature sheet containing Nos. 2120/1 issued on the same date was sold at 45r., a 20r. premium over the face value.

(Des Nihal Sangabo Dias. Litho Dept of Govt Printing, Sri Lanka)

2011 (28 Nov). Most Ven. Kotagama Wachissara Thero (educationist) Commemoration. P 13½×12½ (with one notched elliptical hole on each vert side).

2122	**981**	5r. multicoloured	40	30

982 Emblem

983 Eddy Jayamanna (actor, singer and director)

(Des Rathnapala de Silva. Litho Dept of Govt Printing, Sri Lanka)

2011 (1 Dec). World AIDS Day. P 13½×12½ (with one notched elliptical hole on each vert side).

2123	**982**	5r. multicoloured	75	35

(Des Pulasthi Ediriweera and Indranatha Thenuara. Litho Dept of Govt Printing, Sri Lanka)

2012 (21 Jan). Legends of Sinhala Cinema. T **983** and similar vert designs. P 14×13½.

2124		5r. deep claret, dull mauve and reddish-brown	40	40
2125		5r. deep rose-lilac, violet-grey and reddish-brown (Gamini Fonseka)	40	40
2126		5r. deep turquoise-blue, slate-blue and reddish-brown (Joe Abeywickrama)	40	40
2127		10r. bottle-green, dull blue-green and reddish-brown (Titus Totawatta)	70	70

2128		15r. deep reddish-brown and grey-brown (Malani Fonseka)	1·00	1·25
2129		20r. brown-olive, grey-brown and reddish-brown (Sandya Kumari)	1·10	1·40
2124/29 Set of 6			3·50	4·00
MS2130 109×160 mm. Nos. 2124/9			3·50	4·00

No. **MS**2130 also exists imperforate.

984 Sailing Ship, Liner and Container Ship

(Des Ruwan Upasena. Litho Dept of Govt Printing, Sri Lanka)

2012 (9 Feb). Centenary of Institute of Chartered Shipbrokers UK and 25th Anniv of Sri Lanka Branch. P 12½×13 (with two notched elliptical holes on each horiz side).

2131	**984**	5r. reddish-brown and black	1·00	60

985 '100', Tent and Backpack

(Des Mevan Fonseka. Litho Dept of Govt Printing, Sri Lanka)

2012 (22 Feb). Centenary of Sri Lanka Scouting. P 13 (2132) or imperf (**MS**2133).

2132	**985**	5r. multicoloured	50	30
MS2133 159×120 mm. As No. 2132 but imperf×4			1·75	2·00

986 Guardstone

987 Peony Flower

(Des Piyaratne Hewabatage. Litho Dept of Govt Printing, Sri Lanka)

2012 (10 Mar). Guardstone of Chapter House of the Rathanaprasadaya, Abhayagiri Monastery Complex, Anuradhapura. P 13 (with one notched elliptical hole on each side).

2134	**986**	50r. multicoloured	2·75	2·75
2135	**986**	100r. multicoloured	5·00	6·00

(Des Studio Labranda. Litho Austrian State Ptg Wks, Vienna)

2012 (10 Mar). Peony Flower. Sheet 125×185 mm containing T **987** and similar vert design. Multicoloured. P 13½×14.

MS2136 125×185 mm. 30r. Type **987**×3; 30r. As Type **987** but inscriptions at right×3			3·00	3·50

988 Wind Turbines

(Des Mevan Fonseka. Litho Dept of Govt Printing, Sri Lanka)

2012 (20 Mar). Sustainable Energy for All. P 13½×12.

2137	**988**	5r. multicoloured	40	30

989 Asian-Pacific Postal Union

(Des Isuru Chathuranga. Litho Dept of Govt Printing, Sri Lanka)

2012 (1 Apr). 50th Anniv of the Asian-Pacific Postal Union. P 13½×14.

2138	**989**	5r. multicoloured	40	30

990 New Year Rituals

(Des Piyaratne Hewabatage. Litho Dept of Govt Printing, Sri Lanka)

2012 (10 Apr). Sinhala-Hindu New Year. T **990** and similar square designs. Multicoloured. P 13.

2139		5r. Type **990**	40	40
		a. Block of four. Nos. 2139/42	1·40	1·40
2140		5r. Village temple and couple leaving for work at auspicious time	40	40
2141		5r. Woman giving sweetmeats to boy and women playing board game	40	40
2142		5r. Anointing with oil and women playing board game	40	40
2139/42		Set of 4	1·40	1·40

Nos. 2139/42 were printed together, *se-tenant*, as blocks of four stamps in sheetlets of 16, each block forming a composite design.

991 Sapugaskanda Oil Refinery

992 Sri Lanka on Globe Emblem

(Des Isuru Chathuranga. Litho Dept of Govt Printing, Sri Lanka)

2012 (30 Apr). 50th Anniv of Ceylon Petroleum Corporation. P 13½×14.

2143	**991**	5r. multicoloured	1·00	60

(Des Isuru Chathuranga. Litho Dept of Govt Printing, Sri Lanka)

2012 (3 May). 2600th Sambuddhatva Jayantiya. P 13×12.

2144	**992**	5r. multicoloured	40	30

993 Pandols depicting Jataka Stories

(Des Isuru Chathuranga. Litho Dept of Govt Printing, Sri Lanka)

2012 (6 May). Vesak. T **993** and similar horiz design. Multicoloured. P 13½×14.

2145		5r. Type **993**	40	25
2146		12r. Lanterns	85	1·00
MS2147		161×102 mm. Nos. 2145/6	1·25	1·40

994 Prof. Walpola Sri Rahula Thero

995 St. Philip Neri's Church

(Des Pulasthi Ediriweera. Litho Dept of Govt Printing, Sri Lanka)

2012 (15 May). Prof. Walpola Sri Rahula Thero (Buddhist scholar) Commemoration. P 14×13½.

2148	**994**	5r. multicoloured	40	30

(Des Mevan Fonseka. Litho Dept of Govt Printing, Sri Lanka)

2012 (26 May). 225th Anniv of St. Philip Neri's Church, Udammita South, Ja-ela. P 14×13½.

2149	**995**	5r. multicoloured	40	30

996 Kusuma Gunawardena

997 Asgiri Gedige Rajamaha Viharaya

(Des Isuru Chathuranga. Litho Dept of Govt Printing, Sri Lanka)

2012 (28 May). Birth Centenary of Mrs. Kusuma Gunawardena (MP 1947–59). P 14×13½.

2150	**996**	5r. multicoloured	40	30

(Des Ruwan Upasena. Litho Dept of Govt Printing, Sri Lanka)

2012 (12 June). 700th Anniv of Asgiri Maha Viharaya. P 13½×14.

2151	**997**	5r. multicoloured	40	30

998 '100', Girl Signing and Blind Boy with Cane

(Des Isuru Chathuranga. Litho Dept of Govt Printing, Sri Lanka)

2012 (17 June). Centenary of Ceylon School for the Deaf and Blind, Ratmalana. P 12½×13½ (with two notched elliptical holes in each horiz side).

2152	**998**	5r. multicoloured	40	30

No. 2152 has Braille inscriptions.

999 Terracotta Figure from Sigiriya

(Litho)

2012 (16 July). National Archaeological Week. P 13½×12½ (with one notched elliptical hole in each vert side).

2153	**999**	5r. multicoloured	40	30

1000 Farmer's Hands (gateway of Bata Atha Agriculture Technology Park) and Field Workers

(Des Ruwan Upasena. Litho Dept of Govt Printing, Sri Lanka)

2012 (22 July). Centenary of the Department of Agriculture. P 13½×12.

2154	**1000**	5r. multicoloured	40	30

1001 Athlete running and Big Ben

1002 Sri Lanka Parliament Building

(Des Pulasthi Ediriweera. Litho Dept of Govt Printing, Sri Lanka)

2012 (23 July). Olympic Games, London. T **1001** and similar vert designs, each showing Big Ben. Multicoloured. P 13½×12½ (with one notched elliptical hole in each vert side) (2155/8) or 14×13½ (**MS**2159).

2155		5r. Type **1001**	40	25
2156		15r. Swimmer	1·00	85
2157		25r. Shooting	1·50	1·50
2158		75r. Badminton player	4·25	4·75
2155/2158		Set of 4	6·50	6·50
MS2159	163×103 mm. As Nos. 2155/8		6·50	7·00

(Des Ruwan Upasena. Litho Dept of Govt Printing, Sri Lanka)

2012 (11 Sept). 58th Commonwealth Parliamentary Conference, Colombo. P 12½×13 (with one notched elliptical hole in each horiz side).

2160	**1002**	5r. multicoloured	40	30

1003 Galle Face Hotel

(Des Vasantha Perera. Litho Dept of Govt Printing, Sri Lanka)

2012 (11 Sept). Colonial Buildings of Sri Lanka. T **1003** and similar horiz designs. P 13½×12 (2161/4) or 13½ (**MS**2165).

2161	**1003**	15r. black and azure	1·00	1·10
2162	–	15r. black and dull mauve	1·00	1·10
2163	–	15r. black and pale green	1·00	1·10
2164	–	15r. black and buff	1·00	1·10
2161/64		Set of 4	3·50	4·00
MS2165	174×84 mm. As Nos. 2161/2		2·00	2·25
MS2166	174×84 mm. As Nos. 2163/4		2·00	2·25

Designs: 2162, National Museum; 2163, Municipal Council, Colombo; 2164, Old Parliament.

1004 Children

(Des Isuru Chathuranga. Litho Dept of Govt Printing, Sri Lanka)

2012 (1 Oct). World Children's Day. P 13.

2167	**1004**	5r. multicoloured	40	30

1005 Emblems

1006 Binara Flower (*Exacum trinervium*)

(Des Mevan Fonseka. Litho Dept of Govt Printing, Sri Lanka)

2012 (6 Oct). World Post Day. P 12×13.

2168	**1005**	5r. multicoloured	40	30

(Des Vasantha Perera. Litho Dept of Govt Printing, Sri Lanka)

2012 (7 Oct). Flowers of Sri Lanka. T **1006** and similar horiz designs. Multicoloured. P 13½×14.

2169		5r. Type **1006**	45	45
2170		5r. Frangipani (*Plumeria rubra*)	45	45
2171		5r. 'Shoe Flower' (*Hibiscus rosa-sinensis*)	45	45
2172		5r. Sun flower (*Helianthus annuus*)	45	45
2169/72	Set of 4		1·60	1·60
MS2173	161×112 mm. Nos. 2169/72		1·60	1·75

No. **MS**2173 is inscr 'World Post Day Stamp Exhibition - 2012'.

1007 Woman with her Children

1008 Sri Lanka Insurance Building

(Des Ruwan Upasena. Litho Dept of Govt Printing, Sri Lanka)

2012 (16 Oct). 60th Anniv of World Health Organization in Sri Lanka. P 14×13½.

2174	**1007**	12r. multicoloured	1·00	1·00

(Des Isuru Chaturanga. Litho Dept of Govt Printing, Sri Lanka)

2012 (31 Oct). 50th Anniv of Sri Lanka Insurance. P 12½×13½ (with one notched elliptical hole in each horiz side).

2175	**1008**	5r. multicoloured	40	30

1009 Nativity Scene and Peace Doves flying to Family (Vojitha Heshan Herath)

(Des Isuru Chaturanga (**MS**2178). Litho Dept of Govt Printing, Sri Lanka)

2012 (2 Dec). Christmas. Children's Paintings. T **1009** and similar horiz design. Multicoloured. P 12½×13 (with one notched elliptical hole in each horiz side) (2176/7) or 13½×14 (**MS**2178).

2176		5r. Type **1009**	40	15
2177		25r. Man pulling family in cart and nativity scene (K. G. Morini Anjela Thalis)	1·75	2·00
MS2178	170×93 mm. Nos. 2176/7		2·10	2·40

1010 Early Monoplane

(Des Sudath Jayawardena. Litho Dept of Govt Printing, Sri Lanka)

2012 (7 Dec). Centenary of Aviation. T **1010** and similar horiz designs. Multicoloured. P 12½×13½ (with one notched elliptical hole in each horiz side) (2179/82) or 13½×14 (**MS**2183).

2179	5r. Type **1010**..........................	1·00	30
2180	12r. Air Ceylon (1947–78) plane........	1·75	1·25
2181	15r. Sri Lankan Airlines airliner..........	1·75	1·40
2182	25r. Mihin Lanka airliner...................	2·75	3·25
2179/82 Set of 4....................................		6·50	5·50
MS2183 178×91 mm. Nos. 2179/82		6·50	6·50

1011 Moonstone,
Vishnu Devale, Kandy

(Des Priyaratne Hewabatage and Ruwan Indrajith Upasena. Litho Dept of Govt Printing, Sri Lanka)

2012 (12 Dec). Moonstones, Guardstones and Balustrades of Sri Lanka. T **1011** and similar multicoloured designs. P 12½×13 (with one elliptical hole in each vert side and one notched elliptical hole in each horiz side) (horiz) or 13×12½ (with one elliptical hole in each horiz side and one notched elliptical hole in each vert side) (vert).

2184	50c. Type **1011**..........................	20	10
2185	1r. Moonstone, Watadage, Polonnaruwa.....	25	15
2186	2r. Moonstone, Rajmaha Vihara, Beligala....	30	15
2187	3r. Moonstone, Abayagiri Vihara, Anuradhapura..............	35	20
2188	4r. Guard stone, Jethawana Vihara, Anuradhapura (vert)............	40	20
2189	4r.50 Guard stone, Rajmaha Vihara, Arattana (vert)............	40	20
2190	5r. Guard stone, Tissamaharamaya (vert).....	40	20
2191	10r. Guard stone, Abayagiri Rathnaprasadaya, Anuradhapura (vert).	70	60
2192	12r. Guard stone, Abayagiri Stupa, Anuradhapura (vert).............	75	65
2193	15r. Guard stone, Dematamal Vihara, Buttala (vert)............	1·00	80
2194	20r. Balustrade with dragon's tongue supported by dwarf carving, Mahavihara, Anuradhapura (bright carmine borders)............	1·10	1·00
2195	25r. Balustrade, Lankathilaka Image House, Polonnaruwa.............	1·25	1·25
2196	30r. Balustrade, Jethawanarama Vihara, Anuradhapura.............	1·40	1·40
2197	40r. Balustrade, Mahavihara, Anuradhapura (orange-red borders).........	1·75	1·75
2198	55r. Balustrade, Mahavihara, Anuradhapura (green borders).............	2·50	2·75
2199	75r. Balustrade, Yapahuwa.............	3·75	4·25
2184/99 Set of 16....................................		15·00	14·00
MS2200 75×60 mm. Nos. 2184/7.............		1·50	1·50
MS2201 59×99 mm. Nos. 2188/93.............		3·50	3·50
MS2202 102×61 mm. Nos. 2194/9.............		10·00	11·00

1012 Lotus Flowers

(Des Kumudu Tharaka. Litho Dept of Govt Printing, Sri Lanka)

2013 (18 Jan). 60th Anniv of Sri Lanka-Japan Diplomatic Relations. T **1012** and similar horiz design. Multicoloured. P 12½×13 (with one notched elliptical hole in each horiz side) (3203/4) or 13½×14 (**MS**3205).

2203	5r. Type **1012**..........................	40	20
2204	65r. Cherry blossom....................	3·25	3·75
MS2205 152×95 mm. Nos. 3203/4.............		3·50	4·00

1013 Scout Camp

1014 Airliner, Control Tower and Passenger Terminal

(Des Piyaratna Hewabatage. Litho Dept of Govt Printing, Sri Lanka)

2013 (18 Feb). RISGO (Rajans International Scout Gathering) Centennial International Scout Jamboree, Kandy. P 12½×13½ (with one notched elliptical perf on each horiz side).

2206	**1013**	25r. multicoloured........	1·40	1·60

(Des D. G. Sudath Jayawardena. Litho Dept of Govt Printing, Sri Lanka)

2013 (18 Mar). Inauguration of Mattala Rajapaksa International Airport. P 12½×13 (with one notched elliptical hole on each horiz side).

2207	**1014**	5r. multicoloured........	1·00	60

1015 Pilgrims and Shrines

(Des P. Isuru Chathuranga. Litho Dept of Govt Printing, Sri Lanka)

2013 (5 Apr). Sixth Peace Pada Yatra, Sri Lanka. P 13½×12.

2208	**1015**	5r. multicoloured........	40	30

1016 Dharmasoka College, Ambalagoda

1017 Prince Siddhartha encountered an Old Man

(Des P. Isuru Chathuranga. Litho Dept of Govt Printing, Sri Lanka)

2013 (4 May). Centenary of Dharmasoka College, Ambalagoda. P 12½×13½ (with one notched elliptical hole on each horiz side).

2209	**1016**	5r. multicoloured........	40	30

(Des Kumudu Tharaka. Litho Dept of Govt Printing, Sri Lanka)

2013 (18 May). Vesak. Sathera Pera Nimithi (Four Omens). T **1017** and similar horiz designs. Multicoloured. P 12½×13 (with one notched elliptical hole in each horiz side) (2210/13) or 13½×14 (**MS**2214).

2210	4r. Type **1017**..........................	35	20
2211	5r. Prince Siddhartha encountered a diseased man....................	40	20
2212	15r. Prince Siddhartha encountered a corpse.	1·00	80
2213	50r. Prince Siddhartha encountered an ascetic	3·00	4·00
2210/13 Set of 4....................................		4·25	4·75
MS2214 121×185 mm. As Nos. 2210/13		4·25	4·75

1018 Dambegoda Bodhisattva Statue

1019 Swami Vivekananda

(Des Mevan Fonseka. Litho Dept of Govt Printing, Sri Lanka)

2013 (25 May). Dambegoda Bodhisattva Statue. P 12×13.

2215	**1018**	5r. multicoloured	40	30

(Des Pulasthi Ediriweera. Litho Dept of Govt Printing, Sri Lanka)

2013 (7 June). 150th Birth Anniv of Swami Vivekananda (1863–1902, Hindu monk and spiritual leader, founder of Ramakrishna Mission). P 13×12½ (with one notched elliptical hole in each vert side).

2216	**1019**	25r. multicoloured	1·40	1·60

1020 Christ Church Girls' College

(Des Ruwan Indrajith Upasena. Litho Dept of Govt Printing, Sri Lanka)

2013 (5 July). 125th Anniv of Christ Church Girls' College, Baddegama. P 12½×13 (with one notched elliptical hole in each horiz side).

2217	**1020**	5r. multicoloured	40	30

1021 Hawksbill Turtle
(*Eretmochelys imbricata*)

(Des Kelum A. Gunasekara (5, 15, 30r.) or D. G. Sudath Jayawardhana (25, 40, 50r.). Litho Dept of Govt Printing, Sri Lanka)

2013 (28 July). National Parks of Sri Lanka (4th series). Yala National Park. T **1021** and similar multicoloured designs. P 13½×14.

2218	5r. Type **1021**	55	25
2219	15r. Swamp Crocodile (*Crocodylus palustris*)	1·00	80
2220	25r. Elephant (*Elephas maximus*) - tusker (vert)	1·75	1·40
2221	30r. Black-necked Stork (*Ephippiorhynchus asiaticus*) (vert)	1·75	1·75
2222	40r. Wild Boar (*Sus scrofa*)	2·25	2·50
2223	50r. Spotted Deer (*Axis axis*)	2·50	2·75
2218/23	Set of 6	9·00	8·50
MS2224	144×97 mm. Nos. 2218 and 2223	3·00	3·50
MS2225	144×97 mm. Nos. 2219 and 2222	3·00	3·50
MS2226	145×96 mm. Nos. 2220/1	3·50	3·50

Miniature sheets as Nos. **MS**2224/6 with Thailand 2013 World Stamp Exhibition emblem on the sheet margins were sold for 200r. each, a premium of 145r. above face value of each sheet.

1022 Rev. Fr. Tissa Balasuriya

1023 Villagers using Leaves for Umbrellas and Kirimama buying Umbrella

(Des P. Isuru Chathuranga. Litho Dept of Govt Printing, Sri Lanka)

2013 (29 Aug). Rev. Fr. Tissa Balasuriya (1924 - 2013, priest and founder of Centre for Society and Religion) Commemoration. P 13½×12½ (with one notched elliptical hole in each vert side).

2227	**1022**	5r. multicoloured	40	30

(Des Cybil Wettasinghe. Litho Dept of Govt Printing, Sri Lanka)

2013 (1 Oct). World Children's Day. *The Umbrella Thief* by Cybil Wettasinghe. T **1023** and similar horiz designs. Multicoloured. P 12½×13 (with one notched elliptical hole in each horiz side).

2228	5r. Type **1023**	45	45
	a. Horiz strip of three. Nos. 2228/30	1·25	1·25
2229	5r. Kirimama searching for stolen umbrellas	45	45

2230	5r. Stolen umbrellas hanging from tree and Monkey curled up in umbrella	45	45
2228/30	Set of 3	1·25	1·25

Nos. 2228/30 were printed together, *se-tenant*, as horizontal strips of three stamps in sheetlets of 15 (3×5), each horizontal strip forming a composite design.

1024 Letters, Parcels, Arrows and Globe

(Des Givantha Arthasad. Litho Dept of Govt Printing, Sri Lanka)

2013 (9 Oct). World Post Day. P 12×13.

2231	**1024**	5r. multicoloured	40	30

1025 Colombo - Katunayake Expressway

(Des Mevan Fonseka. Litho Dept of Govt Printing, Sri Lanka)

2013 (27 Oct). Inauguration of Colombo-Katunayake Expressway. P 13½×13 (with two diamond-shaped holes in each horiz side and one notched elliptical hole in each vert side).

2232	**1025**	5r. multicoloured	50	30

1026 Deshabandu Alec Robertson

1027 Dr. Premasiri Khemadasa

(Des P. Isuru Chathuranga. Litho Dept of Govt Printing, Sri Lanka)

2013 (30 Oct). Deshabandu Alec Robertson (1928–2002, Buddhist preacher and lecturer) Commemoration. P 13×12½ (with one notched elliptical hole in each vert side).

2233	**1026**	5r. multicoloured	40	30

(Des P. Isuru Chathuranga. Litho Dept of Govt Printing, Sri Lanka)

2013 (1 Nov). Dr. Premasiri Khemadasa (1937–2002, composer) Commemoration. P 13×12½ (with one notched elliptical hole in each vert side).

2234	**1027**	5r. multicoloured	40	30

1028 Emblem of Ceylon Excise Department

1029 Girl and Emblem

(Des Kelum A. Gunasekara. Litho Dept of Govt Printing, Sri Lanka)

2013 (6 Nov). Centenary of Excise Department. P 12½×13½ (with one notched elliptical hole in each horiz side and one diamond-shaped hole in each vert side).

2235	**1028**	5r. multicoloured	40	30

(Des Kumudu Tharaka. Litho Dept of Govt Printing, Sri Lanka)

2013 (14 Nov). Commonwealth Heads of Government Meeting, Colombo. P 13½×14.
2236 **1029** 5r. multicoloured 40 20
2237 **1029** 25r. multicoloured .... 1·75 2·00
MS2238 170×106 mm. Nos. 2236/7 .... 2·10 2·25

1030 Dr. Tissa Abeysekara **1031** Nativity

(Des P. Isuru Chathuranga. Litho Dept of Govt Printing, Sri Lanka)

2013 (27 Nov). Dr. Tissa Abeysekara (1939–2009, writer and film director) Commemoration. P 12½×13 (with one notched elliptical hole in each horiz side).
2239 **1030** 5r. multicoloured 40 30

(Des Ruwan Upasena. Litho Dept of Govt Printing, Sri Lanka)

2013 (1 Dec). Christmas. T **1031** and similar vert design. Multicoloured. P 14×13½.
2240 **1031** 5r. Type **1031**...................................... 40 15
2241 30r. Madonna and Child and worshippers ... 1·90 2·25
MS2242 106×139 mm. Nos. 2240/1 .... 2·25 2·40

1032 Emblem **1033** Dharmadasa Walpola

(Des P. Isuru Chathuranga. Litho Dept of Govt Printing, Sri Lanka)

2013 (2 Dec). Centenary of All Ceylon Moor's Association. P 12½×13 (with one notched elliptical hole in each horiz side and one diamond-shaped hole in each vert side).
2243 **1032** 5r. lake-brown and black 40 30

(Des Kumudu Tharaka. Litho Dept of Govt Printing, Sri Lanka)

2013 (19 Dec). Dharmadasa Walpola (1927–83, singer and musician) Commemoration. P 13½×12½ (with one notched elliptical hole in each vert side).
2244 **1033** 5r. multicoloured 40 30

1034 Ven. Baddegama Wimalawansa Nayaka Thero **1035** Emblem

(Des Pulasthi Ediriweera. Litho Dept of Govt Printing, Sri Lanka)

2013 (21 Dec). Ven. Baddegama Wimalawansa Nayaka Thero (Buddhist monk) Commemoration. P 13½×12½ (with one notched elliptical hole in each vert side).
2245 **1034** 5r. multicoloured 40 30

(Des D. G. Sudath Jayawardena. Litho Dept of Govt Printing, Sri Lanka)

2013 (23 Dec). 50th Anniv of Sri Lanka Administrative Service. P 13½×12½.
2246 **1035** 5r. multicoloured 40 30

1036 Farmer Ploughing **1037** Raised Fists and Landscape

(Des Pulasthi Ediriweera. Litho Dept of Govt Printing, Sri Lanka)

2014 (12 Jan). Thai Pongal - Farmers Festival. T **1036** and similar horiz design. Multicoloured. P 13½×14.
2247 5r. Type **1036**...................................... 40 20
2248 25r. Couple cooking traditional pongal (rice pudding).. 1·75 2·00
MS2249 157×115 mm. Nos. 2247/8 .... 2·10 2·25

(Des Sudath Jayawardena. Litho)

2014 (21 Feb). Deyata Kirula National Development Exhibition, Kuliyapitiya. P 13½×12½ (with one notched elliptical hole in each vert side).
2250 **1037** 5r. multicoloured 40 30

1038 Spiral Railway at Demodara

(Des Mevan Fonseka. Litho)

2014 (28 Feb). Civil Engineering Marvels of Sri Lanka Railway. T **1038** and similar diamond-shaped design. Granite paper. P 13.
2251 5r. Type **1038**...................................... 70 70
2252 5r. Nine Arch Viaduct at Gotuwala 70 70

1039 Mountain Hourglass Tree Frog (*Taruga eques*) **1040** Anniversary Emblem and Growing Crop

(Des Palitha Gunasinghe. Litho)

2014 (3 Mar). World Wildlife Day. P 13½×12½ (with one notched elliptical hole in each vert side).
2253 **1039** 5r. multicoloured 70 35

(Des Gamini Abekoon. Litho Dept of Govt Printing, Sri Lanka)

2014 (4 Apr). 50th Anniv of Ceylon Fertiliser Company Ltd. P 12½×13 (with one notched elliptical hole in each horiz side).
2254 **1040** 5r. multicoloured 40 30

1041 H. Sri Nissanka

1042 Ho Chi Minh

(Des P. Isuru Chathuranga. Litho Dept of Govt Printing, Sri Lanka)

2014 (4 Apr). H. Sri Nissanka (1898–1954, Kings Counsel) Commemoration. P 13½×12½ (with one notched elliptical hole in each vert side).

2255 **1041** 5r. multicoloured 40 30

(Des Kumudu Tharaka. Litho Dept of Govt Printing, Sri Lanka)

2014 (28 Apr). Ho Chi Minh (1890–1969, Vietnamese leader) Commemoration. P 12×13½.

2256 **1042** 5r. multicoloured 40 30

1043 Emblem

1044 Prince Siddhartha repelled by the Sight of Sleeping Dancers

(Des Sanath Rohan Wickramasinghe. Litho Dept of Govt Printing, Sri Lanka)

2014 (7 May). World Conference on Youth, Colombo. P 12½×13 with one notched elliptical hole in each horiz side).

2257 **1043** 5r. multicoloured 40 30

(Des Kumudu Tharaka. Litho Dept of Govt Printing, Sri Lanka)

2014 (12 May). Vesak. The Great Renunciation of Prince Siddhartha. T **1044** and similar vert designs. Multicoloured. P 14×13½.

2258 5r. Type **1044** 40 20
2259 10r. Prince Siddhartha looking at his sleeping wife Yasodhara and baby son Pahula on the eve of Renunciation 70 55
2260 15r. Prince Siddhartha and courtier Channa leaping the river Anoma on Prince's horse Kanthaka .... 1·00 1·00
2261 20r. Prince Siddhartha cutting off his hair with his sword after giving all royal ornaments to Channa .... 1·10 1·40
2258/61 *Set of 4* .... 3·00 2·75
MS2262 155×93 mm. Nos. 2258/61 .... 3·00 3·00

STAMP BOOKLETS

1905 (Oct). Black on grey (No. SB1) or black on buff (No. SB1a) covers. Stapled.
SB1 1r.21, booklet containing twenty-four 5c. (No. 280) in blocks of 12 ....
SB1a 1r.45, booklet containing twenty-four 6c. (No. 281) in blocks of 6 .... £4750

1908. Black on grey cover. Advertisement on back cover. Stapled.
SB2 1r.20, booklet containing twenty-four 5c. (No. 289) in blocks of 12 ....

1912. Black on grey cover. Advertisement on back cover. Stapled.
SB2a 1r.20, booklet containing twenty-four 5c. (No. 304) in blocks of 12 ....

1919. Black on orange covers. Telegraph details on back cover. Stapled.
SB3 1r.44, booklet containing twenty-four 6c. (No. 309) in blocks of 6 ....
a. Black on grey cover. Advertisement on back cover.
SB4 1r.44, booklet containing twenty-four 3c. and twelve 6c. (Nos. 308/9) in blocks of 6 ....
a. Advertisement on back cover ....

1919 (?). Black on cream cover. Advertisement on back. Stapled.
SB4b 1r.45, booklet containing twenty-four 3c. (No. 302) and twelve 6c. (No. 305) ....

1922. Black on green covers. "Fiat" advertisement on back cover. Stapled.
SB5 1r.44, booklet containing twenty-four 6c. (No. 343) in blocks of 6 ....
SB6 1r.46, booklet containing twenty-four 6c. (No. 343) in blocks of 6 .... £3500
SB6a 1r.46, booklet containing twenty-four 3c. and twelve 6c. (Nos. 340/3) in blocks of 6 .... £3750
b. Black on orange cover. "Colombo Jewelry Store" advertisement on back cover ....

1926. Black on green covers. Kennedy & Co. (No. SB7) or Fiat (No. SB8) advertisements on back cover. Stapled.
SB7 2r.06, booklet containing twelve 3c., 5c. on 6c. and 9c. (Nos. 340, 362 and 345) in blocks of 6 .... £3250
SB8 2r.16, booklet containing twenty-four 9c. (No. 345) in blocks of 6 ....

1932. Black on green covers. Stapled.
SB9 1r.80, booklet containing thirty 6c. (No. 343) in blocks of 6 and pane of three airmail labels £1500
SB10 2r.70, booklet containing thirty 9c. (No. 345) in blocks of 6 and pane of three airmail labels £1900

1935 (May). Silver Jubilee of King George V. Black on light blue (No. SB11) or light green (No. SB12) covers. Stapled.
SB11 1r.80, booklet containing thirty 6c. (No. 379) in blocks of 6 .... £1400
SB12 2r.70, booklet containing thirty 9c. (No. 380) in blocks of 6 .... £1800

1935 (Dec)–**36**. Black on blue (No. SB13) or green (No. SB14) covers. Stapled.
SB13 1r.80, booklet containing thirty 6c. (No. 370) in blocks of 6 and pane of four airmail labels £900
a. Stamps in blocks of 10 .... £900
SB14 2r.70, booklet containing thirty 9c. (No. 371) in blocks of 6 and pane of four airmail labels £1100
a. Stamps in blocks of 10 (1936) £1100

1937 (Apr–June). Coronation of King George VI. Black on blue (No. SB15) or olive-green (No. SB16) covers. Stapled.
SB15 1r.80, booklet containing thirty 6c. (No. 383) in blocks of 10 and pane of four airmail labels (June) £1200
SB16 2r.70, booklet containing thirty 9c. (No. 384) in blocks of 10 and pane of four airmail labels £1300

1938. Black on blue (No. SB17) or grey (No. SB18) covers. Stapled.
SB17 1r.80, booklet containing thirty 6c. (No. 388) in blocks of 10 and pane of four airmail labels £1400
SB18 3r. booklet containing fifteen 20c. (No. 391) in blocks of 5 or 10 and pane of four airmail labels .. £1500

1941. Black on pink cover, with contents amended in manuscript. Stapled.
SB19 1r.80, booklet containing sixty 3c. on 6c. (No. 398) in blocks of 10 ....
a. Black on blue cover ....

1951 (5 Dec). Black on buff cover. Stitched.
SB20 1r. booklet containing twenty 5c. (No. 414) in blocks of four and pane of airmail labels .... 20·00
a. Containing two blocks of ten 5c. stamps and no airmail labels .... 50·00

1952 (21 Jan). Black on green cover. Stitched.
SB21 6r. booklet containing eight 75c. (No. 417) in blocks of 4 and two panes of four airmail labels 20·00

1999 (3 Feb). Multicoloured cover. Stamps attached by selvedge.
SB22 10r. booklet containing ten 1r. (No. 1422) in blocks of ten .... 1·00

B **2** 'Viceroy Special' Steam Locomotive B8 240

2012 (6 Oct). 25th Anniv (2011) of Viceroy Special Steam Train. Multicoloured covers, 49×97 mm, as Type B **2**. Stamps attached by selvedge.

SB23 25r. booklet containing five 5r. (No. 2073) in vert
      strip (Type B **2**)... 3·50
SB24 25r. booklet containing five 5r. (No. 2074) in vert
      strip ('Viceroy Special' locomotive B2 213)........... 3·50
SB25 25r. booklet containing five 5r. (No. 2075) in vert
      strip (Sentinel Camel steam rail car V2 331)........ 3·50
SB26 25r. booklet containing five 5r. (No. 2076) in vert
      strip (Narrow gauge steam locomotive J1 220). 3·50

The cover of No. SB25 is inscr 'Stream Rail Car' in error.

B **3** Gamini Fonseka, Joe Abewickrama, Malini Fonseka, Sandaya Kumari, Titus Thotawatta and Eddy Jayamanna

2012 (6 Oct). Legends of Sinhala Cinema. Multicoloured cover, 63×112 mm, as Type B **3**. Stamps attached by selvedge.

SB27 60r. booklet containing Nos. 2124/6 and 2127/9 in
      two vert strips of three................................. 4·00

B **4** Binara Flower

2012 (7 Oct). Flowers of Sri Lanka. Multicoloured covers, 49×97 mm, as Type B **4**. Stamps attached by selvedge.

SB28 25r. booklet containing five 5r. (No. 2169) in vert
      strip (Type B **4**).. 2·25
SB29 25r. booklet containing five 5r. (No. 2170) in vert
      strip (Frangipani)... 2·25
SB30 25r. booklet containing five 5r. (No. 2171) in vert
      strip (Hibiscus).. 2·25
SB31 25r. booklet containing five 5r. (No. 2172) in vert
      strip (Sunflower).. 2·25

OFFICIAL STAMPS

1869. Issues of 1867–68 overprinted "SERVICE" in block letters. Although these stamps were prepared for use and sent out to the colony, they were never issued.

SERVICE

Type O **1**

Optd with Type O **1** by D.L.R. Wmk **6**. P 12½.

O1	**1**	2d. yellow	75·00	
		x. Wmk reversed	£225	
O2		6d. deep brown (R.)	75·00	
O3	**2**	8d. chocolate	75·00	
O4	**1**	1s. pale lilac	£170	
O5	**2**	2s. deep blue (R.)	£120	
		a. Imperf	£1100	

SERVICE

Type O **2**

Optd with Type O **2** by D.L.R. Wmk Crown CC. P 14.

| O6 | **8** | 1d. blue | 75·00 | |
| O7 | **7** | 3d. carmine-rose | £150 | |

Until 1 October 1895 all Official mail was carried free. After that date postage was paid on Official letters to the general public, on certain interdepartmental mail and on all packets over 1lb in weight. Nos. O11/27 were provided for this purpose.

On

Service

(O **3**)

1895. Optd with Type O **3** by the Govt Printer, Colombo.

O11	**9**	2c. green (No. 147)	20·00	70
		w. Wmk inverted	†	—
O12	**39**	3c. terracotta and blue-green (No. 245)	12·00	2·75
O13	**28**	5c. dull purple (No. 195)	5·50	30
O14	**29**	15c. sage-green (No. 196)	24·00	65
		x. Wmk reversed	†	£325
O15		25c. yellow-brown (No. 198)	13·00	3·25
O16		30c. bright mauve and chestnut (No. 247)	13·00	60
O17	**30**	1r.12 dull rose (*wmk sideways*) (No. 201)	95·00	65·00
		a. Opt double, one albino	£300	
		b. Wmk upright	£100	80·00
O11/17 *Set of 7*			£160	65·00

1899 (June)–**1900**. Nos. 256/7 and 261/2 optd with Type O **3**.

O18	**9**	2c. pale orange-brown (3.00)	12·00	60
O19	**39**	3c. deep green (9.00)	13·00	4·75
O20	**29**	15c. blue (9.00)	27·00	60
O21	**39**	75c. black and red-brown (R.)	9·00	10·00
O18/21 *Set of 4*			55·00	14·00

1903 (26 Nov)–**04**. Nos. 265/6, 268 and 271/3 optd with Type O **3**.

O22	**44**	2c. red-brown (4.1.04)	23·00	1·00
O23	**45**	3c. green	16·00	2·00
O24	**46**	5c. dull purple	32·00	1·50
O25	**48**	15c. blue	42·00	2·50
O26		25c. bistre (15.7.04)	38·00	18·00
O27		30c. dull violet and green (14.3.04)	21·00	1·50
O22/27 *Set of 6*			£150	25·00

Stamps overprinted "On Service" were withdrawn on 1 October 1904.

POSTAL FISCALS

1952 (1 Dec). As T **72** but inscr "REVENUE" at sides. Chalk-surfaced paper.

F1 10r. dull green and yellow-orange.................. £100 50·00

This revenue stamp was on sale for postal use from 1 December 1952 until 14 March 1954.

Used price for stamp with identifiable postal cancellation.

F **1** Republic Crest

F **2**

(Recess Harrison)

1979 (28 May)–**83**. As Type F **1**, but with additional Sinhala and Tamil inscrs on either side of crest. W F **2**. P 13×12.

F2	20r. blackish green	5·00	2·75
F3	50r. deep slate-violet	13·00	7·00
F4	100r. deep carmine-red (14.10.83)	23·00	25·00
F2/4 *Set of 3*		38·00	32·00

The above, together with a 500r. dark blue and 1000r. chestnut, were originally released for fiscal purposes on 24 June 1974. The dates quoted are those on which they were validated for postal use. All three were withdrawn on 6 August 1984.

(Litho Harrison)

1984 (15 Aug). Wmk F **2**. P 14½×14.

| F5 | F **1** | 50r. orange | 45·00 | 16·00 |
| F6 | | 100r. dull chocolate | 60·00 | 55·00 |

A 500r. value in light green also exists, but was not valid for postal purposes.

(Recess Harrison)

1984 (21 Sept). Wmk F **2**. P 14½×14.

F7	F **1**	50r. orange-vermilion	1·00	1·50
		a. No watermark (1996)		
F8		100r. deep reddish purple	2·00	3·00
		a. No watermark (1996)		

Stamps in this series with face values of 500r. (in green) and 1000r. (in light blue) were not valid for postal purposes.

There were a number of printings of these stamps between 1984 and the appearance of Nos. F9/10 with the result that the shades vary considerably.

F **3**

(Recess D.L.R.)

1998 (16 Dec)–**99**. Wmk F **3**. P 14½×14.

| F9 | F **1** | 50r. orange (28.9.99) | 4·00 | 2·75 |
| F10 | | 100r. deep reddish brown | 5·50 | 6·00 |

The 500r. green and 1000r. light blue in this series were not valid for postal purposes. The latter value also exists with wavy line watermark.

F **4**   F **5**

(Des D. Sudath Jayawardena. Recess Banknote Corporation of America Inc., USA)

2002 (28 May). Granite paper. P 12½ (with one elliptical hole on each vertical side).

| F11 | F **4** | 50r. deep blue and yellow-brown | 4·00 | 2·50 |
| F12 | | 100r. deep blue and emerald | 6·00 | 6·50 |

The 500r. deep and light blue and 1000r. deep blue and pink in this series were not valid for postal purposes.

(Des Pulasthi Ediriweera. Photo and recess Garsu Pasaulis, Lithuania)

2007 (23 Nov). Granite paper with fluorescent fibres. P 12½ (with one elliptical hole on each side).

F13	F **5**	50r. multicoloured	55	60
		a. Imperf (pair)		
F14		100r. multicoloured	1·10	1·25
		a. Imperf (pair)		
F15		200r. multicoloured	2·25	2·40
F13/15 *Set of 3*			3·50	3·75

Stamps in this series with face values of 500r. and 1000r. were not valid for postal purposes.

PARLIAMENT STAMPS

M **1** Arms and Parliament Building,
Sri Jayawardenapura Kotte

(Des P. Ediriweera. Litho Dept of Govt Printing, Sri Lanka)

2005 (8 June). Postal Facilities for the Members of Parliament. P 14.

| M1 | M **1** | 5r. multicoloured | 3·00 | 70 |

M **2** Arms and Parliament Building,
Sri Jayawardenapura Kotte

2008 (8 July). Postal Facilities for the Members of Parliament. Litho. P 12½×13 (with one notched elliptical hole on each horiz side).

M2	M **2**	5r. multicoloured	35	40
M3		10r. multicoloured	70	80
M4		15r. multicoloured	1·10	1·25
M5		25r. multicoloured	1·75	2·00
M6		30r. multicoloured	2·10	2·40
M2/6 *Set of 5*			5·50	6·25

Nos. M1/6 were only issued to Members of Parliament.

TELEGRAPH STAMPS
Telegraph Stamps of INDIA used in Ceylon

1869 (1 July)–**78**. Telegraph stamps of India (Nos. T5/20) used in Ceylon.

ZT1	2a. maroon	5·00
ZT2	4a. blue	4·00
ZT3	8a. brown	3·00
	a. Imperf (10.78)	£750
ZT4	1r. grey (Die I)	60·00
ZT5	1r. grey (Die II)	3·00
ZT6	2r.8a. orange-yellow (Die I)	5·00
ZT7	2r.8a. orange (Die II) (1878)	40·00
ZT8	5r. orange-brown	5·50
ZT9	10r. green (Die I)	5·00
ZT10	10r. green (Die II) (1878)	30·00
ZT11	14r.4a. lilac (1870)	40·00
ZT12	25r. violet (Die I)	15·00
ZT13	25r. violet (Die II) (1878)	30·00
ZT14	28r.8a. yellow-green (1870)	40·00
ZT15	50r. rose (Die I)	40·00

The prices quoted above are for used upper halves with clearly identifiable cancels of offices in Ceylon. The large block letters used in these straight-line cancels are such that only three or four letters usually appear on a single stamp, and multiples or examples on piece may be needed to confirm identification. Usage is recorded at the following offices, with Colombo being the most frequently seen : ANURADHAPURA, BADULLA, BATTICALOA, COLOMBO, GALLE, GAMPOLA, JAFFNA (or JAFFRA, in error), KALATURA, KANDY, MANAAR, MATALLE, NAWALAPITYA, NEWARAELIYA or NEWARAELLYA, PANADURE and TRINCOMALEE.

The use of Indian telegraph stamps in Ceylon ceased with the release of the following optd issue (Nos. T1/9).

PRICES. For Nos. T1/164 prices are quoted for unused whole stamps and used upper halves. Used lower halves (often with punched holes) are worth from ×2. Used whole stamps are rare and for many issues unknown.

(T **1**)

1880 (1 July). Telegraph stamps of India (1869–78 issue) optd with Type T **1** twice (on upper and lower halves).

T1	2a. maroon	†	50·00
T2	4a. blue	£1100	40·00
T3	8a. brown	†	20·00
T4	1r. grey (Die II)	†	15·00
T5	2r.8a. orange (Die II)	†	35·00
T6	5r. orange-brown	†	45·00

T7   10r. green (Die II)..   †   30·00
T8   25r. violet (Die II)..   —   40·00
T9   50r. rose-carmine (Die II).................................   †   £450
    The Type T **1** opt has been extensively forged.

T **2**   T **3**   T **4**

T **5**   T **6**   T **7**

T **8**   T **9**   T **10**

T **11**   T **12**   T **13**

T **14** ("CA" in narrow letters)

(Typo, De La Rue)

1881 (14 Feb)–**82**. W T **14**. Perf 14.

T10	T **2**	12c. bistre	18·00	1·00
		w. Wmk inverted	60·00	10·00
T11	T **3**	25c. blue-green	£250	25·00
T12	T **4**	25c. green (3.82)	18·00	50
		w. Wmk inverted	—	45·00
T13	T **5**	50c. blue	18·00	50
		w. Wmk inverted	60·00	10·00
T14	T **6**	1r. red-brown	£150	7·00
T15	T **7**	1r. red-brown (3.82)	18·00	50
		w. Wmk inverted	£100	30·00
T16	T **8**	2r.50c. grey	35·00	1·00
		w. Wmk inverted	—	30·00
T17	T **9**	5r. orange	75·00	1·25
		w. Wmk inverted	—	35·00
T18	T **10**	10r. reddish lilac	£300	16·00
T19	T **11**	10r. rose-lilac (3.82)	—	3·00
		a. Claret	£300	3·00
		b. Reddish purple	£200	2·00
T20	T **12**	25r. bright rose	£1000	2·00
		a. Carmine	£1000	2·00
		w. Wmk inverted	—	35·00
T21	T **13**	50r. brown-rose	£1500	6·00
		a. Brown-lilac	£1500	6·00

    The original types of the 25c. (T **3**), 1r. (T **6**) and 10r. (T **10**) were withdrawn and replaced after it was found that the face value could become difficult to determine after horizontal bisection in use. In the other designs the face value was clearly stated on both top and bottom halves.
    For later printings in these types, but wmk T **129**, see Nos. T139/47.

(T **15**)

1882 (7 Feb). Fiscal stamp inscr "STAMP DUTY" opt as Type T **15**. Wmk T **14**. Perf 14.
T22   T **15**   25c. lilac...   †   £600
    Alternate horizontal rows were optd "TELE" and "GRAPH", to provide vertical pairs for separation. No unused examples, or used examples with "TELE", have been reported.

(T **16**)   (T **17**)   (T **18**)

(T **19**) (T **20**)

(T **29**) (T **30**)

(T **21**) (T **22**)

1882 (1 Jan)–**94**. Nos. T 12/17 and T 19/21 surch with new values by Ceylon Govt Printer, as Types T **16/121**.

(a) Surch 12c.

T23	T **16**	12c. on 25c. green (20.4.87)	£275	55·00
T24	T **17**	12c. on 25c. green (16.1.89)	£300	22·00
		a. Small "12", "2" with straight foot (Type T **18**)	—	60·00
T25	T **19**	12c. on 50c. blue (20.4.87)	£100	5·00
T26	T **20**	12c. on 50c. blue (7.5.88)	55·00	5·00
T27	T **21**	12c. on 50c. blue (16.1.89)	—	27·00
		a. Small "12", "2" with straight foot (Type T **22**)	—	70·00

(T **31**) (T **32**)

(b) Surch 20c.

T28	T **23**	20c. on 25c. green (9.7.86)	£120	6·00
		a. Surch double	†	£500
T29	T **24**	20c. on 25c. green (7.4.87)	£120	6·00
T30	T **25**	20c. on 25c. green (13.4.88)	80·00	10·00
T31	T **26**	20c. on 25c. green (1.4.92)	£150	15·00
		a. "2" in upper "20 cents" with straight foot	†	75·00
T32	T **27**	20c. on 50c. blue (7.4.87)	£110	5·00
		a. Surch double	†	£500
		w. Wmk inverted	—	55·00
T33	T **28**	20c. on 50c. blue (16.1.89)	80·00	5·00
T34	T **29**	20c. on 50c. blue (2.8.89)	80·00	5·00
T35	T **30**	20c. on 50c. blue (18.1.90)	65·00	5·00
T36	T **31**	20c. on 50c. blue (26.9.90)	65·00	5·00
T37	T **32**	20c. on 1r. red-brown (2.92)	£110	6·00

(T **23**) (T **24**) (T **25**)

(T **26**) (T **27**) (T **28**)

(T **33**) (T **34**) (T **35**)

(c) Surch 25c.

T38	T **33**	25c. on 50c. blue (20.1.92)	—	55·00
T39	T **34**	25c. on 1r. red-brown (T **7**) (3.2.92)	—	75·00
T40	T **35**	25c. on 50r. brown-lilac (26.2.92)	£2750	70·00

| (T 36) | (T 37) | (T 38) |

| (T 50) | (T 51) | (T 52) |

T **39** is as T **50** but surcharged in black.

| (T 40) | (T 41) | (T 42) |

| (T 53) | (T 54) | (T 55) |

| (T 43) | (T 44) (14½ mm between words and figures) | (T 45) |

Type **46** is as Type **44** but with 18 mm between words and figures.

| (T 47) | (T 48) (single bar) | (T 49) (double bar) |

| (T 56) | (T 57) | (T 58) |

T **59** is surcharged "60 cents" as T **56/8** but at top *and* centre.

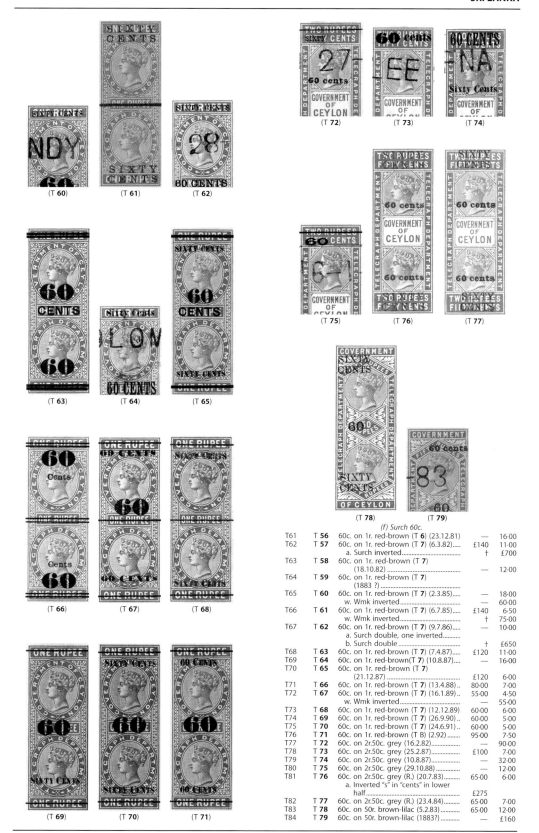

(T 60)　(T 61)　(T 62)
(T 63)　(T 64)　(T 65)
(T 66)　(T 67)　(T 68)
(T 69)　(T 70)　(T 71)
(T 72)　(T 73)　(T 74)
(T 75)　(T 76)　(T 77)
(T 78)　(T 79)

(f) Surch 60c.

T61	T 56	60c. on 1r. red-brown (T 6) (23.12.81)	—	16·00
T62	T 57	60c. on 1r. red-brown (T 7) (6.3.82)	£140	11·00
		a. Surch inverted	†	£700
T63	T 58	60c. on 1r. red-brown (T 7) (18.10.82)	—	12·00
T64	T 59	60c. on 1r. red-brown (T 7) (1883 ?)		
T65	T 60	60c. on 1r. red-brown (T 7) (2.3.85)	—	18·00
		w. Wmk inverted	—	60·00
T66	T 61	60c. on 1r. red-brown (T 7) (6.7.85)	£140	6·50
		w. Wmk inverted	†	75·00
T67	T 62	60c. on 1r. red-brown (T 7) (9.7.86)	—	10·00
		a. Surch double, one inverted		
		b. Surch double	†	£650
T68	T 63	60c. on 1r. red-brown (T 7) (7.4.87)	£120	11·00
T69	T 64	60c. on 1r. red-brown(T 7) (10.8.87)	—	16·00
T70	T 65	60c. on 1r. red-brown (T 7) (21.12.87)	£120	6·00
T71	T 66	60c. on 1r. red-brown (T 7) (13.4.88)	80·00	7·00
T72	T 67	60c. on 1r. red-brown (T 7) (16.1.89)	55·00	4·50
		w. Wmk inverted	—	55·00
T73	T 68	60c. on 1r. red-brown (T 7) (12.12.89)	60·00	6·00
T74	T 69	60c. on 1r. red-brown (T 7) (26.9.90)	60·00	5·00
T75	T 70	60c. on 1r. red-brown (T 7) (24.6.91)	60·00	5·00
T76	T 71	60c. on 1r. red-brown (T B) (2.92)	95·00	7·50
T77	T 72	60c. on 2r.50c. grey (16.2.82)	—	90·00
T78	T 73	60c. on 2r.50c. grey (25.2.87)	£100	7·00
T79	T 74	60c. on 2r.50c. grey (10.8.87)	—	32·00
T80	T 75	60c. on 2r.50c. grey (29.10.88)	—	12·00
T81	T 76	60c. on 2r.50c. grey (R.) (20.7.83)	65·00	6·00
		a. Inverted "s" in "cents" in lower half	£275	
T82	T 77	60c. on 2r.50c. grey (R.) (23.4.84)	65·00	7·00
T83	T 78	60c. on 50r. brown-lilac (5.2.83)	65·00	12·00
T84	T 79	60c. on 50r. brown-lilac (1883?)	—	£160

(T 80)   (T 81)   (T 82)   (T 92)   (T 93)   (T 94)

(T 83)   (T 84)   (T 85)   (T 95)   (T 96)   (T 97)

(T 86)   (T 87)   (T 88)   (T 98)   (T 99)   (T 100)

(T 89)   (T 90)   (T 91)   (T 101)   (T 102)   (T 103)

(T 104)

T **105** is surcharged "80 Cents" similar to T **87**, but at top *and* centre.

(T **106**)   (T **107**)   (T **108**)

(T **109**)   (T **110**)   (T **111**)

(T **112**)   (T **113**)   (T **114**)

(T **115**)   (T **116**)   (T **117**)

(T **118**)   (T **119**)

(g) Surch 80c.

T85	T **80**	80c. on 1r. red-brown (T **6**) (10.1.82) ..	—	13·00
T86	T **81**	80c. on 1r. red-brown (T **7**) (6.3.82).....	£180	16·00
T87	T **82**	80c. on 1r. red-brown (T **7**) (18.10.82)	£110	14·00
T88	T **83**	80c. on 1r. red-brown (T **7**) (6.7.85)	£140	6·00
		a. Surch double		
T89	T **84**	80c. on 1r. red-brown (T **7**) (13.4.88) ..	80·00	8·00
T90	T **85**	80c. on 1r. red-brown (T **7**) (16.1.89) ..	70·00	7·00
		w. Wmk inverted	£140	27·00
T91	T **86**	80c. on 1r. red-brown (T **7**) (16.1.89) ..	—	15·00
T92	T **87**	80c. on 1r. red-brown (T **7**) (2.8.89)....	—	11·00
T93	T **88**	80c. on 1r. red-brown (T **7**) (18.1.90) ..	75·00	4·00
T94	T **89**	80c. on 1r. red-brown (T **7**) (3.92)........	95·00	13·00
T95	T **90**	80c. on 2r.50c. grey (2.3.85)..................	£180	21·00
T96	T **91**	80c. on 2r.50c. grey (9.7.86)..................	£130	6·00
		a. Surch double	†	£400
T97	T **92**	80c. on 2r.50c. grey (26.9.88)	—	8·00
		a. "CENTS" above "80"...........................	—	£350
T98	T **93**	80c. on 2r.50c. grey (16.1.89)	£120	10·00
T99	T **94**	80c. on 2r.50c. grey (18.1.90)	80·00	8·00
T100	T **95**	80c. on 2r.50c. grey (16.9.90)	£275	10·00
T101	T **96**	80c. on 2r.50c. grey (3.2.92)	—	16·00
T102	T **97**	80c. on 5r. orange (3.9.84)	—	38·00
T103	T **98**	80c. on 5r. orange (7.4.87)	£170	27·00
T104	T **99**	80c. on 5r. orange (10.8.87)	—	32·00
		w. Wmk inverted	—	32·00
T105	T **100**	80c. on 5r. orange (21.12.87)	—	21·00
T106	T **101**	80c. on 5r. orange (26.9.90)	£130	12·00
		a. "00" for "80"......................................	£5500	£375
T107	T **102**	80c. on 10r. rose-lilac (T **11**) (3.9.84) ...	—	70·00
T108	T **103**	80c. on 10r. rose-lilac (T **11**) (7.4.87) ...	—	11·00
		w. Wmk inverted	£275	
T109	T **104**	80c. on 10r. rose-lilac (T **11**) (10.8.87).	—	22·00
T110	T **105**	80c. on 10r. rose-lilac (T **11**) (1887?) ...		
T111	T **106**	80c. on 10r. rose-lilac (T **11**)		
		(21.12.87)..	£160	21·00
T112	T **107**	80c. on 10r. reddish purple (T **11**)		
		(26.9.90)..	£120	12·00
		a. "00" for "80"......................................	£6000	£425
T113	T **108**	80c. on 25r. bright rose (5.2.83).............	80·00	13·00
		a. Inverted "s" in "80 cents" on		
		lower half...	£300	
T114	T **109**	80c. on 25r. bright rose (20.7.83)	£160	17·00
T115	T **110**	80c. on 25r. bright rose (23.4.84)	£120	16·00
T116	T **111**	80c. on 25r. bright rose (10.8.87)	£170	21·00
T117	T **112**	80c. on 25r. bright rose (21.12.87).........	—	15·00
T118	T **113**	80c. on 25r. carmine (26.9.90)	—	15·00
T119	T **114**	80c. on 25r. carmine (3.92).....................	—	35·00
T120	T **115**	80c. on 50r. brown-rose (20.7.83)	—	32·00
T121	T **116**	80c. on 50r. brown-lilac (3.9.84).............	—	90·00
T122	T **117**	80c. on 50r. brown-lilac (7.4.87)	—	£130
T123	T **118**	80c. on 50r. brown-lilac (21.12.87)	—	20·00
T124	T **119**	80c. on 50r. brown-lilac (3.92)................	—	50·00

(T **120**)   (T **121**)

(h) Surch 5r.

T125	T **120**	5r. on 25r. carmine (1.4.92)	£250	11·00
		a. Small "s" in "RUPEES"........................	—	70·00
T126	T **121**	5r. on 50r. brown-lilac (13.8.94)..........	—	£100

The dates quoted above for Nos. T23/126 refer to printing dates, where known. For stamps similar to Nos. T125/6, but wmk T **129**, see Nos. T148/49.

T 122

T 123

T 124

T 125

T 126

T 127

T 128

(Typo, Govt Printer, Colombo)

1892 (1 April)–**1903**. T **122/8** (different frame ornaments for each value). No wmk. Date and control figures in black. Perf 12.

(a) Date numerals separated by oblique lines. Large control figures

T127	T **122**	20c. green (1/4/92)	—	10·00
		a. Small control figures	£300	4·00
T128	T **123**	40c. blue (1/4/92)	—	7·00
		a. Small control figures	£300	3·00
T129	T **124**	60c. brown (1/4/92)	—	10·00
		a. Small control figures	£325	4·00
T130	T **125**	80c. olive (1/4/92)	—	10·00
		a. Small control figures	£300	4·00

The 80c. exists imperforate, with date "1/4/92", and the 40c. and 80c. also imperforate with date "1/5/92" but the latter were not issued.

(b) Date numerals separated by dashes

T131	T **126**	5c. lilac-rose (1-4-97)	65·00	3·00
		a. Date 1-11-97	55·00	3·00
		b. Date 1-7-98	—	5·00
		c. Date 1-12-98	60·00	3·00
		d. Date 1-12-99	75·00	2·50
T132		5c. deep purple (1-12-00)	55·00	2·50
		a. Date 1-12-01	60·00	3·00
		b. Date 1-12-02	—	3·00
		c. Bluish paper. Date 18-5-03	—	6·00
T133	T **127**	10c. yellow (1-4-97)	75·00	3·00
		a. Date 1-11-97	70·00	3·00
		b. Date 1-12-98	—	3·00

		c. Date 1-12-99	70·00	2·50
		d. Date 1-12-00	85·00	8·00
		e. Date 1-12-01	65·00	3·00
		f. Bluish paper. Date 18-5-03	—	6·00
T134	T **122**	20c. green (1-9-92)	70·00	5·00
		a. Date 9-1-93	75·00	3·00
		b. Date 1-5-94	65·00	3·00
		c. Date 1-11-94	60·00	3·00
		d. Date 1-11-95	—	3·00
		e. Date 1-9-96	—	3·00
		f. Date 1-11-97	60·00	2·50
		g. Date 1-12-98	—	3·00
		h. Date 1-12-99	55·00	3·00
		i. Date 1-12-00	75·00	4·50
		j. Date 1-12-01	65·00	4·50
		k. Bluish paper. Date 18-5-03	—	6·00
T135	T **128**	25c. deep olive (1-12-97. Date in blue, without control figures)	£350	8·00
T136	T **123**	40c. blue (1-9-92)	75·00	3·00
		a. Date 9-1-93	65·00	3·00
		b. Date 1-5-94	55·00	2·50
		c. Date 1-11-94	65·00	2·00
		d. Date 1-11-95	—	3·00
		e. Date 1-9-96	50·00	2·00
		f. Date 1-12-99	—	6·00
		g. Date 1-12-00	80·00	4·50
		h. Date 1-12-01	80·00	6·00
		i. Bluish paper. Date 18-5-03	—	7·00
T137	T **124**	60c. dark brown (1-9-92)	70·00	5·00
		a. Date 9-1-93	—	3·00
		b. Date 1-5-94	£120	8·00
		c. Date 1-11-94	65·00	3·00
		d. Date 1-11-95	—	3·00
		e. Date 1-9-96	65·00	3·00
		f. Date 1-7-98	55·00	3·00
		g. Date 1-12-98	—	8·00
		h. Date 1-12-99	—	6·00
		i. Date 1-12-00	—	5·00
		j. Date 1-12-01	80·00	5·00
		k. Date 1-12-02	—	6·00
		l. Bluish paper. Date 18-5-03	—	6·00
T138	T **125**	80c. olive (1-9-92)	75·00	5·00
		a. Date 9-1-93	—	3·00
		b. Date 1-5-94	—	3·50
		c. Date 1-11-94	60·00	3·00
		d. Date 1-11-95	—	3·00
		e. Date 1-9-96	70·00	2·50
		f. Date 1-7-98	70·00	3·00
		g. Date 1-12-98	—	12·00
		h. Date 1-12-99	—	6·00
		i. Date 1-12-00	70·00	5·00
		j. Date 1-12-01	70·00	4·00
		k. Date 1-12-02	—	6·00
		l. Bluish paper. Date 18-5-03	—	8·00

The plates used to print the 5c., 10c. and 25c. values (Nos. T131/3, 135) each included two different 'dies', which can be found in *se-tenant* pairs.

T **129** ("CA" in wide letters)

1894. Typo, De La Rue. As Nos. T10, T12/13, T15/17, T19/21, but wmk T **129**. Perf 14.

T139	T **2**	12c. olive-bistre	18·00	1·25
T140	T **4**	25c. green	18·00	75
T141	T **5**	50c. blue	18·00	1·00
T142	T **7**	1r. red-brown	20·00	75
T143	T **8**	2r.50c. slate	40·00	1·00
T144	T **9**	5r. orange	60·00	1·25
T145	T **11**	10r. purple	£190	2·50
		a. Claret	—	2·50
		b. Dull magenta	—	2·50
T146	T **12**	25r. carmine	£1000	2·00
T147	T **13**	50r. lake	£1500	15·00

1894. Nos. T146/7 surch with new values as T T **121** and T **130** by Ceylon Govt Printer, Colombo.

T148	T **130**	5r. on 25r. carmine (26.11.94)	—	38·00
T149	T **121**	5r. on 50r. lake (13.8.94)	—	22·00

(T **130**)	T **131**	T **132**

(Typo, De La Rue)

1903 (June)–**04**. T T **131** or T **132** (25c.). Wmk T **129**. Perf 14.

T150	T **131**	5c. brown and green	95·00	2·50
T151		10c. bluish green and ochre	95·00	3·50
T152		12c. olive-bistre and green (1.04)	£170	7·00
T153		20c. drab and purple	95·00	4·00
T154	T **132**	25c. green (1.04)	95·00	2·50
		w. Wmk inverted	†	40·00
T155	T **131**	40c. purple and brown	95·00	5·00
T156		50c. blue and purple	95·00	3·00
T157		60c. olive and ochre	95·00	4·00
T158		75c. pale blue and blue	95·00	3·00
T159		1r. red-brown	95·00	1·00
T160		2r.50c. slate and ochre	£250	5·00
T161		5r. orange and carmine	£250	8·00
T162		10r. reddish purple and green	£400	15·00
T163		25r. carmine and scarlet	£1400	10·00
T164		50r. claret and blue	£2250	60·00

1905. As Nos. T150/64, but Wmk Mult Crown CA (sideways)*.

			Unused	Used whole	Used upper half
T165	T **131**	5c. brown and green	10·00	2·00	50
T166		10c. bluish green and ochre..	12·00	3·00	50
T167		12c. olive-bistre and green	12·00	8·50	75
T168		20c. drab and purple	10·00	5·00	75
T169	T **132**	25c. green	14·00	3·00	50
T170	T **131**	40c. purple and brown	12·00	8·00	60
T171		50c. blue and purple	15·00	6·00	75
T172		60c. olive and ochre	14·00	6·50	75
T173		75c. pale blue and blue	15·00	6·50	75
T174		1r. red-brown	14·00	4·00	75
T175		2r.50c. slate and ochre	30·00	7·00	1·00
		w. Wmk Crown to right of CA	†	—	55·00
T176		5r. orange and carmine	75·00	10·00	1·00
T177		10r. reddish purple and green	£130	15·00	1·50
T178		25r. carmine and scarlet	£450	80·00	5·00
T179		50r. claret and blue	£650	£200	32·00

*The normal sideways watermark shows Crown to left of CA, *as seen from the back of the stamp.*

During the currency of Nos. T165/79 changes in administrative practice meant that horizontal bisection of the stamps largely ceased. Prices are accordingly quoted both for used whole stamps and used upper halves.

1910 (May–July). Nos T167, T169 and T174 surch with new values in words as T T **133** or T **134** (No. T181) by Ceylon Govt Printer, Colombo.

T180	T **133**	20c. on 12c. olive-bistre and green	75·00
T181	T **134**	20c. on 25c. green (7.10)	75·00
T182	T **133**	40c. on 12c. olive-bistre and green	75·00
T183		40c. on 1r. red-brown (7.10)	75·00
T184		60c. on 12c. olive-bistre and green	75·00
T185		5r. on 12c. olive-bistre and green	£3500
T186		5r. on 1r. red-brown (7.10)	£3500
T187		10r. on 12c. olive-bistre and green	£3500

No used examples of Nos. T180/7 have been seen. Forged surcharges exist.

The telegraph stamps of Ceylon were withdrawn from use on 1 August 1910.

(T **133**)	(T **134**)

Britannia Albums

The perfect solution for housing stamp from any country

From Afghanistan to Zimbabwe...

Whichever country you collect, the Britannia range of albums contains something suitable for you. The binders are made from the best quality vinyl and come with polypropylene pockets, complete with 160gsm white acid free paper used are top quality products.

Each A4 (210mm x 297mm) page is specifically designed, having a space for each stamp with the date, title, and value of the stamp shown. These albums are compiled using the Scott (rather than SG) numbering system. Binders are available in blue or maroon.

There are over 900 volumes available including single countries, states, used abroad and omnibus issues. If you are looking for something in particular or would like a full list of Britannia albums, please contact us on the details at the bottom of the page and we will do all we can to help.

Code	Country	Vol	Period	Pages	Retail	Code	Country	Vol	Period	Pages	Retail
BAN1	Bangladesh	Vol 1	1973-1994	77	£41.36	PKS2	Pakistan	Vol 2	1982-2005	80	£41.36
BAN2	Bangladesh	Vol 2	1995-2012	80	£41.36	PKS3	Pakistan	Vol 3	2006-2013	28	£24.70
CEYL	Ceylon		1857-1972	42	£30.65	SRI1	Sri Lanka	Vol 1	1972-1991	93	£41.36
PKS1	Pakistan - Inc Bahawaluper					SRI2	Sri Lanka	Vol 2	1992-2005	94	£41.36
		Vol 1	1947-1981	80	£36.54	SRI3	Sri Lanka	Vol 3	2006-2011	55	£30.65

Please note: Delivery of these items will take a minimum of 21 days and are only printed to order. If you are unsure about the content of these albums, please contact us prior to ordering.

For a list of Britannia albums, visit **www.stanleygibbons.com/britannia**

Est 1856

STANLEY GIBBONS

Stanley Gibbons Limited
7 Parkside, Christchurch Road, Ringwood, Hants, BH24 3SH
+44 (0)1425 472 363
www.stanleygibbons.com

STANLEY GIBBONS

Dear Catalogue User,

As a collector and Stanley Gibbons catalogue user for many years myself, I am only too aware of the need to provide you with the information you seek in an accurate, timely and easily accessible manner. Naturally, I have my own views on where changes could be made, but one thing I learned long ago is that we all have different opinions and requirements.

I would therefore be most grateful if you would complete the form overleaf and return it to me. Please contact Lorraine Holcombe (lholcombe@stanleygibbons.co.uk) if you would like to be emailed the questionnaire.

Very many thanks for your help.

Yours sincerely,

Hugh Jefferies,
Editor.

Hugh Jefferies (Catalogue Editor)
Catalogue Questionnaire Responses
Stanley Gibbons Limited
7 Parkside, Ringwood
Hampshire BH24 3SH
United Kingdom

Questionnaire

2015 Bangladesh, Burma, Pakistan & Sri Lanka Catalogue

1. Level of detail

   Do you feel that the level of detail in this catalogue is:
   a. too specialised   O
   b. about right   O
   c. inadequate   O

2. Frequency of issue

   How often would you purchase a new edition of this catalogue?
   a. Annually   O
   b. Every two years   O
   c. Every three to five years   O
   d. Less frequently   O

3. Design and Quality

   How would you describe the layout and appearance of this catalogue?
   a. Excellent   O
   b. Good   O
   c. Adequate   O
   d. Poor   O

4. How important to you are the prices given in the catalogue:
   a. Important   O
   b. Quite important   O
   c. Of little interest   O
   d. Of no interest   O

5. Would you be interested in an online version of this catalogue?
   a. Yes   O
   b. No   O

6. Do you like the new format?
   a. Yes   O
   b. No   O

7. What changes would you suggest to improve the catalogue? E.g. Which other indices would you like to see included?

   ....
   ....
   ....
   ....

8. Which other Stanley Gibbons Catalogues do you buy?

   ....
   ....
   ....
   ....

9. Would you like us to let you know when the next edition of this catalogue is due to be published?
   a. Yes   O
   b. No   O

   If so please give your contact details below.

   Name: ....
   Address:..
   ....
   ....
   ....

   Email: ....
   Telephone:...

10. Which other Stanley Gibbons Catalogues are you interested in?
    a. ....
    b. ....
    c. ....

Many thanks for your comments.

Please complete and return it to: Hugh Jefferies (Catalogue Editor)
Stanley Gibbons Limited, 7 Parkside, Ringwood, Hampshire BH24 3SH, United Kingdom
or email: lholcombe@stanleygibbons.co.uk to request a soft copy

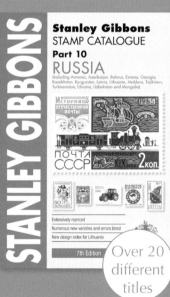
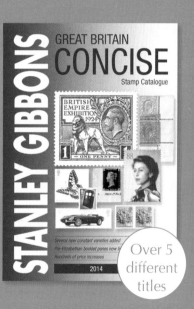

YOUR ORDER

Stanley Gibbons account number

Condition (mint/UM/ used)	Country	SG No.	Description	Price	Office use only
			POSTAGE & PACKING	£3.60	
			TOTAL		

The lowest price charged for individual stamps or sets purchased from Stanley Gibbons Ltd, is £1.

Payment & address details

Name

Address (We cannot deliver to PO Boxes)

Postcode

Tel No.

Email

PLEASE NOTE Overseas customers MUST quote a telephone number or the order cannot be dispatched. Please complete ALL sections of this form to allow us to process the order.

☐ Cheque (made payable to Stanley Gibbons)

☐ I authorise you to charge my

☐ Mastercard ☐ Visa ☐ Diners ☐ Amex ☐ Maestro

Card No.   (Maestro only)

Valid from   Expiry date   Issue No. (Maestro only)   CVC No. (4 if Amex)

CVC No. is the last three digits on the back of your card (4 if Amex)

Signature   Date

4 EASY WAYS TO ORDER

Post to
Lesley Mourne,
Stamp Mail Order
Department, Stanley
Gibbons Ltd, 399
Strand, London,
WC2R 0LX, England

Call
020 7836 8444
+44 (0)20 7836 8444

Fax
020 7557 4499
+44 (0)20 7557 4499

Click
lmourne@
stanleygibbons.com/
co.uk?

If YOU Buy at Auction this is How You Can Save £250+ EACH Year

BURMA / CEYLON INCLUDED

... I'll Give You £55 to get you started

(... some Collectors Save thousands of pounds)

By Andrew McGavin, Managing Director, Universal Philatelic Auctions (UPA)

ANDREW PROMOTING PHILATELY ON THE ALAN TITCHMARSH SHOW ITV

In all my 40+ years in the trade I have never seen an introductory offer to new clients like this .. so you may be wondering the reason why my company UPA can afford to make this offer to you?

In *'plain talk'* most auctions charge 'Buyers Premiums' –YES! You have to pay up to 25% (some charge more) **on top of the *winning price you paid***. That is Simply an Incredible surcharge. Apparently this significant premium is justified by charging the seller a lower fee in order to entice consignments for sale.

My company UPA does not charge any premiums which is one of the reasons why we hold the UK record of 1,975 different bidders in our last auction – an amazing 89% of whom were successful. Fortunately the average bidder spends an average of £250+ per auction...so that with 4 auctions a year offering 80,000+/- lots from £1 to £100,000 for you to choose from ....

with NO Buyer's Premium You Save up to £250+ <u>EACH YEAR</u> PLUS You take NO RISK with our 28 day unconditional Guarantee

So How can UPA offer You £55 OFF too?

1. **Our Business Model is Different.** Fundamentally I believe that if a stamp/philatelic item is not selling then it is too expensive. Compare that with the stamp business whose stock is the same each time you see or hear from them. At the risk of boring you …

2. **Stamp Industry's BIGGEST problem.** … twenty years ago I started to ponder upon what is the biggest problem faced by the average stamp dealer? The answer came back loud and clear. The biggest problem faced by a stamp dealer is not what sells … **but what does not sell**. This is the reason why most stamp dealers have lots of unsold stock you have seen time and time again – worse still this is what prevents that dealer from buying new stock to offer you.

3. **Surface Sell.** There is an actual name for this – it is called 'surface sell' – good material 'floats' on the surface and sells. Less desirable stock sinks so that unless a dealer pays almost nothing to replace his stock then the profit in the business becomes stagnant and bound in less saleable stock. If only that dealer could move this stock he would have more money to invest in new stock to offer to you.

4. **Cover-up.** Twenty years ago almost the entire stamp industry spent its time disguising what did not sell – in those days so pernicious were 'unsolds' that it was common practice for one auction house to sell batches of 'unsolds' to another auction where the new auction could present them to (hopefully) different collectors as new lots. 'Passing the Philatelic Parcel' was common practice.

5. **E-Bay.** Today the philatelic world is almost unrecognisably different. In large part courtesy of the internet. How things have changed. Few 'pass the parcel'. Really active Dealers - these days they **also** sell on eBay - large lots, small lots, all manner of stamps, covers, down to fakes and forgeries – today's equivalent of the Wild West – there's philatelic 'gold' to be mined in those hills … but Boy – you have to work to find it and sadly 'all that glistens is not gold' – you pays your money and you takes your chance often with little support or recourse. UPA too sells surpluses on eBay backed by support and our guarantee – access eBay links via *www.upastampauctions.co.uk*

Continued overleaf ☞